THE CAMBRIDGE HISTORY OF ISLAM

VOLUME 2B

THE CAMBRIDGE HISTORY OF ISLAM

VOLUME 2B

ISLAMIC SOCIETY AND CIVILIZATION

EDITED BY

P. M. HOLT

Professor of Arab History in the University of London

ANN K. S. LAMBTON

Emeritus Professor of Persian in the University of London

BERNARD LEWIS

Institute for Advanced Study, Princeton

CAMBRIDGE
UNIVERSITY PRESS

Published by the Press Syndicate of the University of Cambridge
The Pitt Building, Trumpington Street, Cambridge CB2 1RP
40 West 20th Street, New York, NY 10011-4211, USA
10 Stamford Road, Oakleigh, Melbourne 3166, Australia

Library of Congress catalogue card number: 73-77291

First published in two volumes 1970
First paperback edition (four volumes) 1977
First four-volume hardcover edition 1978
Volume 2B reprinted 1980, 1981, 1985, 1988, 1990, 1995

Printed in Great Britain by Athenæum Press Ltd, Gateshead, Tyne & Wear

ISBN 0 521 21949 3 hardback
ISBN 0 521 29138 0 paperback

CONTENTS

LIST OF PLATES

The plates appear between pages 708 and 709.

ACKNOWLEDGMENTS

The editors are grateful to the following for granting permission to reproduce these illustrations:

The Trustees of the British Museum for plates 12b and 18b.

Victoria and Albert Museum. Crown Copyright for plates 29a, 31b, 32a and 32b.

The Department of Eastern Art, The Ashmolean Museum for plates 6a, 6b, 17a, 17b, 17c and 17d.

Edinburgh University Library for plate 25a.

The Metropolitan Museum of Art, Bequest of Cora Timken Burnett, 1957 for plate 19a.

The Metropolitan Museum of Art, Bequest of Cora Timken Burnett, 1957 for plate 25b.

The Metropolitan Museum of Art, Rogers Fund, 1917 for plate 26.

Courtesy of the Smithsonian Institution, Freer Gallery of Art, Washington, D.C. for plates 6d and 22a.

A Survey of Persian Art, Oxford, 1939, Re-issue Asia Institute Shiraz, 1966 for plates 3b and 18a.

Dr Edmund de Unger for plates 6c, 8b, 12a, 28a and 31a.

Mr David Stronach for plates 10b and 13.

Paul Hamlyn Publishers Ltd., for plate 20a.

Dr J. Ellman for plate 23a.

Mr R. Hillenbrand for plates 24a and 24b.

Professor Oktay Aslanapa for plate 20b.

Mr Nuri Arlasez for plate 29b.

Mr R. Jairazbhoy for plate 10a.

Dr Abdul Aziz Hameed for plate 5a.

Dr G. Fehervari for plates 1a, 1b, 2a, 4a, 4b, 5c, 7a, 7b, 8a, 9b, 11, 14a, 14b, 15a, 15b, 16a, 16b, 21a, 21b, 22b, 23b, 27a, 28b, 30 and 27b.

PREFACE

The aim of these volumes is to present the history of Islam as a cultural whole. It is hoped that in a single concise work the reader will be able to follow all the main threads: political, theological, philosophical, economic, scientific, military, artistic. But *The Cambridge history of Islam* is not a repository of facts, names and dates; it is not intended primarily for reference, but as a book for continuous reading. The editors believe that, while it will not be despised by the expert orientalist, it will be useful to students in other fields of history, and particularly to university students of oriental subjects, and will also appeal to those who read history for intellectual pleasure.

A standardized system of translation has been employed for proper names and technical terms in the three principal Islamic languages—Arabic, Persian and Turkish. Some anomalies have, however, been inevitable, and place-names which have a widely accepted conventional spelling have been given in that form. Dates before the nineteenth century have normally been given according to both the Islamic (*Hijrī*) and Christian eras. Footnotes have been used sparingly; principally to give references for quotations or authority for conclusions in the text. The bibliographies are not intended as an exhaustive documentation of the subjects to which they refer, but as a guide to further reading. For this reason, and to avoid extensive repetition of titles, many of the bibliographies have been consolidated to cover two or more related contributions.

The editors are responsible for the planning and organisation of the work as a whole. They have tried to avoid gaps and overlaps, and have given general guidance to contributors, designed to secure some consistency of form and presentation. The individual authors are, of course, responsible for their own opinions and interpretations.

The editors wish to express their thanks to all who have assisted in the preparation of this work. They are particularly grateful to those who undertook the translation of contributions or gave advice and sub-editorial assistance, especially Mr J. G. Burton-Page, Professor C. D. Cowan, Dr J. F. P. Hopkins, Dr A. I. Sabra, Professor H. R. Tinker, Col. Geoffrey Wheeler and Dr D. T. Whiteside. They would also like to thank members of the staff of the Cambridge University Press for their invariable patience and helpfulness.

THE EDITORS

PREFACE

INTRODUCTION

P. M. HOLT[1]

A reader taking up a work entitled *The Cambridge history of Islam* may reasonably ask, 'What is Islam? In what sense is Islam an appropriate field for historical enquiry?' Primarily, of course, Islam is, like Christianity, a religion, the antecedents, origin and development of which may, without prejudice to its transcendental aspects, be a legitimate concern of historians. Religious history in the narrow sense is not, however, the only, or even the main, concern of the contributors to these volumes. For the faith of Islam has, again like Christianity, been a great synthesizing agent. From its earliest days it displayed features of kinship with the earlier monotheisms of Judaism and Christianity. Implanted in the former provinces of the Byzantine and Sasanian empires, it was compelled to maintain and define its autonomy against older and more developed faiths. Like Judaism and Christianity before it, it met the challenge of Greek philosophy, and adopted the conceptual and logical tools of this opponent to expand, to deepen, and to render articulate its self-consciousness. In this connexion, the first three centuries of Islam, like the first three centuries of Christianity, were critical for establishing the norms of belief and practice, and for embodying them in a tradition which was, or which purported to be, historical.

The Islamic synthesis did not stop at this stage. The external frontier of Islam has continued to move until our own day. For the most part, this movement has been one of expansion—into Central Asia, into the Indian sub-continent and south-east Asia, and into trans-Saharan Africa—but there have also been phases of retreat and withdrawal, notably in Spain, and in central and south-eastern Europe. But besides this external frontier, which has largely been the creation of conquering armies, (although with important exceptions in Central and south-east Asia and Africa) there has also been throughout Islamic history an internal frontier—the invisible line of division between Muslim and non-Muslim. Here also over the centuries there has been an expansion of Islam, so that, for example, in the former Byzantine and Sasanian lands the Christian and Zoroastrian communities were reduced to numerical insignificance, and became minority-groups like the Jews. This two-fold expansion has brought new elements into the Islamic synthesis,

[1] I should like to thank my co-editors, Professors Lambton and Lewis, for reading and commenting on this Introduction in draft.

some permanent and widely accepted, others more transient or local in their effects.

The process of synthesization has not gone forward in a political vacuum. Unlike the early Christian Church, the Islamic *Umma*, or community of believers, achieved political power from the outset, and was organized for mutual support in the maintenance of the faith. This concern of the community for the faith survived the break-up of the caliphate and the emergence of new and often transitory régimes. It has taken various forms. Two of the principal institutions of Islam, *Sharīʿa* and *Jihād*, the Holy Law and the Holy War, are expressions of the concern in its conservative and militant aspects respectively—aspects moreover which are not wholly distinct, since the Holy War is fought in defence of the Holy Law against its external and internal enemies. In political matters as in others, Islam adopted and incorporated contributions from many sources. The successors of the Prophet as heads of his community drew on the customs of Arab tribal leadership, as well as the usages of the Meccan trading oligarchy. They inherited the legacy of Byzantine administration, as well as the traditions of the Sasanian monarchy. Later rulers were influenced by other political concepts: those brought into the medieval Islamic world by Turkish and Mongol immigrants from the steppes, and in the latest age the constitutional and legal doctrines of liberal Europe, followed by the seductive panaceas of totalitarianism.

Islam, then, as it will be examined in the following chapters, is a complex cultural synthesis, centred in a distinctive religious faith, and necessarily set in the framework of a continuing political life. The religion, the culture, and the political structures alike present many features which seem familiar to an observer whose own background is that of Christian Europe. It could hardly be otherwise, since elements derived from Judaism and Hellenism are common to both the Islamic and the Christian syntheses; since, furthermore, the histories of the Islamic community and of Christendom have touched so often and at so many points. But consciousness of the similarities must always be balanced by an awareness of the characteristic and substantial differences. Like Christianity, Islam is a monotheism with an historical founder and a sacred book; although its theology in regard to both differs essentially from Christian theology. There is also a perceptible difference in the criteria of membership of the community. Whereas in Christianity acceptance of the catholic creeds has been the basic criterion, in Islam credal theology has been of less relative importance; adherence to the Holy Law is the characteristic manifestation of faith, and hence orthopraxy rather than orthodoxy has been the usual token of membership. Another difference is that Islam has no equivalent to the Christian sacraments (although certain practices, notably the Fast of Ramaḍān and the Pilgrimage, appear to have an unacknowledged quasi-sacramental character), and no priesthood, although the '*ulamā*' (the religious scholars) and the leaders of the Ṣūfī orders (two groups at some times and in some places closely interconnected) have often played a part in Muslim societies analogous to that of the clergy amongst Christians. The absence of a sacerdotal hierarchy, or of any conciliar system, to define the faith, linked with the primacy ascribed to orthopraxy, has made Islam more tolerant of variations of belief than Christianity. It is in general true to say that heresy (to use a term not quite appropriate in Islam) has been repressed only when it has been manifested as political subversion: it is also true to say that, since Islam is both a religious and a political community, the distinction between religious and political dissent is not clearcut.

Another question which the reader of this work may ask is, 'What are the sources on which knowledge of the history of Islam is based?' The Islamic civilization of the first three centuries (in this as in other respects the seminal period) evolved two characteristic types of historical writing. The first of these was the chronicle, of which the outstanding classical example is that composed by al-Ṭabarī (d. 310/923). But behind the chronicle lay diverse historiographical elements—the sagas and genealogies of the pre-Islamic Arab tribes, the semi-legendary narratives of the Persian kings, and, serving as the central theme to which all others were subservient, the career of the Prophet and the vicissitudes of the *Umma* which he founded. The early historians were primarily religious scholars: the traditions which they recorded were in part Traditions in the technical Islamic sense, i.e. *Ḥadīth,* the memorials of the alleged acts and sayings of the Prophet, as transmitted by a chain of informants. There was no formal distinction between the historical *Ḥadīth* and the main body of Traditions which formed a principal element in the elaboration of the Holy Law; indeed it is clear that many items ostensibly of an historical nature had in fact legal and social purposes. There is also a fundamental problem of criticism; namely, the difficulty of establishing how much of this copious *Ḥadīth* material is a veritable record of Muḥammad's activities, and how much is of subsequent and extraneous origin, assimilated in this form into Islam. The early Muslim scholars were keenly aware of the problem, although the criteria they adopted for discriminating between the authentic and the feigned Traditions seem artificial and insufficiently rigorous by modern standards of historical investigation. The whole subject is highly controversial at the present day, with, on the whole, non-Muslim scholars adopting a more radical, and Muslim scholars a more conservative attitude in *Ḥadīth* criticism.

Thus the motive which led to the development of Islamic historiography was primarily religious. In nothing does Islam so clearly demonstrate its kinship with Judaism and Christianity as in its sense of, and attitude towards, history; its consciousness of the existence of the world under a divine dispensation, and its emphasis on the significance of human lives and acts. Muḥammad saw himself as the last in a sequence of prophets who were God's apostles to mankind. The Qur'ān abounds in references to sacred history. Hence Islamic historiography assumes as axiomatic the pattern already evolved in Judaeo-Christian thought: a succession of events in time, opening with the creation, culminating in a point of supreme divine revelation (when, in effect, there is a new creation of a holy community), and looking prospectively to a Last Day and the end of history. In this connexion, it is significant that, in spite of the contacts between Islamic and late Hellenistic civilization, and of the Muslim reception of much of the Graeco-Roman cultural heritage, the Islamic historians were almost totally uninterested in their Classical predecessors, whether as sources of information, or as models of historiography. The Roman Empire played no part in the *praeparatio evangelica* for Islam as it did for Christianity.

This conception of Islamic history as sacred history was a factor in the development of the second characteristic type of historical writing, a type original in Islam—the biographical dictionary. The earliest of these to survive is a collection of lives of Companions of the Prophet, and, in the words of Sir Hamilton Gibb:

> it is clear that the conception that underlies the oldest biographical dictionaries is that the history of the Islamic Community is essentially the contribution of individual men and women to the building up and transmission of its specific culture; that it is these persons (rather than the political governors) who represent or reflect the active forces in Muslim society in their respective spheres; and that their individual contributions are worthy of being recorded for future generations.[1]

[1] H. A. R. Gibb, 'Islamic biographical literature', in *Historians of the Middle East*, ed. B. Lewis and P. M. Holt (London, 1962), p. 54.

Although both the chronicle and the biographical dictionary changed and developed as, after the third Islamic century, historical writing ceased to be the special field of the religious scholars, as the caliphate was fragmented, and as new states and dynasties arose, the two persisted as the standard forms of historical writing until recent times. From Arabic they were carried over into the Persian and Turkish literatures, and from the heartlands of the Middle East to the fringes of Islam. Only during the last century, and partly at least in consequence of the reception of Western historical objectives and techniques by Muslim scholars, have they become moribund.

One important class of source-material, familiar to the student of Western history, is almost completely lacking for the history of Islam—namely, archives. Certain documents are to be found transcribed in chronicles, as well as in collections of model letters and the encyclopaedic handbooks written for the guidance of government officials, but these are at least at one remove from their originals, and as isolated pieces are of diminished evidential value. Climatic conditions in Egypt, and chancery practice in Europe, have preserved some documents, more or less at random, but only with the records of the Ottoman Empire does a rich and systematically maintained government archive become available. With the nineteenth century, archival material increases. As in other fields of historical study, important contributions have been made by the auxiliary sciences of archaeology, epigraphy, palaeography, diplomatic and numismatics.

The modern study of Islamic history goes back to developments in Europe during the sixteenth and seventeenth centuries. Throughout the previous millennium, the peoples in the lands of Western Christendom and Islam had remained in almost total ignorance of each other's history; but whereas the Muslims almost without exception chose to ignore events which seemed to them extraneous and irrelevant, the Christian writers elaborated what has rightly been called a 'deformed image' of Islam and its founder.[1] In the sixteenth and seventeenth centuries, this came to be challenged. The contacts of trade and diplomacy were increasing between Muslim and Christian states. The study of Arabic was established in European universities for a variety of reasons, not least that it was seen to be the key to the writings of the Muslim philosophers and scientists, hitherto known only in imperfect medieval Latin translations. A knowledge of Arabic was also important in the

[1] See N. Daniel, *Islam and the West: the making of an image* (Edinburgh, 1960).

study of the Hebrew Bible—a study which flourished in the age of the Renaissance and the Reformation. During the same period in Western Europe, the foundations of critical historical enquiry were being laid: ancient texts were being published, old documents were being brought out of neglected archives. The motive behind much of this activity was ardently polemic; nevertheless, controversialists both in Britain and on the Continent were fashioning the instruments and devising the methods of modern research.

A new approach to the study of Islam was one aspect of this 'historical revolution', as it has been called.[1] It was demonstrated in two principal respects. The first of these was the publication of texts. Here the initiative was taken by Dutch scholars, Erpenius and Golius, in the first half of the seventeenth century, to be followed shortly by the Englishman, Edward Pococke (1604–91). The greatness of Pococke, however, lies mainly in a second respect. He had for his time an unrivalled knowledge of Muslim history and Arab antiquities, of which he gave an exposition in a short but very influential work, *Specimen historiae Arabum* (1650). The book remained authoritative for a century and a half, during which time it served as a quarry for a succession of writers. Resting on an encyclopaedic range of Arabic sources, the *Specimen*, implicitly by its scholarship, as well as by the occasional explicit comment, prepared the way for a more accurate and dispassionate view of Islam than the 'deformed image', which was still commonly accepted—and indeed lingered for two centuries. A later generation of orientalists extended the new understanding of Islam, and, by writing in modern languages, conveyed it to a less academic readership. Three highly important works in this connexion were the *Bibliothèque orientale* (1697) of Bartholomé d'Herbelot, *The history of the Saracens* (1708, 1718) of Simon Ockley, and George Sale's Preliminary Discourse to his translation of the Qur'ān (1734). Besides the information thus made available on the Islamic (and especially the Arab) past, there was in the same period a growing body of literature on the contemporary Muslim powers, especially the Ottomans and the Safavids. Through such publications, as well as others which were works of controversy rather than of scholarship, Islamic history became more familiar to educated Europeans, and was established beside ancient and modern history as an accepted field of study. This expansion of the world-view of European historians is

[1] See F. S. Fussner, *The historical revolution: English historical writing and thought, 1580–1640* (London, 1962).

demonstrated by Edward Gibbon, who, in his *Decline and fall of the Roman Empire* (1776–88) devoted nine out of seventy-one chapters to Islamic history, ranging from Arabia in the time of the Prophet to the Mongol and Ottoman conquests, and viewed its course with the same ironical detachment as he did the establishment of Christianity and the barbarian invasions of the West.

In the space of nearly two hundred years that have elapsed since Gibbon wrote, the Renaissance, the Reformation and the Enlightenment have themselves passed into history, and new forces have emerged in the development of European society. Political, social and economic change, the new ideologies of liberalism, nationalism and Marxism, have contributed to form the outlook and to define the preoccupations of historians in the nineteenth and twentieth centuries. At the same time, the methods of historical study have continued to evolve. The source-materials available for research have immensely increased, and the range of techniques at the historian's disposal has been extended. The aims of the historian have changed in response to both of these factors. Where the pioneers in the field sought primarily to construct, from the best sources they could find, the essential framework of political history, and to chronicle as accurately as possible the acts of rulers, historians today are more conscious of the need to evaluate their materials—a critique all the more important in Islamic history since the control supplied by archives is so largely deficient. They seek to penetrate the dynastic screen, to trace the real sites and shifts of power in the capitals and the camps, and to identify, not merely the leaders and figure-heads, but the ethnic, religious, social or economic groups of anonymous individuals who supported constituted authority or promoted subversion. It is no longer possible, therefore, to segregate the political history of Islam from its social and economic history—although in the latter field especially materials are notably sparse over wide regions and long periods. As the study of Islamic history is now developing, many of the apparent certainties of the older Western historiography (often reflecting the assertions and interpretations of the Muslim traditional historians) have dissolved, and it is only gradually through detailed research that a truer understanding of the past may be attained. At the same time, the range of investigation has been extended from its older foci, the heyday of classical Islam, the great dynastic empires, and the areas of confrontation with Christendom, to other periods and regions, which as recently as ten or twenty years ago aroused little interest among serious historians.

The Cambridge history of Islam cannot therefore pretend to supply a definitive conspectus of its field: it seeks rather to offer an authoritative guide to the state of knowledge at the present day, and to provide a sound foundation on which to build. The majority of its chapters are devoted to political history—this is inevitable in view of the relative abundance of source-material, and of the comparatively large amount of work that has been done here. Similar reasons explain the generous proportion of space allotted to the Muslim lands of the Middle East—which were, moreover, the region in which the classical Islamic synthesis evolved. Yet the picture which the work as a whole seeks to present is of the great and diversified community of Islam, evolving and expanding throughout thirteen centuries, creating its characteristic religious, political and social institutions, and making through its philosophy, literature and art a notable contribution to civilizations outside its own household of faith.

PART VIII

ISLAMIC SOCIETY AND CIVILIZATION

CHAPTER I

THE GEOGRAPHICAL SETTING

There is a closer relationship between Islam and its geographical setting, than that of any other of the great monotheistic religions. Glance at a general map of the distribution of Muslims throughout the world, and a pattern is revealed which coincides extensively, at least in its principal features, with the arid zone of the Old World. From the Atlantic to Central Asia, Islam found its primary field of expansion in and around the great desert. There is only one, though important, exception: those additional areas, sometimes very densely populated, which spread all round the Indian Ocean, on the eastern shores of Africa, the coasts of south India, and especially in eastern Pakistan and Indonesia. This coincidence of zone and religion is the more remarkable in comparison with the universal spread of Christianity, which was born in an environment, rather of the Mediterranean than of the desert, but not in reality far from that of Islam and in an area which was easily to be submerged in the Muslim torrent. We are brought therefore to ask two sets of questions: (a) How are we to explain such a notable geographical restriction of this religion, in view of its undoubted universal mission, at least from the time of Muḥammad's successors? What factors were at work, what historical, social, and psychological mechanisms? How is the map of Islam to be explained? (b) On the other hand, what effect has this restriction had on Muslim life? How has the face of Islam been modified as a consequence of the geographical setting in which it spread?

THE GEOGRAPHICAL CONDITIONS FOR THE SPREAD OF ISLAM

The geographical setting and the birth of Islam

The Muslim faith drew the essence of its initial drive from the very setting in which it arose. The two characteristic elements in this setting are the sedentary life of the oases and the pastoral nomads, the bedouin. Between the 27th and 24th parallels, the relative subsidence of the elevated edge of the rocky mountains which overlook from the east the rift of the Red Sea, with the interior slope broken up into long tectonic trenches, partially filled with volcanic deposits, created crossroads; in a generally very arid region where the rainfall appears nowhere to exceed 100 millimetres annually, great springs rising from the base of the lava plateaux gave birth to favourable sites for the development of great oases such as Medina. At the time of Muḥammad, the oases of the Ḥijāz were prosperous market towns; these cities were caravan centres which had organized the relations between southern Arabia and the Mediterranean world ever since the decline of the former, towards the end of the fifth Christian century, had permitted them to take up the reins and assume the directing role. Their atmosphere was already that of an active mercantile economy which favoured private enterprise and large profits. The bedouin constituted the other half of the picture and had done ever since the spread of the dromedary in the desert, probably from the beginning of the first millennium B.C. onwards, had secured the gradual expansion and domination of wide-ranging nomads. These bedouin were a basically aggressive people, their life founded on raiding and consequently on tribal solidarity combined with protective structures. Their political structure was highly unstable and subject to continual regroupings with the rise and fall of those outstanding personalities who are at the root of all tribal organization.

Such a situation was not unusual. It was repeated to some extent throughout the arid zone and on its edges, in all the areas of contact between nomadic and sedentary peoples. In such a context there is nothing abnormal about the dynamic power displayed by the new religion. It follows the pattern of other great expansive movements which have set out from arid zones to conquer the areas of cultivation, profiting from the forces available as a constant result of the population surplus. The nomads multiply in the relatively healthy setting of the desert since they are less subject to the epidemics which, until recent years, have limited the progress of sedentary populations. Apart from the remarkable personality of the Prophet, one factor in triggering off the great movement of the Muslim conquest was probably the climatic oscillation, and the series of great droughts occurring between 591 and 640. These made available to the military and religious leaders of the new faith human resources whose aggressive instincts had been strengthened and who were fully prepared to follow them to the promised lands. An expressive couple of lines from Abū Tammām (A.D. 806–47)[1] says:

'No, not for Paradise didst thou the nomad life forsake;
Rather, I believe, it was thy yearning after bread and dates'

[1] Quoted from P. K. Hitti, *History of the Arabs* (London, 1937), 144.

and the Persian general, Rustam, said the same thing to a Muslim envoy in 637: 'I have observed that it is simply poverty and the miserable life you have led which have induced you to undertake so much'.[1]

The singularity of Islam is, however, obvious. In contrast to what has occurred elsewhere, in Islam it is the town-dwellers who were set above the nomads. From this point of view, the turning-point in Muslim history was the battle of Ḥunayn, where, in Shawwāl 8/January 630, victory was won over a tribal coalition led by the Hawāzin, and the nomads were finally brought to follow the flag of the townsmen. The underlying reason for the supremacy of the latter may be found in the actual characteristics of the Near Eastern climate. Central Arabia bears no resemblance to High Central Asia, with its cold winters and rainy summers where sedentary life was literally strangled by the fact that the areas suitable for cultivation were the same as those which offered grazing for the nomads, whether in summer time it was the higher ground suitable for rain-fed agriculture or in winter the irrigable piedmonts. In the Sahara too the routes for commerce across the desert were never sufficiently active, the distances being so immense, to sustain great cities. But central Arabia is situated in the zone of rainy and relatively warm winters and the oases need not necessarily suffer disadvantage from the proximity of the nomads, since these are dispersed in the winter and driven in the summer towards the marginal sub-desert regions; furthermore, the desert being restricted in area, and regularly crossed by incense routes in active use, secured the basis for urban development of a size adequate to explain this triumph of the cities.

Whatever the cause, the Muslim conquest, even in its earliest stages, went far beyond the scope of a crisis of expansion among the Arab nomads. The Iranian plateau was largely impenetrable to the bedouin and the conquest of the Maghrib was a purely military and political enterprise in which there was no recourse to them. The nomads in any case were never more than second-rate recruits for Islam, often of indispensable help in the armed struggle as soldiers and warriors but, apart from their military merits, regarded as of bad character and poor religion, uproarious and impious. A celebrated *Ḥadīth* forbids milk in these terms: 'What I fear for my people is milk, where the devil lurks

[1] Balādhurī, *Kitāb futūḥ al-buldān*; cf. trans. P. K. Hitti, *The origins of the Islamic state* (New York, 1916), 411–12.

between the froth and the cream. They will love to drink it and will return to the desert, leaving the places where men pray together.'[1] And the Qur'ān adds: 'The desert Arabs are the most hardened in their impiety and hypocrisy.'[2] The bedouin were merely tools at best. In fact, the politico-religious apparatus of the new faith was incomparably superior in its complexity to the potentialities of the rough bedouin. Islam needs the city to effect its religious and social aims. The creation of a town is a highly praiseworthy act, and pious legends about their foundation are innumerable. Blessings have always been associated with a stay at Medina. Special permission was needed to leave it. Contrariwise, the meritious act *par excellence* was the *hijra*, the departure for Medina, the flight to the town.

The basis of Islam is primarily communal prayer. The most significant is the Friday prayer, that of the whole community (*umma*) assembled together. This demands fixed and permanent mosques where this important assembly can take place. The town is in the first place the site of the great Friday mosque, in opposition to the little mosques for daily prayer which lack the same permanence and fixity. The theologians have discussed at length the exact definition of the places where the Friday prayer can be made, but their subject is really the rigorous description of a city. There are disputes over the importance of the localities meriting this honour, which we should call towns, villages, or large hamlets. The mosque must be fixed and fully built. Certain strict authors consider the Friday prayer null and void if made in a place of worship which is left open momentarily to the sky through a fall from the ceiling. Even apart from the great Friday prayer, the rhythm of Muslim practices is designed for town dwellers. The mosque with its pool for ablutions and the complex installations this demands; the five daily prayers in response to the call of the muezzin; the Ramaḍān fast with its active nights: these are all urban in character. Secondly, town life is not only essential to collective prayer, it is necessary to the dignified life which Islam demands. The *imām* needs to live the life of a townsman. Women should be veiled, which conflicts with the requirements of nomadic, or even rural, existence. This rigorous prudish ideal is that of the austere merchants of the Ḥijāz. There still, Islam resorts to the decorum of the cities rather than the disorder of the fields or the desert. Its social

[1] Quoted from W. Marçais, 'L'Islamisme et la vie urbaine,' *Comptes-rendus de l'Académie des Inscriptions* (1928), 86–100.

[2] Qur'ān 9. 98.

constraints, just as much as its spiritual demands, make Islam an urban religion.

It should also be emphasized that this association of townsfolk and nomads puts agricultural activity in the lowest place in the Muslim ideal of society. In the oases of the Ḥijāz, cultivation of the soil was basically servile, in contrast with the outstandingly noble occupation of commerce. In the Qur'ān the growth of the crops is never seen as the fruit of human labour but as the straightforward expression of the Divine will (e.g. 26. 33–36, or 56. 64–65–God is the real sower) and antagonism against peasants is expressed even more freely in the *Ḥadīths*. The Prophet, seeing a ploughshare, is recorded as saying: 'That never enters the house of the faithful without degradation entering at the same time.' The peasants were the last to be able to assimilate Islam.

PROCESS AND LIMITS OF ISLAMIZATION

Islam is thus a religion which finds its most complete expression in an urban setting, but which, on the other hand, was spread by nomads in the course of vast movements of warlike conquest, while the peasants could hardly be other than strangers to it at the beginning. This threefold description affords the basis for an analysis of the mechanisms at work in its expansion, as well as the limits which that expansion reached.

Bedouinization and peasant resistance

As has already been noted, the Muslim conquests exceeded the compass of the nomadic invasions, and were not necessarily associated with them. But from the viewpoint of world history the most significant feature of the new religion was certainly, even though it was not everywhere simultaneous, the triumph of the nomads and the decline of sedentary life—a general 'bedouinization', the more pregnant with consequences since it affected those countries which had survived the Germanic invasions of the northern shores of the Mediterranean as the greatest centres of urban and civilized life.

It is not difficult to explain from this angle the general line of most of the frontiers of the Muslim world, at least where its realm is continuous. The enlistment of the nomads by Islam facilitated the conquest of all the arid or semi-arid zones of the ancient world and its expansion throughout the climatically marginal zones where rural life was precarious and pastoral life could easily acquire supremacy. Limits were met on the tropical fringe of the arid zone, in the forests which pastoral cultures could not penetrate because of the cattle trypanosomiasis; in contrast, the nomadic Peul were the main impetus for its diffusion in the savannahs of Negro West Africa. The north-west frontier of India is equally typical as a climatic and pastoral frontier, which expresses the military balance between the Islamic shepherds of the arid zone and the dense peasant population of the Indo-Gangetic plain. In the direction of Europe, the boundary, in the final reckoning, was in fact the sea; the sea prevented practically any nomadic penetration into the Iberian peninsula and limited it considerably in the Balkans; the resistance of the peasant societies was thus strengthened, particularly since here, in the temperate zone, they were much more firmly entrenched. On the Russian plain, the forest turned out to be an equally decisive obstacle, north of the steppe covered by the Golden Horde.

This general picture requires some modification in detail. Two very different families of nomadic peoples, the Arabs and the Turks, undertook the diffusion of Islam, and the imprint left on the human landscape differed in each case. The Arab nomads, who in particular poured over the whole Maghrib in the middle of the eleventh century (in the phase known as the Hilālī invasions) were people of the hot deserts, who used as their principal means of transport the dromedary, which has sensitive feet, suffers from the cold and can only be habituated to mountain life with difficulty. The Turkish nomads originated from the coldest part of High Asia, and possessed in the Bactrian camel an animal with a thick pelt, infinitely more hardy and tough, which adapted itself well to a mountain setting even though by origin as much a creature of the sands. The consequences of this contrast were decisive.

Throughout the Arab world the tide of nomads covering the deserts and the steppes lapped at the foot of the mountains without managing to make any serious breach in them. Only the skeletal mountains were open to bedouinization, those reduced to rocky outcrops hardly rising above the wide alluvial valleys, like the Saharan Atlas in Algeria, from the Ksour mountains to those of the Ouled Naïl (and even there traces of a previous way of life are to be found among the Berber mountaineers, with a short pastoral season, using load-carrying oxen, but more or less assimilated to the nomadic Arabs), or those reduced to broad grassy plateaux, like the Middle Atlas, roamed by Berbers, whose primarily nomadic life developed in the universal insecurity which followed the

Hilālī invasions. In general, the more important ranges rising above the deserts remained untouched, like the ancient massif of the western High Atlas in Morocco, the principal seat of Chleuh settlement, or the Aurès, the only mountain in the Maghrib which has kept unchanged its Classical name (Aurasius mons), itself a speaking witness to the continuity of the occupation of its soil, or, again, the highlands of 'Asīr and the Yemen in south-eastern Arabia. The ancient way of life, with crops irrigated in terraces in the bottom of the valleys in association with rain-fed agriculture on the higher slopes and with pasturage nearby, has been maintained in such areas without great change. This category also includes the Ethiopian highlands, where the dromedary cannot live; this is undoubtedly one of the main reasons for the failure of the various attempts to establish islamized nomads from the surrounding lowlands on the plateau. Elsewhere, Mediterranean coastal ranges—the Lebanon, the Alawite mountains, the Grande Kabylie—which until the medieval invasions had remained wooded and thinly populated, witnessed an influx of enormous numbers of peoples fleeing from the neighbouring plains. These mountains, whether they remained intact, preserving their ancient pattern of settlement or became refuges, transformed by the upheavals of the Middle Ages, constituted throughout the Arab world decisive obstacles to bedouinization, often to arabization, and even to islamization. We may cite the example of those mountains in the Maghrib where the speech is Berber, the religion is Islam, and the religious setting is pre-Islamic, undoubtedly fairly primitive and never fully converted to Christianity; or, again, the Lebanon or the Ethiopian highlands, which resisted Islam; or the various mountains which have nurtured heresies indicating the inadequacy of any conversion to Islam, like those of the Alawites of the Jabal Anṣāriyya, or the Druzes of the Jabal al-Durūz or the Zaydīs of the Yemen. In these mountainous refuges, Islam found the most stubborn barriers to its triumph.

Nothing similar could occur in the Turkish areas where the nomads had the zoological means to penetrate the mountains. Furthermore, the deep attraction for them of the freshness of summer quarters (*yayla*) drew them irresistibly to the mountains, while the cross-breeding of the Bactrian camel with the dromedary also progressively opened up the low-lying plains to serve them as winter quarters. On all the coastal plains of the Aegean and the Mediterranean, the havoc they brought meant that peasant life practically disappeared, with greater or less speed. The majority of the mountains were bedouinized, either directly, or indirectly by the reversion of their settled inhabitants to nomadic life, extending their previous brief pastoral migrations, as in Kurdistān and Luristān. The only geographically coherent and extended centres of resistance, apart from a few oases and towns, were the coastal forests of Pontus and the Caspian Sea, where the nomads were opposed by insurmountable difficulties in the thick cover of vegetation and the sultry climate, rather than in the sheer slopes. The late survival of the empire of Trebizond (up to 1461) in the first-named area, and the prolonged Iranian resistance to Islam in the Elburz and the heretical communities (particularly Ismā'īlīs) who established themselves there are witness to the exceptional character of these areas, which ensured their escape from the general decay of the deforested highlands and the Mediterranean plains alike, and which produced the great densities of population which mark them out today.

Town-dwellers and merchants: the urban centres of islamization

The essential instruments for the conversion of the countryside to Islam were therefore the nomads rather than the peasants. The towns, as we have seen, were of themselves an especially favourable setting for the new religion to flourish in. We cannot dissociate from this setting the part played by the merchants and traders of every kind, or even the urban artisans, all representatives of those activities which in Muslim eyes ranked highest and deserved most merit. Islam spread along the caravan and sea routes; the web of commercial relations among the towns formed the framework for its progress. It spread throughout the interior of the vanquished countries, where the towns with peculiar speed and intensity made themselves centres for the missionary effort from which Islam spread slowly through the neighbouring countryside. The religion also leapt beyond the border of the continuous territory of Islam, in the pioneering form of colonies of merchants scattered in ports and cities. While the nomadic conquests were limited to the edges of the arid zone, proselytization through commercial expansion was much more widespread and universal. It was responsible for the numerous outgrowths which mark the advance of Islam, far beyond its principal realms. In contrast to the warlike expansion, inseparable from the concept of *jihād* and based on the nomads, this advance was essentially pacific, at least in origin, even if it prepared the way for the organization

Islamic states. This means of progress was to remain active long after ıe disappearance of the political conditions which permitted conquest ·y war, and was to function even within those states under Christian ule. It alone is still an active force today.

On a world scale, however, we note at once the distorted pattern of Islam, for which this process is responsible. It had free play only in one direction. The Mediterranean acted like a great moat dug to separate the two religions and reduced to a minimum any human exchange between the two shores. Quite soon Muslim urban life in this area was unable to attract the swiftly progressing Christian world. In the end, the powers of resistance of the Christian peasant communities, supporting a stubborn political reconquest, destroyed, or at least considerably reduced, the Muslim urbanized settlements established by the Islamic powers in the Balkan and Iberian peninsulas.

By contrast, on its Asian and African fronts Islam often appeared in essence as the peaceful bearer of a superior social organization. Throughout Negro West Africa, since the period of colonial pacification, the role of the Muslim states in the propagation of Islam has passed to the traders, Mande-Dioulas in the west and Hausas in the east. Following them, came marabouts and schoolmasters, and so innumerable Muslim groups were diffused right into the true forest zone along the coasts. In central, east and south-east Africa, a region which had hardly ever been touched by Islamic invasion, except in the repellent guise of slave raiding, Islam is expanding dynamically in the same manner along the trade-routes which have carried it with Swahili traders as far as the Congo basin; and it is taking root fast in the recently established detribalized mining centres. In Central Asia too, where religion did not deflect the Turkish expansion from its general pressures towards the West, Islam did not in the main bring the *jihād*; it was the traders and the teachers who spread it along the roads of Turkistān, whence it penetrated into China. Between Buddhist Tibet and Buddhist Mongolia, the Muslim advance into Turkistān represents more than anything else the existence of the transcontinental trade-route to China, along the strings of oases of the Tarim basin; and it is extended by the numerous colonies of Chinese Muslims, composed basically of merchants and carriers.

The most typical successes were to be gained all round the Indian Ocean. The great navigational currents from the Ḥaḍramawt to Indonesia, and from the Deccan to Zanzibar or the northern cape of Madagascar, which put the great rhythm of the monsoons to profit long before Islam, ensured a perpetual flux entirely favourable to cultural interchange. The movement grew by degrees; the Muslim colonies established in the ports of south India sent out their own swarms; and the Indian merchants spread the new religion in this manner throughout the Malay world; meanwhile, the Arabs dominated the east coast of Africa down to Mozambique. This seaborne form of Islam remained basically coastal; only the fairly narrow coastal strips became completely converted, as a general rule. The very intense islamization of certain islands like Zanzibar or the Comoro Islands marks the importance of these landfalls for the seamen, as well as, on occasion, their early capture by trading cultures faced with a massive and hardly penetrable continent. The islamization of the Malay world is similar, though more spectacular numerically. The Malay sultanates were always basically coastal, being located especially at the mouths of the rivers, linked with the favoured sites for settlements which the spits or the sandy alluvial embankments of the rivers offered them above the level of the mudflats and the mangrove swamps, and taking advantage of the opportunities for rice paddies which the major flood-beds offered them lower down. These isolated centres of development, hardly communicating except by sea, produced the Malay synthesis, the result of the superimposition of numerous cultural layers of external origin, crowned by the islamization which the merchant colonies gradually spread among the rulers and which seems the normal product of such a situation. Its expansion into the interior thereafter followed the stages of the progress of the principalities and peoples of the littoral. It was resisted only by the backward and isolated groups in the interior of the large islands—the Batak country in Sumatra and the Dayak country in Borneo. Meanwhile the Hindus took refuge in islands like Bali and gathered together beyond the open sea which acted as a frontier east of Java. The same pattern could not be reproduced in Madagascar, although the north was subject to a very strong influx of Muslim culture, since the political centre of gravity remained fixed in the highlands of the interior. Finally, the islamization of Bengal, exceptional in size and continental sweep, resulted from the coincidence of the presence at the same time of proselyte Muslim merchants and a floating population of outcastes, only loosely attached to Hinduism, who from the middle of the first Christian millennium had gradually settled in the immense forest of the delta of Bengal which the Aryan shepherds had long shunned. Success was rapid in this pioneer fringe, throughout which the habitations were scattered, the markets being the only centres of social flux.

THE HUMAN LANDSCAPE OF ISLAM

Town and country

Muslim cities. The most distinctive feature of the Muslim countries is the appearance of their cities. The place of these towns in the landscape of these Muslim lands is the more important in that the urban ideal of the religion led to the proliferation of urban foundations. Although these countries knew no industrial revolution until very recent times, although the bedouinization of the countryside rendered the bases of regional life very precarious throughout enormous areas, the towns multiplied. Sometimes entrepôt trade and the intermediary function played by these countries in great international commerce, sometimes the organization of caravans on the borders of the arid zone, furnished them with economic support. On occasion the Islamic ideal itself demanded their establishment. So cantonments of the new conquerors, developed at an early date facing the pre-Islamic cities (as Fusṭāṭ, adjoining the later Cairo, faces pre-Islamic Bābilyūn), like an expression of the Muslim personality. So, too, the *ribāṭ* (a kind of fortified convent for soldiers of the Holy War) was scattered in particular all along the sea-frontiers of the eastern and western shores of the Maghrib, and gave rise to many cities. In addition to these, the rulers founded towns which increased in number, both through the instability of the dynasties and, perhaps, through the incompatibility of court life with the austere ideal of the life of a Muslim town-dweller, and, hence, the wish to separate the prince and his courtiers from the mass of the people.

These towns certainly offer a very singular aspect. European towns were early organized in authoritarian fashion by watchful corporations; Indian towns have a structure designed for the juxtaposition of the castes; Chinese towns were carefully planned by the government. But traditional Muslim cities are marked by an apparently disorderly layout, a tangle of blocks hardly ventilated by a labyrinth of winding lanes and dark alleys, low houses, stretching into the distance between closed courtyards with high walls, and the vivacity of a narrowly circumscribed bazaar contrasting with the silence of the residential quarters.

Nevertheless, this apparently confused picture is not lacking in overall plan. The basic elements of its organization are well defined.

The various quarters are disposed concentrically in an ordered arrangement. The central position of the main mosque stems from the primacy of the religious functions of the city. In its immediate neighbourhood stands the commercial quarter, the bazaar; normally this contains the public baths, which Islam finally adopted in view of their usefulness for the major ablutions, in spite of their associations with debauchery. The official quarter with the public buildings lies not far from this central kernel; it is not normal for it to be at the heart of this area, but on its edge, prepared for defence against popular disturbances. The Jewish quarter is often established in the immediate vicinity, under the shadow of the mighty, for protection against the wrath of mobs. Round these public quarters in the centre come the residential districts; then semi-rural areas, still town-like in appearance but inhabited by cultivators, or often sheltering newcomers in improvised dwellings, shacks or straw huts. The whole is enclosed in a grim cincture of graveyards. This outer border is vast, since the family tomb is unknown in Muslim lands; it offers a striking contrast with the churchyards of medieval Christendom.

As well as this regular concentric arrangement, there is also a strict organization of the various elements of trade and craft, and of the residential quarters. The sellers of different goods are rigidly ranked, separated topographically and usually grouped in guilds, following an order which places the noblest of them nearest to the main mosque: first, the candle, incense and perfume merchants, then the booksellers and bookbinders, followed closely by the clothsellers grouped in the *qayṣariyya*, then the tailors, carpet and blanket merchants, jewellers and leather-workers. The purveyors of food, the workers in wood and metal, the blacksmiths and the potters, are set farther away, even at the city gates, where there are usually also to be found the basket-workers and saddlers, who sell mainly to the peasants and the caravans. In the residential quarters, segregation of the different ethnic and religious groups is observed. These are everywhere split up into enclosed units, built up round an axial street which is closed at each end by great gates, from which blind alleys run on each side. The city of the Levant, where the mosaic of cultures and confessions reaches its greatest complexity, has deserved its description as a conglomeration of separate cities, each living under the spectre of massacre. The Muslim town seems cruelly lacking in unity, an assemblage of disparate elements set side by side without any real links.

However, this thoroughly system-ridden framework disappears often enough at first encounter into an inextricable disorder, in which it is extremely difficult to find one's way. Above all in the residential districts the streets are always very tortuous and narrow. Everywhere there are multitudinous projections from the houses, overhangs, *mashrabiyyas*; covered lanes and bridges over the street proliferate; and in many places the roof-tops of opposite houses touch each other. Squares and unappropriated open spaces are correspondingly rare. All this does nothing to assist circulation; Islam has never designed the street for vehicles, but only at most for pack-animals; even they pass each other at times with difficulty. This diminution of the space for public traffic contrasts with the importance of the space devoted to family life. The houses, which are generally low, frequently contain interior courtyards or patios on which life centres. The anarchic maze of streets is left behind, and order and unity are found within the house.

This urban landscape is easily understood in the light of the fundamental ideals of Muslim life. The anarchy in the detailed plan is never the result of design. The Muslim towns generally had an organized plan when they were founded, often of chess-board pattern more or less under the influence of Hellenistic designs, sometimes radial-concentric. But usually this initial plan was quickly obliterated. The Muslim town, in fact, bears the marks of an almost total absence of municipal organization. Whereas the Classical city, like the medieval Western town, is characterized by a lively feeling of solidarity and notable municipal pride, and by various forms of close understanding and co-operation, the Muslim town offers nothing of the kind. It enjoys no exceptional privileges, no particular rights. The price of the supremacy of religious concepts in social organization is the absence of any political interest in the community. Nothing tempers the absolutism of the ruler. The Muslim town boasts no municipal official or magistrate, except the *muḥtasib*, who has hardly any responsibility but the oversight and policing of the markets. In consequence, the communal spaces are devoured rapidly and completely by individual encroachment. Squatters' rights are quickly effective in questions of occupation of the public highway and there is great tolerance in this respect. This point was already well-observed by a seventeenth-century French traveller: 'There is not a single fine street in Cairo, but a mass of little ones turning hither and thither, which clearly demonstrates that all the houses were built without design, each one choosing all those places which pleased him to build on, without considering whether he stop up a street or no.'[1] In the case of ancient towns converted to Islam, the deterioration of the plan had perhaps already begun before the Muslim conquest—in the Byzantine era at Aleppo and Damascus. In Anatolia, it was certainly facilitated by the occurrence of a first period of decadence of urban life, linked with the nomadic conquest, the population dwindling and buildings being abandoned, to be followed by a new disorderly expansion which ignored the previous alignments. Whether their evolution was thus produced in one or two periods, the Muslim towns never experienced the regular reorganizations which constantly remodel Western towns and direct their development.

The rigid segregation by districts, and the cloistered family life, are expressions of the same principle. The unity of the city is replaced by the cohesion of the district or the group, while the aim is to keep the family away from contamination and dispersal, and to keep the authorities away from private life. Even the house itself bears the signs of a similar frame of mind. The avoidance of many-storeyed houses denotes a rejection of luxury and ostentation, since the raising-up of high dwellings seemed a symbol of pride and arrogance. The architecture is further marked by the fragility of its materials, the preponderance of mud and wood, a sign of individualism and the absence of any materialistic group-feeling, while the durable stone house was linked with Mediterranean city-life, and the prospect of centuries before it. At Istanbul, the little wooden houses of the Turks, scattered at random, quickly took the place of the solid brick constructions of the Byzantines, and effaced the network of main roads of the city. The persistence of the pre-Islamic house-plan with a central court, derived from the Greek peristyle house, was furthered in a remarkable way by this simultaneous proscription of tall houses, and use of fragile materials unsuitable for multistoreyed buildings.

This almost complete absence of any real integration of the diverse elements of city life seems to have had important consequences. The urban ideal of Islam created no forms, no urban structure; its role in the urban landscape was only conservative and negative: conservative in that it preserved the fundamental organs of town life in the same shape which they had received in Classical times, the *sūqs* deriving from the colonnaded avenue, the *qayṣariyya* and the caravanserai from the basilica, the *ḥammām* from the baths, the bazaar from ancient Near Eastern prac-

[1] Thévenot, *Relation d'un voyage fait au Levant* (Paris, 1664), 239.

tices which were no more invented by Islam than segregation into districts; negative in that it replaced the solidarity of a collective community with an anomalous disorganized heap of disparate quarters and elements. Seen on a world scale, it resulted in the persistence over a large area of an outworn pattern of urban life. By a really very remarkable paradox, this religion endowed with the ideal of urban life produced the very negation of urban order.

The traditional exceptions to this general rule were very rare. Some schismatic towns, like the cities of the Kharijites of the Mzab, built with defence needs in mind, pushed out to the edge their economic centre, the market, which had to be accessible to the caravans and the people from outside. The pilgrim towns of Arabia, Jedda and Mecca, are towns without blind alleys, cut everywhere by right-angled crossroads, designed in accordance with the need for space in which large crowds could move about, and dominated by great edifices divided into numerous tiny lodgings and built to function as hostels. Elsewhere serious changes had to await European intervention, by colonization or progressive Westernization.

The traditional urban landscape has been affected by this, but has not in general by any means disappeared. The first signs of evolution hardly appear before the end of the eighteenth and the beginning of the nineteenth century, the main impulse deriving from Muḥammad ʻAlī in Egypt, from the Tanẓīmāt in Turkey, from French colonization in North Africa and, in Persia, delayed until about 1930 under the rule of Riżā Shāh. The phases are well marked. First, the additions to the buildings are attacked, the projections and overhangs of every kind are removed and efforts are made to ease traffic in the old streets by every means possible. Very soon great roads have to be cut through, especially when inter-urban road-traffic develops and demands a way across the built-up areas. This phase was particularly spectacular in Persia, where Riżā Shāh cut open a gigantic chessboard in Tehran, for instance, relegating its traditional aspect to the little side-streets. The third stage is the opening up of the commercial quarters and laying bare the public monuments, frequently concealed until then beneath an undergrowth of private houses. The last stage is that of a change in the style of dwellings, with the very slow modification of the old residential districts. Whereas the first efforts to regularize the pattern are not often characterized by europeanization of the appearance of the city, since the buildings remain traditional in style, there gradually appear thereafter Western-type constructions of greater height. This transformation often remains incomplete and frequently buildings differing greatly in appearance and height stand side by side, and offer a ragged and unfinished impression. The aspect of these towns seems to be caught in the middle of rebuilding operations, paradoxically more like American town-centres, which are quickly rebuilt, than the more uniform and stable appearance of the centre of European cities.

These changes have not been distributed at all equally. Regional types can be distinguished. Algeria is marked by radical alterations, since the European occupation was originally considered to be precarious, and the colonizers establishing themselves in already existing towns thereupon rebuilt them from foundation to roof-tree. Similarly, in the Balkans, the Christian reoccupation came at exactly the same point in time as the beginning of a new era in transport. The most extreme case was Sofia, where the Ottoman town, of 30,000 inhabitants in 1878, was practically razed to the ground. But this is characteristic also of the Pontic regions of Anatolia, and of Istanbul, where the widespread wooden houses constituted excellent fuel for repeated and destructive fires, and equal opportunity for extensive clearances. Thus the areas of Istanbul which were burnt down at the end of the nineteenth and the beginning of the twentieth centuries were rebuilt in a modern style which contrasts strongly with the ancient islands still surviving in the quarters which were spared. On the other hand, Tunisia and Morocco are marked by more modest changes, since there the colonists established themselves beside the older cities and treated them with respect; the same is true almost everywhere in the Arab Near East and in Persia. Beyond the great avenues, the original city centres were generally spared and the introduction of modernity is primarily marked by the development of new towns beside the old. The former centres are gradually abandoned by the middle classes for the newer districts and fall into rapid social devaluation, taking on a proletarian character which radically transforms the social balance of the city. The ethnic and cultural divisions of former days favoured a mingling of the classes and hence a certain harmony in social relations; the new segregation is based on wealth. The previous concentric structure is replaced by bilateral contrasts, as in Tehran, where there is a growing opposition between the comfortable town in the north, near the foot of the mountain, with fresh air and pure water, and the town of the poor which stretches to the south in the dust of the desert. So now principles of internal differentiation make themselves felt in these Muslim cities, while their appearance is remarkably altered. Nevertheless, the heritage of the traditional plan is visible everywhere to a greater or lesser degree.

The rural landscape of Islam. It is much more difficult in the Muslim countryside to distinguish what comes from man and what from nature. The impact of the religion was more limited here.

The dietary regulations of Islam are hardly responsible for more than details. The prohibition of alcoholic beverages, particularly wine, resulted in a displacement of the centre of gravity of wine production from the eastern Mediterranean to the north-western coast. In the Muslim countries the vine, grown primarily for its grapes, became garden rather than field produce; it left the plains, where it had been grown as a dry monoculture, for the hill regions where it persisted, more or less integrated into Mediterranean polyculture. There are rare exceptions, like the Turkish vineyards which were re-established towards the end of the Ottoman period, mainly in Christian villages, under the influence of the Administration of the Public Debt; the Turkish government inherited these at the time of the exchange of populations after the Greco-Turkish War of 1922. The prohibition of pork had more important geographical consequences. It led to the grazing of sheep and goats in the wooded mountains, and certainly accelerated deforestation, which was catastrophic in these arid and semi-arid countries. This factor in the turning of the Muslim countries into deserts should not be underestimated, as may be shown by the significant contrasts in relative areas under timber in the Muslim and Christian sectors on the Balkan frontiers of Islam in Albania. But, equally, its influence should not be exaggerated. The main period of deforestation in the greater part of the Mediterranean and Near Eastern region must considerably antedate Islam, and goes back primarily to the Neolithic or Classical periods of peasant expansion and demographic pressure. In many cases bedouinization, in bringing about a regression of sedentary life, probably encouraged some return to natural vegetation rather than the reverse.

Islam affected the condition of agriculture most through its landowning structure and laws of real property. The basic principles of these are the state ownership and inalienability of land and the system of pious foundations, *waqf* or *ḥubus*. The origins of this system do not go back to the Prophet, who gave land to his warriors, but traditionally to ʿUmar, who reverted to the old principle of collective tribal property under the form of appropriation to the central authority—the original meaning of the word *waqf* before it took on that of mortmain or religious trust. Although the attitude of the various schools of jurisprudence differs on the status of land acquired by conquest, and the Hanafite in particular permits the *imām* to choose between state ownership and distribution, the land-system in force throughout the Ottoman empire was in fact founded on almost universal state ownership. As in the land policy of 'Umar, Muslim ideas combined with pre-Islamic traditions—in this case the old traditions of tribal ownership of the Turks of Central Asia. In the last analysis the Muslim preference that land should be owned impersonally is also due to the spread of the religion by nomadic peoples.

The consequences of this were important. The system of state ownership was accompanied by the organization of the land into *iqṭā'*, concessions granted to soldier-officials in return for military service. The peculiarity of the *iqṭā'* is that the grant is practically detached from the land, which owes no duty in service or labour, but merely a fixed payment determined by the central authority. Thus the possessor has no real interest in the improvement of the working of the soil; the Oriental system of lordship displays hardly any of those personal bonds which constitute the better feature of the Western feudal system, the lord's interest in his vassal, and use of him as a worker and not simply as a payer of taxes. On the other hand, the system of inheritance does not recognize primogeniture, another guarantee against state absolutism. Joint possession by the heirs is the customary usage, frequently pushed to extremes. Although the Muslim law of inheritance therefore is not favourable to the establishment of personal latifundia, its combination with a system of lordship definitely separated from the soil, and with the joint possession of large estates by families, ends in encouraging absentee landlordism. The state ownership of the land, in the form in which the Ottoman Turks pushed it to its most extreme limits, proved disastrous for the shape of rural society, since the progressive influence of great estates run directly by their owners was missing. In the last phase, as the absolute Ottoman system was declining, the developments towards a pattern of great estates, fully appropriated to their owners, of the *chiftlik* type, were certainly of some value, but they came too late, and in a situation of generalized economic disorder which did not favour real progress. The pattern of land-tenure inherited from this system, in which the rights of individuals are always more or less open to question, appears moreover to be everywhere almost impossible to disentangle. In the middle of the nineteenth century, Michaud wrote in his *Correspondance d'Orient*: 'Throughout Turkey the ownership of land is an unknown concept... The village population live in the countryside they till without knowing much about whom the soil that nourishes them belongs to.' In contrast with urban property, ownership of rural land seems burdened with a basic doubt. There is a complete contrast with Western ideas here. While in the West the ploughed field is the image of unfettered property, absolute, virtually eternal, fixed to the soil by demarcation, held down by cadastral survey; in the East, rural land never reaches full individual ownership. The anarchy of the land-system leads inevitably to arbitrary procedures. The true status of a piece of land counts for less than the status of its owner. The imprecise nature of the legal system introduces into the land-market a personal element which has an essential part to play in the development of the system of land ownership.

This is based above all on the large, or even very large, estates which are normally the vast majority (or were so at least before the modern attempts of agrarian reform, still frequently hesitant); this is as much the case in the Levant as in Persia, in eastern Anatolia as in north-western India. It is the result of the joint influence of two factors: the political and social primacy of the cities, and the economic primacy of income from land. The latter is due on the one hand to the lack of industrialization and of opportunities for substantial investment in handicrafts, and on the other to the Qur'anic prohibition of usury, which prevented the establishment of a legal system of return on liquid capital, and meant that it played a restricted part in economic life, so that the acquisition of land was the only normal use for capital. The town-dwellers continually sought to buy up rural properties. They had two principal means of action to hand. The first, in the immediate neighbourhood of the cities, in rich and properly policed areas, was usury, since the religious ban on lending at interest was in fact easily evaded by a notional increase in the sum advanced, so that it had little effect except to render more burdensome the practice it was designed to remove. Secondly, there was the relationship of client and protector in the more distant plains, merging into the great estates of the nomad aristocracy, or of the various powers set up in the anarchic social structure of the mountain ranges; such estates always appeared as a zone of legally defined territorial influence, founded on more or less disguised violence.

The system of exploitation is dominated entirely by its radical dissociation from the principal proprietor. The agrarian system of the Near Eastern countryside has been described with apt brevity: 'The cultivator does not own and the owner does not cultivate.'[1] Here again the basic reasons are to be found in that contempt for land and that flight from agricultural matters characteristic of Islam. The plough brings dishonour. It is a social, almost a moral, victory to free oneself from it. This collective economic renunciation by persons of standing results almost everywhere in the form of exploitation known as share-cropping (*métayage*), by which the farmer pays rent in kind, the owner furnishing stock and seed, which corresponds perfectly to the climate of social subordination. The condemnation in principle which certain *Ḥadīths* bring to bear on contracts for indirect exploitation was quickly evaded and the severity of the '*ulamā*' was most often concentrated on tenant-farming at a fixed rent, which they regarded as too hazardous a contract for the tenant, yet which in the West has been an undeniable factor in capital formation and peasant progress.

Altogether this is a heavy curse weighing on the Muslim lands. In this depressing picture of rural society condemned to mediocrity and sclerosis, only rare sections are lit by a somewhat brighter light. The areas of careful agriculture are really limited in general to the immediate surroundings of the towns, in the suburban zone of gardens and orchards, where property is fragmented and exploitation is intensified in the hands of the working people of the towns. It is there, particularly in the Spanish *huertas*, that are to be found the most positive contributions from Islam to the cultivation of the soil: the exotic trees and plants which it conveyed and introduced into the interior of the Muslim world by means of its far-flung commercial relations; and the irrigation techniques which it perfected, identifying itself with, and spreading, the knowledge of ancient Near Eastern techniques much older than itself. Similarly on its African frontier, Islam has been able at times to appear productive of agricultural progress, in view of the relatively fixed way of life which it recommends instead of the shifting cultivation of burnt clearings typical of the inter-tropical zone; and in view of the influence of agrarian sects like the Murids of Senegal whose collective discipline has worked wonders and has been responsible for great developments, notably in ground-nut growing. But this attraction to the soil is quite exceptional, and specific only to Negro Islam; this preference for agriculture has

[1] Weulersse, *Paysans de Syrie et du Proche-Orient* (Paris, 1946), 121.

only been able to develop to any extent away from orthodox influences.

State and region

Political forms. The very structure of the political forms arises from the economic and moral pre-eminence of the cities which we have already described. The urban state is typical. A Muslim state is first of all a dynasty and a capital, a city where the ruler can have the Friday prayers said on his behalf at the main mosque. Around this capital the authority of his rule extends for a varying distance, normally without interruption, until finally it becomes more and more vague and nominal. Beyond the plain, kept in hand and regularly policed, which serves as a victualling base for the city and the army, one gradually enters the areas of peasant dissidence, especially when control of the country is hampered by hills and mountains. The contrast is perhaps nowhere more striking than in pre-colonial Morocco. In opposition to *bled el-makhzen*, submissive to governmental authority, there stands *bled el-siba* 'the land of insolence', which consists essentially of the Berber mountains. A fragile balance, continually reset, is established between the central power and more or less autonomous tribes. The most extreme case is that of city states by the sea isolated in the middle of an immense tribal hinterland, where their influence is very weak and can only be exercised by full-scale expeditions, such as those which the deys of Algiers mounted annually with their Janissaries to raise taxes in the interior, with the more or less interested complicity of the *Makhzan* tribes. There is nothing comparable here with the Western state which long ago seemed founded, in essence, on territorial possessions, which might often, like those of the House of Austria, be fragmented and discontinuous, but were strictly defined.

A further type of Muslim state should, however, also be noted. Frequently the nomads constituted the main spearhead of advance, and it is here that the ascendancy of a number of dynasties originated, both in early and later times. From the Almoravids of Morocco to the Turkish dynasties of the Near East, 'the land of insolence' produced rulers as frequently as did palace revolutions. The rhythm of Moroccan history is dominated by dynasties, rising in the south, if not in the desert itself, who from time to time come and lay their hands on the rich *Makhzan* plains of the region of Fez. Before the Pahlavī dynasty of the twentieth century, practically all the Persian dynasties were also furnished by Turkish-speaking nomads. These nomad powers even laid the first foundations of certain states, not satisfied with conquering prey already prepared for them. The dynasty which, from the end of the eighteenth century onwards, gradually established the Afghan state, represented the nomadic tribes of Durrānī and Ghilzāy, which achieved the unification of the country for their own benefit, in spite of its being based on mountains mainly inhabited by peasants. Even when the new controlling personalities appear to come from an urban setting, from among scholars or theologians, they can frequently only consolidate their success by reliance on new groupings of nomads. Thus the Safavids in Persia were only able to establish themselves because of the progress of Shīʿī propaganda among the Turcoman tribes of Āẕarbāyjān, although they actually emerged from the urban setting of Ardabīl; and the victory of the Wahhābīs over the urban dynasties of the Ḥijāz can only be explained by the support they received from the nomads.

These nomadic states, more than others, reflect transitory situations. Once raised to the throne, the nomad ruler becomes urbanized, takes up permanent residence in the city, and gradually takes on the mentality of the townspeople who surround him. This change takes place by degrees however and may take a long time in some cases, while in others it occurs quite rapidly. Throughout the nineteenth century the Qājār shahs, true descendants of the great Turkish tribe of that name who wandered in the north, preferred to spend the summer in tents enjoying the fresh air of the Elburz mountains in camps, moving from hunting-ground to hunting-ground, and their ministers had to follow them. Nevertheless, the problems and the methods of political control do not differ fundamentally so much from those common to the states specifically based on cities. The nomad ruler has as much difficulty as the urban prince in extending his influence over the tribes, apart from the actual tribe from which he sprang. And he is subject to the constant threat of intervention by hostile tribes or tribal confederations. The decisive role which the Bakhtiyārīs played in the constitutional crisis of 1907 is well known, when these traditional enemies of the Qājārs marched on Tehran. Nevertheless there is force in the view that the state founded on nomadic power often has a greater facility and greater knack of controlling the 'land of insolence.' It can deploy its supporters more easily than a mercenary army, reluctant to go far from the city gates.

Though the urban state may better fulfil the Muslim ideal, the nomadic state is therefore probably more efficient in the administration of an empire of substantial size. The basic problem in the present-day political life of many Muslim states remains therefore the establishment of effective control and a modern type of administration in many places in their territory. Very often it was not till the colonial period that the 'lands of insolence' were definitely brought under the aegis of the central power. Here the methods of the British and the French colonizers differed profoundly, both in spirit and in manner. The French preferred subjugation, aiming at complete obedience, followed by direct administration; while the British set up military boundaries and then reduced their effective intervention to the minimum by administering indirectly through the medium of the chieftains; but the results of both methods were much the same as far as apparent pacification is concerned. The states which escaped colonization have frequently had to wait until very recent years to attain the same ends, as for instance Persia, in the case of the great Qāshqā'ī confederation in the Zagros mountains. The process of unification has proved relatively easier in those states where urban civilization has long been preponderant, as in Egypt, or Tunisia; it has offered rather more problems for states which, while equally well policed, contain large schismatic or mountain-dwelling minorities and important fringes, like Syria struggling with the 'Alawite problem, or Iraq with the Kurds; for the 'empires', from Afghanistan and Persia to Morocco, it has proved particularly arduous.

Principles of regional organization. The dynamic of regional evolution may be analysed in the light of this political situation. The traditional regional structure of Islam was founded on discontinuity, mainly after the bedouinization which occurred in medieval times. Restricted centres, where a satisfying rural life had been preserved, were separated by immense areas devoted to wandering, decay, and rapine. This preponderance of areas unnaturally turned into deserts prevented the fabrication of those local interconnexions which build up the complex web of regional units, and offer the only basis for any attempt to exploit differing environments on a rational basis. The only kind of regional organization was the urban district, the zone in which a town exercised influence and control over the surrounding countryside, finding its political expression in the urban state. This situation was the natural product of an arid or semi-arid geographical setting, where the intrinsic weakness of rural life, outside the irrigated areas under intensive cultivation, permitted the development of such a state of affairs. It offers a ready explanation for the difficulties found in converting the countryside to Islam beyond the limited range of the cities' influence. The coastal strips converted by the merchants, in a different natural and political setting, were no exception to the rule when set against a hostile hinterland. The great deltaic rice-growing plains, like Bengal or the Javanese plains in monsoon Asia, or like the Nile Delta, belong to the same category. Human organization was only established effectively in a framework of homogeneous natural conditions, though in these cases on a much more considerable scale. The Muslim lands hardly ever produced any regional unity based on the association of areas with complementary economies, such as mountain and plain. It is noteworthy that the sites chosen for towns in Muslim countries are normally linked with the crossroads of long-distance international, or intercontinental routes, or with decisive physical resources at the centre of homogeneous natural units. The towns form the capitals of little isolated basins, or autonomous plains, or oases associated with exceptional water supplies, like Damascus or Fez. The little market-town which acts as a point of contact between differing natural units, along an axis between a mountain and the plain for example, which is so common in Western Europe, is practically unknown in Islam. The rarity of names for districts, which are the most tangible expression of intimacy and intensity in the relationship between men and the land, underlines the inadequacy of regional life in Islam. There used to be a very large number of district-names in Persia, but most of them disappeared from popular speech at the time of the medieval bedouinization.

The diminution of these gaps between centres of intensive occupation is a prerequisite of the progressive development of organized and centralized states. Demographic pressure, which has increased so sharply in contemporary times, since the end of the last century, has been a major influence in this direction by necessitating the utilization of new land. The significant feature of recent developments has therefore been the steady expansion of the ancient centres, and the colonization, or rather the recolonization of the intervening areas. It is the success of this vast movement to conquer new ground which is a precondition of achieving regional balance and satisfying national organization, and which today has become general. Central and eastern Tunisia, where after the Hilālī invasions sedentary life had become confined to the narrow strip of the Sahel—a chain of large villages strung along the coast among their olive groves—has witnessed an astonishing resumption of human occupation of the neighbouring low-lying steppe since the end of the nineteenth century. On the northern border of the Syrian desert, at the foot of the Taurus mountains, in the Jazīra, a cultivable area reserved since the Middle Ages as a kind of winter quarters for the nomads who spent the summer in the highlands, considerable cereal production has been developed from the time of the French mandate onwards. The ʿAlawites, leaving their mountains, are in process of exploiting the Maʿmūra steppe, east of Ḥimṣ and Ḥamāh and south of Aleppo. And in the Mesopotamian plains, where cultivation was confined until recently to narrow irrigated borders beside the rivers, the cultivated area has more than doubled since the middle of the nineteenth century. Everywhere the peasant has become a pioneer.

The human material for this spatial expansion has certainly been supplied to a great extent by the constant demographic surplus of the older centres of population. But a considerable part derives from the settlement of nomads. Their survival in any appreciable numbers is rendered more and more precarious through the progressive colonization of the marginal areas which still offer opportunities for cultivation; this deprives them of their most attractive grazing grounds and pushes them back towards the desert. Settlement is their only recourse, permitting an incomparably higher proportion of human beings to use a given area of land. In this way the settlement of the nomads is an integral part of the process of reconquering the soil. Furthermore, it has been possible for it to figure as a primary goal in the establishment of state control and administration throughout the state territory. It is the most striking manifestation of the revenge of the settled communities against the bedouin which characterizes the present political situation. This attitude is particularly clear in a number of Near Eastern states. Article 158 of the 1950 Syrian constitution laid down the settlement of all the nomads as a fundamental aim to be achieved. Similarly, one of the essential features of Suʿūdī policy has been the settlement of the nomads, and new centres of habitation have been multiplied throughout Arabia, particularly for the *ikhwān*, the companions of the king in battle. Everywhere today the nomadic way of life is retreating rapidly. The sole exception is Afghanistan, where policy is still dominated by the recent nomadic origin of the dynasty, and by the desire to spread Afghan ways through the whole country as quickly as possible. There the state is fostering the spread of those nomads properly called Afghans over the whole of the central arc of mountains, where, if there is not a real bedouinization, the annexation of land by the nomads is making steady progress.

The result of this gigantic movement is a certain change in the economic and social structure of the Muslim countries. The original Islam of towns and nomads is more and more giving way to an Islam of peasants. The old oases are being submerged, and the nomads absorbed by expanding rural societies, swept on in an irresistible movement to conquer the soil, which must be the main activity of these countries where the pace of industrialization remains slow. This acquisition by Islam of a rural character can in itself only be beneficial, and this precisely to the extent to which it destroys the inhibitions imposed by the traditional ideal. The tragedy of the Muslim countries is that this agricultural expansion is being carried out in an unfavourable natural setting, in the marginal areas where rain-fed agriculture is always uncertain. Peasant resistance has generally been concentrated in the mountains and the irrigable districts. The margin for expansion was thus primarily situated in the sub-arid steppes, and the development of irrigated land, even when substantial, cannot follow the rhythm of demographic progress. The economy of these countries is more and more subject to the whims of the weather and the hazards of a particularly variable climate. In these circumstances soil erosion does considerable damage. Gigantic efforts in economic planning and development will be required if this spatial expansion of soil occupation is truly to bring forth stability and progress.

CHAPTER 2

THE SOURCES OF ISLAMIC CIVILIZATION

The spiritual force which suddenly arises as concrete phenomenon before our eyes in unimagined uniqueness cannot be derived from a higher principle. (LEOPOLD VON RANKE)[1]

I

That a civilization should have neatly identifiable sources is a concept of a more limited validity than recent intellectual habituation and customary techniques of scholarship would suggest. It presupposes the notion of developmental units of sufficiently consistent and individual character to be capable of isolation within, though not separable from, the stream of history, and it tends to imply, at least as a metaphor, the idea of a cultural compound resulting from the blending, amalgamation or coalescence of a number of pre-existing historic ingredients. Since obviously these ingredients can be recognized only in retrospect, that is to say, through the analysis of the unit in which they are submerged or active, a teleological outlook is apt to guide the eye of the diagnostician, who also may find it difficult to pry himself loose from the organicism inherent in the image whose persuasiveness only too readily obscures its purely nominalist function as a principle of order.

The concept of sources becomes meaningless in a context in which cultures or civilizations are perceived as essentially changeless, belonging to the world of ideas and withdrawn from historical process which affects or moulds only their surface manifestations. When 'Islamic culture and civilization' are seen to be 'as old as the human race itself', and 'Islamic culture' is defined as 'an interpretation of the will of God as conveyed to humanity through the agency of the prophets starting with Adam and culminating in Muḥammad', it is taken out of history, to which it is not really restored by the statement that 'With Prophet Muḥammad, however, Islamic culture got an extraordinary impetus, attaining to the zenith of its grandeur.'[2]

[1] *Politisches Gespräch* (1836), *Sämmtliche Werke* (Leipzig, 1865–90), 49–50, 325; tr. Th. H. Von Laue, *Leopold Ranke: the formative years* (Princeton, 1950) as *A dialogue on politics* (pp. 152–80), 165.

[2] Abdur Rauf, *Renaissance of Islamic culture and civilization in Pakistan* (Lahore, 1964). Unpublished typescript, 1, 2.

The concept becomes equally devoid of meaning when a civilization is seen if not as all-embracing at least as an absolute without reference to specific historical situations—the component particulars to receive their validation and value (be it positive or negative) from a global verdict of acceptance or rejection. In our period of historicist and post-historicist thinking, this outlook has become rather rare, and it is for this reason that a poem quoted in 1931 as sung by the school children of Baghdād deserves partial mention.

Children of Islam, the world is short of well directed people...Show it your religion for it to follow, that religion of reason and conscience, self-evident as the laws of nature....For us Heaven has lowered itself on to earth when, with the Qur'ān, it has sent down the virtues of the sublime man, star of the earth, Muḥammad, even as every generous aspiration.[1]

Within such an ahistoric perception of cultural environment that implies total acception or rejection, almost like that of the physical reality into which man finds himself thrown, the question of sources, if posed at all, enters consciousness as part either of the sustaining doctrine or of an argument to glorify or deprecate. Thus earliest Islam was rendered aware of preceding revelations and the continuity of God's plan for mankind culminating in the mission of Muḥammad, and soon became alive, owing to circumstances not necessarily connected with the Qur'anic message, to the possibility, even the need, to use the allegation of foreign origin as a tool in its effort at consolidation, be it to substantiate, welcome or to eliminate incongruous patterns of thought and behaviour. Here the 'other' serves but as a means to identify or justify the self and receives its significance solely from its usefulness for self-assertion.

To the historian, whether he arise from within or without that civilization become sure of itself, the temptation is ever-present to unravel results as though they were the inevitable effect of an interplay of vectors, and to reconstruct the development as the successful or miscarried outcome of planning made respectable by the positing of an inner logic which, it is overlooked, is inescapable only in retrospect. There are no doubt intellectual and emotional premisses, as it were, with which the Arabs left the peninsula and which affected their ability to respond to their new environments, and these environments on their

[1] A. Memmi, *La Poésie algérienne de 1830 à nos jours* (Paris, 1963), 48; tr. from *al-Balāgh* and *ash-Shihāb* (Algeria), where the poem is recommended as being recited by *les écoliers de Baghdād*.

part were limited in the possibilities and dangers to which they exposed the conquerors. But the interaction of Arab and non-Arab, Muslim and non-Muslim, never was a constant, but oscillated without cease as new concerns unveiled neglected factors that thus turned into 'sources' and newly encountered circumstances disclosed hitherto dormant concerns which again would be activated into 'sources'.

The establishment of Arab Islam in the alien world from Spain to the Oxus marks one of those periods in history when man loses his contact with his ancestors, and when the psychological continuity appears almost, even totally, broken. The new civilization, which represents the means and the goal of recovering lost bearings, creates a common memory constituted by a selection of shared *memorabilia*, largely historical events and judgments on the one hand, human and doctrinal assumptions on the other. That these *memorabilia* were, for the most part, situated in an Arab milieu was to give the new civilization an Arab cachet. There is incessant interaction between the subjective impulses of individual and society, and the objective factors of the cosmic and the social environments. It is certainly true that the Arabs adopted in large measure the civilizations of the conquered, but the formative process of Islamic civilization is to be understood adequately only when it is realized that this civilization is merely the 'dominant average' of many subcultures, and more particularly that associated with the ruling and authoritatively literate groups. More important still, this process may be seen as the clustering about a mobile magnetic centre of particles, large or small, which by design, by accident or by their proper motion, entered its field. Thus the task of the cultural historian becomes the reconciliation of the concept of sources, fundamentally static, with genetic analysis; in other words, of structure with process.

The nature of the power nucleus around which the civilization of Islam was to precipitate is perhaps most graphically described when it is contrasted with comparable power centres that had formed intermittently, not too long before the emergence of the Muslims from the peninsula, on West Roman soil over a period of some three hundred years. The Germanic tribes or agglomerations of tribes which had taken over control in various forms endeavoured without exception to integrate with the *imperium Romanum*. Not only did they allow Roman administration to continue—the Arabs, too, had no thought of dismantling the administrative cadres and only began to modify them in any serious sense more than a generation after the conquest. But the

Germanic nations accepted Christianity as soon as the empire had become *imperium Christianum*, and this acceptance of a new faith, coupled as it was with a network of attitudes and *mores*, was only one aspect of a general readiness to accept the imperial culture. Like the Arabs after them they were but a minority precariously perched on a complex alien substructure, and again like the Arabs, they endeavoured to keep aloof from their subjects, curtailing intermarriage, monopolizing to a large extent military service and remaining content to perpetuate their identity as the exploiting and policy-making stratum. But in sharp contrast to their Germanic predecessors in the West the Arabs had no inclination to exchange their language, however incomplete in terms of their new tasks, for that of the vanquished, and even less did they think of yielding their faith.

The Prophet had imbued them with the certainty of spiritual superiority; victory added the certainty of racial superiority. The depreciation of the intellectual and material achievements of the conquered may have been less pervasive than complacent anecdotes would suggest. In fact, the realization of the existential and practical possibilities that rulership added to the outreach of a Muslim's life occurred early and widely. Yet there never was felt the temptation to yield the Arab, let alone the Muslim identity and to aspire to leadership, in the mode traditional in the Eastern Empire, as the *élite* of a Christian state of Greek tongue. Islam had made the converted Arabs the centre of a universal world-view and hence, when the time came, the centre of a universal state. In contrast to the Germanic peoples who were in need of legitimation and thus of continuing what they displaced, the Muslim Arab had his centre of gravity within himself. His people were chosen and rule belonged as of right to the elect.

Neither his faith nor the law by which he lived needed to be imposed on the subjects. Rather did he feel a certain reluctance to admit the non-Arab to a full share in heaven and earth. A small caste of saved warriors and their kin, possessors of the last word God was to address to humankind and cultivating a spiritual arrogance which, together with their power, fascinated rather than repelled the exploited, the early Muslims had eliminated the hegemony of the christianized world-view of the ancient universe before they had ever realized its implications, not to say its existence. The cutting certainty of the Iraqi student song of 1931 with its artless assertion 'We are the pure, the glorious, the *élite*. Everything good in this world goes back to us alone' could anachronistically be transferred to the sense of collective superiority that propelled the society of the early caliphate.

This interplay of analogy and contrast can be followed further. History was vindicating Islam. In the most literal manner, truth was conquering. Many of the conquered felt relieved from heterodox, alien pressures. Victory and its stabilization in political control sealed for good and all the coalescence of the religious and the political community as it had been forecast by the Prophet's own conceptions and arrangements. The Arab Muslims were an *umma*, unified body, a *jamā'a*, community, and by modern criteria of linguistic and racial identity, they were clearly a nation. Eusebius, too, in the intoxication of the Christian victory under Constantine, saw the Christians as a nation, albeit of transcendental origin. The illusion was cherished in the fourth century that Christianity would bring steady material advance. It took the object lesson of the falling apart of the Western empire to disabuse the enthusiasts of the confusion between a nation and a religious community, and an Augustine to separate, in Western Christian minds, the power of Rome from the growth of Christianity. Islam was spared the political disappointment at the outset only to pay in heartbreak a thousand years later.

Unlike the wandering Germanic peoples, the Muslims had a geographically fixed political centre. Damascus controlled, at least nominally, expansion and rule. Yet for a long time to come there was, strictly speaking, no Muslim state. Where the Frankish king was *rex Francorum* and his territory *regnum Francorum*, the Muslim ruler was *amīr al-mu'minīn* and his territory actually lacked a designation until the lawyers came up with the term of *dār al-Islām*—a concept depending for its meaning on the complementary *dār al-ḥarb*—the lands under and beyond Muslim control. Some one hundred and fifty years after the conquests the great legist and adviser of Hārūn al-Rashīd, Abū Yūsuf (d. 182/798) discusses at length the concept and the role of the ruler without having a word to say of the state.[1] But where in the Germanic states the law of the ruling population was in competition with the more fully developed Roman codes, the revealed character of the fundamentals of Muslim law (and the naïve intransigence of the Muslims) constituted it the *Reichsrecht* that overarched the laws of the subject peoples even as the ruling community overarched those peoples themselves.

The most important analogy, however, lies in the fact that the

[1] Abū Yūsuf Ya'qūb, *Kitāb al-kharāj* (Cairo, 1352), 5–6, 8, 10, 19; tr. E. Fagnan as *Le livre de l'impôt foncier* (Paris, 1921), 5–6, 11, 14, 19–20.

Classical culture which the Germanic intruders of the fifth or sixth, and the Arabs of the seventh and eighth, centuries are supposed to have combated, dislodged or destroyed, had ceased fully to exist before the first invader appeared. Element after element had, as it were, dropped out, sooner perhaps in the West, and neither the intellectual nor the social structure was any more sufficiently rich and compact to offer that resistance or appeal which we, inured to the picture of an earlier phase of ancient civilization, tend to see before us as option and victim of the barbarians. The crumbling was slower in the West; the Germanic yoke was repeatedly shaken off. In the East, the provinces that fell to the Arabs remained Muslim for centuries, if not to the present. The very suddenness of the conquest and the absence of violent reactions on the part of the defeated civilization did, paradoxically enough, preserve relatively more of the ancient institutional heritage under the Arabs than, for instance, under Lombards and Franks. It is merely the language curtain and the selectiveness of the chronicler that tend to conceal this all important fact. Greek certainly receded under Islam, but it practically died out in the West, and the elimination of Latin under Islam is paralleled by an identical, if possibly somewhat slower, decline of Latin in Byzantium. In any event, neither the rapid victory of a rudimentary Islamic civilization nor the failure of maturing Islam to develop certain facets of its potential, e.g., in literature, could be accounted for without the realization that the 'ancient' civilization it encountered had itself already become fragmentary, 'medievalized', and unproductive.

Incontestably, the cultural level and the outreach of experience accessible in the Arabian peninsula at the rise of Islam, were lower and narrower than in the areas that fell to the first Muslim attacks. This differential, however, must not be allowed to blur the fact that Islam strode forth from its homeland with the essential determinations and decisions already made. It had placed itself in the line of the Abrahamic religions, and although at first its distinctiveness went largely unnoticed and unheeded by its Christian subjects, it entered the lands of ancient civilization already marked with that onesidedness which, in the words of Wilhelm von Humboldt, is the goal of any individual, be it person, nation or epoch.[1]

[1] *Ideen über Staatsverfassung* (1791), in *Werke*, ed. A. Leitzmann (*et al.*) (Berlin, 1903–36), I, 81; analysed by F. Meinecke, *Weltbürgertum und Nationalstaat* (Munich, 1962; first published in 1907), 40. For the initial reaction of the subjected Christians cf. C. Cahen, 'Note sur l'accueil des chrétiens d'Orient à l'Islam', *Revue de l'histoire des religions*, CLXVI (1964), 51–8.

Insofar as they conditioned both receptiveness and creativeness in its new environments a certain number of those 'decisions'—as determinants of what elements would enter its orbit as problems and sources—must be specifically identified. (1) Radical monotheism as understood by Muḥammad had laid down irrevocably a dividing line against trinitarian Christianity, and at the same time defined equally irrevocably the nature of the basic kinship of the two faiths. In a parallel manner, the fundamental agreement with Judaism and Christianity on the facts of prophecy and revelation was never to be shaken, while the role assigned to the historic person of Muḥammad b. 'Abd Allāh was to remain an irremovable stumbling-block. Abrahamic monotheism, i.e., monotheism with a personal creator God, revelation and prophecy, carries its distinctive problematics; in the milieu of the Near Eastern tradition, the resolution of this remains linked with a limited choice of intellectual styles, of which the most advanced and most characteristic are the binomial argument by analogy, formally clad as *Ḥadīth* and the Midrashic narrative from which it stems, and the trinomial syllogism of Greek philosophy as naturalized into Christian theology (and philosophy) by the Fathers and thence into Islam.

(2) Although the Qur'anic texts emphasize the specifically Arab mission of the Prophet as much as the oneness of all revealed truth, and although the invading Arabs were less than anxious to share the privilege of their affiliation, there was nothing in the structure of the new religion to block its spread. In fact, the possession of ultimate truth came to be felt by many as an obligation to assist those on the outside in bridging the abyss between unbelief and belief. Where the social organization of power proved recalcitrant, the attraction of power helped to breach it, and although the racial pride of the converts of the first hour left a lasting imprint on religiously sanctioned social regulations and the law—from the privilege reserving the caliphate to Quraysh to the intricate rules of *kafā'a* affecting intermarriage of Arabs and non-Arabs of different status—the attraction of the Muslim faith as such, whatever the supporting motivations, vindicated a universalism which in his last years may have moved close to becoming a factor in the Prophet's self-view and political planning.

The unwelcome influx of non-Arab converts preserved Islam from being submerged by the older faiths or from surviving as the caste-mark of a comparatively small stratum set apart from their surroundings by an ethnically determined, 'private' religion. But what saved Islam undermined the political power of the Arabs, which was soon to decline, in part at least under the impact of the newcomers' discontent at being debarred from an equality within the community which Revelation had assured them. That the disintegration of Arab control furthered rather than impeded the spread of the Arab language, of Islam, and of a civilization identified in its roots with Arab Islam, is even more remarkable than the conscious universalism with which in the 'Abbasid age Islam came to set itself against provincially confined truths such as that of Zoroastrianism.

The possession of a sacred language proved a source of strength. Zoroastrians and Christians had sacred texts but there was no obstacle to translation, and translation would, in cultural terms, tend to become one important step toward assimilation. Parallelisms of the religious tradition such as the view of Zoroaster as the end of a long line of depositaries of *X^varnah* and the prophetic *charisma*, or the kindred view which placed him in the centre of a chain of prophecy from Gayōmart to Sōshyans, could not but work in favour of Muslim ideology, confirming as they did the basic assumptions of the faith to which both intellectual and political initiative had passed, and which the kindred metahistoric constructions of older religions appeared to legitimize, and in any event consolidated.

The idea of the corruption of Scripture by Jews and Christians put forward in Muḥammad's Medinese period and developed in various ways under the empire proved a strong defensive weapon against corroding influences, and must be counted among the basic armament that permitted the Muslims to face with confidence the older religious learning.

(3) Confidence again was lent to the Muslim by his concept of man. The absolute subjection of creature to Creator, the infinite distance separating man from his God, predisposed some pious circles to contrition and humility as a pervasive attitude, but in the community as a whole the sense of election and collective perfection, at least relative to earlier religious groups, more than balanced the quietism which surrender to a supernatural will might have engendered. Any member of the best community knew himself privileged by nature or destiny over against the heathen from whom he had dissociated himself, and this sentiment was to persist in confrontation with the more advanced communities outside the Arabian peninsula. Obedience to the Lord, fulfilment of His order, justified the individual existence, the more so that no inner

rent called for atonement and redemption—the Muslim was a man without original sin, in need of guidance but not of regeneration. He was used also from time immemorial to see and value himself in the context of a collective, his clan and his tribe; and when in later days the legists proclaimed the infallibility of community consensus, this assertion was little else but an adapted restatement of the inherited self-view in which the nobility or meanness, power or weakness of the group inhered in the individual as a personal quality. But despite this dependence of man on the group, the pagan Arab bequeathed to his Muslim heir an aristocratic self-reliance, bravado and occasional *hubris*, a confident conviction of inalienable excellence grounded in descent and gesture, but most of all in the knowledge of his embodying the norms and expectations of his people. This composite inheritance gave the Muslim conqueror his peculiar invulnerability comparable in kind to that of the Western pioneer in East and South a century ago.

Whatever his defects and however painful his fragility, man was the noblest of existent beings, endowed with command over the other creatures of this earth, beyond whom he had grown and above whom he had been set by the Creator's will.

Built into this attitude and its inevitable adjustment to the restraining values of religion was the seed of the future conflict between two outlooks on man—one putting faith in his excellence, which it would find confirmed in the attunement of the moral law to standards innate in him, and gravitating toward a humanism that would shape and measure the world by his needs and accomplishments; the other, holding to his mediocrity, to the derived character of all his works, his dependence on the supernatural for success and defeat, and looking for protection behind the walls of the community, itself to be enclosed within the walls of the Law.

(4) *'Ilm* and *ma'rifa*, systematic and intuitive, or acquired and vouchsafed, knowledge—to retroject later terminology into the times of the Prophet—were not, as yet, neatly separated. Access to supernatural truth of sorts was conceded to the dreamer, and in a more specialized manner, to the professional soothsayer. An admirably precise observation of the *Lebenswelt* had not led to a clean division between empirical and speculative insights; differently put, it had not resulted in the establishment of criteria to distinguish the possible from the impossible, the material from the spiritual, technique from magic. Truth was concrete and definitive; so was falsehood, both manifest in theoretical

positions as much as in behaviour understood as ancestral custom. In fact, this truth was subject to adaptation in its practical aspect no less than its theoretical formulations; but the collective memory manipulated the past to buttress and harmonize present view and usage. For truth was not self-sustaining, nor was man by his own effort able to sustain it. It rested on authority, and the strength of authority in turn, rested on its age. The personal authority of Muḥammad and the divinity who had chosen him constituted an innovation which the Prophet did everything he could to divest of its unprecedentedness without, however, destroying the sense that a new order had come replacing outmoded truth now become error by new truth and safety everlasting.

The extent is noteworthy to which this concept of truth and its psychological and social function resembled the concept and function of truth as it had come to be accepted 'outside'—in dying Hellenism even more than in a Christianity that was still fighting to define itself. Even the disposition to forgo what we may call a Pelagian concern for free will as the primary motivation for the honour of God in His power and providence, was curiously shared by the Muslims and the tired world they were taking in hand, in which the Platonic idea of philosophy as an unquenchable thirst for comprehension, an indefatigable effort to go further and further, beyond the present limits of the self, in an ever renewing urge to break the deadly grip of acquiescence in an achievement threatening to be accepted as delimitative, was still proclaimed though increasingly introverted. With this expectation of truth goes a readiness to search for mystical experience, for loving absorption into the deity, a longing not yet understood in its dangers for the postulate of divine remoteness. Perhaps it would be more accurate to speak of a search for the mystery rather than of mysticism. In any event, the later development of mystical piety by way of several 'dialogues' with primarily Christian articulations of such experience, would be distorted without recognition of its adumbration in earliest Islam. The vocabulary of mature Muslim mysticism remains to testify to the indelible imprint of certain Qur'anic verses on adepts and advocates.

(5) More than seems to be commonly assumed does the Muslim empire represent an extension of the socio-political concepts prevailing in Arabia among the early community and before. The Arab Muslims as an aristocratic warrior class with weak roots in agriculture and some connexion with commerce continued the part played by a dominant tribe providing protection to weaker groupings. As those weaker

groups retained their own leaders and 'internal autonomy', so the weaker groupings in the conquered territories were under the 'protection' of the Muslim rulers to retain their community organization and their *élite*. The representative of the caliph was to be the military commander on behalf of the 'dominant tribe'.[1] The Muslim community was unstructured as between religious and profane tasks and functions, somewhat like the undifferentiated unity of the family. Divine guidance was always near and unspecialized in regard to the sphere of life which it regulated. Even as membership in a nation will, today, possess the whole person, although it may, in the West at least, leave the individual free to decide and arrange some areas of his existence, so membership in the Islamic 'nation' meant, in principle and increasingly in fact, total submergence, a total 'islamization' of being, thinking and acting.

(6) Less stringently but still noticeably the dominant interests of the Muslim beginnings and of heathendom carried over into Islamic civilization—negatively, an unconcern for architecture and the arts, an almost inevitable concomitant of the physical and social milieu of the peninsula; positively, a passionate dedication to poetry and to the Arabic language altogether. The cult of form coupled with comparative indifference to content variation, an aesthetic of the detail, a sober passion for imagery—these traits were to remain as creative dispositions as well as a specific bequest from pagan times.

Islam thus provided a framework for expansion and integration; it canonized certain limitations of the Arab tradition but deepened and widened the zones of psychological experience and intellectual as much as political activity. The small numbers of the early conquerors guaranteed the continuance of regional differences; the communication problems of the period neutralized the yearning for an all-embracing, uniform Islamic life, and induced the community to ratify a good deal of local custom. The speed of the Muslim expansion, and the speed of the subsequent growth of Islamic civilization, prevented fundamental social changes below the highest level and apart from such arrangements which followed logically from the basic rationale of Muslim community structure. Even when every allowance is made for the contingent character of historical developments, it still remains safe to state that on their exodus from the peninsula the Arab Muslims had made the

[1] Cf. W. M. Watt, 'The Tribal Basis of the Islamic State', *Dalla tribù allo stato* (Rome, 1962), 154–60.

'governing decisions' in regard to what they considered their physical and spiritual ancestry; hence they had, so to speak, predetermined what, on being exposed to a large spectrum of cultural possibilities, was to fit in with their sense of cultural affiliation, and thus, too, the sources on which they might draw to solve problems and fill gaps of which, as yet, they were, for the most part, unaware.

II

What were the intellectual temptations Islam encountered in its new world, and what resources to meet them did this world put at its disposal? The temptations may be described summarily as the availability of, and forced acquaintance with, more fully developed edifices of thought erected with the help of a logical technique of extraordinary subtlety, a rational science, a larger and more varied accumulation of texts to serve as an authoritative basis for deductive reasoning, a wider range of admissible and assimilated experience, and quite generally a higher level of training and sophistication. This sophistication was manifest not least in acute awareness of the implications and problems of a given philosophical or religious position; and it may be argued that the foremost effect of the plunge into the milieux of ancient hellenization was a rise in self-consciousness regarding the meaning of the Muslim postulates, and an inner compulsion of increasing force to think through, articulate and harmonize the accepted religious data. It has frequently and correctly been stated that the dialogue of Christian and Muslim controversialists—which, incidently, began only some fifty or sixty years after the conquest and remained more often than one is wont to assume in actual fact a monologue addressed to the community of the spokesman—impelled the Muslim intelligentsia to consider and reformulate moot points as they were brought up (and, one may add, as the internal development of the community made such points into critical and always, at least indirectly, political issues). But surpassing by far in ultimate importance the impact of competition and polemical discourse, the mere presence of the Hellenic heritage—in Greek, Syriac and Persian garb—brought about a transformation in the conquerors' outlook without which the civilization of classical Islam with its ambitious and successful outreach into the sciences and into philosophy never could have matured. And it may equally be doubted whether the possibilities of a mystical piety, and again those of building a religious law overarching the total structure of life, would have been realized without the model of the Christian mystics, and the tangible existence of Jewish law as model for the aspiration underlying the *Sharī'a*, and that of Roman and Syrian ecclesiastical law as partial model of axiomatics and elaboration.

As the thought draws the word, so the word the thought. 'Le mot entraîne l'idée malgré elle.'[1] Systematization of Islamic doctrine would have occurred in any environment of an advanced civilization, but the conceptual apparatus into which the Muslims grew did indeed exercise a decisive influence on the nature of this systematization, and probably also on the problems through the discussion of which systematization was approached. The habituation of the milieu to paired notions such as substance and accident, eternity (pre-existence) and creation in time, the neo-Platonic ideology of mediated descent from the One to the many, the spiritual to the material, together with the redeeming ascent of the striving soul, predetermined in large measure the problems to be faced, and, given the fundamental insights of the Qur'anic revelation and the ratiocinative methods traditionally utilized in the region, the solutions as well. Fear of the inevitable is ever-present, so is the fear of losing what its very fluidity and indistinctness makes appear as unsullied truth. Only rarely does the faithful realize that the naïve directness of unclarified devotion, unless protected by the kind of intellectual armour that is strong enough to withstand the most advanced questioning of the day, is bound to lose its hold on all but the simple; only a theology adequate to the existential and critical needs of a time will maintain alive for the cultured the religious experience it protects; this is true in spite of the fact that to the believer, and often to the theologically schooled believer too, definition and derivation will threaten to chill, not to say kill, spontaneous devotion.

The reaction of many a Muslim *'ālim* to any movement toward scholasticism could almost be couched in the words of Saint Jerome writing in A.D. 414: 'Unskilled heretics are hard to find... Theirs is not the net of the Apostolic fishermen, but the little chains of dialectic.' The reference is to Aristotelian dialectics—the fear of Aristotle ever paralleled his authority. Al-Tawḥīdī (d. 414/1023) angrily rises against the orthodox and, more particularly, the Hanbalite position, that logic has no right to meddle in law, as little as philosophy has any nexus with

[1] Alfred de Vigny, *Chatterton*, Act III, Scene 1; in *Théâtre*, II (Paris, 1927), 306. The passage is quoted by L. Brunschvicg, *Héritage de mots, héritage d'idées* (2nd ed.; Paris, 1950), 6.

religion or Greek wisdom with the formulation of statutes, *aḥkām*. The tolerance which Revelation and prophetic precedent bespoke for mysticism, that is to say, for the individual seizing his God in a personal intuitive experience, seemingly unmediated by the community or its institutions, made possible a rather rapid growth of Sufism, in part as a reaction to the consolidation of the *Umma* in doctrine and organization. One may wonder how much access the early mystics would have had to Indian practices and theories—despite the conquest of Sind and the presence in 'Irāq of Indian traders and travellers, effective contacts with Hindu spirituality remained slight down to the days of Maḥmūd of Ghazna and beyond—even if the experience aspired to had been more closely akin to them. With Western mysticism as a whole, early Islamic mysticism, where it went beyond ascetic self-discipline, was most of all a theory of cognition, in other words, an intellectual movement with anti-legalistic and anti-scholastic overtones. This thirst for intuitive knowledge of the divinity, where knowledge implies approach, and vision, unification, as well as the procedures cleansing the seeker in preparation for illuminating grace, were in keeping with Christian endeavours which naturally inspired a major share of the descriptive terminology and, as importantly, of the systematization of the *sālik*'s progress to perfection.

The more sober and, in a measure, community-oriented mysticism of al-Muḥāsibī (d. 243/857), while rejected by many as much for its philosophical implications as for its limited devaluation of the law, found more ready acceptance than the self-centred, pantheizing mysticism of Eastern affinities represented by Bāyazīd al-Bisṭāmī (d. probably in 261/874).

If medieval Islam, despite its leaning on the Hellenic heritage, appears to the modern observer in many important ways estranged from what, to us, are some of the dominant features of this heritage, it must be remembered that our image of Hellenic civilization is a composite one, in which the Periclean Age, the great days of the Hellenistic kingdoms, and selected traits of later antiquity tend to blend; an image moreover that is inseparable from its political forms (especially the *polis*), its outreach into rational science, and its literature. Although a good deal survived of ancient political thinking, the *polis* as a concrete historical phenomenon never did enter the purview of Islam; empirical science had suffered a decline at least from the second Christian century; in fact, the rise to the surface of popular religious ideas had, as early as the first century B.C., begun to sap the drive toward research and a rational critique of natural phenomena, while strengthening the need for authority and the belief in miracles with the comfortable abdication of exploratory effort it implied. What remained as science in areas such as meteorology was little more than crude and arbitrary speculation. Already Lactantius (*c.* 240–*c.* 320) had condemned the natural sciences as 'sacrilegious folly', neo-Platonists like Iamblichus (*c.*250–*c.*330) followed in the same track. When many centuries later, al-Niẓāmī (d. 606/1209) derides the same Iamblichus as an impious philosopher he puts opinions in his mouth which drastically show that the comprehension of the nature of empirical investigation in the natural sciences had long disappeared, in part no doubt because it was felt to be an attack on divine prerogative, an intrusion by an inferior mind into the mysteries of the Lord's government of the world.

The principal centres of Hellenic learning in the countries the Muslims were to overrun in the first wave of conquest were (apart from the Greek schools in Alexandria, Caesarea and Berytos), Edessa, Nisibis and Seleucia near Ctesiphon (Nestorian), and Antioch with Amida (Jacobite) in Syriac-speaking and Gondēshāpūr (Khūzistān, again Nestorian) in Pahlavī-speaking territory. The Syriac institutions, destined to become highly influential in the formation of Muslim civilization, were primarily theological schools. For the most part, profane learning was admitted as an endeavour of secondary importance and limited to grammar and rhetoric, philosophy, medicine, music, mathematics and astronomy. The actual restriction, not to say the loss, of profane learning will not be correctly assessed unless it be realized that philosophy, for example, meant little more than parts of the Aristotelian *Organon*, and medicine, the principal works of Hippocrates and Galen. In Gondēshāpūr, whose Academy goes back to A.D. 530, theoretical instruction was supplemented by practice in a hospital, *bīmāristān*, a method adopted later by the physicians of Baghdad. Through Gondēshāpūr a measure of Indian influence was to reach the Arabs; but it was not to become effective before the 'Abbasid age. It was thus on a depleted ancient heritage that the Arabs had to draw; where they felt the urge to supplement it, the impulse had to come from themselves and those within their orbit who had fallen under the sway and the spell of the *'arabiyya*.

Whether or not the Muslim message was originally intended for the Arabians, or even for the north-western and central Arabians alone, or whether its universalism was at the outset metaphysical rather than political and this-wordly, the empire made Islam, once and for all, a universal faith. Universal versus local, or more precisely, national validity, had long been an issue. The concept of a cultural universalism rendered effective and embodied in a political structure, the world had inherited from the Stoics; the idea of an empire held together by a state religion had become familiar through the Sasanian state, even before the adoption of Christianity as the mortar and the soul of declining Rome and rising Byzantium. Religious universalism had been an issue before the Muslims entered upon the scene. The Christians had followed the Manichaeans in criticizing Zoroastrianism for its restricted validity. The fourth book of the *Dēnkart*, in substance a product of the third/ninth century but incorporating older materials, lists, perhaps in defence, some of the works accepted by Persia from the outside—the *Almagest* as well as rhetorical, astronomical and sociological books of India—all of them reformulated to fit the Persian environment and highly esteemed. More consciously is the defence undertaken in Book Five where the political and civilizing mission of Persia is invoked as assurance that the Zoroastrian message with which Persia is entrusted would be spread throughout the world. In fact, however, the all too narrow link between Sasanian royalty and the *dēn* of the Zoroastrian Church inhibited rather than furthered the acceptance of the Mazdaean faith, even though the concept of the twinship of *dawla* and *dīn*, royalty and religion, was to be taken over by Muslim political thinking, together with a number of other elements of Persian political ethics and wisdom as these had been fixed in the Middle Persian *andarz* works, Books of Council, that were to become highly popular in the form of Mirrors for Princes or as parts of general tracts on *adab* from the second/eighth century onward.

The looseness and early disintegration of the gigantic imperial structure of the caliphate helped rather than harmed the universalism of Islam, enabling it to absorb a healthy localism where the cultural self-consciousness of a region was still alive and creative (as was the case above all in Persian-speaking territory), while safeguarding Arabic as the common language of religion and learning, and therewith, to a considerable extent, a common literature and more particularly a common Arabic prose in the service of religion, the law and the sciences in the widest sense of the word. The universal availability of Islam in its definitive Arabic formulations, together with its wide-meshed permeability for the concerns of local tradition, that could be legitimized and incorporated through the *ijmāʿ* of the local *prudentes*, counteracted the 'nationalistic' reaction of some of the conquered—remarkably strong among the Persians, remarkably weak among the Greek- and Syriac-speaking—who, by and large, aspired not to the displacement of Islam by their ancestral faith but to the acceptance within Islam of the cultural heritage and its moral and intellectual attitudes. It deserves notice that the Zoroastrian reaction of the third/ninth century appeals to the superiority of the Persians, allegedly recognized by their neighbours, in point of beautiful speech (or the beauty of their language) and the cultivation of measure, reflecting, or at any rate recalling, the even more emphatic claims of the Arabs to the perfection of their tongue, and to Islam as the religion of the mean.

On the level of seemingly unconditioned or spontaneous religious reaction, expanding Islam would encounter kindred attitudes that were effective below and behind doctrinal formulations. Thus, for example, the uncertainty which the Qur'ān is wont to attach to assurances of divine reward or human comprehension. 'He admonisheth you, mayhap ye will be reminded' (7. 92).—'Thus doth He perfect His goodness upon you, mayhap ye will become Muslims' (7. 83).—'And this is a Book which We have sent down; [it is] blessed, so follow it and show piety, mayhap mercy will be shown you' (6. 156; it must be appreciated that God is speaking). The uncertainty veils not only the human reaction but also that of the Lord, who is introduced as though wishing to reserve His freedom over against the implied commitment of the command. The same 'absence of "certainty of belief" is typical of Israelite religion' and more particularly of that of the prophets. 'In the relation to Yahweh there was always a *perhaps*. Amos exhorted his people to hate evil and love good. *Perhaps*, he says, Yahweh will be gracious to the descendents of Joseph' (Amos 5 : 15).[1]

A certain kinship is unmistakable, too, in the Hebrew prophets' shunning of miracle-working and the insistence of Muḥammad on his character as a mere instrument of revelation—both attitudes soon to be overlaid by the popular craving for the wonder as the ultimate testimony to election. On a strictly theological plane, Christianity and Islam maintain the miracle as a witness, or symbol, of the Lord's freedom. God retains unlimited sovereignty and in breaking through the limitations inherent in His creatures and His order, or perhaps merely habitual to

[1] J. Lindblom, *Prophecy in ancient Israel* (Philadelphia, 1962), 340; the italics are Lindblom's.

them, He manifests His redemptive creativeness, and allows man to comprehend that His order subserves His purpose. Wherever possible, early Islam endeavours to remove the miracle from the grasp of man—God uses it to make the unbeliever aware of His messenger's truthfulness, He allows it as testimony of His friends' closeness to Himself, to help and to warn, but like Christianity and, to a somewhat less extent, Judaism, Islam succumbed to the traditional longing to have faith confirmed and made useful by realizations of the impossible, for the most part very modest, at the hand of religious heroes of various sorts. Inevitably, the frame of mind of the elect, supported as it was by a millenary tradition, frayed its way into Muslim thought. The freedom of divine choice provides the precarious justification in Islamic terms of the esoteric pride of the Perfect, who may be classifiable as prophet or saint, and whose overdimensionality comes to be hesitantly accepted in the wake of Gnostic ideas of his cosmic role. The Hellenistic and Gnostic inspiration is audible in the hubristic description of the Perfect Man, who, tenuously integrated in the Islamic experience of God and creation, 'becomes a world unto himself, comparable to the macrocosm, and merits to be called a "microcosm". Thus he becomes Almighty God's vicegerent among His creatures, entering among His particular saints, and standing as a Complete, Absolute Man... At length, between him and his Master no veil intervenes, but he receives the ennoblement of proximity to the Divine Presence.'[1]

Parallelism of approaches in fundamentals not only promoted permeability by newly experienced influences but, in a number of cases, makes it delicate to decide between an organic and a stimulated development. Thus it will have to remain uncertain whether the preponderant concept of reason as an instrument of deduction from authoritatively given premises, rather than for induction with a view to opening new areas of knowledge, a concept which prevailed, though not exclusively, at least as a programme throughout the medieval world, was brought from the peninsula or acquired on settling outside. The inclination to follow authority, be it that of the ancestors or that of the Prophet, was no doubt indigenous to Arab society. But the identification of greater age with greater closeness to truth had been common and commonplace in pagan Greece and Rome and, in fact, had been used as a stock argument in anti-Christian polemics after having played its part in Jewish endeavours to win respectability, not to mention the authority accorded

[1] The Nasirean Ethics by Naṣīr ad-Dīn Ṭūst, tr. G. M. Wickens (London, 1964), 52.

to the Egyptians by the Greeks on the ground of the antiquity of their religion and culture. 'The most ancient cannot be false,' and consequently, 'later invention cannot be held true,' to use the beautifully concise formulations of Ambrosiaster (*c.* 380).[1] Hence the inclination to develop the rules of the Qur'ān first as the *sunna* of the Prophet, supplementing it then by the *sunnat Abī Bakr wa- 'Umar* (later designated as *sīra* or *fi'l*), and toward the end of the seventh century, placing the *sunna* of the Prophet as an independent norm by the side of the Qur'ān. Hence also the inclination to view the sequence of generations in history after the appearance of Islam as one of necessary decline—an outlook rather than an empirically substantiated verdict since it proved effective despite the victories of Islam, presumably rationalized on a sense of moral decay, but an outlook, in any case, that had been familiar to the Near Eastern environment at least since the Book of Daniel (cf. 2:31 ff.) and reflected even in Genesis 47:9.

The first generation of Muslims showed a dynamism, will and ability to adjust and to take risks that went well with a vision of the world's course as a drama in which God took an active part, a vision not too far removed from that of the Hebrew prophets. Accompanying perhaps the increasing sense of the distance between God and man, and His abstention from direct and miraculous interference in the details of history, this self-confident dynamism gradually tapered off, and the depreciation of becoming over against being, the dominant attitude of classical antiquity, obtained an ever stronger hold, anchored it seems in the need to safeguard the feeling for Allāh's immutable and monumental majesty as the formative experience of the community. What is subject to change and 'becoming' is necessarily subject to degradation and decay. Rank and value hinge on participation in being, which man cannot increase even for himself. So historical action remains inevitably stained with imperfection; besides, man merely executes while will *stricto sensu* belongs to God alone. If Muslims of today are given to depict the first thirty years of the *Umma* as the ideal period, it is, in the last analysis, its dynamism which they hope to recapture and which had been so soon corroded by, or yielded in response to, an identification of the perfect with the changeless desirable as much within the fundamental religious experience of their faith as within the atmosphere which conquered them as they took over their erstwhile Hellenic provinces.

[1] *Quaestiones* CXIV, 10, and LXXXIV, 3, in *MPL*, XVII, 314, 2 and 145, 15.

The invasion and subsequent integration into Muslim consciousness —not always lastingly nor even briefly effective—of ancient Oriental, Jewish and Christian materials would frequently occur on the level of the popular tale, of which the so-called *Isrā'īliyyāt,* stories attributed to the Children of Israel, are probably the best-known example. Stories of earlier prophets abound: the Muslim concept of numerous prophets and messengers allowing the growth of legendary traditions on the fringes of orthodox doctrine. A good many ideas and customs of the earlier civilizations penetrated more deeply by being formulated as *Ḥadīth*, sayings of or about the Prophet and his Companions, when if accepted they would wield a more significant influence, possibly even entering the sphere of the Law as a precept, its precedent or corroboration. In a sense, the Law must be seen as a symbol of the Muslim identification and hence of Muslim cohesiveness, rather than as a practical tool of everyday legal life—a certain analogy to one of the functions of classical Jewish law is not hard to discover. Both *Ḥadīth* and *qiṣaṣ al-anbiyā'* (tales of the prophets) represent basically arabizations of traditional forms of expression. The Qur'ān, on the other hand, differs notably in many places from religious speech as known and accepted by Muḥammad's contemporaries. It would, however, be erroneous to suspect its style (to the Christian less polished, less varied, occasionally disturbing in the abruptness of its narrative technique and in the limiting topicality of reference) to have been a hindrance to the adoption of Islam. As controversy abundantly shows, knowledge of each others' holy books was confined to an insignificant proportion of Muslims and Christians; the same could be said of Muslims and Jews, and, even more emphatically, of Muslims and Zoroastrians. On the whole, the new Muslim would touch the Qur'ān only after his conversion—the decision to accept Islam preceding its study such as it may have been. It may be useful to remember that the Bible had not been read by the pagan world. Acquaintance at first hand with the Jewish and Christian scriptures, with Jewish and Christian history came, as a rule, only with or after conversion to Judaism or Christianity. One could hardly claim the *apartheid* of Christian and pagan, Christian and early Muslim has lost its validity as *types* for the present-day *apartheid* of members of different faiths in the Near East as elsewhere in the Islamic world.

To see the Arab conquests in their true perspective it must be noted that the invaders did not bring in a superior material or technological equipment. Nor is there any indication of a significant innovation in armament or tactics—speed and mobility were made brilliantly effective but can hardly be thought of as something new—with the possible exception that the early Arab army could be held over in the field as long as required without adding extravagantly to the public expense or without infringement of a customary right to break off the campaign after a certain number of days or months. As it was neither a peasant nor a mercenary army, it represented more of an independent instrument in the hands of the community than medieval armies usually did. The Arab Muslim fought, the conquered sowed and traded; only the dynamism of expansion could bear the cost of the initial establishment.

The separation of populations by religious and ethnic differences was a legal fact in the successor-states of the Western Empire; it was less clearly insisted upon by statute in the East, but nonetheless was generally accepted practice. Community differentiation was stabilized by recognition of community law; the personality of the law, as against its territoriality, congenial as it was to Arab attitudes, must nevertheless be included among the first cluster of foreign elements which the requirements of the situation attached to Arab Muslim cultural and political possessions. Payments in lieu of military service as an impost on the non-Muslim, limited *connubium* between different population groups, graduated blood-wit as between rulers and ruled—all these features, which to later ages no longer alive to the rationale of such discrimination would become disturbing, were anything but unprecedented in the world into which the Arabs came to play their part. Parallel institutions would exist in varying forms throughout the *aikumene*; let it suffice to refer to the Merovingian *hostilitium*, the ban on intermarriage between Romans and Goths, and to the fact that alone among all Germanic conquerors the Visigoths, in 654, introduced a unified territorial law for their Spanish state. The near-monopoly of the 'Roman' population on civil service posts has its parallel in the Muslim state, where the administrative cadres continue both in formerly Byzantine and in formerly Sasanian territory. When in the second generation the government undertakes to arabicize the administration, the personnel itself is less affected than the formal changes would lead one to expect. Where the first echelon was reserved for the Arab, the subordinate ranks continued to be the preserve of the native population—an observation, which must however, be appreciated in the light of the slowly but ceaselessly progressing linguistic amalgamation of old and new settlers.

It is this continuity of the administrative tradition which kept the Muslim state from following its contemporaries in the West all the way in their development from what has been called the 'prohibitive' to the 'repressive' state.[1] Where it is no longer possible—or perhaps not even desired—to maintain the authority of the state as both regular and pervasive by means of a bureaucratic apparatus which, in the long run, will remain effective only by being dependent on the ruler's payments in money, this authority will operate fitfully and, for the most part, only with a view to repressing disorders and to re-establishing itself against disregard or rebellion. Authority is not evenly effective throughout the territory or the communities claimed for it, but tends to assert itself forcefully only in the immediate surroundings of the ruler, who may habitually be moving about his realm, and to thin out toward the fringes or toward such areas as do not command special attention or again, that are, in terms of the logistics of the day, too distant from the power-centre to be kept in consistent dependence. The medieval state in Europe, but not Byzantium, and increasingly, the state of the caliphs exemplify the 'repressive' type with its characteristic restorative and punitive interventions and the loose-meshed network of military and financial controls. The Umayyad state and its 'Abbasid successor in its beginnings accepted the inherited machinery where it still existed. It was governing with its aid that alienated Mu'āwiya from the pious opposition with its apprehension of godless power, and led to the distinction between the *imāma* or *khilāfa* of the first Muslim rulers and the 'kingship', *mulk*, of the new dynasty. Wherever the power of the state exceeded its function to protect and expand the domain of Islam and its believers, and consolidated by means of long-term fiscal and administrative policies, which inevitably threatened to impinge on the group individualism of Arab tradition, tribal sentiment and, more significantly, the scruples of the pious, protested and counteracted.

Fearful of an arbitrariness which they never allowed to be contained by formalizing, under God, the means which the maintenance of the *Umma* imperiously demanded, mistaking also Qur'anic directive for immutable statutory precept, the pious pushed the ruler into permanent

[1] For these concepts cf. L. Hartmann, *Ein Kapital vom spätantiken und frühmittelalterlichen Staate* (Berlin, etc., 1913), 16, who follows A. Wagner, *Handbuch der Staatswissenschaften* (3rd ed.), *s.v.* Staat (in nationalökonomischer Hinsicht). See also H. Aubin, *Vom Altertum zum Mittelalter. Absterben, Fortleben und Erneuerung* (Munich, 1949), 24–5.

illegality by refusing, for example, to enlarge the scope of lawful taxation, and, more generally, to identify themselves with the machinery of government, well knowing that the state would be compelled to exceed the functional limits and hence the application of executive power which they were prepared to read into the revealed texts.

Strictly speaking, for them there existed only the community and its commander; the state as such had no place in their scheme of things. The heritage of Byzantium and the Sasanians would win in large measure *de facto* but scarcely *de jure* recognition. Nor did the concept of the 'juristic person' survive from Roman law. The consequences of this elimination were rather far-reaching. Thus, for example, stealing from the public treasury was not held subject to the *ḥadd* punishment for theft, because the illegal act was not committed against a juristic agent independent of the thief, who was, along with every other Muslim, considered part owner of the *māl Allāh* and thus part owner of what he had stolen. Ultimate authority was with God, who holds sovereignty but does not exercise it; His will, according to the sentiment of a majority of the faithful, permeates the charismatic community, which is apt to split over the legitimacy of institutionalization, with the Kharijites' insistence on personal sanctity and their consequent tendency to divide over the question of a ruler's personal morality, recalling the attitude of the Donatists in North Africa toward the Catholics in the fourth and fifth Christian centuries. In time, the caliph came to embody, as it were, the community not only in its political but also in its religious aspect; in fact, he was to wield rather unrestricted control over the religious 'establishment'; but theory kept him at bay. It would require him to be able to make legal decisions and to act as a judge of no appeal, but it would not allow him to legislate, i.e., to add to, or subtract from the *Sharī'a*. The Byzantine emperor and the Sasanian king were less restrained; hence the distinction between the law of the doctors and the law of the land, which, in proportion to the progress in depth of islamization, was to become ever more characteristic of Muslim territories, existed (or had existed) on their soil only in the shape of special legislation and judicial procedures applicable to clerics—but those exemptive privileges in turn were subject to sanction by the head of the state. Here then is an instance in which a basic 'decision' of early Islam led to rejection of the dominant concept of a political and administrative structure which, in most other facets, was taken over into the mechanism of the Muslim state. The separation of *Umma* and 'state', toward which the community gravitated while simultaneously insisting on the service function of the state *vis-à-vis* the *Umma*, repeats to a remarkable extent the Augustinian vision of the community of believers as the *civitas Dei*, untouchable as it is by the fate of the *civitas terrena* whose ultimate justification yet lies in upholding and defending it. On the other hand, the notion that 'the kingdom of the Divine law and the external order could, presumably, be coterminous',[1] that there can be identity between a particular form of political organization and the kingdom of God, is incompatible with any Christian view of society: this 'standard' Muslim belief about fulfilment in history, with the 'Islamicity' of the state as an enduring characteristic, recurs in Christendom only in marginal millenarianisms as exemplified by the Anabaptists of Münster.

Pious tradition makes the Caliph 'Umar define his function in these words: 'Our duty it is to command you to obey the orders which Allāh has imposed on you, to forbid you such disobedience as God has forbidden you, and to establish the order of Allāh among the people, near and far, without caring on whom the punishment may fall.'[2] A saying is ascribed to the Prophet in which the paradox of the ruler is traced and where he appears as a sacrificial victim as much as a necessary punishment for the community.

> Do not revile the rulers; if they act well, they will be rewarded, and for you it is to be grateful; if they do ill, the burden is theirs, and for you it is to be patient. They are nothing if not a visitation [or 'punishment', *niqma*] which God sends to punish whom He wills; do not accept the visitation of God with rage and fury, accept it with humility and submission.[3]

The limitations which this ambivalent attitude to rulership was to impose on the integration of state and community were not to be overcome, however enticing the available models of other solutions as offered by the traditions of Byzantium, Persia and the ancient Near East.

To protect itself, the state maintained the separation of the non-Muslim communities in so far as feasible, not only from the Muslims but from one another. An alliance of the non-Muslims to shake off Muslim rule

[1] To borrow the formulation of K. Cragg, *Sandals at the mosque* (London, 1965), 124.

[2] Abū Yūsuf, *Kitāb al-kharāj*, 13^{13-15}; Fagnan, *Le livre*, 19–20, translates somewhat differently.

[3] Abū Yūsuf, *Kitāb al-kharāj*, 10^{8-11}; Fagnan, *Le livre*, 14, again has the passage somewhat differently.

was hardly within the ideas of the times, and such isolation as the Muslims sustained or established was no doubt congenial to the spirit of the epoch. In fact, isolation was the best safeguard against encroachments. In spite of occasional endeavours of the rulers not to devalue their privileges by having them shared too widely, conversion to Islam could not and would not be curbed. The institution of *walā'*, or clientship, made integration on the social level possible, not very satisfactorily perhaps, but sufficiently so as to surround the Arab Muslims rapidly with a significant number of 'Arabs' *de seconde zone*, the *mawālī*. In a centre like Baṣra of the early second/eighth century one has already the right to speak of people with 'double nationality',[1] Arab and Muslim, or Persian and Muslim—double community affiliations, double loyalties, a measure of bilingualism, and a sampling of that cultural amalgamation to which Islam owes its susceptibility to Persian ideas and ways.

By the cumulative effect of historical connection with, and the centring of the Umayyad state within, the area of its domination, the elements attracted by the new political-cultural entity were preponderantly of Hellenic or, better, hellenized Near Eastern origin. Down to the disappointments due to the dogged resistance of the Isaurian dynasty and the rise to prominence of the Arabs settled in the eastern provinces together with the Persian and Mesopotamian converts and *mawālī*, the orientation of the leading circles was toward Byzantium, at least in the sense that it was from the Byzantine tradition that architecture and the arts drew inspiration and technicians, that it was a hellenized version of alchemy which, perhaps soon followed by medicine, became the first natural science evoking the concern of a Muslim prince (Khālid b. Yazīd, d. *c.* 85/704) and offered the first material to be translated into Arabic, and that the beginnings of Arab grammar (although as far as we can see owed to natives or residents of the eastern areas and largely Persians by descent) built on concepts and categories that are traceable to the Greek rather than the Indian tradition—an indigenous Persian grammar does not seem to have existed.

This orientation toward the resources of the hellenized provinces—it must be realized that 'hellenization' no longer implies, at this period, the actual use of Greek as a vernacular—will make it at times difficult to decide in individual instances if a parallelism is to be accounted for as a

[1] The expression is C. Pellat's; cf. his *Le Milieu baṣrien et la formation de Ǧāḥiẓ* (Paris, 1953), 34.

newly attracted element or as a trait germane to the literary or intellectual style of the region. Comparisons like that of the generous with the Nile or the ocean, as found, for example in John Chrysostom, are of little significance as *loca probantia*. More problematic is God's oath 'by Me' which is fairly frequent in the *Ḥadīth* and occurs one single time in the Old Testament (Genesis 22:16). Very striking is the coincidence, feature by feature, of the Muslim (or at any rate, of Muḥammad's) idea of a prophet with the portrayal drawn by Philo:

A prophet does not utter anything whatever of his own, but is only an interpreter, another suggesting to him all he utters; he is enraptured and in an ecstasy; his own reasoning power has departed and has quitted the citadel of his soul, while the divine spirit has entered in and taken up its abode there, playing the instrument of his voice in order to make clear and manifest the prophecies that the prophet is delivering.[1]

The stability of the religious motif is as remarkable as the secular effectiveness which was, at the time, the Muslim contribution to its development. The unsteadying availability of religious ideas in the newly won lands added to the uncertainties of the doctrines of the countless minor conventicles and often abortive sects, whose uncontrolled teeming is characteristic of the first century of the empire. The fluidity of viewpoints is not to be gauged from the systematic or partisan presentation of sources that originated later in a period of considerable intellectual consolidation, and more surely established communal and governmental control. The essential factor in our context is the untrammelled experimentation with every bit of religious thought and mythological imagery which the older faiths and their splinter groups, and the debris of even more ancient systems, put in the way of religiously and politically excited, in many ways uprooted and puzzled people, who found themselves the masters of their superiors in intellectual experience.

The most dramatic achievement of the age, Umayyad art, in mosques and 'desert' castles—actually royal palaces at the centre of domain lands and sedentary settlements, which have long since reverted to the desert in consequence of breakdowns resulting in (or from) the destruction of irrigation—was often combated or passed over by the self-authorized spokesmen for Islam, because they would resent it as anti-Islamic, as an

[1] *De specialibus legibus* iv, 49; paraphrased by Lindblom, *Prophecy in Ancient Israel*, 29. Even more poignant perhaps is the passage *De spec. leg.* i, 65.

excessive yielding to the needs and standards of a profane royalty. It remains true nevertheless, and Muslim consciousness has come to accept this for the Dome of the Rock, that these ambitious buildings were erected, with inherited technical and artistic means, 'to postulate altogether the pre-eminence of the Arab and Muslim aspect of the new state *vis-à-vis* the claims of the older civilizations and especially of the more ancient religions now thought to be superseded by Islam'.[1] The representations of crowns and other imperial jewellery suspended around the rock in the Dome of the Rock are intended to make manifest the defeat of Byzantium and Persia; they are supported by inscriptions proclaiming the new faith and attacking the ancient religions, and in particular, Christian trinitarianism. This technique of propagandistic pronouncement by pictures, half declaratory, half symbolic, has its precedents not merely in Byzantium but in the coinage of the Roman empire, especially its later phases, and before it, in that of the Hellenistic kingdoms. Significantly, the turning away from Byzantium and toward Persia which is by far the most important development of the last decades of Umayyad rule, is adumbrated by a change in style, a partial relinquishing of Byzantine, and fuller utilization of Eastern elements and motifs in the 'declaratory' art of the Caliph Hishām (105–25/724–43).

Less dramatic, but of incalculable consequences, was the move toward full urbanization of the Muslim rulers and the location in urban centres, old and new, adapted and created, of the developments that were leading toward a specifically Islamic civilization—not least the symbiosis of early and later converts, of Arab and non-Arab Muslims, and its corollary, the drifting into *apartheid* of the Muslim and the non-Muslim communities. Islam had been an urban growth from its inception, in spirit as well as in its actual centres of gravity; but this 'inborn' trait had been immeasurably strengthened by the *hijra* into settlement, and the relocation of its political capital into the old culture areas of the Middle East. Soon, Muslim conquest would mean, in peasant or steppe country, the foundation of an urban focus—military and administrative—rapidly to take the cultural lead, and to become the radiating centre of islamization and, on occasion of attempted arabization. Obviously, the Syrian, Mesopotamian or Persian environment called for such concentration, and provided traditions that would facilitate the transition from nomadism to city-dwelling, yet it would be somewhat

[1] R. Ettinghausen, *Arab painting* (Lausanne, 1962), 19.

misleading without serious qualifications to put down the urbanization of Islam to the impact of the milieu and the expediencies of rulership. In later phases of the Islamic development, ruling Muslim groups did endeavour to remain aloof from urbanism, and the Umayyads themselves remained, as persons, astraddle the two ways of life; only the 'Abbasids were entirely committed to an urban mode of living. So once again, an innate tendency, spurred by political and military preferences, finds itself accommodated and encouraged by the prevailing attitudes and habits of the conquered.

To point to a rudimentary habituation to urban life in parts of Arabia is not to deny the fact that Muslim city administration was in many ways patterned after Byzantine, and presumably Persian models, but of the latter we have little tangible evidence. Hippodrome, water conduit and walls which F. Dölger notes as the essential components of the Byzantine town,[1] are replaced in the Muslim view by mosque, market and bath; but the concentration of crafts in one quarter or street, the attachment to the town of a rural district to be exploited by the 'citizens', as well as the office of the *agoranomos* (paralleling and succeeding to the *aedilis curulis*), under the name first of *ṣāḥib al-sūq* and later of *muḥtasib*, testify to continuity, as does, in a more general fashion, the Byzantine origin of the typical square ground-plan of Arab and Berber fortifications. The warring circus parties of the sixth Christian century show a peculiar similarity to the *'ayyārūn* of the Muslim towns, both in function and organizational structure. The Muslim town did not, however, possess a special *Stadtrecht*; but it is doubtful whether the Byzantine town maintained its city statute after Justinian I, in whose reign it is still attested. As it is patterned on a Byzantine model of organization, the creation by the caliphs in the second half of the ninth century of a *ra'īs al-aṭibbā' wa'l-falāsifa*, in imitation of the *archiatros* and *scholarchos*, warrants mention in this context.

III

The victory of the 'Abbasids ushered in the century that brought about that first synthesis of heterogeneous elements, unified in a measure by their purposeful attachment to an Islamic core, which may be called an Islamic civilization. The eastward turn of the period affected state and administration, rulership and *mores*, more than the development of

[1] 'Die frühbyzantinische und byzantinisch beeinflusste Stadt,' *Terzo Congresso internazionale di studi sull'alto medioevo* (Spoleto, 1959), 65–100, at 73–74.

knowledge as a whole, where directly obtained and mediated Greek materials remained the dominant formative factor. The principal aspirations and consequences of the 'Abbasid revolution were the replacement of Syria by 'Irāq as the heartland of the caliphate, the admission of the Persian Muslims on a level of equality with the Arab Muslims to government and social hierarchy, and the implementation of a tendency toward a more profound islamization of institutions, law and life as a whole.

Islam lost much, or most, of its original ethnic connotation; not, however, to the detriment of the Arabic language and the patterns of expression transmitted in it. In fact, the decline of Arab executive power was, curiously enough, accompanied by a consolidation of Arabic as the culture language of Islam, and while islamization had long left behind the range of Arabism it continued to establish an indissoluble tie with it. In theology, philology, the sciences, nothing would be absorbed into the bloodstream of Islamic civilization to the end of the third/ninth century unless it had first received an Arabic formulation. This is true even though Syriac continued the language at Gondēshāpūr into 'Abbasid times, and remained as late as the fourth/tenth century the mother-tongue of many of the scholars who won fame in Baghdād. But translation into Arabic from Greek, Syriac, Sanskrit, and to a more limited extent, Pahlavī, was the order of the day. The philosopher al-Kindī (d. 259/873) professes to labour for *ahl lisāninā*, 'the people of our tongue',[1] and the assimilation of the highest secular thinking to Islam, as far as it went, was throughout accompanied by an almost systematic enrichment of Arab vocabulary, and a gradual increase in the hypotactic possibilities of Arabic syntax.

Under the levelling blanket of the Arabic language, a new scientific terminology and the style and imagery of the Qur'ān (and soon the *Ḥadīth*), the continuity as well as the accretions remain concealed. When it did not directly contravene scriptural ordinance, the Muslim jurists took the substantive heritage of Byzantine or Sasanian law for granted. What needs to be traced is therefore less the substratum of older legal ideas and institutions than the transformations by which they were brought into harmony with the times and theology, with the postulates of Islam itself. The survival of the Zoroastrian *čakar-ẓanīh*, 'Zwischen-

[1] Cf. F. Rosenthal, 'Al-Kindī and Ptolemy', *Studi orientalistici in onore di Giorgio Levi Della Vida* (Rome, 1956), II, 436–56, at 445; also Kindī, *Rasā'il falsafiyya*, ed. M. 'A. Abū Rīda (1369–72/1950–3), I, 260.

ehe', as the *mut'a* marriage of principally Shī'ī Islam is remarkable especially for the place it received within a concept of marriage with which, at first glance, it would appear incompatible. The islamization of commercial law, and the preservation of its applicability to changing economic conditions, in part by 'fictions' or devices, *ḥiyal*, are examples of the same process on a larger and more significant scale. Procedural habits were adopted, presumably without full awareness of the process. Looking backwards from Muslim law, one cannot but note that, from the third Christian century the private law of the Roman empire, and in particular the law of marriage and divorce, had undergone an 'orientalization', and that the position of women had been shifting in the direction which, much more markedly, we rediscover in classical Islam. Similarly, trial by jury had disappeared; the single judge had become the rule. Mutilation, on the other hand, though widely applied as a punishment in late Roman law, would seem to have its Islamic base more directly in Qur'anic regulations.

General principles, too—such as *al-walad li'l-firāsh*—or on the level of *uṣūl*, the use of *al-maṣlaḥa al-'āmma* or *utilitas publica*, persist; so do methods of interpretation which from Roman law had entered the thinking of the rabbis by way of Hellenistic rhetoric, to continue their efficacy in Islam, with 'Irāqī Jewry acting as transmitter. It is, I believe, only our lack of familiarity with Sasanian law which prevents us from uncovering its traces in the *fiqh*. In any event, it was a Persian, only recently converted to Islam, who proposed to the Caliph al-Manṣūr the establishment of a unified, imperial law (or law for the Muslim empire) to displace the regionalism of prevailing laws, in the interest of the firmness of the caliphal state. Some sixty years after Ibn al-Muqaffa' (d. 139/756) and with the same lack of success, Bishop Agobard of Lyons (*c.* 817) addressed to the Emperor Louis the Pious the demand to do away with personal law and to establish a universal Christian law for the universal Christian commonwealth. Neither the caliph nor the emperor would have been in a position to promulgate a unified code; all the caliphs could and would do was to encourage the elaboration of administrative law (e.g., tax law), and to look with favour on such systematizations of the bases of law as came within their purview and seemed to tend towards stabilizing a rationale for, and consolidating, both community and state. The forty years between Ibn al-Muqaffa' and the compilation of Abū Yūsuf's book on taxes witnessed the elaboration of classical Muslim law, more serviceable in the end as the mortar of the community than as the tool of imperial practice for which it must have been intended.

To understand the constant interweaving of problems arising out of the Muslim tradition itself, the built-in challenges of the milieu and the more conscious challenges of religious adversaries, it must be remembered that the period from *c.* 750 to the end of the third/ninth century was a time of great creativity—in some areas against the desire of the most independent minds, who, like Aḥmad b. Ḥanbal, saw their task as the conservation of the conditions and ethos of the early community, and remained blind to the innovatory character of their own resistance to change. The science of *Ḥadīth*, of which the modern, whether indigenous reformer or Western observer, is apt to perceive above all the critical weaknesses and the formalistic results, was actually in its beginnings, a movement toward the expansion of the materials with which a Muslim could in good conscience operate, whether in the field of law, theology or any other area of direct and burning concern to the times. While disclaiming innovation and even tending to erase the suspicion of innovation from ideas and institutions which *Ḥadīth* would justify by the authority of the origins, the *muḥaddith* actually did innovate by creating a firm framework for the Islamic way of thought and life he aspired to, and he was, because of the novelty of his endeavour, the object of attacks by the practitioners of law.

Originality was noted and encouraged in the 'modern' poetry of Abū Tammām (d. 232/846) or al-Buḥturī (d. 284/897); the acceptance of originality in certain circles at least, is accompanied by the realization that progress is cumulative. The translator of Dioscorides, Iṣṭifān b. Basīl, in the days of the Caliph al-Mutawakkil, replaced what Greek terms he knew by Arabic ones; the others he left untranslated 'in the hope God would later send someone who would know them and be able to translate them'.[1] Al-Rāzī (d. 313/925 or 323/935) insists on the continuous progress of the sciences and the consequent superiority of the later scientists. A century later, Abu'l-Faraj 'Abd Allāh b. al-Ṭayyib (d. 435/1043) still professes the same approach and claims that his own observations go beyond what he had gathered from his predecessors. We are in a period of rationalization, which does not necessarily mean that methods of analytical empiricism will dominate, but that the phenomena are to be put into reasoned order, and, more significantly perhaps, that problems are being recognized as such, and explicitly posed, rather

[1] Cf. F. Rosenthal, *Das Fortleben der Antike im Islam* (Zurich and Stuttgart, 1965), 265.

than being answered by myth, rite or revealed citation without being identified as problems, i.e., as fissures in the shell containing and restraining an unruly experience of the universe.

The similarity of the problems of the Christian Logos and the Uncreate Qur'ān has often been noted. Less attention has been paid to other *cruces theologicae* which beset both faiths because potentially germane to them. Whether stimulated by Christian contacts, or whether Christian contacts were merely utilized to develop and solve problems that may be considered inherent in Muslim doctrine itself, will have to be examined from case to case. Thus a theological opinion like Jahm b. Ṣafwān's (executed 128/745–6) denial of the eternity of Paradise and Hell is *qua* problem explicable as Islamic (even though orthodox opinion would reject this on good grounds)—Jahm's starting-point is Qur'ān 57.3, 'He is the first and the last'—it is, however, impossible, to overlook its earlier treatment by Origen (*c.* 185–*c.* 254) and its resumption by Stephen bar Ṣudhailē (*fl.* end of fifth century). A similar statement could be made regarding the distinction between innate and revealed knowledge of God, where Christian antecedents would include St Paul (Romans 1:18–20; 2:15), Clement of Alexandria (*c.* 150–*c.* 215), Tertullian (*c.* 160–*c.* 220) and again Origen, and which *qua* problem was introduced to Islam by Ghaylān b. Marwān (executed in 124/742); the ethical-legal principle of *al-a'māl bi'l-niyyāt*; or again the 'determinist' use of *al-qaḍā' wa'l-qadar* in analogy with Syriac precedent.

The early ninth century exhibits an increased interest in the Christian Scriptures, which is almost immediately countered by a movement to avoid such direct contacts with Christian documents, or even discussion with Christian representatives. The political implications of this kind of contacts, as well as of the famed dispute on *qadar*, are too well known to need detailing. Less familiar are influences of Christianity—rejected by the wider community—affecting the concept of God itself. Thus Aḥmad b. Ḥā'it (d. before 232/846) and Faḍl al-Ḥadathī, associates of the Mu'tazilite al-Naẓẓām ascribe divinity to Jesus and arrive at a doctrine of two Lords: Allāh, the uncreated, and Jesus, the created, son of God by adoption, who had been Reason, *logos*, before taking on flesh. In reverse, one may note not only the instructions given by St John of Damascus to his fellow Christians ('When the Saracen says to you such then you will reply...'),[1] but the intrusion of Islamic terms into

[1] M. S. Seale, *Muslim theology* (London, 1964), 2–3; D. B. Macdonald, *Development of Muslim Theology, Jurisprudence and Constitutional Theory* (New York, 1903), 132.

Christian phraseology as in Elia al-Jawharī's identification of the *kāhin* of the Old Testament with the *imām* and his reference to Adam's *khilāfa* of God (cf. Qur'ān 2.28). And one must equally point to a certain affinity between Muslim and Jewish thought as expressed at a much later period in Maimonides's advice to Samuel b. Tibbon to read al-Fārābī: 'all he did is excellent'.[1]

In a different sphere of religious experience we find Ḥunayn b. Isḥāq drawing a parallel between the Muslim way of ornamenting mosques with the pedagogical purpose pursued by Greeks, Jews and Christians in adorning their houses of god with statues and pictures. Where Islam seems to go more determinedly its own way, it is due to the blend of the religious and the political aspects of a theological problem; thus notably in the treatment of the distinction between *islām*, adherence to the Muslim religion, and *īmān*, faith (in the Muslim revelation), and the further distinction between *īmān* and *kufr*, unbelief, or non-belief, in both of which cases the definitions will bear on the individual's affiliation with the *Umma* and hence on his privileged position in this world and the next. There is needed a justification of the elevated rank of the believer, an explanation both legally and metaphysically satisfactory; apart from the criticism of the non-Muslims, an answer must be found to the puzzle why non-believers choose the inferior truth and the inferior rank that goes with it. The elaboration given to a number of Qur'anic verses which show the unbelievers incapable of conversion, and thus fulfilling by their recalcitrance the true will and plan of God, reflects the complex of sentiments and practical problems which were inherent in the symbiosis of Muslims and *dhimmīs*.[2]

In some ways, the Persian components of Islamic civilization are more difficult to separate out than the Hellenic precisely because they are more fully integrated, and have become effective on so many levels. In fact, the Muslim world itself, without necessarily putting this judgment in analytical terms, has long since come to accept Islamic civilization as a 'Perso-Islamic synthesis'. From the third/ninth, and certainly the fourth/tenth, century onwards, the educated assumed the essential 'identity and continuity'[3] of Sasanian and Islamic political institutions—

[1] M. Meyerhof, 'Von Alexandrien nach Bagdad', *Preussische Akad. d. Wiss., Sitzungsberichte* 1930, *philos.-hist. kl.*, 389–429, at 417, quoting S. Munk, *Mélanges de philosophie juive et arabe* (Paris, 1857), 344.

[2] The most important pertinent verses are Qur'ān 2. 7; 10. 88–89; 11. 20; 18. 101; Sūra 101. Cf. R. Brunschvig, 'Devoir et pouvoir', in *Studia Islamica*, XX (1964), 5–46, esp. 8–9.

[3] To use the expression of F. R. C. Bagley, *Ghazālī's Book of counsel for kings* (London, New York, Toronto, 1964), Introduction, ix.

from the 'twinship' of *dīn* and *dawla* to the role in which caliph and *wazīr* were cast,[1] administrative techniques, the style of official documents, the social prejudices imputed to the ruler, and the sententious exchanges between him and his counsellors. The upsurge of Persian self-consciousness, to avoid the phrase 'national feeling', which gave body to the *Shu'ūbiyya* and in the fourth/tenth century to the rise of Persian as one of the great literary languages of Islam and of the world, fostered rather than disrupted the process of integration of Iranian elements. As far as Spain, Persian materials became a habitual part of *adab* literature, as witness the first book of Ibn 'Abd Rabbihi's (d. 328/940) *al-'Iqd al-farīd*, and, in a different sphere, the earlier adoption of Persian manners by the court of Cordova under the impact of the singer-courtier Ziryāb (arrived in Cordova in 207/822).

As the *Shu'ūbiyya*, despite a sympathetic approach to Mazdaism, had striven after a more prominent place within Arab Muslim civilization rather than the establishment of a separatist Persian Islam, so the north Persian Samanids and the north-west Persian Buyids retained Arabic as the language of government. We may recall that in the *Dēnkart* Persia's superiority over India and Rūm is based on the beauty of its language and the appreciation of measure, *patmān*. Almost simultaneously, we find Jāḥiẓ defining beauty as *wazn*, *Ebenmass*, referring to physical beauty as much as to the 'beauty' of a man's behaviour and religion.[2] The interlocking of influences becomes strikingly clear when one sees *patmān*, in the best Aristotelian manner, placed in contrast with *frēhbūtīh*, 'to be too much', and *aβēbūtīh*, 'to be defective'. It is perhaps not sufficiently appreciated that, parallel to the building in Arabic of a philological and theological terminology capable of rendering the concepts of Greek thinking, the world of Mazdaism undertook successfully a labour of comparable scope (if perhaps less completely carried through), in creating a Pahlavī terminology in the areas needed for a restatement, a revitalization of its faith. The outsider is left with the impression that, stylistically at least, the Arab effort was more fully successful; but the 'purity' of enriched Pahlavī remains a remarkable feat. Modern Persian, as it emerges as a literary language under the Samanids, appears more flexible, more clearly structured, less

[1] This is said regardless of the actual origin of the vizier's office; on which cf. D. Sourdel, *Le Vizirat 'abbāside de 749 à 936* (Damascus, 1959–1960), I, 41–61; also S. D. Goitein, 'The origin of the vizierate and its true character', *Studies in Islamic history and institutions* (Leiden, 1966), 168–96.

[2] Jāḥiẓ, *Risālat al-qiyān*, tr. C. Pellat, *Arabica*, X (1963), 121–47, at 135–6.

ambiguous in its pliability to the requirements of hypotactic grouping of thought—Ibn Sīnā himself was sensible to certain advantages, in logical terms, of Persian over Arabic, although Arabic must be judged superior in his time in its ability to cope with abstract strands of ideas.

The dominant concerns of Muslim civilization had originated in the Arab milieu—the style of the law, of *Ḥadīth*, was never persianized: that of *tafsīr*, on the other hand, especially insofar as it confined itself to word-by-word interpretation has its stylistic antecedents almost everywhere in the ancient Near East, from the Accadian dream books to the commentaries of the Avesta and the Jewish tradition. By contrast, the outlook on the outside world was more open to Persian inspiration: the geographical world-view of Islam in the fifth/eleventh century was not only formed by the Sasanian tradition (itself it is true not wholly separable from the Hellenistic) but formulated in Arabic by scholars of Persian background. Remarkably, prosodical forms such as the *Urform* of the metre *mutaqārib* seeped through the language curtain into Arabic; narrative motifs and techniques penetrated the core-stories of the *Thousand and One Nights*; but the epic did not take root, and the lives and legends of the Persian kings came to the Arabs through the Pahlavī prose chronicles, the sources of Firdawsī; neither they nor the Homeric poems in at least partial translation inspired a comparable treatment of the heroic age of Islam. But together with the pre-Islamic tales of the Battle-Days of the Arabs, *ayyām al-ʿArab*, and the Christian *vita* of the *miles Christi*, the Persian *siyar al-mulūk* stimulated historical biography—later to shade off into popular fiction—of which the first and greatest representative is the celebrated *Sīra* of the Prophet by Muḥammad b. Isḥāq (d. 151/768).

Every religion of universal aspiration, and more particularly, a religion which has captured the dominant sectors of society, must sooner or later come to terms with, integrate, explain itself by means of, the highest non-religious thought of the times. The obsolescence of science forms a parallel to the weakening of the specific experience to which a given religion owes its existence; but on the whole, this experience, its adaptations and successors within the organized religious community, remain effective longer than any one phase of scientific thought. The obsolescence of science in late antiquity and most of the Middle Ages was slowed by the prevailing anti-empiricism, and the readiness to accept the conceptual apparatus of Aristotelianism for example, without too much regard for the continued adequacy of the contents which it had been designed to scaffold.

It was the great opportunity of the major religions dominating the first millennium of our era that Aristotelian logic was available as a means of explicit rational self-statement. It was their tragedy that the metaphysics which it undergirded was atheistic in the eyes of the religions concerned, in virtue of its rejection of a personal creator God, the createdness of the world in time, its incompatibility with the doctrine of resurrection, and so forth. Even in the neo-Platonizing form given it by the later commentators, which was to gain undisputed sway over Muslim philosophy since al-Fārābī at the latest, it was a highly uncomfortable bed-fellow for a Qur'anic theology. Nevertheless the wave of Aristotelianism which swept, from *c.* 800, over the thinkers of oriental Judaism and Zoroastrianism as well as those of Islam was not to be arrested. Interestingly enough, the first translator of whom we know seems to have been Muḥammad b. ʿAbd Allāh b. al-Muqaffaʿ, the son of the great writer who more than anybody else represented the Persian tradition in his time. As a result of consistent and long drawn out labours, the Arabs came to have a much richer *corpus* of *Aristotelica* than did the Latins before the thirteenth century. Already before the *Bayt al-ḥikma*, toward the end of al-Ma'mūn's reign, took up the translation of his non-logical works, Aristotle's influence had begun to make itself felt, not only in the capital but in Baṣra where it had reached from Gondēshāpūr. The hunger for facts about the outside world notwithstanding, the logical and the metaphysical writings evoked by far the most intense interest. The peculiar way in which the introduction of Aristotelian concepts affected, or could be utilized in, internal Muslim debates, is well illustrated by the role of 'power' and 'act' (*qudra* and *fiʿl*), in the defining of the complementary ideas of divine omnipotence and human decision. Where, as with the Hanbalites and, in more subtle shadings, the Ashʿarites, *potentia* and *actus* are seen to coincide—man never is potentially capable of doing anything except what he actually does—*potentia* becomes compelling (*mujabbira*): omnipotence is saved in its most rigorous interpretation, but human freedom disappears; on the other hand, where, as with the Muʿtazilites, *potentia* is understood not only as preceding the act but as implying the power to act or not to act or to choose between two different acts or actions, man's freedom is safeguarded but divine omnipotence is self-limited; and this limitation is to be understood as in accordance with divine justice and human reason (*'aql*), implanted in man by his Creator as in harmony with the reason that governs the universe, in other words, with divine Reason itself. Beyond the obvious ethical implications there are almost equally obvious political implications—determinism entails the necessity of governmental actions as well as the necessity of their acceptance by the subjects. The bearing which the understanding of *qudra* (or *istiṭā'a*) and *fi'l* has on the problem of *imān* and *kufr*, the wider context of which has already been indicated, hardly requires development. Characteristically enough, Maimonides was to identify both Ash'ariyya and Mu'tazila as inspired by the debates, in Greek and Syriac, between the philosophers and their opponents.[1] The Greek philosophers themselves and their Muslim followers had generally to be charged with unbelief; at the same time Greek doctrines were indispensable as the foil against which Islamic doctrine had to be formulated, quite apart from the numerous verities contained side by side with destructive misconceptions. Impregnation with the Classical heritage was facilitated by the temporary breakdown of political and community controls in the fourth/tenth century, when the freedom of the curious to steep themselves in Greek thought was effectively impeded only by inaccessibility of materials. The community might frown, the *'ulamā'* disapprove, but the authorities would bring pressure on the individual solely when his endeavours threatened to entangle him with sectarian revolt or court factions of sectarian recruitment. The limitations lay in the rejection of the literary bequest of the ancients, which was, in a formal sense, complete, in spite of the admission of Greek categories into literary and rhetorical theory, and the favour enjoyed by ancient didactic and biographical writings. For a brief span, when originality was understood as creativeness and prized, and when the multiplicity and relative weakness of power centres functioning as foci of culture protected the intellectual, the beautiful description by Gregory Thaumaturgos (*c.* 213 – *c.* 270) of the atmosphere in which he grew up, would have given an accurate picture of Islamic 'Irāq. 'No subject was forbidden us, nothing hidden or inaccessible. We were allowed to become acquainted with every doctrine, barbarian or Greek, with things spiritual and secular, divine and human, traversing with all confidence (cf. Acts 28:31) and investigating the whole circuit of knowledge, and satisfying ourselves with the full enjoyment of all pleasures of the soul.'[2]

[1] *The Guide of the perplexed* I, 71; tr. S. Pines (Chicago, 1963), 176–9 Ref. in Seale, *Muslim Theology* 129–30.

[2] Trans. M. L. W. Laistner, *Christianity and pagan culture*, 61, from *In Originem oratio panegyrica* xv, 31–33, in *MPL*, X, 1096AB.

Similarity of problems, shared sources and intellectual assumptions, resulted in the adoption of methods of presentation which, regardless of language, link the philosophical-theological and much of the scientific writing of the Latin, the Byzantine and the Arab Middle Ages. Objections are introduced by *qāla* or *qālū*—as practised already by Arnobius *Adversus nationes* (probably 296–7) with his stereotyped *inquit*, *inquiunt*; this minimal formula is developed into *in qāla*...*qultu*, in keeping with the custom of Christian scholastics. More profoundly symptomatic of continuing thought-habits is the recurrence, in the Islamic environment, of the Western medieval propensity towards elaborate classification and towards a full spelling out of even simple syllogisms with no conceivable consequence or implication omitted or left to the imagination, not to say commonplace reasoning on the part of the reader.

The learned men of this science (i.e. scholastic theology) should confine their instruction to men who have the three following traits:...;...the secrets which they (i.e. the favorites of God, al-*muqarrabūn*) do not divulge to the masses may be divided in five categories...;...(the *salaf*) have known that faith is founded upon four pillars each of which involves ten principles.[1]

Classification of the sciences, or the systematic organization of all branches of learning accessible and deemed worth pursuing, become frequent in the fourth/tenth century. That proposed by al-Khuwārizmī (*c.* 366/976) is inserted here because—although not complete, and hence not fully representative of the Islamic scientific effort—it indicates with particular clarity not merely the range but also the origin of the Arab-Muslim sciences and, by implication, suggests the rationale of selecting and ordering the *scibile*.

1. The Sciences of the Religious Law, *'ulūm al-Sharī'a*
   - A. Jurisprudence, *fiqh*
   - B. Dogmatic theology, *kalām* (defined to cover the doctrines of orthodox Islam, the Muslim sects, and non-Muslim religions)
   - C. Grammar, *naḥw*
   - D. The art of the secretary, *kitāba*
   - E. Poetry and prosody, *shi'r* and *'arūḍ*
   - F. History, *al-akhbār*

[1] Ghazālī, *Iḥyā' 'ulūm al-dīn*, Book II, tr. N. A. Faris, *Al-Ghazzālī: the foundations of the faith* (Lahore, 1963), 33, 39, 56.

II. Foreign Sciences, *'ulūm al-'ajam*, equated with philosophy, *falsafa*

A. Theoretical part, *al-juz' al-nazarī*, including physics (with medicine); zoology; mathematics (with astronomy and music); theology

B. Practical philosophy, i.e. ethics, domestic economy, politics

Other classifications give logic a prominent place apart.

Measured by its permeability to Hellenistic and Persian elements, the profit drawn by Islamic civilization from India appears slight. This is not to play down the quantity of materials, from the *Pančatantra* to the *Rājanīti*, which, mostly by way of Persia, did enter Arabic literature, nor to deny the kinship of the Indian and Tibetan *mantra* with the Muslim *dhikr* (perhaps a case of 'archetypal' kinship rather than diffusion or derivation), and least of all the significance of Indian astronomy and medicine for the Muslims since the days of al-Manṣūr or of the adoption, under al-Ma'mūn, of the positional system of numbers, and so forth. The statement is rather to suggest that with its 'primary decisions' made before leaving the Arabian peninsula the Islamic world in formation had opted for the Mediterranean and Persian orbit, and cut itself off from even an adequate understanding of, let alone a productive dialogue with, Hindu and Buddhist India. The reaction of Sulaymān al-Manṭiqī to Yaḥyā b. 'Adī's expression of respect for Indian philosophy is typical. 'Ibn 'Adī told me the Indians had accomplished great things in the philosophical sciences, and the thought had occurred to him, science had reached the Greeks from there...I do not know how this notion could have occurred to him.'[1] Travellers to India who have left reports are few and far between, but among them are such notable men as the geographers al-Iṣṭakhrī (*fl. c.* 340/951) and Ibn Ḥawqal (*fl.* 367/977) and the famous geographer-historian al-Mas'ūdī (d. 346/956–7); yet of the three only al-Mas'ūdī shows any real interest in Hindu India; it is also he who has preserved for us the title of the earliest study made in Arabic of Hindu sects. It is true that concern for other cultures was generally weak, and research and exploratory travel but rarely undertaken. Yet the objective importance of India might have induced a different attitude—of contacts with the subcontinent there had been no dearth since the earliest days of Muslim expansion.

[1] Ibn Abī Uṣaybi'a, *'Uyūn al-anbā' fī ṭabaqāt al-aṭibbā'*, ed. A. Müller (Cairo, 1882; Königsberg, 1884), I. 9[10ff.]; cf. Meyerhof, *Von Alexandrien nach Bagdad*, 418.

Although Indian astronomical works were translated into Arabic earlier than Greek ones, and although the *Sindhind* (Brahmagupta's *Siddhānta*) held scholarly attention as far away as Spain into the fifth/eleventh century, the borrowings from that source remained minor. With Sind slipping away from 'Abbasid control (in the third/ninth century), India soon became to the public a remote land of mystery, whose inhabitants were ranked with the Rūm and Chinese among the three or four major civilized peoples outside the Muslim sphere, but whose contribution was only superficially and scantily taken note of, with astronomy, chess, and perfumery figuring prominently in the catalogue of their accomplishments.

Sufism may have absorbed more of Indian mentality than the terminology of its self-statements would indicate. Elements in Bāyazīd al-Bisṭāmī's teachings are at least compatible with the Indian aspiration after self-identification with God; other features in the Ṣūfī movement are reminiscent of Indian ideas, such as the concept of the path and of 'concentration,' which present analogies to the noble path and the *dhyāna* of the Buddhists. Older places of Buddhist worship in Central Asia were islamized as tombs of Muslim saints. In fact, a good many individual parallels in doctrine, disciplinary technique, mystical *Brauchtum*, pantheistic rationalization of the unitive experience can without difficulty be assembled. But behind these formal and verbal parallels there is little resemblance in the spirit that animates the mystical movements in Hinduism or Buddhism and Islam. We can agree with al-Bīrūnī (d. 440/1048) who noticed similarities between certain heterodox Ṣūfīs and Hinduistic ideas, among them metempsychosis; but we must also agree with him, the greatest of the medieval Muslims studying India, when he asserts that 'we (i.e. the Muslims) believe in nothing in which they believe and vice-versa' and 'if ever a custom of theirs resembles one of ours, it has certainly just the opposite meaning'.[1]

Julian had chided the Jews for having done nothing for culture; they as the Christians had been forced to take over Hellenic science. Uttered in a different tone of voice this reproach turns to praise, and may certainly be extended to the Muslims—not that they had 'done nothing' for culture, but rather that they, as their Jewish and Christian predecessors, had gone to the only source which, in the Mediterranean basin and beyond, would yield the tools to cultural ascent. The contact with Hellenism, mediated largely in the form it had assumed in serving

[1] *Alberuni's India*, trans. E. Sachau (London, 1910), i, 19; 179; 62–67.

Christian needs, helped to shape a mentality into a civilization. The blessed origins receded into an inspiring dream which has preserved its potency to this very day.

Know that this [the Muslim state under the first caliphs] was not a state after the fashion of the states of the world, but rather resembling the conditions of the world to come. And the truth concerning it is that its fashion was after the model of the Prophets, and its conduct after the model of the Saints, while its conquests were as those of mighty kings.[1]

But while this state grew, its counterpart in history shrank, to be replaced in its service to Islam by the community and its civilization, that became the greater the more it exceeded its denominational limits. The texture of Revelation and Tradition as woven together by Law was strong enough to permit of joyful enrichment. The meshes were wide enough for a pride to assert itself in the fabric. Where the simple believer and the religious spokesman saw all legitimate strands issue from Revelation, those captivated by an Islamic civilization they had helped to make would jubilantly proclaim their own, often remote, heritage turned contribution.

We are the heirs and offspring of paganism which has spread gloriously over the world. Happy is he who for the sake of paganism bears his burden without growing weary. Who has civilized the world and built its cities, but the chieftains and kings of paganism? Who has made the ports and dug the canals? The glorious pagans have founded all these things. It is they who have discovered the art of healing souls, and they too have made known the art of curing the body and have filled the world with civil institutions and with wisdom which is the greatest of goods. Without paganism the world would be empty and plunged in poverty.[2]

The reference, needless to say, is to the Graeco-Roman, not to the Indian tradition of which Thābit b. Qurra had no knowledge. Sophistication rapidly grew. As early as the fourth/tenth century al-Fārābī obtained that distance between himself and his world which led him to observe that the laws of the victors are not necessarily better than those of the vanquished—a guarded way of casting doubt on the absolute

[1] Ibn al-Ṭiqṭaqā, *Kitāb al-Fakhrī* (written in 1302), ed. H. Dérenbourg (Paris, 1895), p. 102; trans. E. G. Browne, *A Literary History of Persia*, I (London, 1902), 188, slightly adjusted in accordance with C. E. J. Whiting, *Al Fakhri* (London, 1947), 69. For reasons of suggestiveness I have left the somewhat anachronistic 'state' where 'dynasty' would have been more literally correct.

[2] Thābit b. Qurra, a 'Sabian' of Ḥarrān (826–901), quoted by Carra de Vaux, *Les penseurs de l'Islam* (Paris, 1921–6), II, 145–6, from whom L. Dawson, *Making of Europe* (London, 1932), 154, reproduces the reference.

superiority of the Islamic order. And al-Bīrūnī was to comprehend that Islam gathered together the various nations on the basis of mutual understanding. Its mental habit and its scientific tradition range it with the Greeks. But the religion and the state are Arabic. It is the Arab strain that gives the sense of oneness to a pluralistic civilization that has come to express itself in many a language—universalism does not destroy specific character. For 'all life carries its ideal in itself'.[1]

[1] L. von Ranke, *op. cit.*, p. 178.

CHAPTER 3

ECONOMY, SOCIETY, INSTITUTIONS

In the vast empire conquered by the Arabs, it is true that the different regions were later to develop or retain their own more or less pronounced characteristics, but, for all that, they were to be not less deeply marked by the unifying imprint of Islam. However, to appreciate the even greater complexity of Muslim society than of Islam considered as a religion, it is important to understand from the outset that both alike resulted from the increasing symbiosis between the conquerors and the original inhabitants, that they preserved a continuity with the traditions of the latter just as much as with those of the former, and that the coming of the new régime did not bring any real social break with the immediate past. Arab immigration into neighbouring territories to the north of their peninsula had started many centuries before Muḥammad, and the conquest, if it extended this process, did not modify all the basic factors as much as one might be led to believe—far less than the Germanic invasions modified European society. It occurred in two different forms, bedouin immigration and military colonization, certain features of which must be carefully defined.

To understand these correctly, it must be borne in mind that the settlement of immigrants was generally effected on the basis of a distinction between indigenous private properties, the owners of which remained on them to ensure the maintenance of cultivation and which were respected, and domains of the former states, with the addition of private properties whose owners had been killed or had fled, and which were distributed as emphyteutic concessions (*qaṭīʿa*; plur., *qaṭāʾiʿ*) to Arab notables who were responsible for their development. This being so, the bedouin at no time received the right to settle on cultivated land, nor did their masters, when they acquired residential estates, do so with a view to threatening agricultural exploitation. In general, the pastoral nomadic economy took possession of the areas which for geographical reasons had necessarily been left vacant between blocks of cultivated land, made possible the utilization of ground which would otherwise have remained unproductive, and enabled mutually beneficial exchanges to be made on the basis of the complementary needs and produce of the stockbreeders and agriculturalists. It is necessary to emphasize this positive aspect of bedouin immigration during the period, because the devastation caused by later nomadic invasions, both in the Near East and in the Maghrib, is liable to give a false impression of the character of the Muslim conquest. In exceptional cases, of course, it did prove harmful to some cultivation closely linked with export to Byzantium, but more often it merely modified the markets that were supplied (for example by diverting to the large garrisons inland and to the Holy Cities of Arabia supplies previously sent from Egypt to Constantinople). Still more generally (as, among other things, the extraordinary stability in the price of Egyptian wheat from the sixth to the ninth century suggests) it can be said that, apart from a temporary crisis in places where the maintenance of cultivation also involved the upkeep of the irrigation canals (which were quickly reconditioned and even extended), agriculture as a whole was not disturbed by the coming of the Arab conquest.

In urban life the changes were possibly somewhat greater, but perhaps not exactly in the way suggested in certain over-simplified accounts. We can agree that the coming of Islam was accompanied by a development of urbanization, as we see, for example, from the founding of Baṣra and Kūfa in 'Irāq, Fusṭāṭ (Old Cairo) in Egypt, Qayrawān in the Maghrib shortly afterwards, Baghdād rather later. We shall return to this point later, but for the moment we must emphasize that these new cities were not founded in all regions (there were practically none in Syria) and that, where they did occur, it was sometimes a matter of the re-siting of towns nearer to the edge of the desert rather than of any increase in importance, Baṣra and Kūfa replacing the decayed Sasanid capital, Ctesiphon, while Baghdād rose near its ruins, Qayrawān replacing Carthage, Damascus, an ancient city, developing at the expense of Antioch, and so forth. What is incontestable is that, whatever their social provenance in Arabia may have been, the settlement of the Arabs was essentially effected in the form of occupation-garrisons in camps which, with the passing of years, naturally acquired an urban character; the original aim had been to make the military occupation secure and, a necessary condition, to enforce a relative separation between conquerors and conquered. But, of course, it must also not be forgotten that the majority of the towns which were to become Muslim had in fact existed before Islam, nor must we fail to note that the way of life in the Arab towns themselves had become civil rather than military, that natives crowded in, and that consequently a certain affiliation with their own urban traditions came into being.

The Arab immigrants did not at once forget their former tribal structure. Among the bedouin, however, it has remained a reality up to our own time, and, in the Umayyad period, the importance of these issues aggravated the strife that divided them to such an extent that the 'Abbasid régime rejected the tribesmen. In the towns, on the other hand, elements from different tribes became intermixed and forms of a new way of life were tried out; inevitably, these soon reduced the ancient tribal pattern to a sentimental link which became even further removed from social reality as the natives, whose importance was steadily increasing, did not adhere to it.

It was in fact through the medium of the towns that the two ethnic categories of the population came into contact reasonably quickly. For a considerable period a religious barrier (the social importance of which must not be overestimated, as we shall see) continued indeed to stand between them. But very soon an intermediate group was formed, the *mawālī* (sing., *mawlā*), whose importance during the first two centuries of Islam was considerable. This name was given either to liberated prisoners of war, or else to free non-Arabs who put themselves under the protection of Arab notables; in either case they were native inhabitants living under Muslim patronage. The necessary condition was that they should have adopted the conquerors' religion, into which, however, they could not help bringing, in some measure, the preoccupations derived from their own cultural heritage. Furthermore, the relationship of patronage made it possible to integrate within Arabo-Muslim society men who, knowing nothing of tribal structure, would but for this have been wretched individuals lost in the community of the faithful. In fact, by learning Arabic, by performing for their masters all kinds of services from the humblest to the highest, and bringing them knowledge of every kind, especially in technical or administrative fields which were unknown to the newcomers, the *mawālī*, even when the Arabs looked down on them with a certain racial pride, quickly became a fundamental element of the new social structure at all levels. The unconverted natives were of course able to participate in public life to a certain extent, but more remotely, less completely. It was indeed among the *mawālī* that what later became Muslim thought and Muslim society, during the centuries when the supremacy of the Arab race had disappeared, took shape. The result of the 'Abbasid revolution was in fact to transform a certain section of them, those who came from Khurāsān, into the military bulwark and source of administrative personnel for the new régime. From that time onwards the two aristocracies, the Arab and that of the *mawālī* natives, were fused together in the towns, with the consequence that, by the third century of the *Hijra*, the term *mawālī* had lost its significance and therefore disappeared.

For the remaining natives who had not been granted patronage or had not adopted the new faith, the principal problems to be faced were of a fiscal nature. Freedom of worship, conditional upon the safeguarding of public order and respect for the conquerors' religion, was guaranteed to them, though subject to the primary requirement of the payment of taxes which symbolized in concrete form their subjection to Islam. The effective regulation of these taxes varied with the traditions of the subject peoples and the conditions of their submission. In a number of cases, particularly in Syria, it seems, tribute was exacted from communities in the form of a lump sum, collected under their own auspices, and paid to the conqueror, without any distinction being made by him between the various sources of payment. But the most usual procedure, especially in Persia and 'Irāq, and, in a different way, in Egypt, was that the subject peoples paid on the one hand a tax on their lands, the *kharāj*, and on the other hand a poll-tax on their persons, the *jizya*. As each local community was entirely responsible for the total amount either of the collective tribute, or at least of the land-tax calculated on its own land, it was in principle laid down that the conversion of certain individuals to Islam, an eventuality not at first envisaged, should not modify it in any way whatsoever. But the attraction of the Arab towns and the desire to escape from this tax did, however, encourage the peasants to flee; in 'Irāq, if not in Egypt, they sought refuge in the chief cities of the various regions and got themselves registered as Muslims. At first, attempts were made to put a stop to these desertions, which were detrimental both to the exploitation of the land and also to the collection of taxes; this also involved resisting conversions to Islam. This paradoxical situation very soon led to a solution which consisted of making a systematic distinction everywhere between the tax on land, which was unaffected by the religious status of the peasants, and the poll-tax, which was waived in the event of conversion (or, more accurately, replaced by the devotional alms, the *zakāt* of the believer). Conversion, which retained the advantage, if not of a clear fiscal gain, at least of placing the converted among the ranks of the dominant faith of society, henceforward took place among the peasants without flight and as in whole communities—with, until modern times, certain zones of resistance, mostly Christian, in Syria-Palestine, the eastern Fertile

Crescent and Egypt. In the towns, where the tax had a more personal character (whether in the case of *zakāt*, *jizya* or the multiple taxes on economic life, which were added to them), conversion, which was accompanied by a more pronounced rise in the social scale, was made individually. The groups remaining faithful to the religion of their fathers *ipso facto* retained their own laws and customs, under the control of their own dignitaries or ecclesiastics, matters of public order and of relations between communities naturally depending upon the Muslim law. To some extent, this was the so-called law of personal status, common in almost all medieval societies in which unfused groups co-existed.

Under the ʿAbbasid Caliphate, through the progressive fusion of the elements enumerated above, a new society thus came into being. As its documentation is less scanty, it is possible to give a rather fuller description of it. Naturally, social hierarchies existed, and disparity of wealth was considerable, but, apart from a limited internal autonomy enjoyed by the whole body of the Prophet's kin, the ʿAlids and ʿAbbasids, the Law did not recognize any legal privilege on the part of any individuals or groups; theoretically, all individuals were equal, and between them and the community as a whole the only body to be interposed was that of the family, as a result of which, by a kind of compensation, there was often a strong though unorganized feeling of solidarity between believers (and, where relevant, between members of the same tribe) which the historian Ibn Khaldūn was to study under the name of *ʿaṣabiyya*.

In the tribe and in the urban aristocracy, the family could easily include two or three generations, but among the poorer classes it was more divided. The law recognized the right of those who were sufficiently rich to have four legitimate wives (and also slave concubines), but these concessions were as a rule not equally operative and clearly the ordinary citizens could not afford them. Polygamy was in conformity with Persian, but not with Christian, tradition, while in Judaism it was unusual but not forbidden; the democratic sects who were accused of wanting to have women in common were apparently protesting against the shortage of wives resulting from the cornering of women by the aristocracy.

If the rich lived surrounded by their dependents, there were few urban families apart from the very poorest who did not have at least one or two slaves. This is not an original feature of Islam, since Christianity itself, at the time of its origin, also retained it, but slavery has had particular importance and has proved particularly enduring in the Muslim countries. But there must be no misunderstanding: although the troops of slaves on the latifundia in the Roman empire were also found on the sugar-plantations of Lower ʿIrāq (Negroes imported from Africa by the merchants of Baṣra), until their celebrated revolt (the revolt of the Zanj) in the middle of the third/ninth century, this is an exceptional case. In general slaves were employed exclusively for household duties or urban crafts, not for agricultural labour; being incorporated in their master's family, they in fact enjoyed certain rights and guarantees, and were not necessarily more unhappy than they would have been in the poverty-stricken African, Turkish or Slavonic communities from which they had been taken. Work in the service of the great and of princes was a special case and could even confer power on certain individuals when, like the Turks in the East, they happened to serve in the army or, at a lower level, like the Slavs or Negroes according to the country, acted as eunuchs for harems or as factors for the management of estates. Manumission, especially by testament, was frequent. The female slave generally was, or had been, her master's concubine; but, as the mother of a child, she could no longer be alienated, was set free on the death of her master, and her children by him were free.

The mixed marriages and servile unions explain why, apart from a certain pride taken by the bedouin in the purity of their blood, there was comparatively little racial prejudice in a medieval society in which the caliphs themselves were for the most part the sons of mothers who were slaves from every sort of origin.

In the economic-social structure, the principal distinction to be noted is that between the town and the countryside. In urbanized areas the rural estates were, it is true, in the ownership of town-dwellers, and produce from them supplied the town; but this picture ceases to be accurate when no town was near, and in any case the link holds good in one direction only, the country receiving practically nothing from the town except for tax-collectors and men-at-arms, while trade, when it existed, passed through the countryside without contributing anything to it. This being said, whatever may be the importance of urban crafts and of commerce in the medieval Muslim world, for individuals as for the state the land remained the principal source, in certain zones indeed the almost unique source, of wealth, and it was moreover in land that successful merchants invested a part of their profits.

The medieval Muslim world was situated almost exclusively within the subtropical zone; in general, therefore, it was characterized by the contrast between desert or sub-desert regions which could only support a limited amount of grazing, and, in places where there was water, rich oases or strips of fertile land (for example, along the Nile and Tigris) sometimes capable of producing two harvests a year. The problem of water was naturally vital, and the East had long before developed a vast network of irrigation canals as well as a variety of machines for raising water (particularly wheels with buckets along the water-courses), introduced by the Muslims into their possessions in the West, for instance the gardens (Sp. *huertas*) of Andalusia. Customary law assured the fair distribution of water among users, and the state maintained public works which, even in times of insurrections or wars, were usually respected by the armies.

It is not necessary to repeat what has been said on the question of the economically positive role of nomadism in the waterless zones; we need only make a distinction between large-scale camel-nomadism, found only in the deserts, and nomadism on a smaller scale, especially with sheep; other kinds of animals were bred by settled populations as a subsidiary or complementary part of their cultivation, but less than in Europe. Later, in the East, there was also the nomadism of the Turcomans, whose camels were better adapted to withstand the winters on the cold plateaux of northern Persia and Anatolia than were those of the Arabs. At the end of the Middle Ages, came the Mongol invasions, which disrupted agriculture and led to a diminution of the land under cultivation, in the same way as was to some extent brought about in the Maghrib, from the fifth/eleventh century, by the penetration of the Hilālī Arabs from the Egyptian borders. But the central period of the Middle Ages must not be depicted in the light of this succeeding period.

The agriculture of the Muslim countries has given rise to a special literature, the forerunner of which appeared in ʿIrāq (*c.* 291/904), the 'Nabataean agriculture' (*Kitāb al-filāḥa al-Nabaṭiyya*) of Ibn Waḥshiyya, a mixture of oral traditions and borrowings from ancient treatises. The later study of agronomy was developed chiefly in Spain in a number of works, several of which such as that of Ibn al-ʿAwwām (sixth/twelfth century) were to inspire later Latino-Spanish writings. But we also find works on this subject in Persia, even in the Yemen and elsewhere; an indication of the interest taken by notables and princes in the exploitation of their estates and the laying out of pleasure-gardens. In general, the Muslims did no more than continue the traditions of ancient agriculture;

but they introduced into other regions—this applies particularly to the West—crops or techniques, such as mills and sugar-cane, previously known only in the East; they imported from the remoter parts of Asia certain crops hitherto unknown in the Near East, such as oranges, and, lastly, considerably developed the cultivation of certain products including sugar, flax and cotton. The basic food for human beings was almost everywhere wheat, and for animals barley. In addition to these there appeared, in gardens, a great profusion of vegetables, leguminous and cucurbitaceous plants, and condiments. In the oases, alongside the vegetables, there grew all kinds of Mediterranean fruit-trees and, on the edge of the desert, there were also date-palms, providing the staple food of the poor. Vines yielded grapes and, in localities where there were many Christians, also wine; and olive-trees, planted in arid soil, produced oil, as did sesame. Cane sugar could only be grown on land belonging to the state or to great landowners, on account of the high cost of production. The main industrial crops other than foodstuffs were flax and cotton, which supplemented wool and silk as textile materials, the vast range of flowers used to make scent, and, until the spread of paper brought it to an end in the fourth/tenth century, the papyrus that was exported from Egypt throughout the Mediterranean.

Gardens were cultivated with the spade, fields with the light Mediterranean swing-plough, not the heavy plough of the North. Rotation of crops was known, but this did not prevent land from frequently being left fallow, and the system of annual redistribution of the community's land among the peasants was often practised. Whether or not the management of the land was conducted by a large estate, the method used was generally that of small-scale exploitation. In some places windmills were known, but water-mills were mainly used and in great numbers, on the smallest *wādī*, less for grinding corn, which was a domestic task, than for working oil and sugar presses.

Estates can be roughly divided, in respect of the status of the property, into three categories: land subject to *kharāj*, land subject to tithe (*ʿushr*), and *waqf* or *ḥubus*. As we have seen, all the land of the countries conquered by the Arabs outside Arabia which remained in the hands of the descendants of the owners at the time of the conquest was subject to *kharāj*. The amount of tax that these lands paid varied according to conditions of cultivation, from a half to about a fifth. The lands subject to tithe were, besides the ancient Arab estates in Arabia, those which had been distributed or acknowledged as *qaṭāʾiʿ* from public or abandoned estates, and which, like all categories of wealth among the Muslims, paid a theoretical tax of a tenth. Unlike the first, which were often of modest size and worked by the owners themselves, these were cultivated by peasants, and it was the difference between the dues that they paid and the tax owed by the owner that constituted the latter's income. As for *waqf* or *ḥubus*, which could in general apply, though not everywhere originally, to rural estates as well as to urban sources of income, these consisted of religious foundations set up in principle for the benefit of a group of 'poor men' or of an institution of public interest. Conceived in such a way that the administration of the *waqf*, together with the salary that it involved, was often reserved until the founder's line of descent became extinct, they were often set up as an indirect way of avoiding too strict a division of property under the terms of the law of succession, and of retaining for the male members of the family, and in undivided form, estates which otherwise would have been split up or alienated. The collective character of the right to the income, and the control which the *qāḍī* of the district consequently maintained over the management of the estate, impeded any individual initiative in the exploitation of the land, but it is only in modern times that the inconveniences of the institution in this respect have been clearly revealed.

The relationship between the large and small estates is difficult to define. The only certain factor is that the large estates developed throughout Muslim history, though without succeeding in destroying either the small estates (especially the gardens) owned by townsmen in the vicinity of cities, or those belonging to country gentry (*dihqāns* in Persia), or held jointly by certain rural communities. In all large properties, the land was cultivated by peasants (sing. *fallāḥ*), the majority of whom paid rent in kind and whose tenure of the land was, in theory, based on a contract of *muzāra'a*. By the terms of this contract, the peasant, who usually had only his labour to offer, paid the owner a proportion of his harvest, generally in its natural state. In the case of fertile land, this could be as much as four-fifths. However, other types of contracts also existed, such as the *musāqāt* which, for land requiring irrigation work and including plantations of trees, divided the proceeds equally between cultivator and owner, and the *mughārasa*, a planting contract, under the terms of which the cultivator had to plant orchards and, when they came into bearing, would receive one-half of the property itself. If one is to take the lawbooks literally, these contracts were said to be concluded for a short term, to avoid any risks; in practice, however, it is certain that in most cases not only were they tacitly renewed, the peasant was in fact by various means bound even more closely to the soil. The hostility of the peasants to the great landowners can be seen in a number of episodes related by the chronicles. However, the point has already been emphasized that labour in the country was in general free from slavery in the strict sense.

It was also in the country—though mostly for the benefit of the towns—that mineral resources were exploited. These were very unevenly distributed and, as a whole, were relatively scarce, though perhaps quantities were sufficient for the needs of the time. Iron was rarer than copper which, apart from the armourers' requirements for which importation had to be relied on, was the basis of metallurgy in the majority of the Muslim countries. Of the other metals, silver was mainly produced in Central Asia and Persia, and gold in Nubia, with monetary consequences to be noted below. Necessary for gold industry, mercury had been produced in Spain since Roman times. Eastern Persia, and India in particular, were rich in precious stones. Quarries supplied the Mediterranean countries with building-stone ('Irāq and Persia used bricks instead), and Egypt had extensive supplies of alum and natron, materials of importance in the manufacture of dyes for textiles and other chemical preparations. It was possible to obtain rock salt, but for the most part salt came from salt-pans along the coast or from inland lakes. From the waters of the Persian Gulf divers collected the celebrated pearls, and coral was also found in the Mediterranean and the Red Sea.

Very little information exists with regard to the techniques used in mining. In regard to status, some mines were the property of the state, and the state (at least in Egypt) held the monopoly of sale of their output; even from private mines and quarries the state exacted a duty of one-fifth, as on all treasure-trove.

The town as such is unknown in Muslim law. It does not possess the individuality either of the ancient city or of the Western commune of the later Middle Ages. However, this distinction must not be misinterpreted, or attributed to Islam. The Muslim town naturally took its place in continuity with the town of late antiquity, which, against the background of empires that became more and more centralized, had lost almost all autonomy; and the European communes came into being in under-organized states, a thing which, by comparison, the medieval Muslim world had never been. Generally speaking, true urban autonomies would have been unthinkable in that world but, as we shall see, it does not follow that the towns formed amorphous and passive communities.

In the first place, and a point of common knowledge, if the town as an individuality was unknown, it is nevertheless true that, in the Muslim world as in the ancient world, but unlike medieval Western Europe, the whole of civilization was found in the town; it was only there that administration, law, religion and culture existed; and from our own point of view, it is consequently from there only that all our records derive. It was pointed out earlier that neither the suddenness nor the extent of Muslim urbanization must be exaggerated; some countries such as Syria were as urbanized before Islam as afterwards, others remained with relatively little urbanization. Nevertheless, the sense of evolution and, still more, the universal dissimilarity of the Muslim world, if not from the Byzantine empire, at least from the Western world before the twelfth and thirteenth Christian centuries, cannot be contested. The majority of the Arabs had become sedentary, and had settled in towns, almost never in the country. And the natives had been attracted to the towns by the courts, business activities and administrative careers. It is quite impossible for us to assess the population of any town; it is no less certain that Baghdād in the third/ninth century and Cairo from the fifth/eleventh were towns which in size could be rivalled only by Constantinople and certain towns in the Far East; and apart from these a multitude of small towns could challenge the largest in the West.

A contrast has also been made between the beautiful orderliness of the Hellenistic-Roman town and the jumble of the medieval Muslim town. This contrast too has been overstressed, since at the time of the conquest many of the towns were vastly different from the theoretical order of the urbanists, while in the Muslim towns municipal dispositions were not entirely lacking. It was not by chance that the various trades and markets were located in relation to the chief mosque, and when necessary to the ramparts; the baths and water-supplies, aids to cleanliness, the maintenance of a certain width in the principal thoroughfares, these and many other matters attest the existence of some form of urban administration. And no doubt many medieval Western towns would have developed features similar to the Eastern ones if they had reached the same dimensions—has it not been said that ancient Rome was already an oriental city? This being said, the medieval Muslim town appears as a conglomeration of a certain number of closed and even hostile quarters separated by undefined stretches of land or by ruins, the one or two principal streets being surrounded by a maze of blind alleys in which the leading citizens mustered their retainers; each was invisible from outside, and the only parts open to the air were the inner courtyards and the roofs, where the nights could be spent in such houses as did not have several storeys. However each trade had its own locality (except, in the large towns, for dealers in foodstuffs who were necessarily represented in all quarters), dealers in textiles, with their central warehouse or *qayṣariyya*, banking and goldsmith's work being nearest to the chief mosque; near the ramparts were located the markets for trade with the nomads, and also the *funduq* or caravanserai for foreign merchants.

In these towns the interrelated rise of commerce and the merchant bourgeoisie was the dominant economico-social factor. However, one must not exaggerate; the officials, the other bourgeois category, in the third/ninth century held an equally important place, while from the fourth/tenth century the soldiers, soon to be joined by the *'ulamā'*, took a more exalted place than the merchant bourgeoisie. The infrequency of direct references to the latter in any kind of literature (in which, for example, as compared with the tens of thousands of biographies of *'ulamā'*, not a single true biography of a merchant has survived), while not expressly proving anything, does nevertheless suggest that it should be given a subordinate place. However, it is still correct to emphasize the rise of commerce for the general repercussions it had on the economy, by comparison with Western Europe at the same time, and even, though to a lesser extent, with the East in late antiquity.

The legitimacy of profit in trade, which, especially at the beginning of the economic decline, some were later to dispute, was never seriously questioned—so long as certain prohibitions were respected—by the founders of Islam, several of whom, starting with the Prophet himself, had been merchants. To the pious souls some writers explained under what conditions one could devote oneself to trade; but for the majority of merchants, considerations of piety remained distinct from professional life. In any case, after a century in which trade sought to adapt itself to the conditions ensuing from the conquest, it is clear that from the beginning of the third/ninth century it was flourishing.

We must make the distinction, here even more systematically than elsewhere, between local small-scale commerce and the commerce organized by powerful merchants (*tājir*; plur., *tujjār*) which not only differs from it, as is obvious, but is indeed essentially distinct from it. All merchandise imported from abroad had to be housed in a *funduq* (cf. shortly afterwards the Italian *fondaco*) where, once duties had been paid to the state, local dealers came to get supplies, the great merchants not being permitted for the most part to make any direct entry into the internal market. It is almost exclusively with this internal market that the legal treatises and summaries of *ḥisba* deal, concerning themselves with day-to-day business, and for the subject of large-scale trade we are reduced to items of information gleaned here and there, in particular from the geographers and from certain descriptions of travels.

In the ʿAbbasid period, the great centre for the whole of the East was Baghdād, to be replaced after the fifth/eleventh century by Cairo, while the distant countries of the Muslim West also had their own activities, though on a smaller scale. From ʿIrāq and Persia, embarking either from Baṣra in the Persian Gulf (or, more accurately, from its port, Ubulla) or from Sīrāf on the Persian coast, and usually with a call at ʿUmān, on the coast of Arabia, their ships sailed to the Yemen and on to East Africa, where they went beyond Zanzibar and the Comoro Islands. Sailing eastwards, they reached India and eventually Malaysia and China (Canton). The Hindus and Chinese, for their part, occasionally visited the Muslim ports or, more often, came to Ceylon or Malaysia to meet merchants from the West. After the disturbances in China which led to the massacre of the merchant colony in Canton at the end of the third/ninth century, these intermediate meeting-places became customary for a time although direct links with China were gradually re-established. Merchandise brought to ʿIrāq was largely absorbed by the court and the wealthy local aristocracy; a certain proportion however was sent on by caravan to the ports of Syria or Egypt, destined for the Christian and Muslim countries of the Mediterranean; some goods were also sent by land or sea from Syria direct to Constantinople, and from there redistributed to eastern Europe and Byzantine Italy. In addition, an overland caravan route led to Muslim Central Asia another centre of international relations from pre-Islamic times; from it, in one direction the traditional Silk Road led to China, in another the Volga lands could be reached. In the fifth/eleventh century the disturbances in the East, Fatimid policy and the rise of Italy led to a re-orientation of the Indian Ocean trade, for which the Yemen became the centre, and the Red Sea the route to the Mediterranean via Egypt. Elsewhere, in the West, relations were maintained with southern Italy and the Nigerian Sudan through the Maghrib, and with the Carolingian countries through Spain.

The goods carried were mostly valuable products of small weight and volume, such as spices (especially pepper) for culinary use, drugs, perfumes, precious stones and pearls, and delicate fabrics such as silks from China. Among the imports, however, certain commodities of greater economic significance were included. From Europe the Muslim countries imported not only hides and furs, but also part of the timber needed for ship-building and the iron for making arms, as well as their indispensable stock of slaves (Slavs, as the word indicates), supplied by merchants, sometimes Jewish, from Verdun, Venice or elsewhere in Italy. Other slaves were brought from black Africa, eastern Europe and Turkish Central Asia; the Indian Ocean also provided the teak and coconut-palm timber that was then indispensable for ship-building. In its turn Europe gradually began to import from the Muslim countries, not only luxury articles and foodstuffs, but also commodities needed for its own manufactures, for example alum from Egypt. Nevertheless, for both parties the basis of the trade resided mainly in speculation on the differences in prices between the countries supplying the goods and those that purchased them, and the question of winning a market never entered the calculations of a merchant, or indeed of a state, in the Middle Ages. The import-export balance which could seldom be achieved purely by merchandise was secured by payments in coin.

The merchants devoting themselves to this trade belonged for the most part to the various creeds to be found in the Muslim East, Muslims, Jews, Christians and Zoroastrians, apparently without any general distinction between them. The Arabs and Persians divided the navigation of the Indian Ocean between themselves, but they carried Jews and Christians coming from beyond the Persian Gulf. Their courage took them among non-Muslim peoples, not to say barbarians in the Sudan and Russia. Nevertheless neither the Muslims nor even the Christians maintained the ancient tradition of relations with the West, which in so far as they existed were kept up, until the fourth/tenth century, either by southern Italians and Venetians or by the problematic Jews from France and Spain known as Radanites whose network of operations extended to the Far East. On the subject of Jewish trade, particularly of North Africa, with the East in the next two centuries, information of great value is being made available by the gradual publication of the treasure of Judaeo-Arabic documents known as the Cairo Geniza. In the time of the Crusades, control of the Mediterranean passed increasingly to the Western Christians; the economic partition of the world left trade with Africa and Asia to the now mainly Muslim East, until the Portuguese discoveries. It was generally in the Egyptian or Syrian ports that the obligatory exchange between Western and Eastern merchants took place, in the same way as at Constantinople in the Byzantine empire. Perhaps Jews used habitually to travel from one end of a trade-route to the other, but we have no evidence that they handled business directly from the Asiatic sphere to the Mediterranean sphere: for this purpose Cairo was always used as the stopping-place.

Whatever their religion, merchants followed the same commercial methods. The capital that they employed for their trade was not theirs alone. Whether they had entered into partnership agreements, or had received goods on *commenda* (*qirāḍ*, *muḍāraba*), they thus combined their own resources with those of others or, conversely, made their own capital multiply in the hands of others, with the object of widening their business activities and spreading the risk. The 'capitalists' whose wealth was used in this way were not other merchants only; just as the merchants invested a part of their profits in land, so all men of substance, from the caliph or sultan downwards, invested part of the income that they drew from their landed properties in trade of this kind, to increase their wealth. Moreover, the merchants often secured the right to farm taxes under conditions that allowed them to use in private business money that in fact belonged to the state. This procedure foreshadows the practice of eminent Italian financiers three or four centuries later.

It has been said that the conditions governing trade compelled merchants to carry hard cash with them. Nevertheless, when they did not go beyond the limits of the Muslim world or the known and established merchant colonies, they took measures to restrict this carrying of money by making agreements with known correspondents. Over sometimes vast distances they thus developed, though they did not entirely invent, the letter of credit (*suftaja*, a Persian word) which allowed someone to have the necessary sum of money advanced to an associate or partner by a third party at some distant place, on a reciprocal basis, a procedure which implied the maintenance of regular accounts and correspondence, which indeed fast couriers often carried. It was of course also possible to contract ordinary loans and make deposits, and private individuals and governments alike made wide use of promissory notes, (*ṣakk*, from which the word cheque may be derived) to be used for payments. Finally, in certain places, in the same way as later at the fairs of Champagne in France, clearing-house procedure was in existence among the bankers; it is known to have been practised in Baṣra in the fifth/eleventh century.

Nevertheless, money naturally played its part. Apart from copper coins, which were only used for local retail trading, there were two others—silver coinage, the unit being the *dirham*, and gold coinage, the unit of which was the *dīnār*. It came to be agreed, in the fourth/tenth century, that their respective legal value was 7/100, corresponding to a ratio by weight of 7 : 10 (or, in metric units, 4 gr. 25 for the *dīnār* and 2 gr. 87 for the *dirham*) and a gold/silver rate of exchange of 10. In reality, neither the market price of precious metals nor the metal content of the coins in circulation regularly corresponded with these definitions. In international markets up to the fifth/eleventh century the *dīnār*, like the Byzantine *solidus* had the prestige now enjoyed by the dollar. But cash payments, made with variable currencies, called for the frequent use of scales. In addition, exchange operations were often necessary, both for the treasury and for trade; they were in the hands of money-changers (sing., *ṣayrafī*) who, as in Europe a little later, formed a special guild; the other operations now performed by bankers were at that time usually carried out by the great merchants themselves. In general, a monometallic system, based on silver, prevailed in the Muslim East until the end of the fourth/tenth century, and also in Spain, while the intermediate countries had a monometallic system based on gold. As a result, the stocks of treasure amassed by the Northmen and discovered on Russian territory and as far as the Baltic are principally of silver. In the fifth/eleventh century silver almost disappeared, and in the seventh/thirteenth gold became a European monopoly, but formerly it was the Muslim currency that was at a premium. The term *mancus* which, in Italy before the Crusades, denoted the principal unit of currency, probably derives from the epithet *manqūsh*, struck, applied to the Muslim *dīnār* as defined by the Caliph ʿAbd al-Malik (65-86/685–705). Certain authors have dwelt on the repercussions of these facts on the European economy, but it would be premature to postulate so unified a market.

In theory, foreign trade was subject to differential tariffs according to the politico-religious status of the merchants, and customs duties were only levied at the frontiers of the Muslim world as a whole. In reality, political and economic requirements resulted, even before the Crusades and still more afterwards, in the conclusion of commercial treaties between Muslim states and others, in which the utility of the merchandise was the prime consideration. The political dismemberment of the Muslim world from the third/ninth century and, even within the principalities then set up, the power of local notables, multiplied the levying of tolls and 'protection' payments. If these did not develop to the same extent as in feudal Europe, the contrast must not be exaggerated. And there was no longer any unity of weights and measures. The relative unity of Law and language, the sense of the community of the faithful had indeed the effect of facilitating exchanges throughout the whole Muslim world; but one must not infer the existence of a single economic market covering the whole world of Islam.

Local trade was not systematically distinguished from industry, many small artisans themselves selling their own products, and the same organization generally including them all. In regard to the character of manufactured goods, the technical contribution of the Muslim world has not been studied sufficiently, and is difficult to define. Its significance seems to have been its unparalleled diffusion, rather than any true inventiveness. No doubt the most important innovation, which was taken from the Chinese in the middle of the second/eighth century, was the making of paper; it quickly spread to the Mediterranean where it superseded the less practical and more costly Egyptian papyrus before reaching Christian Europe. But progress was also made in other fields, though its effectiveness in a slowly developing world is difficult to define; there were advances in metallurgy (the so-called 'damascene' steel, in reality Hindu), in ceramics and glassware, in the textile industry (as is shown by the number of names of fabrics that have passed into the European languages) and the chemical industry (which also has given us its vocabulary), with particular reference to the making of scent and soap, and dyeing.

In industry, a distinction has to be made between the free crafts and the state industries. The dividing line is perhaps not the same everywhere since Egypt, throughout her history, has been more étatist than other countries. Between these two types there were crafts that could be exercised freely, but which were regulated and under compulsion to supply the state. The greater part of the manufacture of arms, the maritime arsenals and even part of the Egyptian merchant fleet were naturally dependent on the state. The same was true of papyrus and paper, and also of certain luxury fabrics, gold brocades intended for princely clothing or gifts, and made in what were known as *ṭirāz* (literally embroidery) workshops. Originally woven according to Byzantine or Sasanid traditions, in the time of ʿAbd al-Malik they were given Muslim inscriptions at the same time as the coinage; there were protests from the foreign clientele, but these did not really restrict their sale. Coinage was naturally a state monopoly, the mints for gold coins being very centralized, while those for silver were more scattered.

The free crafts were extremely numerous and varied. In general, artisans themselves disposed of their products, but there seems to have been a more complex hierarchy in the textile industry in which the powerful merchants (sing., *bazzāz*) employed weavers, spinners and launderers, and, as was the case everywhere during the Middle Ages, represented the merchant aristocracy (sometimes the same men were also *tujjār*). Although naturally there were few collective operations in this work, in the textile industry in particular it was possible for workers to be grouped together in quite large workshops. In the small workshops, artisans worked surrounded by apprentices and slaves; the latter could occupy a shop in their master's name, or indeed even in their own.

As in most medieval towns in all civilizations, and as can still be seen in the traditional quarters of Muslim towns, trades were mostly grouped together, each one in a street or group of streets, (sing., *sūq*) confined to that trade, and often roofed to keep off sun and rain. In addition, there was a corporate organization, the exact nature of which is difficult to specify. What is certain is that in various ways all the artisans of the same trade were organized and grouped, but it is difficult to see whether, as in Byzantium and earlier in Rome, they were set up by state control, or, as in the guilds in the later Middle Ages in Europe, they were spontaneous associations playing an important part in the general lives, both public and private, of their members. The second characteristic is to some extent that of the professional associations which can be studied from the end of the Middle Ages; for the earlier periods, the arguments that have been adduced and that lead to this conclusion rest on analogies which are not proved or have been misinterpreted. It is not possible to confirm the existence of a craft as a collective body except on the ground of the pride that members of a distinguished calling would take in belonging to it, and, more generally, the equivalence that penal law instituted for the definition of rightful claimants to pecuniary compensation, within the tribe, for such of the Arabs as had one, the military administration for soldiers, and the professional collective bodies (sing., *ṣinf*) for those who were neither Arabs nor soldiers. But it is impossible in classical times to ascribe any important role in general life to the truly professional corporate organizations, and those which play that part are not of that character.

An official specially appointed by the police and responsible for trades and local commerce, under the supervision of the *qāḍī*, existed in all towns of any size At first known merely as 'head of the *sūq*', probably a reference to an ancient antecedent, he was later given the more religious title of *muḥtasib*, that is to say, the officer responsible for the *ḥisba*, i.e. the duty to promote good and to repress evil by concerning himself in theory with all questions of public morals, the behaviour of non-Muslims and women, the observance of ritual obligations and the rules of professional ethics. Besides the legal treatises and the *responsa* of the jurisconsults which elaborated these rules during the earliest centuries of Islam, administrative summaries for the special guidance of these *muḥtasibs* also made their appearance in the Arab countries, in both West and East, from the fifth/eleventh or sixth/twelfth century. The regulations which had to be observed were for the most part concerned with honesty in manufacture and selling, protection of the client from fraud, and of the manufacturer from competition, in the same way as in the regulations of the guilds during the late Middle Ages in Europe. On the other hand, apart from basic products in time of famine, and certain objects in which there was a monopoly, the medieval Muslim (but not the Ottoman) state—apparently under the merchants' influence—considered that it did not have the right to fix prices.

If not outside the working population, it was at least outside the framework of the professional system that the only associations which flourished in urban public life existed, namely those which it has become customary to call organizations of *futuwwa*. The references to them in literature are very varied and often obscure, and differ from one period and one country to another, with the result that it is difficult to form any definite idea of their real character. This much is certain, that they always consisted of fairly large solidarity groups, mainly, but not exclusively, recruited from the poorer classes and the young, and of males only. They readily adopted an attitude of hostility to the rich and powerful which resulted, at times when authority was poorly enforced, in violent disorders. One of their principal aims, for the particular purpose of neutralizing repression, was to be enrolled in the police; sometimes they obtained temporary satisfaction of this aim, sometimes powerful leaders recruited henchmen among them, for use in their quarrels, and thus the activities of the *futuwwa* became involved in the general factional strife, which, under various pretexts, sundered many Muslim towns. Entry into the groups of *futuwwa* in the strict sense took place with initiatory rites roughly comparable with those found in other societies, and, in the Muslim world, other associations such as the secret Ismāʿīlī ones; but there seem to be no grounds for concluding that the latter had any specific influence upon the former. Nor is it possible to trace back to the central Middle Ages the influence exercised by the *futuwwa* from the eighth/fourteenth century over trades in the Perso-Turkish countries. Incidentally, the *futuwwa* was always more prominent in the territories of the former Sasanid empire than in the Arab countries, in which we find urban militias of popular *aḥdāth*, without the ritual and ideological developments that characterize the true *futuwwa*. In the Muslim West nothing approaching these *aḥdāth* has as yet been recorded.

From about the fifth/eleventh century certain reciprocal influences came into being between the *futuwwa* associations and the communities of Ṣūfīs. From them resulted a literature of *futuwwa* which, in that it presented only their ritual and mystical aspects, has for a long time prevented us from seeing their real social significance. In a large well-policed town such as Baghdād, this significance might reside in a kind of class opposition to the rich and the rulers, but more generally it appeared as an expression of the latent hostility felt by the whole population of the town towards the usually foreign (or so regarded) governors to whom they were subject. In certain limited cases, by reliance on the strength of the *futuwwa* some notables succeeded in gaining temporary autonomy in a town.

If the subject of government in Muslim society has been left almost until the end, that is because it was never, or almost never, anything other than superimposed; never, or almost never, the emanation or expression of that society. It is in its solidarities at the individual level that the true social coherences and structures of Islam are to be found, not in the princes, their soldiers and their tax-collectors. This was so at least from the time when, in the third/ninth or fourth/tenth century, experience imposed the conclusion that one was obliged to submit to those who were in fact governing, rather than to maintain the idealistic aspirations of the first generations to establish a power expressing in social terms the Islam of the community of believers. This does not alter the fact that, on another level, the political and administrative institutions of the Muslim world are among the most highly developed that had hitherto been known.

The Muslim faith does not distinguish the political from the religious, thereby differing from medieval Christianity with its theory of the Two Powers and even more from Roman tradition or the modern Western world. Consequently, rulers were expected to possess moral and religious qualities, and the religious attitude entailed certain political choices. At the very beginning of Islam the political problem was conceived in terms of a religious problem, indeed the fundamental religious problem.

At the head of the community stood the caliph, that is to say the representative, the successor of the Prophet and, through him, of God. Naturally he had absolute power in principle, absolute however in order that he might apply a Law which was anterior to himself, and for the interpretation of which he had no particular prerogative. The initiatives that he could make must therefore in theory aim only at assuring respect for the Law. The Shīʿa, it is true—and especially the Fatimids in the fourth/tenth century—were to endow their *imām* with more complete authority, in keeping with their belief that in some way God was continuing in him His revelation to the Prophet. But, both before and after the Fatimids, the great majority of Muslims always refused to recognize that the caliph had any claim to interpret the Law outside the consensus of specialists, and that is one of the main lessons of the failure of the Muʿtazilite attempt. This being said, and all true legislation being thus excluded, it nevertheless remains true that, in practice, everyday political activity and the organization of military and financial institutions do in fact imply initiatives which owe nothing to the Law, and that even here, as in every state, there is thus a certain sector which is in effect 'secular'. But the ʿAbbasid Caliphate which sternly rebuked its Umayyad predecessor for having too easily decided in favour of this 'secular' character, itself endeavoured to define its own conduct of government in Muslim terms and consequently, so far as it could do so, to impart a religious orientation to it. We shall see presently how this attempt also finally failed.

In the Umayyad period, the governmental and administrative institutions were still relatively simple. Very broadly speaking, they consisted of an organization of subjects, for the most part governed according to their own traditions and led by agents who came from among themselves—non-Muslim, non-Arab—and, superimposed upon this foundation, the corps of Arab and Muslim rulers whose primary function was to govern the Muslim Arabs, leading them to war, guiding their cultural life and distributing pensions paid for by taxes on non-Muslim subjects. The arabization and islamization which took place from the time of the caliphate of ʿAbd al-Malik were not completed in a day, and did not prevent the institutions from retaining their simple character. In this way of life the caliph, who was easily approached, was no more than *primus inter pares*. In the provinces he left almost all power to the governors whom he appointed, and to whom the local administration was subordinate, with a corresponding limitation of tasks for the central government. Thus, apart from war and religion, the central government hardly needed more than secretary heads of departments who cannot be said to have had any real power.

The evolution which took shape under the Umayyads, and which was accelerated under the ʿAbbasids, was to bring about a profound change in the character of the régime. A considerable effort was made to achieve centralization and control (incidentally, causing uprisings in the provinces in protest), which implies an extensive bureaucracy. In this way, certain traditions of the Romano-Byzantine and Sasanid empires were resumed and developed still further. Offices in which a vast amount of writing was done proliferated and became more complex, with the result that an actual specialized class of officials came into being, the *kuttāb* (literally 'scribes', plur. of *kātib*), mostly arabized and islamized Persians, who also took an influential part in the field of culture and formed a counterpoise to the doctors of the Law. Under the first ʿAbbasids, it was still the caliph alone who co-ordinated the activities of these various departments, and none of the departmental heads had the rank of a real minister. Nevertheless, the caliph gradually gave more and more authority to a personage close to him, the *wazīr*, who originally was no more than a private assistant who helped him to carry his burden—that is the meaning of the word which is Arabic, not Persian as has been stated. The first ʿAbbasids put the *wazīr* in charge of certain departments, and when necessary also made him tutor to their heirs. To the consequent growth of power came reactions, the most famous and spectacular being the fall of the Barmecides, under Hārūn al-Rashīd. But in proportion as the effective power of the caliphate declined, so did that of the wazirate increase and, from the middle of the fifth/eleventh century, the *wazīrs*, who were now recruited from the professional class of the *kuttāb*, were the real heads of the administration, and even played an increasing part in the conduct of purely political activities. Writers were now producing not only biographies of caliphs but also biographies of *wazīrs*.

The principal administrative departments were those of the chancery, the exchequer and the army. Justice, which derives from religion, had a different status and a different personnel, with which we need not concern ourselves here. These departments were all denoted by the Persian word *dīwān*, which passed into European languages (*douane, dogana, aduana*, in the sense of customs-house. It was from the chancery (*dīwān al-rasā'il* or *dīwān al-inshā'*) that all political correspondence emanated, for which a formulary, and later an authentic literary style, were, little by little, perfected, with the result that the work could only be performed by the highly literate. The *dīwān al-jaysh* concerned itself with all matters connected with army recruitment, structure, armament and, of course, payment. The department for *'arḍ* held reviews of the troops, checked the identity of the soldiers and the upkeep of arms and animals and, when that was done, distributed the pay, or awarded the concessions that took its place. These, in the form of *iqṭā's* which will be defined shortly, later constituted an independent department. But it was above all upon the exchequer (*dīwān al-māl*) that everything depended. The central organization, with equivalent departments corresponding to it in every province, consisted of offices which established the bases for taxes particularly by checking and upkeep of the cadastral surveys, among which the *dīwān al-kharāj* and the *dīwān al-ḍiyā'* (the latter for estates or *qaṭā'i'* paying the tenth) should be noted; then the *zimām* (later called *istīfā'*, the head of which was the *mustawfī*) which verified the accuracy of the accounts for taxes actually paid; the department for disbursements, which paid out salaries; the treasury (*bayt al-māl*) to which revenues that were not immediately expended on the spot were brought, and with which the shops for valuable clothing, and jewels were associated. Among the officials or agents attached to these departments a special part was played by the *jahbadh*, who was often a merchant by origin and who verified and exchanged the two variable currencies. Taxation was sometimes levied directly, sometimes farmed out to merchants or influential men, sometimes conceded as a *muqāṭa'a*, that is to say left to some important man who simply paid a lump sum for it or undertook responsibility for some military service at his own expense, or sometimes, particularly after the fourth/tenth century, given as *iqṭā'* in return for service and without any payment being made, as the equivalent of army pay. Varying according to the different regions, periods, kinds of cultivation and status of the land, the land-tax was paid in kind, in cash or with a mixture of the two. It was possible to estimate it in advance; extremely accurately in Egypt where all agriculture was governed by the Nile flood, less precisely in other places where estimates were made nevertheless. We still possess actual 'Abbasid budgets covering the period from the end of the second/eighth century to the beginning of the fourth/tenth. But in these budgets there is no mention of *jizya*, *zakāt* or of local duties on commerce and industry, which were allocated compulsorily for public works in the area where they were collected, or for the salaries (which were regarded as forming part of these) of the police and various agents. This signifies that, at the very time of the rise of the merchant economy, it was less easy for the state to make use of the profits for its own advantage than it was for the merchants to benefit from the public taxes. We shall return in a moment to the consequences of this fact.

The early army was composed of Muslim Arabs fighting in the name of the Holy War, and maintained less by regular pay than by booty. The ending of the conquests dried up this source, and made necessary the establishment of a paid army on the basis of service, not of family and religious standing as at first. The original army had owed its successes to its constant mobility and preparedness, as well as to the disloyalty of the native populations towards the régimes to which they had previously been subjected; but it did not possess the technical aptitude of the old Byzantine and Sasanid armies and in particular lacked any kind of siege weapons. From the last Umayyad days, the need for reform was imperative; the 'Abbasid revolution achieved this. In the sense that as the new régime relied mainly on its immediate Khurāsānī supporters, for the future it was Persian rather than Arab traditions that prevailed, at least in the East and around the caliph. Henceforward there was a professional army, the only one recorded in the rolls of the *dīwān*—with the exception of the West—to which were attached only light corps of voluntary *ghāzīs* and bedouin Arabs on the frontiers of Anatolia or Central Asia, the latter living on the fruits of their raids, the former benefiting also from pious foundations of believers who were themselves unable to participate in the Holy War and who were anxious at least to win Allāh's mercy for themselves in this way. Besides individual warriors, the army henceforward acquired all that military science then knew in the way of siege engines, Greek fire, and soon afterwards crossbows. But even this régime did not remain unchanged. Quite soon there came a time when the exclusive guardianship of the Khurāsānīs proved irksome to the caliphs, while at the same time their recruitment became more difficult on account of the increasing concessions of autonomy that had had to be made to the governors of Khurāsān and the surrounding regions. It was thus necessary to summon new populations, such as the semi-islamized Turks of Transoxania, or Daylamites from the south Caspian provinces, the latter as infantrymen, the former as cavalry. But the idea also came to the caliphs, especially to al-Muʿtaṣim (218–27/833–42) that the fidelity of the troops would be more certain if they were recruited from among foreign personal slaves rather than from indigenous freemen who were involved in party conflicts, and that, if acquired while still young, they could also be given technical training more successfully. In fact, the same thing happened that had happened to the Praetorians of Rome. The new soldiers were not slow to see that the caliphate was powerless but for themselves; moreover the leaders whom they really recognized were not the caliphs, who stayed immured in their palaces, but the generals who commanded them. Conflicts occurred between factions, or against the reigning caliph, with the object of bringing to effective power, in the name of a new caliph, a military commander who would show favour to his adherents, and moreover a prince whose first act would be to grant higher pensions to those to whom he owed his power. It was to no advantage, very much the contrary, that such manoeuvres should replace the former ethnic or politico-religious divisions, with which incidentally they were occasionally combined.

The new army was naturally far more costly to maintain than the old one, since the soldiers had to rely entirely on their pay for their maintenance; the arms and instruments being developed entailed additional expenditure, and the commanders being aware of their own strength demanded more; moreover, for some obscure reasons, it appears that the cost of living became generally very much higher during the third/ninth century. The budget therefore became much more heavily burdened, and for that reason the regular disbursements to the army became more difficult to fulfil, while the harshness of taxation and its unpopularity with the populace increased in proportion. Some of the commanders then demanded direct rule over the provinces where they were to maintain their forces; they themselves were so highly esteemed that it was impossible to refuse them, at least in every case. When their *de facto* autonomy merged with the increasing local feeling of the inhabitants, the political dismemberment of the empire soon followed; and what remained of it consequently suffered from yet another increase in taxation since, to save this residue at least, it was essential to avoid cutting down the army. The whole process was a vicious circle which, in the fourth/tenth century, in the very centre of the caliphate, led to the direct seizure of power by the military commanders, and thereafter it was upon them, after their investiture by a caliph, representing and conferring legitimacy, that the whole administration depended, including the *wazīr*, together with all the revenues of the state.

The *de facto* substitution of military commanders—by popular usage, and later, from the fifth/eleventh century, in the official terminology, these were known as sultans—in place of the caliph did not thereby solve the military-financial problem. Some degree of success was reached by the creation of the system of the *iqṭāʿ* (to be distinguished from the early *qaṭīʿa*, which has often been confused with it on account of the common root) which consisted in making a direct allocation to officers of the right to the taxes from a district where the revenue was approximately equivalent to the pay due to the army units—thus in fact removing them from the control of the state administration. The full consequences of this innovation were not immediately revealed, because the officers, being ignorant of the conditions of sound business, at first had their *iqṭāʿs* constantly changed; but later, especially when the system worked for the benefit of the Turks who arrived with the Seljuks in the fifth/eleventh century, they settled on territory which they became accustomed to regard as their own. With the help of protection and commendation, a method that had existed from the beginnings of Islam, if not before, but which now played in their favour, they also acquired an increasing share of the free property. In this way a régime was established in the East which in certain respects resembled Western feudalism. It never acquired the solidity of that system because the law of succession, ignoring the right of primogeniture, divided the inheritances, and because the recruitment of new slaves allowed the princes to fight against former freedmen until such time as one of the invasions which devastated the East temporarily replaced one aristocracy by another. Nevertheless, the inhabitants became accustomed to think that they were ruled by foreign military aristocracies; hence the development of urban discontent which in the long view was inevitably doomed to failure.

The slowing-down of commerce in certain regions and, in others, the fact that the Europeans were henceforward to take their share of profits, effectively reduced the strength of resistance of the merchant class, which was also severely tested by the political troubles. The new masters only asked that their capital should be made to multiply, but in an emergency they did not hesitate to confiscate the merchants' wealth, and in any case it was largely they who disposed of the funds upon which the merchants lived. The result was that the apogee of Muslim trade in the fourth/tenth century was immediately followed by a partial decline, and by what amounts to a form of tutelage exercised by the ruler over the merchants. This requires the historian to be cautious in estimating the social forces at work. Anxiety to protect their descendants from hazards of this sort, as well as to safeguard public foundations, sentiments that no doubt were shared by the new aristocrats, led to the development of the hitherto modest institution of the *waqf* or *ḥubus* which from that time took the form of large foundations for the benefit of mosques, establishments of Ṣūfī devotees, religious schools, and so forth. As a result, a new class of men appeared, living on these foundations, individually of modest wealth but collectively powerful. If they too, in the final analysis, were materially dependent upon the armed forces, the converse was also partly true, in the sense that it was in their interest to support those army leaders who favoured the religious groups to which they belonged against others, and that they possessed great moral influence over the populace of which they themselves formed part. Thus at the end of the so-called Middle Ages, and even more as the bourgeoisie declined, there was to a certain extent a kind of condominium of the army and the religious; this condominium was to be a characteristic feature of the majority of Muslim countries until the dawn of the modern period.

Though necessarily very brief, the foregoing chapter, it is hoped, will nevertheless have shown that Muslim society in its various aspects, from its economy to its political institutions, while displaying certain specific characteristics, continued constantly to evolve, until the time when those who professed to represent the Law stood as guarantors for a régime which in fact no longer owed anything to it. We have been at pains to emphasize this evolution on account of the legendary idea of Oriental conservatism, for which there is no foundation. That Europe in modern times should have accelerated its rhythm and, in so doing, should have retarded that of the very nations whom its competition was overwhelming, does not mean that they too had not earlier developed like others. For this reason it has not been possible to make the present account follow a static pattern, and the reader may thus have found it difficult to assimilate. But if he has absorbed this lesson at least from it, his time will not have been wasted.

CHAPTER 4

LAW AND JUSTICE

The sacred law of Islam, the *Sharīʿa*, occupies a central place in Muslim society, and its history runs parallel with the history of Islamic civilization. It has often been said that Islamic law represents the core and kernel of Islam itself and, certainly, religious law is incomparably more important in the religion of Islam than theology. As recently as 1959, the then rector of al-Azhar University, Shaykh Maḥmūd Shaltūt, published a book entitled 'Islam, a faith and a law' (*al-Islām, ʿaqīda wa-sharīʿa*), and by far the greater part of its pages is devoted to an exposé of the religious law of Islam, down to some technicalities, whereas the statement of the Islamic faith occupies less than one-tenth of the whole. It seems that in the eyes of this high Islamic dignitary the essential bond that unites the Muslims is not so much a common simple creed as a common way of life, a common ideal of society. The development of all religious sciences, and therefore of a considerable part of intellectual life in Islam, takes its rhythm from the development of religious law. Even in modern times, the main intellectual effort of the Muslims as Muslims is aimed not at proving the truth of Islamic dogma but at justifying the validity of Islamic law as they understand it. It will therefore be indicated for us to survey the development of Islamic law within the framework of Islamic society and civilization, tentative as this survey is bound to be. Islamic law itself is one of our most important sources for the investigation of Islamic society, and explaining Islamic law in terms of Islamic society risks using a circular argument. Besides, the scarcity of expert historical and sociological studies of Islamic law has more often been deplored than it has inspired efforts to fill this gap.

Islamic law had its roots in pre-Islamic Arab society. This society and its law showed both profane and magical features. The law was magical in so far as the rules of investigation and evidence were dominated by sacral procedures, such as divination, oath, and curse; and it was profane in so far as even penal law was reduced to questions of compensation and payment. There are no indications that a sacred law existed among the pagan Arabs; this was an innovation of Islam. The magical element left only faint traces, but Islamic law preserved the profane character of a considerable portion of penal law. It also preserved the essential features of the law of personal status, family, and inheritance as it existed, no doubt with considerable variations of detail, both in the cities and among the bedouin of Arabia. All these subjects were dominated by the ancient Arabian tribal system, combined with a patriarchal structure of the family. Under this system, the individual lacked legal protection outside his tribe, the concept of criminal justice was absent and crimes were reduced to torts, and the tribal group was responsible for the acts of its members. This led to blood feuds, but blood feuds were not an institution of ancient Arab tribal law, they stood outside the law and came under the purview of the law only when they were mitigated by the payment of blood-money, and at this moment the profane character of ancient Arabian law asserted itself again. There was no organized political authority in pre-Islamic Arab society, and also no organized judicial system. However, if disputes arose concerning rights of property, succession, and torts other than homicide, they were not normally decided by self-help but, if negotiation between the parties was unsuccessful, by recourse to an arbitrator. Because one of the essential qualifications of an arbitrator was that he should possess supernatural powers, arbitrators were most frequently chosen from among soothsayers. The decision of the arbitrator was obviously not an enforceable judgment, but a statement of what the customary law was, or ought to be; the function of the arbitrator merged into that of a lawmaker, an authoritative expounder of the normative legal custom or *sunna*. Transposed into an Islamic context, this concept of *sunna* was to become one of the most important agents, if not the most important, in the formation of Islamic law, and the *'ulamā'*, the authoritative expounders of the law, became not in theory but in fact the lawmakers of Islam.

Muḥammad began his public activity in Mecca as a religious reformer, and in Medina he became the ruler and lawgiver of a new society on a religious basis, a society which was meant, and at once began, to replace and supersede Arabian tribal society. Already in Mecca, Muḥammad had had occasion to protest against being regarded as merely another soothsayer by his pagan countrymen, and this brought about, in the early period of Medina, the rejection of arbitration as practised by the pagan Arabs. But when Muḥammad was called upon to decide disputes in his own community, he continued to act as an arbitrator, and the Qur'ān, in a roughly contemporaneous passage, prescribed the appointment of an arbitrator each from the families of husband and wife in the case of marital disputes. In a single verse only, which again is roughly contemporaneous with the preceding passage, the ancient Arab term for arbitration appears side by side with, and is in fact superseded by, a new Islamic one for a judicial decision: 'But no, by thy Lord, they will not (really) believe until they make thee an arbitrator of what is in dispute between them and find within themselves no dislike of that which thou decidest, and submit with (full) submission' (*Sūra* 4. 65). Here the first verb refers to the arbitrating aspect of Muḥammad's activity, and the second, 'to decide', from which the Arabic term *qāḍī* is derived, emphasizes the authoritative character of his decision. This is the first indication of the emergence of a new, Islamic, concept of the administration of justice. Numerous passages in the Qur'ān show that this ideal demand was slow to be fulfilled, but Muḥammad's position as a prophet, backed in the later stages of his career in Medina by a considerable political and military power, gave him a much greater authority than could be claimed by an arbitrator; he became a 'Prophet-Lawgiver'. But he wielded his almost absolute power not within but without the existing legal system; his authority was not legal but, for the believers, religious, and, for the lukewarm, political. He was essentially a townsman, and the bitterest tirades in the Qur'ān are directed against the bedouin.

Muḥammad's legislation, too, was a complete innovation in the law of Arabia. Muḥammad, as a prophet, had little reason to change the existing customary law. His aim was not to establish a new legal order, but to teach men what to do in order to achieve their salvation. This is why Islamic law is a system of duties, of ritual, legal, and moral obligations, all of which are sanctioned by the authority of the same religious command. Thus the Qur'ān commands to arbitrate with justice, to give true evidence, to fulfil one's contracts, and, especially, to return a trust or deposit to its owner. As regards the law of family, which is fairly exhaustively treated in the Qur'ān, the main emphasis is laid on how one should act towards women and children, orphans and relatives, dependants and slaves. In the field of penal law, it is easy to understand that the Qur'ān laid down sanctions for transgressions, but again they are essentially moral and only incidentally penal, so much so that the Qur'ān prohibited wine-drinking but did not enact any penalty, and the penalty was determined only at a later stage of Islamic law. The reasons for Qur'anic legislation on all these matters were, in the first place, the desire to improve the position of women, of orphans and of the weak in general, to restrict the laxity of sexual morals and to strengthen the marriage tie, to restrict private vengeance and retaliation and to eliminate blood feuds altogether; the prohibition of gambling, of drinking wine and of taking interest are directly aimed at ancient Arabian standards of behaviour. The main political aim of the Prophet, the dissolution of the ancient bedouin tribal organization and the creation of an essentially urban community of believers in its stead, gave rise to new problems in family law, in the law of retaliation and in the law of war, and these had to be dealt with. The encouragement of polygamy by the Qur'ān is a case in point. A similar need seems to have called for extensive modifications of the ancient law of inheritance, the broad outlines of which were, however, preserved; here, too, the underlying tendency of the Qur'anic legislation was to favour the underprivileged; it started with enunciating ethical principles which the testators ought to follow, and even in its final stage, when fixed shares in the inheritance were allotted to persons previously excluded from succession, the element of moral exhortation had not disappeared. This feature of Qur'anic legislation was preserved by Islamic law, and the purely legal attitude, which attaches legal consequences to relevant acts, is often superseded by the tendency to impose ethical standards on the believer.

Islamic law as we know it today cannot be said to have existed as yet in the time of Muḥammad; it came gradually into existence during the first century of Islam. It was during this period that nascent Islamic society created its own legal institutions. The ancient Arab system of arbitration, and Arab customary law in general, continued under the first successors of Muḥammad, the caliphs of Medina. In their function as supreme rulers and administrators, the early caliphs acted to a great extent as the lawgivers of the Islamic community; during the whole of this first century the administrative and legislative functions of the Islamic government cannot be separated. But the object of this administrative legislation was not to modify the existing customary law beyond what the Qur'ān had done; it was to organize the newly conquered territories for the benefit of the Arabs, and to assure the viability of the enormously expanded Islamic state. The first caliphs did not, for instance, hesitate to repress severely any manifestation of disloyalty, and even to punish with flogging the authors of satirical poems directed against rival tribes, a recognized form of poetic expression which, however, might have threatened the internal security of the state. This particular decision did not become part of Islamic law, but other enactments of the caliphs of Medina gained official recognition, not as decisions of the caliphs, but because they could be subsumed under one or the other of the official sources of Islamic law which later theory came to recognize. The introduction of stoning to death as a punishment for unchastity under certain conditions is one such enactment. In the theory of Islamic law, its authority derives from alleged commands of the Prophet; there also exists an alleged verse of the Qur'ān to this effect which, however, does not form part of the official text and must be considered spurious. Traditions reporting alleged acts and sayings of the Prophet came into use as proof-texts in law not earlier than the end of the first century of Islam, and the spurious verse of the Qur'ān represents an earlier effort to establish the validity of the penal enactment in question. That the need of this kind of validation was felt at all, shows how exceptional a phenomenon the legislation of Muḥammad had been in the eyes of his contemporaries.

The political schisms which rent the Islamic community when it was still less than forty years old, led to the secession of the two dissident, and later 'heterodox', movements of the Kharijites and of the Shī'a, but they did not lead to significant new developments in Islamic law; the essentials of a system of religious law did not as yet exist and the political theory of the Shī'a, which more than anything else might have been expected to lead to the elaboration of quite a different system of law, was developed only later. In fact, those two groups took over Islamic law from the 'orthodox' or Sunnī community as it was being developed there, making only such essentially superficial modifications as were required by their particular political and dogmatic tenets. In one respect, however, the exclusive, and therefore 'sectarian', character of the two secessionist movements influenced not so much the positive contents as the emphasis and presentation of their doctrines of religious law; the law of the Shī'a is dominated by the concept of *taqiyya*, 'dissimulation' (a practice which, it is true, was forced upon them by the persecutions which they had to suffer), and by the distinction between esoteric and exoteric doctrines in some of their schools of thought; and that of the Kharijites is dominated by the complementary concepts of *walāya*, 'solidarity', and *barā'a*, 'exclusion', 'excommunication'.

At an early period, the ancient Arab idea of *sunna*, precedent or normative custom, reasserted itself in Islam. Whatever was customary was right and proper, whatever their forefathers had done deserved to be imitated, and in the idea of precedent or *sunna* the whole conservatism of

Arabs found expression. This idea presented a formidable obstacle to every innovation, including Islam itself. But once Islam had prevailed, the old conservatism reasserted itself within the new community, and the idea of *sunna* became one of the central concepts of Islamic law.

Sunna in its Islamic context originally had a political rather than a legal connotation. The question whether the administrative acts of the first two caliphs, Abū Bakr and ʻUmar, should be regarded as binding precedents, arose probably when a successor to ʻUmar had to be appointed in 23/644, and the discontent with the policy of the third caliph, ʻUthmān, which led to his assassination in 35/655, took the form of a charge that he, in his turn, had diverged from the policy of his predecessors and, implicitly, from the Qur'ān. In this connexion, there arose the concept of the '*sunna* of the Prophet', not yet identified with any set of positive rules, but providing a doctrinal link between the '*sunna* of Abū Bakr and ʻUmar' and the Qur'ān. The earliest evidence for this use of the term '*sunna* of the Prophet' dates from about 76/695, and we shall see later how it was introduced into the theory of Islamic law.

The thirty years of the caliphs of Medina later appeared, in the picture that the Muslims formed of their own history, as the golden age of Islam. This is far from having been the case. On the contrary, the period of the caliphs of Medina was rather in the nature of a turbulent interval between the first years of Islam under Muḥammad and the Arab kingdom of the Umayyads. Not even the rulings of the Qur'ān were applied without restriction. It can be shown from the development of Islamic legal doctrines that any but the most perfunctory attention given to the Qur'anic norms, and any but the most elementary conclusions drawn from them, belong almost invariably to a secondary and therefore later stage. In several cases the early doctrine of Islamic law is in direct conflict with the clear and explicit wording of the Qur'ān. *Sūra* 5. 6, for instance, says clearly: 'O you who believe, when you rise up for worship, wash your faces and your hands up to the elbows, and wipe over your heads and your feet up to the ankles'; the law nevertheless insists on washing the feet, and this is harmonized with the text by various means. *Sūra* 2. 282 endorsed the current practice of putting contracts, particularly those which provided for performance in the future, into writing, and this practice did in fact persist in Islam. Islamic law, however, emptied the Qur'anic command of all binding force, denied validity to written documents, and insisted on the evidence of eye-witnesses, who in the Qur'anic passage play only a subsidiary part. It is, of course, true that many rules of Islamic law, particularly in the law of family and in the law of inheritance, not to mention worship and ritual, were, in the nature of things, based on the Qur'ān and, we must assume, on the example of Muḥammad from the very beginning. But even here we notice (as far as we are able to draw conclusions on this early period from the somewhat later doctrines of Islamic law) a regression, in so far as pagan and tribal Arab ideas and attitudes succeeded in overriding the intention, if not the wording, of the Qur'anic legislation. This went parallel to, and was indeed caused by, the exacerbation of tribal attitudes in the turbulence created by the Arab wars of conquest and their success. The Qur'ān, in a particular situation, had encouraged polygamy, and this, from being an exception, now became one of the essential features of the Islamic law of marriage. It led to a definite deterioration in the position of married women in society, compared with that which they had enjoyed in pre-Islamic Arabia, and this was only emphasized by the fact that many perfectly respectable sexual relationships of pre-Islamic Arabia had been outlawed by Islam. As against tribal pride and exclusiveness, the Qur'ān had emphasized the fraternity rather than the equality of all Muslims; nevertheless, social discrimination and Arab pride immediately reasserted themselves in Islam. Non-Arab converts to Islam, whatever their previous social standing, were regarded as second-class citizens (*mawālī*) during the first hundred and fifty years of Islam, and all schools of law had to recognize degrees of social rank which did not amount to impediments to marriage but nevertheless, in certain cases, enabled the interested party to demand the dissolution of the marriage by the *qāḍī*. The Qur'ān had taken concubinage for granted, but in the main passage concerning it (*Sūra* 4. 3) concubinage appears as a less expensive alternative to polygamy, a concept far removed from the practice of unlimited concubinage in addition to polygamy which prevailed as early as the first generation after Muḥammad and was sanctioned by all schools of law. Also, the Qur'anic rules concerning repudiation, which had been aimed at safeguarding the interests of the wife, lost much of their value by the way in which they were applied in practice. Early Islamic practice, influenced no doubt by the insecurity which prevailed in the recently founded garrison-cities with their mixed population, extended the seclusion and the veiling of women far beyond what had been envisaged in the Qur'ān, but in doing this it merely applied the clearly formulated intention of the Qur'ān to new conditions. Taking these modifications into account, the pre-Islamic structure of the family survived into Islamic law.

During the greater part of the first/seventh century, Islamic law, in the technical meaning of the term, did not as yet exist. As had been the case in the time of Muḥammad, law as such fell outside the sphere of religion; if no religious or moral objections were involved, the technical aspects of law were a matter of indifference to the Muslims. This accounts for the widespread adoption, or rather survival, of certain legal and administrative institutions and practices of the conquered territories, such as the treatment of the tolerated religions which was closely modelled on the treatment of the Jews in the Byzantine empire, methods of taxation, the institution of *emphyteusis*, and so forth. The principle of the retention of pre-Islamic legal practices under Islam was sometimes openly acknowledged, e.g. by the historian al-Balādhurī (d. 279/892), but generally speaking fictitious Islamic precedents were later invented as a justification.

The acceptance of foreign legal concepts and maxims, extending to methods of reasoning and even to fundamental ideas of legal science, however, demands a more specific explanation. Here the intermediaries were the cultured converts to Islam. During the first two centuries of the *Hijra*, these converts belonged mainly to the higher social classes, they were the only ones to whom admission to Islamic society, even as second-class citizens, promised considerable advantages, and they were the people who (or whose fathers) had enjoyed a liberal education, that is to say, an education in Hellenistic rhetoric, which was the normal one in the countries of the Near East which the Arabs had conquered. This education invariably led to some acquaintance with the rudiments of law. The educated converts brought their familiar ideas with them into their new religion. In fact, the concepts and maxims in question were of that general kind which would be familiar not only to lawyers but to all educated persons. In this way, elements originating from Roman and Byzantine law, from the canon law of the Eastern Churches, from Talmudic and rabbinic law, and from Sasanian law, infiltrated into the nascent religious law of Islam during its period of incubation, to appear in the doctrines of the second/eighth century.

The rule of the caliphs of Medina was supplanted by that of the Umayyads in 41/661. The Umayyads and their governors were responsible for developing a number of the essential features of Islamic worship and ritual. Their main concern, it is true, was not with religion and religious law, but with political administration, and here they represented the centralizing and increasingly bureaucratic tendency of an orderly administration as against bedouin individualism and the anarchy of the Arab way of life. Both Islamic religious ideals and Umayyad administration co-operated in creating a new framework for Arab Muslim society. In many respects Umayyad rule represents the consummation, after the turbulent interval of the caliphate of Medina, of tendencies which were inherent in the nature of the community of Muslims under Muḥammad. It was the period of incubation of Islamic civilization and, within it, of the religious law of Islam.

The administration of the Umayyads concentrated on waging war against the Byzantines and other external enemies, on assuring the internal security of the state, and on collecting revenue from the subject populations and paying subventions in money or in kind to the Arab beneficiaries. We therefore find evidence of Umayyad regulations or administrative law mainly in the fields of the law of war and of fiscal law. All this covered essentially the same ground as the administrative legislation of the caliphs of Medina, but the social background was sensibly different. The Umayyads did not interfere with the working of retaliation as it had been regulated by the Qur'ān, but they tried to prevent the recurrence of Arab tribal feuds and assumed the accountancy for payments of blood-money, which were effected in connexion with the payment of subventions. On the other hand, they supervised the application of the purely Islamic penalties, not always in strict conformity with the rules laid down in the Qur'ān.

The Umayyads, or rather their governors, also took the important step of appointing Islamic judges or *qāḍīs*. The office of *qāḍī* was created in and for the new Islamic society which came into being, under the new conditions resulting from the Arab conquest, in the urban centres of the Arab kingdom. For this new society, the arbitration of pre-Islamic Arabia and of the earliest period of Islam was no longer adequate, and the Arab arbitrator was superseded by the Islamic *qāḍī*. It was only natural for the *qāḍī* to take over the seat and wand of the arbitrator, but, in contrast with the latter, the *qāḍī* was a delegate of the governor. The governor, within the limits set for him by the caliph, had full authority over his province, administrative, legislative, and judicial, without any conscious distinction of functions; and he could, and in fact regularly did, delegate his judicial authority to his 'legal secretary', the *qāḍī*. The governor retained, however, the power of reserving for his own decision any lawsuit he wished, and, of course, of dismissing his *qāḍī* at will. The contemporary Christian author, John of Damascus, refers to these governors and their delegates, the *qāḍīs*, as the lawgivers of Islam. By their decisions, the earliest Islamic *qāḍīs*, did indeed lay the basic foundations of what was to become Islamic law. They gave judgment according to their own discretion or 'sound opinion' (*ra'y*), basing themselves on customary practice which in the nature of things incorporated administrative regulations, and taking the letter and the spirit of the Qur'anic regulations and other recognized Islamic religious norms into account as much as they thought fit. Whereas the legal subject-matter had not as yet been islamized to any great extent beyond the stage reached in the Qur'ān, the office of *qāḍī* itself was an Islamic institution typical of the Umayyad period, in which care for elementary administrative efficiency and the tendency to islamize went hand in hand. The subsequent development of Islamic law, however, brought it about that the part played by the earliest *qāḍīs* in creating it did not achieve recognition in the legal theory which finally prevailed.

A typical example of the way in which the activity of the early *qāḍīs* influenced Islamic law is provided by the law of procedure. The Qur'ān had not only endorsed the use of written documents as evidence; it had also provided for putting the witnesses on oath in certain circumstances (*Sūra* 5. 106–8). Islamic law rejected the first, and neglected the second provision, and had it not been for the early *qāḍīs*, the hard and fast rule that evidence by witnesses, who are not put on oath, has to be produced by the plaintiff, and if no such evidence is produced, the oath in denial has to be taken by the defendant, would have been applied to the letter. The early *qāḍīs*, however, constantly tried to impose safeguards on the exclusive use of the testimony of witnesses as evidence, and this tendency has left more or less extensive traces in several schools of Islamic law.

The jurisdiction of the *qāḍī* extended to Muslims only; the non-Muslim subject populations retained their own traditional legal institutions, including the ecclesiastical and rabbinical tribunals, which in the last few centuries before the Arab conquest had to a great extent duplicated the judicial organization of the Byzantine state. This is the basis of the factual legal autonomy of the non-Muslims which was extensive in the Middle Ages, and has survived in part down to the present generation. The Byzantine magistrates themselves had left the lost provinces at the time of the conquest, but an office of local administration, the functions of which were partly judicial, was adopted by the Muslims: the office of the 'inspector of the market' or agoranome, of which the Arabic designation *'āmil al-suq* or *ṣāḥib al-sūq* is a literal translation. In the last few centuries before the Muslim conquest this office had lost its originally high status, but had remained a popular institution among the settled populations of the Near East. Later, under the early 'Abbasids, it developed into the Islamic office of the *muḥtasib*. Similarly, the Muslims took over the office of the 'clerk of the court' from the Sasanian administration.

The work of the *qāḍīs* became inevitably more and more specialized, and we may take it for granted that from the turn of the first/seventh century onwards appointments as a rule went to specialists, to persons sufficiently interested in the subject to have given it serious thought in their spare time. Their main concern, in the intellectual climate of the late Umayyad period, was naturally to know whether the customary law which they administered conformed to the Qur'anic and generally Islamic norms; in other words, the specialists would be found normally within that group of pious persons who were at the same time working out an Islamic way of life. Once more, the care for efficient administration of justice and the tendency to islamize went hand in hand. Their interest in religion caused them to survey, either individually or in discussion with like-minded friends, all fields of contemporary activities, including the field of law, from an Islamic angle, and to impregnate the sphere of law with religious and ethical ideas. Their reasoning, which in the nature of things expressed their own individual opinion (*ra'y*), represents the beginnings of Islamic jurisprudence. In doing this, they achieved on a much wider scale and in a vastly more detailed manner what Muḥammad had tried to do for the early Islamic community of Medina. As a result, the popular and administrative practice of the late Umayyad period was transformed into the religious law of Islam. But the close personal connexion between the groups of pious persons and the *qāḍīs* notwithstanding, Islamic law did not grow out of the practice, it came into being as the expression of a religious ideal in opposition to it.

The pious specialists on the sacred law were held in respect both by the public and the rulers, and they owed their authority to their single-minded concern with the ideal of a life according to the tenets of Islam. They stood outside the political structure of the Arab kingdom of the Umayyads, and their main function was to give cautelary advice on the correct way of acting to those of their co-religionists who asked for it; in other words, they were the first *muftīs* in Islam. Islamic law has preserved much of this cautelary character over the centuries; it is dominant in the teaching of Mālik in Medina in the second/eighth century, and it recurs in strength in the medieval *ḥiyal* or 'legal devices'. The pious specialists often had occasion to criticize the acts and regulations of the government, just as they had to declare undesirable many popular practices, but they were not in political opposition to the Umayyads and to the established Islamic state; on the contrary, the whole of the Umayyad period was, at a certain distance, viewed as part of the 'good old time'; this idealizing of things past was the first manifestation in Islam of a tendency which, a few decades later, was to lead to one of the most thorough and most successful of literary fictions. The attitude of the pious specialists to the Umayyad government anticipates the attitude of the religious scholars of Islam to any Islamic government.

As the groups of pious specialists grew in numbers and in cohesion, they developed, in the first decades of the second/eighth century, into what may be called the ancient schools of law, a term which implies neither any definite organization, nor a strict uniformity of doctrine within each school, nor any formal teaching, nor even the existence of a body of law in the usual meaning of the term. Their members continued to be private individuals, singled out from the great mass of the Muslims by their special interest, the resultant reverence of the people, and the recognition as kindred spirits which they themselves accorded to one another. It can be said that the division of the Muslims into two classes, the *élite* and the *vulgus*, dates from the emergence of the ancient schools of law. The more important ancient schools of which we have knowledge are those of Kūfa and of Baṣra in 'Irāq, of Medina and of Mecca in the Ḥijāz, and of Syria. The differences between them were caused, in the first place, by geographical factors, such as local variations in social conditions, customary law, and practice, but they were not based on any noticeable disagreement on principles and methods. On principle, the ancient schools were inclined to disturb the practice as little as possible; because of the nature of our documentation, this can be particularly clearly observed in the case of the Medinese and of the Syrians.

The doctrines of the several schools enable us to discern the contrast between the social realities in that ancient Arab land that was the Ḥijāz, and the newly conquered territory of old civilization that was 'Irāq, as well as the various reactions of the ancient lawyers of Islam to them.

The legal integration of the wife into the family of the husband had begun with the Qur'ān, when the wife was guaranteed a share in the inheritance, and the ancient lawyers followed the same tendency by giving the right to inherit to certain female relatives who did not possess it originally. But the school of Kūfa alone went so far as to extend the right to inherit, after the agnates, to a group roughly corresponding to the cognates. The school of Medina rejected this absolutely. On the other hand, the tendency expressed by the school of Kūfa found its consummation only in the doctrine of the Twelver Shīʿīs who unite the agnates and the cognates in one single group. The Twelver Shīʿīs lay emphasis also on the narrowly defined family, consisting of father, mother and their children and grandchildren, against the broader concept of family, merging into the old Arabian tribal system, which forms the background of the Sunnī law of inheritance. ʿIrāq was indeed the intellectual centre of early Shiʿism, and Shīʿī law (and, for that matter, Kharijite law) has occasionally preserved early ʿIrāqī doctrines which were later abandoned by the orthodox. The legal position of the unmarried girl and of the wife within the family, and their legal capacity, were decidedly more favourable in ʿIrāq than in the Ḥijāz. On the other hand, the marriage bond was more rigid there, in so far as in ʿIrāq the wife was inadequately protected even against grave derelictions of duty by the husband, such as failure to provide maintenance, or grave maltreatment; the school of Medina gave her the possibility of suing for divorce in these two cases, a rule which continued, it seems, a practice of Arab customary law which allowed the abandoned or maltreated wife to recover her freedom. As regards the status of the slave, the doctrines of the school of Medina show a certain paternalism which seems to derive from the social conditions in the cities of the Ḥijāz not less than from the civilizing influence of Islam. The Muslim slave, within the patriarchal family, enjoys a status similar to that of a free man; he may conclude a valid marriage by himself, without having secured the previous approval of his master (although the master may subsequently dissolve it); he may marry four wives just as a free man may (in contrast with the general rule which reduces all numbers given in the Qur'ān by half for the slave); he has (notwithstanding certain restrictions) a real right of ownership; if he is authorized to trade, his transactions engage only his stock-in-trade and not his person so that he cannot be sold to pay off a debt; and if he is gravely maltreated he can demand his freedom. None of this is accepted by the school of Kūfa;

in addition, according to the latter, he cannot act as leader of the ritual prayer if it is performed in common, he is not entitled to the Qur'anic procedure of *li'ān* if he suspects his wife of adultery, his blood-money must always be less than that of a free man, and the master is in no case obliged to acknowledge the paternity of children which his female slave has borne. (The rule that children born by a concubine to her master and acknowledged by him as his own are free and in all respects equal to his children by a marriage with a free wife, goes beyond pre-Islamic practice, and is not explicitly laid down in the Qur'ān; it must have asserted itself early in the first century, and it became of great importance in the development of Islamic society.) This hardening shows, no doubt, a more rigid and more differentiated society in which the social classes were more firmly separated, the result, in short, of a certain evolution. On the other hand, the school of Kūfa was more ready to set free certain categories of slaves, to reduce the rigours of penal law for the slave, and to protect his life by making a free man who had murdered him, liable to retaliation. The *'āqila*, the group of persons called upon to pay the blood-money in a case of unintentional killing or wounding, consisted originally, and still consists according to the doctrine of the school of Medina, of the agnates. According to the doctrine of the school of Kūfa, however, it consists of those whose names, as members of the Muslim army, are inscribed in the same army list or pay-roll, alternatively of the members of the same tribe, or alternatively of the fellow-workers in the same craft. This shows most clearly the result of profound social changes. The *qasāma*, the collective oath in criminal procedure when the person of the murderer is unknown, is, in the doctrine of the school of Medina, an affirmative oath by the members of the tribe of the victim which is sufficient to make the accused liable to retaliation. The Umayyad caliphs tried to mitigate its effect. The doctrine of the Kufans, however, recognized only a contradictory oath, not by the members of a tribe but by the inhabitants of the locality in question. Concerning pre-emption, the school of Medina was satisfied with laying down the rule that the co-owner was entitled to it; this was normally sufficient to ensure that strangers did not infiltrate the property owned by members of the same family or clan. In 'Irāq, however, this formula was not found sufficient, and in order to preclude the intrusion of strangers, it was found necessary to extend the right of pre-emption to neighbours, that is to say, owners of adjoining plots even if they were not technically co-owners of the property in question, provided their respective plots were entered by a common gate from a lane or thoroughfare, a kind of settlement common in the new cities of Islam which nevertheless preserved the identity of tribal associations. This provides a vivid picture of the lay-out of building plots in 'Irāq in the second/eighth century. It was only later that the Ḥijāzī and the 'Irāqī doctrines were crystallized into the propositions that the right of pre-emption belonged to any co-owner or to any neighbour, whoever he might be. It is also not by accident that the degrees of social rank which aimed at perpetuating the social superiority of the Arabs over the *mawālī* were elaborated outside Arabia, in 'Irāq, and that the procedure of becoming a *mawlā* by contract was recognized by the school of 'Irāq, where it was of great practical importance, but ignored by that of Medina. The law of property and of obligations, too, as formulated by the schools of Kūfa and of Medina respectively, shows society in 'Irāq more differentiated and more closely controlled by the state than in Medina.

Whereas the ancient schools of law reflected different social realities, their general attitude to popular practice and administrative regulations was essentially the same, and it was certainly not the case, as has often, and recently too, been asserted, that the school of Medina was more traditional in its outlook and the school of 'Irāq more given to individual reasoning. It is true that, apart from differences in social development which are reflected in the doctrine, the doctrines of the school of Medina represent, generally speaking, an earlier stage of development of legal thought. But this means merely that the doctrinal development of the school of Medina often lagged behind that of the school of Kūfa. 'Irāq was the intellectual centre of the first theorizing and systematizing efforts which were to transform Umayyad popular and administrative practice into Islamic law, and the ascendancy of 'Irāq in the development of religious law and jurisprudence continued during the whole of the second/eighth century. This is in keeping with intellectual development generally during the period.

The ancient schools shared not only a common attitude to Umayyad practice and, of course, a considerable body of positive religious law but the essentials of a legal theory, the central concept of which was the 'living tradition of the school'. This idea dominated the development of Islamic law and jurisprudence during the whole of the second/eighth century. Retrospectively it appears as the *sunna* or 'well-established precedent', or 'practice' ('*amal*), or 'ancient practice' (*amr qadīm*). This 'practice' partly reflected the actual custom of the local community of Muslims, but it also contained a theoretical or ideal element, so that it came to mean normative *sunna*, the usage as it ought to be. Already at this early stage, a divergence between theory and practice manifested itself. The ideal practice was found in the unanimous doctrine of the representative religious scholars of each centre. This consensus of the scholars, representing the common denominator of doctrine achieved in each generation, expresses the synchronous aspect of the living tradition of each school. It is significant that the real basis of the doctrine of each school is not the consensus of all Muslims (which also exists) but of the scholars; the function of the class of *'ulamā'* in Islamic society was firmly established in that early period.

The need of creating some kind of theoretical justification for what so far had been an instinctive reliance on the opinions of the majority, led, from the first decades of the second/eighth century onwards, to the living tradition being retrojected, and to its being ascribed to some of the great figures of the past. This process, too, began in Kūfa, where the stage of doctrine achieved in the time of Ḥammād b. Abī Sulaymān (d. 120/738) was attributed to Ibrāhīm al-Nakha'ī (d. 95–6/713–15). The Medinese followed suit and retrojected their own teaching to a number of ancient authorities who had died about the turn of the century, some of whom later became known as the 'seven jurists of Medina'. At the same time as the doctrine of the school of Kūfa was retrospectively attributed to Ibrāhīm al-Nakha'ī, a similar body of doctrine was directly connected with the very beginnings of Islam in Kūfa by being attributed to Ibn Mas'ūd, a Companion of the Prophet who had come to live in that city, and Ibrāhīm al-Nakha'ī became the main transmitter of that body of doctrine, too. In the same way, other Companions of the Prophet became the eponyms of the schools of Medina and of Mecca. One further step in the search for a solid theoretical foundation of the doctrine of the ancient schools was taken in 'Irāq, very early in the second/eighth century, when the term '*sunna* of the Prophet' was transferred from its political and theological into a legal context, and identified with the *sunna*, the ideal practice of the local community and the corresponding doctrine of its scholars. This term, which was taken over by the school of Syria, expressed the axiom that the practice of the Muslims derived from the practice of the Prophet, but it did not as yet imply the existence of positive information in the form of 'Traditions' (*Ḥadīth*), that the Prophet by his words or acts had in fact originated or approved any particular practice. It was not long before these Traditions, too, came into existence, and the persons who put them into circulation were the Traditionists.

The ancient schools of law themselves represented, in one aspect, an Islamic opposition to popular and administrative practice under the later Umayyads, and the opposition group which developed into the Traditionist movement emphasized this tendency. As long as a Companion of the Prophet had been the final authority for the doctrine of a school on a particular point, it was sufficient for a divergent doctrine to be put under the aegis of another Companion of equal or even higher authority, as happened in Kūfa where all kinds of minority opinions were attributed to the Caliph 'Alī, who had made Kūfa his capital. But after the general authority of the Prophet himself had been invoked by identifying the established doctrine with his *sunna*, a more specific reference to him was needed, and there appeared detailed statements or 'Traditions' which claimed to be the reports of ear- or eye-witnesses on the words or acts of the Prophet, handed down orally by an uninterrupted chain of trustworthy persons. Very soon the emphasis shifted from proposing certain opinions in opposition to the ancient schools to disseminating Traditions from the Prophet as such, and the movement of the Traditionists, which was to develop into a separate branch of Islamic religious learning, came into being. It was the main thesis of the Traditionists that formal Traditions from the Prophet superseded the living tradition of the school. The Traditionists existed in all great centres of Islam, where they formed groups in opposition to, but nevertheless in contact with, the local schools of law. Initially the ancient schools offered strong resistance to the disturbing element represented by the Traditions, but they had no real defence against their rising tide; they had to express their own doctrines in Traditions which allegedly went back to the Prophet, and to take increasing notice of the Traditions produced by their opponents. Finally the outlines and many details of Islamic law were cast into the form of Traditions from the Prophet. In this way, one of the greatest and most successful literary fictions came into being.

When the Umayyads were overthrown by the 'Abbasids in 132/750, Islamic law, though still in its formative stage, had acquired its essential features; the need of Arab Muslim society for a new legal system had been filled. The early 'Abbasids continued and reinforced the islamizing trend which had become more and more noticeable under the later Umayyads. For reasons of dynastic policy, and in order to differentiate themselves from their predecessors, the 'Abbasids posed as the protagonists of Islam, attracted specialists in religious law to their court, consulted them on problems within their competence, and set out to translate their doctrines into practice. But this effort was shortlived. The early specialists who had formulated their doctrine not on the basis of, but in a certain opposition to, Umayyad popular and administrative practice, had been ahead of realities, and now the early 'Abbasids and their religious advisers were unable to carry the whole of society with them. This double-sided effect of the 'Abbasid revolution shows itself clearly in the development of the office of *qāḍī*. The *qāḍī* was not any more the legal secretary of the governor; he was normally appointed by the caliph, and until relieved of his office, he must apply nothing but the sacred law, without interference from the government. But theoretically independent though they were, the *qāḍīs* had to rely on the political authorities for the execution of their judgments, and being bound by the formal rules of the Islamic law of evidence, their inability to deal with criminal cases became apparent. (Under the Umayyads, they or the governors themselves had exercised whatever criminal justice came within their competence.) Therefore the administration of the greater part of criminal justice was taken over by the police, and it remained outside the sphere of practical application of Islamic law. The centralizing tendency of the early 'Abbasids also led, perhaps under the influence of a feature of Sasanian administration, to the creation of the office of chief *qāḍī*. It was originally an honorific title given to the *qāḍī* of the capital, but the chief *qāḍī* soon became one of the most important counsellors of the caliph, and the appointment and dismissal of the other *qāḍīs*, under the authority of the caliph, became the main function of his office.

An institution which the early 'Abbasids, and perhaps already the later Umayyads, borrowed from the administrative tradition of the Sasanian kings was the 'investigation of complaints' concerning miscarriage or denial of justice, or other allegedly unlawful acts of the *qāḍīs*, difficulties in securing the execution of judgments, wrongs committed by government officials or by powerful individuals, and similar matters. Very soon, formal courts of complaints (*al-naẓar fi'l-maẓālim*) were set up, and their jurisdiction became to a great extent concurrent with that of the *qāḍīs*' tribunals. The very existence of these tribunals, which were established ostensibly in order to supplement the deficiencies of the jurisdiction of the *qāḍīs*, shows that their administration of justice had largely broken down at an early period. Since then, there has been a double administration of justice, one religious and the other secular, in practically the whole of the Islamic world.

At the same time, the office of the 'inspector of the market' was islamized. Its holder, in addition to his ancient functions, was now entrusted with discharging the collective obligations of enforcing Islamic morals, and he was given the Islamic title of *muḥtasib*; it was now part of his duties to bring transgressors to justice and to impose summary punishments, which on occasion came to include the flogging of the drunk and the unchaste, and even the amputation of the hands of thieves caught in the act; but the eagerness of the rulers to enforce these provisions commonly made them overlook the fact that the procedure of the *muḥtasib* did not always satisfy the strict demands of the law.

The caliph, too, was given a place in the religious law of Islam. He was endowed with the attributes of a religious scholar and lawyer, bound to the sacred law in the same way as *qāḍīs* were bound to it, and given the same right to the exercise of personal opinion as was admitted by the schools of law. The caliph retained full judicial power, the *qāḍīs* were merely his delegates, but he did not have the right to legislate; he could only make administrative regulations within the limits laid down by the sacred law, and the *qāḍīs* were obliged to follow his instructions within those limits. This doctrine disregarded the fact that what was actually legislation on the part of the caliphs of Medina, and particularly of the Umayyads, had to a great extent entered the fabric of Islamic law. The later caliphs and other secular rulers often enacted new rules; but although this was in fact legislation, the rulers used to call it administration, and they maintained the fiction that their regulations served only to apply, to supplement, and to enforce the sacred law. This ambiguity pervaded the whole of Islamic administration during the Middle Ages and beyond. In practice, the rulers were generally content with making regulations on matters which had escaped the control of the *qāḍīs*, such as police, taxation and criminal justice. The most important examples of this kind of secular law are the *siyāsa* of the Mamluk sultans of Egypt which applied to the military ruling class, and, later, the *qānūn-nāmes* of the Ottoman sultans. Only in the present generation has a secular, modernist legislation, directly aimed at modifying Islamic law in its traditional form, come into being; this became possible only through the reception of Western political ideas. But the postulate that law, as well as other human relationships, must be ruled by religion, has become an essential part of the outlook of the Muslim Arabs, including the modernists among them.

Notwithstanding all this, the office of *qāḍī* in the form which it essentially acquired under the early 'Abbasids, proved to be one of the most vigorous institutions evolved by Islamic society. *Qāḍīs* were often made military commanders, and examples are particularly numerous in Muslim Spain and in the Maghrib in general. They often played important political parts, although it is not always possible to distinguish the purely personal element from the prestige inherent in the office. Particularly in the Ayyubid and in the Mamluk periods, they were appointed to various administrative offices. They even became heads of principalities and founders of small dynasties from the fifth/eleventh century onwards, when the central power had disintegrated; there are especially numerous examples in Muslim Spain in the time of the *Mulūk al-Ṭawā'if* (Party Kings) and others occur in Syria, Anatolia and Central Asia. In the Ottoman system of provincial administration, the *qāḍī* was the main authority in the area of his jurisdiction, and elsewhere, as in medieval Persia, he became the main representative of what is called the religious institution. To some extent the *qāḍīs* (and the other religious scholars, too) were the spokesmen of the people; they played an important part not only in preserving the balance of the state but also in maintaining Islamic civilization, and in times of disorder they constituted an element of stability. Nevertheless, as far as the essence of the *qāḍī*'s office was concerned, a real independence of the judiciary, though recognized in theory, was hardly ever achieved in practice.

Very soon after the 'Abbasid revolution, Islamic Spain broke away and became, under a surviving member of the Umayyad family and his descendants, an independent amirate and later caliphate. It is therefore not surprising that Islamic law and justice as applied in Spain should have diverged in some respects (not very essential ones, it is true) from their counterparts in the East. Whereas the *qāḍī* was always in principle a single judge, it was taken for granted in Spain that he should sit 'in council' (*shūrā*). The 'Abbasid institution of the chief *qāḍī* took a long time to become acclimatized in Spain. Although the adoption of the Sasanian 'investigation of complaints' by Islamic law probably dated from the end of the Umayyad period in the East, it had no real parallel in Spain. The 'inspector of the market' retained his ancient title in Spain for centuries, and the theory of his functions was somewhat different there from that of the functions of the *muḥtasib* in the East.

The first half of the second/eighth century was a period of particularly rapid development for Islamic law, and this is well shown by the memorandum which the secretary of state, Ibn al-Muqaffaʿ, presented to the ʿAbbasid caliph, al-Manṣūr, at some time during the last few years of his life (he was cruelly put to death in 139/756). Written by an intelligent and observant outsider, a Persian convert to Islam, it shows us aspects of the stage reached by Islamic law about 140/757–8 which we should not be able to deduce from more conventional sources. Ibn al-Muqaffaʿ deplored the wide divergencies in the administration of justice which existed between the several great cities and even (a completely unexpected piece of information) between their several quarters, and between the main schools of law. He suggested therefore that the caliph should review the different doctrines, codify and enact his own decisions in the interest of uniformity, and make this code binding on the *qāḍīs*. This code ought to be revised by successive caliphs. The caliph alone had the right to decide at his discretion; he could give binding orders on military and on civil administration, but he must be guided by Qurʾān and *sunna*. This *sunna*, Ibn al-Muqaffaʿ realized, was based to a great extent on administrative regulations of the Umayyads. Therefore, he concluded the caliph was free to determine and codify the *sunna* as he thought fit. The plea of Ibn al-Muqaffaʿ for state control over law (and, incidentally, over religion, too) was in full accord with the tendencies prevailing at the very beginning of the ʿAbbasid era. But this was merely a passing phase, and orthodox Islam refused to be drawn into too close a connexion with the state. The result was that Islamic law grew away from practice, but in the long run gained more in power over the minds than it lost in control over the bodies of the Muslims.

A little later, towards the end of the second/eighth century, al-Shāfiʿī made the essential thesis of the Traditionists prevail in Islamic law. For him, *sunna* was not the idealized practice as recognized by the representative scholars; it was identical with the contents of formal 'Traditions' going back to the Prophet, even if such a Tradition was transmitted by only one person in each generation (a fact which, of course, made it very suspect to the ancient schools). This new concept of *sunna*, the *sunna* of the Prophet embodied in formal Traditions from him, superseded the concept of the living tradition of the ancient schools. According to al-Shāfiʿī, even the Qurʾān had to be interpreted in the light of these Traditions, and not vice versa. The consensus of the scholars, too, became irrelevant for him; he fell back on the thesis that the community of Muslims at large could never agree on an error, a thesis sufficiently vague for his purpose. All this left no room for the discretionary exercise of personal opinion, and human reasoning was restricted, in al-Shāfiʿī's thesis, to making correct inferences and drawing systematic conclusions from Traditions. In accepting the thesis of the Traditionists, al-Shāfiʿī cut himself off from the natural and continuous development of doctrine in the ancient schools, and adopted a principle which, in the long run, could only lead to inflexibility. Also, the positive solutions of problems which he proposed were often, sociologically speaking, less advanced than those advocated by the contemporary ʿIrāqīs and Medinese; his reasoning, dominated as it was by a retrospective point of view, could hardly be productive of progressive solutions. Al-Shāfiʿī's was a personal achievement, and his disciples and followers formed from the very beginning the 'personal' school (*madhhab*) of the Shāfiʿīs. The schools of Kūfa and Medina, too, had seen the formation of groups or circles within each school, and early in the third/ninth century the geographical character of the ancient schools gradually disappeared, and personal allegiance to a master and his doctrine became preponderant.

Whereas the Ḥanafīs and the Mālikīs, who continued the ancient schools of Kūfa and of Medina (their names are derived from Abū Ḥanīfa and from Mālik, respectively), did not change their positive legal doctrines appreciably from what they had been when al-Shāfiʿī appeared, they finally adopted in the course of the third/ninth century, together with the Shāfiʿīs, a legal theory of Traditionist inspiration. This theory differed from al-Shāfiʿī's own thesis in one essential respect, in that it returned to the concept of the consensus of the scholars, which it considered infallible. It endorsed al-Shāfiʿī's identification of the *sunna* with the contents of Traditions from the Prophet, but the legal rules which were to be derived from the Traditions were to be determined by the consensus of the scholars, which left the representatives of each school free to determine them for themselves, by interpretation and so forth. The fact that the Shāfiʿī school itself had to accept this modification of the doctrine of its founder shows the hold which the idea of the consensus of the scholars, embodying the living tradition of the ancient schools, had gained over Islamic law, and, by implication, how strong the position of the class of specialists had become.

Islamic law reached its full development in early ʿAbbasid times, and its institutions reflect the social and economic conditions of Islamic society in that period more than any other. The various social backgrounds of the doctrines of the Medinese and of the 'Irāqīs have already been mentioned. A feature which may, perhaps, reflect conditions proper to the early 'Abbasid period is the detailed treatment of 'usurpation' of the property of another, neither theft nor robbery, but high-handed appropriation. The provisions of Islamic law aim at protecting the rightful owner as much as possible, but at the same time make the frequency of similar acts, and the inability of the *qāḍī* to deal with them, painfully clear. The *waqf* or mortmain, too, found its final regulation at that time. The roots of this institution are various. One, which left only faint traces in Islamic law, and in the Mālikī school more than in the Ḥanafī, can be traced to certain kinds of annuity, to use a modern, roughly approximate term, in use among the ancient Arabs; another, still very important at the beginning of the third/ninth century, though later quite pushed into the background, consisted of contributions to the Holy War, the object of innumerable exhortations in the Qur'ān; a third, particular to Egypt during the first few centuries of Islam, seems to derive from the example of the Byzantine *piae causae*; and a fourth, which expanded enormously, particularly in 'Irāq, in the first half of the third/ninth century, and which was, perhaps, most decisive in shaping the final doctrine of Islamic law concerning *waqf*, arose from the desire of the Muslim middle classes to exclude the daughters and, even more so, the descendants of daughters from the benefits of the Qur'anic law of succession; in other words, to strengthen the old Arab patriarchal family system, and also to provide for the *mawālī* in order to make them reliable dependants of the family of the founder; both aims being in conflict with the purpose of the Qur'anic legislation. The *waqf*, and this may be counted its fifth and last root, also enjoyed a degree of security unknown to any other form of tenure, and its use became popular as a guarantee against confiscation. So was another procedure known to Islamic law, the fictitious sale or *talji'a*. Two things are significant here: confiscation with its concomitant procedure of torture, which had become almost a fixed institution of the Islamic state at the end of the Umayyad and particularly at the beginning of the 'Abbasid period, was not taken into consideration at all by Islamic law; in other words, the pious specialists averted their eyes from procedures which they knew were wrong but which they felt they could not, without material damage to themselves, openly criticize. On the other hand, even the early 'Abbasid caliphs and their highhanded and powerful dignitaries were averse to interfering openly with transactions which on the face of it, were valid under the religious law of Islam. Ibn Qutayba (d. 276/889), Traditionist and man of letters, held that the injustice of rulers and the highhandedness of overweening persons, and even the insistence of a creditor on being paid, justified lies and perjury. At a slightly later period, the poet and philologist Ibn Durayd (d. 321/933) composed a treatise on equivocal expressions for the benefit of people who were forced to take an oath against their will, so as to enable them 'to mean something different from what they appear to say, and to save them from the injustice of the oppressor'.

Another omission of Islamic law is more difficult to explain, that of practically all reference to wholesale trade. The activities of wholesale merchants covered the whole of the Islamic world and extended beyond it, and they have left permanent traces in the merchant law of the early Middle Ages. Islamic law treats in great detail of many commercial transactions, but they are, as a rule, envisaged exclusively as transactions of retail trade, and the background of wholesale trading can only be inferred from occasional remarks and from isolated chapters such as those on the contract of *muḍāraba* or *qirāḍ* (*commenda*, which, incidentally, seems to have come to Western Europe from Islamic law). It is true that Islamic law is in the first place concerned with laying down ethical rules for the behaviour of the individual in a society the composition of which is taken for granted, but it is equally true that the wholesale trader, by the nature of his activities, is exposed, from the point of view of Islamic law, to particular moral hazards, which that law might have been expected to point out and safeguard against with the same interest in details as it does with regard to those involved in a householder sending out a minor to buy a loaf of bread. Generally speaking, Islamic law pays particular attention to transactions involving the middle or the lower-middle class; for instance, it appears clearly from legal terminology that the economic reality underlying the contract of *salam*, the ordering of goods to be delivered later for a price paid in advance, was the financing of the business of a small trader or artisan by his customers. A saying attributed to the Caliph 'Umar, which occurs in Mālik's *Muwaṭṭa'*, is specifically directed against the activities of the rich speculators, who buy up supplies of food, anticipating a rise in prices, but exempts the small importer, who carries merchandise 'on his back in summer and in winter'. Merchants are also forbidden to meet caravans outside the town and to buy up what they bring, and a sedentary ought not to act as a sales agent of a bedouin. On the other hand, the *Ḥamāsa* of al-Buḥturī (d. 284/897) contains numerous extracts from the poetic effusions of bedouin, who boasted of having cheated the merchants from whom they had bought.

We are particularly well-informed concerning relations between neighbours in Mālikī law. As interpreted by this school, Islamic law shows itself more humane than juridical. It puts the interest of certain social groups first; but these groups are, as a rule, neither state nor province nor city; in the last resort it is the family which matters, and this concern is reinforced by an easy-going acceptance of the *fait accompli*. The society envisaged by Islamic law is mainly urban, just as medieval Islam was essentially an urban civilization, but Islamic law did not recognize the city as such, nor did it admit corporate bodies. The doctrine of Islamic law does not attach great importance to differences of social status between free, male Muslims except, to some extent, in the requirement of the bridegroom's rank being equal to that of the bride, and, more important, the disqualification of members of certain low trades as witnesses. The doctrines of the several schools differ in details, and have undergone certain changes in the course of time. In a society in which the most highly respected economic activity was not that of the producer but of the merchant, the moralists tried to enhance the functions of the farmer and of the artisan, without, however, quite succeeding. Trade in cloth is generally regarded as the most honourable of professions, and sometimes trade in spices is associated with it. The professions of money-changer and of grain merchant are generally discredited, the first because it risks transgressing the complicated rules devised against 'usury', and the second because it leads to speculation on rising prices of food. The two 'low trades' *par excellence* were those of cupper and of weaver, and the contempt in which they were held seems to go back, in each case, to pre-Islamic times.

The early 'Abbasid period saw the end of the formative stage of Islamic law, and by the beginning of the fourth/tenth century a point had been reached when the scholars of all schools felt that all essential questions had been thoroughly discussed and finally settled (albeit with a choice of answers provided by the several schools); hence a consensus gradually established itself to the effect that from that time onwards no one could be deemed to have the necessary qualifications for independent reasoning in religious law, and that all future activity would have to be confined to the explanation, application, and, at the most, interpretation of the doctrine as it had been laid down once and for all. This is the 'closing of the gate of *ijtihād*', of independent reasoning in Islamic law. It is only in the present century that the reopening of this gate has been seriously envisaged by a number of *'ulamā'* and by Islamic society at large. The doctrine of the 'closing of the gate of *ijtihād*' was not the cause but a symptom of a state of mind which had been induced by the fear of doctrinal disintegration, a fear which was not far-fetched at a time when orthodox Islam was threatened by the esoteric propaganda of the Bāṭiniyya. When this propaganda had brought the Fatimid caliphs to power, first in Ifrīqiya and then in Egypt, they too felt the need of a doctrine of religious law of their own, and their great lawyer, the *Qāḍī* Nu'mān, provided it for them. It was a learned production which drew largely on the doctrines of the existing orthodox schools of law, rather than the result of organic growth, and it confirms the absence of a genuine Shī'ī (as opposed to the general Islamic) tradition of religious law. Whatever the theory might say on the closing of the gate of *ijtihād*, the activity of the later scholars was no less creative, within the limits set by the very nature of their work, than that of their predecessors. New sets of facts constantly arose in life, and they had to be mastered and moulded with the traditional tools provided by legal science. This activity was carried out by the *muftīs*, specialists on religious law who were qualified to give authoritative opinions on points of doctrine. The earliest specialists on religious law had been essentially religious advisers, *muftīs*, and the later *muftīs* only continued their advisory and cautelary activity. Their function was essentially private, and although *muftīs* could be, and often were, appointed officially, it did not add to their authority. The most important officially appointed *muftī* in later times was the Ottoman *shaykh al-Islām*. The doctrinal development of Islamic law owes much to the activity of the *muftīs*, and their advices, or *fatwās*, show us the most urgent problems which arose from practice in certain places and at certain times. Their decisions, if found acceptable, were generally incorporated into the later handbooks, and, generally speaking, the accretion of new cases and decisions in the interval between two comparable works of Islamic law represents the outcome of the discussion in the meantime.

Whereas Islamic law had been adaptable and growing until the early 'Abbasid period, from then onwards it became increasingly rigid and set in its final mould. A doctrine which had to be derived exclusively from the Qur'ān and, even more important, from a number of detailed Traditions from the Prophet, and became more and more hedged in by the ever growing area of the consensus of the scholars, and by the closing of the gate of *ijtihād*, was unable to keep pace with the changing demands of society and commerce. This essential rigidity of Islamic law helped it to maintain its stability over the centuries which saw the decay of the political institutions of Islam. From the early ʿAbbasid period onwards, we notice an increasing gap between theory and practice. This discordance and mutual interference dominated the history of Islamic law during the whole of the period here under review. This does not mean that Islamic law is entirely utopian. Apart from worship, ritual, and other purely religious duties, where in the nature of things the sacred law was the only possible norm, its hold was strongest on the law of family, of inheritance, and of *waqf*; it was weakest, and in some respects even non-existent, on penal law, taxation, constitutional law and the law of war; the law of contracts and obligations stands in the middle. The law of family and inheritance has always been, in the conscience of the Muslims, more closely connected with religion than other legal matters because the greater part of Qur'anic legislation is concerned with it. But even here, practice has been strong enough to prevail over the spirit, and in certain cases over the letter, of strict religious law. The legal position of women with respect to marriage and inheritance was occasionally improved in practice, but more often it deteriorated by comparison with Islamic law. Also, the institution of *waqf* was used to produce this last result, as has been mentioned above. It is not the most important and essential rules of religious law which are observed most faithfully but rather those which for some reason or other have become part of popular practice, and practice sometimes insists on refinements unknown to Islamic law. The institution of pre-emption in its extended, Ḥanafī form proved extremely popular among the Muslims who followed that school of law, and in India it became part of the matters sanctioned by religion, concerning which the continued validity of Islamic law for Muslims was guaranteed at the beginning of British rule in 1772; but the *Sharīʿa* itself does not attach great importance to it, and the more detailed handbooks describe ways by which it can be avoided. The field of contracts and obligations was ruled by a customary law which respected the main principles and institutions of the *Sharīʿa* but showed a greater flexibility and adaptability and supplemented it in many ways, and the same is true of the special rules concerning real estate, of which only a few rudiments exist in the *Sharīʿa*. The customary commercial law was brought into agreement with the theory of the

Sharīʿa by the *ḥiyal* of 'legal devices' which were often legal fictions, transactions by which the parties might achieve, through legal means, ends which were made desirable by the economic and social conditions of the time, but which could not be achieved directly with the means provided by the *Sharīʿa*. The earliest devices were merely simple evasions of irksome prohibitions by merchants and others, but very soon the specialists in religious law themselves started creating little masterpieces of elaborate juridical constructions and advising interested parties in their use.

Another important area of contact between theory and practice was provided by the continued use of written documents which became the subject of a voluminous and highly technical literature. Islamic jurisprudence ignores custom as an official source of law, however much customs of varied provenance had contributed to forming it. But the Mālikī school in Morocco in the later Middle Ages, where it developed in relative isolation from the rest of the Islamic world, took considerable notice of conditions prevailing in fact, not by changing the ideal doctrine of the law in any respect, but by recognizing that actual conditions did not allow the strict theory to be translated into practice, and that it was better to control the practice as much as possible than to abandon it completely. It therefore upheld the principle that 'judicial practice (*ʿamal*) prevails over the best attested doctrine', and it allowed a number of institutions unknown to strict theory. This Moroccan Mālikī *ʿamal* is not customary law; it is an alternative doctrine valid as long as conditions make it necessary.

We must think of the relationship of theory and practice in Islamic law, not as a clear division of spheres, but as one of interaction and mutual interference. The assimilation of the non-Islamic elements by the Islamic core in the formative period, and the assimilation of the practice by the theory in the Middle Ages, are really stages of one and the same process. This process, seen from outside, appears as a modification of the positive contents of Islamic law; whereas, seen from the inside, it appears as an expansion, a conquest of new fields by the ever dominant influence of Islamic law and jurisprudence. The ideal theory showed a great assimilating power, the power of imposing its spiritual ascendancy, even when it could not control the material conditions. Thus an equilibrium established itself between legal theory and legal practice, an equilibrium delicate in fact but seemingly unshakable in a closed society. As long as the sacred law received formal recognition as a religious ideal, it did not insist on being fully applied in practice. But it could not abandon its claim to exclusive theoretical validity, and acknowledge the existence of an autonomous secular law; its representatives, the *'ulamā'*, were the only qualified interpreters of the religious conscience of the Muslims; and the idea that law must be ruled by religion has remained an essential assumption even of modern Muslims. The works of Islamic law, during the whole of the medieval period, properly interpreted in relation to their place and time, are one of the most important sources for the investigation of Islamic society. The hold which the religious law of Islam had gained over the minds of the Muslims by the fifth/eleventh century can be gauged from the writings of al-Ghazālī (d. 505/1111), who, whilst deploring the ascendancy of legalism which threatened to extinguish religious life, and firmly restricting the subject-matter of the law to matters of this world, nevertheless protested that this did not imply reducing it to a secular subject of knowledge, and was unable to envisage secular rules for what he had insisted were matters which had nothing to do with religion.

The general and normal conditions described in the preceding paragraphs were occasionally disturbed by violent religious reform movements, such as that of the Almoravids in north-west Africa and Spain in the fifth-sixth/eleventh-twelfth centuries, that of the Fulbe in West Africa in the nineteenth century, and that of the Wahhābīs in Arabia in the nineteenth and again in the present century. All these movements made it their aim, in the states which they set up, to enforce Islamic law exclusively, to abolish the double system of administration of justice, and to outlaw administrative and customary law. The effects of these religious reform movements as a rule tended to wear off gradually, until a new equilibrium between theory and practice established itself. Of essentially the same kind, though sensibly different in their effects, were the efforts of established states (later than the early 'Abbasid period) to subject actual practice to the rule of the sacred law. The two most remarkable of these efforts were made in the Ottoman empire and in the Indian empire of the Mughals, whilst the Safavid empire in Persia provides an instructive parallel.

The Ottoman empire in the tenth/sixteenth century is characterized by strenuous efforts on the part of the sultans to translate Islamic law in its Ḥanafī form into actual practice; this was accompanied by the enactment of *qānūn-nāmes* which, though professing merely to supplement Islamic law, in fact superseded it. On the part of the representatives of religious law we find, naturally enough, uncompromising rejection of everything that went against the letter of religious law, but at the same time unquestioning acceptance of the directives of the sultans concerning its administration, and, on the part of the chief *muftīs*, a distinctive eagerness to harmonize the rules of the *Sharīʿa* with the administrative practice of the Ottoman state. A parallel effort in the Mughal empire in the seventeenth century was part of the orthodox reaction against the ephemeral religious experiment of the emperor Akbar. In the Persia of the Safavids, the religious institution, including the scholars and *qāḍīs*, was controlled by the *ṣadr*, who exercised control over it on behalf of the political institution, thereby reducing the importance of the *qāḍīs*. The Safavids' supervision of the religious institution was more thorough than had been that of the preceding Sunnī rulers, and by the second half of the eleventh/seventeenth century the subordination of the religious institution to the political was officially recognized. This whole development had already begun under the later Timurids.

CHAPTER 5

RELIGION AND CULTURE

PREFATORY REMARKS

Islam is a religion. It is also, almost inseparably from this, a community, a civilization and a culture. It is true that many of the countries through which the Qur'anic faith spread already possessed ancient and important cultures. Islam absorbed these cultures, and assimilated itself to them in various ways, to a far greater extent than it attempted to supplant them. But in doing this, it provided them with attributes in common, with a common attitude to God, to men and to the world, and thus ensured, through the diversities of language, of history and of race, the complex unity of the *dār al-Islām*, the 'house' or 'world' of Islam.

The history of the Muslim peoples and countries is thus a unique example of a culture with a religious foundation, uniting the spiritual and the temporal, sometimes existing side by side with 'secular' cultures, but most often absorbing them by becoming very closely interlinked with them. It is with the relations between this existing culture and the strictly religious features concerned that we shall try to concern ourselves in this chapter.

Historical landmarks

Between the first/seventh and the ninth/fifteenth centuries, Islamic lands reached great cultural heights. We shall not attempt to outline here all the background of this, still less to draw up an exhaustive catalogue of works and of names. At certain periods the researches, the arguments of the schools and the political repercussions to which they gave rise, the intellectual achievements and the works of art were so abundant that to try to record them in a few pages would be to give an unjust picture of their dynamic qualities. The names which we shall mention therefore will be cited only as examples.

We shall, however, give a few landmarks. The Medinese period and the Umayyad age, particularly the latter, saw the establishment of the first Muslim culture, in which were combined the influences of ancient Arabia and of Byzantium. The Baghdād of the 'Abbasids continually absorbed Persian influences. The greatest advance took place in the third/ninth century when the advent of Greek thought and learning caused the Arabo-Muslim, and soon afterwards the Perso-Muslim, cultures to embrace new methods of thought. The period of the Caliph al-Ma'mūn, the son of Hārūn al-Rashīd and a Persian mother, can be proclaimed as an age of brilliant humanism. More than once Sunnism and Shi'ism overlapped.

The reaction of al-Mutawakkil attempted to re-orientate the 'Abbasid empire, and particularly 'Irāq, towards a deliberately Sunnī domination. The triumph of Sunnism did not take place in a day, and under the Buyid *wazīrs* Muslim thought continued, either directly or through the Hellenistic *falsafa* (philosophy), to receive Shī'ī, and more precisely Ismā'īlī, currents. Samanid Khurāsān and its brilliant capital of Nīshāpūr, Hamadān under the Daylamī Buyids, Iṣfahān under the Kakuyid Kurds, were centres of intense cultural influence. Such was the background of Ibn Sīnā (Avicenna). The Aghlabid kingdom of Sicily in the third/ninth century was followed by the appearance, in the next two centuries, of the influence of the Cairo of the neo-Ismā'īlī Fatimids and its al-Azhar university. In the extreme west, Sunnī and Umayyad Cordova of the third/ninth to the fifth/eleventh centuries rivalled 'Abbasid Baghdād in brilliance. The Caliph 'Abd al-Raḥmān III and later the *wazīr* al-Manṣūr Muḥammad b. Abī 'Āmir (Almanzor) made the Umayyad court at Cordova into a centre of patronage of letters and arts. To borrow an expression from Sir Hamilton Gibb, it can be said that from the end of the second/eighth to the beginning of the fifth/eleventh century was a truly golden age, in east and west alike, not only of Arabic literature but also of Arabo-Muslim culture considered as a whole.

It is possible to consider the following period, from the fifth/eleventh to the seventh/thirteenth century, as only a silver age, to quote Gibb again. This is true if it is a question only of Arabic literature; but Muslim culture proper, at least Sunnī Muslim culture, established itself during this period with increased vigour. The second half of the fifth/eleventh and the whole of the sixth/twelfth century saw in the east the triumph of Sunnism with the Seljuk Turks and the arrival of the Turcoman tribes. Shi'ism remained active, but firmly supplanted and condemned this time in Baghdād, in Syria, and even in Persia by the Sunnī revival. This was the period when religious teaching was spread by the *madrasas*. The fall of the Fatimids finally took place in 567/1171, while the rigorist

Almoravid and then Almohad dynasties reigned in Morocco and Andalus.

This was the period of Abū Ḥāmid al-Ghazālī, the famous Algazel, 'the reviver of religion', the period also when there were produced vast numbers of encyclopaedias and historical and geographical works. Sufism produced at this time the most noteworthy poetry. In Almohad Spain, where some Ismā'īlī tendencies surreptitiously insinuated themselves, there took place, with Ibn Ṭufayl and Ibn Rushd (Averroes), the last flowering of Hellenistic *falsafa*.

While the point should not be over-stressed, it can be said that the great classical age barely survived the Spanish capture of Seville (646/1248) and the decline of the Almohads in the west, and the capture of Baghdād by the Mongols in the east (656/1258). From the second half of the seventh/thirteenth century and throughout the eighth/fourteenth there were certainly cultural movements of great value but nothing to equal those of Baghdād or Cordova, or the writers patronized by the *wazīrs* and the *amīrs* of the east. This period did not lack great names, however. The Syrian Ḥanbalī jurist, Ibn Taymiyya, who played such an important part in the Muslim revival of this time, the Maghribī social historian Ibn Khaldūn, who has achieved a following in the Western world, and the 'theological' work of 'Aḍud al-Ījī and of al-Taftāzānī all belong to the ninth/fifteenth century. Although there was an increase in the minor genres of annals, commentaries and glosses, it was also an age of syntheses and of wide perspectives.

Within this very broadly outlined historical framework, what were the dominant cultural values? And to what extent were they in accord or in conflict with the fundamental religious ideas?

MUSLIM CULTURE: ITS BACKGROUND AND ITS CONSTITUENTS

The Qur'ān as a religious cultural value

'. . . And this is speech Arabic, manifest.'[1] To the Muslim this is not a simple question of fact. The Qur'anic text emphasizes that God sent down to Muḥammad a revelation, or a preaching in the Arabic language,[2] 'wherein there is no crookedness'.[3] If we consider the veneration in

[1] Qur'ān, 16. 103.
[2] Qur'ān, 41. 3; 42. 7; 43. 3 etc.
[3] Qur'ān, 39. 28. R. Blachère translates this: 'exempte de tortuosité'.

which from the beginning Muslims have held their Book, it is possible to understand that for the devout believer every phenomenon of arabization is of directly religious significance.

In fact this 'preaching in clear language' was the first great Arabic prose text. The respect accorded to it by the Faithful, the incessant repetition of it (*dhikr*), and the recognition of it as the Word of God, were to have a profound influence on ways of thought. At the time of the lightning campaigns of the Umayyads, the Qur'ān was certainly not the only factor of arabization, but it was nevertheless an essential factor. To it the Arabic language owed the distinctively religious cadences which for centuries were to characterize so many expressions and vocables, and to impregnate it down to the primary meaning of the triliteral roots.

It is true that pre-Islamic Arabia, with its poets and its orators and with the whole organization of the life of its tribes, had an inchoate but authentic culture. The state of *Jāhiliyya* (Ignorance), which Islam attributed to it[1] is essentially a religious concept and takes no account of the human riches of this time of heathendom. There is no need to stress the attachment of the first generations of Muslims to their Arab past, to the forms of the ancient poetry, *qaṣīda* and *ghazal*, or to the essentially bedouin virtue of *muruwwa*[2] of which the Umayyad period continually boasted. It is probable that the development and establishment of an Arab culture would have been possible without the appearance of Islam, but it nevertheless remains that Islam gave its own form to the Arab culture which already existed historically. It does not seem that the borderline cases of its poetry and of its secular arts on the one hand, and of its wide acceptance of the foreign sciences on the other, disprove this statement.

It was in fact in an atmosphere which was already made up of Arabo-Muslim culture that the foreign sciences were received; and furthermore a secular literature, some poetic forms and some minor arts could not by themselves have given birth to a culture. If culture is in itself 'the flowering of the earthly city', and 'as such depends upon human effort on earth'[3], yet its development is normally accompanied by an awareness of human destiny, both personal and collective. At other points in

[1] Qur'ān, 33. 33; 48. 26, etc.

[2] Translated by L. Massignon, *Parole donnée* (Paris, 1962), 350, as 'considération, honorabilité mondaine (à l'intérieur du clan)'.

[3] Olivier Lacombe, *Existence de l'homme* (Paris, 1951), 114.

history an Arabo-Christian culture, for example, had been, and would be, possible. It may be that there will arise an Arabic secular de-islamized culture, just as in Europe there has been for several centuries a tendency towards a Western secular de-christianized culture. This is all hypothetical. In fact, and chiefly during the five or six centuries with which we are here concerned, it was in a Muslim atmosphere, or linked to Muslim values, that Arabic culture developed.

For it was the Qur'ān which was the primary vehicle of Arabic culture. Was this accidental? Or does the very expression of the Muslim faith necessarily entail arabization?

Certainly the Muslim faith presents itself as a universal religion. Every man, without distinction of race or language, is called to witness to the Oneness of God and to the mission of Muḥammad by the *Shahāda* sincerely pronounced. Consequently every man is called to adopt the *sha'ā'ir al-Islām* (the marks of Islam): that is, the personal obligations determined by the 'four pillars', prayer, statutory alms-giving, the Ramaḍān fast, the Pilgrimage to Mecca; and those rules concerning food, circumcision, family life, wills, cemeteries etc., with which the life of the believer is surrounded from birth to death. The statement of faith is simple, consisting of the four Qur'anic affirmations: 'The believers believe in God, in His angels, in His books, in His messengers'[1]—these will be explained in *Ḥadīths* which mention the future life, the resurrection, and the Divine decree.

But it was the fact that this *credo* was accepted and lived first by the Arab tribes, and according to the Arabic expression of the Qur'ān and the Traditions, which was to give to the Muslim religion the special direction of its religious culture. There appear to be discernible in it three strands:

1. The cult which surrounded the text of the Qur'ān was to make Arabic the only liturgical language of Islam. It is possible to conceive an arabization which is not also islamization; the existence and the vitality of the Christian groups in the Middle East who adopted Arabic as a cultural language prove this. But all islamization of any depth is accompanied by a greater or less degree of arabization—an arabization which progresses sometimes rapidly and sometimes slowly, and which decreases proportionately as the native language and the past of the peoples to whom the message of the Qur'ān is preached make them less directly accessible to Arab influence. And the language of the Qur'ān,

[1] Qur'ān, 2. 285.

the only language in which prayer is liturgically valid, is nevertheless one of the chief factors in the cohesion of the Muslim world.

2. It would be a patent exaggeration to state either that every religious truth expressed in Arabic must necessarily concern the Muslim faith, or that a Muslim tenet can be expressed only in Arabic; but it is nevertheless once again a question of fact. The Arabic language, centred as it is on the verb, the extreme flexibility of the verbal forms, the frequent involutions of meaning, the correlatives which are simultaneously both complementary and opposite, the contrasting ambivalence of many roots in which opposites are joined, the probative value of allusion or metaphor which becomes a parable; all this combined to form a means of expression dedicated to the service of that relationship of radical discontinuity between the creature and the Creator, who is at the same time both close and remote, which is at the heart of the Muslim religious attitude. Future borrowings from the 'foreign sciences' were certainly to modify and sometimes to enlarge the basic vocabulary. It is none the less true that there is no religious statement in classical Arabic which does not suggest some reference to the Qur'ān.

3. This, then, is why the very early period, that of Medina and the beginning of the Umayyad era, began its religious culture, as it were, in terms of the scriptural text itself. It was not until the second and third centuries of the *Hijra* that there were developed as organized disciplines the readings of the Qur'ān (*qirā'āt*) and commentaries on it (*tafsīr*), and that in 'Irāq the schools of the grammarians of Baṣra and of Kūfa could attempt to pursue free researches and analyses. While the Kūfa school concentrated on exceptions and irregularities, that of Baṣra stressed 'systematization and analogy'.[1] In fact Baṣra, through the school of Gondēshāpūr, was to a certain extent influenced by Aristotelian logic. Khalīl, one of the few grammarians of Arab origin, was to remain the accepted authority on poetics and lexicography, and the grammar of his pupil Sībawayh was to remain a standard work. But whatever the long-term influences may have been, all Muslim reflection originated primarily from the aim to read and to understand the text of the Qur'ān.

The truly cultural ferment which the Qur'ān produced therefore cannot be overemphasized. It was of course the ferment of a religious culture, but of one which, through the semantic values involved, spread to inform all literary expression in its widest sense. Furthermore, the Qur'anic preaching does not deal only with the dogmas of the faith.

[1] R. Blachère, *Le Coran* (*Introduction*) (Paris, 1947), 110.

Great Muslim thinkers, such as al-Ghazālī in the fifth/eleventh century, and Ibn Taymiyya in the eighth/fourteenth century, were to distinguish in the text on the one hand the teaching of the religious truths (*'aqā'id*) and the regulations concerning worship (*'ibādāt*), both of them unalterable; and on the other hand a moral teaching and regulations concerning human actions (*akhlāq*), the application of which may vary according to circumstances; and finally everything connected with 'social relations' (*mu'āmalāt*) which to a certain extent depend on times and places. Although the first concern of non-Arab scholars, who had become arabized with their conversion to Islam, was with grammatical studies, the formulation of juridical rules occupied the attention of the Arabs of Medina as well as of the schools of 'Irāq or Egypt, though the 'Irāqī school of Abū Ḥanīfa and his disciples was chronologically the first. This was a matter of an intellectual application (*fiqh*) in which there was applied to the authoritative argument of the inviolable Text, either the judgment based on opinion (*ra'y*) of the *prudens*, or a reasoning by analogy (*qiyās*). *Qiyās* must be understood here as a mental activity bringing together or separating two terms, like to like or to its opposite, greater to less, less to greater; to which the Ḥanafī school would add the search for the cause (*'illa*), the first attempt to find a universal middle term. One has no hesitation, therefore, in considering the first impetus of Arabo-Muslim culture as being dominated by a style of thought which was indivisibly both juridical and semantic. These two methods of analysis are very typical of the Semitic spirit and the spheres which they cover are very much wider and more diverse than those comprehended by law and grammar in western cultures.

Therefore, although it is possible to speak of a Muslim religious culture, it is not merely a question of religious values which form part of the life of the believer and which may find many different modes of expression (rather as though we were to speak of a Christian culture expressing itself through a whole range of national cultures); it is not even a question of a culture whose first expression borrowed its vocables, adapting them, from the Arabic poetry and rhetoric of the *Jāhiliyya*; it is a question of a culture which was commanded by a text considered as directly dictated by God, and it was to be centuries before any translation of it was to be fully permitted. Or rather: a 'translation' of the Qur'ān can be nothing more than a commentary intended for teaching purposes. A devout Muslim, of whatever race, owes it to himself to approach it in the immutable text of its 'lucid' Arabic language. Furthermore, it was from this Qur'anic foundation that there was to develop in the following centuries the corpus of the religious sciences and their subsidiary sciences, which was to become the main axis of Muslim culture. But in order to assess these sciences, we must first consider according to which dialectic, of integration or of opposition, other Arabic or 'foreign' contributions were added to the Qur'anic basis.

The contributions of Arabic secular poetry and prose

The Qur'ān treats severely poets accused of forgery.[1] Nevertheless the dominant of a religious culture linked to the expansion of the Islamic faith was to welcome the coexistence of a secular Arabic poetry and fairly soon of a secular prose also.

In poetry, until the arrival of the freer forms of the *muwashshaḥ* or the *zajal*, the two forms most used were the *qaṣīda* and the *ghazal*. In the Umayyad period many pre-Islamic customs continued. The lyricism of the ancient *Mu'allaqāt*, the Suspended Poems of the fairs at Mecca, was revived in *qaṣīdas* which combined the praise of bedouin customs and virtues with panegyrics of the reigning caliphs. Nor were there forgotten the great troubadours of the past, above all Imru'l-Qays and Labīd. It was thus that there were produced the *qaṣīdas* of the three great masters, Akhṭal the Monophysite Christian, and Farazdaq and Jarīr the bedouin satirists, or the *ghazals* of Jamīl and of Dhu'l-Rumma. The *Kitāb al-aghānī* ('The book of songs') of Abu'l-Faraj 'Alī, an indispensable source for knowledge of the arts and letters of the first centuries of the *Hijra*, describes an Umayyad army which has left Khurāsān to oppose a Kharijite revolt, but is mainly preoccupied with deciding who is the greater poet: Farazdaq, who mingled satires with bawdy songs, or Jarīr, who sang of bedouin honour, and whose poems show at least some religious impulses.

The beginning of the 'Abbasid period, in which the influence of Persian sensitivity and of the minor arts of Persia was so obvious in the amusements of the court of Hārūn al-Rashīd, was delighted by the chivalrous *ghazals* of 'Abbās b. al-Aḥnaf and by the brilliant satires and bacchic or erotic poems of Abū Nuwās (d. 187/803); while Abu'l-'Atāhiya (d. 211/826), a contemporary of Abū Nuwās, expressed himself in didactic and moral poems in which, perhaps for the first time, there appeared a direct concern with religious values.

[1] Cf. Qur'ān, 26. 224–6; 37. 36; 61. 41.

In the following century, poetry and politics (and very active politics) were to form the two extremes of the career of Abu' l-Ṭayyib, called al-Mutanabbī (d. 354/965), a wandering troubadour when he chose to be, also an agitator and rebel, tainted with Carmathianism (without belonging to the Carmathian movement), and patronized at the end of his life by the *amīr* of Aleppo, the Hamdanid Sayf al-Dawla, becoming his official poet. Al-Mutanabbī's *qaṣīdas*, which are his greatest works, combine with the classical form freer and more personal developments. A century later, they were to influence Abu'l-'Alā' al-Ma'arrī (d. 450/1058), a solitary, even a hermit, and a very great poet, who was hardly at all faithful to the Sunnī teaching and faith. His constant meditations on human destiny and his pessimism show very probable Hindu influences, and he seems to have considered all positive religion as merely a human creation. With Abu'l-'Atāhiya, the great Arabic poetry had changed from secular to religious, or at least it had a religious accent; with al-Mutanabbī it returned to Shī'ī inspiration; with al-Ma'arrī, in spite of certain prudent statements, it reached a vision of men and of the world whose most profound inspiration it would be difficult to call Muslim.

Prose literature was also held in high esteem. Under the Caliph al-Ma'mūn, the great writer al-Jāḥiẓ began a series of prose works in which descriptions, anecdotes, poetic quotations, proverbs, one might say a whole popular humanism, became the occasion for brilliant variations and pungent exercises in style. The master of classical Arabic prose was to be his contemporary Ibn Qutayba (d. 276/889), who belonged to the Kūfa school of grammarians, and whose work, *'Uyūn al-akhbār* ('The fountains of story'), was to be for centuries a source of examples and references. Although in his *Ma'ārif* he was able to combine Persian with Arabic traditions, he nevertheless defended the Arabs and the Arabic language against the claims of the non-Arabs. In the following century, the solitary pessimism of al-Ma'arrī produced *Risālat al-ghufrān* ('The treatise of pardon'). But it is certainly in narrative, either mixed with poetry as in the *qiṣṣa*, or in the form of *saj'*, assonant prose, or in accounts of real or imaginary travels, that Arabic prose reached its highest level. From the fourth/tenth to the sixth/twelfth century there developed the genre of the famous *maqāmāt* (sessions), which very distantly foreshadowed modern short stories or novels. Al-Hamadhānī, and more especially al-Ḥarīrī, excelled in this.

There should also be mentioned works—poetry or prose—of a more flexible and more popular nature: the epic of 'Antar, the love-poem of

Laylā and Majnūn, and the stories of the *Thousand and one Nights*. Although these were much enjoyed, devout believers were always willing to criticize the moral and religious laxity of the poets and prose-writers—particularly the poets. More than once the theologians stirred up opinion against them in the towns; and more than once famous writers owed their freedom of speech to the protection of the rulers alone. The rebellious attitude of al-Mutanabbī, and still more the haughty indifference of al-Ma'arrī, to all established religious values, were censured.

Nevertheless it is not possible to speak of a secular Arabic culture developing in radical opposition to all religious culture. Even the most secular works contained echoes of the Qur'ān. The bedouin poet Jarīr owed the patronage of 'Umar II to his reputation for piety; and it is said that the bacchic and erotic poet Abū Nuwās adopted asceticism (*zuhd*) in his old age. The prose-writer al-Jāḥiẓ was also a Mu'tazilite theologian. In fifth/eleventh century Andalusia, the very strict Ibn Ḥazm was to add to his Zahirite theology the courtly genre of his 'Necklace of the dove'. In contrast to this, the cult of the Arabic language, the language of the revelation, was to inspire commentators on the Qur'ān or theologians diligently to fathom out the precise meaning of the words, and in order to do this to turn to the famous poets, and especially to the pre-Islamic poets, to provide a verse or couplet as an example.

The way in which the two fields are interdependent may be summarized thus: in any history of Arabic culture, Islamic religious sciences must occupy an important place, while no study of *Muslim* culture as such would be complete without taking into account a certain *marginal* contribution made to it by secular literature.

The arts

The growth in the culture of the Muslim countries would not have been complete if the development of Arabic literature and religious thought had not been accompanied by a flowering of the arts.

In its strict sense Muslim art consists for the one part of the architecture and ornamentation of the mosques and *madrasas*, for the other part of the austere and very beautiful cantillation of the Qur'ān. Strictly speaking, these are the only arts which are fully permitted in Islam.

Religious architecture was affected by many influences—Byzantine, Persian and later Mongol—and there are many different styles of Muslim architecture. Nevertheless the adaptation of the buildings to the liturgical prayer of Islam, and even a certain harmony between the basic pattern of this 'liturgy' and the very flexible use of arcs, vaults and columns, between the affirmation of the One God and the minarets which were necessitated by the call to prayer, created a unity characteristic of its kind, running through the different styles and schools, which can be said in one sense to have reconciled Sunnism and Shi'ism.

The simplicity of the Medina mosque was followed, among others, during the Umayyad period by the Great Mosque at Damascus with its integration of Byzantine influences, or the Dome of the Rock at Jerusalem. In the 'Abbasid era architecture also was subject to Persian influences. The primitive 'Abbasid mosques of Baghdād and Raqqa have unfortunately disappeared, but there is the mosque of 'Amr in Cairo and above all the astonishingly successful mosque of Ibn Ṭūlūn (third/ninth century). Fatimid architecture (in the great mosque of al-Azhar) at one time joined to Persian inspiration influences from Umayyad Andalusia and particularly also from Tulunid art. There should also be mentioned the Turkish art of the Seljuks in the fifth–sixth/eleventh–twelfth centuries; and in the sixth–seventh/twelfth–thirteenth centuries the Mamluk art of Cairo with its many mosques and its City of the Dead or Tombs of the Caliphs.

In Ifrīqiya, the mosques of al-Zaytūna at Tunis, of Sīdī 'Uqba at Qayrawān, and of Sūs were to appear at the same time as the Umayyad art of the east and the beginnings of the 'Abbasid era. And here in the extreme west there appeared the sober harmony of Hispano-Moorish art, with its austere interlacing ornament, which is certainly one of the finest products of Muslim art, and one most characteristic of the spirit which inspires it. Muslim and Christian architects and craftsmen worked on it together. Berber, Byzantine and medieval European influences mingled with Eastern traditions to produce the almost unequalled masterpieces of the mosques of Cordova (second–third/eighth–ninth centuries) and Tlemcen (sixth/twelfth century), of the Kutubiyya at Marrakesh and the Giralda at Seville (sixth/twelfth century) and of the *madrasas* of Fez (eighth/fourteenth century).

The ornamentation of the mosques had to take into account the fact that the Muslim faith forbade any painting, and still more sculpture, which represented the figures of humans or of animals, in order the better to worship the Unique God and not to run the risk of even the smallest representation of idols. Who has not heard the pungent anecdote attributed to the Rightly-guided Caliph 'Umar b. al-Khaṭṭāb?

To a Persian artist who, having become a Muslim, was lamenting the fact that he must renounce his art, ʿUmar is said to have replied: 'Come now; you have only to give your figures the shape of a flower and cut off their heads.' Hence the triumph of a decorative art which tended all the time rather to dissolve the floral motifs themselves into a suggestive interlacing of geometrical lines, supported by, and sometimes themselves shaped by the splendid designs of the Arabic letters. In this, as in almost everything, the Maghrib paid more heed to the strict regulations; and it was perhaps this which enabled it to achieve in the interlacing of its bas-reliefs such a degree of perfection that without them there would be a gap in the history of sculpture.

This architectural and decorative art extended from the mosques and other religious buildings to the secular buildings. It is true that the architect of the Umayyad palace at Mshattā did not hesitate to use friezes representing animals and there is also the very beautiful 'Court of the Lions' in the Alhambra at Granada (seventh–ninth/thirteenth–fifteenth century), but the Alhambra as a whole remains as the witness (anticipating, perhaps, Indo-Muslim architecture) of a Muslim view of the world which concerned itself with the palaces of the rulers as well as the places of prayer. The same could be said of the minor arts: ceramics, pottery, metalwork. There were scarcely any beside the Persian miniature painters who refused to cut off the heads of their [human] characters. This miniature-painting, also a minor art, was accepted in eastern Islam so long as there was no question of using it in the decoration of mosques, and so long as the figures reproduced had no volume so as to cast a shadow. But it must be admitted that these minor arts, which included also the weaving of carpets and the ornamentation of rich silks and brocades—although they were forbidden by the strict jurists—went with a way of life which was dominated by the quest for pleasure and luxury.

Qur'anic cantillation (*tajwīd*), linked to the science of the readings (*qirā'āt*) and bound by precise rules, is not music in the true sense of the term, for all music was and still is set apart from liturgical prayer. This led the jurists and devout believers to regard the art of music itself with a kind of suspicion. However, the *samāʿ*, the 'spiritual oratorio', spread in Ṣūfī circles. In spite of the attacks of the offended traditionalists, al-Ghazālī defended its legality. It is an unaccompanied religious chant, purely modal and devoted to entirely spiritual themes. It is possible to speak of a Muslim religious chant but not of Muslim music.

The same al-Ghazālī in fact considered it a pious action to enter a house where profane music and songs were being performed in order to smash the instruments and scatter the singers. But in spite of this rigorism, the refined atmosphere of the courts of the caliphs was often lulled by the sound of harps, lutes, rebecs and flutes, and they were accompanied by very profane songs. The *Kitāb al-aghānī*, which preserves details of the most famous songs of the third/ninth century, gives much information on the composers and the male and female singers of the period.

Music (*mūsīqī*, or, especially in the Maghrib, *mūsīqā*) moreover was considered as a 'foreign science' in which the Greek tradition of the schools of Pythagoras lent its structure to the Iranian influences. The *faylasūf* (philosopher) al-Fārābī devoted a whole work to this, Ibn Sīnā was careful not to neglect the study of musical rhythms and numbers, and the encyclopaedia of the *Ikhwān al-Ṣafā'* devotes a large section to musical theory. All this contributed to the formation of the two schools, Eastern and Western, of classical Arab music—we no longer refer to Muslim music. Although it made no real use of harmony it devoted itself all the more to the endless ornamentation of variations on the melodic theme. The court at Baghdād in the third *hijrī* century had its own official musicians, the Mawṣilīs. Ziryāb, one of their pupils, fled to the Umayyad court at Cordova under 'Abd al-Raḥmān II, where he became both court musician and *arbiter elegantiarum*. It was this meeting of East and West which produced Andalusian music.

The 'foreign sciences'

An event of primary importance was the penetration of Greek thought into the Baghdād of the early 'Abbasid era. The aptitude of the Arab spirit for absorbing other ideas and its capacity for assimilation here received full scope, and there was a lively enthusiasm for translations of Greek philosophical and scientific works.

Even before the coming of Islam, translations from Greek into Syriac were not unusual, and the arrival of Islam was to give rise to many Arabic translations, either through the intermediary of Syriac or directly from Greek. At Baghdād, there were teams of translators, at first Christians, later Muslims, under the patronage of the caliphs. The most famous is that of the Nestorian Ḥunayn b. Isḥāq, his son Isḥāq, and his nephew Ḥubaysh. There was also the Jacobite Qusṭā b. Lūqā, a little later Abū Bishr Mattā b. Yūnus (a Nestorian), Ibn 'Adī, Yaḥyā b. Biṭrīq, and others. These groups of translators enriched the Arabic language with works translated from Plato and Aristotle—and from Plotinus confused with Aristotle[1]—from Ptolemy, Galen, Hippocrates and many others besides. The libraries multiplied: among them were the *Bayt al-ḥikma* ('House of Wisdom') of the Caliph al-Ma'mūn at Baghdād with its many Greek manuscripts, and the *Dār al-kutub* ('House of Books') at Baṣra, with scholarships which students could hold there. A century later Fatimid Cairo was enriched by the huge Palace Library with 18,000 works of 'foreign sciences', and by the *Dār al-'ilm* ('House of learning') or *Dār al-ḥikma* founded by al-Ḥākim in the fourth/tenth century.

This directly Hellenistic influence, added to the Perso-Greek (and Hindu) contributions of Gondēshāpūr, produced a whole activity of scientific research in the modern meaning of the word: mathematics, astronomy, physics and chemistry, medicine. Although astronomy was still mixed with astrology and chemistry with alchemy, it was in the Arab and Persian Muslim countries that very remarkable progress was made in science at this time, and for several centuries following. Whole chapters and monographs have been written on Arabian science and its riches are still far from having been fully listed.

The sciences continued to be interwoven with philosophy. The impetus thus given encouraged a whole intelligentsia in the exercise of a free thought which took little account of the literal interpretation of the Qur'ān, and which was, moreover, anxious to break out of the entirely semantic and juridical bounds of the earlier culture. In certain milieux, Greek influences existed side by side with dualist Mazdean and Manichaean influences. They are found actively at work within some more or less esoteric circles, even those which were to be denounced as *zanādiqa* (sing. *zindīq*, a term, adapted from Sasanid usage), which can be understood to mean both 'unbelievers' and 'agitators', and hence blameworthy and sometimes condemned by the authorities. One of the best examples of these extremist tendencies was, in the third–fourth/ninth–tenth centuries, Abū Bakr al-Rāzī, the medieval physician Rhazes. His thesis of the Five Eternals (the Creator, the Soul,

[1] It was probably in the sixth Christian century that a Jacobite Christian translated into Syriac some glossed extracts from *Enneads* IV–VI. The Syriac work, translated in its turn into Arabic, was to become the *Theology of Aristotle* (*Uthūlūjiyā Arisṭūṭalīs*). It was to have a profound influence on Avicenna, who wrote a commentary on it.

Matter, Time, Space) makes God into nothing more than a demiurge, and his atomistic cosmology is very close to that of Democritus, while his treatise *Fī naqd al-adyān* ('On the refutation [or destruction] of religions') is a protest against all positive religion. The esotericism of the Ismā'īlīs or the Carmathians was influenced by al-Rāzī. He certainly professed a radicalism far more absolute than that professed in the following century by 'the three great *zanādiqa* of Islam', as they were to be called: the philosopher Ibn al-Rāwandī, the gnostic Abū Ḥayyān al-Tawḥīdī and the poet Abu'l-'Alā' al-Ma'arrī.

The jurists and moralists had reproached the court poets and prose-writers for their lack of any sense of religion and for the sensuality of the themes they chose. Secular Arabic literature was criticized by the developing Arabo-Muslim culture. But it cannot be said that there was organized opposition between them. Rather did the massive arrival of the influences of ancient Persia and of classical Greece create, within the same Muslim culture, as it were a state of tension which was constantly being renewed, and which was to govern its future development. The results of this were far from being merely negative. The necessity to defend the beliefs of the faith against doubters and deniers was the origin of all the future philosophico- or theologico-dialectical developments. The whole history of *'ilm al-kalām*, the defensive apologia of Islam, was to be the proof of this.

The influence of Hellenism was the direct source of a discipline, certainly marginal in relation to the 'religious sciences', which the pious and 'people of the *kalām*' continually opposed, but which became one of the finest ornaments of the cultural splendour of the Muslim countries. We have mentioned the *falsafa* (very probably a transcription of φιλοσοφια) of al-Kindī, al-Fārābī and Ibn Sīnā in the east, before Ibn Ṭufayl and Ibn Rushd contributed to its fame in the Maghrib. The attitude of the philosophers (*falāsifa*) was by no means one of opposition or of revolt, like that of the earlier *zanādiqa*. They aimed to establish an agreement between the revealed Law (*shar'*) and their philosophy, both one and the other being accepted as a basic datum and as being on the same level of intelligibility. Hence their tendency to treat the text of the Qur'ān according to a method of interpretation (*ta'wīl*) of which another and very similar example is found in the Shī'ī gnosis. While it is easy to understand the mistrust with which the supporters of official Islam regarded the *falāsifa*, the fact remains that the acuteness of the philosophic thought of the greatest of them, linked with the loyalty to Islam which they retained, led them to the most impressive elaborations and syntheses. From the sixth–seventh/twelfth–thirteenth centuries onwards, through the translations from Arabic into Latin of the period, they had a profound influence on the medieval West.

Languages other than Arabic; the quarrel of the Shu'ūbiyya; *the 'sects'*

Falsafa was written mainly in Arabic, though there exist some important works of Ibn Sīnā in Persian. Addressed to rulers of Persian culture and origin, they usually consist of a compendium of the great Arabic treatises, with which are included some new analyses. In fact Muslim or Muslim-inspired culture extended beyond the Arabic-speaking area. We have already emphasized the process of arabization which accompanied the Islamic conquests, but the degree of its completeness depended on the peoples and countries concerned. Apart from the survival (which continues to the present day) of local languages and dialects, there must be mentioned the considerable cultural importance which was retained by Persian. It certainly became arabized, adopting the Arabic script and borrowing from Arabic its poetic forms and the clearest of its religious terms, but whereas there was no *Muslim culture* in the Greek, Syriac, Kurdish, Coptic or Berber languages, there developed very rapidly a great Perso-Muslim culture. The Turco-Muslim culture, both religious and secular, did not begin to assert itself until the seventh–eighth/thirteenth–fourteenth centuries, and was at first to be under Persian influence.

In addition, the use of Persian was regarded from the second–third/eighth–ninth centuries, as an assertion of rights. This was the phenomenon known as the quarrel or revolt of the *Shu'ūbiyya*. *Shu'ūb* originally meant the non-Arab tribes (the Arab tribes being known as *qabā'il*) and this is the meaning which the commentators were to give it when glossing the Qur'anic text, *Sūra* 49. 13: 'We have formed you in confederacies (*shu'ūb*) and tribes (*qabā'il*).' Later, *Shu'ūbiyya* came to mean the 'foreign' peoples who had embraced Islam and who, themselves invoking Muslim principles, protested against the contempt shown to them by the Arabs. At a later time some of them, proud of their own past, considered themselves in their turn to be superior to the Arabs.

In the Umayyad period, those who had newly embraced Islam (and become arabized) became the clients (*mawālī*) of Arab tribes; their political and social claims hastened the coming to power of the 'Abbasids.

The quarrel of the *Shu'ūbiyya* was a kind of repetition, but now on a cultural rather than a political level, of these early claims. Moreover it appeared in very different forms in the west and in the east of the *dār al-Islām*. The *Shu'ūbiyya* of Andalusia were as active as the true Arabs in promoting the Arabic culture and language. They claimed, and in the name of Islam, their integration with the Arabic ethnic group—that integration which the Syrians and the 'Irāqīs, founders of schools of grammar and of law, had formerly so successfully achieved. But the Syrians and 'Irāqīs were very close to the Arabic ethnic group, and their Syriac language was a sister language to Arabic, while the Andalusians were foreigners. In Persia, on the other hand, the movement aimed to restore the authority of the Persian language; it thus took the form of a claim to cultural autonomy.

The preservation of Persian literature and art was certainly not achieved by the *Shu'ūbī* movement alone. It would undoubtedly be an exaggeration to attribute to it that line of court poets which extends from Rūdakī and Kisā'ī in the fourth/tenth century to Kirmānī in the eighth/fourteenth century, and which reached its zenith in the sixth/twelfth century, under the Seljuk Turks, with Anwarī. It is nevertheless true that the *Shu'ūbī* claims helped to arouse a new interest in the Persia of the Great Kings, in its history and its myths. There need be mentioned only, in the last years of the fourth/tenth century, the great epic work of Firdawsī, the *Shāh-nāma*. Although the *Shāh-nāma* was written in a Muslim atmosphere, it remains a major witness to purely Persian culture. It can hardly be classed as a part of Muslim, or even of Perso-Muslim, culture.

It is otherwise with the Shī'ī works in Persian. For one thing, although Shī'ism expressed through the ages a religious phenomenon which was eminently Persian, it was Arab in origin; and secondly, some very great Shī'ī thinkers who were ethnically Persian, such as the Ismā'īlīs, Abū Ḥātim Rāzī and Sijistānī in the fourth/tenth century, or the Imāmīs, Naṣīr al-Dīn Ṭūsī (seventh/thirteenth century) and 'Allāma Ḥillī (seventh–eighth/thirteenth–fourteenth centuries) and many others, were to continue to write in Arabic. In the fifth/eleventh century, the Ismā'īlī, Mu'ayyad Shīrāzī, was to write sometimes in Arabic and sometimes in Persian, and the Ismā'īlī encyclopaedia of the *Ikhwān al-Ṣafā'* is also written in Arabic. Until the reform of al-Mutawakkil, the Arab atmosphere of 'Abbasid Baghdād was, through its Iranian *wazīrs*, as much Shī'ī as Sunnī, and as often Ismā'īlī Shī'ī as Imāmī. The amirates of Hamadān and of Iṣfahān, where Ibn Sīnā lived, were profoundly impregnated with Shi'ism. To ignore these historical facts would be to fail to understand the significance and the value of the writings of al-Fārābī and of Ibn Sīnā and of the whole of the cultural phenomenon of *falsafa*. In Cairo the dominant culture of the brilliant Fatimid empire was also Arab. And there continued to be expressed in Arabic, in the seventh/thirteenth century, the Western (i.e. Yemeni and Egyptian) Isma'ilism which was forced by the Sunnī repression of Saladin to operate clandestinely.

Nevertheless, in the extent to which Imāmī Shi'ism spread among the Persian people, it was to give rise to a whole Persian religious literature; hymns and poems, and especially dramas, resembling mystery-plays, which recount the sorrow of Fāṭima and the martyrdoms of 'Alī and Ḥusayn. They are all the more remarkable in being the only literature in Islam written for theatrical performances. Furthermore, from the time that they had to dissimulate before established authority, Persian Ismā'īlī groups preferred to express themselves in Persian. Among their most notable representatives was Nāṣir-i Khusraw (fifth/eleventh century).

Finally, the seventh/thirteenth century was to produce some great Ṣūfī works in Persian. It is sufficient to mention 'Azīz al-Dīn Nasafī, Farīd al-Dīn 'Aṭṭār and Sa'dī, and above all Jalāl al-Dīn Rūmī, whose *Mathnawī* remains one of the purest literary glories of Persia. But at the end of this century, the rule of the Īl-Khāns (663–736/1265–1337) was a period of decline for Persian culture. Until the age of the Safavids, the only period during which it came to life again was in the second half of the eighth/fourteenth century, under Tīmūr. This was to be the age of the melodious *ghazals* of Ḥāfiẓ and of Sa'dī and then, in the ninth/fifteenth century, of the mystic Jāmī.

It may be useful to summarize briefly the preceding remarks. Concurrently with Arabic culture, the *dār al-Islām* from the second/eighth to the ninth/fifteenth centuries produced a brilliant Persian culture. But whereas Arabic secular literature remained as though attached to Muslim culture, Persian poetry and literature were intentionally a presentation of purely Persian claims. On the other hand, our knowledge of Muslim culture as such would be incomplete if we did not include as part of it many Shī'ī works (and Ismā'īlī Shi'ism in particular) or Ṣūfī works which were written in Persian. But it would be a historical misinterpretation to consider that the only expression of Shi'ism was in Persian. Some very great Shī'ī works are written in Arabic.

It is nevertheless true that Shi'ism, Arab in origin and born of an Arab fidelity to 'Alī and to the 'People of the House', could not have constituted itself in its 'sapiential theosophy' without the contribution of the 'foreign sciences', i.e. of the Greek and Persian traditions. It thus became one of the acting forces of that tension mentioned above, which was to serve as the very mark of the absorption of non-Arab values by the Muslim world. This tension, far from having a destructive effect, was on the contrary to inspire and to universalize the Muslim culture, and especially the Arabo-Muslim culture, of the classical age.

THE ORGANIZATION OF KNOWLEDGE INTO ITS CONSTITUENT DISCIPLINES

Study of the sources of religion, the Qur'ān and *Sunna*, began from the time of Medina. It was the stimulus exerted by the non-Arabs, especially in 'Irāq, which gave rise to the schools of the grammarians. The invasion of the 'foreign sciences' led the doctors and jurists of Islam to defend the dogmas of their faith by rational methods. Sciences, in the modern sense of the word, and literature were cultivated in profusion. There is the well-known *Ḥadīth* which commands: 'Pursue learning (*'ilm*) from the cradle to the grave even as far away as China.' In the eyes of the believer, this learning or knowledge which is to be acquired is that which is related, directly or indirectly, to God, to the things belonging to God and to the Word of God. But the aphorism was frequently applied to all legitimate human knowledge. It is in any case a proof of the respect which Muslim thought was always to have for intellectual research.

Having analysed the constituents of the historical culture of the Islamic countries, we shall now consider in detail the sum of the traditional achievements thus acquired. We must evidently give the most important place to the 'religious sciences'. To these we shall add a mention of the sciences known as 'instrumental', not omitting others which were, it is true, somewhat marginal, but which brought great honour to the cultural climate in which they originated.

The development of the religious sciences

The progressive development of the 'religious sciences' was an innate characteristic of the Muslim mentality. We have mentioned the libraries, plentifully supplied with the works of the 'foreign sciences'.

But there should, nevertheless, be emphasized the importance, from the fourth–fifth/tenth–eleventh centuries onwards, of the colleges (*madrasas*) in which the strictly Muslim disciplines were taught, the role of the great mosque-universities—and the great mosque of Cairo founded by the Fatimids was the first state university—the bookshops in the vicinity of the great mosques, the corporations of students who frequented them, and their influence on the social and even the political life of the cities. To the brilliant life of the palaces and the courts, where often it was secular art and literature which predominated, there corresponded a cultural life of the markets and mosques, centred round the religious sciences and the debates between their various schools. It was often the literate people of the towns who protested against the freedom of thought or the licence in the habits of the great. The triumphs of Sunnism in the fifth/eleventh century, and especially perhaps the Ḥanbalī reaction, were to have their roots in popular movements.

It is possible to enumerate as constituent disciplines five 'religious sciences': that of the 'readings', of Qur'anic commentary, of *Ḥadīth*, of law, and of *kalām* or defensive apologetics. The first four came into being in the Medinese period and the beginning of the century of the Umayyads, the fifth, which arose from the confrontation of Ṣiffīn, was to come to its full development only under the impetus of the 'foreign sciences'. We shall attempt to characterize each briefly.

The Qur'anic sciences

First we have the Quranic science of the 'readings', *'ilm al-qirā'āt*. The first *qurrā'* ('readers' or 'reciters') were devout believers such as Ibn 'Abbās or Anas b. Mālik, Companions of the Prophet. Many 'readers' were also 'bearers' of the Qur'ān, that is to say, they knew it by heart, and meditated on it. After Ṣiffīn, the reading of the Book sometimes became an occupation performed by freed prisoners, who allowed political intrigues to mingle with religion. It was not until the third/ninth century in Baghdād that the readers formed themselves into a corporation and that their function became once again respected.

The influence of the schools of the grammarians was great. Abū 'Amr b. al-'Alā' and Thaqafī at Baṣra, and, a little later, al-Kisā'ī at Kūfa, were both grammarians and 'readers'. It was towards the middle of the second/eighth century that there had been admitted the principle of a plurality of authorized 'readings'. The early Qur'anic recensions of

Ubayy and of Ibn Mas'ūd were sometimes, under the cover of this pluralism, partially reintegrated into the *corpus* of 'Uthmān. The situation, however, still remained somewhat confused during the second half of the second/eighth century. The Shī'īs continued to prefer the 'Irāqī recension of Ibn Mas'ūd, criticizing the vulgate of 'Uthmān for having suppressed texts favourable to the 'Alids. But towards the middle of the third/ninth century there was established a consensus which avoided any divergence from the Qur'anic vulgate, allowing to remain only some variants connected with the vocalizations and with certain consonants. A list was drawn up of seven canonical readings, each of which was referred to a 'reader' of the early generations of Muslims, only two of whom were Arabs.

The science of the Qur'anic commentaries or *tafsīr* ('explanation') is certainly one of the poles of Muslim culture. If it is true that not only a *corpus* but also a *tafsīr* are to be attributed to Ibn 'Abbās, the cousin of the Prophet who died in 68/687–8, then this science began at a very early date. It was to overlap more than once with other disciplines, especially the science of *kalām*, the schools of which were to vary according to their respective tendencies the interpretation (*ta'wīl*) of certain disputed texts. *Falsafa*, and above all Ismā'īlī gnosticism, were to practise largely an allegorical *ta'wīl*. The Sunnīs, who usually favoured the meaning which was clear and evident (*ẓāhir*), were to be in opposition to the *Bāṭiniyya*, or those who upheld the hidden meaning (*bāṭin*).

Two major rules were later to emerge: first, to make the maximum use of lexicography and grammar in order to grasp the exact significance of sentences and words in the Arabic spoken at Mecca in the time of the Prophet; and, secondly, to ascertain precisely, as far as possible, all the circumstances of the revelation, even if this meant using Jewish or Christian sources (*Isrā'īliyyāt* and *Masīḥiyyāt*). But recourse to these sources was treated with suspicion by strict Traditionists.

We shall limit ourselves to citing a few who were to become accepted as authorities: al-Ṭabarī the annalist (d. 310/923), whose commentary reproduces many *Ḥadīths*, and who was not averse to an apologetic and polemical approach; al-Zamakhsharī (d. 539/1143), who was to have a considerable influence, in spite of the accusation of rationalizing *tafsīr* which was brought against him by his enemies; al-Bayḍāwī (d. 685 or 691/1286 or 1291), whose *tafsīr* was to be the type of manual used in teaching and by ordinary literate people. In addition there should be mentioned *al-Tafsīr al-kabīr* ('The great commentary'), called also

Mafātiḥ al-ghayb ('The keys of the mystery'), of Fakhr al-Dīn al-Rāzī (d. 606/1210), the well-known author of *kalām*, who does not hesitate to apply *ta'wīl* to the anthropomorphisms of the Qur'ān, to raise many philosophical and theological problems, and to sketch out some scientific commentaries inspired by the Greek science. As G. C. Anawati says, 'it belongs to the type of commentary which is both philosophical and *bi'l-ra'y* i.e., it does not rely on tradition alone, but on the considered judgment and reflection of the commentator. Into it al-Rāzī put all his philosophical and religious learning.'

The science of Ḥadith

The science of *Ḥadīth* or of Traditions (*riwāyāt*) arose from the devotional attachment of the Muslims to the 'traces' (*āthār*) of the Prophet and his Companions. The collectors of the *Ḥadīths* were numerous. The expression 'people of the *Ḥadīth*' (*ahl al-Ḥadīth*) is used of those who devoted themselves to this task; it refers also to their concern for accuracy and can be used intentionally as a synonym of *ahl al-sunna wa'l-jamā'a* ('people of the tradition and of the community'). They concentrated all their effort not on the criticism of the text (*matn*), but on the establishment of the chains of transmitters (sing., *isnād*), and on their authenticity. It was a matter of ensuring, first, that it was possible for transmitters to have met one another in a direct line, going back to the Prophet, and secondly, that each one of them was completely truthful and trustworthy. This research was the origin of the *ṭabaqāt*, which were collections of biographical notices of the early Muslims, the most famous collection being that of Ibn Sa'd. The genre was extended to cover later generations, and Arabo-Muslim literature was enriched for example by the *Ṭabaqāt* of Ibn al-Farrā' devoted to the Ḥanbalīs, by those of al-Subkī devoted to the Shafi'ites, and by those of Sulamī on the Ṣūfīs.

The science of *Ḥadīth* had as it were two functions in Muslim religious culture: historical research on the lives and the characters of the men who belonged to the very first generations, those of the Companions and of the Followers; and the attribution of a rating to each *isnād*, the value of which it was to determine. This latter normative function should not cause us to forget its historical function. Thus the *Ḥadīth* was pronounced 'sound' or 'good' or 'weak'; according to another view, it was *mutawātir* (with very many chains of transmitters), or simply 'known' or 'uncommon' or 'unique'; or yet again 'well-founded' or 'interrupted', etc. During the second–third/eighth–ninth centuries, six great bodies of *Ḥadīths* were collected and came to be regarded as reliable: those of Bukhārī, Muslim, Abū Dāwūd, Tirmidhī, Nasā'ī and Ibn Māja. The two first, known as the two *Ṣaḥīḥs*, that is to say those which reproduce only authentic *Ḥadīths*, were accorded a preferential authority. To them should be added the famous *Musnad* (i.e. based on uninterrupted *isnāds*) of Ibn Ḥanbal, collected by disciples after their master's death.

Shī'ī Islam also had its collections of traditions (usually called *akhbār*): some of them admitted also by the Sunnīs, others peculiar to Shī'ism, which stressed the 'Alids and their role in the community. The main Shī'ī collections date from the fourth or fifth/tenth or eleventh century, and were written by Kulīnī, Qummī, Muḥammad al-Ṭūsī, and 'Alī al-Murtaḍā.

The science of law

The fourth religious discipline is *'ilm al-fiqh*, the science of the law. From the cultural point of view, with which we are concerned here, we confine ourselves to two observations.

The schools of law are concerned with a much wider area than that which is strictly juridical in the Western sense of the term. In Islam, each of them is the expression, in addition to certain ways of thought, of a certain attitude, which is both practical and intellectual, with regard to the day-to-day behaviour of the devout believer. Many of the speculative quarrels between the schools of *kalām* can be understood in their historical context only by reference to the various schools of *fiqh*: one need only mention the relations between Hanafism and Maturidism, Shafi'ism and Ash'arism, and the opposition and later the welcome which the last was to encounter in the Malikism of the Maghrib. Finally the Ḥanbalī school, which challenged even the legitimacy of *kalām*, did not hesitate to assume responsibility for the defence of religious beliefs. Ibn Ḥanbal remains the typical figure of the 'Devout Elder', and his six professions of faith (sing., *'aqīda*) were the subject of a great deal of meditation and commentary. The Ḥanbalīs, Barbahārī and Ibn Baṭṭa in the third–fourth/ninth–tenth centuries, and the great Ibn Taymiyya in the seventh–eighth/thirteenth–fourteenth centuries, not to mention the Ḥanbalī Ṣūfīs, al-Jīlānī or al-Anṣārī, are among the most important figures in the history of Muslim religious thought and culture.

In the same connexion should be mentioned the cultural importance from the third/ninth to the sixth/twelfth century of the Ẓāhirī school, made famous by Ibn Ḥazm (d. 1064). It was to be conclusively rejected by official Islam. In it all forms of personal judgment or of reasoning were put aside in the process of juridical elaboration, and the emphasis was placed on the literal meaning of the texts in their most obvious sense (*ẓāhir*). The systems of analysis adopted were specifically semantic, according to a very narrow definition of the meaning of 'name' and 'named' (*ism* and *musamma*) and of their connexions. We have here an extreme example of this double method of analysis, both semantic and juridical, which deeply influenced the early directions in which Muslim culture developed.

Finally there should be noted the not inconsiderable influence of the Ibāḍī and Shī'ī schools of *fiqh*. The *Iqtiṣār* of the neo-Ismā'īlī Nu'mān, the chief *qāḍī* of Fatimid Cairo (fourth/tenth century) belongs to the school of Medina (Malikism), but according to the Shī'ī point of view by which the consensus of the doctors (*ijmā'*) was not considered valid without the approval of the *Imām*.

Defensive apologia

The fifth and last religious science, *'ilm al-kalām*, the science of the word (on God, or of God), or *'ilm al-tawḥīd*, the science of the divine Oneness (or of its proclamation), is generally known in the West as theology. We shall dwell on this briefly.

It seems to us more exact, according to the definitions of it given by its doctors, to consider it to mean a defensive apologia, the function of which 'is firmly to establish religious beliefs by producing proofs, and to cast aside doubts'.[1] If we wish to speak of an 'Islamic theology' in the meaning of this word in the Christian West, it is certainly necessary to add to *'ilm al-kalām* many elements which come from *uṣūl al-fiqh* (the sources of the law), and still more widely, many professions of faith or short catechetic treatises grouped under the title of *uṣūl al-dīn* (the sources of religion). It is certain that the great Ḥanbalīs mentioned in the preceding paragraphs would deserve the title of theologians as much as, if not more than, many of the doctors of *kalām*.

'Ilm al-kalām is a specifically Muslim religious discipline. Its origin goes back to the doctrinal ruptures which resulted from Ṣiffīn. However,

[1] Al-Ījī, *Mawāqif* (*apud Sharḥ al-mawāqif* of al-Jurjānī (Cairo, 1325/1907), I, 34–5).

and in contrast to the *tafsīr* for example, for the treatises and the schools to be organized it required an external stimulus: discussions at Damascus with Christian theologians, the influence of Greek science and thought at Baghdād, and the defence of the values of faith against this influence. From this point of view, it is impossible to dissociate from *kalām* the study of the very numerous treatises on heresies which played an important part in the history of Muslim thought.

In the Umayyad period the first debates took place between Murji'ites (who were faithful to the established power and who committed to God the eternal status of the sinful believer), Qadarites, or supporters of human free-will, the Jabarites, who were linked to the strict Traditionists and defenders of the absolute all-powerfulness of God. The ʿAbbasid second–third/eighth–ninth centuries were to see the formation of the Muʿtazilite schools, in their two great traditions of Baṣra and of Baghdād. The solutions given in various quarters to the problems concerning the divine attributes, divine justice, the respective fate of the believer, the sinner and the unbeliever in the next life ('the promise and the threat'), the intermediate state between faith and impiety, the obligation of the community to order the good and forbid the bad—all these solutions could vary among the Muʿtazilites according to tendencies and the subdivisions of the schools. But they were animated by a common spirit: the recognition of the value of reason (*ʿaql*) in the defence of religious values (*ʿaql* even becoming the criterion of the Law), the anxiety to purify the idea of God from all anthropomorphism, the wish to defend the faith and to justify it against the enticements of Greek thought and the attacks of the *zanādiqa* (free thinkers). The Muʿtazilites called themselves 'the people of Justice and Oneness' (of God). Thus it is seen that this is not, as was formerly thought, a matter of rationalism, but of a religious apologia which aimed to use rational methods. It was in this spirit that the school developed one of its central theses, that of the created (*makhlūq*) Qur'ān, in contrast to that of the 'Elders' who considered it to be the eternal and uncreated (*ghayr makhlūq*) Word of God.

Muʿtazilism triumphed for a time and even appeared as official doctrine under the Caliph al-Ma'mūn. It can be said that it belongs to the great humanist age of third/ninth century Baghdād and Baṣra. Among its great writers were Jāḥiẓ (one of the greatest of all Arabic prose-writers), Naẓẓām and ʿAllāf. As it became successful, it began to persecute its opponents, and this was the period of the great *miḥna*, the great 'trial', when the devout elders who defended the uncreated Qur'ān, chief among them being Ibn Ḥanbal, were dragged before the courts, condemned to corporal punishment, imprisoned, and even executed.

This triumph was to be short-lived. The Ḥanbalī influences, which were firmly entrenched in popular circles of 'Irāq, campaigned for the return of 'the old religion' (*al-dīn al-'atīq*). This was the reaction of al-Mutawakkil. The Mu'tazilites in their turn suffered persecutions, condemnations and exile. It is a great loss to the history of ideas that the majority of their works were destroyed, and for centuries were known only through the attacks of their adversaries. It was only recently that some of them were rediscovered and published. However, a direct Mu'tazilite influence was to continue in the Kharijite and Shī'ī sects.

After this, the teaching in the great mosques was to be shared between two great schools of *'ilm al-kalām*: the Ḥanafī-Māturīdī tradition, which arose from al-Māturīdī of Samarqand (d. 333/944), and particularly the Ash'arī school, founded by Abu'l-Ḥasan al-Ash'arī (d. *c*. 330/941), who was a former adherent of Mu'tazilism, and whose treatise on heresies, *Maqālāt al-Islāmiyyīn* ('The opinions of Muslims') remains a documentary source of primary importance. It is possible to distinguish between Māturīdīs and Ash'arīs by emphasizing the intellectualist and also psychological tendencies of the former, and the absolute divine voluntarism of the latter.

The Ash'arī school had to fight continually on three fronts. Against Hanbalism (and at one time against Zahirism), it had to defend the legitimacy of a certain use of reason in matters concerning faith. In his *credo*, al-Ash'arī stated his reverence for the teachings of Ibn Ḥanbal. Nevertheless the Ḥanbalīs were formidable enemies, who, on the day following the death of al-Ash'arī, went so far as to overturn his tombstone in the graveyard at Baghdād. Against Mu'tazilism the school challenged the ontological validity of human free-will and of secondary causes, condemned the theory of the created Qur'ān, and affirmed the separate reality of the divine attributes. Finally, from the fifth/eleventh century, it denounced as tainted with impiety the emanationist theories of the *falāsifa*, their theory of cognition, their tendency to treat allegorically (at least in the cases of al-Fārābī and Ibn Sīnā) beliefs as fundamental as the resurrection of the body.

These arguments were not carried on without borrowing from the *falāsifa* many methods of reasoning or of procedure, and the later

Ash'arīs in their analyses, and even in certain of their conclusions, are sometimes very far removed from their master and founder. They had no hesitation in taking up on their own account the logical, cosmological and ontological problems which *falsafa* had propounded. Nevertheless the philosophies proper to *'ilm al-kalām* could be formulated around either the occasionalist theory of 'atoms' or the conceptualist theory of 'modes', and it is most striking that these two theses, so consonant with the Ash'arī vision of the world, should both be of Mu'tazilī origin.

We should not omit to mention some writers belonging to the Ash'arī school, such as the *qāḍī*, al-Baqillānī (d. 403/1013), his contemporary, al-Baghdādī (d. 429/1037), famous especially for his survey of the sects, and al-Juwaynī (d. 478/1085). The latter was the teacher in *kalām* of the celebrated Abū Ḥāmid al-Ghazālī (450–505/1058–1111), who produced a treatise of *kalām*, the *Iqtiṣād*, and is famous for his *Tahāfut al-falāsifa* ('The incoherence of the philosophers'). In it he refuted al-Fārābī and Ibn Sīnā after having faithfully and objectively set out their principal theses in the *Maqāṣid*.[1] Al-Shahrastānī, his contemporary, was to attack the same adversaries so successfully that he earned the nickname of 'the overthrower of the *falāsifa*'.

One of the last truly original works of the Ash'arī school was to be the *Muḥaṣṣal* of Fakhr al-Dīn al-Rāzī, the only manual of *kalām* studied by Ibn al-'Arabī. Then in the eighth and ninth/fourteenth and fifteenth centuries there appeared the treatises of al-Taftāzānī—perhaps more Māturīdī than Ash'arī—and of al-Ījī with commentary by al-Jurjānī. At this period, and in the following centuries, the Ash'arī school known as 'of the moderns'[2] continually added to its philosophical preambles so as to produce a sort of mixed genre, belonging both to *kalām* and to *falsafa*, which became lost in the endless labyrinths of constantly renewed discussions.

'Instrumental sciences' and related subjects

Many Muslim writers, Sunnīs and Shī'īs, *falāsifa* or people of the *kalām*, or librarians such as Ibn al-Nadīm, have left catalogues of sciences. They frequently mention sciences which may be called 'instrumental', i.e. knowledge which in itself is secular put to the use of the 'religious sciences'. The study of the Arabic language and of its

[1] Whence the contradiction of the Latin Middle Ages which, knowing only the *Maqāṣid*, made 'Algazel' into an Aristotelian.

[2] The expression is Ibn Khaldūn's, in *Muqaddima*, Cairo, 327.

resources is indispensable in order to penetrate the meaning of the texts, and thus is justified the great influence exerted by the grammarians, and even the renown of the poets and prose writers. Astronomy is essential to establish the lunar calendar, the dates of the fast of Ramaḍān and of the Pilgrimage; without recourse to arithmetic, the jurists would not be able to divide legally the shares of an inheritance, and so on.

But these sciences, instrumental though they were, were in fact to develop widely in their own right. We have already mentioned the schools of the grammarians. There should be noted, in the second–third/eighth–ninth centuries, the work of two philologians of Baṣra: the Sunnī al-Aṣmāʿī (d. *c.* 213/828), renowned for his knowledge of poetics, and his rival, the Kharijite Abū ʿUbayda (d. 209/825), who drew attention to the traditions of the pre-Islamic Arab tribes and was one of the authorities cited by the *Shuʿūbiyya*. It should be particularly emphasized that in mathematics, astronomy, chemistry and medicine the Muslim world had no difficulty in continuing the work done by the Indians, the Persians and the Greeks; and that its original contribution was to have an irreplaceable effect on the advancement of science. One need only mention for example Gondēshāpūr, the lively centre of learning at Khūzistān in the second/eighth century, the invention of algebra by al-Khuwārizmī in the third/ninth century, or the works on astronomy by the majority of the *falāsifa*. Yaḥyā al-Khayyāṭ and al-Kindī himself had been preceded by, and prepared by, astrology; algebra had been preceded by gnostic speculations on letters and numbers, such as the famous work attributed to Jaʿfar al-Ṣādiq, the sixth Shīʿī *Imām*; and alchemy was held in much esteem. But distinctions were made. Ibn Sīnā devoted himself to astronomy at the request of ʿAlāʾ al-Dawla, *amīr* of Iṣfahān, adding to it also researches and discoveries in cosmography, geometry and arithmetic. He was able to make progress in chemistry, which, unlike al-Kindī, he clearly distinguished from alchemy, and his great medical work, *al-Qānūn fiʾl-ṭibb*, was still regarded as authoritative by medieval Latin scholars. In the fifth/eleventh century, the mathematician al-Bīrūnī was famous not only for his contribution to the science of numbers and to astronomy, but for his knowledge of Indian culture and his glossed translation of the *yoga-sūtra* of Patanjali. The list of the principal scholars writing in Arabic would be a long one. The apologists freely concede their right to exist in Islam, since the Qurʾān commands to 'reflect on the signs of the universe'[1]; they regard them

[1] Cf. Qurʾān, 2. 164; 3. 190; 6. 99; 13. 2–3; 24. 43–54, etc.

with suspicion only in so far as hypotheses advanced by them contradict the professions of faith.

Finally we must not omit history and geography. The *ṭabaqāt* which we mentioned in connexion with the science of *Ḥadīth* was perhaps the first form of historical narrative in Islam. There were very soon added to it many monographs, which were, however, more annals than history proper, and it was not until the eighth/fourteenth century, with the masterly work of Ibn Khaldūn, thathi story took on the dimension of an explanatory synthesis of the facts. On the other hand, the Muslims, being great travellers, discoverers of countries, organizers of empires and experienced traders, were very early in inaugurating a scientific type of geography. The influence of Greece, of the translations of Ptolemy among others, was decisive. We often find in geography the same names as in astronomy or mathematics: al-Khuwārizmī, al-Bīrūnī and others. In addition we shall confine ourselves to mentioning al-Ya'qūbī (d. 284/897), al-Maqdisī (or al-Muqaddasī) and in particular al-Mas'ūdī (d. 345/956), al-Idrīsī (d. 549/1154), Yāqūt (d. 626/1229), and Ibn Baṭṭūṭa (d. 770/1368–9). This list is by no means exhaustive. Such geographical works as studies on latitudes and longitudes, the science of 'climates' (the Greek κλίμα) and the making of maps (it was in Islamic territory that scientific cartography developed) sometimes turned into travel journals in which much space was devoted to the descriptions of the inhabitants of various countries and their customs. These descriptions were mixed with legends and they are still reflected in popular literature, such as the tales of Sinbad the Sailor.

Two 'marginal sciences'

To complete our investigation a brief excursus may be permitted. In fact the traditional classification of knowledge into 'religious sciences', 'instrumental sciences' and 'foreign sciences' is by itself inadequate to express the complexity of the facts.

For example it risks leaving in obscurity that 'marginal' science, which was at times condemned and even brought before the courts, and at times accepted—*'ilm al-taṣawwuf* or Muslim mysticism. We shall not deal with it directly here. It suffices to mention the very great importance of many Ṣūfī works, and even of the life led by the Ṣūfī circles, in the cultural history of the Islamic countries. There are Ṣūfī poems and prose, analyses of spiritual states or gnostic meditations, and even didactic manuals, which are most certainly the highest expression of Arabic or Persian literature. At the time when Sufism was being attacked by established Islam, the second and third/eighth and ninth centuries produced the incomparable testimonies of al-Ḥasan al-Baṣrī, Rābiʿa, al-Muḥāsibī, al-Bisṭāmī, al-Ḥallāj and others. The manuals of the following age, and especially the *Iḥyāʾ* of al-Ghazālī were to procure them acceptance. The sixth–seventh/twelfth–thirteenth centuries produced the masterly work of Ibn al-ʿArabī and the very fine poems of ʿUmar b. al-Fāriḍ, and we have already mentioned the influence at the same time of Persian Ṣūfī writings. It was no longer a question only of that chiefly formal beauty which characterizes classical poetry and prose; this was a transcription sometimes of personal experiences, sometimes of broadly gnostic evocations, but expressed with such a poetic and literary gift that Arabo-Muslim or Perso-Muslim humanism can be justly proud of it.

Let us reconsider briefly that other 'marginal' discipline, *falsafa*. It belongs so to speak to a fringe-position between the 'religious sciences' and the 'foreign sciences'. Its chief exponents were, as we have seen, both philosophers and scholars, or physicians, and were often involved in the political affairs of their time. The early relations between *falsafa* and *kalām* were far from being hostile. Al-Kindī, the first of the 'philosophers', was often considered as belonging also to the Muʿtazilī *kalām*, and *ʿilm al-kalām* has its place in the 'Catalogue of the sciences' (*Iḥṣāʾ al-ʿulūm*) of al-Fārābī. It was after the triumph of Ashʿarism in *kalām* that the break between the two disciplines occurred.

It is easy to understand how this rupture came about. Only al-Kindī, but still in a very inchoate fashion, gives us a kind of first outline of what could be called a Muslim philosophy in its true sense. From al-Fārābī onwards, the vision of the world of the *falāsifa* was built on an eternal creation, willed certainly by the First Being (God), but necessarily emanating from Him; and if it is possible to speak of an agreement between the prophetic revelation and the intelligible apprehension of the philosopher, it is, we are told, that the first expresses the second according to the usage of the 'vulgar' (*ʿawāmm*) in the form of symbols and allegories. It is only the field of worship which specifically belongs to it.

Such an attitude of mind raised no acute problem at the time of the Eastern *falsafa*, from the third/ninth to the beginning of the fifth/eleventh century; but matters were not to continue thus. Eastern *falsafa* in fact existed in an atmosphere profoundly impregnated with Shiʿism; Western *falsafa* in the sixth/twelfth century was under the patronage of the

Almohads, and it was Sultan Abū Ya'qūb Yūsuf who asked Ibn Rushd to produce a commentary on Aristotle. Not only did al-Fārābī and Ibn Sīnā enjoy the patronage of princes, but the milieu in which they lived, accustomed to Ismā'īlī ideas, was not likely to take offence either at their emanationist cosmology, or at the kind of intellectualist mystique which coloured their theory of knowledge, or at their secret preference for an interpretation (*ta'wīl*) which found in the texts of the Qur'ān their own view of the world. On the contrary, the Almohad milieu obliged the Western *falsafa* to present a defence of its Sunnī Muslim faith. Certainly it is true that the philosophy of Ibn Ṭufayl, and in particular that of Ibn Rushd, sometimes opposed some theses of Ibn Sīnā; beyond Ibn Sīnā, he often ended by agreeing with al-Fārābī, though not without affirming his own originality. Also, Ibn Rushd was often faithful to Aristotle, whereas al-Fārābī and Ibn Sīnā were open to neo-Platonic influences and even to influences from ancient Persia. But they all retained essentially the same basic attitude to established religion. The apologia undertaken by Ibn Rushd in his works of self-defence should not be allowed to deceive us over this.

The hundred and fifty years which separate Ibn Sīnā from Ibn Rushd had seen the triumph of Sunnism over Shi'ism, and the launching of the massive attacks of the 'people of the Tradition' or the doctors of *kalām* against *falsafa*. The *Tahāfut* denounced as dangerous seventeen propositions drawn from the works of the eastern *falāsifa* and declared four of their theses to be tainted with impiety (*takfīr*): the double eternity of the world *ante* and *post*, the denial of a true divine knowledge of singular realities, and the denial of the bodily resurrection. The Shī'ī disciple of Ibn Sīna, Naṣīr al-Dīn Ṭūsī, undertook the task of justifying his master. Ibn Rushd, in his *Tahāfut al-tahāfut* and in his *Faṣl al-maqāl* concentrated his efforts on the defence of *falsafa* itself, though not without some criticism of Ibn Sīnā. In the latter work he openly expresses his contempt for the dialectic of the people of the *kalām*, 'sick minds' who do nothing but 'shatter the law of religion in pieces'.[1]

The 'quarrel of the *Tahāfut*' is justly famous, but the rejoinder of the second *Tahāfut* was by no means decisive. In fact the traces of Shī'ī influence, which had marked the beginning of the Almohad reform, had been forced to give way in the face of official severity. The position of the Western *falsafa* was always to be an uncomfortable one, placed as

[1] *Faṣl al-maqāl*, Fr. ed. and trans. by L. Gauthier, (Algiers, 1942), 29; cf. again Ibn Rushd, *Kashf 'an manāhij . . .*, *apud Falsafat Ibn Rushd* (Cairo A.H. 1313 and 1328), 68.

it was between the intermittent favour of the rulers and the easily offended strict codes of the jurists. Ibn Rushd's self-justification, such an important document in the history of ideas, did nothing at all to disarm the latter. His works were burned in his own lifetime and this Cordovan ended his life in exile at Marrakesh. In short (and unlike al-Fārābī and Ibn Sīnā) Western *falsafa* had scarcely any influence on Muslim thought but was to exert all its influence on medieval Europe.

Broadly speaking, it can be said that the conqueror in the quarrel of the *Tahāfut* was al-Ghazālī, and we should not end this chapter without returning, however briefly, to this interesting figure. Abū Ḥāmid al-Ghazālī is without doubt one of the most famous figures in the history of Muslim culture. His biography is well known: his period of scepticism, then his finding certainty again in first principles, his investigations in *kalām* and *falsafa*, his refutation of the Ismā'īlī extremists, and finally his conversion to Sufism considered as a personal experience. His great work *Iḥyā' 'ulūm al-dīn* ('Revival of the religious sciences') goes beyond the traditional cadres of the 'religious sciences', and concerns them all. The modern Ḥanbalī tendency represented by Ibn Taymiyya was to accuse al-Ghazālī of having watered down Islam first by his broad eclecticism—in which were mingled Christian, Jewish and neo-Platonic influences—and secondly by the affective values which he incorporated in his faith. Some of them even, rather hastily, cast doubts on his sincerity. However, being a Shafi'ite by allegiance, he found among the Shafi'ites passionate supporters, such as al-Subkī, and he was to retain the title of 'Proof of Islam' (*Ḥujjat al-Islām*). It is true that he failed in his task as reformer, and that he failed in the last resort to promote a reasoned understanding of the faith; but after his conversion to Sufism in 488/1095, he produced many pages of spiritual writings on repentance, humility, surrender to God, and the love of God which continue to foster in Islam a genuine piety. They reach beyond the age in which they were written to remain a priceless heritage for men of all time.

CONCLUSION

Thus the cultural movement in the Islamic countries from the first/seventh to the ninth/fifteenth century appears as an extremely rich and complex collection of disciplines. It has its religious field—its 'religious sciences' or learning; it has its field of free philosophical and scientific research, which was at times permitted and protected by the authorities and at times regarded with suspicion by official Islam; and it has its field of the religious and secular arts, and of secular poetry and prose. The question arises whether a distinction should be made between a *Muslim* culture proper, inspired by Islamic values and particularly by the text of the Qur'ān, and a culture which existed *in Muslim territory*, and which either interpreted the religious beliefs of Islam in its own way, or ignored them or even opposed them.

It is certainly true that this distinction has some correspondence with the facts and it can serve as a useful principle for the classification of works and genres, with the proviso however that one should not attribute to it such a sharpness as it would possess, *mutatis mutandis*, in the Christian world. Although the Islam of the jurists and the doctors condemned the licence of the Umayyad or 'Abbasid courts or of the *amīrs* of Syria and Persia, yet the patronage of the princes produced literary and artistic masterpieces, and a way of life which contributed to the brilliance of one of the great civilizations.

Nevertheless the fact is that Islam is, in its deepest sense, *dīn wa-dawla*, 'religion and city', and too rigid a classification into separate sections would not be true to the historic reality. In the Muslim countries neither science nor secular literature or art were separated from religion in the way that certain branches of modern humanism have been in Europe. They were affected by Muslim values. To make again the distinction between *dīn* (religion) and *Islām*, it could be said that they belonged to Islam considered as a community, as a temporal city, without being attached, nevertheless, to the sphere of religion.

Taken as a whole, both religious and secular, Muslim culture of the classical age was always by preference to be Arabic in expression, and even exclusively Arabic in the region from Baghdād to Cordova. There should not be ignored, however, the authentic Persian culture which was contemporary with it. The Turkish culture was not to begin its development until the eighth/fourteenth century; even then it must be remarked that, until the ninth–tenth/fifteenth–sixteenth centuries, in the islamized Turkish countries Arabic was to remain in current use in the field of religion and Persian in that of literature.

Similarly Persian territory should not always be identified with Persian culture. According to the periods and the authors, the chosen language of culture would sometimes be Arabic and sometimes Persian, even within one amirate. In the fourth–fifth/tenth–eleventh centuries, Ibn Sīnā, a native of distant Bukhārā, wrote all his great works in Arabic but adopted Persian for his *Dānesh-nāma* composed at the request of the *amīr* 'Alā' al-Dawla. Firdawsī and al-Ghazālī were born in the same town of Ṭūs. Firdawsī, who wrote of ancient Persia, and only in Persian, seems to have intended to manifest his attachment to the Muslim religion by composing after the *Shāh-nāma* the poem of *Yūsuf u-Zulaykhā*. Nevertheless on his death he was excluded from the Muslim cemetery. Yet a hundred and thirty years later, al-Ghazālī, also a native of Ṭūs, of Shafi'ite and Ash'arite allegiance, was to earn the name of 'Proof of Islam', and his influence was to extend as far as the Almohad reform in the Maghrib.

The third/ninth century saw the development of the basic religious sciences of *tafsīr*, *Ḥadīth* and *fiqh*; the fourth/tenth century produced the great schools of *kalām*, and these two centuries were at the same time the golden age of the freest philosophical and scientific research. In this, Shi'ism, chiefly in its Ismā'īlī branches, played its usual role of catalyst. *Falsafa* cannot be called a Muslim philosophy in the strict meaning of the term: it was rather a Hellenistic philosophy, Arabic or Persian in expression, and with Muslim influences. But it became a vigorous leaven, through its influence, direct or indirect, and through the very refutations which it provoked. The triumph of Sunnism from the fifth/eleventh century onwards is paradoxically a proof of this. Although al-Ghazālī declared himself to be primarily a spiritual writer whose concern was with interior religious experience, yet without *falsafa* his work would have lacked an entire philosophical dimension. In order to oppose *falsafa* effectively, he studied it closely, and carried the debate even into the territory of his adversaries. In this way he had to introduce neo-Platonic elements into the very structure of the traditional problematic. Traces of it are found in the objective summary of the 'religious sciences' to which Ibn Khaldūn devotes several chapters of his *Muqaddima*.

It is probably possible to see in the powerful Ḥanbalī influence one of the most profound and sustained expressions of Sunnī Muslim thought as such. But Ḥanbalī thought was continually enriched by its struggles, sometimes against Shi'ism, and at other times against all trends of *'ilm al-kalām*. A prime example of this is the *Dhamm al-kalām* of the Ḥanbalī Ṣūfī, al-Anṣārī; and even Ibn Taymiyya himself owes many refinements of his analyses to his principal Shī'ī adversaries Ṭūsī and Ḥillī.

The great cultures which came later, the Safavid restoration in Persia and the Mughal civilization in India, were no longer involved in the same way with the *dār al-Islām* in its entirety. It seems, on the contrary, that it was to the combination of its basically Muslim inspiration, to the predominance of the Arabic language, to the patronage accorded (though not always unreservedly) to the arts and literature, and finally to the extensive welcome given to the 'foreign sciences', that the culture of the classical age owed its specific character and influence, and its own complex unity from the Indus to the shores of the Atlantic.

From the ninth/fifteenth century onwards, the 'religious sciences' scarcely developed at all. We cannot consider here the reasons for this. But it is possible to suggest that it was the tension between secular and religious elements which produced the greatness of the Arabo- and Perso-Muslim classicism, and that the presence of both of them was necessary for this. And it may be that a clearer recognition of unity of contrasts will enable Islam as a culture to be accorded its rightful place in the history of universal culture.

CHAPTER 6

MYSTICISM

'Religious mysticism,' wrote W. R. Inge in his classic *Christian mysticism*, 'may be defined as the attempt to realize the presence of the living God in the soul and in nature, or, more generally, as the attempt to realize, in thought and feeling, the immanence of the temporal in the eternal, and of the eternal in the temporal.' Many other definitions of mysticism have been formulated, and some of these have been re-examined with critical acumen by Professor R. C. Zaehner in his *Mysticism sacred and profane*. It is worth recalling that the mystics of Islam were equally at a loss to reach a precise and satisfactory description of the undescribable; Professor R. A. Nicholson once collected a very large list of definitions of Sufism by practising Ṣūfīs.[1] If mysticism in general is beyond accurate and concise definition, the particular variety of mysticism known as Sufism may perhaps be described briefly as the attempt of individual Muslims to realize in their personal experience the living presence of Allāh.

The Christian mystic in his quest for union with God relies first upon the person of Jesus Christ who, being of the Godhead, is Himself both the object of worship, the supreme model, and the goal of attainment. Next he studies the nature of God and His purpose in the world as revealed in the Holy Scriptures. For examples of mystical endeavour he turns to the lives of the saints and the writings of the mystics. Finally he seeks to prepare himself for the gift of Divine grace by observing the sacraments and acts of public worship, by the assiduous practice of self-denial, and by private meditation and other recommended forms of spiritual exercise. The Muslim mystic has no Christ-figure to mediate and intercede between himself and Allāh. The person of Muḥammad, it is true, idealized in time as the Perfect Man, came partly to supply that want; but Muḥammad was never accorded divine honours. For the Ṣūfī, the Logos was God revealed in His speech (the Qur'ān) and His act (the created world); so the Qur'ān was the focus of his faith and meditation, the physical universe the arena in which he observed God in action. Like his Christian brother, he could follow his prescribed discipline of public ritual and private devotion. The early saints of

[1] R. A. Nicholson, 'A Historical Enquiry concerning the Origin and Development of Sufism', in *JRAS* (1906), 303–48.

Islam furnished him with abundant example, the supreme model being the founder of the faith. Later on, many manuals were written for the instruction of the mystic, and convents were founded to promote the communal life of austerity and the service of God.

The formative period of Sufism extended over the first three centuries of the Muslim era. The term *taṣawwuf* (i.e., Sufism) was derived from *ṣūf* (wool); the Ṣūfī by wearing coarse woollen garments, according to some accounts in emulation of Christian practice,[1] proclaimed his renunciation of the world. Asceticism and quietism characterized the first phase of this movement, which was essentially a reaction against the wealth and luxury that, flooding in from the conquered provinces of Byzantium and Persia, threatened to overwhelm Islam and to destroy its primitive simplicity and other-worldliness. An eloquent spokesman of this protest was Ḥasan al-Baṣrī (d. 110/728), a man equally famous in the history of Muslim theology, for he is reputed a founder of the Muʿtazilī school. Enjoying the confidence of the godly ʿUmar II, he set the fashion, followed by later Ṣūfīs to their great personal risk, of blunt preaching against corruption in high places before the caliph himself. Others through the second/eighth century registered their disapproval by going apart from their fellows: in conscious imitation of the Christian anchorites still scattered through the Levant, they took refuge in caves and deserts where they devoted themselves wholly to the life of self-denial. Such were the men described by a woman ascetic of Syria.[2]

Their every purpose is with God united,
Their high ambitions mount to Him alone;
Their troth is to the Lord and Master plighted—
O noble quest, for the Eternal One!

They do not quarrel over this world's pleasure—
Honours, and children, rich and costly gowns,
All greed and appetite! They do not treasure
The life of ease and joy that dwells in towns.

Facing the far and faint horizon yonder
They seek the Infinite, with purpose strong;
They ever tread where desert runnels wander,
And high on towering mountain-tops they throng.

Still others, and they the great majority, sought to solve their personal problem by earning a bare subsistence in honest and lawful toil in the

[1] See A. J. Arberry, *Sufism* (London, 1950), 34–5; L. Massignon, *Essai sur les origines du lexique technique de la mystique musulmane*, (Paris, 1922), 131.
[2] Quoted in al-Kalābādhī, *Kitāb al-Taʿarruf* (Cairo, 1934), 10.

practise of useful crafts, otherwise keeping to their humble apartments and occupying their days and nights with the service of God.

The ascetic movement spread from Medina to Kūfa and Baṣra, to Damascus and newly founded Baghdād, to the distant provinces of Khurāsān and Sind. Presently two principal centres of Sufism developed; in the capital city of Islam, and in north-eastern Persia. A pioneer in the latter region was Ibrāhīm b. Adham, reputed prince of Balkh, who gave up his kingdom in answer to the heavenly challenge, and wandered abroad; he hired himself out as a jobbing gardener in Syria, and achieved the martyr's crown about 160/776 fighting against Byzantium. Contemporary with him were the learned traditionist Sufyān al-Thawrī of Kūfa (d. 161/778) who founded a short-lived school of jurisprudence, and suffered persecution because he refused public office; and the famous woman-saint Rābi'a of Baṣra (d. 185/801), a lifelong virgin by conviction who preached the new doctrine of Divine love.[1]

Two ways I love Thee: selfishly,
And next, as worthy is of Thee.
'Tis selfish love that I do naught
Save think on Thee with every thought.
'Tis purest love when Thou dost raise
The veil to my adoring gaze.
Not mine the praise in that or this:
Thine is the praise in both, I wis.

The transition from simple asceticism to a complex theory of the mystical discipline, and thereafter to a highly developed theosophy, took place during the third/ninth century. The exact course of this transformation cannot now be traced with confidence, since our knowledge of the leading figures in the first phase depends upon secondary sources. Shaqīq of Balkh (d. 194/810), for instance, is said to have been the first to define trust in God (*tawakkul*) as a mystical state (*ḥāl*). This statement rests on a relatively late authority,[2] and presumes that in his time the distinction had already been drawn between station (*maqām*) and state (*ḥāl*). This differentiation, which belongs to a mature and elaborate theory of the mystic's progress towards his goal of passing away in God (*fanā'*), defines 'station' as a degree attained by personal effort, whereas 'state' represents an advance contingent upon grace.

[1] Translation by R. A. Nicholson, *A literary history of the Arabs* (Cambridge, 1941), 234. For another version see D. S. Margoliouth, *The early development of Mohammedanism* (London, 1914), 175.
[2] Sibṭ Ibn al-Jawzī (d. 654/1257), quoted by Massignon, *Essai*, 228.

'The states are gifts, the stations are earnings' is how the classic theorist of Sufism, al-Qushayrī (d. 465/1072) put the matter. In the sayings attributed to Shaqīq the technical term *ma'rifa* also occurs; this word was used by the Ṣūfīs to denote mystical knowledge of God, as distinct from formal knowledge (*'ilm*) derived from revelation and reason and shared by all thoughtful believers; it is generally translated 'gnosis'. Another respectable fifth/eleventh-century source puts this key word already into the mouth of 'Abd Allāh b. al-Mubārak of Merv (d. 181/797), otherwise known as a Traditionist who collected sayings of the Prophet on the theme of self-denial (*zuhd*). Yet the name commonly associated with the introduction into Ṣūfī doctrine of the idea of gnosis is Dhu'l-Nūn al-Miṣrī (d. 246/861), a more substantial figure for all that much legend of alchemy and unriddling of the hieroglyphs and thaumaturgy has gathered around his powerful personality.

In the life of Dhu'l-Nūn, whose grave is still to be seen near the Pyramids, three streams of the Ṣūfī movement ran together. Visited in Egypt by mystics from Persia, he was summoned to Baghdād to answer charges of heresy, and thus had close personal contact with the two principal schools of theosophy. Supposed, after gnostic fashion, to be in possession of the secret of the Greatest Name of God, in his litanies and poems he exhibits a convincing awareness of the presence of God in the world and within the mystic's soul.

> O God, I never hearken to the voices of the beasts or the rustle of the trees, the splashing of waters or the song of the birds, the whistling of the wind or the rumble of thunder, but I sense in them a testimony to Thy unity, and a proof of Thy incomparableness; that Thou art the All-prevailing, the All-knowing, the All-wise, the All-just, the All-true, and that in Thee is neither overthrow nor ignorance nor folly nor injustice nor lying. O God, I acknowledge Thee in the proof of Thy handiwork and the evidence of Thy acts: grant me, O God, to seek Thy satisfaction with my satisfaction, and the delight of a Father in His child, remembering Thee in my love for Thee, with serene tranquillity and firm resolve.

Dhu'l-Nūn's arraignment before the Caliph al-Mutawakkil, relentless champion of strict orthodoxy in its war against the 'rationalizing' Mu'tazila, was symptomatic of the alarm which the growing boldness and popularity of Ṣūfī preaching had awakened in the hearts of professional divines. The Egyptian gnostic was but one of many Ṣūfīs who faced persecution during this period, culminating in the public scandal and cruel execution of al-Ḥallāj (d. 309/922). More shocking to conservative opinion than Dhu'l-Nūn's poetical utterances was the unrestrained language of Abū Yazīd (Bāyazīd) al-Bisṭāmī (d. 261/875), protagonist of the Khurasanian school of 'intoxicated' mysticism. Whether under Indian influence (as Horten and Zaehner have argued) or independently reaching Vedantist conclusions, Abū Yazīd claimed actually to have achieved union with God. '*Subḥānī! mā aʿẓama sha'nī!*' ('Glory be to me! how great is my majesty!'): this ejaculation of ecstasy, explained away by Ṣūfī apologists as God speaking through the annihilated mystic, sounded to less sympathetic ears very like a claim to divinity. Meditating on the popular story of the Prophet's ascension (*miʿrāj*) to the seventh heaven, Abū Yazīd experienced a like rapture of the spirit and set a precedent which other Ṣūfīs aspired to follow.

When He brought me to the brink of the Divine Unity, I divorced myself and betook myself to my Lord, calling upon Him to succour me. 'Master,' I cried, 'I beseech Thee as one to whom nothing else remains.' When He recognized the sincerity of my prayer, and how I had despaired of myself, the first token that came to me proving that He had answered this prayer was that He caused me to forget myself utterly, and to forget all creatures and all dominions. So I was stripped of all cares, and remained without any care. Then I went on traversing one kingdom after another; whenever I came to them I said to them, 'Stand, and let me pass.' So I would make them stand and I would pass until I reached them all. So He drew me near, appointing for me a way to Him nearer than soul to body. Then He said, 'Abū Yazīd, all of them are My creatures, except thee.' I replied, 'So I am Thou, and Thou art I, and I am Thou.'

The founder of the Baghdād school of speculative mysticism was al-Ḥārith b. Asad al-Muḥāsibī (d. 243/837). Born at Baṣra in 165/781, he moved to the capital early in life and became an accomplished student of Traditions, by then a very flourishing science. His readiness to accept as authentic sayings of the Prophet favourable to Ṣūfī ideas brought upon him the wrath of Aḥmad b. Ḥanbal, formidable inceptor of the conservative Ḥanbalī school of jurisprudence, and for a time he had to flee back to his native city. Presently however he returned to Baghdād, and enlisted a following of disciples to whom he imparted his doctrines in a series of books, most famous of which is *al-Riʿāya li-ḥuqūq Allāh* ('The observance of God's rights'). This work laid the foundations of the 'science' of mysticism; attentively studied, it served as a model for later writers. Al-Muḥāsibī supported his theses with frequent references to the Qur'ān and the Traditions, after the manner of the orthodox lawyer and theologian. In another book, the *Kitāb al-naṣā'iḥ* ('Book of counsels'), he describes his desperate search for the way of salvation out of the seventy-odd sects into which Islam had been split; the 'saved' proved to be the Ṣūfīs, whose company he accordingly joined.

Then the merciful God gave me to know a people in whom I found my godfearing guides, models of piety, that preferred the world to come above this world. They ever counselled patience in hardship and adversity, acquiescence in fate, and gratitude for blessings received; they sought to win men to a love of God, reminding them of His goodness and kindness and urging them to repentance unto Him. These men have elaborated the nature of religious conduct, and have prescribed rules for piety, which are past my power to follow. I therefore knew that religious conduct and true piety are a sea wherein the like of me must needs drown, and which such as I can never explore. Then God opened unto me a knowledge in which both proof was clear and decision shone, and I had hopes that whoever should draw near to this knowledge and adopt it for his own would be saved. I therefore saw that it was necessary for me to adopt this knowledge, and to practise its ordinances; I believed in it in my heart, and embraced it in my mind, and made it the foundation of my faith. Upon this I have built my actions, in it moved in all my doings.

With these words al-Muḥāsibī accepted the challenge flung down by the orthodox, claiming the Ṣūfīs to be the truly orthodox; at the same time he opened the door to that grand reconciliation between theology and mysticism which ensued a century and more after him. He had defended the Ṣūfī cause by using the same weapons as its most rigorous opponents, the powerful coalition of Traditionists and lawyers. His disciple al-Junayd (d. 289/910) resumed the argument and fought it out with the second most influential group, the scholastic theologians. The central problem agitating the minds of the religious learned in this century of decision was to elucidate a comprehensive doctrine of the cardinal dogma of Islam, the Divine Unity (*tawḥīd*). This topic was treated by al-Junayd in a series of subtly-composed epistles (*Rasā'il*) written to or for his fellow-Ṣūfīs, and collected after his death. He summed up his findings in a famous definition which came to be accepted as authoritative by most Ṣūfīs, and commanded the approval of even so strict a Ḥanbalī as Ibn Taymiyya (d. 728/1328): *ifrād al-Qadīm 'an al-muḥdath* ('the separation of the Eternal from what was originated in time'). This formula involved, on the human side, the central point of Ṣūfī theory, that the mystic may hope, by God's grace crowning his own exertions, ultimately to reach a state of self-naughting that he passes away (in *fanā'*) from his human attributes and survives eternally (in *baqā'*) united with God. In this stage 'the servant of God returns to his first state, that he is as he was before he existed'. It has been well pointed out[1] that this idea of a pre-existence of the human soul seems to echo neo-Platonic ideas, specifically as expressed by Plotinus in *Enneads* vi, 4. 14: 'Before we had our becoming here, we existed There, men other than now; we were pure souls . . . Now we are become a dual thing, no longer that which we were at first, dormant, and in a sense no longer present.' If in fact al-Junayd here leaned on what had been already translated of the Greek philosophers, he concealed the borrowing well, citing in proof of his startling theory the celebrated 'Covenant' (*mīthāq*) verse of Qur'ān, 7. 171.

> And when thy Lord took from the Children of Adam,
> from their loins, their seed, and made them testify
> touching themselves, 'Am I not your Lord,'
> They said, 'Yes, we testify.'

Al-Junayd gathered around him a large circle of men of like purpose, mostly learned artisans, and the discussions which enlivened those regular meetings for instruction and meditation bore abundant fruit. One of the leading personalities was Abū Sa'īd al-Kharrāz, author of the surviving *Kitāb al-ṣidq* ('Book of truthfulness'), credited by al-Hujwīrī (d. *c.* 467/1075) with the invention of the doctrine of *fanā'* and *baqā'* which loomed so large in his master's teaching. Some of al-Junayd's followers were inspired by what they heard and witnessed to become poets of the mystical life; the handful of their verses saved from the shipwreck of time is a tantalizing reminder of the much more that is lost. Such a one was Abu'l-Ḥusayn al-Nūrī, so named because he saw the Divine Light (*nūr*).

> O God, I fear Thee: not because
> I dread the wrath to come; for how
> Can such affright, when never was
> A friend more excellent than Thou?
>
> Thou knowest well the heart's design,
> The secret purpose of the mind;
> And I adore Thee, Light Divine,
> Lest lesser lights should make me blind.

Poetry now became an important element in the discipline as well as the literature of Sufism. One of the exercises found most effective in

[1] Ali Abdel Kader, 'The Doctrine of al-Junayd', in *The Islamic Quarterly*, I (1954), 167–77.

stimulating ecstasy was to listen to the recitation of verses, sometimes to musical accompaniment. The practice of 'audition' (*samā'*) reminiscent of the use of music in Christian liturgies, and even dancing, gave rise to fierce controversy which raged for many centuries; the Ḥanbalīs in particular were loud in condemning so dangerous an innovation. One was dealing not merely with metaphysical poetry, which though strange and novel could hardly be denounced on moral grounds. To al-Junayd himself we owe some verses of this character.

Now I have known, O lord,
What lies within my heart;
In secret, from the world apart,
My tongue has talked with my Adored.

So in a manner we
United are, and One;
Yet otherwise disunion
Is our estate eternally.

Though from my gaze profound
Deep awe has hid Thy face,
In wondrous and ecstatic grace
I feel Thee touch my inmost ground.

In like manner another unknown poet-mystic of the Baghdād circle spoke of the transforming union.

When truth its light doth show,
I lose myself in reverence,
And am as one who never travelled thence
To life below.

When I am absented
From self in Him, and Him attain,
Attainment's self thereafter proveth vain
And self is dead.

In union divine
With Him, Him only I do see;
I dwell alone, and that felicity
No more is mine.

This mystic union
From self hath separated me:
Now witness concentration's mystery
Of two made one.

If the verses recited at Ṣūfī concerts had been confined to such compositions, few would have cavilled. The scandal arose from the use of profane literature—the love-poems of an 'Umar b. Abī Rabī'a, the bacchanalian effusions of an Abū Nuwās—chanted by a handsome youth whose beauty was taken as a focus of concentration, being an example of the handiwork of the Divine Artist. This convention, no doubt innocent enough in its inception, gave rise to suspicion of grave misconduct; it also engendered the rich and fine literature of the Persian *ghazal*.

Whilst the Baghdād circle was thus contributing massively to the development of a metaphysic of mysticism, no less important advances were continuing to be made in Persia. Sahl b. 'Abd Allāh al-Tustarī (d. 283/896), to whom is accredited the first Ṣūfī commentary on the Qur'ān, evolved a doctrine of letters and light which later influenced the Spanish school from Ibn Masarra to Ibn al-'Arabī. Abū 'Abd Allāh al-Tirmidhī (*fl.* 285/898) in a long series of books and pamphlets, many of which are extant, elaborated a kind of mystic psychology which was taken up by al-Ghazālī and incorporated into his system; he also enunciated a novel doctrine of sainthood and prophecy which reappeared in the writings of Ibn al-'Arabī. Meanwhile al-Ḥallāj, born about 244/858 in the province of Fārs, wandered through a large part of the Muslim world, reaching as far as India and the borders of China, preaching a form of union with God which outraged the orthodox, and shocked many of his fellow-Ṣūfīs; condemned as an 'incarnationist' and a blasphemer, he was gibbeted in Baghdād in 309/922.

If ye do not recognize God, at least recognize His signs. I am that sign, I am the Creative Truth, because through the Truth I am a truth eternally. My friends and teachers are Iblīs and Pharaoh. Iblīs was threatened with Hell-fire, yet he did not recant. Pharaoh was drowned in the sea, yet he did not recant, for he would not acknowledge anything between him and God. And I, though I am killed and crucified, and though my hands and feet are cut off—I do not recant.

The foregoing extract from his *Kitāb al-ṭawāsīn* places in its context the notorious phrase *Ana'l-Ḥaqq* ('I am the Creative Truth') which the adversaries of al-Ḥallāj fastened on as a claim to personal apotheosis. The legend of his death invites comparison with the Christian story of the Crucifixion, which may well have been in his mind as his torturers made ready to slay him.[1]

[1] This and the preceding citation are from versions made by R. A. Nicholson, *The idea of personality in Sufism* (Cambridge, 1923), 32; 'Mysticism', in T. Arnold and A. Guillaume (edd.), *The legacy of Islam* (Oxford, 1931), 217.

When he was brought to be crucified and saw the cross and the nails, he turned to the people and uttered a prayer, ending with the words: 'And these Thy servants who are gathered to slay me, in zeal for Thy religion and in desire to win Thy favour, forgive them, O Lord, and have mercy upon them; for verily if Thou hadst revealed to them that which Thou hast revealed to me, they would not have done what they have done; and if Thou hadst hidden from me that which Thou hast hidden from them, I should not have suffered this tribulation. Glory unto Thee in whatsoever Thou doest, and glory unto Thee in whatsoever Thou willest.'

The brutal martyrdom of al-Ḥallāj startled into circumspection all but the most God-intoxicated Ṣūfīs, who thereafter strove for a way of reconciliation. The mystics of the fourth/tenth century in the main returned to a safer pattern of behaviour and public utterance. The long life of Ibn Khafīf, who died in Shīrāz in 371/982, was a model of scrupulous piety and a careful regard for orthodoxy. A number of scholars now judged the time ripe to sum up the doctrine and practices of the Ṣūfīs as embodied in the school of al-Junayd, and to argue that these were in harmony with the Sunnī code and creed. Abū Naṣr al-Sarrāj (d. 378/988) in his *Kitāb al-luma'* ('Book of flashes'), and Abū Ṭālib al-Makkī (d. 386/996) in his *Qūt al-qulūb* ('Food for the hearts') produced lengthy and learned treatises which in their sedulous advocacy of moderation went far to allay the suspicions of all but the most conservative theologians. In a shorter work, the *Kitāb al-ta'arruf li-madhhab ahl al-taṣawwuf* ('The doctrine of the Ṣūfīs') Abū Bakr al-Kalābādhī (d. *c.* 385/995), who also wrote a commentary on Traditions, prefaced his description of Ṣūfī mystical theory with an account of their theology which corresponds closely to, and even quotes from, a Ḥanbalī creed published in his own lifetime. Then Abū 'Abd al-Raḥmān al-Sulamī (d. 412/1021), a busy author who wrote an extensive Ṣūfī exegesis of the Qur'ān and many lesser works, compiled in his *Ṭabaqāt al-Ṣūfiyya* ('Classes of Ṣūfīs') the first comprehensive register of Muslim mystics. This pioneering book, aimed at proving the right of the Ṣūfīs to be accorded the same serious treatment as Traditionists, theologians, lawyers, poets, grammarians and the rest of 'classified' notables, was followed shortly afterwards by the encyclopaedic *Ḥilyat al-awliyā'* ('Ornament of the saints') put together by that learned biographer Abū Nu'aym al-Iṣfahānī (d. 430/1038) and published in ten large volumes. Then in 437/1045 Abu'l-Qāsim al-Qushayrī (d. 465/1074), who also wrote a Ṣūfī commentary on the Qur'ān and numerous other books, promulgated his famous *Risāla* ('Epistle') which set the seal on the work of rehabilitation and was accepted as the classical exposition of orthodox Sufism. Not many years later Hujwīrī composed his *Kashf al-maḥjūb* ('Uncovering of the veiled'), the first treatise on Sufism in the Persian language. To round off this summary account of the century of consolidation, we may note the names of two of the greatest figures in medieval Islam: the Persians, ʿAbd Allāh al-Anṣārī (d. 481/1088) and Abū Ḥāmid al-Ghazālī (d. 505/1111).

By the end of the fifth/eleventh century a broad measure of agreement had been reached on the meaning of Sufism and the details of Ṣūfī experience and theory. Sufism was very far from pretending to be an independent sect of Islam, a separatist movement such as those which had broken to fragments the legendary monolithic communion of the early years of the faith. The great teachers of those times were no Luthers or Wesleys, founding breakaway churches. Islam was in dire need of reform and revival, but the Ṣūfīs elected to reform and revive from within; they even succeeded in overriding the embattled frontiers between *Sunna* and Shīʿa. The last obstacle in the path of complete assimilation was swept aside by the gigantic labours of al-Ghazālī, that most eminent theologian and jurist, who demolished the philosophers and philosophizing Ismāʿīlīs, and completed a reconciliation between orthodoxy and mysticism which immensely strengthened both to withstand the battery of adverse circumstance soon to be loosed against the very existence of Islam. His masterpiece of irenic propaganda, the *Iḥyāʾ ʿulūm al-dīn*, proved to be more than what its title claimed, a 'revivification of the religious sciences'; it led to a revival of the religion itself.

As has been stated, the classic description of Sufism, studied as a textbook in the medieval colleges and commented upon by many eminent scholars, was the *Risāla* of al-Qushayrī. Addressed in the form of an epistle general 'to all Ṣūfīs throughout the lands of Islam', the book opens with an eloquent exposition of a familiar theme, lamenting the decay of true religion and calling for a return to true faith and sincere practice. After summarizing the tenets of the Ṣūfīs, with special emphasis on their doctrine of *tawḥīd* (unitarianism), al-Qushayrī lists the leaders of the movement beginning with Ibrāhīm b. Adham and ending with al-Rūdhbārī (d. 369/980). (It is noteworthy that in compiling this catalogue he follows closely the classification established by al-Sulamī; both writers exclude from the register such early figures as Ḥasan al-Baṣrī and Mālik b. Dīnār, admitted to the Ṣūfī canon by Abū Nu'aym and Hujwīrī.)

Next, al-Qushayrī offers to explain the technical terms current amongst the Ṣūfīs; such are *waqt* (mystical moment), *maqām* (station), *ḥāl* (state), *qabḍ* (contraction) and *basṭ* (expansion), *jam'* (concentration) and *farq* (separation), *fanā'* (passing-away) and *baqā'* (continuance), *ghayba* (absence) and *ḥuḍūr* (presence), *ṣaḥw* (sobriety) and *sukr* (intoxication), *qurb* (propinquity) and *bu'd* (remoteness). In defining these terms al-Qushayrī was following in the footsteps of al-Sarrāj, and anticipating the technical dictionaries of al-Kāshānī, al-Jurjānī and al-Tahānawī.

The distinction between *maqām* and *ḥāl*, though not observed with complete rigour by al-Qushayrī, nevertheless enables him to divide the mystic's progress into two parts. The 'stations' come first, being headed by (1) *Tawba* (conversion), as commanded by God in Qur'ān, 24. 31: 'And turn all together to God, O you believers; haply so you will prosper.' (It may be noticed incidentally that this text comes at the end of an exhortation to women to behave with decent propriety.) The primary obligation to repent was stressed by all the Ṣūfī masters; when Farīd al-Dīn 'Aṭṭār came to write his lives of the saints he recounted at the beginning of each biography the circumstances of the mystic's conversion.

Thereafter the mystic progresses through the following stations.

(2) *Mujāhada* (earnest striving), as prescribed in Qur'ān, 29. 69: 'But those who struggle in Our cause, surely We shall guide them in our ways.' The Ṣūfīs liked to quote a Tradition which made the Prophet declare that the 'greater warfare' (*al-jihād al-akbar*) fought against the lusts of the flesh was superior to the 'lesser warfare' (*al-jihād al-aṣghar*) waged in the field against the infidels.

(3) *Khalwa wa-'uzla* (solitariness and withdrawal), the former at the beginning of the neophyte's training and the latter when his initiation is complete, so that he may not be disturbed by his fellows and may be free to attend completely to his inward life with God.

(4) *Taqwā* (the awe of God), for Qur'ān, 49. 13 states: 'Surely the noblest among you in the sight of God is the most godfearing of you.'

(5) *Wara'* (abstention), in the sense meant by the Prophet when he declared, 'One of the signs of a man's excellence as a Muslim is that he abandons what does not concern him.'

(6) *Zuhd* (renunciation), even of permitted indulgences.

(7) *Ṣamt* (silence), as the Prophet said, 'Whoever believes in God and

the Last Day, let him speak good, or else let him be silent.' Silence is both external (the reining of the tongue) and internal (the reining of the heart, so that a man silently accepts God's decree).

(8) *Khawf* (fear). Qur'ān 32. 16 says of true believers that 'their sides shun their couches as they call on their Lord in fear and hope'. The mystic is fearful that God may punish him in the future, whether in this world or the next.

(9) *Rajā'* (hope), the reverse side of the same coin, as Qur'ān, 29. 4 states: 'Whoso hopes to encounter God, God's term is coming.'

(10) *Ḥuzn* (sorrow), for 'God loves every sorrowful heart' that grieves over past sins.

So al-Qushayrī takes us from station to station, until we come to (20) *Riḍā* (satisfaction), according to some Ṣūfīs the last of the 'stations' and the first of the 'states'; they quote in evidence of this Qur'ān, 5. 119, 'God being well-pleased with them and they well-pleased with him' which in its context describes the blessed in Paradise. According to al-Qushayrī, the Khurasanian school held that *riḍā* was a station, being a development out of *tawakkul* (trust in God), whereas the 'Irāqī school maintained that it was a 'stage' since God's good pleasure precedes man's satisfaction; he proposes a compromise, taking the beginning of *riḍā* to be a *maqām* and its conclusion a *ḥāl*.

The transition having been accomplished, the following states then ensue.

(21) *'Ubūdiyya* (servanthood), being constantly aware of God as Lord, as bidden in Qur'ān, 15. 99: 'And serve thy Lord, until the Certain comes to thee.'

(22) *Irāda* (desire), the attitude described in Qur'ān, 6. 52: 'And do not drive away those who call upon their Lord at morning and evening desiring His countenance.'

The last two states enumerated by al-Qushayrī are (44) *Maḥabba* (love) and (45) *Shawq* (yearning), when the imagery of Lover and Beloved is fully applicable. His catalogue is far more extensive than that of al-Sarrāj, who recognized only seven stations and ten states; it differs also substantially from al-Kalābādhī's treatment, and totally from Hujwīrī's. The latter indeed offers a novel classification of the Ṣūfīs into twelve sects, 'of which two are reprobated and ten are approved'. He names these sects, each with its distinctive doctrinal features, as follows.

(1) Muḥāsibīs, the followers of al-Muḥāsibī.

(2) Qaṣṣārīs, the followers of Ḥamdūn al-Qaṣṣār (d. 271/884), named by al-Sulamī as the founder of the heterodox Malāmatī school of those Ṣūfīs who courted blame as a proof of their total detachment from worldly things.

(3) Ṭayfūrīs, the followers of Abū Yazīd al-Bisṭāmī, the 'drunken' school.

(4) Junaydīs, the followers of al-Junayd.

(5) Nūrīs, the followers of Abu'l-Ḥusayn al-Nūrī (d. 295/908).

(6) Sahlīs, the followers of Sahl b. 'Abd Allāh al-Tustarī.

(7) Ḥakīmīs, the followers of Abū 'Abd Allāh al-Tirmidhī.

(8) Kharrāzīs, the followers of Abū Sa'īd al-Kharrāz.

(9) Khafīfīs, the followers of Ibn Khafīf.

(10) Sayyārīs, the followers of Abu'l-'Abbās al-Sayyārī of Merv (d. 342/953). 'His school of Sufism is the only one that has kept its original doctrine unchanged.'

These, according to Hujwīrī, are the ten orthodox Ṣūfī sects. The two 'reprobate' sects, consisting of 'those heretics who have connected themselves with the Ṣūfīs and have adopted Sufiistic phraseology as a means of promulgating their heresy', are lumped together as (11) Ḥulūlīs (Incarnationists), followers of Abū Ḥulmān of Damascus (founder of the Ḥulmāniyya sect, condemned by the Ash'arīs) and of Fāris al-Baghdādī who 'pretends to have derived his doctrine from al-Ḥallāj'.

The pattern of the mystic's progress invented by 'Abd Allāh al-Anṣārī in his celebrated *Manāzil al-sā'irīn* ('Stages of the travellers') is still more formal and elaborate than that of any of his predecessors. Accounted the most eminent Ḥanbalī scholar of his generation, al-Anṣārī published, in the Herati dialect of Persian, biographies of the Ṣūfīs based upon the work of al-Sulamī, and this compilation served in its turn as the foundation of the *Nafaḥāt al-uns* ('Exhalations of intimacy') by the great poet Jāmī. To the classical Persian language he contributed exquisite sentences in rhyming prose in the form of *Munājāt* ('Litanies'), whilst his lectures on the Qur'ān were worked up by a pupil into a massive commentary. Quoting a saying of Abū Bakr al-Kattānī (d. 322/934) that 'between God and the servant there are one thousand stations (*maqām*) of light and darkness', al-Anṣārī announces that in the interest of brevity he will reduce that total drastically. Dividing scholastically the Path into ten sections, he subdivides each section into ten chapters. The following list shows the first and last parts of this methodical and subtle tabulation; each topic is introduced with a quotation from the Qur'ān, further analysed, and supported by appropriate definitions.

I. *Bidāyāt* (Beginnings).

1. *Yaqaẓa* (awaking): Qur'ān, 34. 45: 'Say, "I give you but one admonition, that you stand unto God."'

2. *Tawba* (conversion): Qur'ān, 49. 11: 'And whoso repents not, those—they are the evildoers.'

3. *Muḥāsaba* (self-examination): Qur'ān, 59. 18: 'O believers, fear God. Let every soul consider what it has forwarded for the morrow.'

4. *Ināba* (repentence): Qur'ān, 39. 55: 'Turn unto your Lord.'

5. *Tafakkur* (reflection): Qur'ān, 16. 46: 'And We have sent down to thee the Remembrance that thou mayest make clear to mankind what was sent down to them; and so haply they will reflect.'

6. *Tadhakkur* (recollection): Qur'ān, 40. 13: 'Yet none remembers but he who repents.'

7. *I'tiṣām* (holding fast): Qur'ān, 3. 98: 'And hold you fast to God's bond, together.'

8. *Firār* (fleeing): Qur'ān, 51. 50: 'Therefore flee unto God.'

9. *Riyāḍa* (discipline): Qur'ān, 23. 60: 'And those who give what they give, their hearts quaking.'

10. *Samā'* (listening): Qur'ān, 8. 23: 'If God had known of any good in them He would have made them hear.'

X. *Nihāyāt* (Ends).

91. *Ma'rifa* (gnosis): Qur'ān, 5. 86: 'And when they hear what has been sent down to the Messenger, thou seest their eyes overflow with tears because of the truth they recognize.'

92. *Fanā'* (passing away): Qur'ān, 55. 26: 'All that dwells upon the earth is perishing, yet still abides the Face of thy Lord, majestic, splendid.'

93. *Baqā'* (continuance): Qur'ān, 20. 75: 'God is better, and more abiding.'

94. *Taḥqīq* (verification): Qur'ān, 2. 262: '"Why, dost thou not believe?" "Yes," he said, "but that my heart may be at rest."'

95. *Talbīs* (confusion): Qur'ān, 6. 9: 'And We would have confused for them the thing which they themselves are confusing.'

96. *Wujūd* (discovery): Qur'ān, 4. 110: 'He shall find God is All-forgiving, All-compassionate.'

97. *Tajrīd* (divestiture): Qur'ān, 20. 12: 'Put off thy shoes.'

98. *Tafrīd* (isolation): Qur'ān, 24. 25: 'And they shall know that God is the manifest Truth.'

99. *Jamʿ* (uniting): Qur'ān, 8. 17: 'And when thou threwest, it was not thyself that threw, but God threw.'

100. *Tawḥīd* (unification): Qur'ān, 3. 16: 'God bears witness that there is no god but He.'

In 488/1095 Abū Ḥāmid al-Ghazālī, accounted by many the greatest Ashʿarī theologian since al-Ashʿarī and the greatest Shāfiʿī lawyer since al-Shāfiʿī, at the very height of his powers and fame suddenly resigned from his chair of divinity in the Niẓāmiyya academy in Baghdād and went into retirement. Dissatisfied with the intellectual and legalistic approach to religion, disgusted with the hair-splitting sophistries of the philosophers and the scholastics, he took up the life of a wandering dervish searching for that personal experience of God which alone could resolve his doubts and confusions. He afterwards told the story of his conversion to Sufism in a book, *al-Munqidh min al-ḍalāl* ('Deliverance from error'), which ranks amongst the greatest works of religious literature.[1]

Then I turned my attention to the Way of the Ṣūfīs. I knew that it could not be traversed to the end without both doctrine and practice, and that the gist of the doctrine lies in overcoming the appetites of the flesh and getting rid of its evil dispositions and vile qualities, so that the heart may be cleared of all but God; and the means of clearing it is *dhikr Allah*, i.e. commemoration of God and concentration of every thought upon Him. Now, the doctrine was easier to me than the practice, so I began by learning their doctrine from the books and sayings of their Shaykhs, until I acquired as much of their Way as it is possible to acquire by learning and hearing, and saw plainly that what is most peculiar to them cannot be learned, but can only be reached by immediate experience and ecstasy and inward transformation.... I became convinced that I had now acquired all the knowledge of Ṣūfism that could possibly be obtained by means of study; as for the rest, there was no way of coming to it except by leading the mystical life. I looked on myself as I then was. Worldly interests encompassed me on every side. Even my work as a teacher—the best thing I was engaged in—seemed unimportant and useless in view of the life hereafter. When I considered the intention of my teaching, I perceived that instead of doing it for God's sake alone I had no motive but the desire for glory and reputation. I realized that I stood on the edge of a precipice and would fall into Hell-fire unless I set about to mend my ways.... Conscious of my helplessness and having surrendered my will entirely, I took refuge with God as a man in sore trouble who has no resource left. God answered my prayer and made it easy for me to turn my back on reputation and wealth and wife and children and friends.

[1] The following passage is quoted from R. A. Nicholson, *Idea of personality*, 39–40.

After an interval of self-discipline and meditation al-Ghazālī took up once more his always fluent pen. He applied himself energetically to putting on paper a complete system of belief and practice which embraced all that had been formulated by the moderate Ṣūfīs and incorporated with this the revered teachings of the Fathers of Islam. This great task was accomplished in the *Iḥyā' 'ulūm al-dīn*, later re-presented on a smaller scale for Persian readers in the *Kīmiyā-yi sa'ādat* ('Alchemy of happiness'). These two large works, composed in easy and attractive style, were intended for the edification of the general public. In his last years al-Ghazālī addressed himself to a more select circle of inner initiates, taking into his purview the neo-Platonic doctrine of emanation, thus paving the way for the so-called pantheism of Ibn al-Fāriḍ and Ibn al-'Arabī. The startling conception of the Idea of Muḥammad (*al-ḥaqīqat al-Muḥammadiyya*) as the 'light of lights' (*al-nūr al-Muḥammadī*), present already in the suspect writings of al-Ḥallāj and probably deriving from Shī'ī and ultimately from Gnostic sources, now came into the main stream of Ṣūfī doctrine.

> By ruling that the desire for Lordship, that is, the divine omnipotence, is inherent in man by nature because he is the image of God, Ghazālī smoothed the path for all the pathological excesses that were later to bring Sufism into disrepute . . . It is a matter of regret that Ghazālī should have put the whole weight of his authority in the scale of the monistic brand of Sufism that had invaded the movement in the person of Abū Yazīd; and it is a matter of surprise that a man who, when all is said and done, boasted of an intelligence well above the ordinary, should have shown himself so credulously naïve in his approach to the very questionable practices of the accredited Sufis. After Ghazālī, with but few exceptions, the mystical stream—in Persia at least where little effort was made at systematization—got lost in the sands of religious syncretism in which monism, pantheism, and theism were inextricably mingled; yet this doctrinal confusion, so maddening to the intellect, produced a poetic flowering that has seldom been equalled.'[1]

The sixth/twelfth century saw the beginnings of the full development of an institution which thereafter dominated the Ṣūfī movement and mediated its mass appeal—the *ṭarīqa* or dervish order. Earlier, somewhat ephemeral 'schools' of Ṣūfī teaching had gathered around the leading figures; now the need was felt to perpetuate particular traditions of discipline, the communal life and the shared ritual. Already al-Sulamī had compiled rules of companionship (*ādāb al-ṣuḥba*) which al-Qushayrī and his successors revised. The relationship between spiritual instructor

[1] R. C. Zaehner, *Hindu and Muslim mysticism* (London, 1960), 171, 179–80.

(*shaykh*, *pīr*) and neophyte (*murīd*, *shāgird*) acquired an ecclesiastical aura of authority and infallibility; ceremonies of initiation were devised involving the investiture of a distinguishing robe (*khirqa*) and the bestowal of letters-patent attesting true spiritual descent (*silsila*). Convents (*ribāṭ*, *khānqāh*) to serve as residences and centres of instruction were founded and attracted endowments, much after the pattern of the colleges (*madrasa*, *dār*) of theology and religious jurisprudence.

The oldest of the still surviving orders is the Qādiriyya, so named after its founder 'Abd al-Qādir al-Jīlānī (471–561/1078–1166). Like al-Anṣārī, 'Abd al-Qādir was primarily a strict and learned Ḥanbalī and his chief work, *al-Ghunya li-ṭālibī ṭarīq al-ḥaqq* ('Sufficiency for the seekers after the path of truth'), is composed in the form of a regular Ḥanbalī textbook, except that it concludes with a section on the Ṣūfī way of life. The *ribāṭ* in Baghdād in which he taught passed after his death under the control of his sons, and became the centre of a vigorous propaganda which carried the legend of 'Abd al-Qādir as far afield as Morocco and the East Indies. The saying put into his mouth, 'My foot is on the neck of every saint of God,' was taken to justify his elevation to the rank of a universal mediator with rights of worship not far short of the Divine. To this day his tomb in Baghdād, converted by Sultan Süleymān in 941/1535 into a spectacular shrine, attracts multitudes of pilgrims; its keeper is a direct descendant of the saint.

> The Qādiri order is on the whole amongst the most tolerant and progressive orders, not far removed from orthodoxy, distinguished by philanthropy, piety, and humility, and averse to fanaticism, whether religious or political. It seems unlikely that the founder instituted any rigid system of devotional exercises, and these in fact differ in the various congregations. A typical *dhikr* is the following, to be recited after the daily prayers: 'I ask pardon of the mighty God; Glorified be God; May God bless our Master Mohammed and his household and Companions; There is no God but Allah,' each phrase repeated a hundred times.[1]

Numerous sub-orders developed out of the Qādiriyya, some of which became independent; the most notable is the Rifā'iyya, founded by 'Abd al-Qādir's nephew, Aḥmad al-Rifā'ī (d. 578/1183), and widely distributed through Turkey, Syria and Egypt. 'This order was distinguished by a more fanatical outlook and more extreme practices of self-mortification, as well as extravagant thaumaturgical exercises, such as glass-eating, fire-walking, and playing with serpents, which have

[1] H. A. R. Gibb, *Mohammedanism* (London, 1949), 155–6.

been imputed to the influence of primitive Shamanism during the Mongol occupation of 'Irāq in the thirteenth century.[1]

A second order was presently established in Baghdād by Shihāb al-Dīn al-Suhrawardī (539-632/1144-1234), nephew of a Ṣūfī rector of the Niẓāmiyya academy and himself an accomplished Shāfi'ī scholar, a pupil of 'Abd al-Qādir; his best-known work is the *'Awārif al-ma'ārif* ('Benefits of gnoses'), commonly printed on the margins of al-Ghazālī's *Iḥyā'*. The Suhrawardiyya was carried to India by Bahā' al-Dīn al-Mūltānī. Shortly afterwards Nūr al-Dīn al-Shādhilī, born probably near Ceuta in 593/1196 and a pupil of the Maghribī Ṣūfī, Ibn Mashīsh, instituted his own Shādhiliyya community, whose conservative doctrine and orthodox ritual spread rapidly through North Africa, Arabia and Syria. A little later the Mawlawī (Mevlevi) order of Whirling Dervishes sprang up in Konya under the leadership of the great poet Jalāl al-Dīn Rūmī, its characteristic circling dance symbolising the endless quest for the Divine Beloved. Thereafter the orders and sub-orders proliferated with great speed, so that Massignon was able to catalogue no fewer than 175 separate named *ṭarīqas*, many of them having numerous branches.[2]

The lives of three men of exceptional genius spanned the century 560-672/1165-1273, and cast their shadows over the whole world of Islam. The eldest of the trio, Muḥyī al-Dīn b. al-'Arabī, was born at Murcia in southern Spain in 560/1165, studied in Seville and Ceuta, and was initiated into Sufism in Tunis. In 598/1202 he began a long journey eastwards which took him to Mecca, where he resided for a while, through 'Irāq, Anatolia and Syria; he finally settled in Damascus, where he died in 638/1240. One of the most fertile minds and fluent pens in Islam, Ibn al-'Arabī drew upon every available resource—Sunnī, Shī'ī, Ismā'īlī, Ṣūfī, Neoplatonic, Gnostic, Hermetic—to build up a comprehensive system which he expounded in well over three hundred books and pamphlets and a large quantity of poetry. His two chief works are *al-Futūḥāt al-Makkiyya* ('Meccan revelations'), a monument of his Meccan days printed in four huge volumes and running to 560 closely packed sections, and the *Fuṣūṣ al-ḥikam* ('Bezels of wisdom'), a product of his Damascus period. His doctrines have been summarized as follows.[3]

(1) God is absolute Being, and is the sole source of all existence; in Him alone Being and Existence are one and inseparable.

[1] *Ibid.*, 156. [2] The list is printed in *EI*[1], IV, 668-72.
[3] Summarized from A. E. Affifi, *The mystical philosophy of Muhyid Din-ibnul Arabi* (Cambridge, 1939).

(2) The universe possesses relative being, either actual or potential; it is both eternal-existent and temporal-non-existent; eternal-existent as being in God's knowledge, and temporal-non-existent as being external to God.

(3) God is both Transcendent and Immanent, transcendence and immanence being two fundamental aspects of Reality as man knows it.

(4) Being, apart from God, exists by virtue of God's Will, acting in accordance with the laws proper to the things thus existent; His agents are the Divine Names, or universal concepts.

(5) Before coming into existence, things of the phenomenal world were latent in the Mind of God as fixed prototypes (*a'yān thābita*), and were thus one with the Divine Essence and Consciousness; these prototypes are intermediaries between the One as absolute Reality and the phenomenal world.

(6) There is no such thing as union with God in the sense of becoming one with God, but there is the realization of the already existing fact that the mystic *is* one with God.

(7) The creative, animating and rational principle of the universe, or the First Intellect, is the Reality (Idea) of Muḥammad, also called the Reality of Realities (*ḥaqīqat al-ḥaqā'iq*); this principle finds its fullest manifestation in the Perfect Man (*al-insān al-kāmil*).

(8) Each prophet is *a* logos of God; *the* Logos is Muḥammad, the 'head' of the hierarchy of prophets. All these individual logoi are united in the Reality of Muḥammad.

(9) The Perfect Man is a miniature of Reality; he is the microcosm, in whom are reflected all the perfect attributes of the macrocosm. Just as the Reality of Muḥammad was the *creative principle* of the universe, so the Perfect Man was the *cause* of the universe, being the epiphany of God's desire to be known; for only the Perfect Man knows God, loves God, and is loved by God. For Man alone the world was made.

The second of this trio of great mystics, Ibn al-Fāriḍ, was born in Cairo in 586/1181 and died there in 632/1235; his tomb in the Muqaṭṭam hills is a quiet and beautiful shrine. Unlike Ibn al-'Arabī, Ibn al-Fāriḍ was no traveller, his only journey being the Mecca Pilgrimage. For him that rite was a physical counterpart of the spiritual quest, union with the Spirit of Muḥammad, intermediary between God and the world. He expressed this yearning and its ultimate realization in a series of mannered odes, full of the imagery of love and intoxication, culminating in the longest ode in Arabic literature, the *Naẓm al-sulūk* ('Poem of the way').

In a famous passage the poet compares this world of phenomena with the projections of a shadow-play.

And be thou not all heedless of the play:
The sport of playthings is the earnestness
Of a right earnest soul. Beware: turn not
Thy back on every tinselled form or state
Illogical: for in illusion's sleep
The shadow-phantom's spectre brings to thee
That the translucent curtains do reveal.
Thou seest forms of things in every garb
Displayed before thee from behind the veil
Of ambiguity: the opposites
In them united for a purpose wise:
Their shapes appear in each and every guise:
Silent, they utter speech: though still, they move:
Themselves unluminous, they scatter light . . .
Thou seest how the birds among the boughs
Delight thee with their cooing, when they chant
Their mournful notes to win thy sympathy,
And marvellest at their voices and their words
Expressing uninterpretable speech.
Then on the land the tawny camels race
Benighted through the wilderness; at sea
The tossed ships run amid the billows deep.
Thou gazest on twain armies—now on land,
Anon at sea—in huge battalions
Clad all in mail of steel for valour's sake
And fenced about with points of swords and spears.
The troops of the land-army—some are knights
Upon their chargers, some stout infantry;
The heroes of the sea-force—some bestride
The decks of ships, some swarm the lance-like masts.
Some violently smite with gleaming swords,
Some thrust with spears strong, tawny, quivering;
Some 'neath the arrows' volley drown in fire,
Some burn in water of the flaming flares.
This troop thou seest offering their lives
In reckless onslaught, that with broken ranks
Fleeing humiliated in the rout.
And thou beholdest the great catapult
Set up and fired, to smash the fortresses
And stubborn strongholds. Likewise thou mayest gaze
On phantom shapes with disembodied souls
Cowering darkly in their dim domain,
Apparelled in strange forms that disaccord

Most wildly with the homely guise of men;
For none would call the Jinnis homely folk.
And fishermen cast in the stream their nets
With busy hands, and swiftly bring forth fish;
And cunning fowlers spread their gins, that birds
A-hunger may be trapped there by a grain.
Ravening monsters of the ocean wreck
The fragile ships; the jungle-lions seize
Their slinking prey; birds swoop on other birds
Out of the heavens; in a wilderness
Beasts hunt for other beasts. And thou mayest glimpse
Still other shapes that I have overpassed
To mention, not relying save upon
The best exemplars. Take a single time
For thy consideration—no great while—
And thou shalt find all that appears to thee
And whatsoever thou dost contemplate
The act of one alone, but in the veils
Of occultation wrapt: when he removes
The curtain, thou beholdest none but him,
And in the shapes confusion no more reigns.

Jalāl al-Dīn Rūmī, the third of this trinity of mystical giants, was born at Balkh in 604/1207, son of a man who was himself a master Ṣūfī. The father, Bahā' al-Dīn Walad, left a record of his meditations in a book called *Ma'ārif* ('Gnoses') which contains many striking descriptions of occult experiences.

I said, 'God is greater!' I saw that all corrupt thoughts, and every thought but the thought of God, all were put to rout. The idea occurred to me that until a certain form enters the mind, sincerity of worship does not appear; until the word 'God' is uttered, there is no turning from corruption to well-being; until I conceive the image of God's attributes, and gaze upon the attributes of the creature, ecstasy and tenderness and true adoration do not manifest. Then you might say that the Adored is imaged in form; and that God has so created the utterance 'God' and the names of His attributes, that when these are sensibly expressed men at once enter into worship. God, it seems has made the declaration of His unity to be the means of the cutting off of all hesitations, whereas He has made the ascription of partners to Him to be the cause of bewilderment. He has likewise made all words and thoughts to be as it were pivots.

Beholding this I said, 'Come, let me efface from my gaze all that is perishing and vincible, that when I look I may be able to see only the Victor, the Eternal. I desire that, as much as I efface, my gaze may become fixed on God's attributes as Victor and Eternal, and the true perfection of God.' As much as I effaced,

I found myself to be the prisoner of things vincible, things created in time. It was as if God was turning about the things created in time; and in the midst of this I saw that I was upon God's shoulder. I looked again, and saw that not only I, but heaven too, and the skies, earth and the empyrean, all were upon God's shoulder: whither would He cast us?

Bahā' al-Dīn fled westwards when the Mongol hordes stormed into Persia, and after long wanderings finally settled in Konya. There Jalāl al-Dīn Rūmī spent the rest of his life, apart from a visit to Damascus, dying in 672/1273. When he came to write poetry, which he did reluctantly under the overwhelming compulsion of mystical rapture, he poured out his soul in a vast collection of odes and quatrains, naming his *Dīwān* after his beloved mystagogue, the wandering dervish Shams al-Dīn of Tabrīz. He also compiled a famous directory of Ṣūfī discipline and doctrine in the *Mathnawī*, six volumes of didactic verse relieved with brilliantly written illustrative anecdotes. Rūmī freely acknowledged his debt to two poets who had already composed Persian epics on the Ṣūfī way, Sanā'ī and Farīd al-Dīn 'Aṭṭār; the latter he had met as a boy in Nīshāpūr. 'Aṭṭār indeed contributed massively to the exposition of Sufism in a series of long poems, most celebrated of which is the *Manṭiq al-ṭayr*, based upon a brief allegory composed by Abū Ḥāmid al-Ghazālī or his brother Aḥmad, and epitomized by Edward FitzGerald in his *Bird-Parliament*.

The doctrine expounded by Rūmī differs little from that of Ibn al-'Arabī, but their objectives were widely at variance. 'The Andalusian always writes with a fixed *philosophical* purpose, which may be defined as the *logical* development of a single all-embracing concept, and much of his thought expresses itself in a dialectic bristling with technicalities. Rūmī has no such aim. As E. H. Whinfield said, his mysticism is not 'doctrinal' in the Catholic sense but 'experimental'. He appeals to the heart more than to the head, scorns the logic of the schools, and nowhere does he embody in philosophical language even the elements of a system. The words used by Dante in reference to the *Divina Commedia* would serve excellently as a description of the *Mathnawī*: 'the poem belongs to the moral or ethical branch of philosophy, its quality is not speculative but practical, and its ultimate end is to lead into the state of felicity those now enduring the miserable life of man'. The *Mathnawī* for the most part shows Rūmī as the perfect spiritual guide engaged in making others perfect and furnishing novice and adept alike with matter suitable to their needs. Assuming the general monistic theory to be well known to his readers, he gives them a panoramic view of the Ṣūfī gnosis (direct intuition of God) and kindles their enthusiasm by depicting the rapture of those who 'break through to the Oneness' and see all mysteries revealed'.[1]

An illustration of Rūmī's technique is his treatment of the Christian theme of the Annunciation, based upon Qur'ān, 19. 16–18.

And mention in the Book Mary
when she withdrew from her people
    to an eastern place,
and she took a veil apart from them;
then We sent unto her Our Spirit
that presented himself to her
    a man without fault.
She said, 'I take refuge in
the All-merciful from thee!
    If thou fearest God . . .'

Mary, being privately in her chamber, beheld a life-augmenting, heart-ravishing form: the Trusty Spirit rose up before her from the face of the earth, bright as the moon and the sun. Beauty without a veil rose up from the earth, even like as the sun rising in splendour from the East. Trembling overcame Mary's limbs, for she was naked and feared corruption. Mary became unselfed, and in her selflessness she cried, 'I will leap into the Divine protection.'

For she of the pure bosom was wont to take herself in flight to the Unseen. Seeing this world to be a kingdom without permanence, prudently she made a fortress of the Presence of God, to the end that in the hour of death she might have a stronghold which the Adversary would find no way to assail. No better fortress she saw than the protection of God; she chose a camping-place nigh to that castle.

That Proof of the Divine bounty cried out to her, 'I am the trusty messenger of the Presence. Be not afraid of me. Turn not your head away from the lordly ones of the majesty, do not withdraw yourself from such goodly confidants.'

As he spoke, a candle-wick of pure light spiralled up from his lips straight to the star Arcturus.

'You are fleeing from my being into not-being. In not-being I am king and standard-bearer; verily, my house and home are in not-being, only my graven form is before Our Lady. Mary, look well, for I am a form hard to apprehend; I am both a new moon and a fantasy in the heart. I am of the light of the Lord, like the true dawn, for no night encompasses my day. Daughter of 'Imrān, cry not to God for refuge against me, for I have descended from the refuge of God. The refuge of God has been my origin and sustenance, the light of that refuge which was before ever word was spoken. You are taking refuge from me with God; yet in pre-eternity I am the portrait of that Refuge.

[1] R. A. Nicholson, *Rūmī, poet and mystic* (London), 24–5.

I am the refuge that oft-times has been your deliverance; you are taking refuge, and I myself am that refuge. There is no bane worse than ignorance: you are with the Friend, and know not how to love. You suppose the Friend to be a stranger; you have bestowed the name of sorrow upon joy.

By the end of the seventh/thirteenth century the creative phase of Sufism, as a reconciler of philosophy with theology and of both with personal religion, had been completed. Little remained on the intellectual level but to refine points of doctrine; two names may be singled out, those of ʿAbd al-Karīm al-Jīlī (d. 832/1428) and Jāmī (d. 898/1492. The former, following in the footsteps of Ibn al-ʿArabī, perfected the concept of the Perfect Man in a treatise so entitled (*al-Insān al-kāmil*).[1]

The Perfect Man is the *Quṭb* (axis) on which the spheres of existence revolve from first to last, and since things came into being he is one for ever and ever. He hath various guises and appears in diverse bodily tabernacles: in respect of some of these his name is given to him, while in respect of others it is not given to him. His own original name is Mohammed, his name of honour Abu 'l-Qásim, his description ʿAbdullah, and his title Shamsu'ddín. In every age he bears a name suitable to his guise in that age. I once met him in the form of my Shaykh, Sharafu'ddin Ismá'íl al-Jabartí, but I did not know that he (the Shaykh) was the Prophet, although I knew that he (the Prophet) was the Shaykh. This was one of the visions in which I beheld him at Zabid in A.H. 796. The real meaning of this matter is that the Prophet has the power of assuming every form. When the adept sees him in that form of Mohammed which he wore during his life, he names him by that name, but when he sees him in another form and knows him to be Mohammed, he names him by the name of the form in which he appears. The name Mohammed is not applied except to the Idea of Mohammed.

The identification of Muḥammad with the Perfect Man encouraged a cult of the Prophet which took shape in such works as the *Dalāʾil al-khayrāt* ('Indications of virtues') of the Moroccan al-Jazūlī (d. 870/1465), a collection of litanies and encomia which became the standard prayer-book and rivalled in popularity the famed *Qaṣīdat al-burda* ('Ode of the mantle') of the Egyptian poet al-Būṣīrī (d. 696/1297); finely calligraphed and illuminated copies of both were prized as much for their *baraka* (magical blessing) as their artistic merit. Meanwhile the trinitarian theme of Lover, Love and Beloved, first given formal treatment by Aḥmad al-Ghazālī (d. 517/1123) and developed by ʿAyn al-Quḍāt Hamadānī (d. 525/1131) and the poet Fakhr al-Dīn ʿIrāqī (d. 688/1289), was taken

[1] R. A. Nicholson, *Studies in Islamic mysticism* (Cambridge, 1921), 105.

up again and given metaphysical form by Jāmī in his *Lawā'iḥ* ('Effulgences').[1]

The Absolute does not exist without the relative, and the relative is not formulated without the Absolute; but the relative stands in need of the Absolute, while the Absolute has no need of the relative. Consequently the necessary connection of the two is mutual, but the need is on one side only, as in the case of the motion of a hand holding a key, and that of the key thus held.

O Thou whose sacred precincts none may see,
Unseen Thou makest all things seen to be;
Thou and we are not separate, yet still
Thou hast no need of us, but we of Thee.

It is in regard to His essence that the Absolute has no need of the relative. In other respects the manifestation of the names of His Divinity and the realization of the relations of His Sovereignty are clearly impossible otherwise than by use of the relative.

In me Thy beauty love and longing wrought:
Did I not seek Thee how could'st Thou be sought?
My love is as a mirror in the which
Thy beauty into evidence is brought.

Nay, what is more, it is the 'Truth' who is Himself at once the lover and the beloved, the seeker and the sought. He is loved and sought in His character of the 'One who is all'; and He is lover and seeker when viewed as the sum of all particulars and plurality.

The following extract from the beginning of the *Lawā'iḥ* of 'Ayn al-Quḍāt further illustrates the meditation on the great mystery of creation, first enunciated in a Tradition beloved of the Ṣūfīs, 'I was a hidden treasure and desired to be known, so I created the creation in order that I might be known.'

Spirit and Love came into existence both at one time, being manifested out of the same Creator. Spirit discovered itself to be intermingled with Love, and Love proved to be in suspense upon Spirit. Inasmuch as it was the property of Spirit to be in suspense upon Love, and Love out of its subtlety was intermingled with Spirit, by virtue of that suspense and intermingling union supervened between them. I do not know whether Love became the attribute and Spirit the essence, or Love became the essence and Spirit the attribute; however the matter may have been, the result was that the two became one.

When the radiance of the beauty of the Beloved first manifested out of the Divine Heart, Love began to converse with Spirit. Inasmuch as the one was related to air and the other to fire, the air kindled the fire while the fire consumed the air, so that the fire became the victor and the air received the vanquished;

[1] E. H. Whinfield (ed. and tr.), *Lawā'iḥ* (London, 1907), 36–7.

and God pronounced over Being the words, *It spares not, neither leaves alone* (Qur'ān, 74. 28). Love, which had been the victor, encountering the rays of the lights of the Beloved became vanquished. For this reason it is impossible to know whether Love conforms more with the Lover or with the Beloved, because Love rules over the Lover, whereas Love is a prisoner in the clutches of the Beloved's omnipotence.

Thy love is now the ruler of my soul,
And helplessly I wait on Thy command;
A prisoner in Thy omnipotent hand,
I do not see what cure may make me whole.

Most Persian poetry (apart from political panegyric) from the fifth/eleventh century onwards was impregnated with the ideas and imagery of Sufism. Jāmī, last of the classical poets, being a convinced Ṣūfī, a member indeed of the Naqshbandī order, in his voluminous writings in prose and verse rehearsed again and again the legends of the mystics and the mystical meaning of the legends. His *Nafaḥāt al-uns* brought hagiography down to his own times and teachers; in his graceful idylls, the *Salamān wa-Absāl*, the *Laylā wa-Majnūn*, the *Yūsuf wa-Zulaykhā*, he interpreted stories religious and profane as variations of the same unchanging theme, the agonizing quest of the Lover for the Beloved. This same topic continued to inspire Persian poets down to the nineteenth century, as in verses ascribed to the Bābī heroine, Qurrat al-'Ayn.[1]

The thralls of yearning love constrain in the bonds of pain and calamity
These broken-hearted lovers of thine to yield their lives in their zeal for Thee.
Though with sword in hand my Darling stand with intent to slay,
though I sinless be,
If it pleases Him, this tyrant's whim, I am well content with his tyranny.

Even into the twentieth century the more intellectual bent of the Arab tradition of Sufism found expression in the writings of an Algerian mystic, Shaykh Aḥmad al-'Alawī (d. 1934).[2]

I am Essentially One, Single, Unencroachable
By the least object. Leave I any crevice,
Any space vacant that to another might go?
For the Inside am I of the Essence in Itself
And the Outside of the Quality, Diffuse Concentration.
'Thither' is there none whither I am not turning.
Doth other than Me exist, empty of My Attribute?
My Essence is the Essence of Being, now,

[1] Translation by E. G. Browne, see *A Persian Anthology*, 70–1.
[2] Martin Lings, *A Moslem saint of the twentieth century* (London, 1961), 203.

Always. My Infinity is not limited by the least
Grain of mustard. Where can the creature
Find room to intrude on the Truth's Infinite?
Where other than It, when All is Full?
Union and separation are thus in Principle the same,
And to behold creation is to behold the Truth,
If creation be interpreted as it truly is.

Indeed, the history of creation from beginning to end was summed up long ago in a couple of stanzas by Rūmī, epitomizing the whole intricate but essentially simple Ṣūfī doctrine.

Happy was I
In the pearl's heart to lie;
Till, lashed by life's hurricane,
Like a tossed wave I ran.

The secret of the sea
I uttered thunderously;
Like a spent cloud on the shore
I slept, and stirred no more.

CHAPTER 7

REVIVAL AND REFORM IN ISLAM

THE TRADITION

The period in which formative developments took place in Islam, and at the end of which Muslim orthodoxy crystallized and emerged, roughly covered a period of two centuries and a half. Since this was the formative period, one cannot strictly speak of either revival or reform in Islam during this time, for both revival and reform can logically occur only after an orthodoxy has been established. Nevertheless, it would be a grave error to overlook the developments that occurred during this period since the very emergence of orthodoxy occurred only after long struggle and conflict in the fields of politics, moral ideas and spiritual motifs. Indeed the germs of all the subsequent major developments in Islam, involving moral and spiritual issues, are traceable to this very early period in the history of the Muslim community after the death of the Prophet. The issues as to whether the Muslims should have a state at all, and, if so, what would be its nature and structure; whether the community should be based on a catholic toleration or exclusivism; what type of economic principles should be generally regarded as Islamic; whether man is free and responsible, or whether his actions are pre-determined; whether the community should decide issues in a collective spirit through *ijmāʿ* or whether it should accept the principle of an infallible *Imām*—all these problems were in some form or another raised, and in some sort answered during the earliest generations of Islam.

These conflicts ultimately resulted by the third/ninth century in the acceptance of certain settled attitudes and opinions which, during the course of these centuries, had been given currency in the form of Traditions (sing., *Ḥadīth*) attributed to the Prophet. The 'people of the Tradition' (*ahl al-Ḥadīth*) were responsible for formulating the content of Sunnism which has continued to constitute orthodoxy since then. In these struggles, one can speak of the Shīʿī group as a protest phenomenon for a period, until Shiʿism developed its own theology and independent system. The protest was essentially social and political, against the suppressive attitude of the ascendant Arabs, particularly during the Umayyad period. But Shi'ism soon ceased to be a phenomenon of reform and protest, and hardened into a sect with its doctrines of the infallible imamate and of *taqiyya*, i.e. dissimulation of belief.

The next reform phenomenon is the Ṣūfī movement which started in the second/eighth century, partly as a reaction against the political situation, and partly as a complementary antithesis to the development of the systems of law and theology in Islam. With the natural and rapid expansion of Muslim administration, the speedy development of Muslim law was inevitable. But since law can regulate only the external behaviour of man, some sensitive spirits reacted sharply to these developments, questioning the validity of law as an exhaustive or, indeed, as an adequate expression of Islam. The Ṣūfī movement gathered momentum, and from its original moral and ascetic phase rapidly developed an ideal of ecstatic communion with God, a doctrine of esoteric knowledge—as opposed to external, rational theology—with a system of moral gymnastics as a means to the realization of its final goal. But Sufism, like Shi'ism, threatened to drift from the social and communal ethos of orthodoxy, both by making the individual the centre of its attention, and by its doctrine of esotericism.

Nevertheless, Sufism has exercised, next to orthodoxy, the greatest influence on the Muslim community because of its insistence on the inner reform of the individual, and has, ever since its birth, posed the biggest challenge to orthodoxy down to the dawn of modern times. Since the fourth/tenth century, when Sufism aligned itself intellectually with liberalizing intellectual trends, and combined with its esotericism the philosophic legacy of neo-Platonism, it has exerted a tremendous attraction on some of the best minds in Islam. Orthodoxy, however, did not and could not yield to the ideal of Sufism, which, being incurably individual, ran counter to the ethos of the community. Finally, in the fifth/eleventh century, al-Ghazālī forged a synthesis of Sufism and orthodoxy which has exercised one of the most durable influences on the subsequent development of the community. The substance of al-Ghazālī's reform lies in adopting a Ṣūfī methodology to realize the orthodox ideal. Sufism for al-Ghazāli is a way whereby the verities of the orthodox creed can be both established, and invested with full meaning. This is, of course, not to say that the Sufism of al-Ghazālī is externally and mechanically attached to the truths of the faith; on the contrary, in his book *al-Munqidh min al-ḍalāl*, he tells us how, after having forsaken traditional faith, and having wandered through philosophic thought and Ismāʿīlī doctrines, he *discovered* the truth in orthodox Islam, which, in the hands of its official exponents, had become a mere shell, a set of formal propositions without inner power.[1] While, however, al-Ghazālī's influence has been of the utmost fecundity in the religious history of Islam, and has produced a broad *via media*, developments occurred soon after him which led Sufism and orthodoxy in different directions. Al-Ghazālī is a great watershed of religious ideas in Islam, and his influence has not altogether been in one direction. Although he himself claimed to rediscover the verities of the orthodox creed through Sufism, and many followed him in this path, there are strong elements in his writings which do not yield easily to this synthetic treatment, and he often gives the appearance of being a pure mystic rather than an orthodox mystic. It is certainly difficult to infer an effective societal ethos from his teachings. During the seventh/thirteenth century, the Spanish Muslim Ibn al-ʿArabī developed Sufism into a full-fledged pantheistic doctrine, and became the apostle of the new theosophic Sufism, around which clustered the majority of heterodox Ṣūfīs in the succeeding centuries. From the sixth/twelfth century onwards, Sufism also became a mass movement in the form of organized brotherhoods (sing., *ṭarīqa*) which invaded the entire Muslim world from east to west. The antinomian tendencies, which had often been latent in Sufism, and erupted sporadically in the form of intellectual and spiritual movements, now became rampant in the Muslim world, through their alliance with local religious milieus. Henceforward, this fact constitutes a permanent challenge and a threat to orthodoxy.

The Ṣūfī movement, in fact, gathered up a multifarious and vast stock of ideas, beliefs and practices; and, indeed, threw its mantle over all those trends which either wanted to soften the rigours of the orthodox structure of ideas, or even rebelled against them, whether openly or covertly. Sufism thus not only afforded a haven to certain primitive practices and beliefs from various regions of the gradually islamized world, such as the worship of saints and veneration of tombs; but, in some of its manifestations, looked like being simply a spiritualized version of Ismāʿīlī esotericism, or a philosophical dissipation of the orthodox position through intellectual or pseudo-intellectual arguments.

[1] That al-Ghazālī's mysticism is a purely external and 'methodological' affair is a thesis put forward by Farid Jabre in his *La notion de la maʿrifa chez al-Ghazālī* (Beirut, 1958); for its criticism, see Fazlur Rahman's review of the same in *BSOAS* xxii/2 (1959), 362–4; also his book *Islam* (London, 1966), Ch. VIII.

Whereas, therefore, Sufism, in its moderate forms, became acceptable to, and was even espoused by, the orthodox, its flanks became the focal points of all those trends of varying degrees of intensity which sought either to reform orthodox Islam, or to dissipate it completely. The concentration of all these under cover of Ṣūfī thought and practice offered a challenge, to meet which henceforth absorbed all the energies of the orthodox *'ulamā'*. We thus see a whole complex of reform and counter-reform.

Just as the 'people of the Tradition' had played a decisive role in the early struggles against the Mu'tazila, the Shī'a and the Kharijites, and had helped to crystallize and formulate Sunnī orthodoxy, so once again the same revivalist and reformist zeal appeared with the remarkable Ibn Taymiyya in the seventh–eighth/thirteenth–fourteenth centuries. Ibn Taymiyya was a professed follower of Aḥmad b. Ḥanbal, and a typical representative of the right wing of orthodoxy. The immediate objects of his fiery criticism were Sufism and its representatives, but he was no less vehement against the pure thought of the philosophers, the esotericism of the Shī'a in general and the Ismā'īlīs in particular. Even the orthodox Ash'arite formulation of the Muslim creed receives its share of Ibn Taymiyya's critique.[1] But although Ibn Taymiyya generally gives the impression of being a rigid conservative, uncompromising with either rationalism or Sufism, this impression is not altogether correct. There is discernible in his writings a positive movement of the mind and spirit which genuinely seeks to go behind all historic formulations of Islam by all Muslim groups, to the Qur'ān itself and to the teaching of the Prophet. There is ample evidence that he did not reject all forms of Sufism, and that he in fact regarded the Ṣūfī 'intuition' as being on a par with the *ijtihād* of orthodox *'ulamā'*, both of which, he demanded, must be judged in the light of the Qur'ān and the *Sunna*.[2] Similarly, his critique of existing orthodoxy on some of the fundamental points of the creed, such as the freedom and the efficacy of the human will, almost tilts the balance in favour of the Mu'tazilites against the entrenched orthodoxy, and shows glaringly his boldness in resenting reigning opinions, even when orthodoxy had thrown its mantle upon them. Ibn Taymiyya, therefore, undoubtedly sought, with a large measure of success, to start afresh from the Qur'ān and the *Sunna*, and to

[1] See Fazlur Rahman's article 'Post-Formative Developments in Islam', in *Islamic Studies*, Karachi, I, 4 (1962), 13.
[2] Cf. Fazlur Rahman, *Islam*, Ch. VI.

assign their due places to the subsequent developments in Islam, both orthodox and heterodox.

Nevertheless, however, salutary and fresh the content of Ibn Taymiyya's attempt at the reconstruction of Islam may have been, it had certain serious limitations, which became conspicuous among his followers. These arose essentially from the fact that rationalism is condemned on principle, and insistence is almost entirely laid on the Tradition in understanding Islam. Ibn Taymiyya had acted as a liberalizing force against the authority of the medieval schools, and this was the reason for the unrelenting opposition of the contemporary orthodox *'ulamā'* who wanted to maintain the medieval structure of beliefs and practices of Islam. Nevertheless the effect of his activity was to make rigid the earliest interpretations of Islam, and to entrench them more thoroughly, because of his summons back to the Qur'ān and the *Sunna*. For the *Sunna* was taken in a literalist sense, since Ibn Taymiyya was opposed on principle to rationalism. Secondly, the *Sunna*, as it appears in the form of *Ḥadīth* literature, is not actually the work of the Prophet, but is largely attributable to the early generations of Muslims. The essentially formal and external canons of criticism of *Ḥadīth*, devised by the classical and medieval Muslim authorities, are inadequate for bringing about a genuine historical evaluation of *Ḥadīth* literature. The net result is that, whenever an invitation is given to the Muslims to go back to the *Sunna* of the Prophet, in actual terms it is an invitation to accept the formulations of the early generations of Muslims.[1]

We have dwelt at some length on Ibn Taymiyya's work because, even though he was opposed by his contemporaries, his teaching has not only had historical consequences, in the form of certain major reform movements in recent centuries, but his spirit of free and fresh thinking and enquiry may be said to be alive in much of Modernist Islam.

THE PRE-MODERNIST REFORM MOVEMENTS

The epitome of Ibn Taymiyya's message may be formulated as follows: Man on earth must discover and implement the will of God. The will of God lies enshrined in the Qur'ān and embodied in the *Sunna* of the

[1] I. Goldziher, *Muhammadanische Studien,* Vol. II; J. Schacht, *The Origins of Muhammadan Jurisprudence* (Oxford, 1959); Fazlur Rahman, 'Sunnah, Ijtihād and Ijmā' in the Early period', in *Islamic Studies,* I,/1, (1962); *idem,* 'Sunnah and Ḥadīth', in *Islamic Studies,* I./2, (1962).

Prophet. This will of God is the *Sharī'a*. A community which consciously sets out to implement the *Sharī'a* is a Muslim community. But in order to implement the *Sharī'a*, the Muslim society must set up certain institutions, the most important of which is the state. No form of the state, therefore, has any inherent sanctity: it possesses sanctity only in so far as it is an effective instrument of the Muslim community.[1] This implementation of the will of God is the *'ibāda* or 'service to God'. It will be seen that this message emphasizes not merely the individual, but the collective being of the community, and, therefore, lays greater stress on social virtues and justice than on mere individual virtues. In so doing, Ibn Taymiyya once again captures the essential spirit of the Qur'ān and of the *Sunna* of Muḥammad, and thus goes beyond the *historic* Muslim community. Now the reform movements which burst upon the Muslim world during the seventeenth, eighteenth and nineteenth centuries exhibit this common characteristic, that they bring into the centre of attention the socio-moral reconstruction of Muslim society, as against Sufism, which had stressed primarily the individual and not the society.

It is common to begin an account of these reform movements with Wahhabism, the puritanical, right-wing reform movement led by Muḥammad b. 'Abd al-Wahhāb (d. 1206/1792) in central Arabia. Already in the first quarter of the seventeenth century, however, the Indian divine, Shaykh Aḥmad of Sirhind, had laid the theoretical basis of a similar reform. Shaykh Aḥmad (d. 1034/1625) reacting specifically against the abuses into which Sufism had fallen both theoretically and at the practical level, and working against the background created by the eclecticism of the Mughal Emperor Akbar under the intellectual sponsorship of the two brothers Abu'l-Fażl and Fayżī, vindicated the claims of the *Sharī'a* with its socio-moral ethos, against the latitudinarianism of the Ṣūfīs, and the vague liberalism of the pure intellectuals. As with Ibn Taymiyya, so with Aḥmad Sirhindī, the activism of classical Islam came into full focus with the re-emphasizing of the *Sharī'a*.[2] But political developments in India, and the rapid decline of Muslim power in the subcontinent, could not provide the necessary conditions for the

[1] This question has been more precisely studied in a forthcoming monograph by Mr Qamaruddin Khan, to be published by the Central Institute of Islamic Research, Karachi; in a general way it has been treated by H. Laoust in his *Les doctrines sociales et politiques d'Ibn Taimiya* (Cairo, 1939).

[2] See Fazlur Rahman *Selected letters of Aḥmad Sirhindī*, to be published by the Historical Society of Pakistan, Introduction.

realization of Sirhindī's objectives. Nevertheless, through his work and that of his followers, a reformed spiritual tradition came into existence which played a prominent role in keeping the threads of the community together in the political and social chaos that followed the decay of Mughal power.

But the Wahhābī revolt in the heart of the Arabian peninsula during the next century was much more radical and uncompromising towards the un-Islamic accretions, and the superstitious cults linked with popular Sufism. The movement of Muḥammad b. ʿAbd al-Wahhāb was directly inspired by the ideas of Ibn Taymiyya, but in some major aspects it departed from Ibn Taymiyya himself. Thus, unlike Ibn Taymiyya, the Wahhābīs rejected all forms of Sufism, even though they termed their system *ṭarīqa Muḥammadiyya*. They also rejected, with much more virulence than Ibn Taymiyya or Aḥmad Sirhindī, the intellectualist trends in Islam, which they looked upon with great distrust. Although they rejected the authority of the medieval schools of law, following Ibn Taymiyya, and, like him, insisted on *ijtihād*, or fresh thinking, they did practically everything in their power to discourage the actual tools of positive fresh thinking by rejecting intellectualism. The untiring emphasis of the Wahhābīs (and kindred groups) on *ijtihād* has hence proved fruitless and *practically* they have become 'followers' (*muqallidūn*) of the sum total of the Islamic legacy of the first two centuries and a half, even though being described as 'followers' is anathema to them. The Wahhābīs, however, have done good work by bringing into relief the principles of Islamic egalitarianism and co-operation, and actually founded co-operative farm-villages.

Reform movements, fundamentally of a puritanical character, and seeking to rid the Muslim society of the causes responsible for its degeneration and corruption, grew up in a large part of the Muslim world in the Indian subcontinent. Shāh Walī Allāh of Delhi (d. 1176/1762), following upon Aḥmad Sirhindī, set to work on broadly similar lines. He saw, however, that the political situation in India had radically changed since Sirhindī's time, and he therefore propounded a system which would be congenial to the spiritual environment of the Indian subcontinent, and at the same time calculated to regenerate Islamic forces. His attitude towards Sufism is not one of rejection, but of assimilation as far as possible. But while interpreting the message of Islam in these terms, Shāh Walī Allāh endeavoured to create a social-political substructure for it. He attacked the social and economic injustices prevailing in society, criticized the heavy taxes to which the peasantry was subjected, and called upon the Muslims to build a territorial state which might be integrated into an international Muslim super-state. The thinking of Shāh Walī Allāh, although fundamentally in agreement with other similar reform movements, so far as the social side is concerned, sharply contrasts with the Wahhābī movement in that it seeks to integrate various elements rather than to reject them. Political conditions were unfavourable to him, and his ideas ultimately generated a purely puritanical type of movement, not unlike that of 'Abd al-Wahhāb. This movement, which swept over northern India during the first half of the nineteenth century, was led by Sayyid Aḥmad Barēlwī of Rāe Barēlī and a grandson of Shāh Walī Allāh, Muḥammad Ismā'īl, both of whom were killed in battle against the Sikhs in 1831. It is doubtful, however, whether Sayyid Aḥmad was directly influenced by the Wahhābīs as is generally believed.[1]

The Sanūsī movement of the nineteenth century in Libya exhibits similar characteristics. Although it had the organized form of a Ṣūfī *ṭarīqa* and included some Ṣūfī practices as well, its objectives were radically different. It was basically a social reform movement, aiming at the purification of society from degenerate beliefs, and particularly from corrupting malpractices. Above all, it sought to promote a sense of moral solidarity based on honesty, egalitarianism and economic justice. In spite of the fact that some of the views of the Sanūsī shaykh were attacked by some of the al-Azhar authorities as being heretical, the sociological bases helped its growth, and subsequently it waged a bitter struggle against the expansionist policies of European colonial powers. On more or less similar, but basically more militant lines, were laid the foundations of the Fulanī *Jihād* movement of 'Uthmān dan Fodio and the Mahdist movement in the Sudan. We may sum up the general characteristics of all these movements as follows.

Although the attitudes of these reform phenomena towards Sufism ranged from an outright rejection to a more or less modified acceptance of it, the purely world-negating attitudes of medieval Sufism were combated by them. Those movements, such as the Indian, which integrated Sufism into their system, developed a much more positive

[1] See Fazlur Rahman, *Islam*, Ch. XII. It is noteworthy, however, that Sayyid Aḥmad also called his movement *Ṭarīqa Muḥammadiyya*, cf. Murray Titus, *Indian Islam* (Oxford, 1930, revised edition under the title *Islam in India and Pakistan*, 1960), 181–2.

Sufism, endeavoured to eradicate the socio-moral evils that came in the wake of the spread of Sufism and, on the whole, gave it a more dynamic outlook.

The primary concern of all these movements was with the socio-moral reconstruction and reform of society. Although it would be a bold denial of facts to say that any of these movements gave up or even underplayed the concept of the after-life, yet it is significant to note that the *emphasis* had shifted more towards the positive issues of society, whether in political, moral or spiritual terms. The reason for this is not far to seek. It was the social degeneration of Muslim society that had called forth these movements in the first place. They had not come into existence to rectify or strengthen beliefs about the other world but to reform the socio-moral failures of the Muslim community, through which this society had become petrified.

Because of their very nature, therefore, these movements strengthened, in varying degrees, the activism and the moral dynamism which had been characteristic of pristine Islam. All of these movements were politically active; most of them resorted to *jihād* to realize their ideals. This fact, again, aligns them more directly with pristine Islam rather than with historic Islam.

All of these movements, without exception, emphasized a 'return' to pristine Islam in terms of the Qur'ān and the *Sunna* of the Prophet. In practice, however, as we pointed out in the case of Ibn Taymiyya above, the *Sunna* of the Prophet meant the practice or the doctrines worked out by the earliest generations of Muslims.

For this reason, although all these movements unanimously proclaimed the right of *ijtihād*, and denied final authority to all but the Prophet, they were yet able to make but little headway in the reformulation of the content of Islam. The historical belief that the *Ḥadīth* genuinely contains the *Sunna* of the Prophet, combined with the further belief that the *Sunna* of the Prophet and the Qur'anic rulings on social behaviour have to be more or less *literally* implemented in all ages, stood like a rock in the way of any substantial rethinking of the social content of Islam. When, therefore, the leaders of these movements issued the call 'back to the Qur'ān and the *Sunna*', they literally meant that history should move backwards. For the ideal had already been enacted at a given time in the past, viz. in seventh-century Arabia. We shall subsequently see that this utterly revivalist attitude has undergone a considerable modification under the impact of the Modernist movements in Islam, although what revivalism exactly means still remains unclear to the revivalist himself as we shall see.

MODERN ISLAM

The account given above of the pre-Modernist reform movements which swept over the larger part of the Muslim world during the seventeenth, eighteenth and nineteenth centuries has clearly established that the consciousness of degeneration, and of the corresponding need to remedy social evils and raise moral standards, was generated from the heart of Muslim society itself. This needs to be pointed out emphatically, because there is a common error which leads many observers of present-day Muslim society, and its attempts at rethinking and reconstruction, to regard these as being primarily the result of the impact of the West. There are certain considerations which seem to render such a conclusion plausible. The impact of the modern West upon the Muslim East begins with the political and economic expansionism of the West. In almost every case, the Muslim lands suffered a political and military reverse at the hands of the West, and consequently came under its subjection. Because of this political subjection, and the psychological forces generated by it, the Muslim response to the West on the plane of intellectual and scientific thought, and the religious issues raised by this thought, has not been, in its first phase, as constructive as it would have been if the Muslims had been politically ascendant. An average foreign observer, therefore, tends to look upon the Muslim society as an inert mass suffering from a reaction to the Western impact at all levels, but unable to adopt a positive enough attitude towards it. Worse still, many of the modern educated Muslims themselves have come to believe this. The trouble is that the average modern educated Muslim knows as little about his past heritage as does the average foreign observer. Besides being ignorant of his own cultural background, he is mentally a creature of what is essentially the Western educational system—the projection of the West into the Muslim East. He, therefore, begins to think that in so far as progress is actually being achieved in the Muslim world, or is even conceivably achievable, it will be a mere duplication of the West, and that Islam is either neutral in all this, or is perhaps a positive hindrance.

The reform movements described above naturally owed nothing whatsoever to any foreign influence in their genesis, since to postulate any such influence would be a historical absurdity. From the characteristics common to those movements enumerated at the end of the last section, we must conclude that, in so far as the *fact* and the form of the reformist zeal are concerned, they antedate modern Islam, and that modern Islam is a simple continuation, in these respects, of the pre-Modernist reform movements. Where modern Islam does differ from the legacy of these movements is in its positive content. We have seen above that all these movements laid emphasis on fresh thinking (*ijtihād*), but that they were unable to give any large new content to their thinking, because their actual *intention* was focussed on pristine Islam. What the Modernist Muslim has essentially achieved is the maintenance of pristine Islam as a source of inspiration and motive energy, and to this energy he has sought to attach a Modernist content. The measure of success with which this has been done so far, and the rhythm of this entire movement, are now left for us to describe. But we must once again emphasize the continuity between the pre-Modernist awakening and the Modernist renaissance, inasmuch as both are concerned with society. Even the terrific zest and dynamism displayed by the modern movements of liberation from foreign rule are essentially a continuation of the activism of the pre-Modernist reform movements. It is true that to this early Islamic activism, a new nationalist motif has usually been added; but we shall have to discuss more closely the relationship of the nationalist thrust to the earliest *jihād* motivation in various segments of Muslim society.

Intellectual developments

In the very first reactions of the Muslim leaders towards the West, the political and the intellectual factors have gone hand in hand. Thus, Jamāl al-Dīn al-Afghānī (1839–97) combined both these motives in his powerful appeal to the Muslims to awaken to the current situation, to liberate themselves from Western domination, and to carry out the necessary internal reforms that would make for their regeneration and strength. He not only called upon the Muslims to stand against the West politically, but to establish popular and stable governments at home, and to cultivate modern scientific and philosophical knowledge. Although he was not a thinker of great calibre, his activity has left enduring marks on Muslim Modernism as a whole. Apart from his political agitation, the most salient feature of his spiritual attitude, which he has bequeathed to the Modernist Muslim, is his unbounded humanism. Indeed, there is evidence to the effect that even his appreciation of religion was based upon a humanist *élan*; for religion, including Islam, according to him served human ends. It, therefore, must be concluded that his emphasis on populism was not just a means to an external end, the strengthening of Muslim governments against a foreign enemy, but was possessed of intrinsic value. Indeed al-Afghānī appears to be the sympathetic advocate of the downtrodden and the deprived. This is the reason why al-Afghānī not only stirred up Islamic sentiments to rouse the people to meet the challenge of the West, but even appealed to non-Islamic and pre-Islamic cultural factors for this purpose. In India, Egypt and Turkey, for example, he appealed to past Hindu, Pharaonic and pre-Islamic Turkish greatness, and thereby helped to rouse nationalist side by side with Islamic sentiments.

This brief analysis of al-Afghānī reveals simultaneously the unprecedented challenge faced by the Modernist, the complications latent in the modernist situation, and the magnitude of the intellectual task. Its complications are so great that it looks like a vicious circle; and the breaking of this vicious circle carries with it the inconsistencies and anomalies that are characteristic of Modernist attitudes. We have pointed out that the primary task of the pre-Modernist movements was to reform society. The alliance of the spirit of the modern age with the ethos of the pre-Modernist reformers helped further to weaken the Ṣūfī hold upon the educated classes, and further to accentuate the consciousness of social reform. The criticism of historic Muslim social institutions (like polygamy, unregulated divorce and the status of women in general) by orientalists and Christian missionaries specifies the objectives of social reform for the Modernist. But social reform, on closer examination turns out to be a very complex affair, and begins to assume a purely intellectual aspect, because a mere change in social institutions cannot be carried out without rethinking the social ethic and ideas of social justice. Further, social reform implies legislation, and legislation raises very fundamental issues as to who is to legislate, and by virtue of what authority. The entire philosophy of law becomes involved in this—various theories of *ijtihād* and *ijmāʿ* are put forth. This raises further problems of the political constitution of the state, of representation, and the nature of political authority. But change in political ideas and attitudes not only presupposes legislation but also social change itself. This is what we mean by the vicious circle. For the sake of convenience, however, we shall first outline the intellectual developments in modern Islam, since it is ideas which, when they become objects of conviction, are the most potent moving forces in a society.

The bases of modern reformist thinking are, as we have pointed out above, supplied by the pre-Modernist reform movement. It is, therefore, not an accident that the most important Modernist thinkers of the nineteenth and twentieth centuries come from a purificationist-reformist background. We have quoted the notable example of Jamāl al-Dīn al-Afghānī; similar ones are provided by Muḥammad ʿAbduh (d. 1905) of Egypt and Sayyid Aḥmad Khān (d. 1898) of the Indo-Pakistan subcontinent, even though both of these men propounded somewhat different solutions, as we shall see presently. The purificationist reform-legacy of pre-Modernist days, however, could only have prepared the ground for this Modernist thinking, and in the preceding pages we have brought out its essential limitations. Indeed, in so far as its emphasis was literally on a 'going back' to the Qur'ān and the *Sunna*, it appears a positive hindrance in the way of progressive thinking, and, in fact, most reactionaries or revivalists opposed Modernist thinking on these very grounds. Yet, the unanimous call of all the pre-Modernist reforms to *ijtihād* supplied the requisite inspiration for the Modernist to start his work. The actual purificationist activities of these early movements, and their combined efforts either to reject, or at least to control, the extravagances of Sufism stood the Modernist in good stead. In this connexion too, the objective work of orientalists, which focussed attention on the early centuries of Islam, cannot be denied its value. Even the missionary, with his narrow outlook, did not fail to provoke discussion.

But in spite of continuity with earlier reform phenomena, Modernist thinking had to go far beyond anything achieved by the pre-Modernist reform, both in the nature of the questions raised, and in the content of the answers given. The most fundamental question that was raised in Islam (after a lapse of about nine centuries) was that of the relationship between faith and reason, or of faith and scientific thought. This question had preoccupied the minds of the Western thinkers themselves for centuries, particularly from the beginning of their Renaissance, and one cannot help thinking that, to some extent, they have projected their own preoccupations into Islamic discussions around this particular problem. Nevertheless, this question was not raised in Islam for the first time. The Muʿtazilites and the philosophers had asked the same question, and given their own solutions. But the question as raised in the nineteenth century had acquired a new dimension, because of the fact that the actual or putative conflict was not just between religion and thought, as had been the case previously, but that a new scientific world-view had emerged, or was emerging, which had its own claims for recognition. The answers given to this basic problem, both in their form and content, by Muḥammad ʿAbduh and by Sayyid Aḥmad Khān are highly interesting, and at the same time reveal the different approaches of these two types of Modernist. While both emphasize that there cannot be any conflict between Islamic faith and reason, or the religion of Islam and science, and further maintain that Islam is a positive rational and scientific force in the world, the attitude of Muḥammad ʿAbduh, who was a trained *ʿālim*, is a much more moderate one than that of Sayyid Aḥmad Khān. While Muḥammad ʿAbduh more or less seeks to regenerate the rationalizing spirit of the Muʿtazilite school, Sayyid Aḥmad Khān, on the other hand, espouses the much more radical course of medieval Muslim philosophers, such as Ibn Sīnā and Ibn Rushd. This difference does not stop merely at a general level, but appears in the detailed solutions to specific problems handled by both of them.

While it is the aim of both of these thinkers to encourage belief in the scientific world-view, and consequently to discourage belief in superstitions and miracles, the difference in the formulation of their answers is remarkable. Muḥammad ʿAbduh declares as a general principle that the possibility of miracles is to be accepted, but that every particular miracle claimed may be doubted with impunity, either on rational or historical grounds. Thus, one may reject all the miracles one by one, but one may not reject the possibility of miracles as a principle. Very different is the case with Sayyid Aḥmad Khān. He, first of all, lays down the principle of 'conformity of nature'. Nature he declares to be a closely knit system of causes and effects which allow of no supernatural intervention. Indeed, Sayyid Aḥmad Khān seems to espouse a kind of deism which was fashionable among the nineteenth-century scientific circles of the West, and was also closely related to the spirit and the thinking of the medieval Muslim philosophers. Sayyid Aḥmad Khān, therefore, categorically and on principle, rejects the possibility of miracles. Similarly, in the field of historical criticism, the question of *Ḥadīth* comes under discussion. On this point, again, Muḥammad ʿAbduh maintains that one does not incur infidelity to Islam if one doubts any given *Ḥadīth*, but *Ḥadīth* must be accepted on principle and in general. Sayyid Aḥmad Khān, on the other hand, most probably aided by his colleague, Maulavī Chirāgh 'Alī, rejects all *Ḥadīth*. One may say that the method adopted by Sayyid Aḥmad Khān was more thorough-going and consistent, and its conclusions are more radical than those of Muḥammad 'Abduh. But we must remember that neither of these men was aiming simply at producing scientific thought, but that their basic aim was reformist. Reform imposes its own terms, has its own rhythm; and therefore a reformist may well find that he has to put his conclusions in a way that would be acceptable to a large number, if not the whole, of his community. In this sense, as subsequent developments have shown, Muḥammad 'Abduh's ideas have been more potent, and have taken deeper root in the soil than those of Sayyid Aḥmad Khān, whose educational policies were more acceptable to Muslims than his religious ideas.

Formulation of the principle that Islam not only did not oppose reason and science, but encouraged both, persuaded an ever-increasing number of Muslims to take up the study of modern science. Another attempt made by an Indian Muslim to develop a new rationalist theology was also inspired by the leadership of Sayyid Aḥmad Khān; this was the work of Muḥammad Shiblī Nu'mānī (d. 1914) who is, however, better known as a historian. In his work entitled *'Ilm al-kalām* he described the historical genesis and development of the classical Muslim schools of theology. This was followed by a second work entitled *al-Kalām*, wherein Shiblī endeavoured to restate the theses of classical theology in the light of the general nineteenth-century scientific world-view. In doing so he, like Muḥammad 'Abduh, resurrected the rationalist trends of the Mu'tazilite School. His work was, however, rejected as heretical by the orthodox *'ulamā'* of the Deōband Seminary. Shiblī subsequently left 'Alīgarh School (founded by Sayyid Aḥmad Khān) and joined the *Nadwat al-'Ulamā'* at A'ẓamgarh near Lucknow, where he framed his own syllabus for combining traditional and modern learning. The *Nadwa*, as it is called, however, has not produced any thinker of high calibre, and for all intents and purposes its alumni are indistinguishable from the conservative *'ulamā'*.

An obvious corollary of the principle that Islam encourages scientific and rational enquiry is that Islam is a great civilizing and educative force. The fact that through Islam the Arabs became world conquerors and progenitors of a great civilization, supplies the necessary historical evidence for this. The most effective argument built around this thesis was worked out by the eminent jurist Sayyid Amīr 'Alī (d. 1928), whose main contention was that Islam is inherently a civilizing and progressive force. An inevitable result of this position is that those segments of Muslim history, which represent the decline of the Muslims and their civilization, must be rejected as unrepresentative of *Islamic* history. This is what, in fact, many Islamic historians in the late nineteenth and early twentieth century have done. This procedure has been vehemently criticized by certain Western scholars, who have described it as subjective and betraying a lack of intellectual integrity. Irrespective of this controversy, we may note that the character of the intellectual products of Islamic civilization does exhibit something tangibly different from the ancient period, and we think it undeniable that Muslim thought, especially scientific and philosophic, stands at the threshold of modernity.

As for the charge of selectivity and subjectivity against Amīr 'Alī and others, we must once again remember that these men were not simply historians but implicitly reformers. This explains why they underline those segments of Muslim history which represent greatness and progress in civilization. These are an implicit invitation to the Muslims to re-create parallel history in the future. We must, therefore, distinguish this from strictly descriptive historiography. If a Muslim sees his faith expressed more adequately in one segment of history rather than another, we cannot see any legitimate objection to it. In any case, the idea that all knowledge and progress is *par excellence* Islamic is part of the stock-in-trade of Muslim Modernism, and an inevitable conclusion from the principle that Islam invites man to search and enquire. This is why Muḥammad Iqbāl (1876–1938), when he speaks approvingly of the rapid movement of the Muslim world towards the West, says that by acquiring knowledge from the West the Muslims are only retrieving their lost heritage which they must once again cultivate and develop.

It is obvious, however, that pure Westernism, i.e., the projection of the West into the Muslim society, could not and cannot succeed unless it creates for itself a moral and cultural basis within Muslim society. This means that there must be a process of integration and assimilation of the new forces, and adaptation of their institutional embodiment to the moral-cultural heritage of Islam and vice versa. This vital function is to be performed by Muslim Modernism. But Muslim Modernism, after its initial launching by thinkers like Muḥammad 'Abduh, Sayyid Aḥmad Khān and Sayyid Amīr 'Alī, unfortunately, underwent a rapid transformation, and degenerated, on the one hand, into pure apologetics, and, on the other, developed into a more or less purely secular Westernism. Indeed, the story of the decline of positive Modernist thought, beginning roughly with the second decade of the present century, is both interesting and full of lessons. In the Middle East itself, the synthetic thought-movement of Muḥammad ʿAbduh split itself into three parts. In its main direction, under the leadership of his disciple, Rashīd Riḍā, it developed a fundamentalist character, and, although its reformist zeal remained, it progressively assumed the reactionary features of the original Wahhābī movement. Its reformist programme became really limited to the elimination of differences among the different schools of law; it was essentially a throw-back to eighteenth century pre-Modernist fundamentalism. Secondly, the defensive element in Muḥammad ʿAbduh gave rise to a prolific apologetic literature, particularly at the hands of Farīd Wajdī. On all issues of major reform, this apologetic trend defended the old against the new, and endeavoured to create an effective wall against the influx of modern forces and ideas. From being a defence mechanism, it gradually developed into inhibitionism. When, for example, Qāsim Amīn's book entitled *al-Mar'a al-jadīda* ('The new woman'), arguing for improving the status of women and their emancipation, was published, Farīd Wajdī wrote a reply wherein he defended the traditional place of Muslim women in society; and so on. Thirdly, a more or less unmixed thrust of Westernism developed, among the eminent representatives of which may be counted Dr Ṭāhā Ḥusayn. The truth is that the strength of this pure Westernism is commensurate with the virulence of the resurgent fundamentalism and its defensive arm, the new apologetic; this, in turn, is the full measure of the failure of effective Modernism.

In the Indo-Pakistan subcontinent the same story is repeated. The initial modernism of Sayyid Aḥmad Khān and Sayyid Amīr ʿAlī was subjected to bitter invectives and, in fact, denounced as pure Westernism. Men like Abu'l-Kalām Āzād, and the poet Akbar of Allahabad, attacked uncompromisingly the introduction of new ideas and institutions into Muslim society. While the more learned writings of the former were addressed primarily to the higher classes, the bitter epigrams of Akbar proved very effective at the lower-middle class level. Akbar wrote particularly against the new education, and relentlessly satirized the movement for the emancipation of women. Here is one of his quatrains:

Yesterday, having seen some women without veil,
Akbar sank into the earth out of hurt Islamic pride.
When asked whither their veil had gone, they replied
'The veil has fallen upon men's intelligence'.

The reasons for this vehement reaction, and the submergence and decline of modernist thinking, are manifold, and they can only be briefly indicated here. First, the new ideas brought by modern education needed time to ripen in order to produce mature representatives. The relative immaturity of the representatives of modernity has been a great hindrance to the acceptance of modern ideas, and their consequent assimilation through Modernist thought. Allied to this is the fact that the early exponents of Modernism did not fully grasp the deeper spiritual and moral factors behind the phenomenal flowering of modern Western civilization, and they took mainly into consideration only certain external manifestations of this inner vitality, such as modern democratic institutions, universal education, and the emancipation of women. The deeper fountains of the creative vitality of the West, particularly humanism in its various forms, were not studied properly and given due weight.[1] The result was that an attempt was made to transfer, because of their attractiveness, certain more or less external institutions of the West to a new soil wherein they were not properly adapted to the new conditions. Indeed, the Modernist did not develop traditional Muslim thought from the inside to supply an adequate basis for the new values and institutions. It is perhaps also true that liberalism, as it has grown in the modern West, claims absolute validity for itself, and seeks no compromises or rapprochement with any other system of ideas or values. It is obvious enough that this liberalism, pushed to its logical conclusions, is self-defeating, and that it must impose certain checks upon itself. The early Muslim Modernists, the starting point of whose Modernism lay in Westernism, almost deified liberalism, and sought to impose its categories upon Muslim society. The result was that, when their message penetrated into the interior of the society, it was vehemently rejected.

[1] Muḥammad Iqbāl, in the first chapter of his *Reconstruction of religious thought in Islam*, had warned Muslims against being dazzled by the external glamour of the West and had insisted on a deeper penetration into the spirit that moves the Western civilization. But, despite the fact that Iqbāl himself goes to great lengths to cultivate a humanist spirit at the philosophical level, he rejects it almost uncompromisingly in favour of a pure transcendentalism on the ethical plane. This fact itself demonstrates how difficult it is to change quickly settled habits of thought.

Lastly, Muslim society has had to summon up all its energies and concentrate its force on seeking to liberate itself from the political domination of the West, whether direct or indirect. From approximately the beginning of the Balkan Wars in 1912, the Muslim world became conscious that either it must gain independence of foreign powers, or it must finally go under. In this grim struggle where nationalism and Islam fought hand in hand, unity and solidarity were the overriding dictates. In the history of Islam, whenever unity and solidarity have had to be emphasized, differences of opinion have always been discouraged, since differences of opinion have been seen as creating doubts. Since Modernism involves a strenuous and sustained intellectual effort, and must necessarily breed some difference of opinion (liberalism, in any case, must tolerate difference of opinion and interpretation), intellectualism and Modernism were consequently discouraged, and fundamentalism was proportionately strengthened. It would not be going too far to say that the Muslim community in general has usually tilted the balance in favour of external solidarity at the expense of inner growth. This also explains why the most serious of all intellectuals in modern Islam, Muḥammad Iqbāl, in fact tended to discourage intellectualism by what he wrote. He ceaselessly invited the Muslims to cultivate an unshakable certainty, a firm faith, and derided the claims of the pure intellect. There is little doubt that the genius of Islam is also activist, as we have pointed out earlier in this essay, and Iqbāl largely recaptured that activist spirit; but there is all the difference between saying that knowledge must end in action, and between emphasizing action at the expense of the claims of intellectualism.

Given these trends, it is not surprising that strong groups arose in the Middle East and in the Indo-Pakistan subcontinent which were basically fundamentalist, full of an unbounded zeal for action, and suspicious of both modernity and intellectualism. The Muslim Brotherhood of the Arab Middle East, banned in Egypt in 1956, and the *Jamā'at-i Islāmī* of the Indo-Pakistan subcontinent which became especially powerful in Pakistan, and was banned early in 1964, are similar versions of twentieth-century Muslim revivalism and anti-intellectualist activism. Yet, on closer examination, it appears that the revivalism of these groups is more in spirit than in substance. For whenever the representatives of these movements are pressed on any intellectual issue, it is revealed that their position is characterized not by an actual thought-content from the past, but by hardly any thought at all. They are more suspicious of both Modernism and modernity (making hardly any distinction between these two) than they are committed, in the final analysis, to a literal repetition of any actual segment of past history. What has given them power over the middle (and particularly lower middle) classes is not a systematic and coherent understanding of the past, but their embodiment of a reaction against modernizing trends in the upper strata of society; and the fact that they possess no systematic thinking (despite the fact that they are very vocal), does not count against them, because there is hardly any intellectual Modernism in any case. In terms of thought, therefore, they are not at any real disadvantage *vis-à- vis* the modernized classes.

In the recent past, however, certain important developments have taken place in certain parts of the Muslim world, notably Pakistan and Egypt, where centres for the development of Muslim Modernism have been officially set up. The Council of Islamic Research at al-Azhar is even more recent than the Central Institute of Islamic Research in Pakistan. The extent and depth of impact of these institutions on the intellectual life of the Muslim Society will be revealed only with the passage of time. The real task before the Muslim Modernist intellectual is not so much to integrate any given theory or doctrine of modern science and philosophy, as to create the very postulates under which modern thinking becomes possible. Modern thinking on principle must reject authoritarianism of all kinds and must, therefore, rely upon its own resources, facing its risks and reaping its fruits. Openness to correction and, in this sense, a certain amount of doubt, or rather tentativeness, lie in the very nature of modern thought which is an ever-unfolding process, and always experimental. It is on this crucial point that the very nature of modern knowledge comes into conflict with the mental attitudes inculcated by the modern Muslim revivalist or quasi-revivalist movements. The task is, no doubt, difficult and beset with dangers; but there is no particular reason to be pessimistic about the final result, given the right effort.

Social developments

We have seen above that an adequate Islamic intellectual *milieu* still remains to be created in the Muslim world. Until this is achieved, little can be done to start the necessary debate on socio-moral issues, a debate which must be uninhibited, self-confident, non-controversialist and non-apologetic. Nevertheless, a good deal of writing on social issues has taken place, and much actual social change is taking place in Muslim society. The primary reasons for this are, as we have noted before, first that the actual impact of the modern West on Muslim society has been largely on the socio-political front; and, secondly, that the main criticisms of Islamic society both by Christian missionaries and orientalists have been on these very aspects. The early Westernizing Modernists like Sayyid Aḥmad Khān and Sayyid Amīr ʻAlī advocated almost without demur the adoption of modern Western concepts of the family (particularly with regard to the status of women), and equally of modern Western forms of democracy. Indeed, while speaking about Jamāl al-Dīn al-Afghānī, we also said that the democratization of the state was even seen as an internal necessity, in order to build up strong governments based on the popular will.

So far as reforms in family law in particular and the status of women in general are concerned, a very large number of Muslim states have actually enacted legislation, taking up the threads from the early Modernists, and in spite of the strong reaction which was directed against this early Modernism by the revivalists and the conservatives. In Pakistan, for example, although even the most important thinker of this century, Muḥammad Iqbāl, had thrown his weight practically on the side of the conservatives on social issues, the Family Laws Ordinance was promulgated in 1960. The conservative ʻ*ulamā*ʼ and their followers, no doubt, continue to exert pressure for the restoration of the traditional *status quo*, but the Modernist minority in Muslim countries, relatively small but vigorous, is politically influential, and holds the initiative, and it looks as though it is impossible for the conservatives to reverse this movement. There is no doubt that on this question the Modernist's stand is on surer grounds, and is helped by the conviction that the new legislation will tighten up the conditions of family life in Muslim society. The conservative or the revivalist, therefore, despite his ostensible appeal to Islam, feels in his heart of hearts that he is on shaky moral grounds in defending the traditional pattern.

The main problem before the Modernist is, indeed, not primarily whether he will succeed in actually changing society within an Islamic framework. Here the Modernist's attempts are often vitiated by the fact that, instead of facing the problem squarely and on intellectual grounds, he tries to circumvent it and is forced to rely on external patchwork. For example, he may often try to show that the Qurʼān does not *really* allow polygamy at all, and invents explanations for its apparent permission of polygamy which are unfaithful to history, and sometimes violate Arabic linguistic usage. He is on surer grounds when, for example, he contends that the Qur'ān did allow polygamy, but at the same time put conditions upon it which show that monogamy is better than polygamy, and that, therefore, the *drift* of the Qur'anic doctrine is towards monogamy. He would be on still surer grounds if, on all legislation which touches socio-economic life and political institutions, he were frankly to give due importance to the social and historical conditions of the Prophet's time; and, having thus made full allowance for the particular historical context, he were honestly to attempt to enunciate the genuine values of the Qur'ān, and to re-embody these values in present conditions. But, for one thing, he has not yet developed the adequate intellectual equipment for this task—calling as it does for historical criticism, and, for another, one sometimes suspects that even his conviction that society is really changing fails him. This second factor puts him psychologically in an ambivalent state which further impedes the adoption of an honest and bold stand. It is also true that, to a considerable extent, the development of a genuine Muslim Modernism is hampered by the fact that controversy between the Christian West and the Muslim East, which was started by the Christian West, has befogged the intellectual *milieu*, and even the sincere Modernist is sometimes affected by the attitudes of the revivalists. It is necessary to control this controversial spirit, and to concentrate on the genuine issues facing the community itself.

Whereas the development of social modernization has assumed a clear-cut line, on political philosophy the issues are as yet much less clear. There are two main problems. First, the question of the relationship of nationalism to a universal Islamic *Umma* has neither been faced nor answered. We have noted that, during the struggle for political liberation, local nationalisms have played a very prominent role, but that in that context, nationalism has acted in alliance with the Islamic sentiment. In certain countries, Islamic sentiment has played the more prominent role of the two. In Algeria, for example, and in the Maghrib in general, the doctrine of *jihād* as preached by the militant liberationists to the masses, was of decisive importance. In Turkey, on the other hand, the nationalist sentiment became very strong, and, indeed, it is only in Turkey that a secular nationalist state has been officially established. But in Turkey, again, the Turks cherish a lively sentiment for the larger Islamic community, although the issue has not been seriously tackled on the intellectual level. Nor can anybody seriously think that the doctrine of the 'Three Concentric Circles' enunciated by the Egyptian president, Jamāl 'Abd al-Nāṣir, offers the hope of any real solution. What one can safely say is that among the masses throughout the Muslim countries, there exists a very strong sentiment for some form of unity of the Islamic world.

The second question in regard to the nature of the state is the problem of democracy. The contention of the early Modernists that the governments must be based on the popular will through some form of representation is generally accepted; and in fact the Modernist contends, not without plausibility, that since Islam is democratic in its ethos, the adoption of modern democratic institutions cannot be un-Islamic. But the problem does not stop here, and is further complicated by two important factors. First, in all these countries there is a relatively small minority which is educated in the modern sense, and which controls affairs, while the vast majority are illiterate. It is not easy to implement democracy under such circumstances. On major and clear-cut national questions, it is true, even an uneducated person may be able to perceive the issues clearly, but in a democracy not all issues that are debated are so clear-cut. But even more acute than lack of education, although undoubtedly allied to it, is the question of rapid economic development, which is a common problem in the under-developed countries, including all the Muslim countries. The economic problem has many ramifications, including the moral demands for honesty, integrity and a sense of responsibility. The exigency of the situation further demands a very high degree of centralized planning and control of economic development. This is felt to necessitate much stabler and stronger governments than would be the case if democracy were superficially and nominally allowed to work. It is this ubiquitous phenomenon which results in the appearance of strong men to give stability to these countries, primarily in the interests of economic growth. From the Islamic point of view, there can be no harm in this, provided that, at the same time, the spirit of democracy is genuinely and gradually cultivated among the people.

Education

All Muslim countries have adopted modern educational institutions in the form of universities, academies and colleges. This fact itself constitutes one of the most important, probably the most important, fact of social change. It is almost universally true that when these institutions were first adopted by Muslim peoples, they represented modern Western secular education with primary emphasis on its technological aspects. The idea behind this has been that, since the traditional society of Islam had put too much emphasis on spirituality, the balance should be restored by the inculcation of modern technological skills. A combination of modern technology, with its vast potentiality for the production of goods, and the traditional spiritual heritage would, it was thought, regenerate the classical glory and greatness of Muslim society. It is, however, obviously doubtful whether the superficial thesis of a marriage between Eastern spirituality and modern Western technology is meaningful or tenable. Along with the technical and scientific subjects, modern philosophy and thought were also taught, while the seats of traditional learning continued side by side with modern educational institutions. The first problem arising from this phenomenon that has a direct bearing on social change is the education of women. An increasingly large number of modern colleges and universities are co-educational. Although there is still a certain amount of resistance to the large-scale education of women and particularly to co-education, there is little doubt that female education is a *fait accompli*. Its sociological consequences are, of course, far-reaching and will bear fruit in their fullness in a few decades' time.

But the more important educational problem is the integration of the new and the old; or, rather, the assimilation of the ever increasing content of modern knowledge with Islamic culture and its values. It is primarily a lack of integration that has so far resulted in a fundamental dichotomy of the Muslim society. To begin with, it is obvious that the simple borrowing of a foreign system of education, shorn of the spiritual, moral and cultural basis which gave birth to it, is not likely to produce results, unless a new and adequate basis for it is created from Islamic tradition and its values. As pointed out before, even with regard to pure technology, it is more than doubtful whether it will lead to the material creativity envisaged, unless it is made the proper instrument of a system of values adequately adjusted to it. Among the countries of the East, only Japan seems to make great technological headway while keeping its traditional cultural background. But developments in Japan after the Second World War render this view much less acceptable, since during the past two decades, the religio-cultural heritage of Japan has itself been invaded by new ideas on a large scale. To put the matter quite concretely, an engineer may know how to build a bridge; but why he should build one, and with what efficiency and zeal, depend entirely on the values that motivate him. His skill, therefore, must be made part and parcel of a total cultural pattern. But leaving technology aside, the modern humanities of the West themselves are replete with certain moral and cultural values which may be said to belong to the Western tradition, and some, indeed, may be traced back clearly to Christianity. Indeed, it is doubtful whether such a seemingly purely rational system of philosophy as that of Immanuel Kant would have been possible without the Christian tradition. This raises questions of a fundamental order for Muslim society and for its assimilation, modification, or rejection, of the content even of purely Western thought.

But the Muslim world is not intellectually equipped to undertake this task as yet. It is only when the modern and the traditional systems of education are properly combined and adjusted that intellectuals will arise adequate to meet this challenge. At the moment, by and large, the traditional seats of learning continue to function separately from modern universities. So far it is only at al-Azhar in Cairo that certain subjects of modern humanities are taught side by side with traditional subjects, but it is doubtful if their level is very high or their effects are very deep. In Pakistan, the traditional *madrasas* strongly resist any encroachment upon their time-honoured and age-worn curricula, and the teaching of Islam in the modern universities, which has started since Independence, is very limited in its nature and rather ineffective. The teachers, and certainly the trainees, in these 'Departments of Islāmiyyāt', are not even equipped with the primary instruments of Islamic studies—such as the Arabic language. A real, effective renaissance of Islam is not possible until educational developments reach the point of contributing from an Islamic standpoint to the humanities of the world at large.

CHAPTER 8

LITERATURE

ARABIC LITERATURE

Arabic literature in its entirety and in the restricted sense is the enduring monument both of a civilization and of a people. Originally the creation of the pastoral nomads of the Arabian peninsula, it had been in pre-Islamic times the literature of an isolated Semitic community when the Arab conquests in the first/seventh century gave it a new role and a universal significance. Its linguistic medium, the *ʿarabiyya*, the sacred and administrative language of the Arab Muslim empire, developed into the common literary idiom of the various peoples of that empire, and the literature expressed through this common idiom became the most important cultural constituent in medieval Islamic civilization. This literature stimulated the rise, and influenced the development, of a new literary family, that of Islamic literatures represented by Persian, Turkish and Urdu. Its geographical diffusion in three continents enabled it to leave important traces on several non-Islamic literary traditions; for Europe and the Mediterranean region it became, along with the other two classical literatures, Greek and Latin, an integral part of the medieval complex.

The fortunes of this literature in classical times were closely affected by two external factors. The ruling institution exercised, on the whole, an unsalutary influence on its course, as court patronage restricted the freedom of the literary artist and circumscribed the range of his interests. On the other hand, the religious institution rendered it inestimable services. The doctrine of *iʿjāz*, the inimitability of the Qur'ān, ensured interest in Arabic literature and literary criticism as the key to the understanding of that doctrine, but it was indirectly that the religious institution made its more permanent contribution. Its jealous guardianship of High Arabic, the common idiom of the Qur'ān and Arabic literature, contributed decisively towards maintaining the *ʿarabiyya* as the only standard medium of literary expression. This enabled Arabic literature to be enriched by the talents of non-Arab ethnic groups, and what is more, it ensured its very survival in periods of Arab political eclipse, and preserved the strand of continuity throughout its various literary periods over some fifteen centuries. The very structure of Arabic was a third factor, an internal one, the operation of which may be illustrated by reference to one of the language's most distinctive features, namely, the abundance of rhyming words. This has contributed substantially towards making the structure of Arabic verse atomic rather than organic, while the further exigency of the monorhyme has imposed severe limitations on the composition of long poems.

Shaped by these and other factors, which have stamped it with the genius of Arabic, and imbued it with the spirit of Islam, this literature has acquired an individuality which was heightened by its evolution in relative isolation. No external literary tradition exercised a vital influence on its course until very recent times. This has operated to its disadvantage. The dramatic and epic genres, for instance, remained unknown to medieval Arabic poetry; on the other hand, this isolation has resulted in an intensive internal development of its own 'lyrical' genre to the saturation point.

The pre-Islamic period

The solid foundation of this long literary tradition was laid in the pre-Islamic period, notably in the sixth century A.D., when the shepherds and herdsmen of central and north-eastern Arabia perfected a poetic technique and developed a highly complex metrical system, unique in the literary annals of the Semites and all nomadic societies.

This poetry is important historically, and significant artistically. For the non-literate pre-Islamic Arabs, it has preserved the records of the various aspects of their life and history. For literary art, it has given expression to what might be termed the 'desert scene', with its natural phenomena, its landscapes, its fauna and its flora. It abounds with impressive pictures of *natura maligna*, and with fine descriptions of animals and animal life. It is heavily anthropocentric, even egocentric, but its egocentricity is redeemed by the attractive ideal of *murū'a*, the Arab *vir-tus*, which it blazons, the uplifting tones of heroic encounters, and the chastening notes of chivalrous love.

The atomicity of pre-Islamic verse and the convention of the monorhyme naturally favoured short compositions on single themes. But around A.D. 500, there developed an art-form which represented the supreme effort of the pre-Islamic poet to transcend the confining limits of the short composition towards a more complex and layered artistic structure. The *qaṣīda*, as this new art-form came to be called, is a polythematic ode, the many and diverse motifs of which present a panoramic view of desert life, drawn together and unified by the poet's own personality, as he scans the traces of his mistress's encampment in the elegiac-erotic prelude, then proceeds to describe his mount, the wastelands he has crossed, and other aspects of desert life. The expression of a multiplicity of motifs through a verse system so atomic in structure presented obvious compositional problems for the pre-Islamic poet, and it was given to few poets to master the integrative devices and techniques required by the *qaṣīda*, the tradition of which has dominated the composition of Arabic poetry throughout the ages.

Among the poets of the pre-Islamic period, the foremost position is rightly given to Imru'l-Qays, the vagabond prince of Kinda, whose towering poetic personality clearly divides this period into two parts and whose *floruit* may be assigned to the first quarter of the sixth century A.D. His masterful genius domesticated the metres and rhymes of Arabic verse for the expression of a tempestuous and passionate private and public life. His *qaṣīdas*, with their striking similes, vigorous rhythms and inevitable rhymes, are splendid microcosms of life in sixth-century Arabia, while the poignancy of his lyrical cry *qifā nabki*, '*sunt lacrimae rerum*', has not lost its directness of appeal, even after more than fourteen centuries.

During the second half of the sixth century A.D. a far-reaching change came over the spirit of Arabic poetry. The panegyrical tone already known to it entered the structure of the *qaṣīda* and quickly assumed undue significance as its most important motif; improved economic conditions in sixth-century Arabia drew the poets' attention to the economic benefits which could accrue from composing panegyrics on wealthy chiefs, while the two Arab clients of Persia and Byzantium, the Lakhmids and the Ghassanids, opened spacious opportunities for the Arabian poets to visit their courts, and receive handsome rewards in return for their eulogies. This panegyrical tone which the *qaṣīda* acquired, persisted tenaciously, and affected adversely the course of Arabic poetry in Islamic times.

The Islamic period

It was only natural that the literary achievement of the pre-Islamic Arabs should have been in poetry not in prose. But this imbalance was corrected in the first/seventh century by Muḥammad (d. 11/632), both as the recipient of a divinely revealed Sacred Book, the Qur'ān, and as the composer of many speeches, epistles and convenants. With the authoritative and definitive collection of the Qur'anic revelations during the caliphate of 'Uthmān (23–35/644–55), Arabic literature was endowed with a massive prose work to stimulate the development of its prose literature, and to influence its stylistic varieties in the Islamic period; and indeed, the Qur'ān's influence has been incalculable. It was declared unique and inimitable when it was revealed, and so it has remained throughout the ages, casting its spell over Muslim and non-Muslim alike through a sublimity that grips as its *pluralis majestatis* powerfully transmits to erring humanity the voice of the Deity in measured phrase and confident tone to which all the resources of 'that deep-toned instrument', the *'arabiyya*, are made to contribute. No wonder, then, that poetry was temporarily eclipsed by the new prose during the short period of the Patriarchal Caliphs (11–41/632–61) who, moreover, were opposed to an art from which Muḥammad himself had suffered, and which had been crisply denounced in a Qur'anic revelation.

The Umayyad period (41–132/661–750) witnessed a poetic outburst reminiscent of the pre-Islamic one in sixth-century Arabia. The Umayyads revived the traditions of poetic composition, and for political reasons established a firm relationship between poetry and the caliphal court, which was to persist throughout Islamic times. During this period, Arabic poetry experienced two far-reaching transformations: urbanization and islamization. The literary scene shifted from the deserts of Inner Arabia to the arc which comprises the Fertile Crescent and the Ḥijāz. The poets were mostly city-dwellers or urban in taste, and those who were not, e.g., Dhu'l-Rumma (d. 117/735), were anachronistic. The islamization of Arabic poetry was pervasive, ranging from the superficial employment of Islamic terms and ideas in the poetry of the traditional *qaṣīda*-poets to the expression of deeper religious sentiments in the poetry of the politico-religious parties. Poetry borrowed from Islam three impressive motifs: eschatology, Holy War (*jihād*) and the Pilgrimage. The first two fired the imagination of the Kharijites, whose Islamic *ḥamāsa*, expressed both in prose and in verse, is a vivid and powerful reflection of Islam's militancy and piety of fear, (*taqwā*); while the third, the Pilgrimage, through the rites and place-names associated with it, provided the erotic poets of the period with a new context for setting their plots and dialogues, and a host of entirely new associations, through which they restated and refreshed the old themes of love.

The major poets of the period are a triad, al-Akhtal (d. ?92/710), al-Farazdaq (d. ?110/728), and Jarīr (d. ?114/732) who composed for the Umayyad caliphs and their governors in the Fertile Crescent. The closest to the caliphs was al-Akhtal, who was also the last great Christian poet of classical times. The three wasted their prodigious talents as they divided most of their time between the composition of splendid panegyrics and indulgence in unsavoury invectives, with which they entertained Umayyad society.

Far more interesting were the developments in the Arabian peninsula. A new type of poetry came into being and it is the most attractive of all Umayyad poetry. The erotic motif of the old polythematic ode was disengaged from it, and was now developed independently as a love-lyric. The *ghazal*, as this new love-lyric came to be called, was of two kinds. The first was urban, sensuous and gay; it grew in the two cities of the Ḥijāz, Mecca and Medina, stimulated by music and song, and nourished by the affluence and the luxury wholeheartedly granted by the Umayyads to the unfriendly Ḥijāz. It was simple lexically and metrically, almost conversational, and its master was the somewhat narcissistic Qurayshite, the Meccan 'Umar b. Abī Rabī'a (d. ? 101/719). The second was bedouin, and it spread in the *bādiyas* of Najd and the Ḥijāz. It was chaste, hopeless and languishing, and was known as 'Udhrite, after the tribe of 'Udhra, which produced its most outstanding representative, Jamīl (d. 82/701). But it was the half-legendary Qays from the tribe of 'Āmir, whose love for his inamorata, Layla, cost him his reason and earned him the sobriquet *al-Majnūn*, that has exercised the greatest influence on later Arabic, Persian and Turkish romancers.

The literary art of the Umayyad period was predominantly poetic. Nevertheless, it enriched Arabic with what is undoubtedly its finest oratorical prose, for which a fertile ground was provided by the intense political conflicts and religious passions of the times. Towards the end of the period, 'Abd al-Ḥamīd b. Yaḥyā (d. 132/750), the secretary of the last Umayyad caliph, Marwān II, emerged as the first major *kātib* and preluded the contributions of even more illustrious secretaries to the development of Arabic prose literature in the riper age of the 'Abbasids.

The revolution which brought to power a new dynasty, the 'Abbasids, also opened for Arabic literature its golden age (132–447/750–1055).

New factors began to operate, and literature developed new features and characteristics. Baghdād centralized literary life as Umayyad Damascus had never done, and its prestige persisted even after its fall to the Buyids in 334/945. Through the rise of provincial centres, Arabic literature was no longer restricted to the Semitic homeland in western Asia, but spread east and west to Central Asia and the farthest shores of the Mediterranean. The contributors to this literature were no longer predominantly Arabs, as they had been in Umayyad times, but belonged to various ethnic groups, of whom the Persians were the most important, both by virtue of their numbers and by their mediation and transmission of foreign influences, e.g., Sasanid court-literature and Indian fables. The rapid development of an Islamic civilization under the 'Abbasids, cosmopolitan in its facets but nevertheless Qur'ano-centric, 'matured' that literature as it passed on to it, through the common idiom of High Arabic, some of its terms and concepts. The growth and development of Arabic literary criticism evidences this maturity, but unfortunately criticism exercised no salutary influence on literature, as it remained microscopic in its outlook and preoccupations, perhaps answering to the atomic structure of Arabic verse and artistic prose, and thus only confirmed the involvement of literature with pure form and verbal perfection.

Although the 'Abbasid period is the golden age for both Arabic prose and Arabic poetry, it is the development of the first that is arresting. After being the language of a simple Arab culture in Umayyad times, the *'arabiyya* became the language of a complex Islamic civilization. The various specialized disciplines which constituted that civilization developed their own terminologies and modes of expression, but all this redounded to the benefit of Arabic prose—the confluence of many currents from these tributary disciplines. A variety of styles were brought to maturity, and they fall into three main categories: the *muṭlaq* or *mursal*, the free unadorned style of the second/eighth century represented by Ibn al-Muqaffa'; the *muzdawij* or *mutawāzin*, the assonantal style of the third/ninth century represented by al-Jāḥiẓ; and the *musajja'*, the rhyming style of the fourth/tenth century represented by Badī' al-Zamān. The tendency towards ornateness as prose style progressed from the *muṭlaq* to the *muzdawij* and the *musajja'* was irresistible, encouraged by the very genius of Arabic, by the model of verbal and formal perfection presented by the rival poetic art, and by the views of the literary critics and theorists. It was not so much the *saj'*, which can be effective when judiciously used, but the *badīʿ*, the new style with its ornamental devices and artifices, and particularly one of them, *jinās*, homophony, that deprived Arabic prose of the vigour and functionalism which had characterized it in early ʿAbbasid times.

The first group of writers to contribute to the growth of ʿAbbasid prose literature were the *kuttāb*, the chancery secretaries, a well-defined group who, as state officials, endured in the service of Arabic literature as long as rulers needed secretaries, and who counted among their numbers in later times Ibn al-ʿAmīd (d. 360/970), the famous *wazīr* of the Buyids, and al-Qāḍī al-Fāḍil (d. 596/1200), Saladin's secretary. Their most important representative, however, was Ibn al-Muqaffaʿ (d. *c.* 139/757), who holds a central position not only in the history of Arabic literature, but also in the history of Arabic culture. His *Kalīla wa-Dimna*, an adaptation of the Indian fables of Bidpai from a Pahlavī version, is an Arabic classic which has had a fateful history. The second group of writers were the humanists of the third/ninth century, to whom Arabic prose style, prose literature, and Arabic culture are deeply indebted. They are represented by Jāḥiẓ (d. 255/868) and Ibn Qutayba (d. 276/889). The first is the larger literary personality, a veritable genius who wrote on a wide range of subjects, e.g., 'The book of animals', 'The book of misers'; his Muʿtazilite tastes are reflected even in the intellectual accent of his prose, which ultimately betrays the Hellenic current in the mainstream of his cultural consciousness. To the same group may be added the late figure of al-Tawḥīdī, (d. 414/1023). These humanists enriched the concept of *adab* and enlarged it from the narrow 'secretarial' connotation of 'manners' with its emphasis on the Sasanid tradition, to a wider and fuller one, signifying 'letters', the core of which was the Arabic-Islamic tradition. In so doing, they gave the indigenous Arabic literary tradition a privileged position in the concept of *adab* as it emerged in medieval Islamic times; but they were too much preoccupied with the cultural crisis of their time and with their war against the *Shuʿūbiyya*, and consequently much of their work was educational and didactic.

It was the generation that followed them in the fourth/tenth century, which may be termed the belletrists, that rarefied further the concept of literature—not necessarily to its advantage—and turned it into pure literary art, as is evident from the two prose genres which enjoyed a wide vogue in the fourth/tenth century, namely the *maqāmāt*, 'assemblies' and the *rasāʾil*, 'epistles'. The unsurpassed master of the *maqāmāt*,

Badī' al-Zamān, '*stupor mundi*' (d. 398/1007) was also its originator. His 'assemblies' are vignettes of a vagabond who lives on his wit and wits but they are also valuable documents of social life in the medieval Islamic city. The *rasā'il* are literary essays in highly ornamental prose which treat a wide variety of subjects. They have many masters, including Badī' al-Zamān and his contemporary Abū Bakr al-Khuwārizmī (d. 383/1002). The most celebrated of all these *rasā'il*, however, is the substantial *Risālat al-ghufrān* ('Epistle of Pardon') of Abu'l-'Alā' al-Ma'arrī (d. 339/1058) which describes the journey of a philologist to interview the poets of Heaven and Hell. But its audacity and brilliance of conception are vitiated by the frequent alternation of pedantry and obscurity with which its blind author has, perhaps deliberately, encumbered it.

Unlike prose, Arabic poetry in this, its golden age, presents what might possibly be termed a case of arrested development, as the explosion of intellectual and cultural life touched it peripherally and superficially. It lost the social function it had before, and increased its unwholesome dependence on court patronage. Unable to break away from its atomic structure and unvitalized by any external influence, it ruminated on its own resources and on its pre-'Abbasid heritage. Soon enough it became involved in *badī'* to which the old *qaṣīda* was married; but the marriage was inconvenient as *badī'* encouraged artificiality and tended to drown the fresh impulses and wholesome stirrings which were reaching Arabic poetry from some facets of Islamic civilization, notably philosophy and mysticism.

Bashshār, (d. 167/783) a Persian, heralded the advent of 'Abbasid poetry, just as it was another Persian, Ibn al-Muqaffa', who opened the history of 'Abbasid prose. He and his younger contemporary, Abū Nuwās (d. ?195/810) outraged their age and posterity by their unorthodoxy and profligacy, as much as they fascinated it by their versatility and mastery of all forms of Arabic poetry, old and new; but it is their love-lyrics and their wine-songs that have the most enduring interest, both as literary artefacts, and as documents for the movement towards the 'debedouinization' of Arabic poetry. The third/ninth century is dominated by a trio. The first, Abū Tammām (d. 231/846), is the representative of 'Abbasid neo-classicism, a great poet who strained his poetry by over-intellectualization and a hankering after *badī'*. His famous ode on the conquest of Amorium in 223/838 by the Caliph al-Mu'taṣim reveals equally well the excellencies and failings of his style and technique. A sweeter bard is his disciple and admirer, al-Buḥturī (d. 284/897), a verbal alchemist who avoids the lexical and conceptual difficulties of the master. In him, 'Abbasid palaces and establishments found an eloquent panegyrist, although his most celebrated ode was composed on the Sasanid Īwān Kisrā (the Arch of Ctesiphon). The third, Ibn al-Rūmī (d. 283/896) is a highly introspective and hypersensitive poet who excels in the elaboration of single themes at great length, as in the ode on the songstress Waḥīd. But the greatest of all 'Abbasid poets was yet to come. Al-Mutanabbī (d. 354/965), 'the would-be prophet' as the poet was nicknamed, was the master of almost all the traditional themes of classical poetry, and his firm artistic will imposed on the *qaṣīda* a certain organic unity. But what distinguishes his poetry is a series of splendid epinician odes which may be termed the *Rūmiyyāt*. The Arab conquests of the first/seventh century found no poet to do justice to their epic sweep and heroic character, and it was left to this scion of the old tribe of Kinda, three centuries later, to compose for Arabic its finest heroic poetry. In fiery and sonorous verse, the 'would-be prophet' sang the exploits of his patron, Sayf al-Dawla, the Hamdanid warrior-prince (*reg.* 333–56/944–67) who was fighting a valiant but hopeless war against Byzantium. The belated figure of Abu'l-'Alā' al-Ma'arrī closes this golden age. His *Luzūmiyyāt* with their gratuitously complex rhymes are the philosophical *dīwān* of Arabic literature, where poetry alternates with rhymed philosophy, and where even a highly intellectual man of letters succumbs to the temptations of the meretricious *badī'*.

The political decentralization of the Arab empire in the fourth/tenth century, and the reduction of Baghdād itself in 334/945 to a provincial capital by the Buyids, inevitably affected the course of a literature whose fortunes were closely tied up with court patronage. The linguistic and cultural division of the Islamic empire into a Persian-speaking East and an Arab-speaking West began to tell. Arabic poetry lost its Persian contributors, but Arabic prose, partly owing to the prestige of the hieratic '*arabiyya*, continued to count many Persians among its brightest stars, e.g., Badī' al-Zamān and Ibn al-'Amīd. However, it was becoming amply clear that the future of Arabic literature lay in the western half of the empire, Arabic-speaking and for some time ruled by Arab dynasties, such as the Hamdanids of Syria (at whose court a brilliant circle was formed around Sayf al-Dawla), and the Fatimids of Egypt (358–565/

969–1171) who had their *muqaddam al-shuʿarāʾ*, 'the foremost of the poets' and who gave poetry an important propagandist function. But more important was the Far West, consisting of the African mainland and the two transmarine colonies, Sicily and Spain. It is the last, al-Andalus, a slice of Islam on a highly christianized and romanized substrate, which merits most attention on account of its nature poetry and its exploration of new verse forms.

The moods of *natura benigna* already known to early ʿAbbasid poetry, were reflected in a new type of nature poetry which was developed later by the Syrian school represented by al-Ṣanawbarī, 'he of the pine tree', who belonged to the circle of Sayf al-Dawla. The poets of the Muslim Occident were even more susceptible to these moods: Ibn Ḥamdīs, 'the Arabic Wordsworth' (d. 533/1138), caught them in Sicily, but it was an Andalusian, Ibn Khafāja (d. 533/1138), who became the Occident's most dedicated nature poet. The new forms developed in al-Andalus were the *muwashshaḥ* and the *zajal*, whose connexions with music and song were intimate and whose themes were erotic. The appearance of the *muwashshaḥ*, 'the girdled', towards the end of the third/ninth century is associated with the opaque figure of a certain Muqaddam b. Muʿāfā. It was a novelty in its strophic scheme of composition and it refreshed Arabic poetry by relieving it of the exigency of the monorhyme; but it also encumbered it with verbal arabesque. The *zajal*, 'melody', another form of strophic composition represented by Ibn Quzmān (d. 555/1159) was a more basic innovation, since by its employment of the popular speech it challenged the hitherto unquestioned claims of High Arabic as the sole medium of literary expression. It is not impossible that the spread of vernacular poetry in medieval Romance literature may have been due to the Arabic *zajal*. The two main figures of Andalusian literature are Ibn Zaydūn (d. 463/1070) and Ibn al-Khaṭīb (d. 776/1374). Both were masters of Arabic prose and verse, and composers of some beautiful strophic odes, *mukhammas* and *muwashshaḥ*, respectively. Like much of Andalusian poetry, their art is nostalgic, wistful, and anxious, reflecting the uncertainties and instabilities of Andalusia's political life.

In 447/1055 the Seljuk Turks occupied Baghdād, and ushered in the period of Turkish domination which lasted for almost a millennium, as the Seljuks were followed by the Mamluks and the Mamluks by the Ottomans. Although their services to Islam and the *dār al-Islām* were undoubtedly great, the influence of the Turks on the course of Arabic literature was not salutary. To be sure, religious literature and encyclopaedic compilations abounded during this period, but secular and original composition progressively dried up. This was natural, as the interest of Turkish-speaking dynasts in a literature composed in Arabic was understandably minimal.

The Seljuk period is illumined by three major figures who justify its being called the silver age. In ʿIrāq, al-Ḥarīrī (d. 516/1122) composed his famous *maqāmāt* in which he carried the tradition of *badīʿ* to its farthest limits; in Syria, al-Qāḍī al-Fāḍil (d. 596/1200) continued the tradition of the *kuttāb*, and his association with Saladin ensured an enduring interest for his highly ornate prose; in Egypt, Ibn al-Fāriḍ (d. 632/1235) bestowed on Arabic verse the glitters and whispers of its best mystic poesy. Vastly different in temperament as these three masters were, they were all slaves to *badīʿ* and its conventions.

The fall of Baghdād to the Mongols in 656/1258, was another fateful date for Arabic literature and history alike. Egypt supplanted ʿIrāq as the centre of the Arabic-speaking Muslim West, and its central position under the Mamluks was further accentuated by the fall of Granada in 897/1492. But the Mamluk sultans (648–922/1250–1517) were Turkish- or Circassian-speaking rulers and their courts were no market for Arabic literature, which consequently withered. The scene of literary activity shifted from the sultans' courts to the streets and coffee-houses of Cairo, where professional reciters entertained enchanted audiences with their stories and romances. Ironically enough, it was one of these story-cycles, the famed *Thousand and One Nights*—an earlier version of which had been characterized in 377/988 by the understandably supercilious Ibn al-Nadīm as 'a vulgar and insipid book'—that later, and in translation, was to be the contribution of the Arabs to the World Fair of International Literature.

The defeat of the Mamluks by Sultan Selīm in 922/1516 opened the third and last period of Turkish domination, the Ottoman period which lasted until the First World War. During this period, even more adverse factors operated to the disadvantage of Arabic literature; Egypt, its centre, was reduced to provincial status; Cairo was superseded as capital by Istanbul; and the Ottoman sultans were neither Arabic-speaking, nor even like the Mamluks, resident in Arab lands. This was the golden age of a new Islamic literature, Turkish, just as the preceding period of the Seljuks and the Mongols was the golden age of another

Islamic literature, Persian. The vitality of the Arabic literary tradition was transferred to younger and more vigorous Islamic literatures, whose growth it had directly or indirectly stimulated, namely, Persian, Turkish and Urdu. It was during this period, when the ruling institution was not patronizing Arabic literature, that the religious establishment rendered its greatest service by performing a custodial function which made possible the very survival of the traditions of High Arabic. The significance of the Fatimid foundation, the collegiate mosque of al-Azhar, emerges clearly in this long Ottoman winter which set in on the Arab lands. And once suitable conditions in the nineteenth and twentieth centuries obtained, al-Azhar participated in its own way and through its reformers in the modern Arab renaissance.

The modern period

Modern Arabic literature is but one manifestation of the general Arab awakening for which the stage was set by Bonaparte's dramatic invasion of Egypt in 1798. The decisive factor in its evolution has been that highly complex phenomenon known as the 'impact of the West'. The two processes of democratization and secularization, the operation of which has set modern Arabic literature apart from its classical parent, are part of this phenomenon; the first severed its relations with the ruling institution, the second relaxed its ties with the religious establishment. Among the instruments of these two processes of democratization and secularization, the printing press and the Western-style university have played a major role. The printing press has encouraged the translation of foreign works, and has facilitated the rise of journalism (which has been a most potent force in the development of a straightforward functional prose), and the cultivation of the modern literary essay; furthermore, it has established a relationship between the writer and the reading public which has affected the writer's conception of himself, given him an important social function, and relieved him of the inconvenience of court patronage. The university, as an institution of higher learning, has become the centre of organized literary studies, whence new literary traditions and new critical theories are systematically disseminated; consequently, the university has succeeded in relieving the religious institutions, e.g., al-Azhar in Egypt, of their sole custodianship of Arabic. As a result, literature has lost much of the Islamic tinge which coloured it in classical times, and this tendency towards secularization has been accelerated by one of the most powerful factors in the making of modern Arab history, namely, nationalism. Perhaps nothing is better illustrative of this tendency than the emergence of the Christian Arabs as active contributors to Arabic literature, and the rise of Christian Lebanon as a major literary province, whose enterprising emigrants gave impetus to the Egyptian renaissance in the nineteenth century, and carried the Arabic literary tradition to its farthest geographical limits in the New World. In addition to secularization and democratization, the most significant result of the 'impact' has been the opening of the Arab literary mind to the direct influence of Western literary art and literary theory, a chapter long overdue in the history of cultural encounters between the Arabs and the West. A new conception of literature has arisen which emphasizes experience. New literary genres have been added to both prose and poetry, while the fruitful dialogue between artist and critic, often united in one person, has kept the former conscious of the aesthetic foundations of his literary endeavours. But this modern literature has its problems; e.g. the *'arabiyya* itself, with the classical associations and modes of expression of which the poet has to wrestle, while the divorce between the spoken and the written language presents a problem, not an insoluble one, to the novelist and the dramatist in the composition of dialogue.

For Arabic prose it is the introduction of new literary genres that has been the West's most valuable gift. The short story, the novel and the drama, have all found competent practitioners in various parts of the Arab world. Among the earliest pioneers was a Lebanese immigrant to the United States, Kahlil Gibran (Jubrān Khalīl Jubrān) (d. 1931) whose essays, parables and short stories reveal the complex personality of a poet, painter and mystic. He profoundly influenced the literary taste and fashion of his generation, although he wrote his best known work, *The Prophet*, in English. His contemporary and friend, the prolific Mikhā'īl Naimy (Nu'ayma) (b. 1889) is the other major figure in this Arabo-American School—a master essayist, short story writer and critic, whose *Gibran* is the classic of all Arabic biographical literature. It is, however, in Egypt that prose literature has had its foremost authors, where Ṭāhā Ḥusayn (b. 1889) the doyen of Arabic letters has dominated the literary scene for the last half-century. A versatile genius, blind from early childhood, he has functioned indefatigably as a literary critic, a cultural catalyst, a prose stylist and a creative writer. For Arabic he has fashioned a new prose style possessed of great expressiveness, flexibility and elegance, in which he wrote his autobiographical masterpiece, *al-Ayyām*. In the field of dramatic literature, the short story and the novel, three other Egyptian writers, Tawfīq al-Ḥakīm (b. 1898) Maḥmūd Taymūr (b. 1894) and Najīb Maḥfūẓ (b. 1912) respectively, have distinguished themselves as masters of these literary genres. Farther to the west, the Arab Occident has produced an author, the Tunisian Maḥmūd al-Masʿadī (b. 1900), who has attained celebrity for his existentialist dramatic composition, *al-Sudd*.

Modern Arabic poetry, too, has felt the full impact of the West. It has explored new prosodical dimensions in order to emancipate itself from its bondage to rhyme and to a constricting metrical system, and it has plumbed the depths of poetic experience in its attempt to win free from the embrace of traditional verbal craftsmanship. This new creative outburst was made possible by a school of Revivalist poets who successfully rejuvenated Arabic poetry from within by exploiting its inner resources and drawing on the best elements in its classical tradition. They were heralded by the heroic figure of the soldier-poet, Maḥmūd Sāmī al-Bārūdī (d. 1904), and it was another Egyptian, Aḥmad Shawqī (d. 1932), who incontestably became Revivalism's most brilliant representative, and in a sense the greatest Arab poet of modern times. Shawqī succeeded in adding a new genre to Arabic poetry, although his dramas, e.g. *Majnūn Laylā*, are more remarkable for their lyric power than for their dramatic effect. In his *dīwān*, *al-Shawqiyyāt*, poetry often alternates with verse but the accent of great poetry is always audible. There is nothing better than his best, and he is at his best when he remembers contemporary events which have touched his sensibilities, or 'recollects in tranquillity' the historic past which has moved him as a Muslim, an Ottoman, an Egyptian or an Arab, e.g. the fall of Adrianople, 'Andalusia's sister', the extinction of the Caliphate, the valley of the Nile, the Alcázar of Granada and the sunset glow of Moorish Spain. Having performed its restorative and rejuvenating function, the poetry of the Revivalists began to recede before the new waves which were breaking upon Arabic poetry from the West. The most powerful was that of Romanticism, which in the thirties swept over the whole of the Arab world, both in its traditional centres in the East and in such newly revived and emergent literary provinces as Tunisia and the Sudan which produced Abu'l-Qāsim al-Shābbī (1909–34) and al-Tījānī Bashīr (1912–37). But it was the representative of Symbolism who has been the most strikingly original among the poets of these new literary movements—Lebanon's Saʿīd ʿAql, a consummate literary artist with a lustrous poetic style who has cut for the treasury of modern Arabic verse some of its most precious stones. All these poets, however, composed in the classical idiom of Arabic metrical prosody, and it was left to the youngest of the new schools, the school of Free Verse, to bring about the most revolutionary change in the history of Arabic poetry since pre-Islamic times. A new prosodical form has been evolved; not necessarily a substitute for the traditionally measured and monorhymed verse but an alternative or a complement which has endowed the atomically constituted Arabic poem with an organic structure and a subtler internal cadence. With the advent of Free Verse a new dawn may be said to have broken for Arabic poetry, and this has been Iraq's great achievement where a Pleiad whose bright stars include ʿAbd al-Wahhāb al-Bayātī (b. 1926) and Nāzik al-Malā'ika (b. 1923) have successfully established Free Verse as a legitimate prosodical idiom and in so doing have probably determined the future course of Arabic poetry.

As a result of two World Wars, a new Arab world has risen from the ashes of the old, extending from the Persian Gulf to the Atlantic Ocean. New literary provinces have come into existence such as Jordan, the Sudan and Libya, while old ones have been resuscitated into new life, as Arabia itself, the birthplace of Arabic poetry which has been rather silent since Umayyad times when Arabic literature was still the literature of a people. And it is as such that it has re-emerged in the twentieth century, after it had been the literature of a multi-racial society in medieval Islamic times.

PERSIAN LITERATURE

Of the countries falling completely under Arab rule in the early days of Islam, Persia was the only one which succeeded in preserving her national language, thereby maintaining a separate identity within the Islamic world. The language of the country, however, did not remain static, but gradually adjusted itself to the profound changes which the advent of Islam caused in Persian society. When after two hundred years of Arab rule Persian emerged again as a literary medium, it had assumed a fresh colouring, distinct from that of the Middle Persian of the Sasanian era. It had adopted a simpler morphology and had shed most of the words with Zoroastrian connotations, acquiring instead a considerable Arabic vocabulary.

In imperial Persia secular literature had been of a courtly character, and both its form and content reflected the tastes and interests of the kings and nobles who were its chief patrons. The destruction of Sasanian power brought to an end this system of patronage, and in the subsequent period of disruption, change and readjustment, Muslim Persians began to apply their talents to the enrichment of Arabic writing. Their contributions did much to develop Arabic literature into a diverse and truly living structure.

In the third/ninth century, however, with the weakening of the central power of the caliphs in Baghdād and the establishment of autonomous dynasties on Persian soil, the way was once again open for the emergence of a national literature. Now, once again 'the lively and graceful fancy, elegance of diction, depth and tenderness of feeling and a rich store of ideas' which, in the words of R. A. Nicholson,[1] had characterized the contributions made by the Persians to Arabic literature, could be devoted to the development of their own national literature, destined to become 'one of the great literatures of mankind'.[2]

This renaissance of Persian literature owes much to the encouragement of the enlightened princes of the Samanid dynasty, who brought a period of relative peace and stability to their kingdom in eastern and north-eastern Persia and championed the cause of Persian cultural rebirth. They revived or encouraged many old Persian customs and gave expression to the widespread, if not always vocal, desire of many Persians for a distinct national identity. They devised an adminstrative system and revived cultural patterns, largely based on the Sasanian model, and these survived with little change until the Mongol invasion, and even after. Their learned *wazīrs* and secretaries were the predecessors of a brilliant host of Persian statesmen and administrators who helped to maintain Samanid traditions in later periods.

It was under Samanid patronage that the blind bard Rūdakī (d. 330/940), rightly considered the father of Persian poetry, composed his poems. It was under the Samanids that Abū 'Alī Bal'amī, the erudite *wazīr* of Manṣūr I (350/961–366/976) gave the fledgling Persian prose literature his adaptation of the famous universal history in Arabic by his fellow-countryman al-Ṭabarī. Again it was under the Samanids that Firdawsī (d. *c.* 411/1020), the pre-eminent poet of Persia, composed the bulk of his *Shāh-nāma*, the monumental work which was to become the national epic of Persia.

[1] *A literary history of the Arabs* (Cambridge, 1956), 290.
[2] A. J. Arberry (ed.), *The Legacy of Persia* (Oxford, 1953), 200.

Having made their first strides under the auspices of the Samanids, poetry and prose soon expanded into an impressive literature, which flourished not only in Persia, but in other areas influenced by Persian culture, notably in Turkey, but above all in India, which under the Great Mughals became the second home of Persian literature.

Poetry

The first feature of this literature to attract our attention is the preponderance of poetry. Poetry is the great art of Persia, and it is in poetry that we must seek the most intimate and refined expressions of Persian thought and sentiment. It is only natural, therefore, that in a discussion of Persian literature, poetry should be given pride of place.

Whereas the spirit and the content of poetry in Muslim Persia clearly bear national marks, its formal pattern takes its imprint from Arabic. Over the years, however, within the framework of Arabic metres, the Persians developed forms better suited to their literary temperament. Of these one is the *mathnawī*, based on the rhyming couplet, which, though originally adapted from Arabic, was moulded into a distinctively Persian form, employed mainly for longer poems of a narrative or didactic nature. Another is the *ghazal*, a short poem of some seven to fifteen lines, all having the same rhyme, the last line normally including the signature of the poet. This form, which in some ways resembles the sonnet, is generally used for lyric poetry. Yet another example is the *rubā'ī*, or quatrain, a Persian invention, best exemplified by those of 'Umar Khayyām and employed mostly for epigrammatic expressions of amorous and mystical sentiments and philosophical thought. The *du baytī* is a more homely version of the *rubā'ī*. It is native to the land, and though occurring mainly in folk-lyrics, it is occasionally elevated to the level of high poetry. The *qiṭ'a* is a monorhyme, normally of three to twenty lines, employed mostly for casual subjects, satire, and ethical or moralizing themes.

The *qaṣīda*, the basic form of Arabic poetry, consisting of a long monorhyme, was also adopted. It remained the most favoured form for court poetry, and many poets who flocked to the courts of kings and others wrote poems of praise, congratulation, condolence or of satire in this form. The *qaṣīda* was generally written in the grand style, value being placed above all else on eloquence, polished diction, ingenious expression and resounding phrases. In the course of time excessive embellishment and exaggerated rhetorics led to florid and pedantic panegyrics which afford little pleasure to the reader.

The formal *qaṣīdas* of professional court poets, however, tell us little of the true range and depth of Persian poetry or of its distinctive features. Discussing such features, particularly in relation to those of Arabic poetry, J. Rypka concludes that

> the Arabs, in complete contrast to the Persians, have no sense for the epic. Only in the hand of the Persian poet do the *disjecta membra* of the tales of Laylī and Majnūn become a really unified work of art. The immense number of epics of a narrative nature in Persian literature also leads to the same conclusion. Likewise, Sufism failed to find the same fertile ground in Arab lands as it found in Persia, where the poetry is to a large extent plainly saturated with it, even though at times only superficially or apparently. Whereas the true expression of the Arab spirit is the *qaṣīda* in the broadest sense of the word (and not only in the panegyric sense), the lyrical way of thinking of Persia finds its true form in the *ghazal*.[1]

It is indeed to epic, lyrical, and mystical poetry that we must turn for a true appreciation of Persian literary genius. Before Islamic times several massive compilations in Sasanian Persian dealt not only with the histories and legends of Persian kings and heroes but were concerned also with the institutions of the empire, the orders of its aristocracy, rules of conduct and good government, and the arts and skills cherished by the nobility. Their illustrated folios were the ancestors of Persian miniatures.

The Arab conquest and conversion to Islam failed to suppress the memory of a proud past. The nostalgic perspective of the past gave impetus to a series of attempts to collect, translate or recompose the national history. Ibn al-Muqaffaʿ (d. between 139/757 and 142/759–60), one of the founders of Arabic prose literature, translated into Arabic the *Khwatāynāma* ('Book of kings'), compiled towards the end of Sasanian times.

This work, or Persian editions of it, also attracted the attention of Persian poets. Of several attempts made by the early poets at its versification, that of Firdawsī resulted in the birth of an epic of extraordinary power and dignity. The exploits of Rustam, the invincible Persian Hercules and the indomitable defender of the Persian kingdom, dominate the tales told by the poet. With rare poetic gift Firdawsī creates a heroic atmosphere where his characters move as formidable giants and

[1] *Iranische Literaturgeschichte* (Leipzig, 1959), 109.

their deeds assume cosmic proportions. His pure and lofty language, his vigorous diction and virile tones are eminently suited to the treatment of his heroic theme. His genius as a poet is such that one is often apt to forget that he was bound to a prose text which considerably limited the freedom of his imagination. When the episodes are well constructed in the original and suitable for epic treatment, they are moulded in the hands of Firdawsī into supreme examples of epic art. Such is the case with the episode of Rustam and Suhrāb in which the great hero inadvertently kills his brilliant son, a tragedy which inspired Matthew Arnold's poem 'Sohrab and Rustum'.

Although the *Shāh-nāma* is primarily conceived as a heroic epic, concerning itself mainly with the exploits of warrior heroes, it is by no means devoid of the moralizing comments and philosophical and contemplative asides so characteristic of the main stream of Persian literature. In fact early Persian poetry, if somewhat archaic in its simplicity, exhibits remarkable maturity in thought; for although Persian poetry was young, the Persian people were old, and had a long and eventful history behind them.

The *Shāh-nāma* was written in an era when historical events, particularly in eastern Persia, encouraged a hopeful and spirited mood. The pervasive melancholy and mystical detachment which characterize much of late classical Persian poetry are barely perceptible in the poetry of the fourth/tenth and fifth/eleventh centuries. Persian poetry of this period displays a youthful spirit, with unmistakable delight in nature and its beauties. Love shines in a carefree manner and, more often than not, the songs of the poet display the joys of satisfaction rather than the sorrows of frustration.

As the years go by, poetry gradually progresses from youth to maturity, gaining in depth of sentiment and tenderness of feeling. Mystical views begin to affect the poet's themes and a certain detachment mellows the tone of his meditative lines. The animation of Rūdakī (d. 330/940) and Farrukhī (d. 429/1037) gives way to the tenderness of Sanā'ī (d. 536/1141) and Niẓāmī (d. 613/1217). With 'Aṭṭār (d. 627/1230) and 'Irāqī (d. 688/1289) the tone becomes considerably more passionate and moving. The song of love is now set to a minor key and often reveals a lover with an acute sense of tragedy. He rejoices even in the suffering that love brings. The virile tone, the rigorous diction, and the syncopated rhythms of the earlier poets are now mellowed into suaver songs.

The esteem in which wine, the age-old comfort of all Persian poets, is held, grows, and the poet finds the company of the *sāqī* (the cupbearer) and the ruby rim of the cup a remedy for the afflictions of love and reverses of fortune. To enjoy the moment and forget what the perfidious world may hold in store, is the advice most frequently given.

As lyric poetry develops, a set of conventions with regard to both theme and imagery begin to emerge. The beloved is idealized as the supreme epitome of beauty, ruthless in inflicting the pains of love without much concern for the wretched state of the lover. The lover, passionate and humble on the other hand, is ready to renounce both worlds if the beloved will but deign him a single glance of favour. The interminable hours of separation are a continual motif in his laments. In the sad songs of the nightingale, poured forth to the inconstant rose, he sees a reflection of his own fate; in the perishing of the moth in the consuming flame of the candle, to which it is drawn, he discovers a parallel to his own plight. Wine is his greatest comfort. It frees his mind from the shackles of an inexorable passion and the cares of a perverse world.

With the development of the wine-cult in Persian lyrics, there develops a further set of conventions closely related to social satire. In a world blighted by hypocrisy and pretension, wine-drinkers, with their typical abandon and their lack of concern for the approval of the world, come to symbolize the very idea of sincerity and serenity so dear to the poet's heart. The tavern rather than the mosque is the place in which to gain wisdom. Presently the devoted and daring lover, the carefree drunkard and the honest *qalandar* emerge as the characters admired in the lyrics. In contrast, the preacher, the *muftī*, the Ṣūfī and their like become the frequent targets of subtle, if biting, satire. The poet's unremitting praise is not for those who prescribe the sterile arguments of reason; but for those who answer the call of the heart and follow the path of love.

In its continued criticism of bigotry, fanaticism and misuse or misinterpretation of religious dogma, the *ghaẓal* embodies the most consistent, concise and delicate form of social satire to be found in Persian poetry. It is particularly this satire, often cloaked in the form of irony, that gives Persian lyrics their surprisingly liberal atmosphere.

If the strict forms of Persian poetry and its often conventionalized imagery limit the poet's freedom of expression—a fact that makes his achievements all the more worthy of admiration—he enjoys almost complete freedom in the arrangement of his themes. Each line of a *ghazal* is generally self-contained, expressing a complete idea, and very tenuously connected—if at all—with the next line. The poet is at liberty to jump from one idea to another, now marvelling at the beauty of the beloved, now singing the praise of wine; in one line bewailing his lot, in the next satirizing the pretence of the false preacher, and in the third invoking a metaphor to illustrate the ways of the world. This may appear disparate and lacking in unity and coherence, but a *ghazal* is held together first, as regards form, by its single rhyme and metre; secondly, by the prevailing mood of the *ghazal* which helps to throw an imperceptible bridge over the lines; and thirdly, and most effectively, by the larger context of Persian lyric poetry with its conventional and immediately recognizable themes, concepts and metaphors, related to each other after their own logic, and from among which the poet chooses those which happen to suit his purpose in a given *ghazal*.

One of the main traits of the Persian lyric, and in fact of Persian poetry as a whole, is its abstract character—this despite the predominantly romantic outlook of the Persian poet. We are not allowed to identify any character or gain an intimate knowledge of the circumstances, time, or place of any particular event. It is hardly ever possible to know which particular preacher or *muftī* the poet is satirizing, or how the beloved of Saʿdī (d. 691/1292) differed from that of Rūmī (d. 671/1273) or Majmar (d. 1225/1810). It is equally well-nigh impossible to distinguish the patron praised by Unṣurī (d. between 431/1040 and 441/1050) from that of Qā'ānī (d. 1271/1853).

The characters that a poet treats, are in fact idealized and abstract entities who appear on the stage of poetry with the mask of a type and not with the face of an individual. Even in works of fiction, the treatment is generally that of an allegory. But the types are brought to life by the acute and passionate feelings of individual experience. The combination of abstraction and intense emotion imparts to Persian lyrics a universality and at the same time a moving effect peculiar to themselves.

It is in this genre that the three giants of Persian lyric poetry, Saʿdī, Rūmī and Ḥāfiẓ (d. 792/1390), wrote their best.

Saʿdī, a versatile poet and writer of extraordinary verve and finish, matches wit and humour with a deep sense of humanity. His lyric poetry surpasses all that was written before him in felicity of phrase, ease of diction, melodious rhythm and a sustained level of lively imagination.

It is in the hands of Ḥāfiẓ, however, that lyric poetry reaches the heights of the sublime. He cloaks the creation of his sensitive imagination, his delicate sentiments, his lofty thoughts and his subtle satire in a brocade of words so aesthetically designed and so masterfully woven that his art has proved the joy and despair of the host of poets who have attempted to imitate him. His widespread popularity and the unlimited belief felt in his genius, make him the national poet of Persia, and yet he remains a poet's poet.

Rūmī (d. 671/1273), a contemporary of Sa'dī, is in a class of his own. Although his reputation rests mainly on his discursive mystical poem, the *Mathnawī*, his claim as a great lyric poet must rest on his *ghazals*. He was an impassioned lover and mystic, the burning intensity of whose love knew no respite. His rhapsodical *ghazals* derive much of their moving quality from the sheer intensity of their feeling and the potent music of their words. His genius, like the touch of a magician, is able to turn everything that comes his way into poetry, and let cosmic elements become humble tools to his devouring and restless imagination. In his rapture he often stretches the possibility of words and images to the utmost limit, occasionally approaching a ravishing unintelligibility. At his best, Rūmī surpasses perhaps all Persian poets in the width and breadth of his imagination, the forcible rhythm of his words, depth of emotions and tenderness of feelings. But his work, unlike that of Ḥāfiẓ, Sa'dī and Firdawsī, is not even, and he is too absorbed in his all-consuming passion to care for refinement and polish.

As a mystic poet, Rūmī provides a perfect example of that blending of mystical sentiment and amorous feelings characteristic of so much of Persian literature. The Ṣūfī way of life, which advocated intense love and devotion as the means of attaining truth, found a considerable following in Persia, and Ṣūfī convents grew increasingly popular after the fourth/tenth century. Persian mystics often were men of outstanding sensitivity and employed poetry or poetical diction to express their thoughts and to move their fellow men. It was only natural for a school of thought which distrusted 'reason' and relied on the inspiration of the 'heart', to adopt the language of lyrics and to employ the symbolism of sensuous love.

The spread of certain Ṣūfī doctrines which tended to see in the human form a revelation of the Divine Being, further blurred in a great many Persian lyrics the distinction between mystical and erotic love. The symbol and the idea merged and what had been in earlier periods a rather mundane love poetry, limited in its application, assumed with 'Aṭṭār, Rūmī, and 'Irāqī mystical depth and significance, and was now capable of being interpreted on a spiritual plane and of inspiring devotional feelings. After Ḥāfiẓ, a master of equivocal expressions in this sense, this mystical vein itself became a convention to be followed by a host of poets in Persia, India and Turkey, even though not all of them based their mystical utterances on personal experience.

The *ghazal*, which has been discussed at some length already, is the form that embodies the essence of Persian poetry; it is intimate, intense and concise, and owes very little to courtly patronage. It is not, however, because of its structure, suitable for narrative and coherent discourse. The form employed for this purpose is the *mathnawī* or couplet form, and it is in this that Persian poetry displays its fullest range.

With Firdawsī's *Shāh-nāma* the supreme example had been set up for all subsequent heroic poetry. A little later, Gurgānī (d. 442/1050) gave us an exquisite romance based on a legend of pre-Islamic origins. Next, Niẓāmī (d. 613/1217) composed no less than four epics of a predominantly romantic nature, thus setting the model for a plethora of similar compositions, among which those of Amīr Khusraw of Delhi (d. 726/1325), Jāmī (d. 895/1490) and Vaḥshī (d. 991/1583) attained renown. The celebrated *Mathnawī* of Rūmī gave the Islamic world its greatest monument of mystical thought, while Sa'dī's *Būstān* provided it with a masterpiece of great charm and delight. The latter strings together a series of moralizing and philosophical poems written in a uniformly exquisite, mellow and intimate style, illustrated by anecdotes and stories. An immense number of poems in the *mathnawī* form were written in India under the patronage of the Muslim courts, particularly those of the Mughal emperors.

The style of Persian narrative and discoursive poetry reflects the Persian distaste for constructions which are too rigid and too closely controlled. Such poetry is like the natural meanders of a free-flowing river rather than the controlled flow of a canal. Reading a Persian narrative poem is frequently like taking a stroll through a garden which has been laid out with taste and with great care for detail, but not along strict lines. At intervals the poet makes a halt to reflect on the transcendent significance of views and events, and to contemplate and moralize on what can be seen beyond the immediate aspect of physical forms, but only to return once again with renewed enthusiasm to the sensuous world of shape and colour.

This flexible treatment of themes and tendency to meandering, which in some poems lead to an almost 'centrifugal' style of composition, as is the case of Rūmī's *Mathnawī*, is not confined to works of poetry, but may be seen also in prose fiction and in works of a didactic or moralizing nature.

Prose

Turning to prose literature, it is true that prose was used in Persia predominantly for scholarly writing, but *belles-lettres* were by no means neglected. Much has perished in the course of a turbulent history; what remains in prose, however, is rich and diversified. It is only in comparison with Persian poetry that it loses some of its brilliance.

In the field of fiction there exists, first of all, a whole tradition of tales, stories, and popular epics, many of which have their origin in pre-Islamic Persia. The *Hazār afsāna*, the precursor of the *Arabian nights*, is now lost, but works of a similar character such as the *Sindbād-nāma* (556/1160–61) and *Bakhtyār-nāma*, are still extant. Tales of adventure enjoyed a considerable vogue in Persia, a fact attested by such works as the *Samak-i ʿayyār*, the *Dārāb-nāma* and several versions of the *Iskandar-nāma* ('The tale of Alexander') as well as the more recent *Amīr Arsalān*, belonging to the nineteenth century. To the category of fiction there belongs also a series of fable collections with a strong moral tenor, the most remarkable of which is the *Kalīla va-Dimna* (*c.* 538/1144) of Naṣr Allāh, which goes back to an Indian origin.

Story telling, which was always a popular art in Persia, has found its way into many works which are not primarily concerned with stories; thus a large number of Persian works on practical ethics and rules of government, commentaries on the Qur'ān, literary essays, mystical writings and romances are generously illustrated by anecdotes, stories and parables, and they owe much of their readability to such stories.

The crowning achievement of Persian prose is generally considered to be the *Gulistān* of Saʿdī, a volume of practical wisdom, wit and humour written in elegant rhyming prose, and largely consisting of a series of anecdotes and maxims. It is typical of Persian literary taste in its moralizing, its concern for refinement of form and embellishment of phrase, its play on words, as well as in its frequent recourse to citations of poetic fragments and supporting dicta. To the modern taste, however, many a less elegant work of simpler prose and tenderer feeling might well be more attractive.

The works of many Persian mystics belong to this class of writing, notably 'Aṭṭār's *Tadhkirat al-awliyā'* ('Memorial of the saints'), as well as some commentaries on the Qur'ān which reflect mystical sentiments. Among the latter one may mention Maybudī's copious *Kashf al-asrār* (belonging to the sixth/twelfth century), which has considerable literary merit.

There has always existed in Persia an acute sense of style. For this reason, learned writing, particularly in the humanities (*adab*), generally exhibits a high degree of literary skill, emphasizing, at times excessively, the importance of style. It is not always easy, therefore, to make a clear distinction between works of *belles-lettres* and the works of *adab* in general. This is particularly true of Persian histories which are remarkable for their style, be it straightforward, precise and effective like that of the *Tārīkh-i Bal'amī* (fourth/tenth century) and the *Tārīkh-i Bayhaqī* (fifth/eleventh century), more rhetorical as in Rashīd al-Dīn's *Jāmi' al-tawārīkh* (eighth/fourteenth century), or utterly florid and bombastic as in the *Durra-i Nādirī* (twelfth/eighteenth century).

Of works of literary merit in other fields of the humanities one may mention the *Qābūs-nāma* (fifth/eleventh century), truly a 'mirror for princes', by the sagacious prince Kay Kāvūs; the *Siyāsat-nāma*, a very readable manual of the rules of good government by the able *wazīr* Niẓām al-Mulk; and the *Kīmiyā-yi sa'ādat* ('The elixir of happiness'), a treatise of ethics and philosophy by the outstanding theologian al-Ghazālī (d. 505/1111).

Prose, however, was no more immune than poetry from the inevitable decline whose approach could be sensed in excessive refinement, exaggerated embellishment and turgid amplification. The decline in Persian letters may be said to begin after the holocaust wrought by a succession of Mongol and Tatar invasions of the country beginning in the seventh/thirteenth century. Persian poetry, although still written in abundance, lost its freshness, turning out repetitious configurations of the same old themes in ever more languid tones. Occasionally a bright star like the subtle poet Ṣā'ib (d. 1080/1670) appeared in the sky of Persian letters, but its glow was hardly sufficient to illuminate the once brilliant course of Persian literature.

During the period of the Safavids the main centre of Persian literature was tranferred to India, where it received generous patronage at the courts of the Mughal emperors. A large number of works in both prose and poetry was written in all the familiar old forms, and a tradition was established on Indian soil which continued into our own time and gave to Persian poetry a significant lyric writer in the person of Iqbāl of Lahore (d. 1938).

A new era in Persian literature began in the nineteenth century when a reaction against the stilted and uninspiring style of the previous century brought about a return to the simplicity and vigour of earlier Persian poetry. This literary renaissance produced poems which were both rigorous and delicate, but it was soon to give way to methods and styles which reflected the impact of the West. The modern period of Persian letters which belongs to the present century, has seen the development of fiction in the Western sense, has brought about a healthy, balanced and cultivated style of prose, and has given rise to a lively poetry which at its best is imaginative, original and refined, and can hold its own in comparison with the classical poetry.

TURKISH LITERATURE

Following the general trend and development of Turkish cultural history, it is possible to divide Turkish literature into four main periods:

(1) The literature of the Turks before they accepted Islam (from the origins to the eleventh century).
(2) Islamic Turkish literature (from the eleventh century to the middle of the nineteenth century).
(3) Turkish literature under Western influence (1850–1910).
(4) National and local literature (since 1910).

The first products of the old Turkish literature have not reached our times. We only have Chinese translations of the first examples of epics and lyrics. The extant products of the earliest written literature fall into two main groups. One of these consists of the inscriptions in north-east Asia. The most representative of these which are written in an alphabet developed from Aramaic through Sogdian, not deciphered until the end of the nineteenth century, are the Orhon inscriptions. They are known by this name because they were discovered near the Orhon river, a branch of the Selenga which flows into Lake Baykal. They were erected for Prince Kül (or Köl) and Bilge Khan (d. 731 and 734 respectively) of the Kök-Türk dynasty which flourished between the sixth and eighth Christian centuries. They relate the history of the Kök-Türks, their surrender to the Chinese and liberation under the guidance of Bilge Khan. The Turkish of the inscriptions gives the impression of a mature language and its lively style has in various places an exciting and epic atmosphere.

The second group of writings, largely of a religious nature, was developed in the Uigur territory in eastern Turkistān (present Sinkiang) between the ninth and twelfth Christian centuries, by Turks belonging to various religions. These Turks used the same written language but in different alphabets according to the religions to which they belonged. The Uigur alphabet, which was used by the Buddhist Turks who were in the majority, was developed from Sogdian. This alphabet was later adopted by the Mongols, and continued to be used by the eastern Turks to a limited extent after Islam.

Dīvān lughāt al-Turk, written by Maḥmūd Kāshgharī in 468/1074 when Islam had begun to spread among the Turks, and a struggle between Muslim and non-Muslim Turks had commenced, contains examples of passages pertaining to this transitory stage. Many forms of poetry—epic, romantic, pastoral, elegiac—are represented, if briefly, in this work, giving a good idea of the literary tradition of the pre-Islamic period. We can judge from these examples that there was an original and rich literature, much of which is no longer extant.

Islam came to the Turks through Persia. From the fifth/eleventh century, general Islamic culture was adopted by the Turks in a rather Persian form, and the new Persian literature became the source of inspiration for Turkish writers. Persian prosody was accepted in place of the Turkish syllabic metre, as well as Islamic verse-forms such as the *qaṣīda*, *ghazal* and *mathnawī* (*mes̱nevī*). Islamic culture derived from sources such as the Qur'ān, *Ḥadīth*, stories of the prophets, legends of the saints and mysticism began to dominate Islamic Turkish literature, which was also inspired by the *Shāh-nāma* of Firdawsī.

The Turks spread to many countries of Central and western Asia, the Near East and eastern Europe. Within this wide geographical area, various dialects of the Turkish language were spoken, and a rich oral literature also developed. The written literature developed mainly in two major dialects: Eastern Turkish, which can be considered as the continuation of one kind of Uigur; and Western Turkish, which comprises the Ottoman and Āẕarbāyjānī dialects developed from Oghuz.

Eastern Turkish

Eastern Turkish was used as the literary language from the eleventh century until the end of the nineteenth century in all the countries where Turkish was spoken or where Turks ruled except the Ottoman empire, western Persia and southern Crimea. Later on it was replaced by written languages that developed from local spoken languages. Eastern Turkish has gone through three periods of development.

In the Kara-Khanid period, the language, also called *Hakaniye* and Middle Turkish, developed in the fifth–sixth/eleventh–twelfth centuries from the Uigur language in eastern and western Turkistān, Kashghar being the centre, and became the first literary dialect of the Muslim Turks. Their first known work is the *Kutadgu bilig* ('Knowledge that gives happiness') written in 462/1069–70. Its author, Yūsuf of Balāsāghūn, presented his work to Tapgach Bughra Kara-Khan, sultan of Kashghar, and was made first chamberlain as a reward. Research on the content and the language of this important allegorical-didactic poem which comprises more than 6,000 couplets in the *mutaqārib* metre and in the *mesnevī* style, is yet at a beginning. This work by Yūsuf, who is striving after an ethical and religious ideal, is mainly formed by conversations between the Ruler, the *Vezīr*, the *Vezīr*'s son and his friend. As the government and also relations between rulers and subjects are discussed at length, this work has the nature of a political essay. Even though the general principles of Islamic literature have been adopted in respect to the verse-form and philosophy of life, pre-Islamic traditions appear both in the quatrains scattered in it and in many of the ideas concerning government.

Another work of the fifth/twelfth century is the *'Aybat al-ḥaqā'iq* written by Adīb Aḥmed of Yüknek. This little book in verse records the general moral rules of the Islamic world. It is interesting from the linguistic viewpoint, rather than as literature. The Qur'ān was translated into Turkish in this period. Though all the extant copies are quite late, the linguistic characteristics of one (Istanbul, Türk-Islam Eserleri Müzesi, Number 73) shows that it was made in the sixth/twelfth century.

The second stage in Eastern Turkish literature is the Khwārazm-Golden Horde period. In the seventh/thirteenth century a written language which was the continuation of Kara-Khanid Turkish was developed in Khwārazm in the Sir Darya (Jaxartes) delta, and from here it passed on to the Golden Horde. Unlike Kara-Khanid, this written language was also mixed with Oghuz and Kipchak elements.

Among the abundant products of religious literature of this period *Qiṣaṣ al-anbiyā'* (710/1310) by Rabghūzī and *Nahj al-Farādīs* (761/1360) by Maḥmūd of Kerder are especially worth mentioning. The first one of these belongs to the category of works recording the lives of prophets, and the second belongs to the genre of the Forty *Ḥadīths*. Both these works, which were written in the popular language and with a lively style, were widely read and loved until the end of the last century.

In this period parallels to the works of classical Persian literature for the *élite* also began to be written. Quṭb of Khwārazm wrote *Khusrū u-Shīrīn* (741/1341) for the ruler of the Golden Horde, in parallel to Niẓāmī's well-known *mathnawī*. Its content of much material from local culture and its considerable closeness to the language of the people commands attention. It seems that the *mesnevī* named *Maḥabbet-nāme* in *hazaj* metre, completed by Khwārazmī on the banks of the Sir Darya in 754/1353, was inspired by the *Vīs u-Rāmīn* of Gurgānī.

The third stage in the development of Eastern Turkish literature is the Chaghatay period. This literature which began during the Timurid period in Central Asia in the ninth/fifteenth century, developed in cultural centres such as Samarqand, Herat, Bukhārā, Khīva, Farghānā and Kashghar, and spread to the whole eastern Turkish world and India. Sakkārī, the poet who lived at Ulugh Beg's court in Samarqand during the second half of the century, and later on other poets, especially Luṭfī of Herat (d. 867/1462–3), who worked up this literary dialect in their *dīvāns*, *mesnevīs* and disputations, prepared for the appearance of 'Alī Shīr Navā'ī. In the second half of the fifteenth century, Chaghatay literature enjoyed its golden era at Herat. The sultan of Herat, Ḥusayn Baykara (d. 912/1506), was himself a poet. His court became a sort of academy to which poets, scholars, and artists gathered. 'Alī Shīr Navā'ī (844–906/1441–1501), one of the greatest poets of Eastern Turkish literature and one of the most able in Turkish literature as a whole, was nurtured there. Navā'ī was extremely original and fertile in poetry a worthy scholar and an able statesman. His great service to Chaghatay literature has resulted in this dialect often being called Navā'ī.

In recent times Navā'ī has been regarded both as one of the greatest poets of the world, and as a mere follower of the Persian classics. The truth lies between these two extremes. Like all Turkish classical poets, he was inspired by the great poets of Persian literature, such as Niẓāmī, but more often by Amīr Khusraw of Delhi, who was close to his period, and by Jāmī, his contemporary. However, using the common Islamic themes, the common forms and motives, he developed a very personal and original style. He brought out the ingenuity of the Turkish language with all its fineness and expressiveness. In these respects, together with Yūnus Emre, Fużūlī and Nedīm, he is one of the four great poets of classical Turkish literature, but he is the most fertile of them all. Because the majority of his *ghazals* were woven around the same theme they are different from the common tradition. His *mesnevīs* also vary in many instances from the common themes and display individuality.

Navā'ī also wrote many works on other subjects. Among these *Majālis al-nafā'is* (897/1491) is the first collection of biographies of poets in Turkish and moreover, even though brief, it is illustrative of its period. *Mīzan al-awzān* (898/1493) is an essay that he wrote about metre. It also contains some information about the kinds of poetry peculiar to Eastern Turkish. Although actually taking over Jāmī's *Nafaḥāt al-uns* in his *Nasā'im al-maḥabba min shamā'im al-futuwwa*, Navā'ī enlarged it with appendices and also made use of other sources. It is an excellent source for the biographies of the mystics of Turkistān. In his work named *Muḥākamat al-lughatayn* (905/1499) he makes a comparison of Turkish and Persian, the two competing languages and cultures of the time in Central Asia, and he tries to prove the superiority of the Turkish language.

After Navā'ī there are two great names in eastern Turkish literature, both of rulers. The first one of these, Ẓahīr al-Dīn Muḥammad Bābur, the founder of the Mughal empire in India, is known especially for his memoirs, which represent the prose of Eastern Turkish, as well as for his poems, which are equal to Navā'ī's. In his memoirs, which are probably incomplete, Bābur records his most active and interesting life with a frankness and honesty which is rarely found in this sort of work. Here we find Bābur, not only as a ruler and commander, but also as an artist of quality and as a man not hiding his weaknesses or boasting about his merits. His *Bābur-nāme*, which was translated first into Persian and then into the main Western languages, is a valuable source about his family, his circle and his contemporaries in all kinds of professions. The last notable representative of Eastern Turkish literature, Abu'l-Ghāzī Bahādur Khān, was the ruler of Khīva (1054–74/1644–63) and belonged to the Shaybānī Özbeg dynasty. Before he became khan he visited Turkish countries and collected Turkish, Persian and Mongolian sources of Turkish history. In addition to documents, he also made a collection of stories and legends. Besides these he studied the history of the Shaybānī dynasty. The two works that he wrote as a result of his enquiries, *Shejere-i Terākime* (1070/1659) and *Shajarat al-Atrāk* (left unfinished at his death and completed by his son, in 1076/1665), contain much historical information; but are especially important as examples of Chaghatay prose which are close to the popular language and far from ornamentation or artificiality. The second of these works has been translated into various European languages.

Sufficient study has not yet been made on Chaghatay literature after the eleventh/seventeenth century. It is generally accepted that no more than a mere superficial imitation of the old works was achieved, and the literature eventually began to decline. However, the results of some recent research show that writers of considerable importance lived in this period, but their work could not reach beyond a limited circle. Hence it is too early yet to judge the late Chaghatay period. However towards the end of the nineteenth century this common written language was eventually abandoned, and local dialects became literary languages.

Western Turkish

Even though the Eastern Turks in Central Asia had adopted Islamic literature in the fifth/eleventh century, the formation of a written literature was delayed for about two centuries among the Oghuz (Seljuk) Turks who had settled in Anatolia in continuous waves after the fourth/tenth century, and who eventually turkicized and islamized the area. In fact we see the first examples of written Turkish literature in Anatolia during the time of the principalities (*beyliks*) in Anatolia between the Seljuk and Ottoman periods. The main reason for this is the fact that the Seljuk Turks used Persian as the official language and Arabic for learned works until the very end. The expansion of the Turkish language as the official language in Anatolia starts at the time of Karamanoghlu Meḥmed Bey (660–77/1261–78). The emergence of a written literature with a two centuries time-lag between the Eastern and Western Turks, and in geographical areas far distant from each other, affected the orthography of Eastern and Western Turkish. When the Eastern Turks became Muslim and adopted the Arabic script, they developed a many-vowelled orthography following the Uigur tradition, and this system continued in the Kara-Khanid, Khwārazm and Chaghatay periods. Since Eastern Turkish literature was not brought into Anatolia as a whole, Arabic texts with vowel-points were taken as models for the Turkish written in Anatolia in the seventh/thirteenth century, and a spelling system largely marked with vowel-points but generally few vowels was developed in the period in the succeeding two centuries.

Western Turkish literature, comprising the Āẕarī and Ottoman areas, developed in three separate branches: the *dīvān* literature that followed Persian models, intended for an *élite* with a classical *medrese* or palace-school education; mystical folk-literature or *tekke*-literature that developed as a result of the expansion of mysticism among the people and the increased impact of the religious orders; and secular folk-literature.

The *dīvān* literature meant for the higher social classes took Persian literature as a pattern from the thirteenth to the middle of the nineteenth century, and adopted some local elements. The trend of this literature, especially in language and style, until the mid-ninth/fifteenth century (or to be more exact until the period of Meḥmed the Conqueror) and its development after this date, shows an important difference. In the seventh/thirteenth and eighth/fourteenth centuries the capitals of the principalities in Anatolia, e.g. Kütahya, Kastamonu and Aydın, were centres of culture. Although the literary and artistic life was concentrated around the prince's residence, poets and writers in these small towns joined in the daily lives of the people. They were in contact with them in their homes, in the market-place, in the bazaar or in the mosque. Therefore even though they had accepted the Persian type of forms and content of the common Islamic literature, the language they used was not widely different from the spoken language of the people. To some extent the same thing can be said for the first century and a half of the Ottoman empire. The first capital, Bursa, and the second capital, Edirne, were both medium-sized provincial towns, and the courts of the first Ottoman sultans could not completely divorce the poets and the writers they patronized from the people. But all this changed after the conquest of Istanbul and the establishment of this metropolitan city as the capital of the empire. During Meḥmed the Conqueror's period, the poets of the court eventually became divorced from the people, and Arabic or Persian terms superceded Turkish, even for common and frequently used words.

In Western Turkish, the *élite* literature that began in Anatolia followed especially classical Persian verse, and worked upon the same common themes and motives. We see the products of the *mesnevī* form after the seventh/thirteenth century. These *mesnevīs* took as a subject well-known legendary love-stories, or the principles of mysticism in a symbolic way, or moral ideas, of which sometimes five were written by the same author to form a *khamsa*.

Hundreds of poets whose names are mentioned in the Ottoman biographies of poets have worked upon the same limited *mesnevī* subjects. The most favoured theme in western Turkish literature is the story of Yūsuf and Zulaykhā, which is actually taken from the Qur'ān and from the classical commentaries depending on midrashic material. Some of these *mesnevīs* are based on the simple Qur'anic story, but the majority of them have been worked upon in detail, from those in Persian literature. The theme of Laylā and Majnūn was used by some thirty poets, but the presentation by Fużūlī (d. 963/1556) much surpassed others before and after him, except Navā'ī's, and in Turkish literature this theme has become inseparable from Fużūlī's name. Husrev u-Shīrīn (or Ferhād u-Shīrīn) is one of the most popular *mesnevī* themes in Turkish. The most beautiful example of this theme was by Sheykhī at the beginning of the ninth/fifteenth century. Other themes have also been employed. A special characteristic of the *Iskender-nāme* written by Aḥmedī (d. 815/1413) is that it contains a chronicle of the earlier periods of Ottoman history.

Besides the common subjects of the classical tradition, hundreds of *mesnevīs* were written on religious, mystical, ethical, didactic and other subjects. Two religious *mesnevīs* which are read by great numbers of people up to the present day are the *Mevlit* (*Mawlid*) (812/1409) by Süleymān Chelebi of Bursa, which is about the life of the Prophet and is still read on special occasions, and the mystical *Muḥammediye* (853/1449) of Yazıjıoghlu Meḥmed Bijan.

The *dīvān* poetry employed all the forms of Persian literature, with the *qaṣīda* and the *ghazal* having prime importance. Even after a new literature started to develop under Western influence, there have still been groups and individuals who carried on the taste for *dīvān* poetry.

In *dīvān* poetry where common themes, limited motives, certain forms and clichés are dominant, great poets could only show their personalities by means of characteristics of style and the innovations they could contribute to the common material. Among these poets the most outstanding are: Nesīmī (d. 821/1418), who wrote with a great and sincere mystical emotion and was distinct from his contemporaries by his fluent style and his competence in prosody; Nejatī (d. 914/1509) who was near to the language of the people and who brought a new spirit to *dīvān* poetry; Fużūlī (d. 964/1556) who employed the concept of mystical love in a very original way, though showing loyalty to the conventions of his time, and with a deep sincerity in style and expression, a personality that grasps the reader, and the description of pain and sorrow in a most human form; Bāqī (d. 1008/1600) whose poetry was influenced by the welfare and splendour of the period of Süleymān the Magnificent and who wrote the best elegy for this sultan; Nef'ī (d. 1045/1635) the greatest representative of the eleventh/seventeenth-century Ottoman *dīvān* literature, which was influenced by the new Indo-Persian style, known as the *sabk-i Hindī*, who most successfully reconciled fine images with flowery expressions; Nābī (d. 1124/1712). who became distinguished in the symbolism of wisdom, and Nedīm (d. 1143/1730) who wished to make a real reform in *dīvān* poetry. However neither the environment in which he lived, nor the social and cultural conditions, were convenient for a radical change. In spite of this, Nedīm made many great innovations, without touching the traditional forms and clichés. He tried to change *dīvān* poetry from being abstract by putting his own environment and his period into it. Without reading Nedīm we cannot have a complete idea of the life, traditions, costumes, entertainment and personalities of the time of Aḥmed III. He put the spoken language of Istanbul into his poetry, though among it some old clichés can be found. Besides all this, he was a great poet. But the last great master of *dīvān* poetry, Ghālib Dede (d. 1214/1799), a Mevlevī leader, took a contrary direction as a result of his personal taste, tendencies, education, training and environment, though he was influenced by Nedīm in certain respects. Ghālib did not favour the language of the people, and by combining the *sabk-i Hindī* style of the eleventh/seventeenth century and especially the manner of Nā'ilī (d. 1077/1666) with his own sophistic tendencies, he preferred a style which only a very limited group of people could understand. Thus he brought the *dīvān* literature into a dead-end, despite his power as a great poet, and in a way he prepared the decline that took place in the nineteenth century.

Parallel to the *dīvān* literature, two other movements in poetry developed. One of these, popular mystical poetry, or *tekke* poetry, originated from poetry written in the popular language and in the old Turkish syllabic metre by leaders or members of religious orders propagating Sufism among the people, partly in order to gain sympathy and recognition for this movement. The second of these movements, folk-poetry or *ashık* literature, originated from poems generally also written in syllabic metre and in the popular language by illiterate or little-educated poets who came from the masses of the common people.

One of the greatest poets of all Turkish literature, according to some the greatest of all, Yūnus Emre (d. 720/1320), united these three tendencies and created a poetry in the popular language inspired by local Turkish, by mystical and by Persian classical sources; he generally used the syllabic metre. Yūnus Emre was an ardent, deeply inspired, sincere poet of genius whose life-story became woven into legends and myths. His works are preserved in comparatively late manuscripts, but many of his poems have become confused with the productions of his admirers, who took the name of Yūnus after him. He used the themes of life, religion, mysticism and death in a most effective way and had the finest command of the Turkish language. No poet of a calibre to continue his work has followed him. For many centuries Yūnus was held in veneration all over Turkey. His hymns were sung in ecstasies, and he was the greatest source of inspiration for the young poets during the period of literary revival at the beginning of the twentieth century. However after Yūnus Emre, Turkish poetry developed into the three separate branches which have already been mentioned; that is *dīvān*, *tekke* and folk-poetry.

In *tekke* poetry, Kaygusuz Abdal and Pīr Sulṭān Abdal (both of the ninth/fifteenth century) are names worth mentioning because of their great personalities and originality. Research about the lives and works of these poets is as yet only beginning.

Folk-poetry has many representatives in every century up to our time. These poets generally used the popular language and syllabic metre, but they were rarely original. Mostly they developed into formalization and clichés, and some of them even attempted to imitate the *dīvān* poets within the forms of folk-poetry. The greatest poet of this branch, Karajaoghlan (tenth/sixteenth century), is worth mentioning as one of the distinguished exceptions. His poetry, written in a lively, active, colourful style and a fluent language, describes the life of the Anatolian in his village and in the plateau, the mountains, the rivers, the country, the lakes, with all their animals, birds and trees. His works have greater literary value than any other of their kind. In folk-poetry there are also some successful examples of the epic, pastoral, elegiac, humorous and satirical kinds. Generally, these poems are recited with a musical composition written for them. Dadaloghlu (d. ? 1868), who came from the nomadic tribes living on the Taurus mountains, is the last great name to continue the tradition that came from Karajaoghlan, mainly in the epic field.

In Western Turkish literature classical prose has a very different characteristic from poetry. Though Persian examples fundamentally dominated the poetry, they exerted a very limited effect on Turkish prose, which could therefore develop as the most native and original branch of the literature. Until recent times what was meant by prose was the *inshā'* form where the aesthetics of the *dīvān* poetry and many of its arts were used. Prose other than *inshā'* started to be considered as literature only after the Tanẓīmāt, and even then only to a limited extent. Apart from this, the opinion of the literary Reformers that 'Turkish prose which was formerly pure, became gradually elaborate after the fifteenth century and did not tend towards purity before the nineteenth century' has lasted down to our times, though it is not correct. Actually, this prose developed in three parallel categories, from the beginning to the Tanẓīmāt period.

The first is pure prose based on the popular spoken language; although *inshā'* affected this kind of prose in various degrees. After the seventh/thirteenth century, it included commentaries on the Qur'ān enlarged with popular stories, *Ḥadīth* and Islamic legend. The Dede Korkut stories are believed to have been written down in the ninth/fifteenth century in the present form, but are considered to be remains of the lost Oghuz epics, and form the most original example of Turkish epic literature. Popular religious epics, inspired by the legends of the period of conquest and islamization of Anatolia, accounts of Ottoman campaigns written in an epic way, histories of the House of 'Os̱mān, some anonymous, and books on ethics and politics, were also written in this pure prose. One may also mention in this category *Mir'āt al-mamālik* by Seayyidī 'Alī Re'īs, which relates his travels; ten volumes of *Seyāhat-nāme*, an endless treasury of information, written in a colourful style by Evliya Chelebi, the greatest traveller of the eleventh/seventeenth century; an Ottoman history known as *Feẕleke* by Kātib Chelebi, a scholar of a very progressive mind for his time, together with his various essays on current controversial problems or containing his proposals for reform within the empire; the histories of Pechevi (1059/1649) and Silaḥdār Meḥmed (1136/1723) which describe their own times, written realistically and with very vivid scenes; and finally, hundreds of works in this prose style ending with short stories by Giritli 'Alī 'Azīz (d. 1798) making a bridge between the old popular stories and the modern novel.

The second category is ornamented prose (*inshā'*). This is where a word from the Arabic or Persian vocabularies was taken at random and used according to the grammatical rules of either language, with Turkish words given an unimportant place; many of the verbal tricks of *dīvān* literature were adopted, and rhymed prose regarded as fundamental. Although literature in prose was in general unaffected by the divorce from popular speech which affected poetry, in some small circles *inshā'* still continued as an artificial prose language with the purpose of differentiating it completely from the popular language and showing off the writers' skill. Mainly the *Tevārīkh-i Āl-i 'Os̲mān* by Kemāl Pasha-zāde (941/1531), the well-known *shaykh al-Islām* of Selīm I and also a great scholar and historian, the *Tājal-Tevārīkh*, by Sa'd al-Dīn, a leading *shaykh al-Islām* at the end of the tenth/sixteenth century, also some biographies of poets and some official and private collections of letters have followed this ornamented style of prose. Two classical representatives of this artificial prose carried it to an extreme, Veysī (d. 1037/1628), who wrote a biography of the Prophet and Nergisī (d. 1045/1635), who wrote the only prose *khamsa*. The work of Sinān Pasha, the great prose-writer of the ninth/fifteenth century, is generally classified as *inshā'*, although it actually only resembles this form because of its rhymed prose and symmetry. Otherwise its language is generally pure.

The third category is middle prose, where the popular spoken language was left far behind, but, the desire to show off the writer's skill by mere verbal tricks was not the goal, since he was mainly concerned with what he wanted to relate. The ratio of foreign and compound words varies from one writer to another, and some even show an interest in rhymed prose. In all forms of the old literature, this middle prose preponderates. It includes many of the histories, for instance those of Selānīkī (d. 1009/1600), Gelibolulu 'Alī (d. 1009/1600), and Na'īmā (d. 1129/1716), the last a masterful compilation and one of the most vivid in Ottoman prose, an important source for the eleventh/seventeenth century although the original of the book is lost. A large part of the official correspondence and journals, memorials of reform presented to the sultan, reports of ambassadors, the most colourful and interesting of which is the *Sefāret-nāme* of Yirmisekiz Meḥmed Chelebi, who died in 1145/1732, and some books on ethics and politics, were all written in middle prose.

The political and administrative reform movement known as the Tanẓīmāt, which begin in 1839, had also some effect on literature after

1850. The leader of this movement, called the Tanẓīmāt literature, was Ibrāhīm Shināsī (1821–71), who was educated in Paris. On his return to Turkey he brought back a completely new literary understanding. He made translations of poems from a Western language, French, for the first time. He introduced new concepts in the poems, which he wrote in the old style. He discussed the fatherland, the country, the people and the state, instead of the age-old clichés. He established the first private newspaper. He wrote the first Turkish play, and influenced his environment by his articles and speeches. The modernist spirit that he established with Namıq Kemāl (1840–88) and Żiyā Pasha (1825–80) developed a literature under the influence of the eighteenth-century French writers and the nineteenth-century Romantic poets, who were close to the public and opposed to despotism. After ʿAbd ül-Ḥaqq Ḥāmid (1852–1937) joined this group, the taste for *dīvān* literature was almost completely eliminated, in spite of intense resistance and the forms of Western literature were gradually applied to Turkish. The literary movement started by the *S̲ervet-i Fünūn* journal run by Tevfīq Fikret (1867–1915), Jenāb Shihāb al-Dīn (1870–1934) and Khālid Żiyā Uşaklıgil (1866–1945), who came together at the end of the century, saved the Turkish literature from the effects of Persian culture and created a fully Western (French) literature, although it delayed the formation of a native Turkish literature in Western forms and concepts, which was the real ultimate goal. The three leaders, of which the first was a poet, the second a poet and a prose-writer, and the third a novelist believed in the principle of art for art's sake. They preferred to be read and understood by a very small number of intellectuals rather than come down to the public. By carrying out a complete reaction in the language they created a sort of literary jargon consisting of rarely used words from Arabic and Persian. The literature that had been saved from the influence of Persian culture became a perfect imitation of French literature, again in a language which the public did not understand. Writers such as Aḥmed Midḥat (1844–1912) Aḥmed Rāsim (1864–1932), Ḥüseyin Raḥmī (1864–1944), and poets like Meḥmed Emīn (1869–1944) and Riżā Tevfīq (1869–1949), whose subjects as well as language were close to and addressed to the public, preferred to stay outside the *S̲ervet-i Fünun* movement. Though these writers and poets were underrated by their contemporaries, they established the foundations of a truly native Turkish literature which started in 1910 and obtained its full form and direction after 1930.

URDU LITERATURE

Urdu is the language spoken by the Muslims and by certain non-Muslim elements in the urban areas of West Pakistan and north-western India. It is the chief literary language of the Muslims of the subcontinent. The name 'Urdu' is of Turkish origin, familiarized in Persian by the Il-Khanid historians, and adopted in India by the Sayyid ruler Khiżr Khān (817–24/1414–21) for his army and court under Timurid influence. During the reign of the Great Mughals in India it came to be applied generally to the imperial camp, and during the late eleventh/seventeenth century to the language the camp spoke.

The language itself and its earlier regional literatures are much older than its present name. From the thirteenth to the eighteenth century it was referred to as 'Hindawī' or 'Hindī' or given dialectal names, 'Dakhanī' and 'Gujarātī'. This is rather confusing as its philological and literary growth remained quite distinct from the languages known today as Hindī or Gujarātī.

It is descended from one or more dialects of the Indo-Aryan Śawraseni Prākrit. It was evolved by the Indian Muslims for communication with Hindu fellow-citizens in town and country, and for use in the harems in which were Hindu women as wives, concubines or domestics.

The origins of Urdu date back to the period of Ghaznavid rule in the Panjāb in the sixth/twelfth century. The Muslims wrote it in Persian script. While they retained much of its grammatical structure and essential verbs, adjectives and adverbs, unrestrained borrowings from Persian, and through Persian from Arabic and to some extent Turkish, gave it a pronounced Muslim linguistic and literary character.

Its centre of gravity shifted to Delhi in the seventh/thirteenth century with the establishment of the Sultanate. Under the Khaljīs it was carried by Muslim armies to the Deccan and Gujarāt, where it developed a literary character earlier than in northern India. But it is quite possible that the first experimental literary use of the new language was made in the Ghaznavid Panjāb.

In Delhi from the seventh/thirteenth to the tenth/sixteenth century its literary use appears to have been whimsical and half-serious. Most of the pre-Urdu (Hindawī) work attributed to Amīr Khusraw (651–725/1253–1325) has now been demonstrated to be of apocryphal origin, written much later, possibly in the eleventh/seventeenth century.[1]

[1] Maḥmūd Shērānī, *Punjāb men Urdū* (Lahore, 1928), 128–43.

The only Urdu verses which can be attributed to Khusraw with any certainty are the few he has himself quoted in the introduction to one of his Persian *dīwāns*. These are couplets, half-Persian, half in a 'double' language which could be read either as Persian or Urdu, with a *double entendre*, serving as bantering *jeux d'esprit* written for the amusement of his friends. In this tradition a single bilingual couplet, a quarter Turkish, three-quarters Urdu, is also found in the *Dīwān* of Bābur, reflecting throughout these centuries the arrested growth of Urdu's potentialities as a literary language in the north.

The breakthrough towards the development of Urdu for literary purposes was made during these very centuries, away from the northern court, in the Ṣūfī hospices of outlying provinces. The Ṣūfī shaykhs, engaged in the dual task of converting the non-Muslims around them, and of evolving a technique of religious communication with their ill-educated disciples, used an early form of Urdu for their popular writings, reserving the use of Persian more and more for learned dialectics. The treatise *Mi'rāj al-'āshiqīn* of Sayyid Muḥammad 'Gēsūdarāz' (*c.* 750/1350) is generally considered to be the first prose work in Urdu. Mīrāñjī Shams al-'Ushshāq established Urdu as a recognized medium of Ṣūfī narrative verse. These Ṣūfīs freely transplanted Persian and Arabic religious vocabulary and forms of thought and experience into Urdu.

In the courts of Golkondā and Bījāpur in the Deccan, secular literature developed in the Dakhanī (southern) dialect. Sultan Muḥammad Qulī Quṭb Shāh (989–1020/1581–1611) of Golkondā, founder of the city of Ḥaydarābād, was himself a refined poet who grafted local Dravadian and Hindī loan words on the persianized texture of his Urdu verses with a spontaneous and instinctive artistry. He is one of the rare exceptions among Urdu poets, who chose to write intensely of Indian life and love. Among the luminaries of the Golkondā court was Mullā Wajhī, whose prose allegory *Sab ras* (1635) was a free rendering of Fattāḥī's (d. 852/1448) Persian poem *Dastūr-i 'ushshāq*, an allegory of love which contains interesting parallelisms with the *Roman de la rose*. In the court of Bījāpur, Nuṣratī (*c.* 1060/1650) bestowed a classical maturity upon the Urdu *ghazal*, and gave to the *mathnawī* a remarkable resilience as the vehicle of fabled story or contemporary epic.

In choice of material, as in the cultivation of a poetic diction, the literature of these courts showed an uninhibited exuberance, a momentum of development, and a freedom from the obligations of established tradition. Without fear of the loss of cultural identity, elements were borrowed from Hindu *milieux* and diction;[1] a process which seems to have been halted with Awrangzēb's occupation of these southern Muslim states in the second half of the eleventh/seventeenth century, and with the impact of the highly persianized and islamized *Urdū-i muʿallā*, the 'exalted' (Urdu) language of the imperial camp, on the poet and the intellectual of the Deccan. But the 'exalted' Urdu brought by the Mughal army from the north was only a spoken medium. Its refinements were conversational and social. Inhibited in the north by the undisputed sway of Persian, it had not yet bloomed into literary creativity. With Awrangzēb's conquest of the Deccan the two dialectal growths of Urdu, the literary but demotic southern, and the polished but uncreative northern, interfused. The south accepted the northern norms of persianized sophistication; the north was quickened by the precedent and example of the southern literary genius.

This cultural exchange[2] took place towards the close of the eleventh/seventeenth and the beginning of the twelfth/eighteenth century at Awrangābād, Awrangzēb's secondary capital in the Deccan. Walī (1668–1744), the chief representative of this new school, has two styles, an earlier southern and a later northern. He visited Delhi twice, in 1700 and in 1722, where by then the tradition of Indo-Persian poetry had lost most of its creative activity, as the arrival of fresh talent from Persia had ceased after the embitterment of Mughal-Safavid relations during the reign of Awrangzēb. In this inspirational vacuum, Walī's example almost overnight switched the northern desire for poetic expression from Persian to Urdu. But the north preserved its centuries-old Persian heritage almost intact in Urdu.

The School of Delhi rose in the early twelfth/eighteenth century under very inhospitable circumstances. The Mughal capital was sacked many times by invaders from outside, such as Nādir Shāh and Aḥmad Shāh Durrānī, and by the barbaric indigenous hordes of Jāts and Marāthās. This school shows all the sensitivity of individual and social suffering, and all the fortitude of an almost other-worldly composure. Two of its early representatives, Mīrzā Maẓhar Jān-i Jānān and Khwāja Mīr Dard (1720–84), were venerated Ṣūfīs who impregnated Urdu verse with the sublimation of pained love and resignation. The social disorganization of Delhi and the disintegration of human personality contributed to mould the delicately sensitive and intensely poetic

[1] Rām Bābū Saksena, *A history of Urdu literature* (Allahabad, 1940), 32–44.
[2] Aziz Ahmad, *Studies in Islamic culture in the Indian environment*, 251–2.

genius of Mīr Taqī Mir (1724–1808). His contemporary Mirzā Rafī Sawdā (1717–80) reacted to the surrounding chaos and the general decadence of men and morals with fierce invective in his satires.

These two poets, and several others, migrated from insecure Delhi to Lucknow where the nawabs of Awadh (Oudh) patronized a brilliantly degenerate court. Here the foundations of the School of Lucknow were laid.

The decadence of the Court of Lucknow was not uncreative. A comparative security under the indirect protection of the East India Company gave its social life a semblance of stability, and its *élite* the leisure to cultivate a taste for music, and for the witty, the droll and the banal in poetry, and to appreciate conceit, word play and verbal jugglery. Emigrés from Delhi, like Inshā' (1757–1817), soon fell under the spell of Lucknow; though his contemporary Muṣḥafī (1750–1824) maintained a sedate sensitiveness with a strain of asceticism. Inshā' and one of his friends, Rangīn, experimented in the invention of *Rīkhtī*, a frivolous, but linguistically most valuable genre of verse which used the segregated colloquial vocabulary of women of pleasure. *Rīkhtī* reached its culmination in the effeminate work of Jān Sāḥib (d. 1897).

The School of Lucknow had its redeeming features. Nāsikh (d. 1838) effectively 'purified' the Urdu poetic diction; and presumably as a reaction to the influx of demotic and effeminate expressions in Urdu verse, standardized the idiom and vocabulary of poetry by a ruthless and unimaginative process of linguistic elimination which deprived it of much of its indigenous heritage. His contemporary, Ātish (1778–1846), occasionally rose to heights of true inspiration from a morass of conventional bathos. In the last years of the Shīʿī state of Awadh a great school of martyrological verse arose, and bloomed in the passionate fervour of Anīs.

In 1765 Shāh ʿĀlam, the nominal Mughal emperor of Delhi, appointed the British East India Company his revenue collector. In practice he thus became a pensioner of the Company, his effective régime confined to the four walls of the Red Fort. But this gave the much-tormented Delhi some respite. Here, under him and his successors, the second School of Delhi achieved a dignified style in the panegyrics of Ẕawq (1789–1854) and in the crystal-clear subjective lyricism of Mū'min (1800–51). In this milieu wrote Asad Allāh Khān Gḥālib (1796–1869), the greatest of Urdu poets, moulding emotional verities into concrete image-symbols, balancing the magnitude of his structural intellectuality with tantalizing wit, adding nuance to nuance in externalizing the emotionally intricate, giving the inner content of his verse an unprecedented dimension by a fusion of fancy and feeling. He made any further use of conventional verse seem absurd, and pointed the way to the new intellectual styles which were ushered in by the deadly impact of the events of 1857.

Until the beginning of the nineteenth century, Urdu prose had consisted either of theological literature with an arabicized syntax or of ornate magical romances. The administration of the East India Company was, on the other hand, in pressing need of a simpler vernacular for use at the lower levels of administration. This policy was implemented by John Gilchrist at the Fort William College (founded in 1800) at Calcutta. There he guided his literary employees towards evolving a direct, fluent, almost utilitarian, prose style.

The need for a simpler style was being generally felt and there were other experiments in that direction, chiefly Ghālib's colloquially eloquent letters. Finally, all these elements converged on the genius of Sayyid Aḥmad Khān (1817–98), who elevated Urdu prose to the point of scientific precision of expression, and used it as a vehicle for historical and theological scholarship and for advanced journalism. He and his associates of the ʿAlīgarh Movement raised Urdu in expression and richness of content to a rank equal to other great Islamic languages. In acceptance and transmission of Western ideas Urdu outpaced them. Shiblī Nuʿmānī (1857–1914) shares with Zakā Allāh (d. 1910) the credit of forging a methodology of historiography which was to some extent a synthesis of the Islamic and Western disciplines. Shiblī is also the author of a monumental history of Persian literature, the *Shiʿr al-ʿAjam*, which grafts modern chronological method on the classical *taẕkira* technique. Naẕīr Aḥmad developed the didactic *qiṣṣa* (story) to the artistic level of the modern novel. Alṭāf Ḥusayn Ḥālī (1837–1914), as great a prose-writer as he was a poet, established norms of intellectual criticism in his literary biographies and his Prolegomena on poetry. Muḥammad Ḥusayn Āzād (1834–1910), the only great prose-writer of the age who was almost entirely unconnected with Sayyid Aḥmad Khān's movement, was stylistically, though not as a theorist of poetry, the antithesis of Ḥālī, and wrote in an ornately beautiful style with a fascinating gift for telling an anecdote.

The Mutiny of 1857, its failure, and the liquidation of Muslim supremacy in Delhi, mark a sudden revolution in Urdu poetry. So far the

Urdu *ghazal* had blinded itself to its own geographical and ethical environment. Like its model, Persian, it had used a mathematics of imagery and convention, occasionally corresponding to the nuance of an individual emotional experience, but more often multiplying into infinite combinations of verbal arabesques, symbols of Persian heritage, that were accepted and manipulated, but not actually experienced. As Ḥālī, under the inspiration of Sayyid Aḥmad Khān, broke away from this classical pattern, he made a novel use of much of its familiar didacticism and its wealth of phrase and image in the construction of his forceful and profoundly stirring poem of Islamic revivalism, the *Musaddas*, which marks the rise of the political poem in Urdu as a powerful weapon of religio-political agitation.

Ḥālī thus paved the way for the emergence of Muḥammad Iqbāl (1873–1938), by far the most influential of Urdu poets and the most dynamic intellectual personality in the recent history of Islam in the sub-continent. His popularity began with his early nationalist poems written before 1905; during his pan-Islamic phase which followed he achieved poetic greatness. But for the formulation of his philosophical ideas and for their dissemination more widely in the *dār al-Islām* he turned to Persian. It is principally in his Persian poems that he formulated his doctrine of Self, its relation to society, and the ideal role of both the individual and society in a process of creative evolution, through the values of power and movement, in the ultimate quest of a co-existent association with the Infinite Reality that is God. In 1933 he returned to Urdu again and developed a new style, less lyrical, but of unprecedented intellectual forcefulness. To this period belong some of his finest poetic achievements such as the explosively resplendent imagery of his *Masjid-i Qurṭuba* ('Mosque of Cordova') in which he outlines the metaphysical eternity of artistic creation.

Since Iqbāl, Urdu poetry has produced some lesser luminaries, sensitive writers of the *ghazal* like Ḥasrat and Jigar, exuberantly demotic revolutionaries like Josh, and among younger poets Fayż Aḥmad Fayż, who won the Lenin Prize in 1962. Fayż has evolved for himself a technique of cryptic impregnation of the familiar image with a newer significance occasionally producing a highly artistic political *double entendre* which evades all censorship.

The development of Urdu prose since Ḥālī has been extensive rather than intensive. It has continued to borrow fresh vocabulary from English and Arabic; it has translated concepts and popularized them; it has tried to be the vehicle of modern sciences; it is the source of expression and of momentum to extensive journalistic venture.

Urdu fiction had begun in the later eighteenth century with the *dāstāns* of the Amīr Ḥamza cycle. These were voluminous, labyrinthine magical romances peopled with heroes, *'ayyārs* (*tricheurs*) and demons making and breaking enchanted cities in monotonously identical exploits. At Fort William College Mīr Amman dissolved this technique and *métier* to the simpler preternatural story of the familiar Arabian Nights type in his *Bāgh u-bahār*. European influences came to be established in the didactic novel of Naẓīr Aḥmad in the later nineteenth century. The Hindu mind, more expert in visualizing a three-dimensional human character than the iconoclastic Muslim mind, made a significant contribution to the growth of the Urdu novel in the works of Sarshār and Prem Chand, who placed it firmly in the many-faced Indian milieu. The Muslim historical novel in the hands of 'Abd al-Ḥalīm Sharar romanticized the Muslim past in stereotyped colour and imagery and rather cheap sentimentality. It was in the vindication of the 'noble courtesan' that the Muslim Urdu novel showed a certain lyrical realism in the work of Mirzā Ruswā and Qāżī 'Abd al-Ghaffār. From 1935 the leftist 'Progressive Movement' ushered in the down-to-earth naturalistic short story of exquisite realism. Compared to the short story, the contemporary Urdu novel has so far been of a secondary stature.

Since the partition of the subcontinent in 1947, the emphasis of Muslim writing in Pakistan as well as in India has been overwhelmingly religious. In Pakistan, Abu'l-'Alā' Mawdūdī has a lucid and torrentially eloquent style. The style of Ghulām Aḥmad Parwīz has an element of intellectual persuasion. In Pakistan as in India hagiology is being welded into recent Indo-Muslim history, though with a different distribution of emphasis from divergent political angles. In Abu'l-Kalām Āzād's highly arabicized style, and in his intellectual proximity to Egyptian Islamic modernism, a beginning was made towards a closer understanding of Islamic thought in other parts of the Muslim world. This movement has gathered a certain momentum in Pakistan. Publishers' catalogues in Pakistan reflect a wide fluctuation in the book market, and a growing demand for classical and contemporary Islamic literature at the expense of fiction and *belles lettres*.

CHAPTER 9

ART AND ARCHITECTURE

PRIMITIVE ISLAM

The proper usage of the collective name 'Islamic art' has been seriously questioned by a number of scholars during the past two or three decades. As alternatives 'Arab art', 'Persian art', 'Turkish art' have been suggested. Others have even gone as far as denying any common ground or characteristics in this art, and claimed that it should be simply named after the respective country where the monuments stand or where particular art objects were produced. It seems desirable, therefore, before describing the achievements of Islamic art, to answer these critics; to define, as far as is possible, the common characteristics of Islamic art, to reveal its sources and to throw some light upon the foreign influences which contributed to its evolution.

It is a well-known and accepted fact that the Arabs had hardly anything which could be called art when they set out to invade the territories in the north. There was a highly developed architecture in southern Arabia well before the advent of Islam, but that had hardly anything to do with those primitive tribesmen who were united under Islam, and who constituted the backbone of its victorious army. Neither had the Prophet any intention of giving an impetus to a religious art. Indeed, we cannot talk about Islamic art in a religious sense, as we can talk about Christian or Buddhist art.

It was the helping hand of highly skilled craftsmen and artists of the conquered territories which provided the resources needed to erect and adorn the earliest religious and secular buildings of Islam. The effect of these cultures—Byzantine, Coptic, Sasanian and later on Central Asian—can be clearly recognized and distinguished in the early period. Thus we cannot speak of an Islamic style during the first one or two centuries of the *Hijra*. From the amalgamation of these foreign elements, which can be regarded as the sources of this new type of art, was born a new style which made its imprint on art and architecture throughout the Islamic world. The late Sir Thomas Arnold formulated the concept of Islamic art—or, as he called it, 'Muhammadan art'—in the following way: 'By the term "Muhammadan art" is meant those works of art which were produced under Muhammadan patronage and in Muhammadan countries; the artists themselves were of diverse nationalities and were not always adherents of the faith of Islam'.[1]

No monument has survived from the earliest period of Islam. The earliest mosques, such as the Prophet's mosque at Medina, or those of Kūfa and Baṣra, were primitive structures, erected of perishable material. The Prophet, it seems, had no intention of erecting temples for daily prayer. Yet his house in Medina soon became a public building, a gathering place for Muslims and later a *masjid*, a mosque. A detailed description of his house is preserved by Ibn Sa'd. It was a primitive structure with a central court surrounded by mud-brick walls. It had a roofed portico on the north side, the roof being supported by palm trunks. There were also small huts attached to it on the east side which served as dwelling places for the Prophet's wives.

In the first two years of the *Hijra* the *qibla* or direction of prayer was on the north side of the building, that is towards Jerusalem; but after a sudden revelation the Prophet changed it towards the Ka'ba in Mecca. Orientation of prayer or *qibla* was an accepted custom in many religions, but was particularly important among the Semitic people. In Islam the *qibla* is marked by the *miḥrāb*, which is usually a niche placed in the centre of the *qibla* wall. The *miḥrāb* in niche form was first erected in Medina, when they rebuilt the Prophet's mosque in 88/706–7. Before that it was indicated by a strip of paint on the *qibla* wall or a block of stone placed in the centre.

There was also a simple pulpit or *minbar* in Medina, which was later on generally accepted in Islam. Another important feature of the sanctuary, introduced by the first Umayyad caliph, Mu'āwiya, was the *maqṣūra*, a place reserved for the caliph and surrounded by a wooden screen.

Three more mosques had been erected during the reign of the Patriarchal Caliphs. The first was at Baṣra in 14/635 and the second at Kūfa in 17/638. The third mosque was built by 'Amr b. al-'Āṣ, the conqueror of Egypt, at Fusṭāṭ in 21–2/641–2. Historians also gave account of an early mosque in Jerusalem, built by the Caliph 'Umar in 16/637. All these mosques were again primitive buildings, following generally the plan of the Prophet's mosque at Medina.

THE UMAYYAD PERIOD

It was under the Umayyad Caliph 'Abd al-Malik (65–86/685–705) that the first surviving monument of Islam was erected. It is the Qubbat

[1] *Painting in Islam* (Oxford, 1928), n. 1.

al-Ṣakhra, the Dome of the Rock in Jerusalem. It was built above the Holy Rock where David's altar stood and from where, according to legend, the Prophet made his famous night journey to heaven.

The building is an octagonal structure surrounding the rock. Above there is a huge wooden dome resting on a high drum supported by four piers and twelve columns. Between this colonnade and the outer walls is an intermediate octagon supporting the sloping roof of the building. The outer walls are decorated by eight large bays on each side. Five of these bays have been pierced by windows. The upper part of the walls was coated by faience tiles in the early tenth/sixteenth century. There are four doors in the building facing the four cardinal points. Below the rock there is a small chamber with two small *miḥrābs*.

The decoration inside the arcades and of the drum consists of beautiful glass mosaics, most of which are original. These mosaics display fruits, vine and acanthus scrolls and trees, some of them adorned with jewels. They also include a Kufic inscription giving the date of completion as 72/691. The mosaics reveal both Byzantine and Sasanian influences. They were most likely made by Syrian mosaicists, as there was a famous school in Syria in pre-Islamic times.

ʿAbd al-Malik had a number of reasons, mainly political, for erecting such a splendid mosque for Islam. First of all the new faith had to compete with the beauty of Christian churches in Jerusalem, such as the Holy Sepulchre, which it seemed to imitate. Also he had a rival caliph, Ibn al-Zubayr in Mecca. For this reason he wanted to prevent pilgrims from visiting Mecca. That would explain the unusual plan of the building which makes possible a circumambulation of the holy rock, just as Muslims circumambulate the Kaʿba.

Ibn Taghrī-Birdī mentions that ʿAbd al-Malik even had the intention of turning the *qibla* back from Mecca to Jerusalem.[1] Al-Ḥajjāj's contemporary mosque at Wāsiṭ certainly supports that surmise. Archaeologists, when searching for his mosque and palace, found four different mosques one above the other. The upper three buildings were properly oriented towards Mecca, but the lowest mosque with al-Ḥajjāj's palace attached to it, had a deviation of 34 degrees towards the west. A second mosque, that of Isqaf Banī Junayd, a little north of Baghdād, also attributed to al-Ḥajjāj, had almost the same deviation.[2]

Another important mosque, the Great or Umayyad Mosque in

[1] Ibn Taghrī-Birdī, *al-Nujūm al-ẓāhira*, I, 71.

[2] Verbal information given by my Iraqi colleague, Dr ʿAbdul ʿAzīz Ḥamīd.

Damascus, was erected by the Caliph al-Walīd, son of ʿAbd al-Malik. This huge rectangular building was originally a pagan temple, dedicated to Jupiter. Later it was converted to a Christian church. After the Arab conquest of Damascus the building was jointly used by Muslims and Christians. When Damascus became the capital of the Umayyad empire, and the number of Muslims greatly increased in the city, the entire building was taken over from the Christians. That was in 86/705 when al-Walīd succeeded his father as caliph.

Al-Walīd ordered a complete reconstruction of the building. They demolished the inside walls but left the enclosure walls intact, except that the three main entrances on the south side were walled up and new ones were opened on the north. The original building had a tower at each corner; these were also left untouched and served as the first minarets in Islam. Of these four minarets only one, over the south-west corner, survives today. The minaret over the northern entrance is much later, probably as late as the sixth/twelfth century.

Internally, the courtyard (*ṣaḥn*), is surrounded by porticoes on three sides and by the impressive façade of the sanctuary on the south side. The sanctuary has three aisles running parallel to the *qibla* wall, with a trancept in the centre. There are four semicircular *miḥrābs* in the *qibla* wall. One of them, in the centre of the eastern half of this wall, is known as 'the *miḥrāb* of the Companions of the Prophet'; it is the second concave *miḥrāb* in Islam. The other three are later in date.

The walls of the mosque were decorated with mosaics, parts of which are still preserved. These mosaics, in contrast to those of the Dome of the Rock, display not only floral designs, but mainly architectural elements. The walls of the western portico, which were whitewashed at a later date, revealed the most beautiful mosaic panel, known to scholars as the 'Baradā panel' after the river which flows through Damascus. It represents contemporary Damascus with its palaces and houses and the villages of the Green Valley [pl. l(*a*)].

Umayyad architecture, however, was not confined to religious buildings. The Umayyad caliphs longed for the open spaces of the desert, and therefore erected richly decorated palaces and baths in the Jordanian and Syrian steppe. Several of these buildings have been discovered and excavated during the last sixty years. One of the most impressive, and probably the earliest of them all, is Mshattā, some forty miles south of ʿAmmān. For a long time it was considered a pre-Islamic building. Its Umayyad origin, however, has now been firmly established: a semicircular *miḥrāb* was found in the southern part of the building, and a few years later, during the course of excavations by the Jordanian Department of Antiquities, Kufic inscriptions and an Umayyad coin were found.

Mshattā is a square walled enclosure (473 feet, 144 metres) with semicircular intermediate towers on each side and two octagonal ones flanking the gateway on the south side. Internally the enclosure is divided into three tracts, the central ones being somewhat wider than the outer ones. Work was never completed in Mshattā, with the exception of the northern, or palace part of the central tract. Here there was a large hall ending in three apsidal recesses and probably covered by a dome [pl. 1(*b*)].

The outer face of the enclosure wall on the south was richly carved. The design is mainly based on vine and acanthus scrolls enclosing birds and lions. Most of this decorated façade is now in the East Berlin Museum.

The small bath of Quṣayr ʿAmra, about fifty miles east of ʿAmmān, was attributed to the Caliph al-Walīd [pl. 2(*a*)]. Recent research, however, points to a somewhat later date. The building is composed of a large audience hall with an entrance on its northern side, and a small alcove opposite. The alcove is flanked by two small apsidal rooms on either side. There are two more small rooms attached to the audience hall on the eastern side, continued by a third, domed room which has apsidal recesses.

The building is particularly famous for its frescoes. The frescoes were unfortunately damaged during the last fifty years, but they were copied by an Austrian painter at the beginning of this century.[1] There are in particular, two frescoes which assist us in dating this structure. The first painting is that of an enthroned monarch on the back wall of the little alcove [pl. 2(*b*)]. It has a Kufic inscription which refers to a prince, probably the owner of the building. The second painting represents six kings with four inscriptions underneath in Arabic and Greek. The inscriptions identify the first four figures as those of the Byzantine emperor, the Visigothic king of Spain, the emperor of Persia and the negus of Abyssinia.

The largest and probably the most beautiful Umayyad palace is Khirbat al-Mafjar in Jericho. The vast enclosure includes a number of buildings. The palace areas surround the square courtyard with a monumental entrance on its eastern side. The decoration consisted of richly

[1] *Kuṣejr ʿAmra*, Kaiserliche Akademie der Wissenschaften (Vienna, 1907), 2 vols.

carved stones and stuccoes, but fragments of fresco paintings were also discovered. North of the palace, the excavators discovered a huge bath which was covered with a dome. The floors were covered with mosaics, revealing some unusual designs [pl. 3(*a*)]. Recent excavations by the Department of Antiquities behind the bath uncovered workshops and storerooms, which may prove that Khirbat al-Mafjar was not only a palace, but an Umayyad town, just as ʿAnjarr in Lebanon.

There are two great palaces in the Syrian desert, both attributed to the Caliph Hishām (105–25/724–43), Qaṣr al-Ḥayr al-Sharqī, north-east, and Qaṣr al-Ḥayr al-Gharbī, south-west of Palmyra. In the latter building two frescoes were discovered by the excavators, one of them revealing western, the other Sasanian influences. Excavation in Qaṣr al-Ḥayr al-Sharqī is in progress.

The Caliph Marwān II (127–32/744–50) moved his capital from Damascus to Ḥarrān in northern Mesopotamia (today in southern Turkey). Very little is known about his buildings in Ḥarrān, but the minaret of the Great Mosque may date from that period.

Finally, a small marble *miḥrāb* should be mentioned, which is at present in the Archaeological Museum in Baghdād. It is called the 'Khāṣṣakī *miḥrāb*', because it was found in a mosque bearing that name. Until quite recently it was considered to be an early ʿAbbasid work. The *repertoire* of its decoration, however, rather suggests an Umayyad date and a Syrian origin.

Very little is known about the decorative arts of the Umayyad period. Potteries which were found in the Umayyad palaces were either plain coarse kitchen utensils, or reddish-brown painted unglazed wares. No glazed pottery is known from that period. A metal object, a ewer, should be mentioned here as it is connected with the name of the Caliph Marwān II [pl. 3(*b*)]. It was found with other metal objects near Marwān's tomb in the Fayyūm area in Egypt. The ewer has a globular body with a high tubular neck ending in a pierced decoration, and has a spout in the form of a cock and an elaborate handle. The body has engraved decoration consisting of a row of arches with rosettes and animals. The ewer was definitely made in Persia, and like all other early Islamic metalwork reveals a strong Sasanian influence.

EARLY ʿABBASIDS AND TULUNIDS

The Umayyad dynasty was otherthrown by the ʿAbbasids in the year 132/750. The second ʿAbbasid caliph, al-Manṣūr (136–58/754–75) founded the new capital, Baghdād, on the River Tigris. Nothing has survived of al-Manṣūr's city, as it was destroyed by the Mongols in 656/1258, and modern Baghdād was built upon the ruins. For this reason, excavations are hardly possible. However, we have quite a considerable amount of information from contemporary sources of its ground plan.

It was a round city, enclosed by two parallel walls made of mud bricks. There were four gateways in the walls, roughly facing the four cardinal points: the Baṣra Gate on the south, the Kūfa Gate on the west, the Syrian Gate on the north and the Khurāsān Gate on the east. In the centre of the city stood the caliph's palace, called the Palace of the Green Dome. The Great Mosque was attached to the palace on the south side. It was a simple structure. Later it was enlarged and decorated by Hārūn al-Rashīd (170–93/786–809) and al-Muʿtaḍid (279–89/892–902). The construction of the city was completed by 149/766.

Some 120 miles south-west of Baghdād and roughly thirty miles from Karbalā' lies the fortified rectangular enclosure of Ukhayḍir [pl. 4(*a*)]. It has a gateway on all four sides and ten intermediate half-round towers. In the northern half of the enclosure is the palace area connected with the main entrance. In the centre is the court of honour, flanked by living quarters on each side. There is a small mosque in the western part of the enclosure, which has a small rectangular *miḥrāb*. In the corners of the enclosure are staircases leading up to the gallery on the second floor, which runs right round. The exact date of the building is not yet known, but it is believed to be of the third quarter of the eighth Christian century.

From about the same period dates the earliest surviving mosque of Persia, the Tārī Khāna in Dāmghān. Because of its ground-plan and exceptionally large bricks it was formerly considered to be a Sasanian building. The plan is quite simple: a rectangular enclosure surrounded by a single arcade on three sides and a sanctuary three aisles deep on the fourth. The original *miḥrāb* had a rectangular form, as *miḥrābs* usually have in Persia. At present it has an oblique form, since it had to be stilted so as to correct the *qibla* direction. There is no sign of any decoration in the building. A trial excavation which was made in the middle of the courtyard proved that the building is entirely a Muslim construction.[1]

[1] Erich F. Schmidt, *Excavations at Tepe Hissar, Damghan* (Philadelphia, 1937), 12–16.

1 (*a*) Damascus, the Great or Umayyad Mosque, the so-called '*Baradā*' mosaic panel under the western portico.

(*b*) The Umayyad palace of Mshattā: audience hall with the triple apse.

(*Facing page 708*)

2 (*a*) Quṣayr ʿAmra, view from the north.

(*b*) Quṣayr ʿAmra, painting of the enthroned monarch in the alcove.

3 (*a*) Jericho, Khirbat al-Mafjar, mosaic floor in the bath.

(*b*) Ewer of the Umayyad Caliph Marwān II,
Persian, second/eighth century.

4 (*a*) Ukhayḍir, the eastern gateway, looking from the north.

(*b*) Sāmarrā, the Jawsaq al-Khāqānī palace, the Bāb al-ʿĀmma (221/836).

(*b*) Sāmarrā, Jawsaq al-Khāqānī palace, wall fresco representing dancing girls from the harem.

5 (*a*) Sāmarrā, stucco panel from a recently excavated private house.

(*c*) Sāmarrā, the Great Mosque with the Malwiyya.

6 (*a*) Beaker, splashed and mottled ware, Mesopotamia, third/ninth century.

(*b*) Large dish, tin-glazed cobalt blue painted ware, Mesopotamia, third/ninth century.

(*c*) Small bowl painted in polychrome lustre, Mesopotamia, third/ninth century.

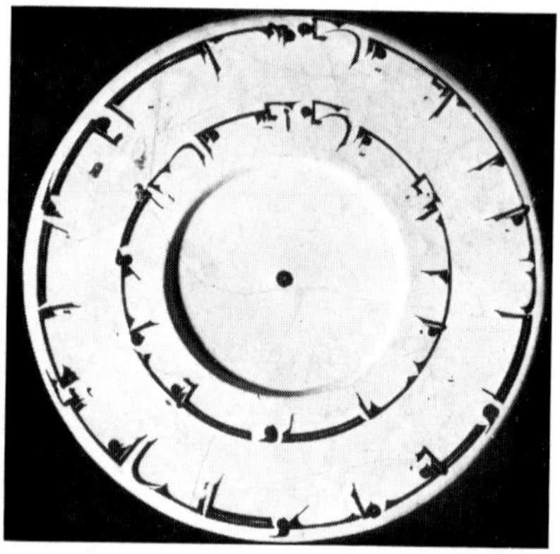

(*d*) Large bowl, slip-painted ware, Nīshāpūr, fourth/tenth century.

7 (*a*) Cairo, mosque of Aḥmad b. Ṭūlūn, 263-5/876-9.

(*b*) Cairo, mosque of Aḥmad b. Ṭūlūn, view of the sanctuary with two stucco flat *miḥrābs* on two pillars in the foreground.

8 (*a*) Cordova, the Great Mosque, the ***miḥrāb***, 354/965.

(*b*) Bukhārā, the mausoleum of Ismāʿīl the Samanid, 295/907.

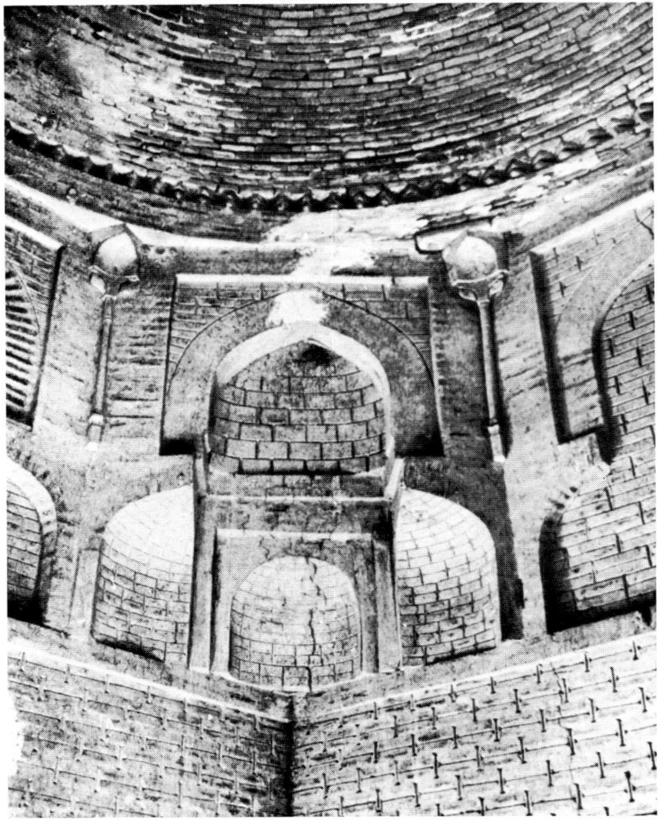

9 (*a*) Tim, Üzbekistan, mausoleum of ʿArab Ata, 367/977-8, zone of transition.

(*b*) Nāʾīn, *miḥrāb* and *minbar* of the Masjid-i Jāmiʿ, late fourth/tenth century.

10 (*a*) Cairo, mosque of al-Azhar, dome over court end of sanctuary with stucco decorations and window grilles, *c.* 545/1150.

(*b*) Kharaqān, a recently discovered Seljuk tomb-tower, 486/1095.

11 Cairo, mosque of al-Juyūshī, the stucco *miḥrāb*, 478/1085.

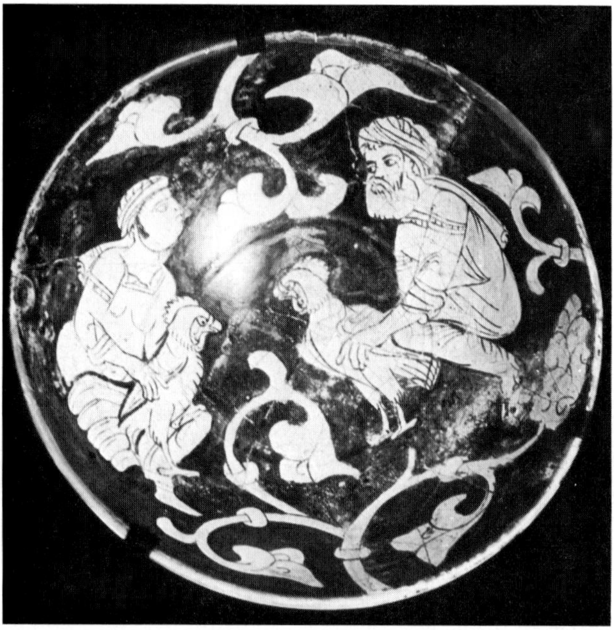

12 (*a*) Large dish, lustre painted, Egypt, fifth/eleventh century.

(*b*) Fatimid painting: siege of a fortress, Egypt, sixth/twelfth century.

13 Damāvand, a recently discovered Seljuk tomb-tower late fifth/eleventh century.

14 (*a*) Ardistān, Masjid-i Jāmi', 553-5/1158-60, zone of transition.

(*b*) Hamadān, Gunbad-i 'Alawiyyān, sixth/twelfth century.

15 (*a*) Naṭanz, Masjid-i Kūchī Mīr, stucco *miḥrāb*, sixth/twelfth century.

(*b*) Mosul, the Great Mosque, 543/1148, the minaret.

16 (*a*) Divrighi, Ulu Jāmiʿ, detail of the main entrance, 626/1229.

(*b*) Ankara, Arslankhāne Jāmiʿ, faience *miḥrāb*, 688–9/1289–90.

17 (*a*) Bowl, decoration in *sgraffiato* technique; Persian, Āmul, late fourth/tenth or early fifth/eleventh century.

(*b*) Jug, so-called 'Seljuk white ware'; Persian, Rayy or Kāshān, late sixth/twelfth century.

(*c*) Large dish, lustre-painted; Persian, Rayy, late sixth/twelfth or early seventh/thirteenth century.

(*d*) Bowl, overglaze, so-called *mīnā'ī* painted; Persian, Rayy, late sixth/twelfth or early seventh/thirteenth century.

18 (*a*) Bucket, inlaid with silver, made in Herat, signed and dated: 559/1163.

(*b*) Ewer, brass, inlaid with silver, signed by Shujāʿ b. Manaʿ, dated: 620/1232

19 (*a*) Miniature painting: the Pharmacy, from Dioscorides's *Materia medica*, Baghdād, 681/1224.

(*b*) Miniature painting: Abū Zayd before the governor of Merv. From the *Maqāmāt* of al-Ḥarīrī, Baghdād, *c*. 622-33/1225-35.

20 (*a*) Islamic calligraphy: (i) simple Kufic, (ii) foliated Kufic, (iii) floriated Kufic, (iv) *Naskhī*, (v) *Thuluth*, (vi) *Nasta'līq*.

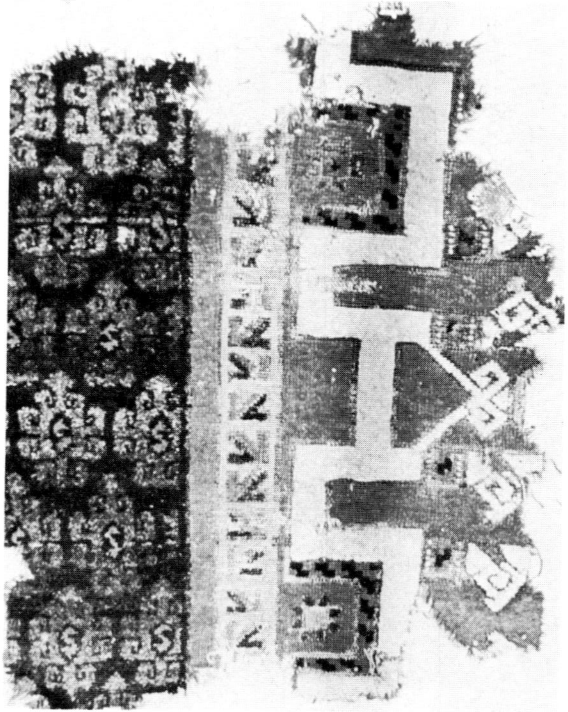

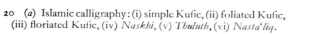

(*b*) Seljuk carpet from Anatolia, seventh/thirteenth century.

21 (*a*) Aleppo, gateway to the citadel, sixth/twelfth century.

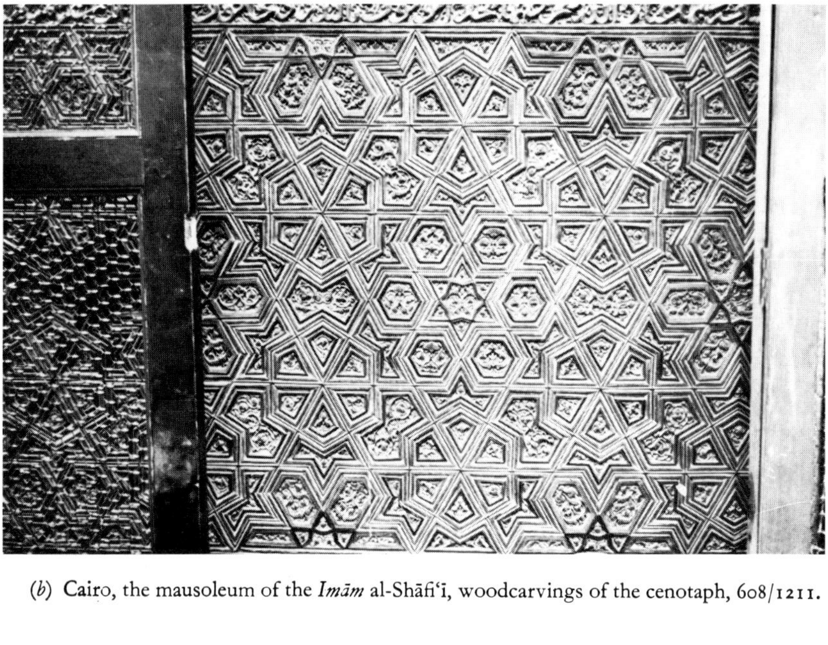

(*b*) Cairo, the mausoleum of the *Imām* al-Shāfiʿī, woodcarvings of the cenotaph, 608/1211.

22 (*a*) Detail of an inlaid bronze canteen, early seventh/thirteenth century.

(*b*) Rabat, minaret of Mosque of Ḥassān.

23 (*a*) Granada, the Alhambra, eighth/fourteenth century.

(*b*) Naṭanz, the minaret of the Masjid-i Jāmiʿ 704-9/1304-9, and the dome of the tomb of Abū Ṣamad, 707/1307.

24 (*a*) Samarqand, Gūr-i Mīr mausoleum, general view, 807/1404.

(*b*) Samarqand, Shāh-i Zinda, detail of portal of Tughluk Tekin's mausoleum, 774/1372.

25 (*a*) Miniature painting from the *Jāmiʿ al-tawārīkh* of Rashīd al-Dīn, 714/1314: Muḥammad replacing the Black Stone in the Kaʿba.

(*b*) Miniature painting from the *Shāh-nāma*: Bahrām Gūr hunting and the death of his mistress, Āzāda; Shirāz school, early eighth/fourteenth century.

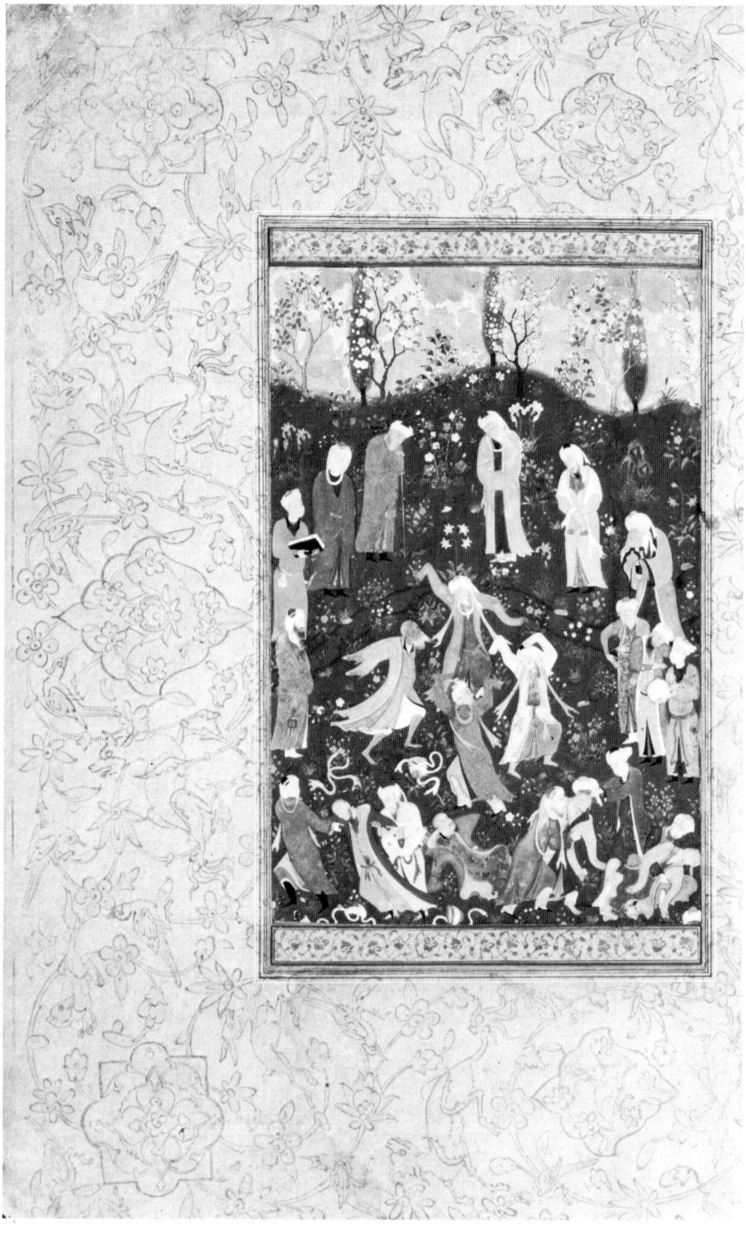

26 Miniature painting from the *Dīwān* of Ḥāfiẓ: Dance of the dervishes; Herat, Bihzād's school, late ninth/fifteenth century.

27 (*a*) Cairo, façade of the mausoleum of Qalawun 683-4/1284-5.

(*b*) Mamluk carpet, Egypt, ninth/fifteenth century.

28 (*a*) Iṣfahān, the ʿAlī Qapu palace, early eleventh/seventeenth century.

(*b*) Edirne, Selīmiye Jāmiʿ, built by Sinān Pasha, 977-83/1569-75.

29 (*a*) Dish, Iznik pottery, third period, early eleventh/seventeenth century. Crown copyright.

(*b*) Turkish embroidery, twelfth/eighteenth century.

30 Iṣfahān, minaret of the Masjid-i Shāh, 1020-48/1612-38.

31 (*a*) The so-called 'Polish rug', silk pile: Persian, eleventh/seventeenth century.

(*b*) Safavid metalwork: covered bowl, dated: 1089/1678. Crown copyright.

32 (*a*) Large dish, so-called 'Kubachi' ware, north-western Persia, eleventh/seventeenth century. Crown copyright.

(*b*) Persian white, so-called 'Gombroon', ware, ewer, late eleventh/ seventeenth century. Crown copyright.

During al-Mu'taṣim's caliphate (218–27/833–42) the riots of the Turkish troops caused so many disturbances in Baghdād that the caliph ordered the erection of a new capital, Sāmarrā, further up the Tigris. Immense palaces and mosques were built there by al-Mu'taṣim and by his successors. The Jawsaq al-Khāqānī palace, erected by al-Mu'taṣim, had a triple-arched entrance, the so-called Bāb al-'Āmma [pl. 4(*b*)]. The throne-room was built in a cross-shaped form, the centre of which was originally covered by a dome. The excavators recovered marble and stucco fragments which originally must have ornamented the walls. The harem was decorated with wall paintings showing dancing figures, birds and large garlands [pl. 5(*b*)].

The Great Mosque of Sāmarrā, built by al-Mutawakkil (232–47/847–61), is the largest mosque in Islam. Only the enclosure walls have survived, along with its helicoid minaret [pl. 5(*c*)]. In the mosque the excavations again revealed stucco fragments and glass mosaics. The Sāmarrā excavations, which were conducted by Ernst Herzfeld and Friedrich Sarre before the First World War, uncovered a second, the Balkuwārā palace, at the southern part of the city. The vast rectangular enclosure included a palace complex and two small mosques richly decorated with stucco and mosaics. This palace is also attributed to al-Mutawakkil.

The same caliph was responsible for the construction of the Ja'fariyya district somewhat north of Sāmarrā. It was here that the second great mosque of the city was erected. That was the mosque of Abū Dulaf, which is better preserved than the Great Mosque. The courtyard is surrounded by arcades, two aisles deep on the north. The sanctuary is divided into seventeen aisles running perpendicular to the *qibla* wall. The *miḥrāb*, for some unknown reason, was doubled. The minaret is similar in form to that of the Great Mosque. Recent excavations by the Iraqi Department of Antiquities uncovered a palace behind the sanctuary.

During the reign of al-Mu'tamid (256–79/870–92), Sāmarrā was abandoned, probably in the year 270/883. Thus its building activities are confined to only forty-seven years, which allows a nearly accurate dating. The great importance of Sāmarrā lies in two facts: first, that the stucco decorations reveal three distinct styles, clearly indicating the main sources of Islamic art [pl. 5(*a*)]; secondly, that it is here that, for the first time, artistic Islamic pottery was found.

Herzfeld recognized the three Sāmarrā styles, and called them the First, Second and Third styles. Professor Creswell, however, realized that the earliest style was Herzfeld's 'Third Style'. He therefore changed the order, the Third Style becoming 'Style A', the Second 'Style B' and the First 'Style C'. In 'Style A' the ornaments are based mainly on floral and plant patterns (vine scrolls, pine-cones, palmettes, etc.), arranged within geometrical compartments. In 'Style B' the patterns are again taken from the plant motives but appear in an abstract form. These first two styles are related to each other, but are totally different from 'Style C'. The latter style displays for the first time Central Asian elements, obviously introduced to Mesopotamia by Turkish artists. Certain elements in this style even reveal Far Eastern motives as well.

Far Eastern influence is, however, more evident in the pottery which has been exposed from the palaces and houses of Sāmarrā. From the excavated material four types of pottery can be distinguished: (1) the unglazed wares with incised or relief decorations; (2) lead-glazed mottled wares [pl. 6(*a*)]; (3) a great variety of tin-glazed vessels which were painted in cobalt blue, yellow or green, sometimes displaying abstract designs [pl. 6(*b*)]; (4) the celebrated lustre technique, which at the beginning started in polychrome [pl 6(*c*)]. No figural subject appears in polychrome lustre, except cocks on some wall-tiles and a peacock on a bowl which is in the Ashmolean Museum, Oxford. By the beginning of the fourth/tenth century lustre became monochrome and vessels from that period display primitively drawn human figures and animals. The production of fine pottery apparently started under Chinese influence, by imitation of the imported T'ang pottery and porcelain. That particularly applies to the mottled and tin-glazed wares. The lustre technique was entirely a Near Eastern invention.

Aḥmad b. Ṭūlūn, who became the governor of Egypt in 254/868 and founded an autonomous dynasty there, built a new city north of Fusṭāṭ. It was here that he erected a congregational mosque which was called after him. Its plan, a rectangular courtyard surrounded by porticoes, two aisles deep on three sides and five aisles on the *qibla* side, the stucco decorations and the form of the minaret, reveal strong stylistic connexion with Sāmarrā [pls. 7(*a*) and (*b*)].

SPAIN AND NORTH AFRICA

The famous mosque of Cordova was erected by 'Abd al-Raḥmān I in 168-9/784-6. In the following century it was enlarged (218/833) and the decoration of the west door was completed in 241–2/855–6. During the fourth/tenth century a new minaret was built, further enlargements were carried out and the decoration of the *miḥrāb* was completed. The mosque is a vast rectangle with a deep covered sanctuary which is divided into nineteen aisles by eighteen arcades. The beauty of the mosque is in the construction of these arcades which have double-tier horse-shoe arches, and in the colourful decoration of its *miḥrāb* [pl. 8(*a*)]. Marble and gold mosaics were used for its lining. The niche itself is seven-sided and is very spacious. The upper part of the niche is decorated by seven trefoil arches. This *miḥrāb* served as a model for other *miḥrābs* in North Africa and Spain.

One of the earliest mosques in North Africa was built at Qayrawān in Tunisia. The original mosque was built in the Umayyad era, but it was demolished, rebuilt and enlarged several times, until Ziyādat Allāh I in 221–2/836 rebuilt the whole structure. It has been preserved in that form up to the present day. It is a great irregular enclosure with eight doorways and a minaret in the middle of the north side. The sanctuary is a deep covered hall of seventeen aisles. The *miḥrāb* has a horseshoe form and, like that of Cordova, is richly decorated. The walls around the niche are coated with polychromed lustre tiles imported from Mesopotamia, while the niche itself is lined by pierced marble panels and the semi-dome has wooden panelling. There is a richly carved wooden *minbar* in the mosque which also dates from the third/ninth century.

THE PRE-SELJUK PERIOD OF PERSIA AND CENTRAL ASIA

During the third/ninth century the power of the ʿAbbasid caliphs started to decline rapidly. Petty dynasties sprang up all over the empire. In the east the most significant among these dynasties were the Samanids (261–389/874–999), who ruled over Transoxania and eastern Persia. They became patrons of the arts. Their capital was at Bukhārā, where one of their earliest surviving monuments was erected: the mausoleum of Ismāʿīl, completed in 295/907.

The mausoleum is a square structure covered by a hemispherical dome. It is as beautiful and perfect as a jewel-box. It was built and decorated entirely of fired bricks, thus being the earliest known building where the decorative brick technique, called *hazārbāf* in Persian, was applied. The mausoleum actually owes its plan to Sasanian architecture. Sasanian fire-altars with their square structures and hemispherical domes served as a model for domed mausoleums of the Islamic period. The plan presented an architectural problem; the transition from square to circle. The earliest successful solution to this problem is known from the fire-altar of Ribāṭ-i Safīd (third Christian century). The problem was solved by the introduction of a series of squinches in the zone of transition.

In the Samanid mausoleum at Bukhārā the zone of transition appears in an elaborated and decorated form [pl. 8(*b*)]. A more complicated zone of transition appears in the recently discovered mausoleum of 'Arab Ata at Tim in Soviet Uzbekistan. The building, which is again square and has a decorated façade, is dated to 367/977–8. In the zone of transition the square squinches were applied in a trefoil form [pl. 9(*a*)]. Previously the earliest of such trefoil squinches were known from the Davāzdah Imām at Yazd, dating from 429/1037.

Excavations by Soviet archaeologists in Samarqand and Afrāsiyāb, and by the Metropolitan Museum at Nīshāpūr, exposed an interesting type of pottery. First it was called Samanid slip-painted ware, or East Persian ware. The decoration is painted with coloured slip under transparent glazes. The body is usually red and has a white, creamy or brownish ground slip. The colours used for decoration were mainly manganese-purple, yellow, tomato-red and green. Kufic inscriptions, stylized birds and floral patterns appear on these vessels, which can be dated to the tenth and early eleventh Christian centuries [pl. 6(*d*)].

There is an early mosque in central Persia, the Masjid-i Jāmi' of Nā'īn, which deserves special attention. The date of the building is not known, but on stylistic ground it is considered to be the second half of the fourth/tenth century. The mosque has a rectangular courtyard surrounded by porticoes, which are deeper on the sanctuary side. There is a small, tapering minaret in one corner. The *miḥrāb* and the surrounding area are coated with richly carved stucco [pl. 9(*b*)], displaying, according to Upham Pope, 'the implicit theme of the age-old concept of fertility'.[1]

In north-east Persia, not far from the Caspian Sea, is the small village of Gunbad-i Qābūs, where, previous to the Mongol invasion, there stood the town of Jurjān. It was here that the earliest Islamic tomb-tower was erected by Qābūs b. Wushmgīr in 347/1006–7. It is a high, cylindrical, slightly tapering tower, capped with a conical top, built

[1] A. U. Pope, *Persian architecture* (London, 1965), 86.

entirely of fired bricks. The sole decoration of the tower is the Kufic inscription which runs around the building above the entrance and below the roof.

A few caravanserais have survived from that period in eastern Persia and Central Asia. The earliest known, that at Āhuwān, near Simnān, dates from 420–41/1029–49. These caravanserais have strong enclosure walls, usually strengthened by buttresses. Inside there are four great *īwāns*[1] opening on to a central court. This cruciform plan with the four *īwāns* goes back to Parthian times, where it first appeared in the palace at Assur (first Christian century).

Meanwhile another dynasty appeared further east, in present-day Afghanistan, the Ghaznavids (351–582/962–1186). The greatest ruler of the dynasty, Maḥmūd (388–421/998–1030), had his capital, Ghazna, near the Indian frontier. Only two polygonal towers survive from this capital. Further south-west, at Lashkar-i Bāzār, palaces and mosques were excavated by the French Archaeological Mission, exposing frescoes, stuccoes and similar slip-painted pottery which were already known from the Samanid period.

The minaret of Jām, in northern Afghanistan, should also be mentioned here, though it is somewhat later in date. It was erected by the Ghurid Ghiyāth al-Dīn Muḥammad between 548/1153 and 599/1203. The minaret has a very fine decoration in stucco, containing Qur'anic and historical inscriptions. The minaret, which was discovered only in 1957, clearly shows its connexion with the Quṭb Mīnār in Delhi, erected in the seventh/thirteenth century.

THE FATIMID PERIOD

The Fatimids came to power in Tunisia and founded their capital Mahdiyya with its Great Mosque. This mosque has the first example of a monumental entrance, recalling in appearance some of the Roman triumphal arches. Later on, in 356/969 the Fatimids conquered Egypt and founded Cairo. Their adherence to Shiʿism marked their religious and political differences with the ʿAbbasid caliphs of Baghdād.

The Fatimids erected several buildings in Cairo, among which the mosque of al-Azhar is the most outstanding example. The original mosque was nearly square in plan, with five aisles in the sanctuary

[1] *Īwān* in Islamic architecture means a portal or a hall, which is usually enclosed on three sides and is roofed by a barrel vault.

running parallel to the *qibla* wall. There were three domes, one in front of the *miḥrāb*, and two more at either end of the *qibla* wall. Later on there were several additions and alterations made in the mosque, and today it looks like a labyrinth. Some of the original stucco decorations in the sanctuary, and a number of window grilles have survived up to the present day [pl. 10(*a*)].

Another Fatimid mosque in Cairo is that of al-Ḥākim, erected between 380/990 and 394/1003. Later on it became the Friday Mosque of the city. It is an immense square building, recalling the mosque of Ibn Ṭūlūn with its arcades supported by brick piers. It also resembles the mosque of al-Azhar with its three domes in the sanctuary. There are two minarets at the corners of the main façade. The decoration of the sanctuary contains a band of beautiful floriated Kufic inscription running the length of the arcades.

Badr al-Jamālī, the commander-in-chief and *wazīr* (466–87/1074–94), rebuilt the walls of the city by replacing the former mud-brick walls with excellent stone masonry, and strengthened them with towers. He also built three monumental gateways: Bāb al-Naṣr which has two great square towers and a beautiful semicircular arch; Bāb al-Futūḥ, where the archway is again flanked by two solid towers; and Bāb Zuwayla, very similar to that of Bāb al-Futūḥ. All three gateways reveal the strong North African influence which is obvious throughout the Fatimid period. This period also witnessed the introduction of a new kind of structure, the *zāwiya* or domed mausoleum with three bays.

The little covered mosque of al-Juyūshī dates from the end of the fifth/eleventh century. It has a remarkable *miḥrāb*, one of the finest stucco works in Egypt [pl. 11]. The mosque of al-Aqmar was built in 519/1125. Its façade is very impressive, with two niches flanking the entrance. The niche-heads are decorated with stalactites or *muqarnas*.

Nothing has survived of Fatimid secular buildings. It is known, however, from literary sources that the Fatimids erected a palace in Cairo. A number of wooden panels from this palace are preserved in the Museum of Islamic Art in Cairo. They show human figures: musicians, dancers, animals and birds against a dense scroll background. In the same Museum there are also a few wooden *miḥrābs* demonstrating the great skill of Fatimid artists in this field.

The potter's art flourished throughout the period, and lustre wares in particular are worth mentioning. At the beginning the same naïvely drawn human figures and animals were represented, like those on Mesopotamian forerunners in the early fourth/tenth century. Later examples, however, reveal great progress in rendering the figures and also in their selection of subjects. Episodes from everyday life appear frequently on dishes and bowls [pl. 12(*a*)]. A number of vessels are signed by the potters, and among them the name of Sa'd appears very often. This potter seems to have been very active at the end of the fifth/eleventh and beginning of the sixth/twelfth century.

Apart from lustre wares, splashed and monochrome, glazed vessels were also produced, probably in Fusṭāṭ and the Fayyūm.

Very little is known of Fatimid metalwork. A small number of engraved vessels, zoomorphic aquamaniles and incense-burners, are attributed with more or less certainty to the period. These are in the Museum of Islamic art in Cairo and in the Benaki Museum of Athens.

The earliest known Islamic paintings on papyri were found at Fusṭāṭ and in the Fayyūm region of Egypt, dating from the fifth/eleventh and sixth/twelfth centuries. Apparently a lively school of painting functioned in the Fayyūm under the Fatimids, as is mentioned by a later Egyptian writer.[1] Very few of these paintings have survived, and these are mostly in Cairo. There is one such painting in the British Museum showing the siege of a fortress, most likely representing a fight between Muslims and Crusaders [pl. 12(*b*)]. It probably dates from the second half of the sixth/twelfth century.

Fatimid painting can be observed on the ceiling of the Capella Palatina of Palermo which was executed by Egyptian painters around 535/1140. The enthroned monarch, musicians, dancers, slave girls and fantastic animals painted on the ceiling clearly resemble the decorations of the lustre-painted vessels or wall frescoes of Sāmarrā, which in turn can be traced back to Central Asia.

The earliest known Islamic textiles are the so-called *ṭirāz* bands which contain inscriptions in beautiful Kufic. These were produced in Egypt, where Tinnis (near Port Said), Damietta and Alexandria were the main centres in the Tulunid and Fatimid era. There are also *ṭirāz* bands decorated in polychrome wool, and lined or embroidered in silk. The Fatimid era produced the finest silk and linen the decoration of which continued the scheme of earlier examples: a broad inscription band followed by narrow fields of animal figures and arabesques.

[1] Al-Maqrīzī, *Khiṭaṭ*, I, 486–7; II, 318. Al-Maqrīzī also wrote a book on the history of painters, which has unfortunately not survived.

THE SELJUKS IN PERSIA, ʿIRĀQ AND ANATOLIA

The Seljuk period is frequently called the 'Persian Renaissance'. Architecture and decorative arts certainly reached a very high apex in their development, but this does not apply only to Persia. The Seljuks, who extended their domination over ʿIrāq and parts of Anatolia, greatly affected the development of arts in these two regions as well. In architecture the period witnessed the perfection of decoration in brick technique. Several ways of brick bondings were invented or further developed.

The earliest monuments of the period, like the recently discovered tomb-tower in Damāvand, express both the power and grace of the brick technique. The Damāvand tomb-tower [pl. 13], which can be dated to the third quarter of the eleventh Christian century, reveals a great variety of designs, all executed in brick. There is an early sixth/twelfth century tomb-tower at Melik Ghāzī, east of Kayseri in Turkey, the decoration of which, but particularly the herringbone patterns of the dome, comes very close to the Damāvand tomb-tower.

Two more tomb-towers were also discovered recently in Persia, not far from the Qazvīn–Hamadān road. Both of these are octagonal buildings capped by double domes [pl. 10 (*b*)]. They reveal the finest brick decoration of the period. According to their inscriptions, they were erected in 460/1067–8 and 486/1093 respectively.

In mosque architecture, a great number of surviving monuments bear witness to Seljuk activity. In Persia the dome over the northern *īwān* in the Masjid-i Jāmiʿ of Iṣfahān, which dates from 480/1088 should be mentioned. The zone of transition here again has trefoil squinches. The Masjid-i Jāmiʿ of Iṣfahān is actually a four-*īwān* building. Other Seljuk mosques in Persia were erected in the same style. In Ardistān, the zone of transition below the dome in the *jāmiʿ* indicates a further development. Within the trefoil squinch appear four niches with pointed arches resting on engaged columns [pl. 14(*a*)]. That trend had actually begun in Iṣfahān in the Masjid-i Jāmiʿ, a hundred years earlier.

Decoration in stucco also reached its apex under the Seljuks. Entire wall surfaces were coated with carved stucco, revealing not only a variety of patterns, but also ingenious application of the design in a number of superimposed layers. In this respect first of all two Seljuk monuments should be referred to: the Madrasa Ḥaydariyya in Qazvīn, and the Gunbad-i 'Alawiyyān in Hamadān [pl. 14(*b*)]. In both buildings the *miḥrāb* and the surrounding areas, the cornice and the zone of transition in part, are decorated in very dense stucco. The richness of the design reminds us of the exaggerations and wildness of the rococo. In Hamadān the façade is also coated with carved stucco, and there is an inscription which runs round the square building.

The Masjid-i Kūchī Mīr in Naṭanz has an entirely different ground-plan. Instead of the cruciform plan with four *īwāns*, it is completely roofed with a small dome in front of the *miḥrāb*. It is one of the earliest known completely roofed mosques in Persia. The actual date of the mosque is not known, but it is considered to be of the sixth/twelfth century. While the building is quite simple and unadorned, its *miḥrāb* [pl. 15(*a*)] is coated with carved stucco. Two small rectangular recesses are set in a rectangular frame. The columns, capitals, spandrels and the back panel of the inner or lower recess are decorated in the Seljuk style.

A great number of Seljuk minarets survive in Persia. All these are tall, round, tapering towers decorated in brick technique. On rare occasions, glazed brick or tiles were used for the decoration of inscriptions or other horizontal patterns. Such a minaret exists in Nigār, south of Kirmān.

Very little is known of Seljuk secular architecture in Persia. So far no palace has been found. There is a Seljuk bath in Nigār, but even that has been drastically altered on several occasions. A few caravanserais are known from the period, among them the most interesting is Ribāṭ-i Malik in eastern Persia, dating from 471/1078. The enclosure walls are of massive bricks, strengthened one side by a row of cylindrical piers which are connected to each other by arches above. Another caravanserai, again in eastern Persia, close to the Afghan frontier, is the Ribāṭ-i Sharīf built by Sultan Sanjar in 447/1055. Inside it has an extensive stucco decoration, including a stucco *miḥrāb* within the mosque.

Seljuk building activity in the Fertile Crescent was associated with the name of Nūr al-Dīn (541–69/1146–73). He ordered the erection of a number of *madrasas*, and was also responsible for the Great Mosque in Mosul. It is better known as the Jāmi' al-Nūrī. Only the sanctuary and the minaret have survived in their original form. The cylindrical minaret has a cubical base [pl. 15(*b*)], and the cylindrical part is divided into seven equal horizontal fields all of which are decorated in different brick designs.

Though the Seljuk empire began to decline in the middle of the sixth/twelfth century, and a number of petty dynasties shared its realm, the vigorous and lively trend and style in art and architecture continued in Persia up to the Mongol invasion in the early seventh/thirteenth century, while in Anatolia it continued until about 700/1300. A great number of Seljuk monuments have survived in Anatolia, particularly in Konya and Kayseri.

Seljuk mosques in Anatolia are different from those of Persia or Mesopotamia. Since they had to be suited to a more severe climate, they were completely roofed. Thus the courtyard disappeared, and was replaced by a large central dome with a fountain beneath. One of the earliest of these Seljuk mosques in Anatolia was erected in Silvan (ancient Mayyāfāriqīn, east of Diyār Bakr), dating from the fourth/eleventh century. Here the zone of transition was formed by stalactites.

The basic element of the stalactite is a quarter dome, unsupported above and applied in several rows. Its origin is still ambiguous, but as far as is known today, the earliest examples are found in Central Asia, dating from the third/ninth and fourth/tenth centuries. From the fifth/eleventh century onwards they were widely used nearly everywhere in Islamic architecture.

Another early Seljuk mosque is in Kızıltepe (ancient Dunaysir, west of Mardin). It is in a ruinous state, and the dome collapsed some time ago. The mosque has a richly carved stone *miḥrāb*. It should be noted here that in Anatolia the building material was stone, while bricks, both fired and unfired, were used in Persia.

The most beautiful of the Seljuk monuments is the Ulu Jāmiʿ and annexed hospital in Divrighi, in central Anatolia. It is without any doubt the masterpiece of Seljuk workmanship. Whatever beauty was achieved in stucco in Persia, appeared in stone at Divrighi. The main entrance of the building [pl. 16(*a*)] displays a great variety of Seljuk patterns, appearing as if it were in a number of superimposed layers.

Another richly carved portal is that of the Inje Mināre in Konya, which was built in 657/1258. It is actually a *medrese*. *Medreses* in Anatolia are different from those of Persia. There are in fact two different types. The first type has an open court with a large *īwān* opposite the entrance. Sometimes even four *īwāns* appear, just as in Persia. The second type is similar to Anatolian Seljuk mosques, that is a small covered building with a central dome and a fountain placed below. *Medreses* in general had minarets, richly decorated either in bricks, or, as an addition, glazed bricks and tiles, which were used for horizontal panels and inscriptions.

The technique of covering large surfaces with glazed tiles was actually a Seljuk innovation. It first appeared on mausoleums at Marāgha in western Persia. In Seljuk Anatolia they were frequently used, particularly for decorating *miḥrābs*. The earliest known examples of these faience *miḥrābs* are in Konya in the 'Alā' al-Dīn Jāmi' (618/1221), Sirjeli Medrese (640/1242), and Laranda Jāmi' and Ṣaḥib Ata Jāmi', both dating from 656/1258. Among the later examples are those of the 'Alaja Jāmi' at Kharput (672/1273), in the Eshrefoghlu Jāmi' at Beyshehir (697–8/1297–8), and probably the most colourful faience *miḥrāb* is in the Arslankhāne Jāmi' of Ankara [pl. 16(*b*)] dating from 688–9/1289–90.

Mausoleums in Anatolia followed the Persian tradition. These were built mainly in stone. Their ground plan varied from octagonal, polygonal to square. One Anatolian mausoleum with a square form, has already been mentioned; that of Melik Ghāzī, on the Kayseri–Malaṭya road. A number of mausoleums survived in Kayseri, among which the Döner Gümbet (675/1276) is probably the most decorative.

The Seljuks built up an entire network of caravanserais. The number of surviving Seljuk caravanserais in Anatolia is even greater than in Persia. Their ground-plan closely follows the Persian models, but here the building material was stone, and they were more richly decorated. The earliest examples are around Konya, such as the Altınapa (598/1201), and the Kızılören khans (601/1204) on the Konya-Beyshehir road. The most famous caravanserai is probably Sulṭān Khān on the Kayseri–Sivas road, dating from 634/1236.

A number of bridges are also known from the period. These were sometimes used for frontier customs or tolls. The finest example of a Seljuk bridge is the Shahristān bridge in Persia which spanned the Zāyanda Rūd river near Iṣfahān. In Anatoliā, the bridge over the Kızılırmak, near Kirshehir, is a monument to the ingenuity of Seljuk engineers.

The Seljuk period was a golden age for decorative arts, particularly for pottery. Previous to the Seljuk invasion, about the beginning of the fifth/eleventh century, new pottery centres sprang up in the northern and north-western mountainous parts of Persia, in the Caspian borderland, in Āẕarbāyjān and Kurdistān. The significance of these kilns in these parts is outstanding, since their products greatly differed from other

Islamic wares. They reveal a strong Sasanian influence. Though the Arabs conquered the Sasanian empire, Sasanian traditions and Zoroastrianism nevertheless lingered, particularly in more remote areas of the country. One of the strongholds of Sasanian and Zoroastrian traditions centred around Ṭabaristān, which was long ruled by native princes.

It was in this part of Persia that pottery making was taken up soon after the decline in Samarqand and Nīshāpūr. These local potters developed special wares of the incised so-called *sgraffiato* technique. It was actually the pottery equivalent of the engraving in metalwork, frequently used in Sasanian metalwork. Even some of the designs were borrowed from Sasanian metalwork, such as the stylized bird in a bowl, which is in the Ashmolean Museum, Oxford [pl. 17(*a*)]. There are three different types of *sgraffiato* wares, which are dated to the fifth–seventh/eleventh–thirteenth centuries.

The coming of the Seljuks brought about great changes in Islamic pottery. First of all, a new white composite material was introduced, and was henceforward used in all parts of the Near and Middle East. Secondly there was a gradual evolution in the methods of decorating the white material by carving, staining the glaze, painting under the glaze, and painting in lustre and polychrome over the glaze.

The wide range of Seljuk pottery starts with monochrome-glazed wares. The glaze might be white, or coloured in different shades of green, turquoise blue, aubergine, purple and brown. The body was very fine and thin. Actually this was an attempt to imitate Chinese porcelains and celadon. Muslim potters of Persia, ʿIrāq and Anatolia produced a variety of finely executed bowls, jugs, ewers, vases and tankards. Occasionally these vessels are so thin that they seem translucent, an impression which is further enhanced by working pierced openwork into them. The jug shown in pl. 17(*b*) was executed in the same way. The field around the moulded inscription was pierced, and the small holes were filled with the glaze which then produced tiny windows giving the impression of glass.

The decoration of these monochromed wares consisted of floral patterns, inscriptions in *naskhī* script or human figures, which had been carved, moulded or incised into the body before the glazing took place. The date of these fine Seljuk wares is considered to be sixth–seventh/twelfth–thirteenth centuries. The main production centres in Persia were Rayy and Kāshān; in Syria, Raqqa and Ruṣāfa. The same types were also produced in several parts of Anatolia.

A further development in the decoration of pottery was the painting in blue, black and turquoise, under a clear glaze of transparent turquoise or deep blue. Underglaze-painting was again a practice which was introduced under the Seljuks but was quickly accepted all over the Middle East.

Lustre painting was also introduced into Persia. Its appearance coincides with the fall of the Fatimids in Egypt. The greatest change in these medieval lustre wares from those of the early period is that while on the earlier examples the decoration was painted in lustres, it is now the background which is lustred in deep brownish or yellow, thus leaving the space open for the decoration. A number of important centres are known to have been producing lustre wares during the second half of the sixth/twelfth century and during the seventh/thirteenth century. Among them Rayy, Kāshān, Sāva and Raqqa should be mentioned. A beautiful large dish (diameter 18½ inches) comes from Rayy, and probably dates from the sixth/twelfth or early seventh/thirteenth century [pl. 17(*c*)]. Human and animal figures, depicted on a floral background, are the favourite subjects.

The last phase of development in pottery decorations was that of painting in polychrome over the glaze. Two kinds of techniques were used: *mīnā'ī* and *lajvardina*. The so-called *mīnā'ī*, meaning enamel, denotes a technique in which the colours are usually blue, green, brown, black, dull red, white and gold, and are painted over an opaque white ground under transparent colourless or turquoise glaze. There was a close connexion between *mīnā'ī* wares and miniature painting, and most likely the decorations were executed by painters. The designs display court-scenes or scenes from Persian legends. A *mīnā'ī* bowl here depicts the meeting of two horsemen under a tree. An inscription outside gives the date of the vessel as 583/1187. It was probably made in Rayy [pl. 17(*d*)].

The other overglaze painted technique, the *lajvardina*, took its name from the cobalt-blue glaze on which the decoration was painted in red and white, and leaf gilding was added. The production of *lajvardina* wares is considered to have taken place in the Sulṭānābād region of Persia.

In metalwork the Seljuk period also brought about a considerable change. Previously, metal vessels in Persia, which was the cradle of Islamic metalwork, appeared as a straight continuation of Sasanian metalwork. Silver dishes, bowls and ewers displayed the same ornaments for another three or four hundred years. On some specimens, however, Kufic inscriptions were added. On ewers the decoration was engraved. As a general trend necks and spouts, or even whole vessels, followed the form of birds or animals. Aquamaniles and incense-burners in zoomorphic forms, are known from the third/ninth to the sixth/twelfth century.

A new technique, inlaying in bronze or brass with silver, copper or gold, was introduced during the sixth/twelfth century. The earliest piece of inlaid metalwork known today is a pen-box made in Herat by 'Umar b. al-Fażl and dated 542/1148. The next inlaid object in chronological order is a large bucket made of bronze and inlaid in silver and copper [pl. 18(*a*)] also made at Herat and signed by the caster, Muḥammad b. 'Abd al-Wāḥid, and by the inlayer, Mas'ūd b. Aḥmad, and dated 559/1163. Both objects are in the Hermitage Museum of Leningrad.

The elaborate inlaid decorations of the bucket are disposed in five registers, out of which three contain inscriptions, while the other two present festive court and hunting scenes. The Kufic inscription deserves special attention. The vertical strokes of the letters end in human and animal heads. This is known as 'animated inscription', common in Islamic metalwork from the end of the seventh/thirteenth century.

There are a great number of ewers, candlesticks, boxes, incense-burners and buckets preserved in public and private collections, dating from the late sixth/twelfth century or early seventh/thirteenth century, decorated in the inlay technique and most likely originating from Khurāsān and Herat.

The approach of the Mongols uprooted these craftsmen, and some of them set up their workshops in Mosul in Mesopotamia. Not long ago, all fine inlaid metalwork was designated as a product of Mosul. But in fact there are only a few specimens which can be attributed to Mosul without any doubt. Among them is a very fine brass ewer signed by a certain Shujā' b. Mana' of Mosul, dated 629/1232 [pl. 18(*b*)]. The medallions depict scenes from Persian legends. The T-fret and swastika patterns among the polylobed medallions and the elaborate star rosettes are characteristic of the new Mosul style.

There was a school of miniature painters in Mesopotamia and Syria during the seventh/thirteenth century. In Mesopotamia, these schools were probably in Baghdād and in Mosul. A number of illuminated manuscripts are preserved from that period, among them the Arabic translation of Dioscorides's *Materia medica*, dating from 621/1224. The paintings of the manuscript reveal the powerful influence of Byzantine art [pl. 19(*a*)].

Among the earliest manuscripts is the *Kalīla wa-Dimna*, a collection of fables about animals. More important, however, are the copies of the *Maqāmāt* of al-Ḥarīrī, which recall the adventures of Abū Zayd. The illustrations give us glimpses of contemporary Arab life. They are not related to Byzantine paintings, figures and all elements being presented in a true Arabic manner [pl. 19(*b*)].

In connexion with painting, calligraphy should be mentioned, as it played an important role in Islamic art. There were two main styles in calligraphy: the angular Kufic and the cursive *naskhī*. Kufic [pl. 20(*a*) (i)], which is alleged to have been invented at Kūfa, was used during the first four or five centuries of Islam. It appears in architecture, tombstones, early Qur'āns, on pottery and in textiles. Foliated Kufic [pl. 20(*a*) (ii)] was a more advanced form, decorating the endings of vertical strokes in lobed leaves or half-palmettes. The floriated Kufic [pl. 20(*a*) (iii)] developed in Egypt and reached its apex under the Fatimids.

Naskhī [pl. 20(*a*) (iv)] was developed in Baghdād, and from the fifth/eleventh century onwards gradually replaced Kufic. In Persia and Anatolia several cursive styles were developed in subsequent centuries, among which *thuluth* [pl. 20(*a*) (v)] should be mentioned. In this style, certain elements, such as the vertical strokes and horizontal lines, are exaggerated. From the second half of the fourteenth century the elegant *nasta'līq* becomes the predominant style in Persian calligraphy [pl. 20(*a*) (vi)].

Carpet weaving was also practised during the Seljuk period, as is attested by a few carpets discovered in the 'Alā al-Dīn Jāmi' of Konya and in the Eshrefoghlu Jāmi' of Beyshehir. Later on more carpet fragments turned up in Fusṭāṭ which betray a close relationship with their Anatolian counterparts. These Seljuk carpets, which are coloured in two shades of blue, green, red and yellow, reveal geometric designs in their central parts and mostly Kufic characters in the borders [pl. 20(*b*)]. The origin of carpet-making must be sought in Central Asia, where they were woven by Turkish nomads who then brought the technique with them to the Middle East.

THE AYYUBID PERIOD

Though the Ayyubids were preoccupied with military campaigns against the Crusaders, they made an important contribution to Islamic architecture and the decorative arts. In architecture, solid stone buildings, expressing strength and durability, are the most characteristic. A unique example is the citadel of Aleppo. Its history goes back to pre-Islamic times, [pl. 21(*a*)]. Saladin, the first Ayyubid ruler, further strengthened the walls of Cairo and erected the citadel on the Muqaṭṭam. He was responsible for the erection of a number of *madrasas* in Damascus and for their introduction into Egypt. These *madrasas* are, however, different from Persian examples, as they have only two *īwāns* instead of the usual four. The most famous *madrasa* in Cairo is that of the Sultan al-Ṣāliḥ Ayyūb built between 640–2/1242–4. It has four *īwāns*, but they are arranged in two separate blocks connected by the archway of the entrance, which at the same time carries a beautiful minaret.

A large number of mausoleums (Arabic sing., *qubba*) were also erected in Damascus and in Cairo, of which quite a number have survived. In Cairo two should be particularly mentioned: that of Shajar al-Durr (648/1250), and the mausoleum and mosque of the *Imām* al-Shāfiʿī, erected in 608/1211. Stucco played an important role in the decoration of Ayyubid mausoleums as is attested by the richly carved stucco *miḥrāb* of the mausoleum of Shajar al-Durr.

The marble decoration of the mosque and mausoleum of the *Imām* al-Shāfiʿī dates from the Mamluk period, but its wooden cenotaph is a very fine example of Ayyubid woodwork. It is decorated with finely carved scrolls and inscriptions placed on a dense scroll background [pl. 21(*b*)].

In metalwork the inlaid tradition of Mosul continued with slight alterations in the style. This was of course due to the migration of Mosul artists to Syria and Egypt. Candlesticks, large basins and incense-burners are known from this period, some of them decorated with Christian scenes. A bronze canteen in the Freer Gallery of Art in Washington is a unique piece of work of a Syrian artist or artists. Among the Christian scenes one represents Christ's entry into Jerusalem [pl. 22(*a*)]. Obviously the scene was borrowed from contemporary miniature paintings. It also seems very probable that most of these objects with Christian scenes were made for Christians, or even that some of the artists themselves must have been Christians.

In pottery, partly Fatimid, partly Persian Seljuk types, were followed. Lustre was produced in Syria. Wares which were underglaze-painted in polychrome, copying Persian *mīnā'ī* ware, decorated with human and animal figures, were made in Ruṣāfa and Damascus. Painted tiles have survived from the period in some of the Damascus mosques. Their decoration is in blue, black and green under a transparent colourless glaze. Ivory and bone carving was also practised both in Egypt and Syria, and reached a very high standard.

SPAIN AND NORTH AFRICA IN MEDIEVAL TIMES

The golden age of Muslim rule in Spain came in the reign of ʿAbd al-Raḥmān III (300–50/912–951), who founded the new capital, Madīnat al-Zahrāʾ near Cordova. A great variety of limestone and marble fragments disclose the strong connexion which still existed between Spanish Umayyad architecture and that of the second/eighth and third/ninth centuries in the eastern half of the Islamic world.

In the first half of the sixth/twelfth century the Almoravid ʿAlī b. Yūsuf ordered the enlargement of the mosque of the Qarawiyyīn at Fez, and the decoration of the Great Mosque at Tlemcen. The Almohads, who succeeded the Almoravids in North Africa, founded a new capital, Tinmāl, in the High Atlas in southern Morocco, and erected there a congregational mosque in 548/1153. This is now in ruins, but its *miḥrāb* is still preserved in good condition. The Kutubiyya mosque at Marrakesh, particularly its *miḥrāb*, resembles that of Tinmāl. The minaret is square, like most minarets in North Africa and Spain. The second largest mosque in Islam, the Mosque of Ḥassān (the Great Mosque of Sāmarrā being the first) was erected in Rabat. It also has a square minaret, opposite the sanctuary [pl. 22(*b*)]. The building is in ruins now. Only the minaret, bases of columns and the enclosure-walls survive. In Spain the Great Mosque of Seville is an Almohad building. Its minaret, the famous Giralda, was completed in 591/1195.

The best-known Islamic structure in the Western countries of the Islamic world is of course the celebrated Alhambra at Granada, erected by the Nasrid, Muḥammad b. Yūsuf. It was completed in its present form in the early eighth/fourteenth century. The palace, which is in the citadel, comprises two complexes, each surrounding a central court [pl. 23(*a*)].

Qalʿat Banī Ḥammād in Algeria was the capital of the Hammadid dynasty for nearly one hundred and fifty years. It was founded in 398/1007–8, and destroyed by the Almohads in 547/1152. Excavations there have revealed a number of palaces. There is also a mosque with a surviving square minaret. Glass and pottery kilns were also uncovered in the course of the recent excavations.

North African and Spanish architecture differs from that of the rest of the Islamic world, yet it seems to be a direct descendant of the earlier Umayyad art in Syria. The horseshoe arch, which originated in Syria, played an important role. After the early second/eighth century it disappeared from Syria and reappeared in the Maghrib, and also at the other extreme of the Islamic world, in Afghanistan. In stucco carvings, the minute and accurate workmanship and the extensive use of the stalactite reached a very high standard.

Pottery is known to have been produced in Spain from early Islamic times. The earliest specimens were excavated in Cordova and at Madīnat al-Zahrā'. Much more is known about later Hispano-Moresque pottery, dating from the ninth/fifteenth and tenth/sixteenth centuries. Potters, even after the Christian reconquest of Spain, continued to decorate their vessels in Moorish style. The pottery centres of Paterna, Málaga and Manisa produced golden and ruby lustre vessels, large dishes, bowls and vases, sometimes adding blue to the decoration. Kufic letters, arabesques and scrolls were the favourite designs. By the late sixteenth century the Moorish style had gradually disappeared and pottery-making had gradually slipped into the hands of Christian artists.

Textiles made in Muslim Spain are also worth mentioning. Almería, Granada, Málaga, Murcia and Seville were the main textile-producing centres, making tapestry-woven bands, silks and golden brocades displaying human figures and animals, usually placed in round medallions. Textile designs were similar to those of ivory carvings. Ivory carving played an important role in Andalusian art and reached a very high standard under the Umayyad rulers. A large number of ivory boxes have survived and can be seen in various public and private collections. The Victoria and Albert Museum possesses a few Moorish ivory carvings which are decorated with vine scrolls, palmettes, human and animal figures and Kufic inscriptions.

Moorish metalwork greatly resembles that of the eastern Islamic world, and uses the same techniques. A great number of engraved and inlaid vessels are preserved in Spanish collections, mostly dating from the tenth to the fourteenth centuries.

Very little is known of Maghribī and Andalusian paintings. A famous seventh/thirteenth-century manuscript, containing the love story of

Bayāḍ and Riyāḍ was illustrated in Ceuta in Morocco. Though the actual story takes place in 'Irāq, the architectural elements depict Maghribī forms. In calligraphy the Maghribī style was quite distinct from the rest of the Islamic world by reason of the round forms of the letters and the placing of the dot under the *fā'*.

PERSIA AFTER THE MONGOL INVASION: ĪL-KHĀNS AND TIMURIDS

The Seljuk period was a golden age for art and architecture in Persia. It was followed by a brief rule of the Khwārazm-Shāhs and by the disaster caused by the successive Mongol invasions during the first half of the seventh/thirteenth century. Recovery from the Mongol devastation was very slow. Some cities, such as Rayy, a former centre of pottery and textile industry, never regained their previous vitality. But the recovery was initiated by a Mongol dynasty, the Īl-Khāns, who later embraced Islam. From their capital at Tabrīz they encouraged artisans and builders to heal the severe wounds caused by their predecessors.

It was Hülegü, the captor and destroyer of Baghdād, who made Tabrīz his capital, and was also responsible for the erection of an observatory in Marāgha. His architect was al-'Urdī, an engineer and astronomer. The real recovery and building activity, however, started under Ghāzān Khān, who became the ruler of the Il-Khanid empire in 694/1295. After his death in 703/1304 his brother, Öljeitü, continued his work. Rashīd al-Dīn, the famous historian, was their contemporary and their minister.

Öljeitü ordered the erection of a new capital, Sulṭāniyya, south of Tabrīz, in 706/1306. Mosques, palaces and a citadel were erected there. The only surviving building today is his own mausoleum. It is an octagonal building partially coated with faience bricks inside and outside. The platform outside carries the huge dome and eight small minarets above each corner. The building today is partially ruined.

Öljeitü was also responsible for the erection of a very fine stucco *miḥrāb* in a prayer-hall in the Masjid-i Jāmi' of Iṣfahān. According to the inscription it was completed in 710/1310. The stucco decoration is arranged in several layers above each other, just as those of the Seljuk period. The details of the design, however, differ from those earlier examples.

The Masjid-i Jāmi' of Tabrīz, better known as the Masjid-i 'Alī

Shāh, with its massive walls, looks rather like a fortress or a citadel. It was erected by Tāj al-Dīn 'Alī Shāh, Öljeitü's *wazīr*, and the rival of Rashīd al-Dīn, between 710/1310 and 720/1320. The building is in ruins to-day. The existing ruins are parts of the *qibla īwān*. There is no sign of any decoration today, but contemporary sources mention a faience-tiled lustre *miḥrāb*.

The most interesting and probably the best preserved monument of the Il-Khanid period is the Masjid-i Jāmi' complex in Naṭanz, in central Persia, east of Iṣfahān. It was built between 704/1304 and 725/1325. The mosque is of the four-*īwān* type with an octagonal dome and a tall slender minaret, partly decorated with enamelled bricks [pl. 23(*b*)]. The building has a faience-tiled portal. The original *miḥrāb* was of faience-lustred tiles. Parts of this are now in the Victoria and Albert Museum.

Faience-tiled lustre *miḥrābs* were made in Kāshān during the second half of the seventh/thirteenth and at the beginning of the eighth/fourteenth centuries. While pottery production came to a halt in Rayy after the Mongol destruction, Kāshān, it seems, quickly recovered. Underglaze-painted and lustre-painted wares were produced there until the end of the eighth/fourteenth century.

New pottery centres emerged in the Sulṭānābād region. Here the main type was the underglaze-painted ware, using grey as the main colour for the background, reserving the designs in white or blue, sometimes in relief. Far Eastern elements are apparent in Sulṭānābād wares.

Large dishes and bowls are known from the eighth/fourteenth and ninth/fifteenth centuries painted in heavy green or purple lines, frequently with cross-hatchings. These are considered as rustic wares. Their actual provenance has not yet been identified.

A more important group of the period is the Persian blue and white, which was produced in Kirmān and Mashhad. It was previously thought that blue and whites were first made in China. Recent research, however, has established that their origin should be sought in Persia. In fact the cobalt ore which was used for the decoration of Chinese blue and whites was imported from Persia. Very little is known of early Persian blue and whites, and no piece can be confidently dated to the eighth/fourteenth century. From the ninth/fifteenth century a number of small bowls are known. Their shapes resemble those of Chinese rice-bowls. The designs are confined to scrolls and palmettes. In one instance a flying crane is depicted. Later Chinese influence becomes more and more apparent, and from the eighteenth century onwards designs are outlined in black.

In 737/1336 the last Il-Khaṇid ruler died. The Il-Khanid empire disintegrated and was divided among a number of petty dynasties. Then in the late eighth/fourteenth century a new and ruthless leader emerged in the east: Tīmūr. He sacked and plundered a number of cities in Māzandarān in the north, and some also in Fārs and Kirmān in the south. Nevertheless, he had great respect for beautiful and sacred monuments. He also systematically collected artists in his capital, Samarqand, to beautify it. Tīmūr's work, the patronage of arts, was continued by his sons and successors, who later on moved the capital to Herat. There was then a new renaissance in Persia. Beautiful buildings were erected, painting, calligraphy and bookbinding, and all the other arts, flourished.

In architecture the most outstandings building can be found in Samarqand. The finest among them are the mausoleum-complex of the Shāh-i Zinda. Some of the buildings date from pre-Timurid times. The buildings are richly decorated with faience mosaics and painted tiles. Dense stalactite semidomes hang over the portals. Openwork is frequently apparent [pl. 24(*b*)].

To the Shāh-i Zinda complex is attached Tīmūr's own mausoleum, the Gūr-i Mīr, which was completed in 807/1404. The building is dominated by a huge bulbous dome, covered with enamelled tiles. Walls and portals are similarly decorated [pl. 24(*a*)].

Other religious buildings in Samarqand, Bukhārā, Herat or in Persia proper, are similarly decorated. Of these the *muṣallā* of Gawhar Shād in Herat, the four-*īwān madrasa* in Khargird and the Masjid-i Gawhar Shād in Mashhad should be mentioned. In western Persia the Blue Mosque of Tabrīz deserves special attention. It is one of the very few completely roofed mosques of Persia. Its inner walls were decorated with cobalt-blue faience tiles. The rectangular building was crowned with a central dome surrounded by smaller ones over the sanctuary and the galleries. The mosque was completed in 869/1465.

Islamic architecture in Persia reached its highest quality during the Timurid period, and this was never surpassed in refinement and elegance. The importance of the period for the history of Islamic art, however, is not due to architecture alone. Great progress was made in the art of painting, development of which had already started under the Il-Khanids. Rashīd al-Dīn compiled his universal history, *Jāmiʿ al-*

tawārīkh, between 707/1307 and 714/1314. One of the manuscripts, which is divided between Edinburgh University Library and the Royal Asiatic Society, has a number of illustrations. These miniatures clearly reveal the new, Far Eastern elements, which are, however, fully incorporated into the pictures. Landscapes, particularly rocks, trees and clouds, appear in Chinese style [pl. 25(*a*)]. The manuscript was executed in Tabrīz, the home of one of the most important schools of painters during the Il-Khanid and Timurid periods. Copies of the *Kalīla wa-Dimna* are also attributed to Tabrīz.

One of the most famous illuminated manuscripts of Tabrīz is the so-called Demotte *Shāh-nāma* of Firdawsī. The manuscript is dated 730/1330. Far Eastern elements are still evident, but Persian features appear somewhat stronger than in the illustrations of the *Jāmiʿ al-tawārīkh*.

A second school of painting existed in Shīrāz. It was a prosperous city during the Il-Khanid period and was the home of great poets like Saʿdī and Ḥāfiẓ. Four *Shāh-nāma* manuscripts are known to have been illustrated in Shīrāz during the first half of the eighth/fourteenth century [pl. 25(*b*)]; as well as a copy of the *Kalīla wa-Dimna*, dating from 733/1333. The pictures are rather naïvely drawn, in comparison with those of Tabrīz. The backgrounds are painted in red, yellow or blue. Architectural elements are represented by a few small features such as arches. Pictures are small and fully incorporated into the text.

During the Timurid period the centre of painting shifted to Herat, where Shāh-Rukh (807–50/1404–47) became the great patron of artists. Several *Shāh-nāma* and *Kalīla wa-Dimna* manuscripts illustrated in Herat during the middle of the ninth/fifteenth century have survived. The great importance of Herat in painting, however, started under the patronage of ʿAlī Shīr Navāʾī, a politician, painter and poet. He patronized Bihzād, the greatest painter in Islamic art.

Bihzād was active from the late ninth/fifteenth century until his death in Tabrīz in *c*. 942/1535–6. He excelled in battle scenes, but was equally outstanding in depicting architectural elements or in the very fine drawing of human figures. Very few signed miniatures are known today. Four of such works illustrate the *Bustān* of Saʿdī. The finest miniatures by Bihzād are, however, in two copies of the *Khamsa* of Niẓāmī in the British Museum. Bihzād had a number of pupils who continued to paint in his style (pl. 26).

In 913/1507 Herat was occupied by the Özbegs and three years later by Shāh Ismāʿīl, the founder of the Safavid dynasty. He made Tabrīz his capital and as a consequence most of the artists, among them Bihzād, followed the new ruler there.

In parallel with book illuminations, bookbinding also reached a very high standard. In Persia, Timurid bookbindings are the finest specimens. Leather was used, the decorations being stamped and incised, and then painted in red, green or blue and gilt. In a number of instances, birds appear against scroll backgrounds.

In calligraphy also great progress was made in Herat. The best calligraphers of the time were working there. The *nasta'līq* script developed in Herat during the Timurid period, as did the *dīwānī* and *dashtī*.

THE MAMLUK PERIOD OF SYRIA AND EGYPT

During the Mamluk period (648–922/1250–1517), Muslim traditions in arts and architecture continued and flourished without any interruption. The Mongols were halted and defeated by the Mamluks. The Mamluk sultans of Egypt and Syria erected a number of significant buildings. A great number of *madrasas*, mausoleums and mosques were built in Cairo. Most of these have survived up to the present day in more or less satisfactory condition.

Among the religious buildings the mosque and *madrasa* of Sultan Baybars I al-Bunduqdārī, erected between 660/1262 and 668/1269, should be mentioned. Here, unfortunately, only the outer enclosure-walls have survived. The complex of Sultan Qalawun (built in 683/1284–85) comprises a *madrasa*, a mausoleum and a hospital. It is one of the most significant buildings of the Mamluk period, because of its monumental façade with the double windows, the beautiful crenellations and the rich stucco carvings [pl. 27(*a*)]. Inside, the stone and marble coatings and the woodcarvings mark the apex of the Mamluk art.

The mosque of al-Azhar was enlarged and altered a number of times by the addition of the Ṭaybarsiyya *madrasa* in 709–10/1309–10, the Aqbuqāwiyya in 741/1340, and the Jawhariyya *madrasa* in 844/1440.

The mausoleums are mostly domed square buildings with usually a stucco *miḥrāb* and a stucco decorative panel running round the inside of the building. The mausoleum of Aḥmad b. Sulaymān al-Rifā'ī is unique with its glass mosaic decorated *miḥrāb*, dating from 689/1290.

Of secular architecture not much has survived. Some Mamluk

alterations and additions in the citadels of Cairo, Aleppo and in Ḥarrān are still visible. The palace of Dār Bashtāk in Cairo, dating from 742/1341, and a few caravanserais in Egypt and Syria are still standing. In private houses and palaces the *mashrabiyyas* or wooden lattices were generally introduced.

Arabesques played a more important role in Mamluk woodcarvings, of which a great number of *minbars* and *miḥrābs* are preserved in Cairo. The decorations of these are divided into small compartments filled either by arabesques or by geometrical patterns. By the end of the period wood-carving started to decline.

Glass-making reached a high standard during the Mamluk period. A number of mosque-lamps decorated with enamel and gilt are known. The decorations are arranged in horizontal bands containing inscriptions, giving the names and titles of sultans, *amīrs* and high officials for whom the particular object was made. Their heraldic blazons are illustrated in round medallions. Leading glass centres were in Damascus. The making of fine enamel and gilt glass came to an end by the end of the eighth/fourteenth or at the beginning of the ninth/fifteenth century.

In pottery, Mamluk artists followed the examples of the Ayyubid period. The main type of pottery was the lead-glazed *sgraffiato* ware. The glaze is usually transparent brownish-yellow. Large inscriptions appear sometimes on a floral background. Official blazons, so common in Mamluk glass and in metalwork, are also frequently depicted. The production of lustre ware was discontinued in Egypt. Polychrome underglaze-painted wares presenting human and animal figures were still produced.

The production of fine metalwork greatly increased, particularly in three towns: Cairo, Damascus and Aleppo. At that time the inlay technique reached its highest quality. Human figures rarely appear; the main decorative theme is the *naskhī* inscription and heraldic blazons. Some new motives were also apparent, resembling Chinese elements. The best pieces were made under the reign of al-Nāṣir Muḥammad b. Qalawun (693–741/1293–1340), and these were mainly bowls, large basins and candlesticks.

It was about at that time or somewhat later, during the fifteenth and sixteenth Christian centuries, that fine metalwork was produced in Venice in the old Islamic style by craftsmen from Syria and Egypt. Overcrowding, the extensive use of silver and the curious round form of vessels are the characteristic and distinguishing features of the Venetian metalwork. The majority of them date from the sixteenth century.

One of the greatest achievements of the period was the weaving of geometrical carpets, which seems to have developed during the ninth/fifteenth century, and continued right up to the tenth/sixteenth century. The design, as its name indicates, is confined to geometrical forms: octagons, stars, triangles, etc. The ground colour is red and the decorations are in golden-yellow, blue and in green [pl. 27(*b*)].

THE OTTOMAN PERIOD

The Ottomans made Bursa their first capital in 727/1326, and the earliest monuments of the period can be found there and at Iznik. Some forty years later the capital was moved to the European territories, to Edirne, the former city of Adrianople, and after the conquest of Constantinople in 857/1453, it became the seat of the new empire.

The earliest Ottoman buildings were modelled on Seljuk architecture, as can clearly be seen in the Ulu Jāmiʿ of Bursa, erected between 799/1396 and 803/1400. This is a rectangular building divided into twenty equal parts by arcades resting on twelve piers. Each part is roofed by a dome. The ground-plan of the Eski Jāmiʿ of Edirne (807–17/1404–14), or that of the Zinjirli Kuyu Jāmiʿ of Istanbul (end of the ninth/fifteenth century) follow the same principle.

These mosques are not characteristic of the period. Ottoman mosques, as a principle, are square buildings, covered by a large central dome. To this main part a number of smaller parts can then be added which are then roofed by smaller domes or semi-domes. Minarets played an important part. These are slender, tall, round or polygonal towers with a balcony on the upper part for the muezzin.

Medreses largely follow the traditional Anatolian types, the cells of students and lecture rooms being connected by an arcade and surrounding the rectangular courtyard. *Türbes* or mausoleums are square or polygonal and are covered by the traditional conical or pyramidal roof.

The inner decoration of religious buildings deserves special attention. Large surfaces were covered by painted faience tiles or faience mosaics, which were mainly produced at Iznik. The earliest known faience *miḥrāb* of the period is in the Green Mosque of Bursa (824/1421), which was signed by a Tabrīzī artist. The building itself is the work of a Turkish architect.

The finest Ottoman religious buildings were erected by Sinān Pasha, one of the greatest Turkish architects (896–997/1490–1588). Some three hundred and fifty buildings are attributed to him, of which the Süleymāniye mosque in Istanbul (965/1557), and the Selīmiye Jāmiʿ of Edirne (977–83/1569–75) [pl. 28(*b*)] are the best known. The mosque of Sultan Aḥmed, or Blue Mosque (so called because of its inner tile decoration), is the last among the great Ottoman mosques (1018–26/1609–17).

In secular architecture the Ottoman caravanserais, which differed somewhat from previous Seljuk models, should be mentioned. Arranged around a central rectangular courtyard the buildings were provided with two floors, the ground floor providing accommodation for shops, workshops and stables, and the upper one rooms for travellers merchants and craftsmen.

Ḥammāms or baths followed the traditional line. These were covered by a number of small domes. Great numbers of Ottoman *ḥammāms* are preserved in Anatolia and in other parts of the former Ottoman empire.

Covered bazaars roughly followed the ground-plan and arrangement of the caravanserais but without the central courtyard. Public fountains were decorated with richly carved stones of Iznik faience tiles. Among the palaces the Topḳapi̊ Sarayi̊ complex in Istanbul should be mentioned. Later palaces, like the Dolmabaghche, Beylerbeyi and many others, were erected in European styles. From the eighteenth century onwards, Turkish architecture, both religious and secular, follows the contemporary European styles, such as baroque and rococo.

In pottery a distinct type was discovered during an excavation some forty years ago by the late Friedrich Sarre at Miletus. Thus the name 'Miletus ware' was wrongly given to them. They are of red clay and are painted on a ground white slip under a clear glaze in blue, green and black. The decorations are presented in a naturalistic style. Rosettes, scrolls, flowers or birds appear on the small bowls, which are the commonest type of this 'Miletus ware'. Excavations by Professor Oktay Aslanapa at Iznik have established that the 'Miletus ware' was produced at Iznik and can be dated to the eighth/fourteenth and ninth/fifteenth centuries.

Later Iznik pottery can be divided into three main groups. The first period, which was previously called the 'Abraham of Kütahya' group, is generally considered to date from 896/1490 to 932/1525. The body in all three groups is white and soft. During the first period vessels like large dishes, mosque-lamps, jars, ewers, and standing-bowls, were painted in cobalt-blue on a white ground. The designation of 'Abraham of Kütahya' derives from a signed piece.

The decorations of the second period specimens were painted, in addition to cobalt-blue, in turquoise-green and sometimes also in purple. They date from 932/1525 until about 963/1555. An outstanding example of this period, a mosque-lamp, which was made for the Dome of the Rock in Jerusalem in 956/1549, is in the British Museum.

In the third period (*c.* 964–1113/1555–1700) a lively red is added to the colour scheme. Wall-tiles belonging to this group are preserved in a number of mosques in Istanbul and in the Selīmiye Jāmi' of Edirne. Carnations, tulips, and roses appear in dishes, and jars. Ships, human and animal figures, and birds are also depicted [pl. 29(*a*)].

After the decline of pottery-making in Iznik, a new pottery centre emerged at Kütahya, producing vessels mainly for the Armenian communities of Anatolia. Kütahya wares are of white earthenware and decorations are painted in yellow, blue, grey and green on a white ground under a clear glaze. Many signed and dated pieces are known from the eighteenth and nineteenth centuries.

Another pottery centre of less importance was at Chanakkale on the Dardanelles. Porcelain was also manufactured in Turkey, but the cheap imported mass-produced European porcelain seems to have put an end to these experiments.

Great progress was made in calligraphy and miniature painting under the Ottomans. There was a school of calligraphists and painters in the palace of Istanbul under the patronage of the sultans. Among them Sultan Meḥmed the Conqueror had the greatest name for supporting the arts. He invited Italian painters to Istanbul and sent Turkish artists to study in Italy. Naqqāsh Sinān Bey also studied in Italy and on his return to Turkey painted, among many other things, the portrait of Sultan Meḥmed.

Turkish calligraphists and illuminators developed a new style and their great achievement and merit was in the fact that they recorded the important historical events of their time. Matraqji, the celebrated geographer and historian, for example narrated the Persian campaign of Sultan Süleymān the Magnificent. 'O̱smān, in his *Hüner-nāme* (dated

957–68/1550–60), recorded the history of the Ottoman sultans in two volumes. In the accounts of the Szigetvár campaign written by Ferīdūn Pasha in 976/1568, events of the campaign and Sultan Süleymān's death are described, and are illustrated by a number of miniatures.

There are about 10,000 or even more illuminated Turkish manuscripts in the Topḳapï Sarayï Müzesi in Istanbul, recording historical events and topography of cities or depicting the portraits of sultans and high officials. Other manuscripts, quite contrary to Islamic tradition, depict scenes from the Prophet Muḥammad's life and of the greatest events of Islamic history.

One of the last great Ottoman painters was Levnī, who lived in the eighteenth century. His greatest work represents the festivities organized for the wedding of Sultan Aḥmed II's daughter. Levnī was already working under the strong influence of European painting, which eventually completely destroyed the real character of Ottoman painting.

Apart from painting it was in the field of textiles and carpets that great progress was made under the Ottomans. The Turks, who had already excelled in carpet making for many centuries, developed many new types during that period. One of the earliest types was the so-called 'animal carpet', which can be dated to the eighth/fourteenth and ninth/fifteenth centuries. The so-called 'Holbein rugs' with arabesque patterns in the field and Kufic characters on the border, are known from Dutch and Italian paintings of the sixteenth and seventeenth centuries.

Several types were produced and developed in Ushak. Among them the medallion and star Ushak and the so-called 'Transylvanian carpets' should be mentioned. Prayer rugs representing *miḥrāb* niches are known to have been made in Ghiordes, Kula, Ladik, Bergama and at Mujur. Rugs made in the Caucasus have distinct geometrical designs. Persian influence on them is apparent. They mostly date from the nineteenth century.

Brocades, velvets and embroideries were made in Bursa, in the neighbourhood of Edirne, and at a number of places along the Aegean coast. On brocades and velvets some Italian influence can be observed. Embroideries are very colourful, sometimes so fine that they give the impression of painting [pl. 29(*b*)]. These are embroidered on linen or silk. They are reversible, and generally represent beautiful flowers and cypress-trees. They mostly date from the eighteenth and nineteenth centuries.

THE SAFAVID PERIOD IN PERSIA

Shāh Ismā'īl (907–30/1502–24), the founder of the Safavid dynasty, occupied Herat in 913/1507, and took a great number of artists with him to his capital in Tabrīz. No monuments survive of his or his immediate successors' time. His palace at Kwuy, north-west of Tabrīz, is known only from the description of European travellers. Later on the capital was moved to Qazvīn, where Shāh Ṭahmāsp (930–84/1524–76) erected the royal mosque and his palace, parts of which can still be seen today.

Great building activity did not really start until the accession to the throne of Shāh 'Abbās I (985–1038/1587–1629). He once again moved the capital to Iṣfahān, and was responsible for the planning and erection of the royal square, the Maydān-i Shāh. The Maydān-i Shāh is surrounded by the royal mosque, the Masjid-i Shāh on the south, the Masjid-i Shaykh Luṭf Allāh on the east, the Qayṣariyya Bazaar on the north and the 'Alī Qapu palace on the west.

The Masjid-i Shāh, one of the greatest achievements of Safavid architecture, is a large four-*iwān* mosque, the walls of which are covered by faience tiles and mosaics. The monumental portal is flanked by two slender minarets with balconies on their top (pl. 30), then the axis of the whole mosque is turned around the entrance hall for the correction of the *qibla* towards the south-west. There is a large dome over the *qibla* *iwān*, decorated inside and outside with faience mosaics, recalling the ornaments of carpets. The building, which was erected between 999/1590 and 1025/1616, bears the signature of the architect, Ustād Abu'l-Qāsim and a number of calligraphers.

The Masjid-i Shaykh Luṭf Allāh is a small covered mosque, again turned behind the entrance hall in order to correct the orientation of the *qibla*. It has a huge dome similarly decorated to that of the Masjid-i Shāh. The building was completed in 1028/1618.

The 'Alī Qapu palace was the seat of Shāh 'Abbās's government, and his official residence. The ground floor provided rooms for offices and for the guards, while on the first floor was a large audience hall and a gallery, a *tālār*, opening into the royal square [pl. 28(*a*)]. There are two more floors, the rooms of which were decorated with mural paintings, openwork and niches for glass and pottery.

The shah's private residence was in the Chihil Sutūn or 'Palace of the forty columns'. There is a large pool in front of the building in which the columns of the gallery, the *tālār*, are reflected. From there opens the audience hall, the walls of which were originally decorated with mural paintings representing hunting scenes and landscapes. The palace originally had a number of lacquer painted doors, which are now scattered in a number of European and American museums. The building was partially destroyed by fire in the eighteenth century..

The Safavids contributed a great deal to the decoration and enlargement of the complex of the *Imām* Riżā's shrine in Mashhad. Work began there under Shāh 'Abbās I in 1010/1601. Oratories, *madrasas*, and libraries were added and richly decorated in faience mosaic and glass.

The last great contribution to Persian architecture was the erection of the Madrasa Mādar-i Shāh in Iṣfahān, at the beginning of the eighteenth century. It is built in the traditional style, having four *īwāns* opening on to a central courtyard. The *qibla īwān* has a dome and a minaret. Walls are covered all over with painted faience tiles. Decorations of later buildings, such as the Vakīl Madrasa in Shīrāz (twelfth/eighteenth century), or the shrines at Karbalā' and Sāmarrā, and the Sipahsālār Mosque in Tehran (nineteenth century), never reach the heights of previous architecture.

In miniature painting, Herat remained the centre only for a few years after Shāh Ismā'īl's occupation of the city. Artists, like Bihzād and many of his pupils, moved to the new capital, Tabrīz. Thus Tabrīz became once more a centre of Persian painting. Another new centre emerged in Bukhārā, which was very active during the tenth/sixteenth and early eleventh/seventeenth centuries. Illumination of manuscripts of the *Shāh-nāma* and *Khamsa* of Niẓāmī continued. Bihzād's style was followed for quite a long time. Upon the moving of the capital to Iṣfahān under Shāh 'Abbās I, a new school of painters was founded there which excelled not only in miniature painting, but also in the production of bookbindings and in lacquer-works as well.

Carpets of the Safavid period were greatly influenced by contemporary miniature-painting and bookbinding. Under Shāh Ismā'īl and Shāh Ṭahmāsp, Tabrīz became an important centre of carpet-weaving, but places like Kāshān, Iṣfahān, Yazd and Kirmān also produced a number of types. Animal and hunting carpets are known from the tenth/sixteenth and eleventh/seventeenth centuries. Large medallion carpets were made in the tenth/sixteenth century. The finest example of that type is the Ardabīl carpet in the Victoria and Albert Museum. It dates from 946/1539. The vase rugs, it seems, were made in north-western Persia in the tenth/sixteenth and eleventh/seventeenth centuries, while the 'garden carpets' may have been the products of south and south-eastern Persia, possibly of the Kirmān region.

Rugs with Chinese cloud-patterns and extensive floral designs came from Khurāsān and Herat, and may date from the tenth/sixteenth and eleventh/seventeenth centuries. Some floral and animal rugs were made in silk in the tenth/sixteenth century. The so-called 'Polish rugs', the name derived from the eagle on them, believed for a long time to be the Polish eagle, were actually made in Persia and sent out as gifts by Shāh 'Abbās I. They were probably manufactured in Kāshān and Iṣfahān [pl. 31(*a*)]. Tapestry-woven silk rugs, *kilims*, of the same period were made in medallion, floral, vase and in animal designs. Carpet-making still flourishes in Persia in the Tabrīz, Hamadān, Kāshān, Iṣfahān and Kirmān regions.

Safavid brocades, velvets and embroideries were influenced by miniature painting just as carpets were. Designs frequently depicted scenes from the *Shāh-nāma* and the *Khamsa* of Niẓāmī. These brocades and velvets were exported to Europe, and a number were presented by Shāh 'Abbās I to European rulers. He supported the weaving-centres, which apparently were located in Kāshān and Iṣfahān.

Metalwork in the Safavid period was still flourishing, and a number of dated and signed pieces are preserved in museums and private collections. Inlaying was not so much favoured, and was used on copper or brasswork. It more often appears on iron and steel vessels, or zoomorphic figures are weapons. These were inlaid in gold and silver, but gold inlay is more characteristic of the period. Brass vessels are engraved or in relief decoration; backgrounds are frequently filled with niello [pl. 31(*b*)]. Metalwork centres were in Tabrīz, Iṣfahān and in Kirmān. Tabrīz was and still is famous for its fine silverware, decorated with minutely drawn engraved designs.

Several new types of pottery appeared during the Safavid period. Among them the earliest and probably the finest was the so-called 'Kubachi ware'. These were most likely made in north-western Persia in the Tabrīz region. Decorations, which often present human figures, animals and birds, are painted in blue, yellow, green and dull brownish-red under a clear glaze on a white ground [pl. 32(*a*)]. There seems to be a connection with or influence by Iznik pottery. The finest specimens date from the tenth/sixteenth century.

During the eleventh/seventeenth century, lustre painting was re-introduced, using brownish or ruby lustre on a very hard, white earthenware. The place of production is not yet known. Fine white wares, similar to those of the Seljuk period, decorated with incised lines, in openwork, or painted in black and blue, appeared again in the eleventh/seventeenth century [pl. 32(*b*)]. These wares are known as 'Gombroon wares', after the harbour (modern Bandar 'Abbās) in the Persian Gulf, whence they were shipped and exported to Europe.

Kirmān seemed to have been responsible for the production of a number of monochrome-glazed wares, mainly of celadon, brown or blue colours. Sometimes these were painted in white, or the design was incised right down to the white body. Underglaze-painted polychrome wares were also made in Kirmān during the eleventh/seventeenth and twelfth/eighteenth century.

In later times, Iṣfahān and Tehran produced underglaze-painted vessels and tiles. Decorations often appeared in relief. Figures were naïvely drawn, and the quality was far inferior to those of the earlier types. Import of mass-produced European and Far Eastern porcelain caused the final decline of the industry in Persia.

CHAPTER 10

SCIENCE

'Say, shall those who have knowledge and those who have it not be deemed equal?' (Qur'ān 39.12). 'Seek knowledge, in China if necessary.' 'The search after knowledge is obligatory for every Muslim.' 'The ink of the scholars is worth more than the blood of the martyrs'. It would be possible to quote many such texts from the Qur'ān and many from the Tradition (*Ḥadīth*) in which knowledge is extolled, in terse phrases, in the sight of the faithful.

Actually, the knowledge here envisaged is preeminently religious knowledge, which enables man to have a better understanding of the Book of God and the teaching of His Prophet. And it may be maintained, without paradox, that, with the possible exception of its poetry and its proverbs, all Muslim intellectual activity in the widest sense had its starting-point in the Qur'ān: grammar was created by non-Arabs so that they might be able to read the sacred text correctly, rhetoric for the emphasizing of its beauties, the Tradition assembled in order to explain it and supply its omissions, jurisprudence drawn up as a system of principles for moral and social life, and finally theology to defend against sceptics, or even to demonstrate, the truths taught by the Book.

It would have been surprising if this taste for knowledge had not been extended to the 'profane sciences' when the Muslims came into contact with those peoples who had inherited them. Even if there were, here and there and at certain periods, theologians of a narrow and defensive orthodoxy who forbade them, it must be said that Muslims in general, led by their caliphs and princes, showed a great thirst for instruction and were eager to assimilate the treasures of ancient science when it came within their reach. The original religious fervour still remained, for Muslim scientists, whether astronomers, mathematicians or physicians, were not seeking any the less to work for the glory of God and the service of religion when they devoted themselves to the sciences derived from Greece, from Persia or from India.

The actual course of Arab conquests was from the beginning a conducive factor. Leaving a 'canton isolated from the world', to use Pascal's phrase, the Arabs at once found themselves in contact with Syria and its Byzantine culture, with Egypt, heir to the ancient world of the Pharaohs, with the Persia of the Sasanids, with India and before long with North Africa and Spain. Various peoples (Persians, Turks, Berbers, Andalusians, Egyptians, etc.) embraced Islam; other elements, 'the People of the Book' (Christians, Jews and Sabaeans), remained in the midst of the Muslim community, second-class citizens but protected by the law and taking an active part in cultural life. All contributed to the development of the sciences in Islam, and all or nearly all of them wrote their works in Arabic, so that for medieval Western Europe 'Arab' was synonymous with 'Muslim.' It should cause no surprise if both terms are used indiscriminately in the present account when dealing with ancient Islam; in this context it seems hardly likely that national susceptibilities will take it amiss.

The importance of this 'Muslim' or 'Arab' science to the general progress of culture is beyond question, and much evidence of it can be adduced. In the first place, numerous Arabic words have passed into some of the Western languages, especially terms used in chemistry, navigation and astronomy. 'Arabic' figures, which came from India, were transmitted to Europe by the Muslims. An even more significant fact is that in his monumental *Introduction to the history of science* Sarton has given the name of a Muslim scientist to seven chapters of the second volume, deeming that the period under consideration can be designated by him. Finally, the visitor entering the chapel of Princeton University may be somewhat surprised to find there a window representing an outlandish personage: clad in a long eastern robe and a majestic turban, he holds in his hand an unrolled parchment on which can be read in Arabic *Kitāb al-ḥāwī*. That those who inspired or endowed this chapel should have deemed al-Rāzī (Rhazes), the author of the book, worthy to be represented in a place of Christian worship among the great figures of mankind, is a sufficient indication of the position occupied by Muslim science in the history of culture. Its importance has moreover become more apparent as a result of studies accomplished during the past half-century. Thanks to the work of researchers, many unpublished texts have been made available to readers. It may be added that Oriental scientists have also made interesting contributions to the history of science among the Arabs.

The subject under consideration is immense and it is not possible within the narrow limits assigned to deal with more than the essentials. In the first place mention should be made of the interest taken by many Muslim thinkers or historians in classifying the various sciences of their time. This was the treatment accorded to the subject by Ibn al-Nadīm in his *Fihrist*, by al-Fārābī in the *Iḥṣā' al-'ulūm*, in the dissertations of the *Ikhwān al-Ṣafā'*, in the 'Keys of the sciences' of al-Khwārizmī, by al-Ghazālī in several of his writings, by Ibn Khaldūn in his famous 'Prolegomena,' by Tashköprüzādeh in his *Miftāḥ al-sa'āda*, and later by al-Tahānawī in his *Kashshāf*.

From all these classifications it emerges that two kinds of science must be distinguished: (a) the religious sciences, which form to some extent the spinal column of Muslim thought: Qur'anic exegesis, Tradition (*Ḥadīth*), jurisprudence and all the propaedeutic disciplines which enable its depths to be explored; and (b) the 'foreign' or rational sciences, also called the 'sciences of the ancients', which were introduced into Islam as a result of contact with various peoples. The former lie outside the scope of the present chapter; it remains to consider the latter.

The first Muslim thinker to have given an overall picture of the sciences in his time is al-Fārābī (d. 339/950), whose 'Catalogue of Sciences' (*Iḥṣā' al-'ulūm*) known in the Latin Middle Ages by the name of *De Scientiis*, sets out to be an analytical review of all the sciences of his time with their subdivisions. He enumerates them as follows:

1. The linguistic sciences.
2. Logic (containing the eight books of the *Organon* of Aristotle).
3. Mathematics (comprising arithmetic, geometry, optics, astronomy, music, statics, mechanics).
4. Physics, reproducing the Aristotelian divisions.
5. Metaphysics.
6. Politics.
7. Jurisprudence.
8. Theology.

It will be observed that the Muslim sciences take their place beside all the other sciences which form the hierarchy within the framework, enlarged by tradition, of the Aristotelian classification.

Another philosopher, Ibn Sīnā (Avicenna, d. 428/1037), a disciple of al-Fārābī, was to extend the classification further. Confining himself to the rational sciences (*al-'ulūm al-'aqliyya*), he divided them into (a) speculative sciences (seeking after truth), and (b) practical sciences (aimed at wellbeing). Into the former class he relegated physics (eight basic sciences drawn from the works of Aristotle and seven derivative sciences as follows: medicine, astrology, physiognomy, interpretation of dreams, talismans, charms, alchemy); mathematics, including arithmetic, geometry, astronomy and music, with some ten derivative sciences; and metaphysics, which comprised the five great divisions of the *Metaphysics* of Aristotle and two derivatives—prophetic inspiration and eschatology.

Practical science was composed of personal morality, domestic morality and politics, to which Ibn Sīnā also appended prophetology. It is clear that philosophy was the queen of the sciences, and it was indeed by philosophy that they were governed.

In opposition to this philosophical view of the sciences, a mystical theologian like al-Ghazālī was more concerned with the religious aspect. What chiefly interested him was the relationship of these sciences to the ultimate happiness of man and the religious usefulness to be derived from them by the community of believers. It was accordingly this criterion which he was to apply in judging the value of the 'rational sciences'. At the beginning of his great work, *Iḥyā' 'ulūm al-dīn*, he divides the 'science which directs our progress towards the future life' into two main parts: (1) the science of relationship with God and with one's neighbour, and (2) sciences of the 'revelation'. The second category had pure knowledge as its sole object, while the first combined action with knowledge.

In the third chapter of his first volume, al-Ghazālī gives a detailed classification of the sciences from the standpoint of legal obligation: certain sciences are compulsory for each individual (*farḍ 'ayn*) while others are compulsory only for the community (*farḍ kifāya*). The former class concerns only the sciences of relationships; with regard to the communal obligation, al-Ghazālī distinguishes two kinds of sciences, those which are of a juridico-religious nature (*al-'ulūm al-shar'iyya*) and those which are not. The first are those which are communicated by the prophets and cannot be acquired by reasoning (like arithmetic), or by experiment (like medicine), or by ear (like language).

The non-religious sciences may be recommended, culpable or merely permitted. The recommended sciences are those which are closely connected with wordly affairs, like medicine and calculation, and are of two kinds. Some ought to be undertaken by the community (communal obligation): in this category are the sciences without which life in a community becomes impossible, such as medicine and calculation; the others have an optional character and are supererogatory, but devotion to them is laudable since to acquire them increases competence. An example is the pursuit of calculation or medical studies beyond the point required by practical utility. The culpable sciences are such as magic, the science of talismans, and prestidigitation, while the sciences which are merely tolerated are poetry—provided that it is not immoral—and history. The juridico-religious sciences are all recommended and are obligatory only for the community.

In the 'Prolegomena', Ibn Khaldūn, the celebrated historian and sociologist of the eighth/fourteenth century, has given a clear account of the whole field of the sciences as they appeared in his time. The principle of classification is based on the part played by reason or tradition in their acquisition. He distinguishes (a) the sciences which are 'natural' to man, in the sense that he can acquire them by his own reflections; these are the philosophical sciences; and (b) those which are only attainable through 'tradition'; these are the positive sciences of the tradition, all of which are derived from the lawgiver who first established them. He means, of course, the religious sciences, whose sources are to be found in the Qur'ān and the *Sunna*. They are characteristic—and a monopoly—of Islam, as opposed to the rational philosophical sciences which can be found elsewhere, and which, moreover, have always existed, being the natural product of human reason. The latter are called 'philosophy' or 'wisdom' and comprise the four main classical divisions of the Aristotelian tradition. The complete plan of this classification is as follows:

Classification of the Sciences according to the 'Prolegomena' of Ibn Khaldūn[1]

A. *Traditional religious sciences*

1. Exegesis of the Qur'ān.
2. Qur'anic readings.
3. Science of Tradition.
4. Science of the principles of jurisprudence including:
   (a) the science of controversial questions,
   (b) dialectics
5. Science of jurisprudence, which includes the science of the law of inheritance.
6. Speculative theology (*kalām*).
7. Mysticism (*taṣawwuf*).

[1] Ibn Khaldūn, *al-Muqaddima*, Cairo edn., 305 ff.; tr. de Slane, II, 450 ff., III, 1 ff.; tr. Rosenthal, II, 436 ff., III, 1 ff.

8. Interpretation of dreams.

Under provisional heading:

Philological sciences.

B. *Philosophical sciences*

1. Logic (the eight books of the *Organon* of Aristotle).
2. Physics, including:
   - (a) Medicine.
   - (b) Agriculture.
   - (c) Magic.
   - (d) Talismans.
   - (e) Prestidigitation.
   - (f) Alchemy.
3. Metaphysics.
4. Mathematics, comprising:
   - (a) the numerical sciences:
     - (i) arithmetic,
     - (ii) calculation,
     - (iii) algebra,
     - (iv) commercial transactions,
     - (v) partition of inheritances.
   - (b) the geometrical sciences:
     - (i) spherical and conical geometry,
     - (ii) surveying,
     - (iii) optics.
   - (c) astronomy, which also includes:
     - (i) astronomical tables,
     - (ii) judicial astrology
   - (d) music.

Subsequent Muslim authors were not to add anything essential to this classification, though some of them, like Tashköprüzādeh, adopted a different criterion as their starting-point, distinguishing between four kinds of existence: in writing, in speech, in the mind and in external reality, and in this last category differentiating between the speculative and the practical viewpoints, within each of which, finally, that which appertained to religious Law was separated from that which was philosophical. Hence seven major off-shoots were obtained, each containing many sub-sections. Eventually the author reached the point of classifying 316 'sciences', some of which were merely simple techniques, such as phlebotomy, preparation of inks and construction of apparatus.

It would be wrong to regard the work of Muslim scientists simply as an appropriation of the ancient legacy. The Muslims welcomed the great works of Greece, and some from India, with avidity, with love and with infinite respect, and, instigated by powerful patrons, a succession of translators rendered into Arabic the works of Plato and Aristotle, Hippocrates and Galen, Ptolemy, Euclid and Archimedes, Apollonius and Theon, Menelaus and Aristarchus, Hero of Alexandria, Philo of Byzantium and many others. The admirable flexibility of the Arabic language made it possible for them to coin an exact philosophical and scientific vocabulary, capable of expressing the most complicated scientific and technical terms. On this subject it is rewarding to read the penetrating studies of Louis Massignon, who has shown how helpful the Arabic language is to the internal exploration of thought, and for this reason it is 'particularly suitable for the expression of the exact sciences and for their development along the lines of the historical progress of mathematics: the transition from an arithmetic and a geometry which were intuitive and almost contemplative...to a science of algebraic constructions in which arithmetic and geometry were ultimately united.'[1]

From being enthusiastic and industrious disciples, the Muslims proceeded to the second stage of becoming masters, enamoured of research and experiment, exploring not only the books of the ancients, but also nature itself. Islam was soon to produce original scientists in various branches of study, such as astronomy, mathematics and medicine, who were the equals of the greatest known in history. To illustrate this scientific activity, which was at the same time assimilating inherited science, and inclined towards the perfecting of the old and the discovery of the new, mention may be made of three institutions or factors which appear to be characteristic of this medieval Muslim science: the libraries and translation centres, the hospitals, and finally the instruments for observation, especially the astronomical observatories.

With regard to the 'books' (which means, of course, the manuscripts) of Muslim civilization; it is enough to know that there exist at the present day, in spite of many losses by destruction, nearly a quarter of a million manuscripts in the various libraries of the Muslim world, and in the great libraries of Europe and America. A large part of this wealth deals with scientific subjects, and includes both Arabic translations of

[1] L. Massignon and R. Arnaldez, *La science antique et médiévale* (Paris, 1957), 450.

ancient Greek works, and original works written by Muslim scholars themselves.

The history of these libraries is well known. At first religious instruction was given in the mosques; then, very generously, the mosques were put at the disposal of scholars, who were able to teach there not only religious sciences but also related disciplines, and even the profane sciences of the ancients. Gradually the libraries bequeathed by scholars came to be housed in buildings specially intended for the purpose, and soon the scholars themselves were lodged in dwellings reserved for their use.

In 218/833 al-Ma'mūn founded the famous 'House of Wisdom' (*Bayt al-ḥikma*), which was bound to have an important influence on the transmission of ancient learning to the Islamic world, and to stimulate a burst of intellectual activity. This academy was reminiscent of the one which had existed at Gondēshāpūr. It contained an important library and was soon enriched with numerous translations (see below). A later 'Abbasid caliph, al-Mu'taḍid (d. 290/902) installed in his new palace lodgings and rooms for all branches of science, and professors were paid salaries for teaching there. Private individuals followed the example of the caliphs, among them 'Alī b. Yaḥyā known as *al-Munajjim* (d. 275/888) who possessed a palace and a library called *Khizānat al-ḥikma* which he placed at the disposal of scholars, the study of astronomy being especially favoured there. In Mosul there existed a *Dār al-'ilm* with a library, where students were not only able to work without payment, but were even supplied with paper. At Shīrāz a great *Khizānat al-kutub* was administered by a director and his assistant. Yāqūt recounts in his *Mu'jam al-udabā'* that at Rayy a *Bayt al-kutub* contained more than four hundred camel-loads of books, catalogued in a *Fihrist* of ten volumes.

It was in Cairo, however, under the Fatimids that the richest libraries of Islam were established. Al-Maqrīzī describes in his *Khiṭaṭ* a *Khizānat al-kutub* directed by the minister of the Caliph al-Mu'izz. It consisted of forty store-rooms containing books on all branches of science, 18,000 of which dealt with the 'sciences of the ancients'. But the library which surpassed all others was the *Dār al-ḥikma* founded by the Caliph al-Ḥākim in 396/1005, which contained a reading-room and halls of courses of study; efficient service was secured by means of paid librarians, and scholars were given pensions to enable them to pursue their studies. All the sciences were represented there. Other similar institutions were founded at Fusṭāṭ. In the year 435/1043 a traveller saw a library in Cairo containing 6,500 books on astronomy, geometry and philosophy.

It should not, however, be inferred from this extraordinary abundance of written documents that Muslim science was purely a matter of books. It borrowed a great deal from the ancients, but it also applied itself to the direct observation of nature and to experiment, as is demonstrated both by the institution of hospitals, and by the instruments for observation and experimental apparatus.

Like the mosques, tombs, cupolas and sanctuaries, hospitals in Islam were institutions inspired by charity for pious purposes, but they made it possible for medical science to develop experimentally. These hospitals, called by the Persian name of *bīmāristān*, were designed both to care for the sick and to provide theoretical and practical medical training. Special buildings were erected, and considerable funds were assigned to them in *waqf*. Four of the largest of these hospitals are especially well known: al-'Aḍudī in Baghdād, al-Kabīr al-Nūrī in Damascus (both of which bear the names of their founders) and the two in Cairo, al-'Atīq founded by Saladin and, in particular, al-Manṣūrī, founded by Sultan Qalawun with its imposing building which can still be admired in Cairo today.

Each hospital contained one section for men and another for women. Each section contained several wards: one for internal diseases, a second for surgery, a third for opthalmology and finally a fourth for orthopaedics. In addition the ward for internal diseases was divided into subsidiary wards, for fevers, for maniacs, for melancholics, for mental derangement, and for diarrhoea. In every hospital there was a pharmacy under the direction of a head-pharmacist which made up the prescriptions of the doctors. The director of the hospital was assisted by the heads of sections, each a specialist in his own branch. Servants of both sexes watched over the sick, under the supervision of nurses and administrative staff who received fixed salaries paid out of endowments.

The physician had complete freedom for his experiments there, and was able to advocate new treatments. He wrote up the results of his experiments in special reports, which could be consulted by members of the public. Physicians gave courses of instruction to their pupils, and, on the completion of teaching and practical work confirmed by an examination, granted them the *ijāza* which allowed them to practise medicine. Several hospitals had libraries, and students used to travel in pursuit of instruction from celebrated teachers. Spanish sources mention that a physician of Cadiz established a botanical garden in the park of the governor, where he cultivated the rare medical plants which he had brought back from his travels. Some hospitals, or at least infirmaries, were mobile, and were designed specifically to care for casualties of war.

Ultimately the Muslim scientists surpassed their masters in powers of observation and care in verification. When studying the *Materia medica* of Dioscorides, for example, they succeeded in identifying, from observation of nature, the botanical terms which the original translation had left obscure. In the mathematical sciences they checked calculations and measurements, twice measuring afresh, for example, the arc of the terrestrial meridian instead of being satisfied with the figure left by Eratosthenes. From his clinical observations, al-Rāzī succeeded in distinguishing smallpox from measles; the laboratory apparatus which he used for his chemical experiments was unknown to the ancients. Geographers and travellers noted and described the wonders of nature, the riches of the soil, types of agriculture, techniques of craftsmanship. Al-Bīrūnī succeeded in determining specific gravities with an exactitude quite remarkable for his time. Moreover the observatories founded by caliphs and princes were provided with important collections of instruments. Al-Battānī, for example, made use of astrolabes, tubes, a gnomon divided into twelve parts, a celestial sphere with five rings, of which he was perhaps the inventor, parallactic rules, a mural quadrant, horizontal and vertical solar quadrants. These instruments were of considerable size—in fact the Arabs enlarged their instruments as much as possible in order to reduce the margin of error; they then began to make special instruments for certain measurements.

The foregoing account has put into perspective the state of the various sciences in Islam and their relationship with the whole field of learning and has described both their debt to ancient science and the spirit which inspired them. The exact sciences, mathematics and astronomy will now first be discussed and after them, in the second part, the natural sciences.

Arithmetic

Arithmetic (*al-ḥisāb*) was, as Ibn Khaldūn observed in his 'Prolegomena,' the first of the mathematical sciences to be used by the

Muslims, being indeed a means of solving such material problems which present themselves in daily life as assessment of taxes, reckoning of legal compensation, and division of inheritances according to Qur'anic law.

Arabic manuals of arithmetic divide numbers into whole numbers, fractions, and non-rational. Basic principles and definitions are taken from the Greeks. The definitions of certain progressions are mentioned, and the authors give methods for calculating sums, for example the the aggregate of equal numbers, and of certain unequal numbers, but without explaining these in general terms. Al-Karajī (d. 420/1029) nevertheless offers a neat solution of the problem of summing the third powers of the progression $1 + 2 + 3 \ldots + n$, and later al-Kāshī (d. 841/1437) a mathematician, physician and astronomer, was to give the sum of the fourth powers.

Muslim arithmeticians practised exponentiation, and the extraction of square and cube roots, sometimes using the formulae of root approximation borrowed from the Byzantines, although equivalent processes of root-extraction may be found, for example, in Hero's works. The knew the fundamental rules of numerical manipulation: identity, permutation, associativity, combination and distributivity, for example, the laws $am + bm = (a + b)m$; $\sqrt{a} \times \sqrt{b} = \sqrt{ab}$.

They noted that numbers which ended in 2, 3, 7, 8 or in an odd number of noughts were not perfect squares. They constructed abaci to make calculation easier. Without explicitly giving the formula of the rule of three they applied it by means of ratios. The discovery of the proof by casting out nines is sometimes attributed to them, and the procedure known by the name of 'the rule of double false', which is found again among European arithmeticians from Pacioli (1494) onwards.

Being ingenious and spontaneously inquisitive, they studied the properties of the 'amical' numbers, and Thābit b. Qurra (d. 289/901), a Sabaean, discovered their remarkable characteristics. 'Amical' numbers are those in which the sum of the proportional parts of one is equal to the other and *vice versa*. For example, taking the numbers 220 and 284: $220 = 1 + 2 + 4 + 71 + 142$, the parts of 284, and likewise $284 = 1 + 2 + 4 + 5 + 10 + 11 + 20 + 22 + 44 + 55 + 110$, the parts of 220.

Lastly, Muslim authors showed a predilection for the composition of magic squares (called in Arabic *wafq*, pl., *awfāq*), which gave in figures the value of the Divine Names and were used in talismans (cf. the *Sham al-maʿārif* of al-Būnī).[1]

Geometry

Arabic geometry was founded on a deep knowledge of prior Greek works, particularly those of Euclid, Archimedes and Apollonius, and it was also influenced by the Indian *Siddhānta*. In constructing the regular polygons which were included in the design of certain arabesques, they made use of intersecting conic sections. Thus to construct a regular nine-sided polygon, Abu'l-Layth used the meet of a hyperbola and a parabola. Profiting by the researches of Ibn al-Haytham on a theorem not proved by Archimedes in his *On the sphere and the cylinder*, 6–7, al-Kūhī constructed a segment of a sphere equal in volume to the segment of a given sphere and in its surface area to another segment of the same sphere. He resolved the problem very ingeniously with the help of two auxiliary cones and the intersection of two auxiliary conic sections—a hyperbola and a parabola—and then discussed limit cases.

For these problems of the construction of interrelated figures, the Banū Mūsā in particular showed outstanding talent. Another aspect of geometry of especial interest to Arab authors was its use in making calculations. Also to be noted are the works of Ibrāhīm b. Sinān on the quadrature of the parabola; of Abu'l-Wafā' (d. *c.* 387/997) on the construction of regular polygons which led to equations of the third degree; of Abū Kāmil (third/ninth century) on the construction of the pentagon and the decagon, also by means of equations. The commentary of ʿUmar Khayyām (d. 526/1131) on Euclid is an important precursor of non-Euclidean geometry, which may also have been inspired by Naṣīr al-Dīn al-Ṭūsī.

Certain problems gave rise to discussions bordering on natural philosophy, such as the nature of the mathematical point, line, and angle or of space, which was conceived of sometimes as a container or a support (cf. the Aristotelian definition), sometimes as a receptacle (Plato and Abu'l-Barakāt [d. 547/1152]).

[1] With regard to arithmetical notation, the Arab mathematicians used sexagesimals, and after al-Kāshī's time decimals, in their large-scale computations: this was an immense advance upon the standard Greek 'literal' number scale with which even Archimedes had to cope. To point this, there is a world of difference between Archimedes's best inequality $3\frac{1}{7} > \pi > 3\frac{10}{71}$ (which yields π correct only to two decimal places) and al-Kāshī's computation of π correct to 16 decimal places. Without the facilities afforded by the ease of manipulation of sexagesimal (and later decimal) fractions, it is probable that Arab computational astronomy (and perhaps practical optics too) would have been significantly retarded.

Applications of geometry were numerous: problems of surveying, studies of mechanical tools in 'Irāq and in Persia in the fourth/tenth century, the construction of improved mills, of *norias* (from Arabic sing., *nā'ūra*, wheels with scoops for the continuous drawing of water from a watercourse), mangonels (stone-throwing machines), tractors etc.

Algebra

Algebra, as the form of the name indicates, is an Arabic word: *al-jabr*, which signifies the restoration of something broken, the amplifying of something incomplete. The word *jabr* is sometimes associated with the word *ḥaṭṭ*, descent; it expresses the diminution of a number so as to make it equal to another given number. More often *jabr* is associated with *muqābala*, the balancing of the two sides of an equation. In the equation $12x^2 - 6x + 9 = 6x^2 + 18$ for example, it is possible to obtain by *al-jabr*:

$$12x^2 + 9 = 6x^2 + 6x + 18$$

by *al-ḥaṭṭ*:

$$4x^2 + 3 = 2x^2 + 2x + 6$$

by *muqābala*:

$$2x^2 = 2x + 3$$

Muḥammad b. Mūsā al-Khuwārizmī (third/ninth century), the latinized distortion of whose name has produced the word 'algorithm', was chiefly responsible for laying the foundations of Islamic algebra. He began his treatise on the subject with a clear if long-winded exposition of equations of the second degree, after which he discussed algebraic multiplication and division, then the numerical measurement of surfaces, the division of estates and other legal questions. Such problems were always presented in the form of numerical examples.

Perhaps following Diophantus, al-Khuwārizmī distinguished sixty pes of the general quadratic:
$ax^2 = bx; ax^2 = c; bx = c; ax^2 + bx = c; ax^2 + c = bx; bx + c = ax^2$.
Having laid down rules for solving them by verbal means, algebraic notation not yet having been invented, he then proved these rules geometrically in Euclidean style.

With 'Umar Khayyām algebra made considerable progress. In a work which bears this title he classified the equations of third degree into twenty-five categories according to the number and the nature of the terms on each side of the equation, and then attempted to solve them, giving numerical solutions for equations of the first and second degrees and geometrical solutions (by means of conic intersections) for those of third degree. Although he had no knowledge of negative and imaginary solutions, the results which he obtained are noteworthy.

Trigonometry

The Arabs were, according to Carra de Vaux, unquestionably the inventors of plane and spherical trigonometry, which did not, strictly speaking, exist among the Greeks. In fact, Hipparchus had calculated a table of chords, and Ptolemy gave a more elaborate one in Book I of his *Syntax* (ch. 9) for arcs at intervals of half a degree. Computation of this was made in effect, by first calculating the length of the side of a regular polygon with angles of 18°. With the Arabs, the trigonometrical functions of sine, tangent, cosine and cotangent became explicit. They adopted for 'sine' the name *jayb* which signifies an opening, bay, curve of a garment, specifically the opening of an angle. The Latin term 'sinus' is a mere translation of the Arabic *jayb*. It appears in the twelfth Christian century in the translation of *De motu stellarum* of al-Battānī, (d. 317/929), the Albategnius of the Latins. The definition of the cotangent expressed as a function of the sine and of the cosine appears there for the first time, and in ch. III trigonometry begins to assume the appearance of a distinct and independent science.

In spherical trigonometry also al-Battānī presented an important formula (uniting the three sides and one angle of a spherical triangle) which has no equivalent in Ptolemy:

$$\cos a = \cos b \cos c - \sin b \sin c \cos A$$

A further advance was made with Abu'l-Wafā', and he was probably the first to demonstrate the sine theorem for the general spherical triangle. He proposed a new technique for the construction of sine tables, the value of sin 30′ thus computed being correct to the eighth decimal place. He also knew the identities which are, in modern form,

$$\sin (a \pm b) = \sin a \cos b - \cos a \sin b$$

$$2 \sin^2 \frac{a}{2} = 1 - \cos a \qquad \sin a = 2 \sin \frac{a}{2} \times \cos \frac{a}{2}$$

Making a special study of the tangent, he tabulated its values, and introduced the secant and the cosecant; he knew the simple relationships between these six basic trigonometric functions, which are often used even today to define them. Indeed, Carra de Vaux has demonstrated, following Moritz Cantor, that it was Abu'l-Wafā' and not Copernicus who invented the secant; he called it the 'diameter of the shadow' and set out explicitly the ratio (in modern form)

$$\frac{\tan a}{\sec a} = \frac{\sin a}{1}$$

Optics

The application of the principles of geometry to light made possible the construction of mirrors and lenses. A remarkable practitioner of this science among the Arabs is to be found in the person of al-Ḥasan b. al-Haytham (d. *c.* 431/1039), well known to the West under the name of Alhazen. A native of Baṣra, he came to Cairo, and entered the service of the Caliph al-Ḥākim, who set him to find a means of regulating the annual inundation of the Nile. His failure to do so nearly cost him his life, for the Fatimid caliph, who was known for his eccentricities, was prone to dangerous outbursts of anger. It, however, cast no doubt on al-Haytham's scientific ability in the field of optics, and his book *Kitāb al-manāẓir* ('On optics') exercised an important influence in the Middle Ages, prompting the studies of Roger Bacon and of Witelo. Ibn al-Haytham discussed the nature of light, declaring that light emanated from the object. He treated the eye as a dioptric system, by applying the geometry of refraction to it. He had some knowledge of reflection and refraction and brilliantly investigated the phenomenon of atmospheric refraction, calculating the height of the atmosphere (ten English miles). He made a study of lenses, experimenting with different mirrors—flat, spherical, parabolic and cylindrical, concave and convex. He also described experiments which he made on starlight, the rainbow and colours, and observed the semi-lunar form of the sun's image cast during eclipses on a wall set opposite a screen with a tiny hole in it: this is the first known instance of the camera obscura. His catoptrics included the problem known by his name: given object and image by reflection in a spherical mirror, to find the reflection point. Ibn al-Haytham's solution of this is wholly geometrical: the algebraic solution was a discovery of Huygens and Sluse in the mid-seventeenth century.

One of his successors, Kamāl al-Dīn al-Fārisī (d. *c.* 720/1320), repeated and improved the accuracy of the experiments of Ibn al-Haytham on the camera obscura, and also observed the path of the rays in the interior of a glass sphere, hoping to determine the refraction of solar light through raindrops. His findings enabled him to give an explanation of the formation of the primary and secondary rainbows.

Mechanics, hydraulics and technology

The demands of Muslim civilization, which extended from one ocean to the other, obliged rulers to make the maximum use of the resources of the countries which they conquered. Science was required to make its contribution, and technical arts were rapidly developed in the most varied fields: the construction of irrigation works, of canals for the provision of water, of ways of communication, and the erection of hydraulic machines. The first textbook of mechanics dates from 246/860 and is the *Book of Artifices* of the Banū Mūsā, the mathematicians Muḥammad, Aḥmad and Ḥasan, sons of Mūsā b. Shākir, who were all both scientists and enlightened patrons of learning. The work in question contains about a hundred technical constructions, some twenty of which are of practical value: apparatus for hot and cold water, wells of a fixed depth, the lifting of weights by machinery, a whole series of the scientific and automatic toys so much beloved by the courts of princes in the Middle Ages.

In the seventh/thirteenth century al-Jazarī, a native of ʿIrāq, wrote a *Kitāb fī maʿrifat al-ḥiyal al-handasiyya*, 'a great book on mechanics and clocks, the best extant in the Islamic world'.[1] An engineer, Qayṣar, who died in Damascus in 649/1251, constructed irrigation wheels on the Orontes, as well as fortifications, for the prince of Ḥamāh. It was he who set up the celestial globe which is today in the National Museum at Naples. Generally speaking, the mechanical devices encountered in the countries of the Orient were improved and perfected during the Crusades or in Spain.

With regard to measuring devices, al-Khāzinī (*c.* 494/1100), making use of the works of the ancients (he quotes Archimedes, Aristotle, Euclid, Menelaus, Pappus and especially his co-religionist al-Bīrūnī), expounded a detailed theory of balance in his book entitled 'The balance of wisdom' (*Mīzān al-ḥikma*) in which he defined the centre of gravity of a body and conditions for various types of equilibrium. Al-Bīrūnī (d. 442/1050) one of the greatest scientists of Islam, ascer-

[1] M. Meyerhof, 'Science and medicine', in T. Arnold and A. Guillaume (ed.), *The legacy of Islam* (Oxford, 1931), at p. 342.

tained experimentally a certain number of specific gravities, by means of a 'conical instrument' which may be regarded as the earliest pycnometer. Al-Khāzinī, in dealing with liquids, used a hydrometer similar to those used by the Alexandrians. The results obtained by these two scientists 'constituted one of the finest achievements attained by the Arabs in the realm of experimental physics.'[1]

In addition to the balance (*mīzān*), the Muslims were also familiar with the steelyard (*qaristūn*) inherited from antiquity, which they employed both for the measurement of time (by a weight in perpetual equilibrium with an hour-glass), and theoretically to illustrate certain equations, for example those arising in inverse proportions. Likewise al-Bīrūnī used the balance to demonstrate the rules of *jabr* and *muqābala*.

Certain mechanical concepts, such as the nature of time, of the force of movement, were discussed in philosophical terms. Arab atomists revived the theory of rectilinear movement, and envisaged circular motion as an infinite sequence of indefinitely small displacements from the straight line, but this theory was not defined explicitly in scientific terms.

Astronomy

It has been seen above that Muslim authors following the Greeks classified astronomy among the mathematical sciences; it was called *'ilm al-hay'a* (the science of the aspect of the universe) or *'ilm al-aflāk* (the science of the celestial spheres). For the Arabs as for the Greeks, this science had as its sole object the study of the apparent movements in the heavens, and their representation in mathematical terms. It consisted of what we call spherical astronomy, together with the calculation of planetary orbits, with applications to the composition of astronomical tables and the theory of instruments. On the other hand, the study of meteors, of comets, shooting-stars, etc., that is of what might be called elementary celestial physics (origin of celestial movements, nature of the spheres, light of the stars, etc.), was regarded as a part of physics and of metaphysics.

A special branch of the subject called the 'science of fixed moments' (*'ilm al-mīqāt*) determined, by calculation and instrumentally, the hours of the day and night in order to establish the times of the five canonical prayers; a fact which serves to emphasize the close connexion of as-

[1] A. Mieli, *La science arabe* (Paris, 1938), 101.

tronomy with prescribed religious practices. Indeed in the *Jāhiliyya*, the Arabs, as they travelled by night over their peninsula, had had the opportunity of observing the heavens, of noting the names and positions of certain constellations, the rising and setting of the bright stars, from which they were able to tell how many hours of the night had elapsed. They had defined twenty-eight successive groups of stars called 'stations' or 'lunar stages' (*manāzil al-qamar*) and the position of the moon in relation to these groups made it possible to determine the season of the year. The agricultural seasons, the meterological prognostications were linked with the annual rising of certain stars or with the cosmic setting (*naw'*) of the lunar stations.

The new religion borrowed certain elements from this pre-Islamic heritage in order to fix the hours for prayer, in particular that of the night, which had to be carefully determined to comply with the religious law; it was also necessary to ascertain the direction of Mecca for the *qibla*, and the beginning and the end of the month of Ramaḍān by the exact definition of the time of the new moon (from observation, not calculation). Moreover certain ritual prayers were prescribed on the occasion of an eclipse of the sun or moon; for these it was necessary to prepare, and therefore to be able to predict them. In this way religion stimulated research, and when the Muslims came into contact with other civilizations, they did not fail to take immediate advantage of the latter's astronomical knowledge, the more so because it is stated in the Qur'ān that the stars were created for the benefit of man, whom they invite to contemplation. For this reason it is hardly surprising to find astronomy as a kind of science allied to religion, subject, at least ostensibly, to the condition that none of its theories should clash with the assertions of the Sacred Book.

When and how did the study of astronomy as a science begin among the Arabs? Ibn Ṣā'id relates in his *Ṭabaqāt al-umam* that 'the Caliph al-Manṣūr received in audience a native of India who had a thorough knowledge of the calculation called *Sindhind* concerning the movements of the stars'. This occurred in Baghdād in 155/771. From this astronomical treatise, called in fact the *Siddhānta*, Ibrāhīm b. Ḥabīb al-Fazārī extracted the elements and methods of calculation for the astronomical tables (*zīj*, pl. *azyāj*) which he adapted to the Muslim lunar year. At about the same period Ya'qūb b. Ṭāriq composed a similar book, making use both of the Indian *Siddhānta*, and other sources provided by a second mission from that country, while Abu'l-Ḥasan al-Ahwāzī communicated to the Arabs the information concerning the planetary movements which is expounded in the treatise of *al-Argiabhad*. These Indian works, particularly the *Sindhind*, had many imitations in the Muslim world up to the first half of the fifth/eleventh century.

Very shortly after the introduction of the Indian sources and before the end of the second/eighth century, an Arabic translation was made of a Pahlavī work, the 'Astronomical table of the king' (*Zīj al-shāh*), which had been produced in the last years of the Sasanids. The Arab version had a great success among the Muslims. Mā Shā' Allāh (Messahala), an astrologer and astronomer at the beginning of the third/ninth century, used it for his calculations, and in the first half of the third/ninth century Muḥammad b. Mūsā al-Khuwārizmī extracted from it his account of the periodicities of planetary movements. Abū Ma'shar (Abumasar d. 273/886), also availed himself of the *Zīj al-shāh* for his astronomical tables, but after the third/ninth century it came to be referred to less and less in the Orient. In Spain, on the other hand, it remained in use until about half way through the fifth/eleventh century.

The most important sources of all, however, although they became available later than those described above, were the classical Greek authors. At the end of the second/eighth century and the beginning of the third/ninth the Barmecide Yaḥyā b. Khālid, a great patron and protector of scholars and men of letters, caused to be translated into Arabic for the first time the μεγάλη σύνταξις μαθηματική of Ptolemy which, under the contracted and arabized title *al-Majistī* (*Almagest*), had a tremendous success in the Orient in the Middle Ages. It was especially after the production of two new and more accurate versions (notably the later rendering of Ḥunayn b. Isḥāq as revised by Thābit b. Qurra) that its influence superseded that of the works of Indian or Persian origin. Other works of Ptolemy which came to enrich the Muslim heritage were the *Geography*, the *Tabulae manuales*, the *Hypotheses planetarum*, the *Apparitiones stellarum fixarum* and the *Planispherium*.[1] Contributions from other Greek authors included the *Tabulae manuales* of Theon of Alexandria, the book of Aristarchus, *On the size and distances*

[1] While it must be agreed that everything significant in technical Arab astronomy falls within the shadow of Ptolemy's *Almagest* and his minor works, the *Hypotheses* particularly, its originality should also be stressed. For example the Ptolemaic models for the orbits of Mercury and the Moon were particularly inadequate representations of reality, and ingenious improvements were suggested by al-Ṭūsī, al-Shīrāzī and al-Shāṭir in the seventh/thirteenth century. Some of al-Shāṭir's planetary models, in particular, are very close to Copernican models, except that the centre of motion is kept centred on the earth. See E. S. Kennedy, 'Later medieval planetary theory' in *Isis*, 57 (1966), 365–78.

of the sun and of the moon, the *Isagoge* of Geminus, two small works of Autolycus, three of Theodosius, the short study of Hypsicles on ascents and finally the astronomical tables of Ammonius.

The Muslim astronomers in their turn composed treatises in imitation of those which reached them from the outer world: general elementary introductions, such as the compendia of Thābit b. Qurra (d. 289/901), and of al-Farghānī (Alfraganus) who died after 247/861, systematic treatises corresponding to the *Almagest*, treatises of spherical astronomy for use of the calculators and observers, consisting essentially of calculation tables, and finally specialized treatises, such as catalogues of the stars, dissertations on instruments, etc.

What are the characteristics of the Muslim science of astronomy? Speaking generally, it may be said that the only system professed was geocentrism, for a variety of reasons: firstly, out of deference to the authority of the philosophy of the great master Aristotle; then, in astronomy, by reason of the authority of Ptolemy; finally, and somewhat surprisingly, because of the demands of astrology, which was almost unanimously accepted as a true science in the Middle Ages, and which was based on a strict geocentrism. In any case heliocentrism could not be demonstrated irrefutably, nor, in the absence of the telescope, could it be of any use in practical astronomy. The same planets were known to the Arabs as to the Greeks, and also their movements. Moreover the method of representing them was necessarily similar, being eccentric and epicyclic. Only those authors who were more philosophers than astronomers, like Ibn Ṭufayl or al-Biṭrūjī (Alpetragius), tried to substitute an original (although not heliocentric) theory, but one which did not affect the strictly circular movement of the celestial bodies.

Some details may be given of this classical Muslim astronomy. The number of the spheres, which in the medieval West were sometimes called the heavens, amounted in Aristotle and Ptolemy to eight (seven for planets and one for fixed stars), a number which was to be retained by the first Arab astronomers such as al-Farghānī and al-Battānī. Some would have liked to reduce them to seven in order to conform with the Qur'ān (2. 27), but this figure was never accepted by the astronomers. When Ibn al-Haytham introduced into his teaching Aristotle's doctrine of the solid spheres, it was necessary to add a ninth without 'stars', imparting the daily movement to the other spheres, and this was not the first appearance of this doctrine. This ninth sphere, which was subsequently accepted by all astronomers, was called the universal sphere, the greatest sphere, the sphere of spheres, the united sphere (*al falak al-aṭlas*), etc. In general the *falāsifa*, such as Ibn Sīnā and Ibn Ṭufayl, accepted the nine spheres, but Ibn Rushd was not willing to go beyond eight.

Ptolemy's order for the planets was retained, although, like the Hellenic astronomers, Muslims recognized that there was no empirical justification for the relative positions of Mercury and Venus in regard to the sun. Astrological requirements likewise guaranteed the continuing sway of the Ptolemaic system. The following were the Arabic names of the seven planets in the traditional order: *Zuḥal* (Saturn), *al-Mushtarī* (Jupiter), *al-Mirrīkh* (Mars), *al-Shams* (the Sun), *al-Zuhara* (Venus), *'Uṭārid* (Mercury), *al-Qamar* (the Moon).

The obliquity of the ecliptic in relation to the terrestial equator, one of the basic parameters of astronomical calculation, necessarily presented a problem to Muslim astronomers. The Greeks, from the time of Eratosthenes (230 B.C.) on making calculation had found the result 23° 51′ 20″, a figure which they assumed to be constant. Great was the surprise of the Arab astronomers when they subsequently arrived at a lower figure: al-Battānī, for example, made it 23° 35′. Hence the question arose, whether there might have been some diminution in its obliquity or whether the ancient observations had been inaccurate. Al-Battānī supported his own figure, correctly alleging the latter hypothesis, but there were others who, relying in addition on the precession of the equinoxes, conceived the illusory theory of 'trepidation' (or 'libration') of the constant angle which was accepted by Ibn Qurra and, in a slightly different form, by al-Zarqālī. But repeated observations led to the widespread conviction that there was in fact a slight diminution, which was admitted by all the astronomers of the seventh/thirteenth century. Whether its change was continuous or intermittent, and within what limits, was a question Muslim astronomers were unable to decide. On the other hand the astronomers of al-Ma'mūn did discover that the motion of the solar apogee was tied to the movement of the fixed stars and to that of the apogees of the planets, i.e. to the displacement in longitude caused by the gradual precession of the equinoxes.

The general Ptolemaic theory, accepted by nearly all Muslim astronomers, met with opposition only in Spain, where Ibn Bājja, Ibn Ṭufayl and Ibn Rushd rejected, in the name of Aristotle, the Ptolemaic account of the movements of the heavenly bodies. Al-Biṭrūjī (d. *c.* 601/1204), went further, and denied all motion of heavenly bodies from west to east. These theories of the Spanish philosophers did not, however, command any wide credence among contemporary astronomers.

Like Ptolemy, the ancient Muslim astronomers refrained from defining the nature of the celestial sphere, a problem which belonged to physics and metaphysics rather than to astronomy. For their part they were interested only in its mathematical aspect. The Aristotelian theory of solid spheres was introduced to Islam by Ibn al-Haytham, and Muslim authors accordingly came to consider spheres and celestial bodies as composed of a single substance, the fifth element, differing essentially from the four sublunary elements. The solidity of the spheres secured the permanence of the stars, which by their rotation they drew after them.

Complementary to astronomy is geography, the science of lands and their resources. Here too the Muslims were indebted to India and above all to Greece, especially the works of Ptolemy and of Marinos of Tyre. In the third/ninth century, thanks to the labours of such astronomer-geographers as al-Khuwārizmī, al-Farghānī and al-Battānī, geography, which had hitherto been merely a literary subject, was able to develop in the direction of a cosmography. At the same time travellers were making journeys about the vast Muslim empire and bringing back personal observations, and reports of strange and marvellous facts.

This geographical activity in the widest sense may be summarized in the following periods and categories: (a) literary geography, which flourished in the third-fourth/ninth-tenth centuries and consisted of compendiums for the use of secretaries (cf. the books of Ibn Khurradādhbih, Ibn Rusta, Qudāma) and of popular works; (b) the second period, fourth–sixth/tenth–twelfth centuries, saw the expansion of these original types in different directions, either in the form of travellers' reports (Ibn Faḍlān, Buzurg b. Shahriyār) or descriptions of cities and of the high roads connecting them. Works of this kind (al-Ya'qūbī, al-Balkhī, al-Iṣṭakhrī, Ibn Ḥawqal, al-Muqaddasī, al-Bakrī, al-Idrīsī) have, in part, been published in the *Bibliotheca Geographorum Araborum*, and there was a popularization of geography through such works as the *Murūj al-dhahab* ('Fields of gold') of al-Mas'ūdī and the *Qanūn al-Mas'ūdī* of al-Bīrūnī. Finally (c) a third period from the sixth/twelfth century onwards included geographical dictionaries (al-Bakrī, Yāqūt), works on cosmography and universal geography (al-Qazwīnī, Abu'l-Fidā'), the historico-geographical encyclopaedias (al-'Umarī) and detailed and picturesque accounts of travels like those of Ibn Jubayr

(d. 614/1217) and of Ibn Baṭṭūṭa (d. 779/1377). Note must also be taken of maps, some of which, in colour, illustrate several of these works.[1]

Since mention has been made of al-Bīrūnī, it should be added that this first-class scholar was one of the most remarkable personalities of the Muslim world. His 'Chronology' (*al-Āthār al-bāqiya*) is a work devoted to an examination of the calendars of various peoples—Persians, Greeks, Jews, Melkite Christians, Nestorian Christians, Sebaeans, Arabs both pagan and Muslim—and within it are to be found numerous details concerning historical facts and traditions. Besides this treatise, which is equally important for the history of religion, al-Bīrūnī wrote on the astrolabe, the planisphere and the armillary sphere; he also composed tables for Sultan Mas'ūd. His knowledge of Sanskrit allowed him to draw information at first-hand from the sources themselves, which enhances his work on India inestimably; indeed it is still useful today. He also wrote a work on precious stones.

Astrology

After the science of astronomy, the scientific character of which was never questioned in any of the classifications, a few words must be said in respect of a pseudo-science which was very popular in the Middle Ages but which encountered lively opposition among most philosophers and among theologians and was eventually condemned by religious thinkers as being incompatible with itself—the subject of astrology.

It is difficult for people at the present day to understand the important place occupied by such a science in the Middle Ages, after it had, moreover, occupied a similar position in antiquity. In order to comprehend its scope, it is necessary to remember the fundamental principle on which it rested, that the universe is a single whole and that the sublunary world is subject to the movements of the stars, whether by the direct influence of the latter or because there is a certain correspondence, an 'analogy', between changes on earth and the movements of the stars; the latter may, thus, provide signs and indications.

Henceforth the observation of the stars was to permit those who knew how to read these indications to ascertain present or future events, which were taking place, or would take place, in the world below. The astrologer had therefore to make use of a certain number of these 'signs in the sky' and this 'astrological apparatus' was derived essentially

[1] Cf. the articles DJUGHRĀFIYĀ in Supplement to *EI*[1] and in *EI*[2], II.

from the following elements. In the first place the stars themselves and their positions in relation to the earth and to one another, which would give rise to five combinations: conjunction and the five 'aspects' or 'dispositions'. Next, the signs of the zodiac, considered either in isolation or grouped in threes. It was possible to carry the division of the zodiac further, and to imagine a special character for each degree; it would then be possible to distinguish the masculine or feminine signs, the shining ones, the dark, the coloured, the nebulous, those which increased happiness, etc. Certain parts of the zodiac had a particular importance in relation to the sun, to the moon and to the five planets, for they were their 'limits', 'domiciles' and 'detriments', their 'exaltations' and their 'downfalls'.

The horizon and the meridian also played a considerable part; their points of intersection with the ecliptic were called the four pivots: the ascendant (*al-ṭāli'*), which was the point of the ecliptic rising to the horizon, the pivot of the earth, the descendant and the point of culmination. The ecliptic was thus divided into twelve sections, called the twelve celestial mansions (*buyūt*), which were the basis of every astrological exercise. Lastly, since each geographical region was subject to a particular influence, it was necessary also to take account of them.

The combination of these various factors, exactly noted, would enable the astrologer to devote himself to three kinds of exercises, based on different principles. Thus (1) he could, in the first place, reply to 'interrogations' (*masā'il, questiones*)—how some absent person fares, who was responsible for a theft, where would a lost object be found, etc.; (2) he could calculate the propitious moment for undertaking some important course of action or other (*ikhtiyārāt, electiones*). For example, al-Ya'qūbī when writing about the foundation of Baghdād, recounted that the Caliph al-Manṣūr laid the foundations 'at the time appointed by the astrologers Nawbakht and Mā Shā' Allāh'.

Finally (3) he could foresee the future, the genethialogical system making it possible, with the help of data concerning the birth of an individual or the beginning of a reign, of a sect or of a religion, to 'foresee' what would happen to them in the future. This last system, which was different from the two previously mentioned, was based on the principle that at the moment of the birth of a human being or the occurrence of an event the configuration of the celestial sphere fixed irrevocably the destiny of the newly-born or the consequences of the event.

This determinism which regarded man as the mere instrument of cosmic forces was not slow to arouse the censure of religious teachers. Many philosophers likewise attacked its basic principles, particularly al-Fārābī, Ibn Sīnā and Ibn Rushd. Some, however, like al-Kindī, the *Ikhwān al-Ṣafā'*, and theologians like Fakhr al-Dīn al-Rāzī, held it in esteem. One thing is certain, that in spite of all condemnation, astrology remained very popular in daily life. It was only in the modern period, following on the Copernican revolution which undermined its foundations, and the introduction of Western civilization, that astrology lost practically all credence among serious people. A few journals alone draw up horoscopes, perhaps in imitation of those in the West.

What must be mentioned, however, is the superiority of Arab astrology over that of its sources. These sources were, for astrology as for astronomy, Indian, Persian and above all Greek, including especially the works of Ptolemy (*Tetrabiblos*), of Dorotheos Sidonius, Antiochus, Vettius Valens, Teucros and others. But the immense progress achieved in astronomical observation itself, the use of mathematical methods for the calculation of the 'astronomical apparatus' mentioned above, gave to Muslim astrology a 'scientific' turn, especially in the preparatory stages of establishing 'data'. Besides, all these preliminary operations were based on astronomy properly so called and were demonstrated with all the exactitude to be desired in treatises of astronomy, alongside problems of trigonometry.

Natural sciences

According to the classification of the sciences previously considered, it has been seen that the field of the 'natural sciences' includes physics properly so called, in the Aristotelian sense of the word, and a certain number of related sciences. Physics in this sense is based on philosophy and will not be discussed here; only the two sciences which were especially studied by Muslim scholars, medicine and alchemy, will be examined in detail.

Medicine

When the Muslims appeared on the world scene, medicine had already covered a long period of its history, with Hippocrates, Galen and Dioscorides and the doctors of the school of Alexandria, finally becoming concentrated, during the sixth century, in the city of Gondēshāpūr.

This city of south-western Persia had in fact been accepting a succession of refugees—the Nestorians of Edessa when their school was closed in 489, followed by the Neoplatonic philosophers of the school of Athens, when in turn this latter school was closed by Justinian in 529.

The Nestorians brought with them to Gondēshāpūr the Syriac translation which they had already had in Edessa. The city soon became aware of a remarkable intellectual fermentation, and under the reign of Chosroes Anūshirwān, the Kisrā of the Arab chronicles, the school reached the zenith of its activity. Greeks, Jews, Christians, Syrians, Hindus and Persians lived side by side in a splendid atmosphere of toleration, united by the same love of science. Gondēshāpūr became a medical centre of first importance: hospitals were established there where, in addition to the care of the sick, facilities were assured for the theoretical and practical teaching of medicine.

In 17/638 the city was taken by the Arabs. In view of its nearness to the Arab city of Ḥīra it is probable that Arabic was spoken there even before the conquest. At all events doctors must have been speaking the language very soon afterwards, since Ibn Abī Uṣaybi'a, the famous historian of Arab medicine, recounts that on the occasion of the visit of the physician Jurjīs b. Jibrīl of Gondēshāpūr to the Caliph al-Manṣūr, Jūrjīs addressed the caliph in Arabic. In this city there were actual dynasties of medical families, who handed down their scientific knowledge, enriched by personal experience, from father to son. And it was the physicians of Gondēshāpūr who became the teachers of the Muslims in medicine.

Until 132/750, that is to say before the coming of the 'Abbasids and the foundation of Baghdād, this influence was chiefly indirect, inasmuch as there were Arabs who arrived in Gondēshāpūr for the purpose of being initiated into the science of medicine. It is said that the first of the Arabs to have earned the title of physician, Ḥārith b. Kalada, was born at Ṭā'if towards the middle of the sixth Christian century. After being admitted to the court of Chosroes, he had a conversation with him which has been preserved. The basis of his system of hygiene was moderation in eating. What was most harmful, he said, was to introduce food on top of food, that is to say to eat when one was already satisfied. He forbade the taking of baths after meals and sexual relations in a state of drunkenness, and he advocated bed-coverings at night, the drinking of water for preference and the total avoidance of undiluted wine. Meat which was salted or dried, or which came from young animals, he regarded as undesirable. Fruit might be eaten when it first came into season and at the proper stage of ripeness. With regard to the use of medicine, he replied to Chosroes in the following terms: 'So long as your health lasts, leave medicines alone, but, if illness comes, check it by all the means available before it can take root.' He also prescribed methods of combating every ailment individually and recommended the use of enemas. Cupping-glasses should be applied when the moon was waning, in calm weather and when the body was in an active state. He was on close terms with Muḥammad, who sent sick people to him, and his son, al-Nadr, inherited his medical knowledge.

Ibn Abī Uṣaybi'a quotes, according to al-Nadr, a certain Ibn Abī Ramtha of the tribe of Tamīm who practised surgery. When he was with Muḥammad one day he saw that he had between his shoulders the excrescence (*al-khātim*) which was regarded as the attribute of prophets and proposed to remove it by surgery. Muḥammad refused his offer.

Apart from the various physicians mentioned by Ibn Abī Uṣaybi'a, tradition relates a certain number of medical aphorisms attributed to Muḥammad himself which have been collected and annotated in books entitled 'The medicine of the Prophet' (*al-Ṭibb al-nabawī*). These collections embody Traditions of the Prophet in a systematic medical treatise, with notes and additions.

It was, however, in the second/eighth century in Baghdad that the science of medicine began to make rapid progress among the Muslims. The Caliph al-Manṣūr was ill, and demanded that the best physician in his empire should be brought to him. Jurjīs b. Jibrīl, the leading physician in Gondēshāpūr, was recommended, and he at once sent messengers in search of him. From that time these Christian physicians, and particularly the family of the Bukhtīshū', were in firm favour with the ruling princes and in consequence Jibrīl b. Bukhtīshū' remained in the service of Hārūn al-Rashīd for twenty-three years, after which he was successively the physician of al-Amīn and of al-Ma'mūn.

These physicians had free entry into the palace, being consulted constantly by the caliphs on what they should eat or what they should avoid. Many anecdotes are recounted by the historians showing to what extent the caliphs accepted, for the sake of their health, the recommendations, sometimes severe, of their Christian doctors.

The virtual monopoly which the Christians exercised over the medical profession could not fail, after a certain time when the numbers of practitioners had increased, to make life somewhat difficult for non-

Christian physicians. An echo of it is perceptible in a curious anecdote narrated by al-Jāḥiẓ in his 'Book of misers' (*Kitāb al-bukhalā'*). The privileged position of the Christians was not, however, to last indefinitely, and indeed under the powerful influence of the Caliph al-Ma'mūn there was a concentrated attempt to translate scientific and philosophical works inherited from antiquity, which constitutes, from the point of view of the history of thought, one of the most important landmarks in culture.

For the realization of his desires in this field, al Ma'mūn employed a man of genius. Born of a Christian tribe in the neighbourhood of Ḥīra, Ḥunayn b. Isḥāq (d. 260/873) by dint of hard work succeeded in mastering perfectly the four languages of the cultivated world of his age: Arabic, Persian, Greek and Syriac. He also studied medicine under the guidance of the Christian teachers of the day. No one could have been better prepared for the immense work of translation which al-Ma'mūn entrusted to him. After accompanying the mission which was sent to Byzantium in search of good manuscripts, he gathered around him an excellent team of translators, and the task was begun. Ḥunayn's own activity as a translator exceeds imagination. Not only did he translate or revise the works of Plato, Aristotle, Autolycus, Menelaus, Apollonius of Tyana, Alexander of Aphrodisias and Artemidorus, but also the greater part of the three authors who provided the basis of all Greek medical science and who performed the same service for Arab medicine: Hippocrates, Galen and Dioscorides. These works became the reference books of all those who wanted to study medicine, and summaries, commentaries and extracts were made. Enriched by the personal experience of the Arab physicians, they laid the foundations for the great treatises subsequently produced. Ḥunayn, not content with translating a large number of works, also wrote a hundred or so himself, the major part of this output being concerned with medicine. The book which made him famous in the Latin Middle Ages was his *Ars parva Galeni*, also known under the title of *Isagoge Johannitii*.

Those of his books which had the most influence in the Orient were three in number: 'Medical questions,' a general introduction to medicine in the form of questions and answers, which was a favourite method with writers of this period, and two ophthalmological works, 'Ten dissertations on the eye' and 'Questions on the eye.' The 'Ten dissertations' is the most ancient systematic manual of ophthalmology. In the series of ten dissertations, which follow Galen closely, Ḥunayn explains the anatomy of the eye, describes the brain and the optic nerve, examines nosology, aetiology and symptomatology, the diseases of the eye and the properties of useful medicaments. Mention must also be made of the diagrams which accompany the book: they are the first known on the anatomy of the eye, and they are much superior to similar works produced during the Middle Ages in the West.

This intense activity in translation, combined with the application of the principles transmitted by the Greeks, and supplemented by medical traditions derived from Persia and India, was not slow to bear fruit. The art of medicine became more extensive; precious manuscripts were distributed over the vast territories of the Muslim empire and commentaries were made in all the important centres, in Spain, North Africa, Egypt and Syria. Soon there appeared Muslim physicians, who lost no time in attaining the fame of their Christian and Jewish predecessors. Hospitals were built, as was mentioned earlier, and celebrated physicians appointed by the caliphs to direct them. The government even had to supervise the control of medical practice, a function which was exercised under the *ḥisba*. Handbooks of *ḥisba*, drawn up with the object of enabling officials to fulfil their responsibilities conscientiously, contained lists of all the occupations of the time. The medical and para-medical professions had, of course, their special chapters: pharmacists and druggists, perfumers, makers of syrups, veterinary surgeons, phlebotomists and cuppers, finally oculists, surgeons and orthopaedists. These books outlined the questions which should be put to these different experts, and the instruments which they ought to possess.

One of the most eminent physicians, perhaps the greatest clinical doctor of Islam, was without question Abū Bakr al-Rāzī (d. 313/925), the Rhazes of the medieval Latins. Like so many great men, he has become surrounded by legend. It was maintained by some that, when he was attempting to perform certain experiments in alchemy before al-Manṣūr which were not successful, the caliph flew into a passion and hit him on the head, and that as a result of this ill-treatment he lost his sight. Others, however, and especially al-Bīrūnī, who dedicated a short treatise especially to him, declared that it was his own excessive reading which had caused his blindness. Moreover, he did not wish to undergo an operation, and questioned the oculist who proposed to operate on him about the anatomy of the eye, asking him the number of membranes of which it was composed. The answer was not satisfactory and he sent his friend away, adding: 'In any case, I have seen enough of the world and have no desire to see it further.'

In medicine al-Rāzī was the least dogmatic of the Muslim physicians, as is shown by his clinical day-book, which he kept carefully, describing the progress of each malady and the results of treatment. The literary output of al-Rāzī, like that of most of the great authors of the Middle Ages, was enormous and encyclopaedic. The list given by al-Bīrūnī named fifty-six medical treatises, thirty-three dealing with natural sciences, eight on logic, ten on mathematics, seventeen on philosophy, six on metaphysics, fourteen on theology, twenty-two on chemistry, ten on miscellaneous subjects. The three principal medical works will be discussed here; his important work on chemistry will be considered later.

The most famous of the medical works is that which deals with smallpox and measles, known in the medieval Latin translations as *De variolis et morbilis* or sometimes *Liber de pestilentia*. This book is not simply an outline of Hippocrates or of Galen, but is truly original. It is based on al-Rāzī's personal observations, patient and detailed, from which his clinical genius made its deductions, and it is the first treatise in existence on infectious diseases. Al-Rāzī distinguished two kinds, true smallpox and measles, describing them with care and basing their respective diagnoses on signs and symptoms. In examining the course of a disease, al-Rāzī advised paying great attention to heart, pulse, breathing and excrements. He observed that a high temperature helped to bring out the rash, and he enjoined precautions for protecting the eyes, face and mouth and for the avoidance of pockmarks.

The second important book of al-Rāzī is the *Kitāb al-ṭibb al-Manṣūrī*, called in the Latin translations *Liber medicinalis ad al-Mansorem*. It is an encyclopaedia of practical medicine composed of two treatises, derived almost entirely from Greek sources: anatomy, constitution, hygiene, skin diseases, simple medicaments, diet for travellers, surgery, poisons, treatment of various complaints and finally fevers.

Under the title of *Opera parva Abubetri* several minor works of al-Rāzī were printed together with his *al-Manṣūrī*, consisting of: divisions, antidotes, diseases of the joints, children's diseases, aphorisms, prognosis, experimental data, medical observations, diet, the discourses of Hippocrates, who should be a physician, a formulary, prophylactic calculations, cauteries and cuppings, properties, animals.

Finally al-Rāzī's most important work is his celebrated *Kitāb al-ḥāwī fi'l-ṭibb* which in Latin became the *Continens*, that is to say a work containing the whole of medicine.

Before speaking of Ibn Sīnā (Avicenna, d. 429/1037) some mention may be made of medical and pharmacological science in northern Africa and Spain.

A contemporary of al-Rāzī was the Jewish physician, Isḥāq b. Sulaymān al-Isrā'īlī, known to the Latins by the name of Isaac Judaeus. He practised medicine in Qayrawān in Tunisia, and was particularly famous as an oculist. His books on the elements, fevers and on urine were translated into Latin in the Middle Ages by Constantine the African. Another of his works, the 'Physician's guide,' of which the Arabic original is lost, has been preserved in the Hebrew translation. His treatise 'Peculiarities of diet,' printed in Latin at Padua in 1487, is the first printed treatise on dietetics.

The best pupil of Isaac Judaeus was the Muslim, Ibn al-Jazzār, also called Algazirah, a native of Tunisia who died in 1009. His *Zād al-musāfir* was also translated by Constantine the African under the title *Viaticum peregrinantis* and later in Sicily there was a Greek translation with the title *Ephodia*.

In Muslim Spain also there was a ready supply of physicians, pharmacologists and botanists. Under Arab domination numerous useful plants were introduced: date-palms, sugar-cane, rice, cotton, orange trees, etc.; in southern Spain they cultivated a number of medicinal plants which were very successful.

Cordova was pre-eminently the seat of culture and of science, and among the great figures who were illustrious in medicine, three were later than Ibn Sīnā, namely Ibn Zuhr (Avenzoar d. 557/1162), Ibn Rushd (Averroes, d. 595/1198) and Maimonides (d. 601/1204), while Abu'l-Qāsim al-Zahrāwī (Abulcasis d. *c.* 404/1013), was earlier than Ibn Sīnā. He is the leading representative of Arab surgery and his work *al-Taṣrīf* had the same authority in surgery as the *Canon* of Ibn Sīnā had in medicine. The thirtieth dissertation of this work was devoted to surgery; it was produced separately and was the first medical work to contain diagrams of surgical instruments.

The *Taṣrīf* contained three books, the first of which was concerned with cauterization, used generously in Arab medicine since being recommended by the Prophet. Al-Zahrāwī advised it for various surgical disorders, and also for apoplexy, epilepsy and dislocation of the shoulder.

For arterial haemorrhage, he recommended compression with the fingers, followed by cauterization. The second book described operations performed with the scalpel and also ocular and dental surgery, operation for stone, obstetrics, extraction of arrows, etc. It advocated the use of artificial teeth made of bull's bones, and also described methods of treating wounds, and the numerous sutures employed as well as instruments. In conclusion the third book dealt with fractures and dislocations, and mentioned paralysis resulting from fracture of the spine. It also dealt with the gynaecological position known as 'Kalcher's position', with a note on gynaecological dressings.

With Ibn Sīnā, Muslim medicine reached the peak of its achievement. While less of a clinical physician than al-Rāzī, he was more philosophical, more systematic; he tried to rationalize the immense accumulations of medical science which had been inherited from antiquity and enriched by his predecessors. He left behind him a lively autobiography, from which it emerged that he had been a precocious genius, who by the age of sixteen had already mastered the medical science of his time. In spite of a disturbed social and political career, he succeeded in pursuing his studies, writing all the time on his travels, in the evenings after his day's work, and even in prison when the troubled turn of events had brought him there. Since Ibn Sīnā was more of a philosopher than a physician, his biography and his great philosophical work, *al-Shifā'*, which had such a resounding effect on Christian thinkers of the Middle Ages, are discussed in the chapter on Philosophy. Here it will be enough to examine his great medical work, the *Canon of medicine* (*al-Qānūn fi'l-ṭibb*), the Arabic replica in the Middle Ages of the great works of Hippocrates and Galen.

The work consisted of five books, of which the first, *Kitāb al-kulliyāt* (the Latin name being the distorted form *Colliget*), contained generalities of medical science: (1) the elements and fluids, the limbs, muscles, nerves, veins, in a word anatomy; (2) diseases and their causes regarded from a general viewpoint, pulse, digestion; (3) hygiene; (4) general rules for treatment—purges, baths, etc. The second book was devoted to simple medicaments. It was the most complete dissertation of its time, and comprised eight hundred paragraphs describing medicaments of animal, vegetable and mineral origin. The treatises of Galen and of Dioscorides on the subject were systematically reproduced, and a number of new medicaments were included. The third book had as its subject the disorders particularly affecting each limb, both internally and externally. They were classified from head to foot in descending order. The fourth volume dealt with maladies which were not peculiar to any particular members, such as fevers. There was also some discussion of tumours and pustules, poisons, fractured limbs and also of beauty treatment. The fifth and final book was devoted to compounded medicaments—theriacs, electuaries, crushed medicaments, powders and dry drugs, potions, syrups, etc. At the end of this book there was inserted a short fragment on balances and an instrument for measuring taken from Ibn Serapion.

Ibn Sīnā was not satisfied with completing the work of his predecessors: he knew how to supplement it from his own experience. Thus he distinguished between mediastinitis and pleurisy, recognized the contagious nature of tuberculosis, the transmission of epidemics by land and water, and noted that he had tested the efficacy of garlic against snake-bite, etc.

The *Canon* of Ibn Sīnā was studied enthusiastically and lavishly annotated over the centuries by Muslim physicians, who also made summaries of it. One of the most celebrated, *al-Mūjaz*, was that of the seventh/thirteenth-century physician Ibn al-Nafīs, a native of Damascus who practised in Cairo, was appointed leading physician in Egypt and died there in 687/1288. In 1924, Dr Tatawi, a young Egyptian doctor at the University of Freiburg, who was working on the unpublished text of the commentary of Ibn al-Nafīs on the anatomy of Ibn Sīnā, demonstrated in his medical thesis that the Damascus physician took the opposite standpoint to that of Galen and Avicenna, and that he had given an almost exact description of the small or pulmonary circulation nearly three centuries before its discovery by Michael Servetus (1556) and Rinaldo Colombo (1559).

Closely connected with the medical sciences, pharmacology became very fashionable among Muslim authors. In addition to the names of physicians given above, it is necessary to mention in this connexion the book, *Kitāb al-saydala fī'l-ṭibb* ('The science of drugs') by al-Bīrūnī (d. 432/1050), and the important work of Ibn al-Bayṭār, a native of Malaga, the vast *Jāmi' al-mufradāt* ('Collection of simples').

In the field of pharmacology, Muslim physicians enriched the *materia medica* inherited from Greece. They also added valuable remedies, such as camphor, senna, tamarind, the purgative cassia, myrobalans, nutmeg, ergot, rhubarb, galanga root and a host of other drugs which are now obsolete. It is known, moreover, that it was the Arabs who introduced into the West sugar, lemon and other varieties of citrus fruit, mangoes, jasmine, pepper, etc., and that they prepared numerous colorants, including tannins.

If it were not for the strict limitations of space, it might have been possible to discuss here other branches of Muslim achievement connected with the medical sciences, such as hygiene and dietetics, dentistry, ophthalmology, gynaecology, toxicology, physiognomy, as well as other natural sciences such as zoology (the works of al-Jāḥiẓ, al-Damīrī, and al-Qazwīnī), agriculture (cf. 'Nabataean agriculture' of Ibn Waḥshiyya, the *Kitāb al-filāḥa* of Ibn al-'Awwām), botany, horticulture, the veterinary art, hippiatry, falconry, etc. and to demonstrate the part played by Muslims in each of these sciences. Discussion must, however, be confined to a science which was of considerable importance in the Middle Ages and to which Muslim scholars made a decisive contribution—namely alchemy.

According to the *Fihrist* of Ibn al-Nadīm, the first of the Arabs to concern himself with it was the Umayyad prince, Khālid b. Yazīd, who died in 85/704. Enamoured of science in general, he was particularly interested in alchemy, and, adds Ibn al-Nadīm, it was the first time under Islam that the work of translation was begun.

Khālid must have learned alchemy at Alexandria under the guidance of a certain Marianos, who had himself been the disciple of the Alexandrian alchemist Stephanos. According to the Ottoman historiographer Ḥājjī Khalīfa the most celebrated treatise on alchemy attributed to Khālid was the 'Paradise of wisdom,' composed of 2,315 verses. Contrary to Ruska, who is sceptical concerning this attribution, Holmyard regards it as probable.

With Jābir b. Ḥayyān the ground becomes firmer. Jābir, who was born in about 103/721 at Ṭūs in Persia (whence his by-name of al-Ṭūsī), was also called *al-Ṣūfī*, 'the mystic'. Bereaved of his father, he was sent to Arabia, where he studied the Qur'ān, mathematics and other disciplines, then returned to live at Kūfa. He emerges as a personality after being established as alchemist at the court of Hārūn al-Rashīd, and becoming the personal friend of the sixth Shī'ī *Imām*, Ja'far al-Ṣādiq (d. 148/755) whom he regarded as his master. He also was in favour with the celebrated ministers, the Barmecides, one of whom, Ja'far, brought him into contact with the caliph. For him he wrote 'The book of the flower', describing chemical experiments in an elegant style. He had a laboratory at Kūfa, which was rediscovered two centuries after his death, in the quarter near the Damascus gate. A golden mortar was found there, weighing two and a half pounds. In 188/803, with the collapse of the Barmecides, Jābir fell into disgrace. He returned to Kūfa and spent the rest of his life there. According to some, he may have died at Ṭūs in 200/815, with the manuscript of his 'Book of mercy' under his pillow.

There exists an immense corpus of material connected with Jābir which has been closely studied by Paul Kraus; he has shown that a large part of this corpus was written later (?*c.* 900) by a group of Ismā'īlīs, and it is difficult to distinguish what actually belongs to the master.

Jābir's alchemical theory was based on the Aristotelian theory of matter being composed of earth, water, air and fire, but developed it along different lines. There existed in the first place four elemental qualities or 'natures', heat, cold, aridity and humidity. When these were united with a substance, they formed compounds of the first degree, i.e. the hot, the cold, the dry, the wet. The union of two of these properties give:

hot	+	dry	+	substance	=	fire
hot	+	wet	+	,,	=	air
cold	+	wet	+	,,	=	water
cold	+	dry	+	,,	=	earth

In metals, two of these 'natures' were external and two internal. For example, lead was cold and dry externally, hot and wet internally. Gold was hot and wet externally, cold and dry internally.

The sources of these 'natures' were sulphur and mercury—not ordinary sulphur and mercury, but hypothetical substances of which sulphur and mercury represented the nearest equivalents. Sulphur provided the hot and dry 'natures'; mercury the cold and wet 'natures'. Under the influence of the planets, metals were formed in the heart of the earth by the union of sulphur and sugar. This theory was to become general until the appearance of the phlogiston theory of combustion in the seventeenth century.

When sulphur and mercury were completely pure, and were blended together in perfect balance, they produced the most perfect of all metals, gold. Flaws in the purity and especially in the proportions resulted in the production of other metals: silver, lead, tin, iron, copper. Since the elements were the same, however, it was possible to try to remove this impurity and to regain the equilibrium which was characteristic of gold and silver. This process was achieved by means of elixirs. To avoid considerable loss of time in attempting these experiments, Jābir worked out his 'theory of balance', based on the fact that everything in nature contained weight and dimension: it was a question of establishing not equality of mass or of weight, but an equilibrium of 'natures'. According to Jābir, there existed various elixirs for specific conversions, and also a 'master elixir', capable of effecting all conversions.

Jābir was not merely a theorist, but was above all an excellent practitioner, who gave very clear directions for the preparation of certain products. He divided minerals into three groups: (a) spirits, which became volatile when heated (sulphur, arsenic (realgar), mercury, camphor, sal ammoniac); (b) metals, which were fusible, malleable, resonant, lustrous substances (gold, silver, lead, tin, copper, iron and *kharsini*); and finally (c) non-malleable substances, which could be reduced to powder, subdivided into eight groups.

Jābir left some interesting observations. In his *Kitāb ṣundūq al-ḥikma* ('Chest of wisdom') he mentioned nitric acid. Elsewhere he pointed out that copper coloured flame green; he indicated methods of producing steel, of refining other metals, of dyeing clothes and leather, manufacturing a varnish which made clothing waterproof, keeping iron free from rust, dyeing cloth with alum, and of making phosphorescent ink from gilded marcasite instead of from gold, which was too costly. He referred to the use of manganese dioxide in the manufacture of glass, and knew how to concentrate acetic acid in distilling vinegar. In some of his works he gave an exact description of processes such as calcination, crystallization, solution, sublimation and reduction.

With al-Rāzī, who has already been discussed in relation to the medical sciences, alchemy was to take on a more scientific aspect and the descriptions of apparatus and experiments were to be more precise. Like Jābir he accepted the four elements as being at the base of all substances, but did not accept his complicated theory of the 'balance'. For him the object of alchemy was twofold: it taught on the one hand how to transform non-precious metals into silver or gold, on the other hand how to convert quartz or even ordinary glass into precious stones, emeralds, sapphires, rubies, etc. by means of the appropriate elixir. It is remarkable that al-Rāzī never called these elixirs 'the philosopher's stone', but he accepted the theory of Jābir that metals were composed of sulphur and mercury, sometimes adding to them a third element of a saline nature.

The interest of al-Rāzī, however, lies particularly in his practical chemistry. His *Sirr al-asrār* (*Secretum secretorum*) gave for the first time a lucid classification of chemical substances, and he preferred the positive work of the laboratory to unfounded theoretical lucubration. His descriptions of apparatus make it probable that his laboratory was well equipped, since he mentions (1) instruments used for melting substances: fireplace, bellows, crucible, the *botus barbatus* of the medieval chemists, ladle, tongs, scissors, hammer, file; (2) instruments for the preparation of drugs: cucurbit and alembic with evacuation tube, 'blind' alembic (without evacuation tube), receiving mattress, aludel, beakers, flasks, flasks of rose-water, cauldron, pots with covers glazed on the inside, water-bath and sand-bath, furnace, small cylindrical stove for heating the aludel, funnels, sieves, filters, etc.

With regard to chemical processes, al-Rāzī mentions distillation, calcination, solution, evaporation, crystallization, sublimation, filtration, amalgamation, ceration (this last process being the conversion of a substance into a doughy mass or into a fusible solid).

Finally al-Rāzī gives a systematic classification of the products of the three realms of nature employed in alchemy, which really belongs to true chemistry. Thus, for example, mineral substances are divided into six groups: (1) spirits (mercury, sal ammoniac, sulphur of arsenic [orpiment and realgar], sulphur); (2) substances (gold, silver, copper, iron, lead, tin, *kharsini*); (3) stones (pyrites, iron oxide, zinc oxide, azurite, malachite, turquoise, haematite, oxide of arsenic, lead sulphur, mica and asbestos, gypsum, glass); (4) vitriols: (black, alums, white, green, yellow, red); (5) boraxes; (6) salts.

To the 'natural' substances mentioned above, al-Rāzī adds a certain number of substances which are obtained artificially: litharge, oxide of lead, verdigris, oxide of copper, oxide of zinc, cinnabar, caustic soda, polysulphurs of calcium, various alloys.

His great merit was that he rejected magical and astrological practices, while adhering to what could be proved by experiment. Al-Rāzī's insistence on promoting research work in the laboratory did not fail to bear fruit in pharmacology, and Abu'l-Manṣūr Muwaffaq, a Persian of the fourth/tenth century, mentions chemical details about certain medicaments which show real progress in this field. Facts observed with so much care demonstrate, as Holmyard says, 'that a by-product of alchemy was a steadily increasing body of reliable chemical knowledge, a trend which Razi did most to establish and for which he deserves the gratitude of succeeding generations.'

To make a study of the sciences in Islam reasonably complete, it would be necessary to be able to discuss their application to the various techniques in arts and crafts as well as in industry: textiles, cloth, carpets, dyeing, enamels, ceramics, manufacture of various kinds of paper, perfumes, preparation of leather, tempering of steel, extraction of metals, jewellery, embossing, etc.—fields in which the ingenuity of the craftsman profits from the experiments and discoveries of the scientist. The present survey, however, must be terminated here.

In it an attempt has been made to throw into relief the magnificent scientific achievements which distinguished the Muslim Middle Ages but which virtually ceased in the ninth/fifteenth century, and in conclusion it is necessary to face the questions: what were the reasons for what George Sarton was pleased to call 'the Arab miracle', and what were the reasons for its decline? It is indeed a very complex problem, which it is neither easy nor wise to try to dispose of in a few words.

One thing which can be stated with certainty, apparently, is that in the first place questions of race or nationality do not play an essential part. Indeed the emergence has been witnessed, in Baghdād, Cairo, Cordova and Samarqand, of the Persian and the Arab, the Turk and the Andalusian, the Berber and the Sabaean. There appears to be a constant supply of cultural entities, independent of race or nationality, which develop or decline and die according to whether they find a soil which is favourable to them or an environment which destroys them.

Secondly, Islam, of itself, did not offer any kind of opposition to scientific research, in fact quite the contrary. Reference was made at the outset to the stimulus provided by the Qur'ān since God was glorified by wonder at His creation. So long as the interpretation of religious data remains broad enough to enable different theological and philosophical doctrines to confront each other in complete freedom, and, so to speak, on terms of equality, the scientist is living under conditions which are favourable for bringing his researches to a successful conclusion, and for expounding his hypotheses. When the time comes, however, for the triumph of a narrow and defensive theology, which, in the name of official orthodoxy, puts fetters on free research, persecutes the scientists and confines them, then science is not slow to disappear.

In the Middle Ages, Muslim scientists were indisputably at the peak of their progress, scientific curiosity and research. In order to do full justice to the importance of their work, contemporary Western scientists must put into their historical context those who were, in former times, the teachers of their ancestors. In recent years, on the other hand, the movement of the *Nahḍa*, of the Arab renaissance in the Middle East from the middle of the nineteenth century, and, more generally, the awakening of *élites* in all the Muslim countries, has not failed to produce achievements in the scientific field. Modern universities and research institutes have been founded in the great capitals of the Islamic world. There can be nothing but rejoicing at a revival which thus links the present with the glorious past.

CHAPTER II

PHILOSOPHY

Islamic philosophic thought presents a rather greater diversity than medieval Christian philosophy, and the range of the differences of opinion is perhaps wider. For the purposes of the present survey, a division into two main classes may conveniently be adopted. One of these classes comprises the *falāsifa* (this Arabic word for philosophers being used as a technical term) and philosophical theologians whose scheme of reference is provided—whether they acknowledge this fact or not—by the Aristotelian, the Platonic or the neo-Platonic systems of thought. The second main class will comprise the *mutakallimūn* and various other thinkers whose opinions are related to theirs or derived from them. Some of these thinkers profess to be hostile to *kalām*. In contradistinction to the philosophers and the philosophical theologians, the *mutakallimūn* and the other thinkers belonging to this class do not as a rule use the concepts of the Aristotelian, Platonic or neo-Platonic systems as their scheme of reference, though in many cases an influence of these dominant currents of antique philosophy as well as other Greek schools of thought may be discerned. The sociologist and historian Ibn Khaldūn does not belong to either of these two classes. The Ismā'īlī theologians constitute a border case.

FIRST PERIOD: LATER SECOND/EIGHTH TO EARLY FOURTH/TENTH CENTURY

(a) *The translators and the* Falāsifa

The fact that the Arab invasion did not wholly destroy in the conquered countries the continuity of the administrative and economic life has often been remarked upon. Early Islam took over in a certain measure the social fabric of the provinces which were incorporated in the caliphate. It did not seek to operate in a vacuum. A similar explanation might be adduced to account for the adoption of Greek science and philosophy in Islam, and the case for it could be strengthened by a reference to the fact that the Islamic empire included one of the main centres of Greek philosophical and scientific tradition, namely Egypt, and strongly hellenized regions such as Syria. Nevertheless this explanation does not constitute more than a half-truth. For the development of philosophy in Islam, centred at the beginning in provinces which before the Arab conquest belonged either to the Syrian or the Iranian cultural domain, differs considerably in degree and in kind from the philosophical activities which existed in these regions before the rise of Islam.

One of the most noteworthy examples of the cultural continuity which this explanation presupposes is provided by the history of the so-called Alexandrian academy. According to information which may be substantially correct, this institution of Greek philosophical and scientific learning was transferred some time after the beginning of the Islamic era to Antioch, where it was active for a considerable period. Finally, however, the academy dwindled away, and only one professor was left. Its two students left Antioch and in their turn engaged in teaching. In the second half of the third/ninth century, the great Muslim philosopher al-Fārābī, from whom this information derives, received part of his philosophical training from a pupil of one of these two scholars, while the somewhat older Abū Bishr Mattā b. Yūnus, an outstanding Christian translator and commentator of Greek texts, studied in Baghdād with another pupil of the same scholar.

This story admirably illustrates how a small group which, in spite of various political and religious transformations and a change of the linguistic *milieu*, succeeded in maintaining itself for many generations, was able to transmit a knowledge of Greek philosophy to certain select individuals. In a similar way Ibn Sīnā (Avicenna) of Bukhārā got a first notion of philosophy from the teaching of al-Nātilī, a philosopher who took up his abode in the remote far east of the Muslim empire, where Ibn Sīnā grew up.

However, the story of Islamic philosophy is by no means only that of the contacts of isolated individuals; it has also a social and political aspect, which in its beginnings is made evident in the activity of the translators, sponsored and maintained by the caliphs and numerous other powerful and rich patrons, the pillars of society. It was with their help and protection that the great and sustained work of a number of schools of translators was accomplished. Most of the translations, though not all of them, were carried out within a period of roughly two hundred years, ranging from the first half of the third/ninth to the first half of the fifth/eleventh century. In that space of time Arabic versions of a very considerable part of the Greek philosophical and scientific literature were provided. All the principal works of Aristotle were translated (with the possible exception of his *Politics* or of a part of that work) and also many of his less important treatises as well as numerous Greek commentaries on Aristotle, some of which have not come down to us in the original. Arabic translations were also made of paraphrases of many of Plato's dialogues (and perhaps also of the complete text of some dialogues), and of various texts of Plotinus, or deriving from him (these texts being generally attributed by the Arabs to other authors). A sizeable portion of Proclus's writings and certain other neo-Platonic texts were also made known to the Arab intellectuals. In the same period a considerable portion of Greek scientific literature, including mathematical, astronomical, astrological, medical, alchemical and technological texts not preserved in the original, was also translated. On the other hand, Greek poetry and *belles lettres* remained virtually unknown and an object of indifference to the Muslim *élite*, who were keenly interested in the translations referred to above.

In fact the Arabic translations seem to represent the earliest large-scale attempt known in history[1] to take over from an alien civilization its sciences and techniques regarded as universally valid, while other manifestations of that civilization, which were supposed to lack this kind of validity, were more or less neglected. The contrast which this attitude presents to the reception of Greek culture, including the arts in their religious contexts, by the Roman *élite* is instructive, but the point cannot be elaborated here. The fact that philosophy and the sciences, in the form in which they were taken over and developed by the Muslims, had generally speaking no special tie to any particular religion, facilitated their acceptance in Christian Western Europe.

It may be added that the translators created in a remarkably short time a serviceable philosophical vocabulary which was previously totally lacking in Arabic. This vocabulary was enriched and made more accurate, but not essentially altered, by the philosophers who used the translations. This philosophical terminology is to a considerable extent modelled upon the Syriac. There are some Greek loan-words, for which generally an Arabic equivalent is available. A few Persian words, for instance *jawhar*, substance, have also been adopted in the philosophical vocabulary in the strict sense of the term. Words of Persian origin form a a considerable part of the nomenclature of the sciences.

[1] There have been many since, among them that made by the Christian medieval scholars when they became acquainted with the Arabic translations from the Greek.

What was the impulse at work in the translations? As it has already been suggested, they may have continued cultural processes which can be discerned already before the rise of Islam in the countries in which the translations were carried on. Under the auspices of certain monasteries, Greek philosophical and scientific works were being translated into Syriac long before the Arab conquest. Many of the translators who were employed in the incomparably more numerous translations undertaken in the Muslim period were Syriac-speaking Christians, who used in the novel task the traditional technique worked out in turning Greek texts into their native language which, being Semitic, has a certain affinity with Arabic. In fact, these specialists sometimes seem to have found it easier to provide, as a first stage, a Syriac version of a Greek text, and then to translate this version into Arabic, than to attempt a direct translation from Greek to Arabic. This technique seems to have been widely practised in the school of Ḥunayn b. Isḥāq, a Syriac-speaking Christian, who was perhaps the most celebrated of the translators. However, the pre-Islamic monastic Syriac translations appear to have been undertaken mainly to integrate for apologetic purposes certain parts of philosophy, and perhaps also of the sciences, into a syllabus dominated by theology. In fact great prudence was exercised in this integration; for instance, certain portions of Aristotelian logic were judged dangerous to faith, and banned.

In Islam the story is quite different. The translations, which for many successive generations were brought in an unceasing flow to the knowledge of a not inconsiderable public of intellectuals, were clearly not undertaken or patronized for the benefit of Islamic apologetics. Nor were they carried out under the auspices of a traditionalist hierarchy of Sunnī Islam. By contrast, during a long period, zealous religious dignitaries in the main cultural centres had no power to interfere with a relatively free circulation of this dangerous knowledge. Thus, while a certain continuity exists between the Syriac translations carried out under ecclesiastical auspices and the Arabic ones, the impulse behind the latter is quite different. It appears to have been of a purely secular nature.

In this respect a certain analogy may exist between the university of Gondēshāpūr founded in Sasanid Persia and the House of Wisdom (*Bayt al-ḥikma*), the central institute for translations set up by the 'Abbasid Caliph al-Ma'mūn. It is not beyond the bounds of possibility that the latter sought to revive the cultural tradition of pre-Islamic Persia.[1] In the present context, however, it may be more significant to note that—as far as our very incomplete information goes—both the professors of the university of Gondēshāpūr and the early Arabic translators were concerned with the propagation of the practically useful sciences at least as much as, and perhaps more than, with the diffusion of purely theoretical knowledge. Not only Greek philosophy, in Syriac and perhaps also Pahlavī translations, but also Greek (possibly also Indian) medicine seems to have been taught as a main subject at Gondēshāpūr.

It is also certain that treatises dealing with the three practical sciences, astrology, alchemy and medicine constitute a very considerable part of the early Arabic translations.[2] It may accordingly be presumed that the hope to enjoy the advantage of a knowledge of the future, or to possess unlimited wealth and the power over man and nature promised by the alchemists, as well as the wish for scientific medical care, may have been a prime factor in the patronage accorded to the Greek sciences. On this view the reception of the theoretical sciences was favoured because of their close connexion with the practical disciplines.[3] In point of fact, very few Islamic philosophers had any use for alchemy, and belief in astrology was prevalent among those thinkers who may be said to belong to the main stream of philosophical thought only in the first period, i.e. during the third/ninth century. Virtually all philosophers, however, as distinct from the *mutakallimūn*, up to the end of the sixth/twelfth century, and perhaps even later, were practising physicians. Medicine was regarded as a characteristic way in which philosophers earned their living.

This phenomenon and this conception (which is foreign to Christian medieval Europe and also generally speaking to classical antiquity) may be explained by the lack of universities or other officially recognized institutions in which philosophy was studied. Al-Ma'mūn's House of

[1] For that matter, it is not impossible that he may have wished to found an institution rivalling the imperial university of Constantinople or some other Byzantine seat of learning. Some evidence points this way.

[2] Arabic translations of treatises on astrology and medicine were made already before al-Ma'mūn's reign. There is also some, perhaps not quite reliable, evidence that treatises on alchemy had been translated or adapted into Arabic already in the Umayyad period.

[3] Al-Bīrūnī practised astrology, but seems inclined to regard it as largely a pseudo-science. He suggests that it was invented as a protective device by the theoretical astronomers, who wished to be allowed to devote themselves in peace to the pursuit of their science, which was abhorrent to the common run of men. The latter could be brought to accept this theoretical avocation only because of their interest in astrology, which is bound up with scientific astronomy.

Wisdom was not a durable institution, and the religious universities which were founded at certain periods taught as a rule, as far as Sunnī Islam is concerned, the theology of whatever *kalām* school was favoured by the government, and were interested in philosophy only as an object of polemics.

Owing to the absence of such institutions as the ecclesiastically controlled universities of Christian Western Europe, which integrated Greek philosophy into the doctrine approved by the Catholic hierarchy, and ensured its continued study (but required the philosophers to conform to theological doctrine), the philosopher *qua* philosopher had no recognized social function. The hallmark of respectability which he often had was due not to his being a university professor teaching philosophy, but to his practising medicine or some similar avocation. The fact that philosophers as such did not belong to an ecclesiastical or governmental establishment had, of course, from their point of view an advantage. For a long time they could, with some equivocation, escape from tailoring their thoughts to the requirements of a dominant theology. On the other hand, the ambiguity of the position of the philosophers in society may have exacerbated for some of them the preoccupation with the problem of the true political and social function of the philosopher, and of the duties incumbent on him in this field of action, if circumstances permit. This is the main topic of philosophical discussion from the time of al-Fārābī in the first half of the fourth/tenth century till the end of the sixth/twelfth. We have no evidence indicating that this problem engaged the attention of al-Kindī, the main philosophical author of the first period of Islamic thought.

Abū Yūsuf Ya'qūb al-Kindī, a philosopher and author of pure Arab origin, who died probably some years after the middle of the ninth Christian century,[1] was a rich patron of the translators, and sometimes revised their work. As a philosophical author, he is first and foremost a product of the intellectual climate which their activity had created. He is often described as the first Islamic philosopher, and this designation has some justification, provided that it is not understood to mean that he was an original thinker. No such claim can be made for him, if we may judge by his extant treatises, although it is true that they form a very small part of his immense literary output. As far as Greek learning is concerned, his foremost function seems to have consisted in expound-

[1] The exact date is unknown but surmises have been made on the basis of indirect evidence.

ing or adapting texts which the translators had rendered accessible to the Arabic reading public.

As his treatises show, he had a good grasp of the various physical doctrines of Aristotle, and of the concept of mechanical causality on which some of them are based. On the other hand, a probably authentic treatise attributed to him, which as far as is known is extant only in a Latin translation, sets forth a theory of universal radiation, which is foreign to the Greek philosophy. In a treatise on the soul purporting to give the opinion of Plato, Aristotle and other ancient philosophers, he asserts that the soul is immortal, that it is a substance deriving from the substance of the Creator, and, when separated from the body and purged of the latter's dross, omniscient. God as conceived by al-Kindī is principally described by negatives, but his is a moderate form of negative theology. Contrary to what has been sometimes asserted, there is no clear evidence for a strong influence of Muʿtazilite *kalām* on al-Kindī, though his method of interpreting the Qur'ān has some resemblance to that of the Muʿtazila. It is true that he speaks of one God who created the world out of nothing, but this was not only a religious, but also a philosophical doctrine. It was professed by late Greek neo-Platonists, who were mostly Christians. He attributes to the prophets an intuitive immediate knowledge, which contrasts with the knowledge of other men which is acquired step by step. This view, which is also held by later philosophers such as Ibn Sīnā, is by no means characteristic of the Muʿtazila, who generally tend to minimize the difference between the Prophet and other men.

Al-Kindī, who was the author of numerous medical works, seems to have rejected alchemy, but believed in astrology, and composed a certain number of writings dealing with questions pertaining to this science. It is worth noting that one of these treatises deals with a politically explosive subject: it purports to determine by astrological methods the duration of Islamic rule, which at a certain time will come to an end. Obviously al-Kindī did not apply to the claims of astrology the kind of critique which led to the rejection of that science by later Islamic Aristotelians. His largely uncritical acceptance of the heritage of antique civilization that was known to him appears to have led him to see in a favourable light the religion of the *Ṣābi'a* (Sabians). This was a designation of a baptizing sect named in the Qur'ān as one of the three protected religions together with Judaism and Christianity. It came to be applied to a Syriac-speaking pagan community which survived in

Ḥarrān and practised a cult which is reported to have been impregnated with philosophical elements. It is at all events certain that this community included a number of persons acquainted with Greek philosophy. One of its leaders, Thābit b. Qurra, who belongs to the generation after al-Kindī, was a distinguished philosopher and translator of Greek texts. Finally *Ṣābi'a* became a blanket designation for pagan religion, which in Christian polemics was regarded as a single entity including all the various cults, and was called *Hellenismos*. The term 'Sabian religion' was used as an equivalent of the religion of the Hellenes, and had an even wider extension, being applied for instance to Buddhism. For evident reasons it was, however, often associated with the Greek philosophers; at least in one Arabic text it is said to be the religion they professed. It is perhaps on these grounds that al-Kindī in a survey of Sabian beliefs and customs (preserved in a work of his pupil Aḥmad b. Ṭayyib al-Sarakhsī, of which an extract has come down to us) gives an account of the fundamental dogmas, which was clearly calculated to dispel Muslim suspicions; the Sabian dogmas being shown to be virtually identical with the Muslim ones.

Al-Kindī influenced in the course of the third/ninth and fourth/tenth centuries certain Muslim and Jewish writers of compilations, such as the authors of the encyclopedia of the *Ikhwān al-Ṣafā* and Isaac Judaeus. As far as I can see, no strong influence of his can be discerned in the writings of al-Fārābī, who started a new philosophical tradition.

In conclusion of this account of the first period of Islamic *Falsafa*, a brief reference may be made to the Sabian, Thābit b. Qurra, who appears to have had epistolary relations with al-Sarakhsī. In his philosophical writings, composed in Arabic, he affirmed in opposition to Aristotle the existence of an actual infinite. He also wrote in Syriac a work in which he extolled the cultural achievement of paganism.

(b) *The* Mutakallimūn

The various theological doctrines and schools of thought to which the general appellation *kalām* (literally: speech) is applied developed in close connexion with other manifestations of Islamic civilization. The early attempts to meditate upon and to understand the theological meaning implicit in the text of the Qur'ān and to discover the correct Islamic solution for such problems as the relation between God's decree and human actions certainly contributed to the formation of the *kalām* as well as to the origination of Ṣūfī mysticism, which in its inchoate period did not manifest the sharp antagonism to the *kalām* theology which later on often characterized it. Indeed it may be argued, with a certain show of reason, that the Muʿtazilite *kalām* and a dominant Ṣūfī tradition stem from the same school, that of Ḥasan al-Baṣrī (d. 110/728). There is also a close relation between *kalām* in its early period and the Muslim legal science (*fiqh*). To quote but one example, it is more than probable that the Muʿtazilite conception of the role of reason owes a great deal to parallel notions expounded by certain jurists. The impact of various political positions and options on the origin and evolution of the different schools is even more evident.

However, since Islamic civilization, even before its full exposure to the influence of Greek philosophy and science, was by no means self-contained, *kalām* cannot be understood without an inquiry into the relations of its exponents with other religions and theologies, and into the possibly non-Islamic origins of some tenets of its main schools. It is certain that *kalām* is greatly indebted to Christian theology, both because some concepts were taken over from the latter, and because the polemics against the Christians helped to crystallize Islamic theology. Islamic apologetic literature directed against the Manicheans, or perhaps in certain cases against the Zoroastrians, played an analogous, though probably a less important role.

The first beginnings of *kalām* in the proper sense of the word go back at the latest to the end of the Umayyad period, i.e. the first part of the second/eighth century; that being the time when the Muʿtazilite and a great number of other sects appear as separate entities. There are no *kalām* texts dating from this period. Later Muʿtazilite texts however and the accounts of Islamic heresiographers, some of whom are reliable, enable us to have a fair idea of the common doctrines of this sect, and of the formulations of, and variations upon, these doctrines found in the teachings of such outstanding ninth-century Muʿtazilite theologians as Abu'l-Hudhayl ʿAllāf (d. 226/841 or 235/849), Ibrāhīm al-Naẓẓām (d. between 220–30/835–45), al-Muʿammar and others, some of whom seem to have propounded coherent systems of thought.

Wāṣil b. ʿAṭā' and ʿAmr b. ʿUbayd, who, according to tradition, founded the Muʿtazila in the second/eighth century are much more shadowy figures, and so are the founders and chiefs of other early *kalām* sects or schools, such as Jahm b. Ṣafwān, al-Najjār and many others. Seen in historical perspective, the importance of these sects is incomparably less than that of the Mu'tazila; but their members played a certain part in the lively controversies which are characteristic of the history of *kalām* in the third/ninth century and probably also earlier, and which continue in a changed theological atmosphere in the fourth/tenth century.

None of the incipient *kalām* sects of the Umayyad period seems to have whole-heartedly accepted the dynasty and the régime. Their attitudes seem to have greatly varied, running the whole gamut from the toleration shown by the Murji'a, to active hostility. The Mu'tazila do not form an exception to this rule. Indeed it has been maintained that the Mu'tazila contributed to the success of the 'Abbasid insurrection.[1] However that may be, the accession of the 'Abbasids ushered in what was perhaps the intellectually most lively and most uninhibited period in the history of *kalām*. Moreover, the Mu'tazilite doctrine was declared by al-Ma'mūn to be the official theology of the caliphate. Al-Ma'mūn's immediate successors followed suit. It was not until approximately 235/849 that al-Mutawakkil reversed this policy, putting an end to the privileged position of the Mu'tazilite theologians and taking various measures against them. As the heresiographer al-Shahrastānī puts it: 'As for the splendour of *kalām*, it begins with the 'Abbasid Caliphs Hārūn al-Rashīd, al-Ma'mūn, al-Mu'taṣim, al-Wāthiq and al-Mutawakkil.'[2] In this sentence al-Shahrastānī seem to equate—perhaps justifiably, as far as the early period is concerned—*kalām* with Mu'tazilism. The latter's preponderance among the *kalām* schools was jeopardized only with the rise of the Ash'ariyya in the fourth/tenth century.

[1] The appellation Mu'tazila has been interpreted as meaning those who do not take sides either for the Caliph 'Alī or for his adverseries. Nyberg argues that this attitude of the Mu'tazila facilitated their adoption of the 'Abbasid claims, to which, as he thinks, they gave whole-hearted support. It may be noted that Abū Muslim, the military leader of the 'Abbasid insurrection, seems to have used men known as *mutakallimūn* as some kind of field-preachers or missionaries. An anonymous Arabic historian, whose work contains abundant and apparently reliable information on the 'Abbasid revolt states: '[Abū Muslim] ordered the *mutakallimūn* among his partisans to go to Merv to spread information about their opinions (*amrahum*: literally "method") and to describe their position (*mā hum 'alayhi*), in so far as it consists in following the religious tradition (*al-sunna*) and in doing what is right (*al-'amal bi' l-ḥaqq*).' (*Nubdha min kitāb al-ta'rīkh li'l-mu'allif al-majhūl min al-qarn al-ḥādī 'ashar*, ed P. A. Griaznevich (Moscow, 1960), 269b of the Arabic facsimile, 110 of the Russian translation) No further particulars are given about the *mutakallimūn* in question, but the passage rather suggests that, *mutatis mutandis*, they played in Abū Muslim's insurrection, which had a religious side to it, an analogous role to that played later by the missionaries (*du'āt*) of another revolutionary movement, that of the Ismā'īlīs. It is at least arguable that the *mutakallimūn* referred to in this passage may have been some sort of proto-Mu'tazila, or at least close to the sect.

[2] *Kitāb al-milal wa'l-niḥal* (Cairo, 1948), I, 39.

As we have seen, al-Ma'mūn favoured both Greek philosophy and the Mu'tazilite *kalām*. It may be maintained that there is a certain affinity between the two schools of thought; for both accord a preeminent value to reason or to the intellect (both English terms being possible translations of the Arabic word *'aql*). And to a certain limited extent, this contention may be justified. However, the Mu'tazilite conception of reason is very different from that of the Aristotelian philosophers. One aspect of this difference may become clear if one considers the doctrines involved in the principle of justice (*'adl*). This is one of the five main principles (with two of which we shall be concerned here) which were used by the Mu'tazila with a view to a classification of their theological teachings.

Dealing with problems related to this principle, the Mu'tazila assert that it is a primary function of reason to distinguish between good and evil, justice and injustice; these being in their opinion objectively existing qualities inherent in actions. The discernment of what is right and wrong can claim the same degree of universal validity as the perception of a colour. Regarded from the point of view of the Islamic Aristotelians, this doctrine would seem to imply a thesis wholly unacceptable to them, namely that practical reason has the same kind of truth-content, the same universal validity and the same dignity as theoretical reason. The Mu'tazilite view has some affinity with the Stoic idea of natural law and with the cognate Christian conceptions, and may in the last analysis derive from the one or from the other, or from both. But it is very different from either, one reason being that the Mu'tazilites could not have used the expression 'natural law', as it seems to imply the existence of a stable cosmic order, which they denied.

Furthermore certain particularities of their conception may have also been due to the fact that they flouted the popular Muslim idea of the omnipotence of God. To some extent this position was determined by the Mu'tazilite belief that good and evil were independent of God's will, and that human actions could be judged to be right or wrong without any reference to the divine commandments. This doctrine concerning the objective existence of the quality of goodness led them to the belief that God has the same kind of knowledge as men with regard to the distinction between good and evil. As a corollary, He could not be supposed to do evil; all His actions being *sub ratione boni*, which means that a restriction was imposed on His freedom of action. As far as God's dealings with men and, even according to certain theologians, with brute animals are concerned, this means that all suffering is either merited, being a punishment for a transgression, or must entail for the innocent victim a compensation in the other world. All good actions must be rewarded; God cannot act otherwise. This view can of course be derived from Jewish and Christian conceptions, and perhaps also in part from the Qur'ān, but there exists in addition the possibility that the central position held by it in the Mu'tazilite doctrine may be partly due to the necessity of combating Manichean and Zoroastrian dualistic conceptions, which maintain that, in view of the prevalence of evil in the world, an omnipotent God cannot be considered as just.

The fact that men (i.e. as it would appear, all men of sound mind) are held by the Mu'tazilites to have a spontaneous and immediate knowledge of what is good implies that, at least in this important respect, there are no essential differences between human beings. This egalitarian tendency of the Mu'tazilites is clearly opposed to the Shī'ī conception of a strict hierarchy, with, at the top, the prophets and *imāms*. In point of fact the Mu'tazilites are, as has already been stated, generally inclined to reduce to a minimum the differences between the prophets and ordinary people; the former and the latter having one supremely important thing in common; namely the fact that both are endowed with reason. The radicalization of the Mu'tazilite doctrine by such heretics as Ibn al-Rāwandī sets in at this point.

The principle of unification (*tawḥīd*) was as characteristic of the Mu'tazila as the principle of justice. They were currently designated as 'the people of justice and of unification' (*ahl al-'adl wa'l-tawḥīd*). The unification which is referred to is that of God. The principle in question appears to be concerned both with the relation of God to the world, and with God considered in Himself. According to the Mu'tazilite view, which was adopted also by their adversaries the Ash'arites, the existence of God is not, as far as man is concerned, an object of immediate and evident knowledge. It has to be deduced from a consideration of the world, which, being obviously created in time, calls for the conclusion that an eternal Creator must exist. It can also be proved that there is only one Creator. The Mu'tazilites contended that the unity of God would be impaired if there existed divine attributes superadded to God's essence. They accordingly maintained—using various formulations—that such attributes as God's will, God's wisdom and so on are identical with the divine essence. This thesis, the adoption of which may have been facilitated by polemics against the Christian dogma of the

Trinity, was one of the points which provoked the most vehement attacks against the Mu'tazilites on the part of the Ash'arites and others. The Mu'tazilite belief that the Qur'ān was created in time likewise pertains to the principle of unification. This belief too caused them to be stigmatized as heretics.

Most of the Mu'tazila were atomists.[1] This meant that they rejected the Aristotelian idea of an orderly cosmos, and believed in a world which called for incessant direct intervention on the part of God. They posited the existence of indivisible corporeal atoms, a minimum number of which was needed to form a body, of atoms of time and space, of atoms of motion and of atoms of the various categories of accidents, such as of colour. According to them there were atoms of life, and even atoms of belief. In motion a corporeal atom passed in an atom of time from one atom of space to another; the differences in the speed of various motions were due to the lesser or greater number of atoms of rest which were interspersed in the atoms of motion. It is a discontinuous universe and an impermanent one. After having taught that the duration of the existence of the atoms of accidents did not exceed one atom of time, and that at every instant God created new atoms of accidents to replace those which had existed in the instant which had just come to an end, the Mu'tazilites in a later phase of the doctrine extended this conception to the corporeal atom. With every atom of time the world was created anew.

They were consistent in denying as a general rule causality, which appears to be hardly admissible in a discontinuous universe. Using an argumentation which bears a certain resemblance to Hume's, they denied that a causal relation may be proved from the fact that one phenomenon usually follows upon another. Cotton put close to fire generally burns. But this should be regarded merely as a habit. It does not mean that it pertains to the nature of fire to produce this effect. They did not extend this theory to human actions, which, according to them, had within certain limits a causal effect. A man who throws a stone and kills another man was in their opinion the cause of the death. In this case the Mu'tazilite principle of divine justice prevails over the doctrine of discontinuity. This principle posits on one hand that murder is punished by God, and on the other, that such punishment would be unjust if the murderer were not the cause of the victim's death. Thus

[1] The one great exception is Ibrāhīm al-Naẓẓām who believed, like Anaxagoras and the Stoics, that bodies resulted from a total mixture of infinitely small particles of various substances. Al-Naẓẓām's physical theories may have been influenced by the Manicheans.

the principle of justice made it necessary to attribute to man a certain freedom and independent power of action. Owing to their atomism not being consistent the whole way through, God was not the sole agent. Because of the ascription to man of God's prerogative of action, a saying attributed to Muḥammad charges the Mu'tazila with being the Magians (i.e. the dualists) of Islam. It is by no means impossible that the disputations with the Iranian dualists may have contributed to the crystallization of this Mu'tazilite doctrine. On the other hand, the possibility of a Christian influence should also be taken into account. The Oriental Christians with whom the Muslims came into contact appear to have believed in man's freedom of action.

The question of the origin of *kalām* atomism is even harder to answer. The Mu'tazilite theory is very different from all the Greek atomistic doctrines known to us. However, our information as to these doctrines is incomplete. The possibility of one of them bearing a greater resemblance than now seems likely to the *kalām* conception cannot be entirely ruled out. It also seems clear that the *mutakallimūn* are indebted to the Greek atomists for at least some of their views. There exists on the other hand an undeniable similarity between various important points of the *kalām* doctrine and the Indian (Nyāya-Vaishēshika and Buddhist) atomistic doctrines. It is not beyond the bounds of possibility that the *mutakallimūn* may have adopted some Indian concepts, which may have been transmitted to them directly from Indian sources, or through some Iranian intermediary.

The *mutakallimūn*, apparently including the Mu'tazila, were accused by the philosophers from al-Fārābī onwards of putting the power of ratiocination, such as it was, at the service of religion; they were supposed to be wholly indifferent to truth, being exclusively concerned with apologetics. This charge may have been true in some measure with regard to many *mutakallimūn*, both Ash'arites and Mu'tazilites, posterior to al-Fārābī; but it seems a gross misrepresentation, not only of numerous earlier Mu'tazilites, but also of the fourth/tenth century doctors of the sect, al-Jubbā'ī and his son Abū Hāshim, who certainly had genuine theoretical interests not connected with religion. In fact, from the religious point of view, reason as conceived by the Mu'tazila (however superficial it might, rightly or wrongly, appear to the Aristotelian) was a two-edged weapon. It was sometimes used with telling effect against Islam. The most famous case is that of a renegade Mu'tazilite, Ibn al-Rāwandī, who probably died around 250/864.

In a lost work, known only from quotations, Ibn al-Rāwandī put into the mouth of mythical Brahmans, whom he chose to be his spokesmen, arguments in all likelihood suggested by the Mu'tazilite position, which sets up reason as a judge of religion, and distinguishes between the rational and non-rational religious commandments. According to Ibn al-Rāwandī's Brahmans, God, who is assumed to be wise, cannot be supposed to have imposed upon man obligations not legitimated by reason. What the prophets say is either in accordance with reason, in which case no prophets are needed (the common run of men being endowed with the power of reasoning), or it does not conform to reason; in that case it has to be rejected. Ibn al-Rāwandī specifically mentions a number of religious commandments which are not in conformity with reason. All this obviously involves on his part a critique of the current assumption regarding prophetic inspiration, and this critique goes hand in hand with the belief in miracles attributed to Muḥammad. This ex-Mu'tazilite was one of the earliest free-thinkers of Islam and a veritable precursor of the Platonist, Abū Bakr al-Rāzī.

SECOND PERIOD: FOURTH/TENTH TO MID-SIXTH/TWELFTH CENTURY

(a) *The philosophers and the philosophical theologians*

(i) *Al-Fārābī.* Muḥammad b. Muḥammad b. Tarkhān al-Fārābī, a descendant of a Central Asian Turkish family, died, apparently in ripe old age, in 339/950. He is said to have lived for some time in Damascus. The last period of his life was spent in Aleppo, at the pro-Ismā'īlī court of Sayf al-Dawla, a fact which may be significant. Al-Fārābī was not only a product of what Massignon has called the Ismā'īlī century of Islam, which can be said to have begun some time before 287/900; he also appears to have helped to mould its political ideology. In a larger context, he may be said to be the earliest outstanding Islam-minded philosopher (if the term is interpreted as excluding the *mutakallimūn*). I do not of course refer to his reportedly having been an observant Muslim. The statements labouring this point may be correct, but they are irrelevant. His genuine position can only be discovered in his writings.

In these one point stands out clearly: al-Fārābī's preoccupation with a certain category of problems connected with the beliefs, the political institutions, the law and the apologetics of Islam and of other religions set in the same pattern accounts for some of the most important themes of several capital works of his, such as *Ārā' ahl al-Madīna al-Fāḍila* ('The opinions of the people of the Virtuous City'), *al-Siyāsāt al-madaniyya* ('Political régimes'), and others. As has been indicated, this seems to have been a new departure among the Islamic philosophers; it was the religion of the pagans that appears to have engaged al-Kindī's particular interest.

It is, however, clear that al-Fārābī's attitude is a purely philosophical and not a religious one. He is alive to the capital importance of Islam and the other monotheistic prophetic religions as a subject-matter for philosophical study; they have to abide the philosopher's judgment. In al-Fārābī's case this integration of the science dealing with the prophetic religion, complete with its political aspect, into the general system of philosophy was rendered possible by his Platonism, proved by all his political treatises.[1] The reasons he gives for the creation of political societies and for man's need for them derive from those found in Plato's *Republic*. Al-Fārābī points out that in order to subsist and to develop a useful activity, men must co-operate, division of labour being necessary. He does not profess the theory, which seems already to have been current in his time, that unless men's natural instincts were curbed by the authority of religious legislation and of a state founded by a prophet, the human species would run the risk of being destroyed, all men being naturally animals.

A look at the various categories of thought posited by al-Fārābī in the two works mentioned above may give some idea of the complexity of his political thought and of the way he amalgamates, apparently in accordance with a reasoned plan, philosophical (mainly Platonic) and Islamic elements. These categories are: the Virtuous City (*al-Madīna al-Fāḍila*), the existence of which is a philosophical postulate—which may or may not be equated with an actually existent state, e.g. the Islamic. The term is clearly philosophical. It does not belong to the specifically Islamic vocabulary. Opposed to the Virtuous City are the various categories of inferior states which have as their scheme of reference the Virtuous City and may be defined by their particular kind of difference or deviation from it. Differences and deviations from an orthodox conduct of the state can of course be defined by means of terms used in Muslim law, in the Qur'ān or in Islamic tradition, and this is done by al-Fārābī.

[1] He composed a paraphrase of Plato's *Laws*, part of which is pure al-Fārābī.

The categories of the inferior states are: (1) the Ignorant (*al-Jāhiliy-ga*), (2) the Transgressing (*al-Fāsiqa*), (3) the Falsifying (*al-Mubaddila*), and (4) the Erring (*al-Ḍālla*). All of these are Islamic terms: *al-Jāhiliyya* designates the pagan Arabs before Islam. In al-Fārābī's terminology, the term applies to states which have never been 'virtuous', whereas the other categories enumerated above are indicative of deviations from and corruptions of the Virtuous State. *Al-Fāsiqa* is a legal term, supposedly used by Wāṣil b. 'Atā', the founder of Mu'tazilism, to designate the perpetrators of actions contrary to the religious law, which, according to al-Fārābī's scheme of reference, is that of the Virtuous State. *Al-Mubaddila*, refers in Islamic terminology to such communities as the Jewish, which are said to have falsified the prophetic books. *Al-Ḍālla*, can signify in this vocabulary people holding wrong beliefs which are a distortion of the correct ones; this being the meaning which al-Fārābī proposes for this appellation. Al-Fārābī also enumerates the categories into which the Ignorant or Pagan State can be subdivided. These subdivisions correspond in the main to the variety of imperfect states described in Plato's *Republic*: the state providing for the bare necessities of life only, the states whose inhabitants are solely preoccupied with the pursuit of wealth, or with pleasure, or with honours; the democratic state concerned with freedom; and the tyrannical state, the goal of whose inhabitants is power and domination. The Virtuous State, which is opposed to all the others, is characterized by the fact that its inhabitants co-operate with a view to achieving true happiness, the Greek *eudaimonia*.

What is the relation between this more or less ideal state conceived by al-Fārābī and the Islamic commonwealth? The answer to this question hinges to some extent on al-Fārābī's characteristic of the founder of the state, designated by him as the First Chief, the *Imām* (meaning religious leader, the word is not used in this context in the pregnant Shī'ī sense) and the principal Limb; the community being compared to a living organism. This founder, who is the first cause of this state—in this connexion al-Fārābī draws a parallel between this chief and God, the state being analogous to the world[1]—is also a prophet, according to 'The opinions of the people of the Virtuous City,' or at least, may be one.

This treatise discusses the intellectual illumination which comes from an entity called the Active Intellect, this being the last of the incorporeal

[1] Al-Fārābī is a partisan of the world state. This state is, according to him, the most perfect, being more self-sufficient than all the others. According to him, the First Chief is at the head of the whole habitable earth.

Separate Intellects, which in a way are intermediaries between God and the created universe. This illumination actualizes the potentiality for intellection existing in man; and this brings about the production in human beings of the forms of actualized intellect that are called the intellect in act, and the acquired intellect. An intellect belonging to this last category is close to the active Intellect. Man can, however, go beyond this and achieve union with the Active Intellect.[1] If this involves the theoretical and practical rational faculty and also the imagination, the man in question is said to have received a revelation[2] from God through the intermediary of the Active Intellect. Such a man may be called with respect to his intellectual capacity a philosopher and a sage; with respect to his imaginative power (by means of which he is able to have veridical dreams, to see visions and to perceive events in the present and in the future) he may be called a prophet.

The connexion between al-Fārābī's First Chief and Plato's Philosopher-King is quite evident; in fact, al-Fārābī attributes to the former a number of qualities obviously taken over from a description of the rulers of the ideal city in Plato's *Republic*. On the other hand, the fact that the First Chief must be, or at least in many cases is (a passage in 'The opinions of the people of the Virtuous City' seems to imply that there is no necessity about it[3]), endowed with a powerful imagination, enabling him to see visions and to foretell the future, makes it possible to identify him with such prophetic lawgivers as Muḥammad. This would of course imply that the latter was a philosopher.

The First Chief is an originator of religious legislation. The second, who follows him, and the successors of the second, are guardians and students of this tradition. This and other characteristics of theirs enumerated by al-Fārābī seem to have been taken over from an exposition of the qualifications of a caliph set forth in a Sunnī (rather than a Shī'ī) legal treatise, for al-Fārābī does not ascribe to the Second Chief superhuman qualities, such as were attributed to 'Alī and the *Imāms* by all but the most moderate Shī'a.

From a certain point of view, the inhabitants of the Virtuous State possess a common system of belief. There are, however, essential

[1] The verb *ḥalla* is used to describe the descent of the Active Intellect upon the man in question. This verb is applied by theologians to the incarnation of the Deity in Christ, as conceived by the Christians.

[2] As a rule the term is used exclusively of prophetic revelation.

[3] Al-Fārābī's parallel treatise entitled 'Political régimes' does not mention the imaginative faculty of the First Chief, who is described there at some length.

differences between them. The philosophers (*ḥukamā'*, literally, sages) know through the exercise of their intellectual powers the naked, undisguised truth regarding God, the Separate Intellects, the heavenly and terrestrial bodies, the processes of generation and corruption, and finally man, the faculties of his soul, his intelligence, the First Chief, prophecy, the Virtuous State and the other states, and so on. Another category of persons does not profess the truth concerning these matters because of their own capacity for knowledge, but because of their belief in the philosophers. All the other categories have access to these truths only through the parables 'imitating' them. Some of these parables come closer to the undisguised truth than others, but all of them indicate the same truth, and all of them point to one and the same happiness.

In other words, the core of all religions is identical in all of them; whereas the outward manifestations, i.e. myths and stories, vary from one religion to another. It follows from al-Fārābī's definitions that divergences between the religions are not a matter of primary importance, because they do not entail, as far as the philosophers who profess these faiths are concerned, any disagreement as to the scientific and philosophical truths which are the kernel of all religion. Obviously, this system of doctrines gives a philosophical legitimation to the beliefs and institutions of Islam and the other prophetic religions. It also consecrates the principle of the essential inequality of human beings; the prophets, who are also philosophers, and the philosophers, who lack the imaginative power of the prophets, being at the top of the pyramid.

Many elements of these theories, (for instance to some extent what may be called the psychological explanation of prophecy), could be found in philosophical doctrines which antedated al-Fārābī. However, the latter manifested indubitable originality in his interpretation of the primordial facts of the society in which he lived; he used both the concepts of Islamic law and, at least in a certain measure, Plato's political science for his own philosophical purposes.

What are the truths which are known without disguise to the philosophers and may be discovered in the parables of the prophetic religions? The concepts in question are concerned with physics, with metaphysics and with anthropology in general, in particular with politics; i.e. with the human sciences as they are thought of by al-Fārābī, whose more or less Platonic views on some of the problems posed in these sciences have been referred to above.

Al-Fārābī's physical doctrine is Aristotelian. The origin of his metaphysics, on the other hand, cannot be defined with comparable certainty. According to al-Fārābī, who on this point follows Aristotle, God is a pure intellect. In formulae which smack of Mu'tazilite *kalām*, the existence of attributes superadded to the divine essence is denied. On the other hand, the appellation 'The First' (*al-Awwal*) applied to God is of neo-Platonic provenance. It is used in the same sense by Proclus.

All that is not-God emanates from God; this doctrine of al-Fārābī appears to be likewise influenced by neo-Platonism. In expounding this doctrine al-Fārābī stresses the point that there is no difference between being as it is in the substance of God, and being as it is in the emanated things. All being is essentially one. This conception, which in its latter elaborate forms was known as the doctrine of the 'unity of being' (*waḥdat al-wujūd*) was to have a considerable influence on Islamic philosophical and mystic thought.

The first emanations, as far as the order of being is concerned (for the priority is not of a temporal nature, the entities in question as well as the cosmos being eternal) are ten incorporeal intellects, each of which, except the last, produces two emanations: one of them being the intellect which immediately follows in the series, and the other a celestial sphere. The tenth and last of these Intellects was, doubtless, already identified by al-Fārābī with the Active Intellect (see above) which illuminates man's reason.

These Intellects have much in common with Aristotle's prime movers. These are also Intellects, and each sphere has one of them as its mover. This kind of connexion between the Intellects and the spheres is also propounded by the Arab Aristotelians. The main differences are that al-Fārābī restricted the number of the incorporeal Intellects to ten, whereas Aristotle mentioned much greater numbers; and that Aristotle did not speak of the emanation of the Intellects from God. On the other hand, the neo-Platonists referred to emanations, but they did not have the conception of a series of incorporeal Intellects. Al-Fārābī's doctrine is an amalgam of these two elements.

In several passages of his works, al-Fārābī appears to expound the Aristotelian view that there is nothing superior to the achievement of philosophical knowledge. However, he sometimes expresses a somewhat different opinion. Thus, in his treatise *Taḥṣīl al-sa'āda* ('The achievement of happiness') he refers to the false (*bāṭil*) philosopher who has theoretical knowledge, but not the power to engender it in other people. The true philosopher has this power and is for this reason identified by al-Fārābī with the true lawgiver, the true king and the true *imām*. In other words, al-Fārābī considers that the supreme activity of the highest type of man has an educational purpose and is of a political nature. This conception has obvious Platonic overtones—it may also have revolutionary implications. It certainly fits in with the programme of the philosophically minded among the sympathisers and propagandists of the Ismā'īlī movement in the fourth/tenth century.

With regard to the destiny of the soul after death, self-contradictions of al-Fārābī were noted by the Spanish Muslim philosopher Ibn Ṭufayl; one of his opinions, incompatible with the others, being that the soul is annihilated by death. He is also reported to have denied (in a work which is no longer extant) the possibility—which he affirms elsewhere—of man's union with the Active Intellect. We do not know whether these inconsistencies indicate some kind of evolution in al-Fārābī's thought. It might be argued that some of them might be due to considerations of prudence. But this is not certain, though al-Fārābī was certainly not unaware of the necessity of being cautious. In fact, the seemingly deliberate abstractness, which occasionally calls to mind Spinoza's way of expressing himself, may have been meant to mask his intentions and the content of his reflections, many of which must have been unacceptable to even a very tolerant religious and political orthodoxy.

Al-Fārābī disbelieves in astrology. He apparently considers that the prophets, the true philosophers and the *imāms* rule, or should rule, not through recourse to one of the 'practical' natural sciences, but by virtue of personal superiority, which enables them to acquire theoretical knowledge, to transmit it in the most suitable form to the various classes into which the inferiors are divided, and to rule the people as a whole. This was a question which had at that time some measure of actuality. The extremist Shī'a, of which the Ismā'īlī propagandists were in the fourth/tenth and fifth/eleventh centuries the most prominent, but by no means the only representatives, were preoccupied with the promise of personal and political power held out by the sciences of alchemy, astrology and magic.

Al-Fārābī, 'the Second Teacher' after Aristotle, was considered as the greatest Muslim philosopher up to the advent of Ibn Sīnā, who was decisively influenced by him, but who superseded him in the Islamic East as 'the Master of those who know.' In Spain and the Maghrib, al-Fārābī's prestige remained among Aristotelians superior to that of Ibn

Sīnā. There is no doubt that the distinctive Islamic Aristotelianism, which is to some extent Platonism, is in a great measure his personal creation.

(ii) *Al-Rāzī.* The celebrated physician Abū Bakr Muḥammad b. Zakariyā al-Rāzī (i.e. a native of Rayy, near Tehran) who died in the early fourth/tenth century, and was consequently a near-contemporary of al-Fārābī was, as far as his philosophical position is concerned, in many ways the latter's direct opposite. It is true that he too was a Platonist of sorts, but his Platonism derives from the *Timaeus,* and not the *Republic* or the *Laws*, and he was emphatically not an Aristotelian. Of his main philosophical works only two ethical treatises and the partly philosophical, as yet unpublished, *Shukūk ʿalā Jālīnus* ('Doubts concerning Galen') have been preserved. But the polemics which are directed, first and foremost by Ismāʿīlī authors, against other writings of his, notably against his *al-ʿIlm al-ilāhī* ('Divine science'), are of great help in reconstituting his doctrine.

Al-Rāzī is totally opposed to the principle of authority, and is an egalitarian, believing that ordinary people are endowed with the capacity to handle their own affairs, in a reasonable way, and they are even able, with the help of a sort of rational inspiration accorded to everybody, to perceive in an immediate way scientific truths. This view has an obvious resemblance to Ibn al-Rāwandī's conception of reason, but al-Rāzī's theory seems to have been more elaborate and, contrary to his predecessor, he had a profound knowledge of the Greek sciences.

According to al-Rāzī, no authority in philosophy, which includes the sciences, should be beyond the reach of criticism. He considers himself entitled to attack the views of Galen, whom he professes to revere, because having come after him, and being versed in Galen's writings, he can see further than the Greek physician. For al-Rāzī believes in the progress of the sciences through the accretion of knowledge, which occurs in all periods. He is even more opposed to the religious authorities. In his opinion, the Qur'ān and the scriptures of the other religions are a tissue of absurd and inconsistent fables; the miracles of the prophets are based on trickery or the stories regarding them are lies. The people who gather around the religious leaders are either feeble-minded, or they are women and adolescents. Religion stifles truth and fosters enmity. If a book in itself can constitute a demonstration that it is a true revelation, the treatises of geometry, astronomy, medicine and logic can justify such a claim much better than the Qur'ān, the transcendent literary beauty of which, denied by al-Rāzī, was thought by orthodox Muslims to prove the truth of Muḥammad's mission.

Al-Rāzī's extant writings contain no reference to a positive political function of the prophets and of religion. He was obviously not particularly interested in political science; but it is also clear that he considered that human beings did not need to be coerced by the prophets and the religious law into behaving in a manner compatible with the existence of an orderly community. In his only extant, and rather sketchy, *exposé* of the origin of human society, he sets forth the economic reason, i.e. the utility of the division of labour.

Since, in al-Rāzī's opinion, the existence of mankind and the avoidance of anarchy do not depend on respect for religious authority, he does not consider the disclosure of truths that tend to undermine this authority as dangerous—as most Aristotelians believed it to be. Unlike them, he has no use for esotericism.

In physics, he totally rejects the Aristotelian doctrine, professing an atomism which is very different from that of *kalām* and has, in spite of important divergences, some similarity with the doctrines of Democritus and Epicurus. According to al-Rāzī, all bodies are composed of corporeal atoms, which as far as we know he considered to be all alike, and of empty spaces. The qualities of all substances can be accounted for on a quantitative basis; they reflect the proportion in that substance of one of these components to the other.

Contrary to Aristotle, al-Rāzī considers that space (or place) exists independently of the bodies which are in it, and that time is not a function of motion. In arguing against the Peripatetic conceptions, al-Rāzī appeals to the immediate certainties of common people. Their testimony, in accordance with his egalitarian tendencies, he regards as more trustworthy than that of the scholars, who, in the opinion of the Aristotelians, alone have access to philosophic and scientific truths. An ordinary person would in al-Rāzī's view be perfectly clear that outside the world there exists an empty three-dimensional space, and that if the world were to disappear, time would continue to flow. Infinite three-dimensional space is designated by him as absolute space, and infinite time as absolute time; to these he opposes relative space and limited time. There is, *mutatis mutandis*, a curious similarity between his use of these two pairs of antithetical terms and Newton's distinction between absolute and relative time and space.

According to agnostic myth, which al-Rāzī adopted at some stage n the evolution of his thought, there existed before the creation of he world five eternal entities; God, the Soul, Matter, Time and Space. Γhe ignorant Soul having desired Matter, God, in order to ease her misery, created the world conjoining her with matter, but also sent to her the Intellect to teach her that she would be finally delivered from her sufferings only by putting an end to her union with Matter. When the Soul grasps this, the world will be dissolved. This view of the role of matter might appear to entail a rigorous asceticism. Yet one of the ethical treatises of al-Rāzī, perhaps written at a time when he did not profess this myth, is devoted to inculcating moderation in this respect.

Believing as he did that the sciences progressed from generation to generation, and that, consequently, one had to keep an open mind, al-Rāzī was interested in alleged facts, which the Aristotelians, because they could not fit them into the framework of their theories, considered as dubious or untrue. Because of his empirical approach, he wrote a treatise on the sometimes apparently inexplicable properties ascribed to various substances, which, as he admitted, were not always verified. He was a noted alchemist.

(iii) *The Ismā'īlī theologians and 'The Brethren of Purity'.* Al-Rāzī's bitter opponents, the Ismā'īlī missionaries, developed a theory affirming the natural inequality of man. In addition, the doctrine that prophets are needed because the spontaneous impulses of human beings would, if they were left unrestrained, prevent the establishment of a viable society, was currently held, and not only in Shī'ī circles.

In the course of the fourth/tenth century, the Ismā'īlī doctors, many of whom were active propagandists for the Fatimid dynasty, adopted a theology which derives from a perhaps christianized neo-Platonism. Later in the fifth/eleventh century, some of the theologians adopted a doctrine which seems to have been influenced by al-Fārābī's and Ibn Sīnā's theory of the Incorporeal Intellects. Part of their appeal to the intellectuals or the would-be intellectuals, was due to their being popularizers of a predigested science. They were accordingly alive to shifts in philosophical fashions.

These philosophical Ismā'īlī theologies teach the existence of two parallel hierarchies; the spiritual, constituted by cosmic entities (such as the Universal Intellect and the Universal Soul or the separate Incorporeal Intellects), and the corporeal, constituted by the dignitaries of the sect, from the *Imām* downwards. The Ismāʿīlīs did not submit to the tendency found in the Shīʿa from the earliest times to regard human beings, to the exclusion of cosmic entities, as the only intermediaries between God and men, and indeed sometimes as God incarnate.

In the second half of the fourth/tenth century, a small group of Ismāʿīlī sympathizers or propagandists composed the so-called *Rasāʾil Ikhwān al-Ṣafā*, ('Epistles of the Brethren of Purity'), the 'Brethren of Purity' being supposed to be a ubiquitous hierarchical society. These epistles are, in the main, an encyclopaedia of the Greek sciences, with the notable exception of Aristotelian metaphysics. The last epistle deals with the science of magic. This is probably the earliest encyclopaedia composed, like that of Pierre Bayle or that of the eighteenth-century *Encyclopédistes*, with a view to undermining the existing political and religious order. Propaganda for an *imām*, who is not named, occurs frequently in its pages.

The authors of this encyclopaedia drew heavily upon the philosophical literature with which they were acquainted, and incorporated various passages of earlier writers, one of them being al-Fārābī, by whose political doctrines they were manifestly influenced. They quote, without mentioning his name, his list of the qualities which the First Chief (to use al-Fārābī's term) is required to have.

A fable in this encyclopaedia, which was translated or adapted into several languages, tells of an animal rebellion against human domination, and the speeches of their spokesmen and those of their opponents, the human beings, before the arbiter, who is a king of the Jinn. In spite of the telling arguments of the animals, the final verdict affirms the legitimacy of human rule, which will be abolished only after certain periods of time have passed. It may be mentioned in this connection that the authors of these epistles believed in the transmigration of souls. It is, I believe, certain that this verdict is intended to set forth the legitimacy of human social inequality and of authoritarian hierarchical rule.

The authors of the encyclopaedia look forward to an eschatological future which, *inter alia*, holds out the promise of deliverance from religious commandments and from tyrannical rulers.

(iv) *Ibn Sīnā* (*Avicenna*). Abū ʿAlī ibn Sīnā, known in Christian medieval Europe as Avicenna, who is said to have been born thirty years after the death of al-Fārābī and died in ?429/1036, acknowledges the great debt he owes to al-Fārābī's writings, and refers to the respect he felt for that philosopher. And yet, partly at least because of Ibn Sīnā, and also in consequence of a shift in the political and social situation, the specific doctrines of al-Fārābī concerning political science, did not, from the time of Ibn Sīnā onwards, arouse any interest at least in the countries of the Muslim East, as opposed to the Maghrib and Spain. In the thirteenth century, the Spanish Muslim philosopher, Ibn Sab'īn, mentions Ibn Sīnā's Platonism, and, at the time of the Renaissance, Pico della Mirandola makes a similar remark. This characteristic certainly fits an important aspect of Ibn Sīnā's philosophy, but, on the other hand, contrary to Plato and to al-Fārābī, he apparently did not consider that, circumstances permitting, it was the duty of the philosopher to become a ruler or an adviser of rulers. Ibn Sīnā played a certain role in practical politics, but there is no evidence for supposing that in this activity he was impelled by theoretical reasons.

Ibn Sīnā was a native of Bukhārā and familiar with both Persian and Arabic. He mentions in his autobiography that his father and brother had Ismā'īlī sympathies, and this may have aroused his interest in philosophy, which he began to study systematically under the tuition of al-Nātilī, who sojourned at that time in Central Asia. This story seems to be typical of the way in which interest in philosophy was acquired in remote regions of the Islamic world. Ibn Sīnā is said to have become possessed of all his immense book-learning before attaining the age of eighteen, having had in his early youth the run of a great library.

As an adult, he had a position of some eminence at the court of certain sultans in Persia proper, and displayed some political activity. He was a renowned physician and wrote one of the standard medical works of the Middle Ages, namely *al-Qānūn*, which was studied in both Islamic and Christian lands. This work contains a set of rules for experiments to determine the efficacy of medicaments, which seem to be an advance on anything to be found in earlier Greek or Arabic texts.

As a philosopher, he had a number of disciples, who played a certain part in the explanation and propagation of his doctrine, and many adversaries. In particular, he was an antagonist of the Baghdādī, mostly Christian, interpreters of Aristotle. In relation to Ibn Sīnā, who was a native of Bukhārā and lived in Persia, these were Westerners. This is a significant point in view of the fact that Ibn Sīnā opposes to the Greek philosophical tradition an Oriental (*mashriqī*) one, which according to him, is of immemorial antiquity. However, there is not the slightest indication that Ibn Sīnā used, or indeed had a modicum of knowledge of, any ancient Oriental sacred or profane tradition. The evidence tends to show that in speaking of the antique 'Oriental wisdom' or 'philosophy', he had in mind his own contemporary personal philosophy, with which he confronts the Western one, namely the Baghdādī philosophy and perhaps also that of the Greek commentators of Aristotle.

The growing strength of Persian national sentiment, which led in Ibn Sīnā's lifetime, to Persian partly replacing Arabic as the administrative language in Maḥmūd of Ghazna's empire, and which may have been to a certain extent responsible for Ibn Sīnā's composing some philosophical and scientific treatises in Persian, may have been one of the factors which suggested this mystification. As we shall see, the notion of 'Oriental wisdom' (*al-ḥikma al-mashriqiyya*) appealed to later Islamic thinkers, and may have inspired in al-Suhrawardī a new departure in philosophy.

Ibn Sīnā's enormous literary output includes the following major works:

(1) *Kitāb shifā' al-nafs*, ('The book of the healing of the soul'), known in medieval Europe under the title of *Sufficientia*. This voluminous work gives detailed expositions of the Greek sciences, those treatises which are included in the *Corpus Aristotelicum* and some others. Ibn Sīnā's intention in composing this work was to set forth the Peripatetic system, but, as he states in his preface, he himself was no Aristotelian, and the book often expresses his personal view. Its sheer size turns it into the earliest specimen of the new genre of philosophical texts. Neither the extant Greek nor the Arabic writings prior to Ibn Sīnā provide an example, other than the *Corpus Aristotelicum* taken together with its commentaries, of an all-inclusive work of this kind, in which the problems of the various sciences are exhaustively discussed. The fact that *Kitāb shifā' al-nafs* is not a commentary and does not have to refer to the letter of the Aristotelian text is in this connexion of great historical importance. As a direct consequence, this work and other writings of Ibn Sīnā largely superseded in the Muslim East as philosophical textbooks the *Corpus Aristotelicum* and also the treatises of al-Fārābī and other relatively early Islamic authors.

(2) *Kitāb najāt al-nafs* ('The book of the salvation of the soul'), appears to consist of extracts from *Kitāb shifā' al-nafs*.

(3) *Kitāb al-ishārāt wa'l-tanbīhāt* ('The book of indications and hints') composed in the last period of Ibn Sīnā's life, was meant to be

an esoteric work, written for the chosen few. It labours much less than *Kitāb shifā' al-nafs* at demonstration, striving rather (at least this is the impression it makes) to bring about intellectual illumination. Certain parts of the Aristotelian doctrine, which Ibn Sīnā found unconvincing are omitted in this work, and his personal contributions to philosophy are much more in evidence than in the earlier work.

(4) *Kitāb al-mubāḥathāt* is a chaotic mass of notes, made known to the public after the death of Ibn Sīnā, and giving invaluable insight into the philosopher's hesitancy and changes of mind, as he endeavours to fit his novel conception into the rigid framework of medieval Arab Aristotelianism.

A point on which Ibn Sīnā may have been opposed to the Baghdādī Aristotelians of his time, and which he appears to have claimed to be part of the tradition of 'Oriental philosophy', concerns the immortality of the individual soul. This was denied by the post-Avicennian orthodox Aristotelians of Spain and the Maghrib, who probably followed an interpretation of Aristotle adopted in such earlier centres of Muslim philosophy as 'Irāq. From the Aristotelian point of view, an individual soul could not continue to exist after its separation from the body, because it is matter, which is only present in the corporeal substance, that is the principle of individuality. Consequently only the intellect, which has no individuality (an intellectual act performed by Peter being strictly identical with the same intellectual act performed by Paul) can survive death. Ibn Sīnā gets around the difficulty by supposing that the individual soul, which, in his opinion, is created at the same time as his body, acquires through its association with the latter, an individuality which it originally does not possess. This individuality is preserved after death. The details, or even the whole of Ibn Sīnā's solution, may be to some extent a novel contribution to the debate, but the thesis itself is clearly not a new one. The immortality of the individual soul was maintained by al-Kindī, not to speak of the Greek Platonists, Pythagoreans and so forth. However, other conceptions of Ibn Sīnā manifest a marked originality. They struck out new roads for Islamic philosophy, and two of them have exerted a lasting influence on European philosophy by providing it with two of its main themes.

One of these themes, which stems from a conception of Ibn Sīnā, is concerned with the radical division between essence and existence, or being. According to the Muslim philosopher, this duality is to be found in all things except God; existence being superadded in them to the essence. By themselves, the essences are neutral with regard to existence. The domain of essence is in some respects reminiscent of that of the Platonic Idea; but the latter, contrary to the essences of Ibn Sīnā, possesses being. As Ibn Sīnā puts it, existence is an accident that happens to the essences. However, it does not happen by chance, but by necessity; everything that exists, including the activity of God, being subject to a strict determinism. The things that are contingent *per se*, i.e. all things that are composed of essence and of existence, or in other words, all things that are not God, are necessary if referred to Him. This determinism does not derive from Aristotle, according to whom random happenings may occur in the sublunar world.

The second Avicennian theme which became an intrinsic part of European (as well as of the Eastern Islamic) philosophy, derives from what may be described as Ibn Sīnā's discovery of the ego and of man's self-awareness. According to Ibn Sīnā, a man suddenly created in full possession of his faculties would, if he were floating in the air, with no previous knowledge of, and no opportunity to perceive, the external world, and with no possibility to sense his own limbs, yet be fully aware of his personal existence. This immediate certainty as to one's ego is Ibn Sīnā's favourite proof for the existence of the soul; he prefers it to the Aristotelian arguments which cite as evidence the motions of animals. Obviously, this proof tends to imply the identification of the soul with the ego and to attribute paramount importance to consciousness and its immediate certainties. In this approach, Ibn Sīnā may have been influenced by some unknown Greek neo-Platonist. He was certainly unaquainted with Augustine, some of whose conceptions have a certain kinship with his. The impact of this philosophy of the ego and of self-awareness both on Islamic and on medieval Christian philosophy, which influenced Descartes on this point, was immense.

However, Ibn Sīnā would not abandon the Aristotelian distinction between the soul and the actual intellect, which, as his doubts and changes of mind on crucial points of the doctrine indicate, was incompatible with this new insight. Some of the more radical conclusions which seemed to be called for were drawn by Abu'l-Barakāt al-Baghdādī.

As far as we know, no notice was taken by the earlier Aristotelian philosophers of the great Ṣūfī mystics. Accordingly Ibn Sīnā seems to have struck out new ground when he recognized in the last section of *Kitāb al-ishārāt wa' l-tanbīhāt* that their experiences were a valid subject for philosophical study; he integrated the varieties of religious experience into his philosophical system. He also seems to consider that the illuminations of the mystics may be on a par with the cognitions of the philosophers.

Occasionally, he englobes the mystics and the prophets in one category. Thus the mystic experience which the Ṣūfīs attempt to express can be made available for the study of the psychology of the prophets. The persons belonging to the category in question can in Ibn Sīnā's opinion have natural powers which enable them to perform actions called miracles, though they are in conformity with the natural order. For the rest, he assigns to the prophets a political role, in accordance with the current idea that men, because of their natural instincts of domination and aggression, cannot establish a viable society unless they are disciplined by a superior authority which they cannot but obey. According to Ibn Sīnā, the prophets are devices of nature with a view to the preservation of the human species. He shows no trace of the interest manifested by al-Fārābī in the various kinds of pagan or monotheistic communities.

A literary form employed by Ibn Sīnā in three of his smaller works may be noted, because it gave rise to a genre which has some importance in the history of Islamic philosophy. I refer to what Ibn Sīnā himself calls parables, i.e. allegorical tales which are meant to express philosophical truths. The composition of such tales clearly requires both philosophical insight and a recourse to imagination. It is not clear whether Ibn Sīnā paid attention to the fact that these are exactly the requirements, as formulated by the philosophers, needed for prophetic visions and revelations. At all events, he showed by his example that a philosopher could fittingly permit his imagination to help his intellect in communicating abstract concepts. Imagination thus became a useful part of a philosopher's equipment. This lesson was not lost upon some of Ibn Sīnā's successors, in particular the Ishrāqī philosophers.

Within a generation or two of Ibn Sīnā's death, or even before that, his doctrine was dominant among the philosophers of the Muslim East, as is proven by the fact that it was the object of the criticism which Abu'l-Barakāt al-Baghdādī and al-Ghazālī directed against the prevalent philosophical views.

(v) *Abu'l Barakāt al-Baghdādī.* Abu'l-Barakāt Hibat Allāh al-Baghdādī (who died as an octogenarian or nonagenerian in 547/1152) was a physician, and lived most of his life in or near Baghdād. Of Jewish origin, he was converted in old age to Islam. The Jews living in Muslim countries used Arabic as their language of philosophical and scientific writing, and Abu'l-Barakāt was no exception. His *magnum opus, Kitāb al-muʿtabar,* a title, which according to his explanation means 'The book of that which has been established by personal reflection' and all his other works were written in that language. *Kitāb al-muʿtabar* had a great influence on later Islamic philosophy and belongs to its history.

As Abu'l-Barakāt lets us know, this work was composed from a collection of jottings in which he had noted his observations upon, and criticism of, the philosophical texts he read. As has already been stated, he apparently referred, in the first place, to texts by Ibn Sīnā. His work has sections dealing with most Greek sciences except mathematics. In view of its genesis, it is not surprising that *Kitāb al-muʿtabar* does not propound a wholly coherent philosophical doctrine. Sometimes Abu'l-Barakāt takes over without any alteration Avicennian theories which do not fit in with his personal view. However, on some essential points, he perceives and eliminates the inconsistencies in Ibn Sīnā's views. Moreover, as regards certain fundamental questions of physics he seems to follow a quite different tradition, which at least in some details clearly derives from Plato's *Timaeus*. There is a certain kinship between some of Abu'l-Barakāt's physical opinions and those of the professed Platonist, Abū Bakr al-Razī. Like the latter, Abu'l-Barakāt rejects the Aristotelian formulations according to which place (or space, one term is used for both concepts) is a limit, i.e. should be identified with a certain relation between two bodies, and that time is a function of motion. Again, like al-Rāzī, Abu'l-Barakāt considers that space is independent of the existence of bodies and is three-dimensional and infinite. However, he differs from al-Rāzī in his view of time, which he defines as the measure of being; a formulation which is similar to that of the Greek neo-Platonist, Damascius.

Ibn Sīnā's teaching concerning the ego and self-awareness presented an unresolved contradiction. For while it was based on a recourse to the primal certainty of self-awareness, which proves the existence of the ego, Ibn Sīnā, in deference to the Aristotelian separation of the intellect from the soul, differentiates—perhaps only in the last period of his life—between self-awareness accompanying an act of intellection (which alone has the characteristics which he generally attributes to self-awareness *tout court*), and the inferior self-awareness accompanying an act of imagination or any other not strictly intellectual human (and also animal) activity. Abu'l-Barakāt sweeps away this distinction, taking his stand on the fact of one's being certain through self-awareness that all the acts which one performs, whether they be intellectual, imaginative, volitional or sensual, are accomplished by one and the same subject, the ego. This appeal to the self-evident character of one's self-awareness disproves, according to Abu'l-Barakāt, the Aristotelian theory elaborated by Ibn Sīnā as to the multiplicity of the psychic faculties. According to Abu'l-Barakāt, there are no distinct faculties; nor is there a distinction between the intellect and the soul.

God is conceived by Abu'l-Barakāt to some extent after the analogy of the human 'I'. He is not, and obviously cannot be, the pure intellect of the Aristotelians, or the divinity of negative theology, but has pre-eminently the characteristics and the capacity for various activities which are found in a lesser degree in human beings.

Events in our world are determined by causality or by chance, which, as Abu'l-Barakāt defines it, results from the encounter of two independent lines of causation. For instance, a man impelled by certain causes sets out to cross the road, and so does a scorpion impelled by another set of causes. In such a case, their meeting and the fact that the man is stung by the scorpion is an effect of chance. However, God, who *inter alia* has the power to will, sometimes—by no means always—directly intervenes in terrestrial affairs.

(b) *Kalām*

From the point of view of *kalām*, this period is marked by the emergence of the Ash'arite school. This does not mean that with the coming of the fourth/tenth century the Mu'tazilites had lost their intellectual vigour. Abū Hāshim, who was the son of the noted Mu'tazilite al-Jubbā'ī and died in 321/933, i.e. at the beginning of the period we are dealing with, continues the Mu'tazilite tradition of almost uninhibited enquiry into a great variety of such acts. Later on, this kind of intellectual curiosity may have weakened among the Mu'tazilites. Such authors as Abū Rashīd al-Nīshāpūrī (d. after 415/1024) and especially 'Abd al-Jabbār al-Hamadhānī (d. 415/1025), the greatest name among these later Mu'tazilites, seemed to be engaged in taking stock of the idea and discussions of their school; 'Abd al-Jabbār's enormous encyclopaedia of Mu'tazilite opinions is the kind of work which often marks the waning of a movement. It should be recognized that his was a very difficult position. Sunnī Islam, with which he fully identified himself, was not only overwhelmingly anti-Mu'tazilite. It was also, as he believed, in the beginning of the fifth/eleventh century, in desperate straits because of the combined effects of the Byzantine victories and of the subversive activities of the Fatimids and other extremist Shi'ites.

(i) *Al-Ash'arī.* Abu'l-Ḥasan 'Alī b. Ismā'īl al-Ash'arī (d. 324/935 or thereabouts) who is said to have been for forty years a companion of the famous Mu'tazilite al-Jubbā'ī, had, perhaps in 300/912–13, a change of heart, brought about, as one of the stories goes, by three dreams in which the Prophet Muḥammad laid his commands upon him. One of these ordered al-Ash'arī not to give up *kalām*—of which he had an exhaustive knowledge attested by his great doxographical work *Maqālāt al-Islāmiyyīn* ('The views of the Muslims')—but to adapt *kalām* to what was regarded as the orthodox Islamic doctrine. In point of fact, the Ash'arites set a considerable value upon 'knowledge' and rational argument, but they implemented them with a view to the defence of religion. This was the veritable function of *kalām*, as al-Fārābī defined it. But the Mu'tazilites seem occasionally to have pursued knowledge with no reference to religion, whereas the Ash'arites, by and large, lived up to al-Fārābī's definition. They met the need for an official theology which was felt at a certain period by the rulers of Sunnī Islam, who had to oppose the propaganda of the hierarchic Ismā'īlī organization with its several elaborate systems of theology. Al-Ash'arī rejects the Mu'tazilite view on the divine attributes, which he considers as not identical with God's essence, and thus, denies the Mu'tazilite conception of God's unity. He also believes that the Qur'ān, regarded as God's speech, was not created in time.

Al-Ash'arī considers that the agent who produces human actions is not man, but God, and thus lays himself open to the objections stemming from the Mu'tazilite principle of justice. However, the Mu'tazilite arguments are founded upon the idea that good and evil have an objective existence independent of God, and that He is obliged to recognize the difference between them and to do good, whereas according to the Ash'arite view what is good and what is evil is determined by God's will.

While man does not perform his own actions, he can 'acquire' them (*kasb* or *iktisāb*, terms which may be derived from the Qur'ān but which, rather curiously, call to mind a somewhat similar doctrine of 'acquisition', *arj*, of action occurring in the Indian Sāmkhya philosophical system). The *kalām* use of the Arabic terms predates al-Ash'arī. The latter is careful practically to annul the minimal concession to man's freedom implied in the doctrine of acquisition, which may refer to man's acquiescence in the actions he is obliged to do, by affirming that the 'acquisition' of an act can only be brought about in every particular case through a power of acquisition specially created by God in the man in question.

The Ash'arites, and there is every reason to suppose their master before them, took over atomism from the Mu'tazila. Like the latter, they disbelieved in causality as far as natural causes were concerned, and indeed were more consistent than the earlier sect with respect to this doctrine. For they did not believe, as did the Mu'tazilites, that human actions produced a series of causes and effects. The Ash'arites had no need of this doctrine. They were not called upon to justify God for punishing a man for a crime of which the latter was not the author; the reason being that, as we have seen, in their opinion, man does not perform even the actions which proceed from him; and that God is in no need of justification, His Will being the sole criterion of right and wrong.

Al-Ash'arī's doctrine was elaborated by Abū Bakr Muḥammad al-Bāqillānī (d. 403/1013) and by Abu'l-Ma'ālī al-Juwaynī *Imām al-Ḥaramayn*, 'the *Imām* of the Two Sanctuaries', (d. 478/1085), who was al-Ghazālī's teacher.

(ii) *Al-Ghazālī.* Abū Ḥāmid Muḥammad al-Ghazālī (450/1058–505–1111) transcends *kalām*. As his account of the evolution of his ideas shows, his crisis of doubt, a time of anguish, during which he lost faith even in the so-called self-evident truths, was a stage in his spiritual progress towards Ṣūfī mysticism, which gave him, according to his own words, lasting peace.

However, he was also an eminent *mutakallim*, the first who was able to expose from a *kalām* point of view, but with a profound knowledge of the doctrine of his opponents, the heresy and weaknesses of what paased for Aristotelian philosophy. In reality, he attacked the system of Ibn Sīnā, with which he was familiar. In fact, he was the author of an excellent, widely read account of it entitled *Maqāṣid al-falāsifa*, ('The intentions of the philosophers'). It is because of such versatility that Ibn Rushd and others accused al-Ghazālī of wishing to be all things to all men.

His critique of philosophy is set forth in *Tahāfut al-falāsifa* a much-debated title which can be translated as 'The incoherence of the philosophers.' This relatively early work (finished in ?488/1095) starts by pointing out that the partisans of philosophy adopt its doctrines because of a blind belief in authority, and goes on to attack some of these doctrines, starting with the conception of the eternity of the world. Al-Ghazālī uses some of the arguments of John Philoponus, the Greek Christian philosopher of the sixth century, showing that this conception must lead to the absurd conclusion that an infinite number is less than another infinite number. For the number of the revolutions of the sun which have occurred up to the present, must, on the hypothesis of the eternity of the world, be infinite, and the same applies to the revolutions of Saturn, and yet the former number must be greater than the latter, since the sun accomplishes its revolutions in one year, whereas Saturn's period is thirty years. At the end of the work, al-Ghazālī formulates the three points on which the conceptions of the philosophers are radically opposed to the Islamic religion. These are, the belief in the eternity of the world, the denial of God's knowledge of particulars, the denial of resurrection.

'The incoherence of the philosophers' had a considerable impact. It has been occasionally maintained that it brought about the decline or the end of philosophy in the Islamic East. This is a pure legend—the fact being that some of the most interesting philosophers of that region come after al-Ghazālī. It is true that not all of them conformed to the pattern of thought which had been attacked by him, but their deviations are not to be laid at his door. It may be mentioned that some of al-Ghazālī's own late works, belonging to his Ṣūfī period, have strong neo-Platonic elements.

PHILOSOPHY IN SPAIN AND THE MAGHRIB

(a) *The Spanish Aristotelians*

The history of Aristotelian philosophy (to use this convenient, though not in all cases quite accurate, term) in Arab Spain is a short one. It begins and it ends in the sixth/twelfth century, or as near as makes no difference. Yet it produced among the Muslims three outstanding philosophers, and had an immense influence on the history of thought in Christendom and Judaism. This impact can be partly explained by the litical division of Spain, and by the presence in that country of a nsiderable Jewish community. Spain was half-Muslim and half-hristian, and this facilitated intellectual contacts, notably the transla-on by the Latins (often with the co-operation of Jews) of Arabic texts r Arabic versions of Greek texts, into Latin. During the lifetime of n Rushd (Averroes), Arabic texts were being translated into Latin in oledo. The famous Muslim philosophers of Spain who lived in that eriod, were, for obvious reasons, better known to the Latin translators nd to their patrons, and consequently more likely to be translated than e equally famous philosophers of the same period who lived in the Iuslim East.

Thus the accident of biographical proximity accounts for the fact, vhich had incalculable repercussions, that many of Ibn Rushd's com-nentaries were translated into Latin and Hebrew. In the last analysis, his accident is also responsible for an optical error which often causes, ven at present, the later philosophers of the Muslim East, who were not nown in medieval Europe, to be undervalued when compared to the Muslim philosophers of Spain. It may be added in this connexion that Maimonides, the greatest Jewish Aristotelian of the Middle Ages, was a product of the Aristotelian school of Islamic Spain, and occasionally stressed this fact.

Before the sixth/twelfth century, intellectual life in Islamic Spain had been influenced by offshoots of neo-Platonic philosophy, i.e. a philosophy centred on the theory of emanation, and on the formulation of the various planes of being. The theologian Ibn Ḥazm (d. 456/1064), a many-faceted personality, may also be mentioned. While his most popular work is a treatise on love, his *magnum opus, Kitāb al-fiṣal*, is concerned with heresiography and contains bitter attacks both on the Ash'arites and on the Mu'tazila.

At the end of the fifth/eleventh century, Muslim Spain was annexed by the fanatical Almoravids, whose armies came over from Africa and defeated the Christians in 479/1086. In their turn, the Almoravids were defeated in 541/1147 and the territories they ruled taken over by the Almohads, an even more intolerant sect, which, contrary to the Almoravids, had adopted *kalām* doctrines, influenced by al-Ghazālī. The first in the outstanding trio of Spanish Aristotelians, Ibn Bājja, lived under the rule of the Almoravids, the other two, Ibn Ṭufayl and Ibn Rushd, under that of the Almohads. These biographical details may account for a certain resigned awareness on the part of all the three of the practical impossibility of philosophy effecting a change in the state of society, an attitude which contrasts with that of al-Fārābī. In the case of Ibn Rushd, the political situation may account for his profound conviction that the *mutakallimūn* do great harm.

(i) *Ibn Bājja* (*Avempace*) *and* (ii) *Ibn Ṭufayl.* This attitude of resignation is perhaps most clearly expressed by Abū Bakr b. Bājja (d. 533/1138), in his work entitled *Tadbīr al-mutawaḥḥid* ('The governance of the solitary'). His thesis is that in the imperfect and diseased states and societies of his time, as well as in the great majority of those of the past of which we have report, the men dedicated to the pursuit of wisdom, and capable of achieving this aim, 'the happy ones' as he calls them, have, and should have, nothing in common with the ordinary population, except in so far as such communications are required for the necessaries of life. They should regard themselves as solitary strangers. This opinion can only be held on the supposition that man's highest end is not of a political nature. In fact, Ibn Bājja considers that this end consists in union with the Active Intellect. He also holds (contrary to Ibn Sīnā) that the individual soul dies with the death of the body. The intellect which survives it has no individual quality. Only what is universal in man survives.

Abū Bakr Muḥammad b. Ṭufayl (d. 581/1185), a *wazīr* and physician of the Almohad rulers, is known as the author of the philosophical novel *Ḥayy ibn Yaqẓān*, a title taken from one of the philosophical tales of Ibn Sīnā, and meaning 'The Living son of the Waking One'. This refers to the Soul, principle of life, which is supposed to be engendered by the Unsleeping Intellect. The fact that Ibn Ṭufayl borrowed the name from Ibn Sīnā is no accident. He is the only one among the three Spanish Aristotelian philosophers referred to above who professes to be a disciple of the philosopher from Bukhārā. As he makes it clear, he is most interested in the 'Oriental philosophy', which seems to hold out the promise of esoteric lore. Like Ibn Sīnā, he believes that the individual soul is an immaterial substance, which survives the death of the body.

Ḥayy ibn Yaqẓān, the principal character in Ibn Ṭufayl's novel is a solitary who, unlike the philosophers for whom Ibn Bājja prescribes isolation, is not exposed to the vexations and dangers of life in an imperfect society. From his birth onwards he lives alone on a desert island and, after having gradually learned the skills necessary for the preservation and comfort of life, he acquires, without the aid of books or teachers, knowledge of the philosophical sciences and finally achieves a mystic unitive ecstasy. In the last part of the work, Ḥayy receives information about a community of people, living on a neighbouring island and obeying a religious law promulgated by a prophet. He admires the hidden allusions contained in the law, which being interpreted refer to the truths he knows, and wishes to explain to the people of this community the true significance of the prophetic revelation. However, these people are refractory to his teaching. This failure makes him grasp the difference existing between the different kinds of men, most of whom are comparable to animals, being devoid of the faculty of philosophic understanding. He recommends that their minds should not be confused by interpretations of the law that are beyond their intellectual capacity; they should confine themselves to obeying the commandments and honouring the religious tradition. Thereupon he returns to his island. In Ibn Ṭufayl's tale, the solitary, of whom Ibn Bājja spoke, recognizes at least one social duty: he must not disturb the religious way of life of ordinary people.

(iii) *Ibn Rushd* (*Averroes*). This was also the opinion of Ibn Rushd, whom Ibn Ṭufayl protected at the beginning of his career. According to this younger philosopher, there are three categories of people: first, the great multitude of common folk, whose simple religious beliefs should not be disturbed by allegorical interpretations of the prophetic revelation, which, with these unsophisticated people, might lead to the abandonment of religion; secondly, the philosophers who, being capable of grasping the truth, have a twofold legal duty: they must devote themselves to the pursuit of philosophy, and they must take care not to divulge the truth to people who are unfit to understand it; thirdly, the dialecticians, to use Ibd Rushd's term, i.e. the *mutakallimūn*, who on the one hand do not attain truth by the sole correct way of philosophical demonstration, and on the other hand, propagate, with dangerous results, frequently false interpretations of the Qur'ān among the ignorant masses of the first category. Moreover, these semi-intellectuals tend to be intolerant. This is an undisguised attack on the oppressive régime instituted or inspired by the *mutakallimūn*, who had formulated the dogmas of the Almohad movement.

Abu'l-Walīd Muḥammad b. Aḥmad b. Rushd (520–95/1126–98), who was known in medieval Christian Europe under the name of

Averroes, was a practising jurist; it is as such that he was able to answer in the affirmative the question as to whether the study of philosophy by those who have the capacity for it is an obligation imposed by the religious law. For some years he was *qāḍī* in Seville, having received this appointment from an Almohad ruler interested in philosophy. Later he became chief *qāḍī* in his birthplace, Cordova, and in 578/1182 he succeeded Ibn Ṭufayl as the royal physician in the capital, Marrakesh. A few years before his death he fell into disgrace, and was ordered to live in a small town, while many of his books were burnt. However, after a period of one or two years, he was allowed to return to the capital, where he died. Under the Almohads, the pursuit of philosophy entailed certain risks, but it could also procure the favour of the ruler.

It is as a commentator that Ibn Rushd is best known. He wrote three sorts of 'commentaries': a Great, an Intermediate and a Paraphrase, dealing in this way with nearly all the principal works of Aristotle: the most notable omission being that of the *Politics*. As he could not find a manuscript of the Arabic translation of this treatise (although, according to his information, such a translation was available in the Muslim East), he wrote a paraphrase of Plato's *Republic*, which he used as a substitute for Aristotle's *Politics*. In these commentaries, he attempts to set forth Aristotle's authentic opinion, eliminating neo-Platonic and various other accretions, which are found in the writings of earlier Muslim philosophers.

Ibn Rushd's often proclaimed belief in Aristotle's intellectual supremacy naturally provoked rather facile jibes. Thus Ibn Rushd's countryman, Ibn Sabʿīn, observes that the commentator would have agreed with Aristotle even if he had heard him saying that one can be sitting and standing at the same time. In fact, however, Ibn Rushd is characterized by considerable originality of thought, which he sometimes manifests as it were unintentionally, while endeavouring to discover Aristotle's true meaning.

His much-debated thesis concerning the unity of the hylic intellect is a case in point. Intending to clarify a section of Aristotle's *De Anima,* Ibn Rushd puts forward the view that the faculty of intellection, called the hylic or material intellect, is one and the same for the whole of mankind, participated in by the individual human being. This faculty is permanently actualized, which means that the existence of philosophy in every generation is part of the nature of things. The fact that in a given period there seem to be no philosophers at all, is not a decisive objection, for there may be some in the unknown southern part of the habitable earth.

In his paraphrase of Plato's *Republic*, Ibn Rushd indicates the possibility that Plato's ideal state may come into being through the action of a succession of enlightened rulers, who may gradually bring about a transformation of the conduct and the beliefs of their subjects. In spite of the resignation which he sometimes manifests, there is no reason to suppose that he excluded the possibility that this kind of good fortune might befall the Almohad state in which he lived.

A considerable portion of Ibn Rushd's commentaries were translated into Latin, either directly from the Arabic, or from a Hebrew version. Their impact on Christian (and also on Jewish) philosophy, can hardly be overestimated. This influence may have been due in the first place to the knowledge and understanding of Aristotle's thought that could be gained from them. Soon, however, intellectual controversy was centred upon some of Ibn Rushd's own theses, as distinct from those of his master. Latin Averroism became, notwithstanding the opposition of the ecclesiastical authorities, a vigorous philosophical school, the derivation of which from Ibn Rushd is, in spite of many deviations, unmistakable.

Ibn Rushd's thought had incomparably less influence in Islam. The political conditions in the West—in the first place the progressive deterioration of the position of the Muslims in Spain—may perhaps account for the fact that he did not found a lasting school in the countries in which he lived. In the East, people interested in philosophy were mostly partisans of the system of Ibn Sīnā or of that of al-Suhrawardī, or of some amalgam of the two.

(b) *The Ṣūfī current in Spanish philosophy*

Muḥyī al-Dīn b. al-ʿArabī, a native of Murcia (d. 638/1240), who is one of the most influential thinkers of Islam, was first and foremost a Ṣūfī. He believed in the primordial unity of all being.

Abū Muḥammad ibn Sabʿīn, who, according to report, committed suicide in Mecca (in 669/1270) because he wished to achieve union with God, seems to have been greatly influenced by neo-Platonic works currently attributed to Aristotle (such as the *Theology of Aristotle*, deriving from Plotinus's *Enneads*, and *Kitāb al-khayr al-maḥḍ* ('The book of absolute good', known in Europe as *Liber de causis*) which derives from Proclus's *Elements of theology*), and by the unitive experience of the Ṣūfīs. He lays stress on the philosophical doctrines which imply God's immanence in the world. For instance he states that God is the form of every existent thing. His theory of emanation is different from that adopted by al-Fārābī and Ibn Sīnā.

(c) *Ibn Khaldūn*

Abū Zayd 'Abd al-Raḥmān Ibn Khaldūn (733–809/1332–1406), is primarily an historian and a sociologist rather than a philosopher. But the great work which he entitled *al-Muqaddima* ('The introduction', *sc.* to a universal history) may fittingly receive a brief mention in the present chapter, because, from a certain point of view, it draws a line under the history of philosophy in Spain and the Maghrib. It should be noted that Ibn Khaldūn was a descendant of Muslims who had left Spain, a country in which he himself sojourned for two years, and that his personal political and sociological experience was mainly drawn from north-western Africa. He came to live in Egypt in 784/1382 at the age of fifty, when the *Muqaddima*, or a first draft of it, was already written, though he continued working upon it when in Egypt.

Ibn Khaldūn correctly claimed that he had created a new science—which approximates both to sociology and to a sort of philosophy of history. This science is in the last analysis based upon the recognition of the law, established by Ibn Khaldūn, that societies and civilizations are by nature mortal, and that in the course of their existence they go through parallel phases. In the first 'bedouin' phase, life is hard, simple and savage; in order not to perish, people are obliged to be brave and to feel intense loyalty to their family and tribe. This life, which is especially characteristic for a desert habitat, develops the military virtues. In due course the bedouin overrun the civilized countries. This way of life also prepared people, especially the Arabs, to accept the religious truth and the guidance of a prophet.

The second 'sedentary' phase, which is in store for the savage conquerors, is marked by an increase in the comforts and luxuries of life and by the growth of the crafts, arts and sciences. As life becomes easier, the old loyalties and the warlike qualities of the population tend to disappear. The community loses its power of resistance against aggression. It is in its turn ripe for conquest by whatever vigorous uncivilized barbarians yet remain.

Some of the characteristics of the two phases, especially of the first, conform to the schema, found in Greek political philosophy, of the transformation of the natural simple healthy community into a diseased community hankering after luxury.

Ibn Khaldūn applied the philosophical theory of these two phases to the history of the Arab, or the bedouin, people and to the destiny of various Islamic dynasties and régimes. As a result, the description of the two phases had to be somewhat modified in order to make them fit Arab or Islamic history. On the other hand, Arab history was used to illustrate the unchanging historical laws and thus became a paradigm for the course of history in the various kinds of states and communities, some of which have already gone through one or both phases, while others will have this experience in the future.

This historical or sociological approach entails a shift of attention. The problem which concerns Ibn Khaldūn first and foremost is not the truth or falsehood of a particular religion, but its place in the historical process which leads societies from primitive barbarism to civilized effeteness. The arts and the philosophic and other sciences are also regarded from the historic point of view. Their appearance in the second phase is a symptom of the ripeness and approaching senility of a given society. As has sometimes happened in Western civilization, historicity is seen to be an essential element of all theoretical and practical sciences.

ISLAMIC THOUGHT IN THE EAST AFTER THE MID-SIXTH/TWELFTH CENTURY

In the history of Islamic thought in the East, the second half of the sixth/twelfth century is marked by the appearance of a new system of thought, namely the Ishrāqī philosophy (*ḥikmat al-ishrāq*). Its author, Shihāb al-Dīn Yaḥyā al-Suhrawardī (often called *al-Maqtūl*, 'the Slain', because in 578/1191, at the age of thirty-six, he was executed as a heretic in Aleppo), has influenced the evolution of Islamic philosophy in the later period nearly as much as Ibn Sīnā himself.

Al-Suhrawardī himself adapted for his own purposes elements of Ibn Sīnā's thought and vocabulary. There is, for instance, little doubt that the appellation *ḥikmat al-ishrāq* ('The philosophy of [the sun] putting forth its rays') is at least in part meant to be a counterpart to Ibn Sīnā's oriental (*mashriqiyya*) philosophy. Al-Suhrawardī showed that he had a greater interest in, and knowledge of, Eastern wisdom than Ibn Sīnā, to whom he frequently makes disparaging references. While Ibn Sīnā makes no attempt to substantiate his claim that the Oriental philosophy derives from an ancient eastern philosophical tradition, al-Suhrawardī, who was of Persian origin, and some of whose works are written in Persian, incorporates into his own system many Zoroastrian terms and concepts.

As far as philosophical tradition is concerned, he is first and foremost a Platonist, hostile to the Peripatetics (whom he follows in some of his earlier writings), though not to Aristotle himself, and full of respect for the Hermetic writings, which, in his opinion, antedated Plato. He adopts the doctrine of Platonic ideas considered as existent, and not as neutral with respect to existence like Ibn Sīna's essences. These ideas form a part of an elaborate system of incorporeal entities.

Fakhr al-Dīn al-Rāzī (d. 606/1209), a contemporary of al-Suhrawardī, was a philosopher, a *mutakallim* and a commentator on the Qur'ān. Some of his most important works are decisively influenced by Abu'l-Barakāt al-Baghdādī. Fakhr al-Dīn wrote a very critical commentary on Ibn Sīnā's *Kitāb al-ishārāt wa'l-tanbīhāt*. This was countered by another commentary on the same work written by Naṣīr al-Dīn al-Ṭūsī (d. 672/1273), a faithful disciple of Ibn Sīnā. The debate thus inaugurated had many repercussions in Islamic philosophic literature.

As far as philosophy is concerned, the Avicennian and the Ishrāqī doctrines show the greatest vigour in the three centuries that follow upon Naṣīr al-Dīn al-Ṭūsī. The numerous philosophical texts of this period have not yet been sufficiently studied. Nor has the *kalām* literature of the period after 1150, which had several eminent representatives, for instance Hāfiẓ al-Dīn al-Nasafī (d.710/1310), and Mas'ūd al-Taftazānī (d. 792/1390). The Shī'ī theologian, Zayn al-Din al-'Āmilī (d. 966/1558), may also be mentioned in this connexion.

There are grounds for thinking that the most original attack upon philosophical thought made in Islam, perhaps not even excluding al-Ghazālī's, was not made by a professed *mutakallim* but by a Ḥanbalī Taqī al-Dīn b. Taymiyya (d. 729/1328), who from his strictly Traditionalist standpoint opposes *kalām*, the pantheism of the mystics and that inherent in Ibn Sīnā's doctrine. In his great work, *Kitāb al-radd 'ala'l-manṭiqiyyīn* ('The book of the refutation of the logicians') Ibn Taymiyya criticizes Aristotelian logic. He points out the very limited utility of definitions in giving knowledge of the thing defined and the uselessness of logical 'demonstration' in so far as it refers to existent things, for demonstration only concerns universals, which possess reality solely in thought and not in the external world.

The composition of *kalām* texts, and of Ḥanbalī treatises concerned with anti-philosophical polemics or with theology, was not confined in the period with which we are dealing to any one region of the Islamic East. They were written both in the Arab and in the Persian countries, and also in other parts of the Muslim world.

In contrast, a living tradition of philosophical writing can only be discovered during this period, apart from a few exceptions, in the Persian-speaking countries. In Persia this tradition had a last flowering in the Safavid period, in which a great name, Ṣadr al-Dīn al-Shīrāzī (d. 1058/1648) stands out. His 'Four books', *al-Asfār al-arbaʿa*, written in Arabic, which continued to be, to an incomparably greater extent than Persian, the linguistic medium of the philosophers, is a sort of *summa* of the philosophical doctrines of the schools of Ibn Sīnā and of al-Suhrawardī, who, with a touch of Persian patriotism, is called by al-Shīrāzī 'the Reviver of the Traces of the Pahlavī Sages.' This tradition survived to an even later period. It seems not to have been entirely moribund when, in the nineteenth century, Western orientalists began to take a scholarly interest in Islamic philosophy.

CHAPTER 12

WARFARE

The Arabs, within the two decades which followed the death of the Prophet Muḥammad (11/632), won for themselves a large empire embracing Syria, Egypt, ʿIrāq, Persia and much of Arabia itself. The battles at Ajnadayn (13/634), on the river Yarmuk (15/636) and at ʿAyn Shams, i.e. Heliopolis (19/640), foreshadowed for the Byzantines the definitive loss of Syria and Egypt; the battles of al-Qādisiyya and Jalūlāʾ (16/637) and at Nihāvand (20/641) marked crucial moments in the reduction of Sasanid ʿIrāq and Sasanid Persia to Muslim control. It was a conquest at once rapid, astonishing and durable.

The success of the Arabs must be ascribed in no small measure to the circumstances prevailing at that time in the conquered territories. Byzantium and Persia, a little before the Arab assault, had come to the end of a protracted conflict, extending over almost a hundred years and destructive of their resources—neither of these states was in a condition to meet a new and formidable threat from outside. Grievances political, religious and financial made the rule of Byzantium unwelcome to the populations of Syria and Egypt—populations which, being Semitic in origin, were more akin to the Arabs than to their masters at Constantinople. In ʿIrāq, too, there was a population of Semitic descent, also with grievances of a similar nature and little inclined to favour the alien domination of Persia. Throughout the lands constituting the Fertile Crescent the Arabs fought, therefore, with the mass of the local people passive towards their intrusion or, more often, sympathetic towards the Muslim cause.

Of great importance in the campaigns of conquest were the physical toughness of the Arab warriors born and reared in a desert milieu, the high morale deriving from their identification with Islam and the confidence bred of continuing and remarkable success in the field. The tribesmen living adjacent to Syria had acquired no doubt some degree of acquaintance with the art of war practised in Byzantium. Moreover, the tribes located on the western fringes of ʿIrāq must have been familiar to some extent with the methods of warfare used in Persia. None the less, even with due allowance made for these factors of refinement, it remains true that the practice of war common to the mass of the Arab warriors was of an unsophisticated kind: no elaborate organization for warfare, no developed system of tactics and no armament equal to the weapons used in the Byzantine and Sasanid armies. Swift and fluid in movement, mounted on camels but fighting at need on foot, the Arabs excelled in the arts of sudden manoeuvre and of the harassment of their foe. On the field of battle the various tribal elements fought as distinct units arranged often in lines; the usual mode of procedure was an alternation of frontal assault, of withdrawal and of renewed advance, the javelin and the lance being prominent at first, with the sword to follow as the main weapon at close quarters. The campaigns of conquest represented in fact the *Kleinkrieg* of the desert raised to abnormal proportions and carried out with forces of unwonted size—for the Muslim régime at Mecca and Medina acted as a mechanism of concentration, bringing together the Arab tribesmen in numbers far transcending the small bands characteristic of nomad warfare in Arabia.

The warriors who, under the banner of Islam, came out of Najd to win a new empire found themselves perforce separated from their former habitat. With success once gained, the Muslim armies became in effect forces of occupation within the conquered territories—forces located in cantonments which soon developed into large garrison cities, e.g., Kūfa and Baṣra in 'Irāq or Fusṭāṭ in Egypt. Here the Arabs, now constituting a dominant warrior caste in the Muslim empire, lived with their households, enjoying the prestige and profit accruing to them from their imperial role.

Their means of subsistence were, in general, twofold: plunder taken in war (*ghanīma*—a rich reward, as long as the tide of conquest flowed without abatement) and also allowances (*'aṭā'*) paid to active soldiers, Muslim in faith and Arab in descent, from the revenues of the the state. Most of these soldiers received *'aṭā'* amounting perhaps to 500 or even 1,000 dirhams per annum in the time of the Umayyad régime (41–132/661–750), although the higher ranks no doubt obtained much more. As to the average strength of the Arab forces serving in the first hundred years of Muslim rule, no clear estimate is available. A total of 50,000 has been suggested for the reign of the Caliph 'Umar I (13–23/634–644) and of 100,000 for the golden age of the Umayyad state (*c.* 81/700). The value of these figures is, of course, no more than approximate, but even at such a modest level of calculation the payment of *'aṭā'* would have been a serious burden on the finances of the central government.

The burden tended to become heavier as the tide of conquest slowed down and the spoils of war diminished in amount. Warfare itself, more complex than before and waged now on distant frontiers, rose in cost. Of urgent importance, too, was the growing movement of conversion to Islam among the subject peoples of the empire. Of the new converts a large number, known as *mawālī*, stood in a relation of clienthood to the Arab tribal elements constituting the armies of Islam and fought at their side as auxiliaries, but for rates of remuneration and a share in the plunder of war less than the Arabs enjoyed. The *mawālī*, as Muslims, aspired to an equal status with the Arabs—and this on a financial and economic, as on a religious and social, level. A claim of this magnitude, if realized in practice, would perforce undermine the domination of the Arab warrior caste within the empire.

The role, in the armies of Islam, of soldiers Muslim through conversion and non-Arab in ethnic origin grew in importance during the years of Umayyad rule. Of great significance for the Umayyad state was Khurāsān, a vast region embracing north-eastern Persia and much of Turkistān. Here a warlike frontier population, long accustomed to defend itself against the nomads inhabiting the western steppe lands of Central Asia, had come over in large numbers to Islam and, as *mawālī*, had taken service with the Arab armies located in that area. The men of Khurāsān and also of other regions in Persia, conscious of their Iranian origin, of their imperial past and of their cultural pre-eminence over the Arabs, soon become impatient, to an ever increasing degree, of the inferior status which the Arab warriors sought to enforce on them. Also important for the future was the fact that the recrudescence of tribal feuds, so marked within the Arab warrior caste during the later years of Umayyad rule, made itself felt with peculiar violence in Khurāsān. A combination of *mawālī* grievances and Arab feuds offered to the subversive elements ranged against the Umayyads a fertile ground for the dissemination of their propaganda—and it was indeed from Khurāsān that the armies came which, in the great revolution of 132/750, overthrew the house of Umayya and raised to the caliphate the house of al-ʿAbbās.

The events of 132/750 did not at once eliminate the Arabs as a factor of importance in the armies of Islam—indeed, the troops from Khurāsān responsible for the fall of the Umayyads included numerous soldiers of Arab as well as of Iranian origin. It is true, however, that the succeeding hundred years saw the gradual diminution in number of the

Arabs serving in the forces of the ʿAbbasid régime and, at the same time, the progressive limitation—not least for financial reasons—of the ʿ*aṭ ā*ʾ payments.

After 132/750 the Khurāsānīs constituted for some two generations the hard core of the ʿAbbasid armies, having the status of regular and, as it were, professional troops in receipt of pay and maintenance from the central government. It was their fate to be severed from their former *milieu* in Khurāsān and assimilated more and more to their new environment in ʿIrāq—in short, to become identified above all, in outlook and allegiance, with the capital of the empire, Baghdād.

This condition of affairs was altered in the time of the civil war between the sons of the ʿAbbasid Caliph Hārūn al-Rashīd (170–93/786–809)—i.e. between the Caliph al-Amīn (193–8/809–13) and the future Caliph al-Maʾmūn (198–218/813–33). Al-Maʾmūn, victorious over his brother, recruited in Khurāsān and the neighbouring lands the forces which raised him to the throne. The civil war was in fact a conflict of the 'new Khurāsānīs' under al-Maʾmūn against the 'old Khurāsānīs' of 132/750, or rather their descendants, long established at Baghdād as the *élite* troops of the ʿAbbasid régime. Of Arab elements in the armies of al-Maʾmūn there is little mention in the sources—their number was indeed to diminish in the course of his reign and to decline still further in the time of his successor, al-Muʿtaṣim (218–27/833–42). Only rarely in the future would Arab warriors assume once more a role of major importance in military affairs and then only within a restricted sphere, as, for example, in Syria and al-Jazīra, where the local Hamdanid and Mirdasid dynasties, both of Arab origin, flourished during the fourth/tenth and fifth/eleventh centuries.

As the ʿAbbasid caliphate fell into decline, new régimes began to make their appearance in the Muslim empire, each of them maintaining its own separate establishment for war. The composition of the various Muslim armies, in respect of race, was now becoming more diversified than it had been before. A good example can be seen in the Fatimid caliphate of Egypt (356–567/969–1171). The Fatimids had in their service Berber tribesmen from the Maghrib, but also regiments of Turks, black troops from the Sudan and, in addition, though to a lesser degree, contingents of Slavs from the Balkan lands and of Armenians from Asia Minor. An element of serious danger existed in the recruitment of mixed armies, for differences of ethnic origin, of language and of technical competence in war led often to bitter conflict along ethnic lines—a phenomenon well exemplified in the 'time of troubles' which beset Egypt during the years 452–70/1060–77, when the rivalries of the Turks and the Sudanese reduced the land to a state of confusion.

Of all the peoples represented in the armies of Islam none would surpass in importance the Turks, destined to become the warrior race *par excellence* of the Muslim world. There was some recruitment of Turks—though still, no doubt, on a small scale—in the time of the first 'Abbasid caliphs and perhaps even earlier. The 'new Khurāsānīs' of al-Ma'mūn included soldiers described as Farāghina (men from Farghānā), also as Bukhārīs and Khwārazmīs (men from the regions of Bukhārā and Khwārazm)—troops, in short, drawn from the eastern areas of Khurāsān and from Transoxania. Amongst the 'new Khurāsānīs' are numbered, too, the *Atrāk*, i.e. the Turks. The reign of al-Mu'taṣim, the brother of al-Ma'mūn, was to see a large increase in the recruitment of Turkish soldiers. This inflow of Turks must have come at first from districts close to the north-eastern frontiers of the empire. Soon, however, with the gradual consolidation of Muslim influence in Transoxania, it became possible to draw recruits from the steppe lands beyond the border zones—i.e. Turkish children acquired, through war and trade, as slave material, made Muslim, trained as slave soldiers (*mamlūks*) and then manumitted to become the regular, professional troops of the caliphate and of the local dynasties now emerging within the 'Abbasid territories, e.g. the Tulunids in Egypt and Syria (254–92/868–905) or the Samanids in Persia and Transoxania (261–389/874–999). Henceforward the fame and pre-eminence of the Turks as soldiers would be universal in the lands of Islam.

The pattern of warfare which had brought the Arabs success in the time of the great conquests was soon overlaid, as it were, with procedures drawn from the traditions of Byzantium and Persia. It was to be altered still further through the changes of recruitment occurring in the first two centuries of Muslim rule. The Arab warriors had as their main arms the javelin (*ḥarba*) and the lance (*rumḥ*), with the sword (*sayf*) as their chief weapon for close combat. The bow (*qaws*) was also known to them. A superior skill in the use of this arm did not become common, however, in the Muslim world until contact had been made with the Persians and, above all, with the Turks, who excelled as archers, being able to let loose a hail of light arrows while riding their horses at speed. The cross-bow, too, was employed in the armies of the 'Abbasid caliphate. As to means of defence, mention can be made here of the shield (*daraqa*), the cuirass (*tarīka*), the coat of mail (*dir'*) and the helmet (*khūdha*).

To the general in charge of a campaign was given the title of *amīr*—later, under the 'Abbasids, the expression *amīr al-umarā'* came into use with the sense of head of the *amirs*. The troops sent into the field might constitute a number of separate corps reflecting various lines of division, e.g., tribal allegiance or ethnic origin, dependence on a particular general or technical function in war. It was usual for each corps to have its own flags (sing., *rāya*) and sometimes a distinctive mode of dress also. The general in command had a special banner (*liwā'*) located near his tent. On the march the arrangement of the troops (*ta'biyya*) was into a fivefold order known as *khamīs*, i.e. into a vanguard (*muqaddama*), a centre (*qalb*), a right wing (*maymana*), a left wing (*maysara*) and a rearguard (*sāqa*). The *khamīs* was an ideal, a theoretical arrangement which often had to be modified in order to meet the demands of the moment—e.g. to overcome the difficulties of the terrain or to counter the operations of the foe.

The march itself tended to be slow, since the rate of progress was dependent on the speed of the foot-soldiers, of the flocks and herds carried along as food supplies, and of the camels, asses and mules laden with the tents, baggage and munitions of war. Great care was taken to choose suitable encampments in the field, the defensive possibilities of each site and the nearness to water and pasturage being of particular importance. Should the halt be a long one, the camp would be surrounded with a trench (*khandaq*). The fivefold order was often maintained inside the camp, with broad avenues separating the different corps and with the general stationed at the centre. The normal covering for the troops in summer consisted of tents (sing., *khayma*); in winter more solid accommodation was sometimes built of wood.

As to the order of battle, the vanguard and the rearguard might now be combined with the main forces, the actual line of battle comprising a firm centre and two wings. At times the troops would be aligned in small squadrons or companies (sing., *kardūs*). An alternative method was to fight in ranks, often three in number, one behind the other. Of these ranks the first might contain archers and cross-bowmen; the second would be of infantry armed with lances, swords and shields; and the third might consist of the heavy cavalry. At the centre of the battle formation was the standard of the general. The battle itself was in essence a cavalry charge repeated at need several times. To the bowmen fell the task of disrupting the enemy assault at long range; the role of the infantry was to repulse that assault in close combat, should need arise. The cavalry, if successful in breaking through on one sector of the battle front and if well-led and disciplined, would then turn with effect against the flank and rear of the foe.

A manoeuvre sometimes attempted was to ambush the hostile forces along their line of march, or with the battle once engaged, to lure them into terrain subject to attack from positions prepared in advance. Of great advantage here would be not so much the tactics of the Arab horsemen, often wont to charge in line formation, but the tactics of the Turks, i.e. the sudden onset, the feigned flight, the infiltration to the flanks, the arrow bombardment from all sides and the swift renewal of the assault.

The pre-eminence in such warfare rested with the cavalry. Now and again, however, it was the infantry which came to the fore. A good example can be found in the men of Daylam, a mountainous region south of the Caspian Sea. The Daylamīs attained a notable reputation as foot-soldiers. Their expansion southward from Daylam in the third/ninth and fourth/tenth centuries led to the establishment of the Buyid régime in Persia and ʿIrāq, but Daylamī warriors also served as mercenaries in the armies of other Muslim states. A mountain race inured to stress and privation, the Daylamīs fought on foot and exhibited great skill in the use of their own particular weapons, above all the *zhupīn*, a short, two-pronged javelin for thrusting or throwing, and the battleaxe. On ground which allowed them some freedom of manoeuvre their frequent mode of fighting was to link together their tall, painted shields in the form of a wall and then to join combat at close quarters. Often the Daylamīs, seeking to achieve in some degree the mobility characteristic of horsemen, came to the field of battle on camels and mules—a practice also in use among the palace infantry of the sultans of Ghazna in the fourth/tenth and fifth/eleventh centuries.

The Arabs who conquered a great empire for Islam had little acquaintance with the techniques of siege warfare. It was not long, however, before the Muslims took over the methods practised in Byzantium and in Sasanid Persia. Their command of the relevant techniques became, in due course, more refined and elaborate, reaching its highest level of development—at least in the world of medieval Islam—during the time of the Crusades, when siege warfare assumed a decisive importance in the long conflict between Muslim and Christian. None the less, with llowance made for some measure of advance in respect of the siege nstruments themselves, it remains true that the siege warfare of the Muslims—as indeed of the Christians also—was still, with no fundamenal change, the siege warfare of the Ancient World.

The armies of Islam made much use of the *manjanīq* or mangonel, a nachine which involved the swinging of a beam or the movement of a counterpoise to strike and propel a missile with great force; also of the *'arrāda*, a ballista which hurled projectiles through the torsion of ropes. The *qaws al-ziyār*, a large cross-bow machine shooting great arrows and requiring several men to operate it, became known to the Muslims perhaps a little before 597/1200. Of frequent use, too, were the wooden tower (*burj*, *dabbāba*) and the battering ram (*kabsh*). The sources refer, in addition, to multiple-shooting bows, which the Mongols introduced into the Muslim world. A special corps of troops (*naffāṭ*) existed for the employment in siege warfare of naphtha (*nafṭ*), emitted from copper tubes (sing., *naffāṭa*) or thrown in pots (sing., *qārūra*). The art of mining (*naqb*) attained a high standard of excellence in the sixth/twelfth and seventh/thirteenth centuries. Tunnels would be excavated towards a fortress wall, the foundations of which were then hollowed out, wooden beams being inserted to support the stone-work. Once the beams had been set alight, the wall, in due course, would collapse of its own weight.

The period of the 'Abbasid decline (third–seventh/ninth–thirteenth centuries) saw a large increase in the use of *mamlūks* recruited as slaves, trained in the practice of war and freed to serve as professional troops—i.e. as horsemen bearing into combat a considerable weight of armament, but still mobile and far less burdened than the feudal knights of Western Europe who met them in battle during the time of the Crusades. The lands of Islam, in general, bred horses excellent for speed and endurance, but in no wise comparable for size and strength with the horses of Christendom. This factor was of great importance, since it limited the weight of armour that a Muslim soldier might wear in battle.

With the gradual disintegration of the Great Seljuk Sultanate after 485/1092, a number of small states made their appearance, notably in 'Irāq, al-Jazīra (Mesopotamia) and Syria, each having its own *'askar* or establishment of *mamlūk* soldiers. To maintain an effective *'askar*—and above all to maintain it at the highest level of professional excellence—was an expensive business. The state had to make regular payments to its *'askar* and also various donatives granted on special occasions, e.g. after a great success in the field or on the accession of a prince to the throne. It was the state, too, which in large measure bore the cost of the equipment and supplies distributed to the *mamlūks* at the beginning of a campaign. The manufacture of siege machines, the purchase of transport animals, the gathering of provisions—all meant additional expenditure, and on a lavish scale. Finding the expense of its armies more and more difficult to sustain, the central government of the caliphate, long before the rise of the Seljuks, had to abandon the system of cash payments and to replace them with assignments on the taxation due from a given area. The caliphs, failing to meet the cost of the imperial forces, began to make over even whole provinces to individual *amīrs*, on condition that the *amīrs*, and not the state, should maintain the troops essential for the defence of a particular region—a procedure which favoured greatly the emergence of local autonomies within the empire. At the same time it became not uncommon to see grants of taxation allotted to the rank and file amongst the *mamlūks*. This device underwent a long evolution which gave it at length the character of a grant (*iqṭā'*). To each *mamlūk*, after the completion of his training as a slave soldier and his subsequent manumission, was accorded a definite assignment of revenue per annum based on an estimate (*'ibra*) which was calculated in a fictitious unit of account. The actual revenue, comprising payments in kind as well as in cash, came to the *mamlūk* from specific lands ascribed to him—i.e. from the local population cultivating those lands and owing taxation to the state. A grant of *iqṭā'* involved no right of ownership in the estates constituting the grant. The *mamlūk* soldier enjoyed only the unsufruct of the land, the right to receive certain defined revenues from it. He was obliged, from the yield of the fief, to provide for the equipment that he needed to maintain himself as an efficient soldier (tents, arms, beasts of burden, etc.) and also for a personal retinue which would go with him to war. It was advantageous for the *mamlūk* to be at home during harvest-time in order to ensure that he obtained the revenue in cash and in kind due to him from his grant. This recurring need meant that it was almost impossible to keep a *mamlūk* force in the field from one campaign season to the next or even, at times, to bring them to war over a consecutive number of years. It was a signal evidence of the esteem accorded to the great Ayyubid Sultan Saladin (564-89/1168–93) that he was able to sustain unbroken for nearly two years (August 1189–July 1191) his operations against the Christians at 'Akkā (Acre) in Palestine.

The *iqṭā'* system was reaching its full development in the sixth/

twelfth and seventh/thirteenth centuries. Of the troops endowed with these grants two characteristics deserve to be underlined here: their ethnic origin, which was in general Turkish, and their function in war, which was to serve above all as mounted archers. The bow was the dominant weapon in use amongst them, but with the lance, sword, mace and shield (a small round target) also constituting a normal part of their equipment. Their tactics in the field offered little that was new—unless perhaps in their formidable excellence—over the practice of earlier centuries. Combat at a distance with missile weapons, notably the bow, also feigned retreat leading into ambush, pressure on the flank and rear of the opposing forces, and harassment of the foe, while his columns were still on the march—manoeuvres of this sort find ample illustration in the campaigns, for example, of the armies which served Saladin. It was a warfare marked by the indubitable pre-eminence of the cavalry and of the bow, distinguished, too, by mobility, by superb horsemanship and by a skill no less superb in the individual management of arms. A classic expression, as it were, and embodiment of this warfare can be seen in the famous régime known as the Mamluk Sultanate of Syria and Egypt (648–922/1250–1517), a régime composed at first of Turks drawn from the Kıpchak steppe adjacent to the Caspian and Aral Seas, but later of Cherkes (Circassians) recruited from the Caucasus. Here, indeed, was a splendid example of a warrior caste sustaining itself through a continuing inflow of slave material destined to be trained in the arts of war and then manumitted to assume the full status and privileges of a *mamlūk* soldier.

The Mamluks stood at the end of a long evolution already in 648/1250 more than six centuries old. There had been, during that time, notable changes in the composition of the armies of Islam (e.g. the growing importance of the Turks) and in the institutions which sustained those armies (e.g., the rise of the *mamlūk* element or the emergence of the *iqṭāʿ*). On the tactical side, too, there were changes of note. The tactics of nomad warriors—at first of the Arabs and later of the Turks—had been combined with modes of procedure characteristic of more complex societies like Byzantium and Persia to form a Muslim pattern of warfare. One major line of evolution was towards the undeniable dominance of horsemen in war, above all of mounted archers swift and fluid in manoeuvre, adept in the use of the bow. The degree of change was much less marked on the technological front. Here the personal weapons of the Muslim warrior, such as the lance, the sword and the mace, differed little from the weapons familiar, at an earlier date, to the Byzantine or the Sasanid soldier. If there was a change of genuine importance in respect of armament, it is to be found in the gradual rise to pre-eminence of the bow—and also of the tactics appropriate to its efficient use in battle. As to siege operations, the instruments and techniques employed in the armies of Islam were still, in general, the instruments and techniques known to the armies of Byzantium and of Sasanid Persia. A revolution of a technological kind would soon begin, however, to alter in radical fashion the character of warfare. Of this revolution the basic cause was the introduction of gunpowder, cannon and firearms.

No exact date can be given to mark the first use of cannon in the lands of Islam. A broad perspective can be obtained, none the less, from the evidence available in the sources. The Arabic authors al-Qalqashandī and Ibn Khaldūn, describing events which occurred in the time of the Mamluk Sultanate, afford some reason to believe that cannon (sing., *midfaʿ*, *mukḥula*) existed at Alexandria and Cairo in the years *c.* 767–78/1365–76. There was, however, no serious attempt amongst the Mamluks to exploit the possibilities of the new weapon on a large scale, until conflict with the Portuguese in the Indian Ocean after 1498 and with the Ottoman Turks in 890–7/1485–91 and again in 922–3/1516–17 forced them into such a course. The arquebus (*al-bunduq al-raṣāṣ*, *bunduqiyya*) did not make its appearance in Egypt, it would seem, until as late as 895/1489–90 in the reign of the Mamluk Sultan al-Ashraf Qā'it Bāy.

As to the Ottoman empire, a register for Albania, dating from the year 1431, indicates that cannon (*top*) had been introduced at least in the time of Sultan Meḥmed I (816–24/1413–21) and perhaps even somewhat earlier. There are references to the Ottoman use of cannon, e.g. against Constantinople in 825/1422, at Adalia in 827/1424 and against the Hexamilion on the isthmus of Corinth in 849/1446. It is, moreover, well known that Meḥmed II (855–86/1451–81) brought a number of large cannon to the siege of Constantinople in 857/1453. The Ottomans would seem to have used cannon for the first time on a battle-field at Kosova in 852/1448. The arquebus (*tüfenk*) found acceptance amongst them *c.* 1440, i.e. in the course of the Hungarian campaigns fought during the reign of Sultan Murād II (824–55/1421–51).

The employment of cannon and of the arquebus, at least on an appreciable scale, tended to occur a little later in time elsewhere in the Muslim world. Persia came into contact with the new instruments of war during the reign of Uzun Ḥasan (d. 883/1478), the head of the Ak-Koyunlu Turcomans. A number of references bear witness to the use c. 1506–8, of cannon (*tūp*) and of the arquebus (*tufang*) in the first years of the Safavid régime in Persia. Guns would appear to have been well known in northern India under the Lodī sultans (855–930/1451–1526). There is evidence, too, of their employment in the Deccan states before 1500. Cannon had also a considerable role at the battle of Pānīpat (932/1526), which marked the establishment of the Mughal empire in northern India. As to the far western reaches of the Muslim world, guns and fire-arms, although noted in connexion with events of an earlier date, did not come into more general use in Morocco until the rise of the Saʿdid régime (960–1065/1553–1654).

The adoption of the cannon and the arquebus was nowhere more earnest and intensive than in the Ottoman empire. A major role in the transmission of these arms and of the techniques associated with them fell to the peoples of Serbia and Bosnia. Troops skilled in the employ-ment of guns and firearms and recruited in these lands are known to have served under Meḥmed II. No less important was the continuing flow of specialists from Europe, most of them German and Italian at first, but with experts from France, England and Holland becoming more numerous in later times. A specialist of Hungarian origin, by name Urban, cast some of the great cannon that the Ottomans brought to the siege of Constantinople in 857/1453. Artillerists of European descent, Italian, Dutch and English, served the Ottoman guns in 1048/1638, when Sultan Murād IV besieged and retook Baghdād from Shāh Ṣafī of Persia. French officers came to Istanbul on a number of occasions in the late eleventh/seventeenth and twelfth/eighteenth cen-turies in order to advise the Ottomans on the techniques of warfare then current in Europe. Experts of Christian origin constituted, indeed, a permanent and indispensable element in the technical corps of the Ottoman army—i.e. amongst the armourers (*jebejiler*), the artillerists (*topjular*), the transport corps handling guns and munitions of war (*top ʿarabajiları*), the bombardiers (*khumbarajılar*) and the sappers (*laghımjılar*).

Even the names which the Ottomans gave to their cannon derived, to some extent at least, from Europe—e.g. *bajalushka* (cf. Italian *basilisco*), *balyemez* (perhaps from the German *Faule Metze*) and *kolonborna* (cf. Italian *colubrina*—i.e. culverin). The sources also contain expressions of non-European origin, such as the name *ḍarbzāna* indicating (in

Ottoman usage) a falconet type of cannon. *Ḍarbzan* is found, too, as the name employed for a particular kind of gun in the armies of Safavid Persia. How strong, in the field of war, the Ottoman influence was in the lands to the east of Anatolia and ʿIrāq can be seen from the fact that words current in Ottoman Turkish like *bajalushka*, *ḍarbzan*, and *tabanja* found acceptance in the armies of Mughal India. It is well known that artillery experts from the Ottoman empire often took service and rose to high rank in the armies of various Indian states: a Muṣṭafā Rūmī was active under Bābur and a Rūmī Khān under the sultan of Gujarāt. Even the battle order adopted in these armies is said to have been arranged at times in accordance with the custom of Rūm, i.e. of the Ottoman empire.

The dissemination of firearms was often a slow and gradual affair. To the Mamluks, for example, proud of their status, yet also exhibiting the indurated mentality of a cavalry *élite* bred in a tradition now old and over-rigid, skill in horsemanship and in the management of the bow, the lance and the sword was central to their whole lives. The new firearms, if taken over, would involve the relinquishment, at least in no small degree, of their familiar weapons and in addition the need to fight dismounted, since the arquebus was too cumbersome to be used on horseback. The arquebus, indeed, was to them the instrument of a craven and treacherous foe, a device unchivalrous and undignified, against which no warrior could demonstrate with success his valour and his pre-eminence in the art of personal combat. The danger threatening from the Portuguese in the Indian Ocean and also from the Ottomans forced the Mamluks, at a late hour, to countenance the introduction of guns and firearms—not for their own use, but for special corps recruited, however, from elements regarded as of inferior status, e.g. black slaves (*ʿabīd*), Turcomans and Maghāriba (men from the Maghrib). At the same time, care was taken to ensure that these special troops did not become too strong. Their unrestricted growth would have undermined the dominance of the Mamluk *élite*, which was itself of no great numerical strength.

Amongst the Ottomans, too, there was resistance to the adoption of firearms. The mounted regiments of the imperial household, also the *sipahis*, i.e. the horsemen endowed with fiefs in the provinces of the empire, and, in addition, the retinues of the high officials and dignitaries, all constituted a cavalry *élite* not less proud than the Mamluks of their skill in horsemanship and in arms, nor less identified with the older methods of warfare. Ogier Ghiselin de Busbecq, the ambassador of the Emperor Ferdinand I at Istanbul, relates how the Ottoman grand *vezīr*, Rustem Pasha, sought to accustom some of his retinue to the use of firearms, only to see them become engrimed with gunpowder and subjected to the laughter and scorn of the other soldiers, a humiliation which led them to ask—and to receive—from their master permission to end the distasteful experiment. The same author tells also of an Ottoman *deli*, a member of a special corps of horsemen, who, explaining the reasons for a reverse that he and his comrades had undergone, ascribed the misfortune not to the valour of the foe, but to his employment of firearms, adding that the result would have been quite different, with success going to the Ottomans, had the conflict been fought *vera virtute*, i.e. with true courage involving physical prowess and personal skill in the conduct of arms. With the gradual appearance of lighter and more manageable types of hand-gun the reluctance of the Ottoman cavalry to adopt firearms was broken down, although the process was in fact a slow one. Venetian sources relating to the Hungarian War of 1001–15/1593–1606 between Austria and the Ottoman empire note that the *spahi di paga*, i.e. the mounted regiments belonging to the household of the sultan, had begun to arm themselves with the *terzarollo*, a short-barrelled arquebus, but that as yet the pistol was not in use amongst the Ottomans. Paul Rycaut, describing the situation which existed in the time of the first two Köprülü *vezīrs* (1066–87/1656–76), was still able to state that the cavalry of the imperial household, though now armed with carbines and pistols, yet had no great love for the new weapons. A hundred years later soldiers and authors of European origin would confirm this judgment, attributing to the horsemen of the sultan a marked preference for *l'arme blanche* and underlining their incomparable adroitness in this form of warfare.

The arquebus found a much readier acceptance amongst the infantry than amongst the cavalry of the Ottoman sultan. It became well established in the corps of Janissaries during the reign of Meḥmed II. The more general extension of its use, both inside and outside the corps, was, however, a long and gradual affair. The changing pressures of warfare, above all in the Caucasus (986–98/1578–90) and along the Danube (1593–1606), enforced on the Ottomans a rapid increase in the number of foot-soldiers serving the sultan. The increase was achieved through the recruitment, notably from Anatolia, of Muslim-born soldiers into the troops of the imperial household and also as 'irregular' levies known under such names as *levend, sarıja* or *sekban*. These levies served, too, in the retinues of the provincial governors and of other high officials—retinues much larger now than in earlier times. Of the new forces, the main weapon—with the sword and the pistol—would be the arquebus and later the musket.

The fame of the Janissaries as a corps of foot-soldiers expert in the use of firearms extended far and wide throughout the lands of Islam. It is not surprising that other Muslim states should seek to imitate the splendid model set before them. The Safavid régime in Persia had been the creation of Shāh Ismā'īl I (d. 630/1524). Its military strength consisted primarily of warriors drawn from the Turkish tribes long resident in Anatolia. These warriors retained in Persia their tribal identities; their chieftains became governors of provinces under the shah; the young men of the tribes continued to form the mass of the Safavid armies. At the same time there were feuds amongst them and indiscipline arising from tribal enmities and from the conflict for domination centred around the throne; a serious threat, in short, to the well-being of the state. Shāh 'Abbās I (995–1038/1587–1629), the ablest of the Safavids, strove to fashion a counterpoise to the influence of the tribal warriors, a concentration of armed strength under his immediate control. To achieve this aim he established three corps: of arquebusiers, of artillerists, and of horsemen equipped with firearms, all of them recruited from the Circassian and Georgian peoples of the Caucasus. A further example can be found in Morocco. Here the *Sharīfs* of the Sa'did line, moving out of the southern Atlas, employed the tribal forces at their command to subdue almost the whole of Morocco. As a means of defence against enemies at home and abroad the Sa'dids maintained a corps of arquebusiers (*rumāt*) embracing various ethnic elements, e.g. men of Rūmī descent (i.e. from the Ottoman lands) and also renegades from Christendom, often Spanish in origin.

The arquebus of the Ottomans, like that of North Africa, tended to be longer in the barrel than the Christian model and of a calibre enabling it to fire heavier bullets. Its range is not often indicated in the sources, but there is mention of distances as great as five and six hundred paces. The skill of the Ottoman arquebusiers at the siege of Malta in 972–3/1565, even when firing by moonlight, earned special praise in some Christian accounts of the event. As improved versions of the hand-gun made their appearance, the technical expressions used in Turkish reflected the change, e.g. *mushkat tüfenkleri* (muskets), *karabina* (carbine) and *tabanja* (pistol: cf. also *chifte tabanjalı tüfenk*—a double-barrelled pistol). Words and phrases of this kind underline the continuing influence of Europe on the Ottoman practice of war.

The transition in siege warfare from the machines employed in earlier times, such as the *manjanīq* and the *'arrāda*, to the cannon and gunpowder was not abrupt. Old instruments and techniques had still a role in the Ottoman sieges of the ninth/fifteenth and tenth/sixteenth centuries: mantlets, for example, at Otranto in 885/1480 and at Nicosia in 978/1570, also wooden towers at Malta in 972–3/1565. Moreover, the Ottomans—as at Rhodes in 928–9/1522—found it advantageous to continue the ancient method for bringing down the walls of a fortress, i.e. excavation under the walls and the insertion of wooden beams later to be set on fire, so that the stonework would collapse, once the flames had burnt through the supporting timber.

It was in siege warfare, however, that cannon first came into their own. The methods employed to cast guns were still crude, the finished products incapable of a performance at once accurate and predictable over a sustained sequence of firing. As to the procedure for aiming the cannon, it consisted of little more at first than the use of wooden baulks and wedges under the barrel to fix the elevation of the gun and around the loading chamber to control the recoil. Cannon, during the earlier phases of their development, had no great effect, therefore, on objects in motion. The ideal target was something large and immoveable—for example, a fortress which could be bombarded at leisure. The conviction was strong that the bigger the gun and the heavier the projectile that it hurled, then the more devastating its performance would be. It was a belief which, given the primitive character of the metallurgical and ballistic techniques then available, contained some measure of truth; massive cannon-balls did cause much damage on striking their target. Of the large cannon used in siege warfare an excellent example can be found in the *bajalushka* of the Ottomans. One of these guns, present at the siege of Malta, is said to have weighed 180 quintals and to have thrown iron shot one quintal in weight.

A Spanish artillerist, Collado, describes the Ottoman cannon as ill-proportioned and defective, but of sound metal. Chemical analysis of an Ottoman gun made in 1464 and now located at the Tower of London has shown it to be fashioned out of good bronze, although the smelting process was imperfect. The Ottomans often carried supplies of metal into the field, rather than whole cannon, ponderous and difficult to haul. The metal would be cast into guns before the actual fortress under attack and, once the siege was over, might be broken into pieces for convenience of transportation and for re-use on a subsequent occasion.

On the rate of fire the sources offer only scattered information. At Scutari (Ishkodra) in 883/1478–9 the Ottomans, using eleven great guns, fired *per diem* at different times 178, 187, 183, 168, 178, 182, 194, 131, 193 and 173 shots against the town. The extreme range of such cannon is difficult to assess. Some of the Ottoman batteries, however, at Malta began their bombardment from a distance of a thousand paces and more. The technique of the Ottoman gunners was a reflection of the methods current in Europe, e.g. a concentrated fire of batteries at one section of a fortress wall: medium cannon of the *kolonborna* (culverin) type would be used to achieve deep penetration into the stonework along transverse and vertical lines, the large *bajalushka* guns being employed thereafter in salvo to smash down the enfeebled wall with the violent surface impact of their shot.

Of much importance in siege warfare were devices other than cannon, yet depending on the use of gunpowder. Amongst them can be numbered the mortar (*havān*) throwing great shot of stone or metal; the bomb (*khumbara*) filled with explosives and fragmented material, e.g. pieces of iron or glass, and projected from the *havān*; the hand grenade (*el khumbarası*) made of bronze, glass or even earthenware and containing combustible and explosive matter; *sacchi di polvere* provided with a fuse and intended to be thrown at close quarters; also inflammable mixtures used as smoke-screens to cover the digging of trenches or as fire-balls to give illumination at night. Of all the instruments of siege warfare none was more potent, however, than the mine (*laghım*). The Ottomans excelled in this branch of siege-craft, not least because of their command over large resources of human labour, e.g. troops like the *'azab* soldiers, levies from the population of a given area, and also the skilled mining communities of the empire. Montecuccoli, in describing the siege technique of the Ottomans, refers to 'des mines simples, doubles et triples l'une sur l'autre...très profondes...de 120 et de 150 barils de poudre et davantage'.[1] The subterranean mines excavated beneath a fortress often consisted of several galleries each with a terminal chamber holding large amounts of gunpowder.

[1] *Mémoires de Montecuculi* (Paris, 1746), 345.

Although guns soon achieved a dominant role in sieges, their effectiveness was far less marked in battle. It was to be long indeed—in Europe as in the lands of Islam—before a true field artillery came into being as a result of continuing technological advance. The Muslim sources for the ninth/fifteenth and tenth/sixteenth centuries mention several kinds of light cannon, such as the *zanbūrak* used in Persia and in Mughal India, also the Ottoman *chakaloz* (or *shakaloz*: cf. Hungarian *szakállas*) and *pranghi* (or *pranki*: perhaps from the Italian *petriere a braga*). There are numerous references to the *ḍarbzan* or *ḍarbūzan* noted earlier—a light to medium gun, much more mobile than heavier cannon like the *bajalushka*, the *balyemez* and the *kolonborna*. It would seem to have been in the time of Bāyezīd II (886–918/1481–1512), or perhaps a little earlier, that the Ottomans began to make a more extensive use of the lighter types of gun. The Arabic historian Ibn Zunbul, writing about the campaigns of Selīm I (918–26/1512–20) against Syria and Egypt, refers to small Ottoman cannon which he calls *ḍarbzānāt* and which he describes as protected with covers of red felt and travelling in waggons, each having a team of four horses. The ammunition boxes for the guns hung suspended from the underside of the waggons and contained shot large enough to fill the palm of a hand. How effective such cannon were on the field of battle is difficult to see with exactitude. Ibn Zunbul declares that the Ottomans owed to their guns and firearms the victories of Marj Dābiq (922/1516) and Raydāniyya (922/1517) over the Mamluks. At Mohács (932/1526) the cannon massed in the centre of the Ottoman battle line drove back the Hungarian cavalry, but their fire was delivered, it would seem, at almost point-blank range.

The Ottomans sought, in respect of their field guns, to assimilate the advances made in Europe—and not without some degree of success. New words and phrases, or new meanings for old ones, came into use: e.g. *sachma toplar*, cannon firing a form of grape-shot or langrage; *alay topları*, 'regimental' guns, light and mobile; and also *balyemez*, employed now not so much to designate a particular type of cannon, but with the sense of the European *canon de batterie*. The process of standardization which was being carried out in Europe had some effect in the Ottoman empire, but the rate of advance was slow, at least before 1700. To read, for example, the lists of guns taken by the Christians from the Ottomans in the long war of 1094–1110/1683–99 is to encounter still a wide range of different calibres, weights and dimensions—although even here a qualification is advisable: the lists tend to be somewhat misleading, since the Ottomans, in order to make good rapidly the severe losses of cannon sustained by them, during this war, on the field of battle, at times pressed into service guns of ancient type, often well over a hundred years old, and relegated long before to the defence of fortresses far from the frontiers of the empire. Montecuccoli noted that the Ottoman artillery, though effective when it could be brought into action, was cumbersome to handle and transport, and consumed, moreover, large quantities of munitions.[1]

The rapid development of cannon and firearms extended greatly the logistic side of warfare. To prepare now a major campaign was to undertake in effect a full-scale industrial enterprise. The range of material needed was wide and varied: it would of course include guns, muskets, bombs and grenades, but also such items as powder-horns, leather sacks (for gunpowder), saltpetre, quick-match and lead (for bullets); picks, mattocks, shovels, axes, crow-bars, scythes and sickles (to gather forage); carts, axle-trees of iron, waggon-wheels, grease and tallow; cables, ropes, nails, horseshoes, anvils and bellows; and, in addition, pitch, resin, sulphur, tar, petroleum, wool and cotton. A list of this kind reflects in miniature the economic resources of a given state—in this case, of the Ottoman empire. And yet it can, and should, be amplified further. To a great campaign the Ottomans brought transport animals in large numbers: draught horses from Wallachia and Moldavia; oxen from state 'ranches', e.g. in the region of Cilicia; buffaloes from Thrace, Bulgaria and Greece; camels from the desert areas adjacent to Syria and 'Irāq; and mules, above all from Anatolia. The mineral wealth of the empire would also serve the needs of the war machine—lead from the silver mines of Bosnia and Serbia; iron from Bulgaria; copper from Anatolia; and tin, much of this metal coming from sources outside the direct control of the sultan. Of the constituents of gunpowder, sulphur was available in Anatolia, while rich supplies of saltpetre existed in Egypt, Syria and 'Irāq.

An important source of *matériel de guerre* was the contraband traffic flowing from Christendom to the Muslim world. It had long been illicit, under the canon law of the Catholic Church, for Christians to export to the infidel materials useful in war. The Church indeed had tried time and again, though without much success, to prevent the sale, to the Muslims, of horses, arms, iron, copper, tin, sulphur, saltpetre,

[1] *Mémoires*, 280.

timber and the like. At various times this contraband trade assumed a special importance, as it did for the Ottomans during their great wars against Persia (1578–90) and Austria (1593–1606). It was now that the English carried into the Levant numerous cargoes containing tin, lead, copper, saltpetre, sulphur, swords and arquebuses, also broken bells and broken images (i.e. bronze taken from the churches despoiled in England during the course of the Reformation). There is mention, too, in the Ottoman chronicles, of *Ṭalyan tüfenkler*, muskets of Italian origin, produced no doubt in such famous centres as Brescia.

After their conquest of the Mamluk Sultanate in 922–3/1516–17 the Ottomans ruled over most of the central lands of Islam, together with much of North Africa and a large proportion of the Balkan territories. Of other Muslim states strong enough to fill a role of the first importance there remained no more than two, Persia and Mughal India, neither of which could equal the Ottoman empire in extent and resources. Muslim warfare, during this, the last distinctive phase of its development, was to find perhaps its most splendid formulation in the Ottoman procedures of war, and nowhere with more richness of detail than in the spectacle of the Ottomans marching to a great campaign. Much care was taken to render the advance as smooth as possible. Orders went out for the repair of roads and bridges to facilitate the movement of guns and waggons. Piles of stones and wooden stakes might be used to indicate the actual line of march. The crossing of rivers like the Euphrates and the Danube demanded the construction of large pontoon bridges. Often the Ottomans took with them into the field prefabricated parts of the structure, together with quantities of timber, cables and nails. The order of march included an advance screen of light horsemen (Tatars from the Crimea or Turcomans from Anatolia), a vanguard of picked cavalry, a main force embracing the troops of the imperial household (the Janissaries, the mounted regiments of the sultan and the specialist corps, e.g. the artillerists and armourers), two wings of 'feudal' *sipahis*, one on each flank, and a rearguard covering the baggage and supplies.

The day's march began during the small hours of the morning and continued until about noon, when the site of the next encampment would be at hand. Access to water and pasture was of prime importance in the choice of a site. At the centre of the camp stood the sultan, the Janissaries and the other household troops, and here, too, the high dignitaries had their station, with their personal retinues in attendance on them; beyond this nucleus would lie the 'feudal' *sipahis*, a separate quarter being assigned to each provincial contingent. Water-carriers moved through the camp, providing refreshment for all; artisans and craftsmen from the guilds at Istanbul—saddlers, smiths, butchers, bakers, etc.—awaited the frequent call for their services, working in small huts, over each of which floated a pennant indicating the trade practised there. A special enclosure held strayed animals until their owners came to collect them. Herds of cattle and flocks of sheep accompanied the Ottomans to war as sustenance for the troops in the field. The life of the Ottoman soldier on campaign was sober and frugal, dried beef, mutton and rice, onions, bread or biscuit, and water constituting the main ingredients of his diet. To the Christians who saw these great encampments nothing was more remarkable than the wonderful silence prevailing in them and the high level of personal and public hygiene maintained amongst the troops.

A word must here be said about the composition of the Ottoman armies. Of notable importance were the soldiers belonging to the central régime—i.e. the Janissaries, a corps of infantry equipped with firearms and numbering some 12–15,000 men in the time of Süleymān the Magnificent (926–74/1520–66); the six mounted regiments of the imperial household, expert with the bow, the lance and the sword and, at least in later times, trained also in the use of the lighter forms of hand-gun, e.g., the pistol and the carbine; and, in addition, the various technical services—the armourers, the artillerists, the transport corps, the bombardiers and the sappers. Also at the command of the sultan were the *sipahis*, who held grants of small (*timar*) or of large (*ẓiʿāmet*) yield per annum. No right of ownership was granted to them in the lands constituting their grants; as in the *iqṭāʿ* system of earlier times, the soldier holding the grant also enjoyed only the usufruct of the lands assigned to him, i.e. the right to certain revenues in cash and in kind from the population dwelling within the limits of his grant. Out of the annual yield accruing to him the *sipahi* had to maintain himself as an efficient warrior and also, when summoned to war, to bring with him on campaign a retinue, the personnel of which increased in number with the value of his *timar* or *ẓiʿāmet*, as promotion came to him, and the cost of which, in respect of arms, tents, supplies and transport, he himself was obliged to meet from the revenues allotted to him.

The excellence of the Janissaries as infantry made a deep impression on the Christian world of the fifteenth and sixteenth centuries—to such an extent, indeed, that their role in Ottoman warfare, and that of the various technical corps, has tended to receive an emphasis stronger than their undoubted importance perhaps warranted. No force of 12–15,000 men, however formidable their skill, is numerous enough to be the decisive element in the armed forces of a vast empire. The main weight of the Ottoman armies was to be found in the *sipahis*, who far out-numbered the troops of the central régime. This fact determined in large degree the battle order and the field tactics of the Ottomans. Their order of battle, reduced to its essentials, consisted of a firm centre and two wings of *sipahi* cavalry. The centre, embracing the Janissaries and the other corps of the imperial household, was defended with trenches, waggons and with guns placed at intervals along its front—in short, a kind of *Wagenburg* formation. Here was the solid nucleus designed to break the onset of the foe. On either side of this centre stood the powerful formations of the *sipahis*, seeking the moment to infiltrate along the flanks and to the rear of the opposing forces and, if all should go well, to over-run them in a relentless assault and pursuit. The tactics natural to these horsemen differed little from the methods used in the armies of earlier Muslim states. Of the Ottoman cavalry engaged in the war of 1182–88/1768–74 against Russia one Christian author gives a vivid and informative account:

> ...these are light troops of the best kind. They attack in lively fashion, without order, without co-ordination, without a plan devised in relation to the terrain or the position of the enemy: they surround him and fall upon him from all sides. Numerous banners are in the first rank and in front of them to heighten their courage. Their officers set an example by fighting at the head of their troop. One body of horsemen is repulsed; another takes over from it, without more success. They carry away in their flight the horsemen who are hastening up behind them. Cavalry and infantry become inter-mingled. Their attacks weaken; the confusion becomes general and leads to a retreat almost as lively as the first shock of battle.
>
> An assault so confused is of little danger to an army war-hardened and disciplined; but a force which allowed its ranks to be broken by these troops would be lost. Not a man would escape, because of the swiftness of their horses, managed by riders who rarely deliver a blow without effect. To be avoided with them are the skirmishes that they try ceaselessly to induce, small detachments, open ground, and affairs of outposts. In these latter, above all when they are on the defensive, their courage, patience and stubbornness are extreme...[1]

[1] L. F. Guinement de Kéralio, *Histoire de la dernière guerre entre les Russes et les Turcs* (Paris, 1777), I, 113–14.

As to the role of the Ottoman infantry, e.g. the Janissaries, their mode of procedure on the battle-field is well illustrated in yet another Christian source dating from the eighteenth century:

...in flat country they rush in large groups on the foe, with the *enfans perdus* at their head: and, since they keep no order, only the foremost amongst them can use their fire-arms. They hold a sabre or a knife in the right hand, with their musket in the left, before the head, in order to ward off the bayonet and sword thrusts delivered against them. The rearmost of them as a rule carry their musket slung over the shoulder. Some of them also take up in their teeth the hem of their jacket and breeches, which are very ample, and fall like bulls, head down, on the enemy, crying with all their might Alla, Alla: God, God...[1]

There were occasions, however, when the tactics of the Ottoman infantry assumed a different form, and here, with the Janissaries, can be included the troops known as *levend, sarıja* or *sekban* and also the Albanian levies, i.e. troops equipped with firearms, fighting as infantry and serving often under a contract for a given period of time. The Albanians, in particular, gained a high reputation as soldiers in the seventeenth and eighteenth centuries. One Christian source observes of them that

...the Albanians are a militia from Bosnia, Albania and Macedonia, most of them on foot; they are counted amongst the volunteers. They serve by contract...they are recruited in this fashion: a Turkish officer proposes to raise a corps of eight to ten thousand men, whom he will arm and maintain in consideration of ten crowns [*écus*] per month for each man; and this contract is normally for one campaign or five months. If there is further need of these troops, the contract is renewed...[2]

Amongst the Albanians, and also amongst the *sekban* and the Janissaries, there were excellent marksmen, employed frequently to cover the flanks of the Ottoman armies and to harass the foe. Troops of this kind, advancing in open formation through irregular or broken terrain and using independent fire from the protection of trees and the like, fought sometimes with decisive effect as at Gročka in 1739, where their long muskets drove back the Austrian columns in confusion.

The same general pattern of development can be discerned elsewhere than in the Ottoman empire. It is visible in the Persian armies of this time, the main strength of which consisted of horsemen. The

[1] De Warnery, *Remarques sur le militaire des Turcs* (Leipzig and Dresden, 1770), 24.
[2] De Warnery, *op. cit.*, 30.

continuing importance of the mounted soldier is reflected in the career of an able captain like Nādir Shāh (d. 1160/1747), whose military reputation derives largely from his great skill as a cavalry general. He also had at his command, however, a corps of *jazāyirjīs*, i.e. of infantry armed with the long musket known as *jazāyir*, which often did excellent service in the course of his campaigns. Nādir Shāh was less successful in siege warfare, notably because of deficiencies in the amount and quality of his artillery, the difficulties attendant on the transport of guns over arduous terrain, and the relative inexperience of his military engineers.

The manner of warfare which can be described, in a meaningful sense, as Muslim was now entering into the last phase of its evolution. It was becoming in fact out of date. The process of obsolescence can best be understood once more in the context of the Ottoman empire, and this for the simple reason that the Ottomans, standing in close contact with states like Austria and Russia, felt the impact, immediate and sustained, of the innovations wrought in the European practice of war. Even in respect of sieges, a field of endeavour which had seen some of their greatest triumphs, as at Constantinople (857/1453), Rhodes (928–9/1522) and Candia (1078–80/1667–9), the general trend of development was unfavourable to the Ottomans. The art of fortification had been raised to new levels of excellence through the efforts of men like Rimpler and Vauban. Now, although the mines and mortars of the Ottomans and their lavish employment of human labour in siege operations continued to earn the approval of the Europeans, the prospect that the old methods would remain viable was doubtful indeed. As to the defensive side of siege warfare, the technological advance in the casting of guns, especially during the later years of the War of the Austrian Succession (1740–8) in Europe, called into question even the achievements of a Vauban. The great soldier, Maurice de Saxe, was to declare of fortresses in general that the old ones had no value and that the modern were hardly of more worth.

On the field of battle the prospect before the Ottomans was still less reassuring. To keep abreast of developments in Europe, if only to an approximate degree, had never been a simple task for the Ottomans. Already in 1596 a Muslim from Bosnia was lamenting that the Christians, using the latest types of firearm, held a distinct advantage in battle. The European practice of war had begun in fact to take a new and, for the Ottomans, a fateful orientation—one which led at length to the repeated victories of Austria and Russia over the armies of the sultan in the seventeenth and eighteenth centuries.

Of the technical improvements made in Europe at this time none was more notable than the creation of light and mobile cannon built to a few standardized calibres. A soldier of great judgment like the Maréchal Duc de Villars attributed the success of the Austrians in the war of 1683–99 against the Ottomans to their possession of an excellent field artillery. On the Ottoman guns, however, the comment of the Christians was almost unanimous—they were far too cumbersome, difficult to transport, wasteful in their consumption of gunpowder and only rarely effective in the open field. And indeed, time and again in their wars with Austria and Russia, the Ottomans would suffer defeat in battle and lose at once all the cannon and all the equipment gathered together for the campaign.

Important, too, were the developments occurring in Europe with regard to the hand-gun. The arquebus yielded place to the musket, the carbine and the pistol came into more extended use—arms, in short, more manageable than the arquebus, lighter and quicker to load and discharge. All these new weapons made their appearance in due course amongst the Ottomans. In general, however, the Ottoman *tüfenk* or musket was longer in the barrel and heavier, carried farther and gave a more accurate fire than the types common in Europe, but at the same time it was much slower to prepare and use.

An effective combination of all arms was difficult to achieve, while the rates of fire for the cannon and the hand-gun remained low. Technological advances leading to the development of the light field gun and of the musket made possible the elaboration of a tactical system efficient enough to realize in battle the potentialities of firearms. The end result was the square or rectangle, each side composed of alternating groups of horse and foot, with *chevaux de frise* in front of them, the cannon being located at the corners, and the reserve troops and the baggage at the centre of the formation. Changes introduced in the course of time involved a diminution in the size of the squares and an increase in their number, with a view to greater mobility, and also the elimination of the pikemen and the strengthening of the musketeers, in order to ensure a maximum of fire-power. It was Raimondo Montecuccoli who, on the tactical basis of the square, formulated the principles of action which brought Austria and Russia such remarkable success in their wars against the Ottoman empire. Emphasizing that the best means to overcome the

Muslim foe was to force him into a major battle, Montecuccoli urged that the Ottomans, foot and horse alike, be subjected to a continuing bombardment, from the square, with field guns and all available fire-arms; that intensive musket-fire should be used to drive back the *sipahis*; and that cuirassiers be employed to rout the Janissaries, once the cannon had disrupted their advance. Here indeed—though often modified to suit the terrain of a given encounter—was a blueprint for war which, in the hands of able soldiers like Louis of Baden and Prince Eugene for Austria and Münnich, Rumyantsev and Suvorov for Russia, led to a long series of Christian victories over the armies of the Sultan, and which laid bare the fact that the old Muslim pattern of warfare, even in its most developed and elaborate, i.e. its Ottoman exemplification, had become inadequate to meet the demands of the modern age.

It was not that the Ottoman empire lacked the strength, human and material, for war; its wealth and resources were as abundant in the era of defeat as in the golden age of success. Nor, in relation to new elements of warfare from Europe, was the power to assimilate visible in the reign of Sultan Süleymān less evident in the time, for example, of the first Köprülü *vezīrs*. The great change was in the nature of the elements now demanding assimilation. As long as technological developments in Europe connected with cannon and firearms remained below the level at which tactical evolution of a major kind became possible, the Ottomans did not find it difficult to take over the latest advances in equipment and technique. The capture of guns on the battle-field or in a fortress, converse with prisoners of war, the services of renegade experts, these and other means of contact enabled the Ottomans to learn about the new types of cannon or hand-gun and the most recent devices employing gunpowder. And at this 'simple' level of assimilation such borrowings continued to be made during the fifteenth and the sixteenth, but also in the seventeenth and the eighteenth centuries, as the introduction of new terms into Ottoman usage, e.g. *aghaj top* (petard) and *mushkat* (musket), bear witness.

The case was quite different, when the technological progress achieved in Europe called forth tactical systems involving the use, in close interdependence, of cannon and muskets, of infantry and cavalry. The Ottomans might, with ease, borrow from Europe a new instrument of war—but not a new complex of ideas embodied in a tactical formation. The weapon would fit into a pre-existing context, where it would not be out of place; the tactical system had no such context of absorption awaiting it. To attempt the assimilation of the enlarged modes of warfare now developing in Europe meant, for the Ottomans, to recast the whole practice, and indeed the structure itself, of their armies, and even the fabric of their governmental machine. Not until the impact of continuing defeat in battle against Austria and Russia had become unendurable was the need for radical reform at last accepted amongst them. The movement of reform in imitation of European procedure began in earnest with the accession to the Ottoman throne of Selīm III (1789–1807), gathered momentum under Maḥmūd II (1808–39) and found its full expression in the era of the Tanẓīmāt (1839–76). This movement was not confined to the Ottoman empire. It was extended in the course of the nineteenth and twentieth centuries to the other lands of Islam. The Muslim practice of war now lost those features which had given it hitherto a distinctive character—more and more it became identified with the general course of technical advance and performance attained in Europe. With the advent of radical reform *à l'européenne* Islamic warfare had reached in fact the verge of dissolution. A last comment—almost a formal valediction—can be left to Maurice de Saxe: writing of the Ottomans and their traditional mode of war, he was to declare that neither courage, nor number, nor wealth was lacking to them, but order, discipline and 'la manière de combattre'.[1]

[1] Maurice Comte de Saxe, *Mes rêveries*, ed. Pérau (Amsterdam and Leipzig, 1757), I, 87.

CHAPTER 13

THE TRANSMISSION OF LEARNING AND LITERARY INFLUENCES TO WESTERN EUROPE

THE TRANSMISSION OF LEARNING

In the early days the Latin West knew the Arabs only as conquerors and marauders. From the seventh to the ninth Christian century, Muslim invasions and raids in the Mediterranean basin (to which, rightly or wrongly, Pirenne attributes the function of breaking up its old economic and cultural unity), brought Christendom face to face with the warlike and destructive aspect of Islam. It was not until the second phase, when the Arab onslaught had passed its zenith, and these two religious and political worlds began to have contacts other than those of war, that the West became aware of the high level of culture and learning achieved by the 'Saracens' in their own domains. Envoys and individuals travelling for business reasons or as pilgrims were the first to bring news to Europe of the existence of Muslim culture and science. But above all it was the collective contact between Arab Islamic and Christian communities in the areas of mixed population on the borders between the two worlds that revealed to Christendom the wealth of cultural attainments of which the Arabs were now the depositaries, the promoters and the transmitters. A famous and much-quoted passage from the works of Alvaro of Cordova bears witness to the interest felt by Mozarabic circles in ninth-century Spain for Arab literature, including its poetry, ornate prose and epistolography; but from our point of view this is merely an isolated phenomenon. What impressed the West in the intellectual achievements of the Arabs was the role of mediators of Greek philosophy and science which they had assumed, and the impulse they had imparted to the various branches of learning. The attitude of the Latin West towards the ancient heritage, and in particular to Greece, was much the same as that of the Islamic East—indifference to the artistic element, but keen interest and admiration for the philosophic and scientific aspects, direct contact with which, however, was generally precluded by ignorance of the language. Now it was discovered that these barbarian infidels had translated into their own tongue the wisdom of the ancients, the lofty concepts of Plato and Aristotle, the medical lore of Hippocrates and Galen, the astronomical and mathematical teachings of Ptolemy; and in all these fields they had enriched the inheritance with their own speculations and experiments. This twofold aspect, Greek and Arab, of the knowledge which from the eleventh century onwards the Christian West had been eagerly striving to acquire, is clear; clear, too, is the awareness of its hybrid character on the part of the West. This second contact between East and West in the cultural field was a repetition, in Europe after the year 1000, of that which had taken place in Mesopotamia and 'Irāq between Greek and Islamic culture during the third/ninth and fourth/tenth centuries.

Muslim and Mozarabic Spain, before its reconquest by the Christians, was the theatre and the most important centre of this new contact. Contacts between the West and Graeco-Arab culture in other Mediterranean areas such as Sicily and Italy were of secondary importance compared with the intensity and significance of the work accomplished in Spain; and the influence of the Crusades, to which at one time it was customary to attribute a considerable share in these scientific and cultural exchanges, now appears to have been very slight. In reality, so far we know only of one or two cases of Arab texts reaching the West from the *milieu* of the Crusades, and as a result of them. Less negligible, though not so great as might have been expected, was the part played in the translation and transmission of scientific knowledge by southern Italy and Sicily, despite the fact that the latter was under Arab domination for centuries, while the mainland had often been the goal of Arab raids. In this field much is obscure, and will probably remain so, but the little we know brings us back, so far as southern Italy is concerned, to the school of Salerno, where the only clearly identifiable figure of interest to us in this connexion is Constantine the African (d. 1087), a Tunisian Muslim converted to Christianity, a great traveller and translator into barbaric Latin of Graeco-Arab medical works, which he often passed off as his own, such as writings of Hippocrates and Galen, the *Kāmil al-ṣinā'a al-ṭibbiyya* by 'Alī b. 'Abbās al-Majūsī, also known as the *Liber regius,* the *Zād al-musāfir* and other works by Isḥāq al-Isrā'īlī (Isaac Judaeus). Constantine, who ended his life as a monk at Montecassino, was on the whole a mediocre figure, lacking the high ethical standards of a Gerard of Cremona, but so far as we know he was the first in chronological order to produce in Italy Latin translations and adaptations of Arab works. To a much later age, after the efflorescence of these studies in Spain during the twelfth century, belongs the work of Christian and Jewish translators at the courts of Frederick II, Manfred and the first Angevins: Michael Scot (d. 1235), who had previously worked in Spain, the translator for Frederick II of Aristotelian works on natural history with the commentaries of Ibn Rushd and Ibn Sīnā; the astrologer Theodore, the Sicilians John and Moses of Palermo, who all belonged to Frederick's circle; the Jew of Agrigento, Faraj b. Sālim, who for Charles of Anjou translated *al-Ḥāwī* or *Continens,* al-Rāzī's great medical encyclopaedia; the Provençal Jew, Kalonymos ben Kalonymos, translator during the reign of King Robert of the *Tahāfut al-tahāfut* of Ibn Rushd—the polemical defence of Peripatetic philosophy against al-Ghazālī. With these few names and titles we have exhausted the list of what was accomplished in Italy and Sicily in the field of direct translations from Arabic of scientific works, whether it was a matter of purely Arab science and technics or of Greek science—a meagre result when we remember the close political and cultural ties between that part of Italy and the Arab world, from the conquest of Sicily in the ninth century down to the end of the Saracen colony in Lucera in 1300. It is a result which appears even more meagre when we compare it with the superb harvest reaped at the same time in Spain.

Here the cultural contact between Islam and Christendom, which began in the days of the Cordova amirate, was carried on intensively by the Mozarabic and Jewish elements throughout the period of Arab domination, and it yielded its best fruits at the time when this domination was declining. We know that translations from Arabic into Latin were made in Catalonia from the tenth century onwards, and during the first half of the twelfth century Barcelona was the abode of the first translator of those days whose identity can be established—Plato of Tivoli Between 1116 and 1138, with the help of an Andalusian Jew, Abraham bar Ḥiyyā, called Savasorda (*Ṣāḥib al-shurṭa*), Plato of Tivoli translated Jewish and Arab works on astrology and astronomy, including the astronomical tables of al-Battānī. About this time the centre of such activities shifted to Toledo, which had been restored to Christendom a few decades before, and had become a beacon of Graeco-Arab-Hebraic culture for the whole of the Latin West. The praiseworthy activities of the learned men who flocked thither from every part of Europe, in order to study the treasures of Graeco-Arab philosophy and science, were a striking feature of a great part of the twelfth century. In reality we know very little of the part played in the promotion and guidance of this movement by the archbishop of Toledo, Raymund (1125–52), or of the organization of the work and the relations between the various translators. This does not alter the fact that the name of Raymund has become almost a symbol of this noble undertaking, and the term 'Toledo school', applied to this group of translators, expresses the spirit by which they were animated, even if it does not imply institutional organization. In most cases they probably knew no Arabic at all when they arrived in Toledo, and certainly not enough to enable them to understand the original text of the difficult works on philosophy, medicine, mathematics, astronomy, astrology and matural science which they were eager to study. Consequently, most of them availed themselves of the services of Jewish or Mozarabic scholars living in Toledo, who translated the Arabic text literally into Spanish, which they then turned into Latin. It was, however, only natural that after spending some time in this polylingual *milieu* they acquired in the course of their work a knowledge of Arabic sufficient to enable them to read the originals of their beloved texts without outside assistance, and their work thus became more and more personal and independent. This was certainly the case with the leading members of the group, for example Dominicus Gundisalvi, archdeacon of Segovia, and Gerard of Cremona. Nevertheless, collaboration between these Latin scholars and their teachers and advisers on oriental matters—Savasorda in the case of Plato of Tivoli, the Mozarab Galippus (Ghālib) in Gerard's case, and the converted Jew Avendeath (Ibn Dāwūd), better known under the name of Johannes Hispanus, in the case of Gundisalvi—remains a characteristic feature of those times. Johannes Hispanus, whose long collaboration with Gundisalvi made these two a typical example of this method of working, also produced a number of translations on his own account, such as the *Differentia spiritus et animae* of Qusṭā b. Lūqā, the *Fons Vitae* of Ibn Gabirol, several works of Avicenna, and the *Liber de causis*. Nowadays it is customary to separate the work of this Johannes, who died in 1166, from that of the almost homonymous Johannes Hispalensis or John of Seville (d. 1157), who was also a translator, not of philosophical texts, but of works on astrology by Mā Shā' Allāh, al-Farghānī, Abū Ma'shar and al-Zarqālī.[1] The partner of Johannes Hispanus, Dominicus Gundisalvi (d. 1181) was also the principal or sole translator of great Arabic philosophers such as al-Fārābī's *Liber de*

[1] M. Alonso, *Juan Sevillano, sus obras propias y sus traducciones*, in *al-Andalus*, XVIII (1953), 17–50.

scientiis, De intellectu and *Tanbīh ʿalā sabīl al-saʿāda,* al-Kindī's *De intellectu,* al-Ghazālī's *Maqāṣid al-falāsifa,* Ibn Sīnā's *Metaphysics, Physics, De coelo et mundo,* and others.

To these indigenous members of the Toledan group must be added the foreigners, drawn thither by their thirst for knowledge. They include two Englishmen, Adelard of Bath (translator of Euclid, Abū Maʿshar and al-Khuwārizmī) and Robert of Chester, who produced the first Latin version of the Qur'ān, and, independently of Plato of Tivoli, also translated al-Battānī; a Slav, Herman the Dalmatian, who concerned himself with apologetic, astronomical and astrological works; and above all the Lombard Gerard of Cremona (1114–87), whose mighty figure dominates the whole group, not only on account of the extent of his work, but also because of his lofty moral character. A testimony to both is provided by the bio-bibliographical note compiled shortly after his death by his colleagues and pupils in the Toledan circle and inserted in the manuscripts of several of his translations. From this note we learn that Gerard, scorning the worldly riches which he possessed, led an austere life entirely devoted to science, for love of which he learned Arabic and translated from that language more than seventy works, a list of these being given in the note. Prominent among them are the *Almagest,* the search for which appears to have been the reason for his first coming to Spain, and which he finished translating in 1175, perhaps from the version of al-Ḥajjāj b. Yūsuf; Ibn Sīnā's *Canon of medicine,* which with this translation by Gerard began its triumphal progress throughout the Western Mediterranean lands; works of Euclid, Aristotle, Hippocrates, Galen, Alexander of Aphrodisias, Menelaus, Themistius; and, among the Arab writers, Thābit b. Qurra, al-Kindī, al-Fārābī, al-Qabīṣī, al-Khuwārizmī, al-Nayrīzī, al-Rāzī, al-Zahrāwī and al-Zarqālī. In short, the whole range of Hellenistic-Arab science which had inspired the ʿAbbasid culture of the ninth and tenth centuries and later, in the twelfth century, the international circle in the Toledo of Archbishop Raymond, seems to have been included in the vast *opus* of this indefatigable scholar, who, after devoting most of his life to this work of mediation, returned to his Lombard home to die, leaving behind him an imperishable fame in the history of knowledge.

This first great Toledan period, personified in the names of Archbishop Raymund, Gundisalvi and Gerard, was followed in the thirteenth century by a second efflorescence of translations, centring around the figure of another archbishop of Toledo, Rodrigo Jiménez de Rada

(1170–1247), in whose time appeared the second translation of the Qur'ān, by Marcus of Toledo, and Michael Scot translated al-Biṭrūjī, while Herman the German, translator of Aristotle, al-Fārābī and Ibn Rushd, was active a little later. The work of this second group was continued at Seville in the propitious atmosphere of the court of Alfonso the Wise. Here in 1256 Egidio de Tebaldis of Parma and Pietro da Reggio translated the astrological works of Ibn Abi'l-Rijāl and Ptolemy's *Quadripartitum,* while Castilian or Latin translations were also made of works on magic like the *Picatrix* of the pseudo-Majrīṭī, or of literary works in the old Eastern tradition such as the *Kalīla wa-Dimna* and the *Book of the seven wise men*; of the eschatological *Liber scalae* we shall speak below (pp. 879–80). The last famous Spanish translator was Arnald of Villanova (d. 1312), who specialized in medical works, among them those of Ibn Sīnā and Galen. During this later period interest in the Arabic language spread from the purely scientific and philosophical field, as parts of the ancient heritage, to the Muslim religion, the intention being either apologetic or missionary, as is proved by the part played by the Dominican and Franciscan orders in the teaching of Arabic and the works of great apologists like Ramón Martín and Raymund Lull. But this sector of the study of Arabic in Spain and in the rest of Europe is outside the scope of our subject.

Each of these branches of learning was transmitted by this group of translators and commentators in a manner which on the whole was reasonably faithful, if we bear in mind the *gravitas materiae* (which Plato of Tivoli invoked at the beginning of his translation of al-Battānī as an excuse for any obscurities or difficulties of interpretation) and the often mediocre knowledge these Latin interpreters had of the technical terms they found in the Arabic originals. A typical example in philosophical and theological texts is the frequent use of *loquentes* as a translation of *mutakallimūn,* thus using a generic word to express the specialized sense of the Arabic term denoting the speculative Muslim theologians; while even the great Gerard, when translating one of al-Farghānī's astronomical works, *Jawāmi' 'ilm al-nujūm,* called it *De aggregationibus scientiae stellarum* instead of 'elementary notions of astronomy', because he failed to understand the technical meaning of *jawāmi'*. Despite these and other shortcomings, very natural if we remember how little was known of the Arabic language at that time, it can be said that the Latin approach to Graeco-Arab thought through these medieval translators was on the same level as the Arab approach to the heritage of antiquity three centuries earlier. In one respect it may even be said to have surpassed it, owing to a certain affinity of spirit even when technical adequacy was lacking, since both the Arab philosophers and scholars of the 'Abbasid era and their Latin interpreters were men of the Middle Ages, with a mental outlook which on the whole was more closely akin than that of the Arabs to the thinkers and scientists of pagan Antiquity, particularly of the Classical period. This intellectual affinity helped them to bridge the gap created by the unfamiliarity of the language and the different technical level, so that in our opinion it would be wrong to describe what the West received as a sheer travesty of the Graeco-Arab heritage, a term which is frequently applied to the transmission of the antique originals to the medieval East.

THE INFLUENCE OF THE ARAB HERITAGE

Let us now see to what extent this Arab heritage influenced the medieval West and the Renaissance, how much the West came to know of Arab-Islamic thought and through it of Greek thought, and what effect this contact had on the subsequent evolution of Western thinking. The theme is so vast that here we shall have to limit ourselves to a few brief notes on the various branches of philosophy, theology and science.

In the field of philosophy it is generally maintained that what the West knew of Greek thought, and in particular of Aristotle, was transmitted to it by the Arabs. Such a statement needs qualification and a more precise formulation, but on the whole it remains valid. In reality, the direct channel of transmission through Byzantium was never completely closed to the West, and during the twelfth and thirteenth centuries works of Plato and Aristotle were translated directly from Greek into Latin (the *Meno* and the *Phaedo* in Sicily by Enrico Aristippo (d. 1162); the *Metaphysics,* the *Nicomachean ethics,* the *Physics* and the *De anima* during the first half of the thirteenth century). Of some works the medieval Latins received two translations almost at the same time, one from the original Greek and the other from Arabic. Yet, at the end of the thirteenth century, in one of his most famous passages, Roger Bacon could affirm that the knowledge of Aristotelian philosophy had remained hidden from the West since the days of Boethius and had been revived in his own time thanks to Arab mediation, and above all to Ibn Sīnā. And it is a fact that during the late Middle Ages and the Renaissance, Greek philosophy was studied in the West on the basis of Arab re-elaborations, rather than through direct transmission and translation. The logic, physics and metaphysics of Aristotle were studied either in re-translations from Arabic or in the works of Ibn Sīnā. The latter's great encyclopaedia of philosophy, *Kitāb al-shifā'*, was in substance a recapituiation of Aristotelian thought, though with many interpolations, either deliberate or unconscious, of neo-Platonist ideas. It was in this somewhat hybrid form that the Peripatetic doctrines reached the Latins for the first time. With them, amidst misunderstandings and misinterpretations, came the quarrel that had flared up in the East as to the validity of these Aristotelian-Avicennian doctrines and the possibility of reconciling them with Islamic orthodoxy. The two greatest Muslim thinkers after Ibn Sīnā—al-Ghazālī (d. 505/1111) and Ibn Rushd (d. 595/1198)—encountered each other on this field. The former's attack on Peripatetic philosophy, which he had learned through Ibn Sīnā, was formulated in his *Maqāṣid al-falāsifa* (which in reality contained only an exposition of the doctrines he was fighting against, mistaken in the West for his own ideas) and in the *Tahāfut al-falāsifa,* both of which were translated into Latin. Ibn Rushd defended Aristotle in his polemical *Tahāfut al-tahāfut,* and most of the works he wrote in his attempt to give a more faithful picture and interpretation of Aristotelianism were also translated and studied, in fact many of them have survived only in the Latin translations. Consequently, the figure of the philosopher of Cordova soon became the focal point of the attention of the Latin world, as an interpreter of Aristotle and also as an original thinker, more or less faithfully interpreted.

Contrary to historical truth, which has been re-established only as a result of more recent study of the works of Ibn Rushd, the West assigned to this philosopher an attitude of pure rationalism, averse to any form of revelation, and he was made a symbol of impious unbelief—the feeling against him found expression even in the visual arts, in a painting by Traini in Pisa showing Averroes vanquished by St Thomas Aquinas. In reality, as has been shown by Asín Palacios, the positions of Ibn Rushd and Aquinas regarding the substantial accord between reason and faith were identical, and Ibn Rushd explained his own attitude in the little treatise entitled *Faṣl al-maqāl,* which Aquinas may well have got to know through Maimonides and Ramón Martín. For Ibn Rushd, instead of a 'twofold truth' there was only one truth, on which, on different planes and through different channels, philosophical speculation and revelation converge, the former by means of purely rational arguments and the latter with the occasional aid of symbols and images, which can be interpreted allegorically if necessary, but are not for that reason any less cogent or respectable, and moreover are more easily understood by the masses. It is thus legitimate to speak of the existence in Aquinas of a veritable 'theological Averroism', as Asín Palacios calls it; an Averroism which must, of course, be distinguished from the conceptions that spread in the West under that name, had their most illustrious exponent in Siger of Brabant, and were carried on in France, in England and in Italy (at Padua down to the eighteenth century), with clearly defined aspects of antidogmatism and anticlericalism. To this Latin Averroism are due the theories of the twofold truth (a hint of which can be found, on the Islamic side, in the works of Ibn al-'Arabī, who died in 638/1240), of the denial of the immortality of the individual soul and of a future life. The first of these, as we have said, was extraneous, and even directly opposed, to the authentic ideas of Ibn Rushd, while the others are two corollaries (not unjustified, it is true, but which the Muslim philosopher never intended, or had the courage, to deal with explicitly himself) of the principle propounded by Ibn Rushd of the unity of human minds and the generic Aristotelian concept of the eternity of the world.

Such, in brief, is the story of the transmission of Aristotelianism to the West through Arabic mediation. Apart from this general trend, we must not forget the other factor, to a certain extent bound up with it but in other respects opposed to it, of Platonism, or rather neo-Platonism, of which, as we have seen, al-Fārābī was the leading exponent and interpreter in the East. In its Arab form it had already penetrated to the West through Muslim and Jewish thinkers in Spain, like Ibn Masarra (d. 319/931) and Ibn Gabirol (Avicebron, d. *c.* 450/1058). The original text of the former's work has been lost, but it has been reconstructed by Asín Palacios and can be distinguished from Eastern neo-Platonism by the introduction into its emanationist system of a 'prime element' or 'prime matter', purely spiritual and symbolized by the throne of God, considered as having been the prime aim of divine creation. But a far more direct influence on Christian philosophy and theology was exercised by Avicebron, whose *Fons vitae* translated by Gundisalvi and Avendeath was a favourite textbook of the Franciscan school of William of Auvergne, Alexander of Hales and others, whereas it was opposed by the Dominicans under the influence of Aquinas. Nor, in addition to these purely intellectual influences, must we forget that which earlier Muslim writers had exercised in the field of mysticism on the corresponding Christian evolution, a typical example being the one brought to light by Asín Palacios, who in the figure of Ibn ʿAbbād of Ronda (d. 792/1389), in his speculations and even in his vocabulary, identified an Arab precursor of St John of the Cross.

In this way, far from being merely the transmitters of the philosophical ideas of antiquity, the Arabs, and the Muslims in general, became the teachers and inspirers, or else the controverted and confuted adversaries, of the West. The chief factors in the transmission of philosophy and the controversies that followed, regarding questions such as the reconciliation of reason with faith, were in reality extraneous to genuine Classical philosophy, or were at least barely touched upon, since the relationship between these two elements had been completely different in Antiquity. But from its distant cousin, Islam, Christianity inherited the ideal formulation and the dramatic tension of the problem. The Muslim element was reflected in scholasticism, in medieval apologetics and even, elaborated and perhaps adulterated or misunderstood, in the philosophy of the Renaissance and the Enlightenment—we need only mention the success achieved at that time by Ibn Ṭufayl's *Ḥayy ibn Yaqẓān*, originally starting from a standpoint of accord between reason and faith in perfect harmony with that of the authentic Ibn Rushd. Hence the function of Islam as regards this legacy to the West, far from being merely extrinsic and passive, became dynamic and fruitful.

The nexus between philosophy and the sciences, which dates from the origins of Greek thought and can be followed throughout Antiquity, was bequeathed to the Arabs as part of the ancient heritage and was by them transmitted to the Western world. Just as Ḥunayn b. Isḥāq and his successors turned their attention to Greek science, in particular to medicine and mathematics, so did the Latin translators devote themselves to Arab and Greek works of pure theoretical speculation (Aristotle and pseudo-Aristotelian logic and metaphysics, Plato, and their great Muslim commentators) and at the same time to the patrimony of antique science or pseudo-science that Muslim culture had greeted so eagerly and which it had so much enriched. Our own differential specialization tends to make us break down this nexus, and deal separately with each single branch of thought and knowledge, but in the sphere of medieval civilization, whether Eastern or Western, this unity of conception must never be overlooked. The particularly close connexion between philosophy and medicine (of which there is a reflection in the ambiguity of the Arabic word *ḥakīm*, often used indifferently to denote either 'philosopher' or 'physician'), is revealed in the works of the greatest Islamic thinkers, such as al-Rāzī, Ibn Sīnā and Ibn Rushd, whom the Middle Ages ranked as physicians and at the same time philosophers (the first-named essentially as a physician). The importance of Arab medicine, which was not merely an echo of the Greek, but was fortified by its own experiments and conquests, was clearly recognized by the West, and led to the translation not only of Arabic versions of Greek texts, but also of the original works of great Muslim writers, regarded as classics of the art of medicine.

The first great figure in Arabian medicine to achieve canonical status in the West was al-Rāzī, the Rhazes of Latin translations, whose chief work, the *Continens,* as we have seen, appeared in translation, by order of Charles of Anjou, in the thirteenth century, but whose other books and minor writings such as the *Liber Almansoris,* the *De morbis infantium* on smallpox and measles, and the *Aphorisms* had already been turned into Latin during the preceding century by Gerard of Cremona and other anonymous translators. The next in chronological order was 'Alī b. 'Abbās al-Majūsī (d. 384/994), whose *Kāmil al-ṣinā 'a* was one of the first medical works made known to the West through the translation of Constantine the African, while under the other title of *Kitāb malikī* or *Liber regius* it appeared in 1127 in a new and better translation by Stephen of Antioch—one of those rare cases of a translation being known to the Latin East from the *milieu* of the Crusades. For the medieval Latins, another important Arab authority on medicine was Abulcasis (Abu'l-Qāsim al-Zahrāwī, d. 404/1013), the great physician of Umayyad Spain, whose great encyclopaedia of medicine, *al-Taṣrīf,* unlike al-Rāzī's *al-Ḥāwī,* was never translated in its entirety, but only in parts, the most important being the section on surgery, translated by Gerard, which enjoyed a great reputation throughout the Middle Ages. Other Arabic writers on medicine well known to the West were the Maghribīs Isḥāq al-Isrā'īlī, or Isaac Judaeus (d. *c.* 320/932), and Ibn al-Jazzār (d. 395/1004), both of whom were translated by Constantine the African; 'Alī b. Riḍwān, or Haly Rodoam, of Cairo (d. 459/1067) and his contemporary and adversary Ibn Buṭlān of Baghdād (d. after 455/1063), the former being the author of a commentary on Galen translated by Gerard, and the latter of the *Taqwīm al-ṣiḥḥa* (*Tacuinum sanitatis*), translated by an anonymous scribe; the Spaniards, Avenzoar or Ibn Zuhr (d. 557/1162), whose *Taysīr* was translated at Venice in 1280 by Paravicius, and Ibn Rushd, whose *Kulliyyāt fi'l-ṭibb* ('General principles of medicine') was translated in 1255 by the Paduan Jew Bonacossa under the title of *Colliget*. But in the eyes of posterity the names of all these illustrious writers were overshadowed by the fame of Ibn Sīnā.

The *Canon* (*al-Qānūn fi'l-ṭibb*) of the great scholar from Bukhārā was in fact destined to be the bible of the physicians of both East and West for several centuries. In the East, where the native scientific traditions still survive, it is studied and used even to this day; in the West it remained a classic throughout the Middle Ages until the advent of modern medicine with Paracelsus and Vesalius. Translated about the middle of the twelfth century by the omnipresent Gerard, whose version was revised and corrected in the sixteenth century by the Venetian Andrea Alpago, the *Canon* was printed in Latin in more than thirty editions from the beginning of the sixteenth century onwards, while a printed edition of the original Arabic text appeared in Rome in 1593. This remarkable success was due not so much to any special scientific originality in Avicenna's work, but rather, in the words of one competent to judge, to 'the unrivalled methodicalness with which the author welded into an organic whole all the material of the medical traditions of the Greeks and of Islam' (Plessner). The section of the *Canon* dealing with opthalmology has been the subject of special study on the part of modern medicine, which reminds us that this branch of medical science had an illustrious tradition in the East, and was likewise transmitted through the Arab-Latin channel to the medieval West; in fact the *De oculis* of Constantine the African, whom we have already had occasion to mention several times, is nothing but a re-hash of Ḥunayn's *Kitāb al-'ashr maqālāt fi'l-'ayn*, the fruits of that great translator's personal experience as a doctor.

Arab medicine, culminating in Ibn Sīnā, thus remained until the closing years of the Renaissance the most authoritative source of Western theory and praxis. But while, as regards the transmission of the old philosophical doctrines, Arab mediation was relegated to second place after the re-establishment of direct contact with classical tradition, a new phase in the history of medical science was inaugurated by the experimental method, which rapidly outstripped both Greeks and Arabs and set medicine on the path of its great modern progress.

Pharmacology may be considered a kind of appendix to medicine and it was assiduously cultivated by Muslim followers of Dioscorides. Here, since we are dealing only with transmission, we will confine ourselves to mentioning the names of Māsawayh or Mesue of Baghdād

(d. 405/1015),[1] whose *De simplicibus* was translated in the sixteenth century by J. Dubois (Jacobus Sylvius), though his other work, *De medicinis universalibus et particularibus,* had been known since medieval days, and the Spaniard, Ibn Wāfid (d. 466/1074), the Abenguefit of Gerard, who translated his *De medicamentis simplicibus*.

Muslim civilization acted as teacher to medieval Europe of other branches of knowledge as well as philosophy and medicine, these being mathematics, astronomy and astrology. Here too the legacy of Classical and Hellenistic Antiquity was presented to the West enriched with the further studies, comments and experience of Islamic science, one proof of this being the number of technical words that passed from Arabic into Latin and the other languages of Western Europe, e.g., algebra, algorithm, zenith, nadir, azimuth and cipher. The work of the great Arab mathematicians, astronomers and astrologers (it is not always easy to distinguish the three activities) was among the features of Islamic science that appealed to the translators of Toledo or at the court of Alfonso X the Wise of Castile and León, and in general everywhere during the twelfth and thirteenth centuries. Here we can only give a brief list, in chronological order, of the authors who were most widely known and studied in the West. We begin with the great al-Khuwārizmī, whose name, as is well known, as a result of medieval Latin distortions, gave rise to the term *algorithm*; his little treatise on algebra, the earliest of its kind in Arabic, was translated into Latin twice during the twelfth century, by Gerard, who retained the Arabic title, *De jebra et almucabala,* and by Robert of Chester, who gave an exact Latin rendering of it, *Liber restaurationis et oppositionis numeri,* while al-Khuwārizmī's astronomical tables, as rearranged about the year 1000 by Maslama al-Majrīṭī, were translated by Adelard of Bath. With a contemporary of al-Khuwārizmī, Abū Ma'shar (the Albumasar of the Latins, d. 272/886) we pass from pure mathematics to astronomy and astrology; his great introduction to astrology, *al-Madkhal al-kabīr,* was translated by Johannes Hispalensis under the title of *Introductorium maius,* and in abridged form by Herman the Dalmatian; his *Dalālāt al-ashkhāṣ al-'ulwiyya* was also translated by John of Seville under the title *De magnis coniunctionibus et annorum revolutionibus*. Both these works had a great influence on Western astrology, one reflection of them being the representation of the ten degrees of the zodiac as described by Abū Ma'shar on the frieze

[1] This means Mesue 'the younger', often confused, even in the attribution of works, with the ninth-century doctor and translator of the same name.

in the Palazzo Schifanoia at Ferrara. No less famous in medieval times (and mentioned by Dante, among others) was the other great astronomer al-Farghānī or Alfraganus (d. after 247/861), whose compendium *Fī jawāmiʿ ʿilm al-nujūm* was translated by John of Seville and again by Gerard of Cremona. Arabic works on geometry and trigonometry were known to the Latins through translation of the *Liber trium fratrum* (on the measurement of plane and spherical surfaces) written by the three Banū Mūsā, the brothers Aḥmad, Ḥasan and Muḥammad b. Mūsā b. Shākir, whose joint scientific work was one of the glories of the caliphate of al-Ma'mūn (d. 218/833). The two great Sabian scientists of the ninth century, Thābit b. Qurra and al-Battānī, were likewise well known to the medieval West, thanks to the labours of Gerard, John of Seville and Plato of Tivoli. Of the writings of Thābit, Gerard translated the *Liber carastonis* on the mathematical theory of the steelyard, the *De figura sectore* on the theorem of Menelaus, fundamental for the study of spherical trigonometry, and the *De motu accessus et recessus,* which elaborates the theory of the twinkling and oscillation of the fixed stars, and attempts to bring the data given by Greek astronomers into harmony with the observations of the Arabians. On the other hand, John of Seville devoted himself mainly to the astrological works of Thābit, such as the *Liber iudiciorum astrorum.* The chief work of al-Battānī or Albategnius (d. 317/929), the celebrated astronomical tables known as the *Zīj al-Ṣābi'*, was translated several times, either in part or in its entirety, during the Christian Middle Ages: once by Plato of Tivoli in the first half of the twelfth century, once at the court of Alfonso the Wise in Seville (latter half of thirteenth century), and in the early years of the twelfth century by Robert of Chester.

Another medieval astrological classic of Arab origin was the *Introductio in astrologiam,* of al-Qabīṣī (Alcabitius), the fourth/tenth-century astrologer who compiled his manual for the Hamdanid prince of Aleppo, Sayf al-Dawla; in Europe it became known thanks to the translation by John of Seville, to which was added the little treatise entitled *De coniunctionibus planetarum,* and for centuries, together with the *Tetrabiblos* or the *Centiloquium* of Ptolemy (both likewise translated several times from Arabic versions), it constituted an authoritative and handy introduction to the science of astrology. Alhazen, the physicist and mathematician Ibn al-Haytham (d. 430/1039), was made famous in the West by Gerard's translation of his little booklet on astronomy, *De crepusculis et nubium ascensionibus,* and by his great treatise on physico-mathematical optics, *De optica* (translated and revised by a certain Witelo in the thirteenth century from an Arabic original which seems to have disappeared), which in the opinion of competent judges was one of the major glories of the Muslim Middle Ages. On the other hand, the versatile and brilliant al-Bīrūnī (d. 440/1048), nowadays regarded as the leading figure in medieval Muslim science, was practically unknown to the West at that time, even if he can be identified with a certain 'Rinuby', author of a few astronomical writings preserved in Latin translations.

The last effervescence of Arab mathematics and astronomy passed on to the West includes the works of the Spanish scholars al-Zarqālī (Azarquiel), Jābir b. Aflaḥ al-Ishbīlī and al-Biṭrūjī, all of the twelfth century, and almost contemporaries of the great translation period in Toledo and Seville. Al-Zarqālī's treatise explaining the modified form of astrolabe he had invented was translated into Latin by Gerard, and into Castilian by order of Alfonso the Wise. Gerard also translated Jābir's compendium of the *Almagest,* together with the important treatise on trigonometry prefixed to it by the author of the Arabic original, *Gebri filii Affla Hispalensis de Astronomia libri novem.* Lastly, al-Biṭrūjī (Alpetragius, d. 600/1204) with his treatise on astronomy of anti-Ptolemaic tendency evolved a cosmographical system more consonant with pure Aristotelian principles and was for this reason studied and translated by Michael Scot; the work was later translated into Hebrew and in the sixteenth century from Hebrew again into Latin.

It was by such means that Arab knowledge of mathematics, astronomy and astrology gave a helping hand to the early days of scientific activity in the West. In those same early years of the thirteenth century, Leonard of Pisa compiled his *Liber Abbaci,* strongly imbued with Arab algebra, which was a landmark in European mathematics, and introduced the system of 'Arabic' numerals, in reality Indian, which were adapted but used only in part by the Arabs themselves. Arab astronomy and astrology remained in vogue throughout Europe until well on into the Renaissance, down to the days of Regiomontanus and the Copernican revolution.

No less profound was the influence of Islamic culture and science in the field of alchemy and magic, which throughout the Middle Ages and until the eve of the modern era formed a conspicuous part of the intellectual patrimony of mankind. This was derived also from the Hellenistic and late antique legacy, singularly congenial, because of the Eastern elements it already contained, to Muslim culture of the 'Abbasid period, during which it was also cultivated by non-Arab and heterodox circles.

The Latin Middle Ages greeted these speculations and researches with equal enthusiasm, and important Arabic texts on magic and alchemy have come down to us in numerous Latin translations of which the original versions have been lost. For example, the text that might be called the Magna Carta of the earliest Arab alchemy, said to have been found by Apollonius of Tyana in a cave, engraved on a tablet of emerald, is included in a treatise on hermetic cosmology, *Sirr al-khalīqa,* better known by the Latin title of *Tabula smaragdina,* under which it enjoyed wide circulation in the West in early times. Scanty fragments of an Arabic original also exist of another celebrated work on alchemy, very popular in the Middle Ages, of which several versions of an anonymous translation have come down to us. This is the *Turba philosophorum,* the original of which was apparently written about the year 900, containing the description of a conference presided over by a certain Arisleus (Aristeus or Archelaos ?), with numerous speeches by Greek philosophers on subjects connected with alchemy and natural philosophy, the latter being considered as a premiss of alchemy. From such purely theoretical speculations, Arab alchemy passed to praxis with the corpus of writings going under the name of Geber (Jābir b. Ḥayyān); the pseudographical character of these writings has been shown, and the compilation of them, going back to Ismāʿīlī circles, is nowadays attributed to a number of authors of the ninth and tenth centuries. Here we are interested only in the Latin Geber, who soon became classed as an Arab authority, thanks mainly to Gerard of Cremona, who translated at least the first of a group of seventy little treatises attributed to Jābir (*Liber divinitatis de septuaginta*), and later through a whole series of anonymous translations (*Liber adabesi, De arte alchemiae, Flos naturarum, Summa perfectionis metallorum,* etc.), which gave added authority to the mythical Arab alchemist, or rather to the writings passing under his name, and created a vogue for them in the Latin West. Such was the fame of this 'Geber' that works on alchemy of later date and of undoubted Latin origin were attributed to him. The works of the great physician and philosopher al-Rāzī (d. *c.* 320/932), who knew at least the earlier writings of the Geber corpus and gave a vigorous impulse to the experimental side of such researches, were also translated into Latin (*Liber secretorum, Liber experimentorum*) and as a result this original and profound thinker was looked upon as an authority even in this field lying halfway between science and fantasy, which was destined to engage the energies of so many generations to come.

Alchemy as a science soon became chemistry and eventually the most gorous form of modern research, but originally its extravagant aberra-ons and its conception of nature brought it closer to magic. Since the ays of late Antiquity, magic, concentrating on the production of talis-ıans and amulets, which were supposed to counteract the forces of nature ıd the whims of fortune, had undergone extensive development. Its igh priest and grand master was, in Eastern tradition, Apollonius of 'yana (in Arabic, Bālīnās or Bālīnūs), to whose theurgic figure every sort f prodigy was attributed. In the West, Bālīnās became Belenus, and to im were ascribed various writings on alchemy, astrology and magic urrent in Latin translations at that time. But the most comprehensive ırab manual of magic that the West knew was the *Picatrix* (perhaps a orruption of Hippocrates, the name of a suppositious Greek author), he Arabic original of which was entitled *Ghāyat al-ḥakīm* ('The philo-opher's aim'), attributed to a tenth-century mathematician living in pain, Maslama al-Majrīṭī, whereas in reality it would appear to have een compiled about a century later. The Latin version of this encyclo-aedia of magic, based on a mixture of astrology and neo-Platonism, but vith the fundamental practical aim of producing natural phenomena and nvoking spirits at the request of the initiate, was made by order of ılfonso the Wise during the latter half of the thirteenth century, and its nfluence in the Middle Ages and the Renaissance was prolonged and enacious. The survival of this most irrational and extravagant sector of ate antique culture transmitted by the Arabs to Europe, down to the beginning of the modern era, is exemplified in a most significant way in this curious treatise on talismans and magic exhalations; here we touch the lowest level of that cultural heritage which at its apex had the philosophy of Aristotle and Plato, the science of Ptolemy and Galen. Gold and dross were studied and transmitted by Islam in equal parts.

To complete this brief review, we must mention a few Arabic texts on technical subjects, the results of observations and experiments made by Muslims independently of ancient tradition, which eventually reached the West. Among them are treatises on falconry and hunting with dogs, a genre well represented in Arab technical literature. Two authors, 'Moamin' and Ghaṭrīf, are known to us through translations, and it would appear that at least part of the original texts has recently been discovered.[1] 'Moamin' is known to have been a falconer in the service of Frederick II, who had his work translated into Latin by his interpreter,

[1] E. Viré, in *Arabica*, VIII (1961), 273.

Theodore, and certainly made use of it in his own treatise, *De arte venandi cum avibus*. We do not know whether this Latin translation has survived, but what has been preserved and recently published is a Romance translation, in Franco-Italian, of both 'Moamin' and his possible contemporary, Ghaṭrīf, a rare example in its genre, since such works were normally translated only into Latin.

THE TRANSMISSION OF LITERARY INFLUENCES

In the scientific field, the chief function of Islam was the transmission to the West of a goodly portion of the ancient heritage, though it is true that it made certain contributions of its own. In the spheres of literature and art, however, it transmitted far more of its own stock. By saying this we do not mean to imply that in these fields no Classical elements reached the West as a result of Islamic mediation (for example, through the *Thousand and one nights*), but it is nevertheless a fact that apart from such sporadic cases, Eastern influence on Western literature and art presupposes the existence in Islamic civilization of a clearly defined spiritual patrimony evolved in the East in a spirit and in forms peculiar to it, and constituting a counterpart to Classical culture and the continuation of that culture after its transformation in the Romance lands. Here the East acted not only as mediator and elaborator, but also as a creator on its own account; and the West—almost unwittingly during the Middle Ages, but more consciously and systematically in the modern era—received from these contacts and sought in them cultural elements completely extraneous to its own tradition, making experiments in grafting them which were more or less successful, the very fact that they were made being a testimony to the vitality of the Islamic heritage and the contribution it made in this way to the common heritage of all mankind.

There would seem to be no doubt that throughout the Middle Ages and the Renaissance, down to the threshold of the modern era, only Arabic literature need be taken into account when we are dealing with literary contacts with, and influence upon, the Christian world. It was not until the second phase, the spiritual rediscovery of the East by the Enlightenment and European Romanticism, that Persian, and to a lesser degree Turkish and the other minor literatures, took their places by the side of Arabic literature. Differing in language, in their areas of diffusion, in the volume and complexity of their output, all these literatures had nevertheless one common denominator, which was precisely that conferred upon them by Islam, of which they are the expression.[1] The spirit of Islam permeates them all, just as Arabic, the language of the Qur'ān, gave them its vocabulary and its script. But this plurality of Islamic languages and literatures was, we repeat, a phenomenon affecting only the modern phase of the contacts between East and West. During the first thousand years of its existence, Islam was revealed and expressed to Europe almost exclusively through Arabic literature, and in the West, for obvious geographical and historical reasons, 'Arabic' and 'Saracen' were synonyms. Throughout the Middle Ages, the literary position of the two worlds, Islam and Latin Christendom, was thus as follows. On the one side was a supranational language and literature, Arabic, which from being the language of one nation had become the vehicle of culture for a whole civilization. The use of different dialects in the spoken language, of considerable importance for certain aspects of our theme, never led to the formation of autonomous literary languages, and this is true even today. On the other side was a language, medieval Latin, also international, but out of which, by contrast with what happened with Arabic, the Romance vernaculars gradually evolved, each with a thriving literature of its own.

Since we are dealing here only with the influence of Arabic literature on the West, we shall mention only a few of its general characteristics which can be used for purposes of comparison with medieval Latin literature. First and foremost there was poetry, and then prose, carefully cultivated, stylized and codified. From the very beginning the poetry was completely autochthonous, going back in origin to the dim past of pre-Islamic civilization, and remaining for a very long time free from foreign influence—a poetry that soon became a canonical model, little tolerant of new development. The prose, after a first unique and inimitable monument in the shape of the Sacred Book, flourished exceedingly during the Islamic era; it too at first immune from foreign influences, as the language not only of religion, philosophy and science but also of history and jurisprudence, of culture and art. Throughout their evolution, Arabic poetry and prose retained that learned and intellectual character which made them the prerogative of the cultured classes, with an ever-widening gap between them and the life of the people. These characteristics of the Islamic East's major literature have

[1] Cf. F. Gabrieli, 'Literary Tendencies', in the volume *Unity and Variety in Muslim Civilization* (ed. G. E. von Grunebaum) (Chicago, 1955).

a certain affinity with those of medieval Latin and Graeco-Byzantine literature, giving, one might say, a common physiognomy to the literary output of the early Middle Ages in both East and West. But whereas in the West, after the year 1000, the spirit of each of the individual nations made itself more and more felt in literary activity, as a result of the birth of new languages, new forms and new ideas—some of which, as we shall see, were fertilized by contacts with the East—Oriental literature clung tenaciously to its aristocratic character and in the end became fossilized. Between lofty, refined literature and formless, genuinely popular expression there was, in Islam, a gap that was never filled; and so, while medieval literature in the international Latin language gave birth—not only in the linguistic sense—to neo-Latin offshoots, Arabic literature knew no such new development. It paid for this by contracting sclerosis and by centuries of decadent sterility, until the advent of the modern revival, when the trend of influence was reversed and Arabic literature was fertilized and invigorated by the West. But during its golden age, which lasted until the Renaissance, it gave much to the West, and received nothing in return.

The Middle Ages

Until quite recently we were in the dark as to how much literary influence, if any, the Islamic East had on the West in medieval times, when relations between East and West were those of war and commerce, with little opportunity for cultural exchanges. Here too an exception—and at the same time an anticipation—is provided by Spain, where the Arab-Islamic and Latin-Christian elements soon learned to live together in a fruitful symbiosis. Alvaro of Cordova's celebrated testimony shows that as early as the ninth century, only a hundred years after the conquest, his Christian contemporaries were assiduously cultivating Arabic literature. He laments the fact that, instead of poring over the Holy Scriptures, they were reading the poems, the epistles and the stories of their infidel conquerors, vying with one another in imitating them, spending vast sums in acquiring libraries of Arabic books and, though ignorant of Latin, using Arabic with a fluency equal to that of the Arabs themselves. Nothing has survived of this ancient Mozarabic literature, and very few of the originals by which it was inspired, if we except a few fragments of poetry dating from the days of the Cordovan amirate. It should, however, be noted that at that time, and even during the golden century of the Cordovan caliphate, Arab culture in Spain still retained a definitely oriental stamp, and did not until later assume an Andalusian character of its own. In any case, the cultural supremacy of Arabic among the Christian community in Spain in those distant days would seem to be well documented, while traces of translations from Latin into Arabic (for example, of the historical works of Orosius) confirm that there was cultural contact between the two worlds. The most recent and sensational novelty in this field was the discovery of the Romance-Arabic *kharjas,* the early history of which leads us back to this same remote period of Muslim–Christian Spain. But this discovery was only the last chapter in the thorny problem of Arabic poetry and European poetry, which first came to the fore at a much later date and is now the focal point of every controversy on literary influences and the relationship between East and West in medieval times.

The theory that the Arabs had a pre-eminent influence on medieval Romance culture, and in particular on its poetry, was first advanced in the sixteenth century by Barbieri, and then by Andrés in his erudite work on the history of literature written in the days of the Enlightenment, when there was much curiosity concerning the East.[1] As regards poetry, they identified the classical Arabic poets, the only category then known, as the inventors and transmitters to the neo-Latin world of rhyme. Nineteenth-century Romanticism, with Sismondi and Fauriel, shifted the stress from the field of form to that of content, and considered the Arabs as precursors and inspirers of the concept of courtly love elaborated by the troubadours. In this way they laid the double foundation of that 'Arab theory' on the origins of Romance lyric verse—a theory which, though combated and almost shelved by the positivists, was destined to have a vigorous revival in our own century and to become the apple of discord between students of oriental and Romance literatures, giving rise to a violent controversy which is still going on.

We have just spoken of a double foundation, but it would perhaps be better to speak of two threads, often rightly or wrongly intertwined and entangled. One is the question of the influence on metre, of rhyme and later of the strophe, which from Andalusia might have crossed the Pyrenees and entered Provençal, Old French and Italian poetry, while in the Iberian peninsula they might have been adopted by the nascent Gallego-Portuguese and Castilian poetry. The other problem, which

[1] G. Andrés, *Origine, progresso e stato attuale di ogni letteratura,* (Parma, 1782–99); G. M. Barbieri, *Dell'origine della poesia rimata* (ed. by Tiraboschi, 1790).

can be considered as either bound up with the question of metre or else distinct from it, concerns the spiritual background of the sentiments, concepts and images expressed by Romance lyric poets and above all by the troubadours, the real or supposed oriental precedents of which are being sought for and identified. Before Ribera and the more recent studies and discoveries, this latter element of a migration across the Pyrenees to the Romance world of a conception of love and of woman unknown to the Classical world was the most assiduously pursued and asserted. The conception of love as humble service and chaste adoration was rediscovered in the ʿUdhrite poets of the desert, and among city-dwellers in ʿAbbās b. al-Aḥnaf, of the early ʿAbbasid period. It was easy to follow its passage from the East to Arab Spain in the works of poets like Ibn Zaydūn (d. 463/1071) or in treatises on love like those of Ibn Ḥazm (d. 456/1064), whose pleasing little book on the phenomenology and case-histories of love, *Ṭawq al-ḥamāma*, owed most of its success in the West to the fact that it was supposed to be a pre-troubadour manual of courtly love against a Muslim background. The undeniable analogies between the basic concepts and certain stock situations and figures in Arabic and troubadour lyrics (the jealous lover, the *raqīb/guadador*, the *wāshī/lauzenjaire*, etc.) were so striking as inevitably to encourage the idea that the Arab-Andalusian world must have exercised a direct influence on Romance poetry. Borne on the waves of intercourse—diplomatic and commercial, religious and cultural (through pilgrimages), social and even military, since wars also promote contacts—Moorish mentality and literary conventions were believed to have fertilized the nascent poetry in *langue d'oc*, despite the diversity of language, faith and culture. The language difficulty was actually the knottiest problem for these champions of a migration across the Pyrenees of concepts and themes—a stumbling-block which the opponents of the 'Arab theory' did not fail to point out.

In the early years of the present century the whole problem entered upon a new phase, thanks to the Arabic and Hispanic scholar J. Ribera. On the one hand he threw light on the Arabic-Romance bilingualism prevalent in the social life of Muslim Spain and its consequences in the literary field, which subsequent studies were to confirm and extend. On the other hand, by his study of the works of the twelfth-century poet Ibn Quzmān, he opened a new chapter in the history of Arabic literature and its relations with the Romance world. The *dīwān* of Ibn Quzmān was found to have been composed, not in classical Arabic, but in the Arab-

Hispanic vernacular, not in the classical metre of the monorhyme quantitative *qaṣīda,* but in the popular form of the *zajal*—syllabic strophes (though sometimes showing traces of quantitative schemes, or adapted to them) with various combinations of rhymes. Some of these 'zejelesque' strophic forms seemed to Ribera to be almost identical with those of the earliest Provençal troubadours, e.g. William of Poitiers, Cercamon and Marcabru (for example, the simplest and most typical form rhyming *aaab, cccb, dddb,* etc., preceded, like the strophes of the Arabic *zajal,* by a prelude-refrain *bb* and ending with a finale repeating the same rhyme—the famous *kharja*). This identity, however, was not confined to the Provençal poets. Ribera was able to show that the 'zejelesque' strophe in its various combinations is to be found in the early lyrics of other Romance languages—in Galician in the Alfonsine *Cantigas,* in Castilian *villancicos,* in Franco-Provençal popular poetry and in the *laudi* of Jacopone da Todi and of the Franciscans in general. The old and unproven assertion of former scholars that rhyme was introduced into the Romance world by the Arabs, found an unexpected confirmation of a concrete kind in this popular type of poetry, in which the debt of Romance poetry to the Arabs seemed to be supported by chronological data that could not be ignored. According to Arab tradition the inventor of Arabic-Andalusian strophic poetry (the *muwashshaḥa* in classical language, the *zajal* of Ibn Quzmān and other poets being merely a variant in the vernacular) was Muqaddam or Muḥammad of Cabra, who flourished about the year 900. Ibn Quzmān (*c.* 1080–1160) and William of Poitiers (1071–1126) were contemporaries, but the Cordovan poet was only the most illustrious representative of Arabic 'zejelesque' poetry whose work has come down to us, and we have ample documentary evidence of the existence in Arab Spain during the tenth and eleventh centuries of this form as well as of the metrically equivalent *muwashshaḥa.* Even if we exclude—as we should—the possibility of Ibn Quzmān having had any direct influence on the earliest Provençal troubadour, it would seem to be beyond all doubt that the Arab strophic form existed before the days of the troubadours and Romance poetry in general.

As regards form and metre, Ribera's studies certainly gave valid support to the 'Arab theory', but it cannot be said that he contributed anything new to the question of content and concept. In reality, Ibn Quzmān was anything but a singer of courtly love, and his carefree cynicism could be better compared with analogous realistic traits which we find side by side with the prevalent idealistic trend in certain Provençal poets. In any case, Ribera's new formulation of the metrical problem was developed by Arabic scholars like Nykl (editor and first translator of Ibn Quzmān), Tallgren-Tuulio, García Gómez, and above all by that great authority on Romance literature, R. Menéndez Pidal. The last named, in a classic paper, made a profound study of 'zejelesque' metre in Romance poetry and finally accepted the 'Arab theory' when he found that the identity of strophic schemes extended to all seven variants of the original Arabic and corresponding Romance forms, remarking that this Arabic-neo-Latin type of strophic verse constitutes 'a family group that cannot be confused with any other tristich, or with any other strophe having a refrain'. With this precise formulation he took his stand against the tenacious attempts of adversaries of the 'Arab theory' to ascribe the origin of the Romance strophe to the Latin monorhyme tristichs with a *volta,* the only possible alternative to the theory that it was due to the passage of Arabic influence across the Pyrenees. Such tristichs exist, but those which can be dated were not written until after the days of William of Poitiers and cannot therefore constitute a profound substratum of tradition such as the Arabic forms can boast in the country of their origin, as A. Roncaglia, the most recent and most conscientious student of Romance literature to tackle the problem, has to admit. Nevertheless, the reasoned and instinctive objections of the Romance camp have not yet been entirely confuted, and scholars like Spanke and Le Gentil still prefer to resort to an agnostic 'not proven', or to maintain that any analogies are purely casual and extrinsic, instead of bowing to what would now seem to have been convincingly established.[1]

While he is obliged to accept, almost by force of circumstances, the Arabic origin of Romance rhythmics, Roncaglia rightly insists on antedating the actual fertilizing influence to a period before the end of the eleventh century or the early years of the twelfth, to which that typical pair, Ibn Quzmān and William, would otherwise bring us. Between a 'pre-troubadour melic tradition', which might have had a Romance background, and the Arab *milieu* in Spain, one would have to presuppose contacts some time before the year 1000, during a protoliterary phase concerning which we have only very fragmentary documentary

[1] S. M. Stern has recently made a strong case against the theory of the borrowing of rhyme in Western Europe from Arab models. See *L'Occidente e l'Islam nell'Alto Medioevo,* Centro di studi di Spoleto, XII, 1965, II, 639-66.

evidence, but which would provide a better explanation for the slow osmosis of these rhythmical elements, and also of certain *topoi* of Eastern origin in the nascent Romance lyric poetry. This reconstruction and backdating of the process are based in their turn on the most recent phase in the study of Arabic-Andalusian verse, that is to say on the discovery of the existence in the latter of the Romance *kharja,* which has opened up new perspectives in the whole field and raised new problems.

The presence of isolated Romance words in Ibn Quzmān's *zajal* written in colloquial Arabic had already been noticed by Ribera. But since 1948, thanks mainly to S. M. Stern and E. García Gómez, some fifty *kharjas* have been studied and published, taken from *muwashshaḥāt* written in Hebrew (a simple imitation of the Arabic forms) and in Arabic, in which the classical Arabic strophic group ends with a finale that can only be explained as due to a commingling of Arabic and Romance, and sometimes seems to be pure Romance. Most of them are love poems (distant precursors of the *Cantigas de amigo*), in which a girl gives vent to her feelings, her passions and her reproaches; but there are also *kharjas* of a laudatory or descriptive kind, all more or less closely connected with the subject-matter of the *muwashshaḥa* containing them. Ribera's theory of Arabic-Hispanic bilingualism even in the field of popular or would-be popular literature—a theory which also finds support in certain passages in Arabic anthologies and treatises, for example those of Ibn Bassām and Ibn Sanā' al-Mulk—could not have a more striking confirmation. Quite apart from the exceptional importance of such documents dating from the earliest phase of the Iberian vernacular (these *muwashshaḥāt* were written by poets of the tenth, eleventh and twelfth centuries even if the anthologies containing them are of later date), here we seem to have a reversal of the trend of give and take between the Arab and the Romance worlds. We find, namely, the Arabs using and inserting in their poems a very old Mozarabic tradition; perhaps because, as some scholars maintain, such Romance *kharjas* existed before the various *muwashshaḥāt* and were extracted ready-made from their Romance background, or else because the Arab poet composed them himself with all the gusto of a virtuoso for pastiches, deriving them, however, from some familiar tradition of his own milieu. In either case, one thing is now certain. Starting from the type of poetry in rigorously classical language and quantitative metre, which in Spain preserved the Eastern spirit and forms, we arrive at this other type of strophic structure (likewise not without Eastern precedents, but receiving its own characteristic form and development in Spain, whence it later returned to the East), and find a polylingual foundation wherein Arab tradition and the Romance spirit are closely interwoven, so much so that we are left in doubt to which branch individual features are to be attributed. And whereas during the purely literary phase (the only phase we knew until quite recently) there was very probably an Arab influence on the Romance world on both sides of the Pyrenees, its slow maturing in Andalusia reveals a participation of Romance elements the extent of which it is still difficult to estimate. This would be the only exception to the maxim we laid down above, namely that in the literary field during the Middle Ages the East gave everything to the West and received nothing in exchange. But it is certainly difficult to continue to apply the term 'East' to that very remarkable crucible of races and cultures which Muslim Spain, in the light of the most recent discoveries, would more and more appear to have been, down to the centuries of the reconquest.

To conclude our remarks on this fascinating theme, still the subject of study and controversy, we should like to say that to us the 'Arab theory', on a somewhat broader basis, seems to be firmly established, that is to say in so far as concerns form, rhythmic structure and rhyme, transmitted by the Arabs in their 'zejelesque' shape to the Romance lands on either side of the Pyrenees. Likewise undeniable, though with certain limitations and reservations, is the transmission through Arab tradition to the courtly lyric poetry in *langue d'oc* of certain motifs and thematic notions, in an atmosphere, however, of spiritual autonomy, which should be rightly claimed as a counterpoise to the strict adherence to the actual metrical schemes. In other words, the Arabs gave the Romance world the form of the strophe and rhyme, through their happy innovations on Andalusian soil; while the Romance world filled this form with a spirit which, though it too may have been in part of Arab origin, with its complexity, variety and creative originality, opened up new paths for the West.

The great argument, still in progress, about 'Arab poetry and European poetry' has tended to distract attention from the other fields in which Spain, and in general all the medieval West, received Oriental matter from the Arabs and developed it. In the field of literature, we must first of all consider didactic and gnomic works, and then narrative, often connected with them. Interest in, and translation of, such works seems to have awakened in Christian Spain rather later than was the case with works of philosophy and science, and was mainly thanks to the influence of Alfonso X the Wise (1252–84). For example, from Alfonso's time and milieu we have the translation, under the title *Bocados de oro,* of an anthology of maxims of the ancient sages compiled in Egypt during the eleventh century by Mubashshir b. Fātik. The same may be said of the translation from Arabic into Castilian of the *Kalīla wa-Dimna,* probably made by order of Alfonso in 1251, and of the *Book of Sindibād* (the *Syntipas* or *Dolopathos* or *Book of the seven wise men,* to quote the titles of other Western translations), translated about the same time at the behest of Alfonso's brother under the title *Libros de los engannos et los asayamientos de las mujeres.* In all these cases the subject-matter was not specifically Arabic but part of the earliest Hellenistic and Oriental tradition, going back to Persia and India but known to the West through Arabic versions, the earliest originals of many of them, like that of the *Sindibād,* having been lost. The West absorbed all this material eagerly and it had a far wider circle of readers than the works of philosophy and science, which explains the preference in this field for translations into the vernacular. But apart from translations in the strict sense of the term, Arabic didactic works and narrative poured into Spain during the late Middle Ages and the Renaissance in the form of adaptations, re-elaborations and imitations, the Oriental models of which can sometimes be conjectured and often definitely identified. First we have the *Disciplina clericalis* by Petrus Alfonsi, a converted Jew (early twelfth century), which may originally have been written in Arabic, and even in the Latin version shows clear traces of derivation from the *Kalīla,* the *Sindibād* and the *Thousand and one nights,* one of the most popular works in Muslim Spain. Next we have the *Conde Lucanor* by Don Juan Manuel (1282–1349), many of whose stories are drawn from the same sources, and the Catalan *Disputa del ase* by Fra Anselmo of Turmeda (d. 1420 at Tunis, after conversion to Islam), which goes back to an apologue of the Arabic philosophical encyclopaedia of the *Ikhwān al-Ṣafā'*. Lastly there is the *Patrañuelo* by Timoneda (*c.* 1520–*c.* 1583), the curious vicissitudes of which were noted by Cerulli, who points out that the Arabic subject-matter passed from medieval Spain into the Italian *novella,* and later returned to Spain thanks to this Renaissance story-teller. The Arabic element, often transmitted via the narrative traditions of the Moriscos, characterizes all Spanish literature, even that of the classical period, from Cervantes to Gracián (1601–58), whose *Criticón,* as has been shown by García Gómez, refers in its prologue to a Morisco tale, the common source of this seventeenth-century Jesuit and of the twelfth-century Muslim, Ibn

Ṭufayl, author of *Ḥayy ibn Yaqẓān,* which enjoyed such popularity at the time of the Enlightenment.

The fortunes of this Arabic didactic-narrative material as it spread from Spain throughout medieval and Renaissance Europe have hitherto been followed in single threads which it would be premature to try to draw together. The Arabic, or to speak more generically, Eastern, origin of many *fabliaux,* and of old French romances like *Floire et Blanchefleur* and *Aucassin et Nicolette* (in which the first name is the Arabic al-Qāsim) is now generally admitted. In Italy, no adequate study has yet appeared on the more or less direct Arab sources of the *Novellino,* of Fiorenzuola and Doni—all names which remind us of the transmission, nearly always by way of Spain, of Oriental narrative to Italian culture between the thirteenth and the sixteenth centuries. Outside the field of narrative, other points of contact between the Islamic East and the medieval West have been suggested rather than established for literary forms such as the *tenson* and the *contrasto,* for which some scholars, in addition to a more probable derivation from Middle Latin *altercationes,* have thought of a possible influence of the Arabic and Persian *munāẓarāt,*[1] perhaps through Hebrew mediation. During the last few decades, all these matters of purely historical and literary interest have been overshadowed by another question, important for the history of religion as well. This is the problem of the knowledge and interpretation in the West of Arab-Islamic ideas, images and works relating to the other world, which brings Islamic eschatology into touch with the loftiest medieval expression of poetry and spirituality, the great poem of Dante.

The search for Oriental, and in particular Islamic, sources of Dante's vision was, as is well known, a thorough one, and the results were presented in 1919 by M. Asín Palacios in his book *La escatología musulmana en la Divina Comedia.* After establishing a not altogether convincing, but on the whole impressive, series of analogies in structure, concept and details between Dante's portrayal of the other world and certain Arab-Islamic eschatological sources, Asín Palacios reached the conclusion that, while the poetical genius of Dante as creator of the poem remains intact, the subject-matter was to a considerable extent drawn more or less directly from these Islamic sources. Among the texts which he analysed most minutely, and collated with the *Divine Comedy,* were the

[1] Cf. E. Wagner, *Die arabische Rangstreitdichtung und ihre Einordnung in die allgemeine Literaturgeschichte,* Akademie der Wissenschaften und Literatur, Abhandlungen der Geistes- und Sozialwissenschaftlichen Klasse (1962), No. 8.

Risālat al-ghufrān by Abu'l-'Alā' al-Ma'arrī (d. 449/1057), a half-fantastic, half-satirical description of a journey to the other world, and the works of the Spanish mystic Ibn al-'Arabī (d. 638/1240), especially *al-Futūḥāt al-Makkiyya,* abounding in eschatological descriptions accompanied by graphic illustrations. There was, however, and still is, no trace of any medieval translations into a Western language of these literary and religious texts, the interpretation of which is by no means easy even for modern Arabic scholars, and this linguistic barrier made it extremely unlikely that Dante could have had the precise, detailed knowledge of them that Asín Palacios's theory postulated. In addition to Abu'l-'Alā' and Ibn al-'Arabī, the Spanish scholar also mentioned more generally a number of other Islamic eschatological sources in both learned and popular literature, but here the same objection of the language difficulty could be raised, as well as the problem of the cultural *milieu* in which Dante could have got to know them. The spirited opposition to the theory on the part of Romance philologists and students of Dante was based not only on arguments such as the intrinsic improbability of the whole story, and on doubts as to the validity of some of the alleged analogies, but also on the lack of any vehicle through which these Islamic descriptions of the other world could have been transmitted to Europe and Italy in Dante's time.

Round about 1950, however, the discovery of the Romance *kharjas* threw an unsuspected light on the cultural contacts between the Arabs and the Romance lands through Spain, and at the very same time there came to light what seemed to be the missing link, in the transmission of Islamic eschatology to the West. This was the *Liber scalae Machometi* or *Livre de l'eschiele Mahomet,* to give it the titles of the two versions so far discovered, one in Latin and the other in Old French, published independently and simultaneously, in Spain by Muñoz, and in Italy by Cerulli. Both these translations were made by an Italian, Bonaventura da Siena, from a lost Castilian version of an Arabic *Mi'rāj*—a popular religious text describing the journey of Muḥammad to the other world—which Alfonso X had caused to be translated into Castilian, and then into the two languages of the surviving versions. Cerulli's exhaustive researches, published as part of his edition of this text, have thrown light on its fortunes and provide documentary proofs that it was known (and by this we mean more or less directly and completely) in fourteenth-century Italy, and even by followers and imitators of Dante—the *Liber scalae* is mentioned expressly under the Italian title *Libro della scala* by the

Tuscan poet Fazio degli Uberti in his *Dittamondo* and under the Arabic title *Helmaerich* (= *al-Mi'rāj*) by a fifteenth-century Franciscan preacher. With the discovery of this text and of its migration across the Pyrenees and the Alps, the obstacle of the missing link was removed, and we can now disregard the authors of learned works like Abu'l-'Alā' and Ibn al-'Arabī and concentrate our attention on this vein of popular Muslim piety, which Asín Palacios mentioned, though he was unable to produce any evidence of a contact between it and the age and background of Dante. It would now seem to be at least possible, if not probable, that Dante may have known the *Liber scalae* and have taken from it certain images and concepts of Muslim eschatology, thus providing confirmation of Asín Palacios's bold theory. But the function which this presumed knowledge played in the conception and execution of his poem, the manner of his absorption and utilization of these Muslim elements, and their share in the prevailing spirit and tone of his masterpiece, are a very different matter.

In this very delicate field of research, which has to be conducted with due regard for what we know from other sources of Dante's notions of Islamic religion, science and culture, the conclusions drawn by Cerulli and others who accept the new factual elements provided by the *Liber scalae* are extremely cautious. Any data which the poet may have culled through this channel from Muslim eschatological beliefs constitute only one element, a limited portion of his intellectual and cultural preparation, and are of secondary importance compared with the essential elements he drew from the Classical world and the Christian Bible. Moreover, these Islamic elements were inserted and interpreted in his poem in a spirit very different from that of their source—in the spirit of medieval Christendom. Such conclusions, very different from those reached by Asín Palacios in his eagerness to prove his case, and stressed even more forcibly by some of his followers after the discovery of the *Liber scalae*, are curiously close to those of the more discreet supporters of the 'Arab theory' regarding the influence of Islam on Romance lyric verse. In both cases there would seem to have been a utilization of motifs, notions and concepts of Arab-Islamic origin, but these, in the case of Romance poetry, were interpreted by a whole nascent civilization and culture, and in Dante's, by the great individual soul of one poet, in a different spirit and in harmony with a new and different tradition.

To sum up, Dante, notwithstanding the episode of the *Liber scalae*, cannot have known any more about Islam, its literature and civilization, than the average Italian of his day. Did Petrarch, that other great Tuscan who left his mark on the poetry and doctrines of the fourteenth century, know more? A minor nineteenth-century Italian Arabist, P. Valerga, also believed that he could establish some sort of connexion—of ideas, if not of imitation—between the poems of Petrarch and certain aspects of Arabic love-lyrics.[1] But the Arabic poems which he compared with the *Canzoniere* were not songs of earthly love, like those of the poet Jamīl al-'Udhrī or of 'Abbās b. al-Aḥnaf, the 'minstrel of Baghdād', but those of 'Umar b. al-Fāriḍ (d. 633/1235), the leading exponent of mystical poetry in Arabic, in which the poetical form clothes and gives allegorical expression to experiences and passions of divine love. Although, from the strictly aesthetic point of view, even an allegorical poem ought to be judged by the perfection and efficacy of its form, it is obvious that no opinion can be formed nor comparisons made on a cultural and historical basis without having at least some knowledge that one of the two objects compared had an allegorical significance. Valerga knew nothing of this essential characteristic in Ibn al-Fāriḍ and consequently ignored it, so that the parallels he draws between the Arab and the Italian fall to the ground. The former was in reality a religious soul burning with mystical zeal, while the latter was bound to this earth and to mundane emotions, the conflict between these and the call of Heaven being one of the most moving aspects of his poetry.

Another thing that Valerga did not know was that the first person to be astonished and aggrieved by these gratuitous comparisons with the Arabs would have been Petrarch himself. It would seem that he, unlike Dante, really knew something about Arabic poetry, which, if we are to believe what he says in a curious passage in one of his epistles, he did not like at all.[2] Writing to a friend who was a physician, he says: 'Arabes vero quales medici, tu scis. Quales autem poetae, scio ego: nihil blandius, nihil mollius, nihil enervatius, nihil denique turpius. Vix mihi persuadebitur ab Arabia posse aliquid boni esse.' Since Petrarch could not have read the originals, we must suppose that he had seen some samples of Arabic verse translated for his benefit into Latin or Italian by some returned traveller or missionary who knew the language. In the same way, though for a very different reason, Petrarch tried to learn

[1] P. Valerga, *Il Divano di Omar ben al-Fared tradotto e paragonato al canzoniere del Petrarca* (Florence, 1874). It should be noted that Valerga confined his study to the minor odes of Ibn al-Fāriḍ and did not include the great *Tā'iyya*.

[2] *Epistole Senili*, XII, 2.

something of the poetry of Homer through translations. But to what category of Arabic poets was he referring? We are bound to think that it was either Ibn al-Fāriḍ himself (whose personal qualities as an artist, in defiance of general opinion, we do not rate very high) or some later Syrian or Egyptian poet of the Ayyubid or Mamluk period, for example Bahā' al-Dīn Zuhayr or Ibn Sanā' al-Mulk, with their re-hashes of old motifs. Ignorance of the language would have made it impossible for him to judge the form, and in this case the author of the *Canzoniere* can only have been acquainted with Latin or Italian renderings of images which to him must have seemed clumsy and grotesque—images of languishing bedouin love or laudatory baroque hyperbole. Consequently, while some influence of Arabic poetry on the origins of Italian vernacular verse, at least as regards form, could, as we have seen, have existed, this fleeting contact between the Arabic muse and one of the greatest figures of the Tuscan Parnassus remained completely sterile—a case of disappointed curiosity.

The Renaissance and afterwards

At the time of the Renaissance, Islam was a political and religious factor, not a literary problem. The revival in Europe of the cult of Classical Antiquity and the drying up about the same time of the creative genius of Islamic civilization helped to make the period from the fifteenth to the seventeenth century one of the poorest as regards literary contacts between East and West. Ciriaco of Ancona toured the Levant with his eyes fixed only on relics of antiquity, and even Pietro Della Valle, who took such a keen interest in the contemporary Islamic East which he visited, seems to have been hardly aware of its high level of literary culture in Arabic, Persian and Turkish. Not until the advent in the eighteenth century of the Enlightenment and cosmopolitanism did Europe show in the world of Islam an interest not merely political and religious, but also spiritual, sentimental and aesthetic. In the early years of the eighteenth century, almost as a symbol of this new attitude, the *Thousand and one nights*, in Galland's French translation, made their triumphal entry into European culture.

The history of this famous collection of tales reflects in its formation and fortunes an almost stratigraphic succession of cultures in both East and West. Late medieval Egypt had given a more or less definite form to this corpus of narrative, containing, as is known, ingredients of

Indian, Persian and Arab origin, from ʿAbbasid ʿIrāq and from the Egypt of the Mamluks. Muslim Spain also made its contribution (the story of the slave-girl Tawaddud, who in Spanish became the learned damsel Teodor) and transmitted individual themes and incidents from the *Arabian nights* to Castilian literature. But in Galland's incomplete translation, based on material of Oriental origin, this composite medley of stories and folklore of the East with its Arab-Islamic patina acquired full citizenship in the Europe of the Enlightenment. In the course of the same century, Galland's pioneer efforts were continued and imitated, e.g. in the *Mille et un jours* by Pétis de la Croix, and the *Veillées du Sultan Chahriyar* by Chavis and Cazotte; and the early nineteenth century, with the English translation by Edward Lane and the German version by Hammer-Purgstall and Weil, was able to present readers, whether cultured or not, with the whole corpus of the by then famous collection of stories, which for several generations was their chief, or only, introduction to the East.

But even during the latter half of the eighteenth century, the more cultured classes of Europe were offered a broader view of the Muslim East. In addition to the Arab world, which for the medieval West had been the sole representative of Islam, and that of Ottoman Turkey, which had found its way in during the Renaissance, Persia was discovered towards the end of the eighteenth century as a source of literature and culture. As early as the seventeenth century, Olearius had made the *Gulistān* of Saʿdī known to the Germans. In the following century and the early years of the nineteenth, Anquetil Duperron revealed the religion and the sacred texts of the *Avesta,* while Ḥāfiẓ, Firdawsī and the other great poets of Islamic Persia began to be known and appreciated in Europe. To the Europe of the Enlightenment and Romanticism, Persia thus displayed the double aspect of its ancient national religion and civilization and its Islamic phase, in which many scholars have tried to discern the survival of characteristics peculiar to Aryan Iran. To the colourful and fabulous, but in reality shallow and at times puerile, world of the *Thousand and one nights,* which for many, together with the newly accessible Qur'ān (Sale's English translation appeared in 1734), represented the sum of Arabic literature, there were thus added the exquisite flowers of the lyrical, epic and gnomic poetry of Muslim Persia, till then unknown to the West. This new literary harvest from Persia was soon to be supplemented by the discovery of the poetry and wisdom of India. The ethnic and linguistic links between India and

Persia had already been perceived at that time, but were overrated, to the detriment of the historical and religious differences. All these new Eastern literatures joined the choir of the 'voices of the nations' re-echoed by Herder, in the garland of that *Weltliteratur* which was Goethe's dream. Such was this 'Oriental Renaissance', as Schwab calls it, which is one of the most complex and fascinating features in European culture from the late eighteenth to the twentieth century.

Goethe's *West-Östlicher Divan* (first published in 1819), the most illustrious fruit of this new European attitude of curiosity and sympathy for the East, and in particular the Muslim world, was a phase in his versatile experience and gave the German language and German culture the leading place in this field, a place which Germany was destined to retain throughout the nineteenth century. The East in which Goethe sought refuge, with the aid of translations, but above all on the wings of fancy and wisdom, was the East of the Arab-Persian Middle Ages, in which the literary and gnomic Persian element played a leading part. Of the Arab world, in which the figure of the Prophet himself had already attracted Goethe—and to this we owe the magnificent lyric *Mahomet's Gesang,* a fragment of a projected drama—there are but few traces in the *Divan,* but there are more in the accompanying *Noten und Abhandlungen,* among them a forceful translation of Ta'abbaṭa Sharran's 'song of vengeance'. Pride of place is given to the Persia of Ḥāfiẓ and Sa'dī, of sultans and dervishes, of Suleika-Willemer and Hatem-Goethe, because, it is hardly necessary to say, the poetry of the *Divan* is not an antiquary's evocation, but a continuation in an orientalized form of that great autobiographical *Bekenntnis* which the whole of Goethe's work represents. What interests us here is the Oriental dress, a striking testimony to the poet's widespread intellectual interests and to a whole trend in European science and culture. In those same years during which the aged Goethe was assimilating and remoulding the lyrico-gnomic world of medieval Islam, a young man who died at an early age, Wilhelm Hauff (1802–27), was absorbing the Muslim art of storytelling and imitating it in his *Märchen,* which, inspired by the world of the Arabian Nights, are the most colourful echo of them produced by the Romantic movement, and from the artistic point of view are often superior to their models. The fame of Goethe and the fortunes of Hauff marked the entry of the Muslim East into German literature, and though Hauff knew no Arabic or Persian and Goethe contented himself with a superficial attempt—little more than a game—to learn these languages, other poets interested in the

East, like Platen and Rückert, with the inspiration and virtuosity of artists, based their *Nachdichtungen* on a direct acquaintance with the originals—Platen in his *Abbasiden* and the exquisite *Ghaselen* and likewise Rückert in his *Östliche Rosen*, his translations from the *Ḥamāsa*, from al-Ḥarīrī and Firdawsī, and above all his *Morgenländische Sagen und Geschichten*, do not merely re-echo Eastern motifs, but reveal a direct knowledge of the original texts in which they sought inspiration. The Muslim East thus remained a favourite motif in German literature throughout the nineteenth century—from genuine poets like Heine (*Der Asra, Firdusi, Almanzor*) to pleasing rhymesters like Bodenstedt (*Die Lieder des Mirza Schaffy*) and gifted dilettanti like A. von Schack, who used his literary talent to further the cause of Oriental poetry (*Poesie und Kunst der Araber in Spanien und Sizilien*). During the last decades of the nineteenth century, scholarship gradually suffocated this form of poetical evocation, and, as the world of Islam became in Germany the subject of ever more thorough scientific study by Nöldeke, Wellhausen, Goldziher, Brockelmann and others, the roses of this artistic *Nachdichtung* withered. In the troubled days of the twentieth century, Semitic philology, Iranistics and *Islamkunde* have blocked the way to any approach to the East which is not of a strictly scientific, political or journalistic nature.

Literary France, like Germany, had its Oriental phase during the nineteenth century. Heralded by the interest of men of the Enlightenment, such as Boulainvilliers and Voltaire, in Islam and its founder, by the success of the translations of the Arabian Nights published by Galland and his followers, and by the great scientific work of a scholar like Sylvestre de Sacy, the Arab-Persian-Turkish world was appropriated as an integral part of the patrimony of Romanticism. The French pendant to the *West-Östlicher Divan* was Victor Hugo's *Les Orientales* (1829), published just after the Greek rising and on the eve of the Algerian expedition. But unlike Goethe's *Divan*, which is a poetical meditation on mankind and the universe based on Oriental notions, and on what one might almost call 'pretexts', Victor Hugo's little book was more than anything else a colourful fresco of the Levant and the Maghrib of those days, of the splendours and horrors of the tottering Ottoman empire, and of that African colouring which a few years later was to inspire the brush of Delacroix. Interesting, for the light they throw on the author's tastes and his knowledge of Eastern matters, are the notes, a reflection, filtered through Hugo's sensibility, of opinions on Islamic poetry and history current in France during the early nineteenth century. Islamic motifs are also to be found in *La Légende des Siècles* (*L'an neuf de l'Hégire, Mahomet, Les trônes d'Orient*), and again in that Parnassian 'légende des siècles', the *Poèmes* of Leconte de Lisle (*L'apothéose de Mouça-al-Kébyr, Le suaire d'al-Mançour*), but between the youthful Hugo and Leconte de Lisle lies the whole generation of the Romantics, who sought, in a more or less conventionalized East, sensations, experiences and colouring —from the Chateaubriand of the *Itinéraire* and the *Abencérages* to Lamartine, the revealer of the story of 'Antar and of the beauties of Lebanon, to the Flaubert of the letters from the East and the Gobineau of the *Nouvelles asiatiques*, whose aesthetic admiration for the East was coupled with an ideological contempt for its civilizations. Notwithstanding the scientific pretensions of this theoretician of the *Inégalité des races humaines*, the link between Oriental scholarship and literature seems to have been less close in France than it was in Germany, and none of the poets and men of letters we have just mentioned, or of the many others who could be added to the list, can be said to have been himself an orientalist. But thanks to that more rapid circulation of knowledge which is so characteristic of France, these literary roses were nourished by the contemporary labours of the specialists and by their talent for vulgarization. For this reason, the gap, in this field too, between science, art and general knowledge, was narrower in France than elsewhere. The end of the nineteenth century and the early years of the twentieth witnessed an increase in the output of exotic literature and books on travel, e.g. by Pierre Loti, Maurice Barrès, as well as a revival of the vogue for the East, thanks to the translation of the *Thousand and one nights* published by J. C. Mardrus (1899–1904)—fair and faithless indeed, since in conformity with the decadent taste of the time it presented the Muslim East under a refined and precious guise reminiscent of theatrical scenery and the ballet (Bakst's *Scheherazade*) or of Dulac's illustrations.

In Britain, which, like Holland, had had a pioneer role in the modern study of the Arab-Islamic world (we need only recall the names of Pococke, Ockley and Sale), criticism of the old Arabic poetry was inaugurated by William Jones (1746–94), author of the first translation of the *Mu'allaqāt*, which Goethe, among others, found useful. But side by side with this serious approach to real Arabism, English poetry and narrative were swamped by conventionalized travesties of Islamic civilization like Beckford's fantastic but very successful *Vathek* (1786) and, during the Romantic period, certain works of Byron (*The Giaour*, 1813) and Thomas Moore (*Lalla Rookh*, 1817). The *Thousand and one nights*—that barometer of interest in the East in every European country —was translated into English three times in the course of the nineteenth century, by Lane (1839–42), Payne (1882–4) and Burton (1885), the last-named version being the most famous of all on account of its literary quality and abundance of notes. But the most fertile encounter between English literature and the Islamic East was in Persian rather than in Arabic, since the higher aesthetic values of Persian literature had the same fascination for Anglo-Saxons that they had for German culture. That mysterious Asia which as early as 1816 had inspired Coleridge's *Kubla Khan* was revealed by Firdawsī's great epic to Matthew Arnold (*Sohrab and Rustum*, 1853), and by Jāmī, 'Aṭṭār and above all 'Umar Khayyām to Edward Fitzgerald. Every student of English literature knows the extraordinary vicissitudes of this Persian scholar-poet of the eleventh-twelfth centuries, who enjoyed what was practically a second life in Britain and America after the publication in 1859 of the Victorian poet's exquisite and artistic re-interpretation. Ever since that time there has been controversy as to the truthfulness of Fitzgerald's rendering of 'Umar Khayyām. Here we must confine ourselves to the statement that the Persian *Rubā'iyyāt* attributed with more or less certainty to 'Umar provided inspiration in the nineteenth century for a great English poem in the same metrical form—a phenomenon which was not repeated to the same degree in any subsequent translation of 'Umar in the various European languages. To this we would like to add that, according to the most competent judges in Oriental matters—whose opinion we share—Fitzgerald managed to grasp and transmit in a substantially faithful manner one essential aspect of the ambiguous original—that pessimistic and at the same time hedonistic mood which is the most characteristic feature in 'Umar's physiognomy, even if he gave to his interpretation a coherence lacking in the original. This contact with the Eastern world established by Fitzgerald in a work of pure literature was developed during the nineteenth and twentieth centuries in a series of brilliant works by British Oriental scholars and travellers, such as E. G. Browne, R. A. Nicholson, A. J. Arberry and Gertrude Bell, some of whom also turned their attention to Arabic, for example Nicholson, who among other things studied the 'Arab Khayyām', Abu'l-'Alā' al-Ma'arrī. The Arab world attracted the British to an equal degree with its past and present problems, as can be seen in classics of travel like Kinglake's *Eothen*, Doughty's *Travels in Arabia Deserta*, books on customs (Lane's *Manners and customs of the modern Egyptians* or politics and war (T. E. Lawrence's *Revolt in the desert* and *Seven pillars of wisdom*).

The scarcity of material and our own shortcomings prevent us from adding more than an even briefer summary regarding other countries and literatures. In Spain, the scholarly study of Islamic civilization and its influence on literature was naturally bound up with that of Arabism, as a basic factor of national history and culture in the Iberian peninsula. In more recent times, and in our own, it would perhaps be more correct to speak of an increasing interest in the 'Arab problem' in historiography and journalism; above all of the different values assigned to the old Islamic factor in the sociological and historical fields by students of *hispanidad*, e.g. A. Castro, Cl. Sanchez Albornoz. In another Latin country, Italy, which was also for a time partially occupied and frequently raided by the Arabs, we find, on a smaller scale, the same problem. In so far as this problem concerns Sicily, it has already been dealt with in the historical writings of Michele Amari (1806–88), while from the standpoint of literary history and linguistics there is today a revival of interest among Arabic and Romance scholars. But when we pass from this well-defined historical field to the general influence of the Muslim East on Italian literature and modern Italian thought, there seem to be few signs of interest, despite, or perhaps because of, the rigorously scientific tradition of Italian Arabic scholarship. By this we mean that, contrary to what has been the case in other countries, in Italy the scientific study of Islam, of its literary history and civilization, has been the jealously guarded preserve of a small group of scholars. It has hardly ever penetrated into the living literature and culture of the country, this being in contrast to what has happened in other fields of orientalism such as Indology. An exception is to be found in the work of the Iranist Italo Pizzi (1849–1920), translator of the *Shāh-nāma,* who with an enthusiasm more laudable than his talent as an artist tried to popularize in Italy the 'flowers of the East', to quote the title of one of his anthologies. In our own days Pizzi's example has been followed with a more delicate feeling for literary values and a keener historical sense by the living Iranist, A. Bausani.

Before concluding this brief review of the literary impact of Islam on the modern West, there is one general observation which concerns the whole trend of these influences exchanged between the two worlds, for long enemies but each complementary to the other. Whereas during the Middle Ages the trend was almost entirely from East to West, in modern times the direction of influence has been reversed. Europe still continues to seek inspiration and ideas in the East, but these are almost invariably confined to the spheres of landscape and customs (in so far as the East still has customs of its own that can be contrasted with those of Europe), or to the spiritual heritage of the past, when Islam acted as the teacher of the West. Now that this active role of Islam has been eliminated by the paralysis that began in the Middle Ages, the Muslim East, which renewed its contacts with Europe in the nineteenth century, no longer has original elements to transmit; on the contrary, it is the East which now absorbs the myths, the political ideologies and the literary theories of the West.

THE UMAYYADS OF SPAIN

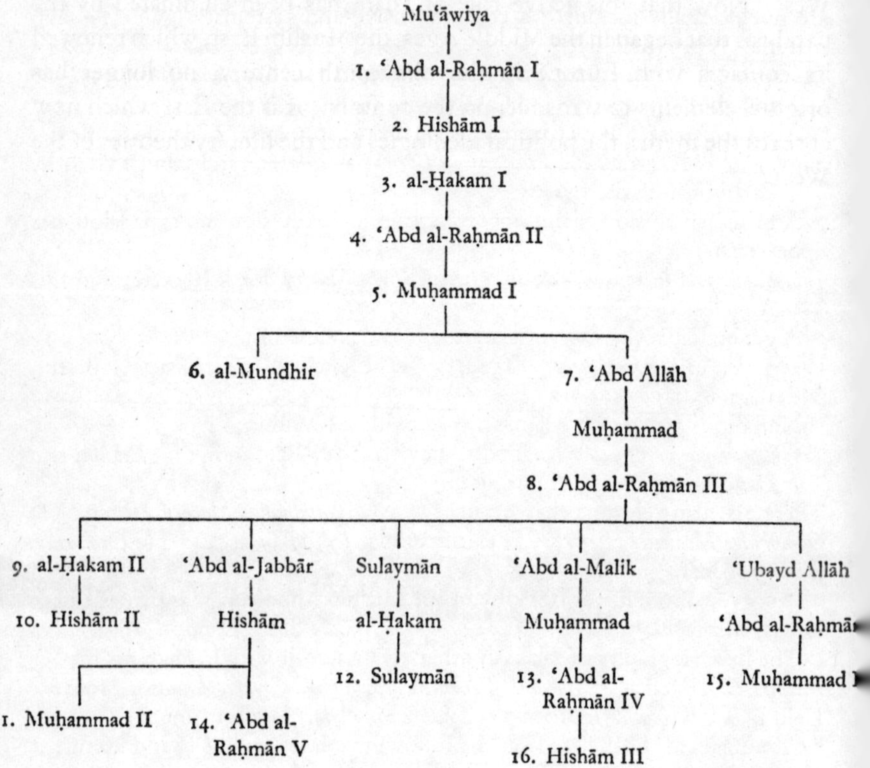
Mu'āwiya
1. 'Abd al-Raḥmān I
2. Hishām I
3. al-Ḥakam I
4. 'Abd al-Raḥmān II
5. Muḥammad I
6. al-Mundhir
7. 'Abd Allāh
Muḥammad
8. 'Abd al-Raḥmān III
9. al-Ḥakam II
'Abd al-Jabbār
Sulaymān
'Abd al-Malik
'Ubayd Allāh
10. Hishām II
Hishām
al-Ḥakam
Muḥammad
'Abd al-Raḥmā
12. Sulaymān
13. 'Abd al-Raḥmān IV
15. Muḥammad
11. Muḥammad II
14. 'Abd al-Raḥmān V
16. Hishām III

BIBLIOGRAPHY

The following book-lists are intended as a guide to further reading, and consist almost entirely of secondary sources in the principal European languages. Articles in learned journals, *Festschriften* and other collective works of the kind are not normally included; a comprehensive and systematic guide to such materials is provided by:

Pearson, J. D. *Index Islamicus 1906–55*, with its two *Supplements* for 1956–60 and 1961–5 respectively. Cambridge, 1958, 1962, 1966.

An indispensable work of reference on the bibliography of Islamic studies is:

Sauvaget, J. *Introduction à l'histoire de l'orient musulman.* 2nd edn. revised by Cahen, Cl. Paris, 1961.

An English version of this, incorporating some revision and expansion, has appeared as:

Jean Sauvaget's Introduction to the History of the Muslim East. Berkeley and Los Angeles, 1965.

A general introduction to Islamic studies is offered by:

Pareja, F. M. *Islamologia.* Rome, 1951. French edn., *Islamologie,* Beirut, 1957–63.

Numerous articles on Islamic history will be found in:

The Encyclopaedia of Islam. 1st edn. Leiden, 1913–42. 2nd edn. Leiden and London, 1960– (in progress).

There are also relevant chapters in *The New Cambridge Modern History, The Cambridge Medieval History, The Cambridge History of India,* and *The Cambridge History of Iran.*

A survey of the historiography of the Muslim Middle East is provided by:

Lewis, B. and Holt, P. M. *Historians of the Middle East.* London, 1962.

The historiography of Islam in other areas is dealt with in chapters in:

Philips, C. H. (ed.). *Historians of India, Pakistan and Ceylon.* London, 1961.

Hall, D. G. E. (ed.). *Historians of South East Asia.* London, 1962.

Amongst aids to the student, the following atlases will be found useful:

Hazard, H. W. *Atlas of Islamic History.* 3rd edn. Princeton, 1954.

Roolvink, R. *Historical Atlas of the Muslim Peoples.* Amsterdam, 1957.

Atlas of the Arab World amd the Middle East. Macmillan; London, 1960.

Oxford Regional Economic Atlas: The Middle East and North Africa. Oxford University Press; London, 1960.

Genealogical and dynastic lists and tables are given by:

Lane-Poole, S. *The Mohammadan Dynasties.* Paris, 1925.

Zambaur, E. de. *Manuel de généalogie et de chronologie pour l'histoire de l'Islam.* Hanover, 1927.

The following works are of basic importance to the student of Islamic history, society and institutions. They have in different ways contributed to the corpus of knowledge about Islam, to its interpretation and understanding, and to the development of methods of research and investigation.

Becker, C. H. *Islamstudien.* Leipzig, 1924–32.

Gibb, H. A. R. *Modern Trends in Islam*. Chicago, 1947.
—— *Mohammedanism: An Historical Survey*. London, 1949.
—— *Studies in the Civilization of Islam*. Ed. Shaw, S. J. and Polk, W. R. Chicago, 1962.
Goitein, S. D. *A Mediterranean Society*. Vol. I. Berkeley and Los Angeles, 1967.
Goldziher, I. *Muhammedanische Studien*. Halle, 1889–90; Hildesheim 1961. Eng. tr. of Vol. I, ed. S. M. Stern, *Muslim Studies*. London, 1967.
—— *Vorlesungen über den Islam*. 1st edn. Heidelberg, 1910. (French tr. by Arin, F. *Le dogme et la loi de l'Islam*. Paris, 1920.)
Grunebaum, G. E. von. *Medieval Islam: A Study in Cultural Orientation*. 2nd. edn. Chicago, 1953.
—— *Islam: Essays in the Nature and Growth of a Cultural Tradition*. London, 1955.
Hurgronje, C. S. *Verspreide geschriften*. Bonn, Leipzig, Leiden, 1923–7.
—— *Selected Works*. Ed. Bousquet, G.-H. and Schacht, J. Leiden, 1957.
Macdonald, D. B. *Development of Muslim Theology, Jurisprudence and Constitutional Theory*. New York, 1903; Beirut, 1964.
—— *The Religious Attitude and Life in Islam*. Chicago, 1906; repr. Beirut, 1965.
Schacht, J. *The Origins of Muhammadan Jurisprudence*. Oxford, 1950.
Wellhausen, J. *Skizzen und Vorarbeiten*. Berlin, 1884–99.

The Indian Sub-continent

A History of the Freedom Movement. Karachi, 1957–61.
Aga Khan. *The Memoirs of Aga Khan*. London, 1954.
Ahmad, A. *Studies in Islamic Culture in the Indian Environment*. Oxford, 1964.
Ahmed, Jamil-ud-Din. *Speeches and Writings of Mr. Jinnah*. Lahore, 1960.
Ali, M. (ed. Iqbal, A.). *My Life: A Fragment*. Lahore, 1946.
—— (ed. Iqbal, A.). *Select Writings and Speeches of Maulana Mohamed Ali*. Lahore, 1944.
Ambedkar, B. R. *Pakistan, or the Partition of India*. Bombay, 1946.
Ayub Khan, M. *Friends Not Masters*. London, 1967.
Azad, A. K. *India Wins Freedom*. Calcutta, 1959.
Baljon, J. M. S. *The Reforms and Religious Ideas of Sir Sayyid Aḥmad Khān*. Leiden, 1949.
Bazaz, P. N. *A History of Struggle for Freedom in Kashmir*. Delhi, 1954.
Bolitho, H. *Jinnah, Creator of Pakistan*. London, 1954.
Brown, P. *Indian Painting under the Mughals*. Oxford, 1924.
Callard, K. *Pakistan; A Political Study*. London, 1957.
Chand, T. *Influence of Islam on Indian Culture*. Allahabad, 1943–6.
Chandra, S. *Parties and Politics at the Mughal Court, 1707–1740*. Aligarh, 1959.
Chandra, T. *Society and State in the Mughal Period*. Delhi, 1961.
Coupland, R. *The Indian Problem 1833–1935*. Oxford, 1942–3.
Das, M. N. *Indian under Morley and Minto*. London, 1964.
Edwardes, M. *British India, 1772–1947*. London, 1967.
Erskine, W. *A History of India Under the First Two Sovereigns of the House of Taimur*. London, 1854.

Faruqi, Z. H. *The Deoband School and the Demand for Pakistan*. Bombay, 1963.
Feldman, H. *Revolution in Pakistan*. London, 1967.
Gopal, R. *Indian Muslims. A Political History, 1858–1947*. Bombay, 1959.
Gopal, S. *British Policy in India, 1858–1905*. Cambridge, 1965.
Graham, G. F. I. *The Life and Work of Sir Syed Ahmed Khan*. London, 1885.
Gwyer, M. and Appadorai, A. *Speeches and Documents on the Indian Constitution, 1921–47*. Bombay, 1957.
Habib, I. *The Agrarian System of Mughal India, 1556–1707*. London, 1963.
Hodivala, S. H. *Studies in Indo-Muslim History*. Bombay, 1939, 1957.
Hunter, W. W. *The Indian Musalmans*. London, 1871.
Husain, S. A. *The Destiny of Indian Muslims*. London, 1965.
Husain, Y. *Medieval Indian Culture*. Bombay, 1957.
Ibn Hasan. *Central Structure of the Mughal Empire*. London, 1936.
Ikram, S. M. *History of Muslim Civilization in India and Pakistan*. Lahore, 1961.
—— *Modern Muslim India and the Birth of Pakistan, 1858–1951*. 2nd edn. Lahore, 1965.
—— and Spear, P. *The cultural heritage of Pakistan*. Karachi, 1955.
Kabir, H. *Muslim politics, 1906–1942*. Calcutta, 1944.
Khan, M. A. *History of the Fara'idi Movement in Bengal*. Karachi, 1965.
Korbel, J. *Danger in Kashmir*. Princeton, 1954.
Majumdar, R. C. (ed.). *The Delhi Sultanate*. Bombay, 1960.
Mallick, A. R. *British Policy and the Muslims in Bengal, 1757–1856*. Dacca, 1961.
Menon, V. P. *The Transfer of Power in India*. Bombay, 1957.
Misra, B. B. *The Indian Middle Classes*. London, 1961.
Moreland, W. H. *The Agrarian System of Moslem India*. Cambridge, 1929.
Mosley, L. *Last Days of the British Raj*. London, 1961.
Mujeeb, M. *The Indian Muslims*. London, 1967.
Palmer, J. A. B. *The Mutiny Outbreak at Meerut in 1857*. Cambridge, 1966.
Philips, C. H. *India*. London, 1949–8.
—— (ed.). *The evolution of India and Pakistan, 1858 to 1947*. London, 1962.
—— (ed.). *Politics and Society in India*. London, 1963.
Prasad, B. *History of Jahangir*. 5th edn. Allahabad, 1962.
Prasad, I. *The Life and Times of Humayun*. Bombay, 1955.
Prasad, R. *India Divided*. Bombay, 1947.
Qureshi, I. H. *The Administration of the Sultanate of Dehlī*. 4th edn. Karachi, 1958.
—— *The Muslim Community of the Indo-Pakistan Subcontinent, 610–1947*. The Hague, 1962.
—— *The Struggle for Pakistan*. Karachi, 1965.
Rizvi, S. A. A. *Muslim Revivalist Movements in Northern India in the Sixteenth and Seventeenth Centuries*. Agra, 1965.
—— and Bhargava, M. L. (ed.). *Freedom Struggle in Uttar Pradesh: source material*. Lucknow, 1957–61.
Saksena, B. P. *History of Shahjehan of Dihli*. Allahabad, 1932.
Sarkar, J. N. *History of Aurangzib*. Calcutta, 1912–24.
—— *Shivaji and His Times*. 2nd edn. London, 1920.

Sarkar, J. N. *Fall of the Mughal Empire*. Calcutta, 1932–4.
Sayeed, K. B. *Pakistan the Formative Phase*. Karachi, 1960.
Sharma, S. R. *Mughal Government and Administration*. Bombay, 1951.
Smith, D. E. *India as a Secular State*. Princeton, 1963.
Smith, V. A. *Akbar, the Great Mogul, 1542–1605*, 2nd edn. Oxford, 1927.
Smith, W. C. *Modern Islam in India*. London, 1946.
Stephens, I. *Pakistan*. London, 1963.
Symonds, R. *The Making of Pakistan*. London, 1950.
Tinker, H. R. *India and Pakistan: A Political Analysis*. 2nd edn. London, 1967.
Tripathi, R. P. *Some Aspects of Muslim Administration*. Allahabad, 1936.
Williams, L. F. R. *The State of Pakistan*. 2nd edn. London, 1966.

South-East Asia

Al-Attas, Sayyid Naguib. *Some Aspects of Sufism as Understood and Practised among the Malays*. Singapore, 1963.
Arnold, T. W. *The Preaching of Islam*. 2nd edn. London, 1913.
Benda, H. J. *The Crescent and the Rising Sun: Indonesian Islam Under the Japanese Occupation, 1942–1945*. The Hague and Bandung, 1958.
Berg, L. W. C. van den. *Le Hadhramout et les colonies arabes dans l'Archipel indien*. Batavia, 1886.
Bousquet, G.-H. *La politique musulmane et coloniale des Pays-Bas*. Paris, 1938.
Burger, D. H. *Structural Changes in Javanese Society: The Supra-village Sphere*. Ithaca, N.Y., 1956.
Drews, G. W. J. 'Indonesia: mysticism and activism', in Grunebaum, G. E. von. (ed.). *Unity and variety in Muslim civilization*. Chicago, 1955.
Geertz, C. *The Religion of Java*. Glencoe, Ill., 1960.
Gullick, J. M. *Indigenous Political Systems of Western Malaya*. London, 1958.
Hurgronje, C. S. *The Achehnese*. Leiden, 1906.
—— *Verspreide geschriften*. Vol. IV, Parts 1, 2. Bonn, Leipzig and Leiden, 1924–6.
—— *Mekka in the Latter Part of the 19th Century*. Leiden and London, 1931.
Itagaki, Y. 'Some aspects of the Japanese policy for Malaya under the occupation, with special reference to nationalism', in Tregonning, K. G. (ed.). *Papers on Malayan History*. Singapore, 1962.
Jay, R. R. *Religion and Politics in Rural Central Java*. New Haven, 1963.
Niel, R. van. *The Emergence of the Modern Indonesian elite*. The Hague and Bandung, 1960.
Nieuwenhuijze, C. A. O. van. *Aspects of Islam in Post-Colonial Indonesia*. The Hague and Bandung, 1958.
Pijper, G. F. *Islam and the Netherlands*. Leiden, 1957.
Roff, W. R. 'Kaum Muda—Kaum Tua: innovation and reaction amongst the Malays, 1900–1941', in Tregonning, K. G. (ed.). *Papers on Malayan History*. Singapore, 1962.
—— *The Origins of Malay Nationalism*. London and New Haven, 1967.
Schrieke, B. J. O. *Indonesian Sociological Studies: Selected Writings of B. Schrieke*. The Hague and Bandung, 1955.

Wertheim, W. F. *Indonesian Society in Transition: A Study of Social Change*. 2nd edn. The Hague and Bandung, 1959.
Wilkinson, R. J. *Malay Beliefs*. London and Leiden, 1906. (Republished as 'Malay customs and beliefs', in *Journal of the Royal Asiatic Society, Malayan Branch*, xxx, 1957).
—— and Winstedt, R. O. *Papers on Malay Subjects: Malay Literature*. Kuala Lumpur, 1907.
—— and Rigby, W. J. *Papers on Malay Subjects: Malay Law*. Kuala Lumpur, 1908.
Winstedt, R. O. *The Malays, a Cultural History*. 6th ed. London, 1961.
Zoetmulder, P. 'L'Islam', in Stöhr, W. and Zoetmulder, P. *Les religions d'Indonesia*. Paris, 1968.

North Africa

Ageron, C. R. *Histoire de l'Algérie contemporaine, 1830–1956*, Paris, 1966.
Ashford, D. E. *Political Change in Morocco*. Princeton, 1961.
Aubin, E. *Le Maroc d'aujourdhui*. Paris, 1904.
Ayache, A. *Le Maroc: bilan d' une colonisation*. Paris, 1956.
Barbour, N. (ed.). *A Survey of North West Africa*. London, 1959.
Behr, E. *The Algerian Problem*. London, 1961.
Bel, A. *Les Benou Ghânya*. Paris, 1903.
—— *La religion musulmane en Berbérie*. Paris, 1938.
Bernard, A. *Le Maroc*. 7th edn. Paris, 1931.
Berque, J. *Le Maghreb entre deux guerres*. Paris, 1962.
—— *Structures sociales du Haut-Atlas*. Paris, 1955.
Boyer, P. *La vie quotidienne à Alger à la veille de l' intervention française*. Paris, 1964.
Braudel, F. *La Méditerranée et le monde méditerranéen à l'époque ce Philippe II*. Paris, 1949.
Brunschvig, R. *La Berbérie orientale sous les Hafsides des origines à la fin du XVe siècle*. Paris, 1940, 1947.
Catroux, G. *Lyautey, le marocain*. Paris, 1952.
Colombe, M. 'L'Algerie turque', *Initiation à l'Algérie*. Paris, 1957.
Corbett, J. S. *England in the Mediterranean (1603–1713)*. London, 1917.
Cour, A. *L'établissement des dynasties des Chérifs au Maroc*. Paris, 1904.
—— *La dynastie marocaine des Beni Wattâs (1420–1554)*. Constantine, 1920.
Debbasch, Y. *La nation française en Tunisie, 1577–1835*. Paris, 1957.
Delmas de Grammont, H. *Histoire d'Alger sous la domination turque (1515–1830)*. Paris, 1887.
Depont, O. and Coppolani, X. *Les confréries religieuses musulmanes*. Algiers, 1897.
Despois, J. *La Tunisie orientale. Sahel et basse steppe*. 2nd edn. Paris, 1955.
—— *La Tunisie: ses régions*. Paris, 1961.
—— *L'Afrique du Nord*. 3rd edn. Paris, 1964.
Deverdun, G. *Marrakech des origines à 1912*. Vol. I. Rabat, 1959.

Dragué, G. *Esquisse d'histoire religieuse de Maroc*. Paris, 1951.
Emerit, M. *L'Algérie à l'époque d'Abd-el-Kader*. Paris, 1951.
Evans-Pritchard, E. E. *The Sanusi of Cyrenaica*. Oxford, 1949.
Favrod, C. H. *Le F.L.N. et l'Algérie*. Paris, 1962.
Fisher, G. *Barbary legend*. Oxford, 1957.
Fitoussie and Benazet, A. *L'état tunisien et le protectorat français*. Paris, 1931.
Fournel, H. *Les Berbères. Etude sur la conquête de l'Afrique par les Arabes d'après les textes arabes imprimés*. Paris, 1875–81.
Ganiage, J. *Les origines du protectorat français en Tunisie, 1861–1881*. Paris, 1959.
Gautier, É.-F. *Le passé de l'Afrique du Nord. Les siècles obscurs*. Paris, 1937.
Golvin, L. *Le Magrib central à l'époque des Zirides*. Paris, 1957.
Grandchamp, P. *La France en Tunisie de la fin du XVIe siècle à 1705*. Tunis, 1920–33.
Hahn, L. *North Africa: Nationalism to Nationhood*. Washington, D.C., 1960.
Huici Miranda, A. *Historia politica del imperio almohade*. Tetuan, 1956–7.
Idris, H. R. *La Berbérie orientale sous les Zīrīdes (Xe–XIIe siècle)*. Paris, 1959.
Julien, C.-A. *Histoire de l'Afrique du Nord (Tunisie, Algérie, Maroc). De la conquête arabe à 1830*. 2nd edn. Paris, 1956.
—— *Histoire de l'Algérie contemporaine I: La conquête et les débuts de la colonization (1827–1871)*. Paris, 1964.
Lacoste, Y., Nouschi, A., Prenant, A. *L'Algérie passé et présent*. Paris, 1960.
Lane-Poole, S. *The Barbary Corsairs*. London, 1890.
Le Coz, J. *Le Rharb, fellahs et colons*. Rabat, 1964.
Leduc, G. and others. *Industrialization de l'Afrique du Nord*. Paris, 1952.
Le Tourneau, R. *Fès avant le protectorat*. Casablanca, 1949.
—— *Fez in the age of the Marinides*. Norman, Oklahoma, 1961.
—— *Évolution politique de l'Afrique du Nord musulmane 1920–1961*. Paris, 1962.
Lévi-Provençal, É. *Les historiens des Chorfa*. Paris, 1922.
Mandouze, A. *La révolution algérienne par les textes*. Paris, 1962.
Marçais, G. *La Berberie musulmane et l'orient au moyen âge*. Paris, 1946.
—— *Les Arabes en Berbérie du XIe au XIVe siècle*. Constantine and Paris, 1913.
—— *Tlemcen*. Paris, 1950.
—— *L'architecture musulmane d'occident. Tunisie, Algérie, Maroc, Espagne, et Sicile*. Paris, 1954.
Marçais, W. 'Comment l'Afrique du Nord a été arabisée', *Articles et conférences*. Paris, 1961.
Massignon, L. *Le Maroc dans les premières années du XVIe siècle*. Algiers, 1906.
Masson, P. *Histoire des établissements et du commerce français dans l'Afrique barbaresque*. Paris, 1903.
Miège, J. L. *Le Maroc et l'Europe, 1830–1894*. Paris, 1961–64.
Monchicourt, Ch. *L'expédition espagnole contre l'île de Djerba*. Paris, 1913.
Montagne, R. *Les Berbères et le Makhzen dans le sud de Maroc*. Paris, 1930.
—— (ed.). *Naissance du prolétariat marocain*. Paris, 1951.

Nouschi, A. *Enquête sur le niveau de vie des populations rurales constantinoises de la conquête jusqu'en 1919*. Paris, 1961.
—— *La naissance du nationalisme algérien*. Paris, 1962.
Pignon, J. 'La Tunisie turque et husséinite', in Basset, A. and others. *Initiation à la Tunisie*. Paris, 1950.
Playfair, R. L. *The Scourge of Christendom: Annals of British Relations with Algiers Prior to the French Conquest*. London, 1884.
Poncet, J. *La colonization et l'agriculture européennes en Tunisie depuis 1881*. Paris, 1962.
Raymond, A. *La Tunisie*. Paris, 1961.
Rézette, R. *Les partis politiques marocains*. Paris, 1955.
Ricard, R. *Études sur l'histoire des Portugais au Maroc*. Coimbra, 1955.
Rinn, L. *Marabouts et Khouan*. Algiers, 1884.
—— *Le royaume d'Alger sous le dernier dey*. Algiers, 1900.
Rossi, E. *Storia di Tripoli e della Tripolitania dalla conquista araba a 1911*. Rome, 1968.
Rousseau, A. *Annales tunisiennes ou aperçu historique de la Régence de Tunis*. Paris-Algiers, 1864.
Sebag, P. *La Tunisie*. Paris, 1951.
Talbi, M. *L'émirat aghlabide 184–296/800–909. Histoire politique*. Paris, 1966.
Terrasse, H. *L'art hispano-mauresque des origines au XIIIe siècle*. Paris, 1932.
—— *Histoire du Maroc des origines à l'établissement du protectorat français*. Casablanca, 1949–50.
Venture de Paradis, J. M. de. *Alger au XVIIIème siècle*. Algiers, 1898.
Vonderheyden, M. *La Berbérie orientale sous la dynastie des Benoû'l-Arlab, 800–909*. Paris, 1927.
Weir, T. H. *The Shaikhs of Morocco in the XVIth Century*. Edinburgh, 1904.
Yacono, X. *Les Bureaux arabes et l'évolution des genres de vie indigènes dans l'ouest du Tell algérois*. Paris, 1953.
—— *La colonization des plaines du Chelif*. Algiers, 1955–6.
Ziadeh, N.A. *Sanūsīyah*. Leiden, 1958.

Trans-Saharan Africa

Abbas, M. *The Sudan Question*. London, 1952.
Abun-Nasr, J. M. *The Tijaniyya*. London, 1965.
Allen, B. M. *Gordon and the Sudan*. London, 1931.
Anderson, J. N. D. *Islamic Law in Africa*. London, 1954.
Ba, A. H. and Daget, J. *L'empire peul du Macina*. Paris, 1962.
Balewa, A. T. *Shaihu Umar*. London, 1967.
Bovill, E. W. *The Golden Trade of the Moors*. 2nd edn. London, 1968.
Collins, R. O. *The Southern Sudan, 1883–1898*. New Haven and London, 1962.
Crawford, O. G. S. *The Fung Kingdom of Sennar*. Gloucester, 1951.
Evans-Pritchard, E. E. *The Sanusi of Cyrenaica*. Oxford, 1949.
Fisher, H. J. *Ahmadiyyah. A Study in Contemporary Islam on the West African Coast*. London, 1963.

Froelich, J.-C. *Les Musulmans d'Afrique noire*. Paris, 1962.
Gray, J. R. *A History of the Southern Sudan, 1839–1889*. London, 1961.
Hasan, Y. F. *The Arabs and the Sudan*. Edinburgh, 1967.
Henderson, K. D. D. *The Making of the Modern Sudan*. London, 1953.
Hill, R. L. *A Biographical Dictionary of the [Anglo-Egyptian] Sudan*. 2nd edn. London, 1967.
—— *Egypt in the Sudan, 1820–1881*. London, 1959.
Hogben, S. J. and Kirk-Greene, A. H. M. *The Emirates of Northern Nigeria*. London, 1966.
Holt, P. M. *The Mahdist State in the Sudan, 1881/1898*. Oxford, 1958.
—— *A Modern History of the Sudan*. 2nd edn. London, 1963.
Klein, M. A. *Islam and Imperialism in Senegal: Sine-Saloum 1847–1914*. Stanford, 1968.
Kritzeck, J. and Lewis, W. H. *Islam in Africa*. Princeton, 1968.
Last, M. *The Sokoto Caliphate*. London, 1967.
Levtzion, N. *Muslims and Chiefs in West Africa: A Study of Islam in the Middle Volta Basin in the Pre-colonial Period*. Oxford, 1968.
Lewis, I. M. *A Pastoral Democracy*. London, 1961.
—— *The Modern History of Somaliland*. London, 1965.
—— (ed.). *Islam in Tropical Africa*. London, 1966.
MacMichael, H. A. *A History of the Arabs in the Sudan*. Cambridge, 1922.
Monteil, V. *L'Islam noir*. Paris, 1964.
Sanderson, G. N. *England, Europe and the Upper Nile, 1882–1899*. Edinburgh 1965.
Smith, M. F. *Baba of Karo: A Woman of the Muslim Hausa*. London, 1954.
Smith, M. G. *Government in Zazzau, 1800–1950*. London, 1960.
Shibeika, M. *British Policy in the Sudan, 1882–1902*. London, 1952.
Theobald, A. B. *'Alī Dīnār, last sultan of Darfur*. London, 1965.
Trimingham, J. S. *Islam in the Sudan*. London, 1949.
—— *Islam in Ethiopia*. London, 1952.
—— *Islam in West Africa*. Oxford, 1959.
—— *The Influence of Islam upon Africa*. London, 1968.

The Iberian Peninsula and Sicily

Amari, M. *Storia dei Musulmani di Sicilia*. Florence, 1854–72. Revised edn. Catania, 1930–9.
Bosch Vilá, J. *Los Almorávides*. Tetuan, 1956.
Cágigas, I. de las. *Los Mozárabes*. Madrid, 1947–48.
Codera y Zaidin, F. *Decadéncia y disparición de los Almorávides en España*. Saragossa, 1899.
—— *Estudios críticos de historia árabe española*. Saragossa-Madrid, 1903–17.
Dozy, R. P. A. *Histoire des musulmans d'Espagne*. 2nd edn. revised by Lévi-Provençal, E. Leiden, 1932.
—— *Recherches sur l'histoire et la littérature des Arabes d'Espagne pendant le moyen âge*. 3rd edn. Leiden, 1881.

Famin, C. *Histoire des invasions des Sarrazins en Italie du VIIe au XIe siècle*. Paris, 1843.
Gabrieli, F. *Aspetti dèlla civiltà arabo-islamica*. Turin, 1956.
Gaspar Remiro, M. *Historia de Murcia musulmana*. Saragossa, 1905.
González Palencia, A. *Historia de la España musulmana*. 4th edn. 1951.
Huici Miranda, A. *Historia política del imperio almohade*. Tetuan, 1956.
—— *Las grandes batallas de la reconquista durante las invasiones africanas. Almorávides, Almohades y Benimerines*. Madrid, 1956.
—— *Estudios de la Edad Media de la corona de Aragón*. 1962.
Lévi-Provençal, E. *L'Espagne musulmane au Xème siècle*. Paris, 1932.
—— *Histoire de l'Espagne musulmane*. 2nd edn. Paris and Leiden, 1950–3.
Menéndez Pidal, R. *La España del Cid*. Madrid, 1956.
Perez de Urbel, J. *Historia del condado de Castilla*. Madrid, 1948.
Pons Boigues, F. *Historiadores y geógrafos arabico-españoles*. Madrid, 1898.
Prieto y Vives, A. *Los reyes de taifas, estúdio histórico-numismatico*. Madrid, 1926.
Primaudie, E. de la. *Arabes et Normands*.
Saavedra, E. *Estudio sobre la invasión de los Árabes en España*. Madrid, 1892.
Watt, W. M. *History of Islamic Spain*. Edinburgh, 1965.

The Geographical Setting

Capot-Rey, R. *Le Sahara français*. Paris, 1953.
Coon, C. S. *Caravan. The Story of the Middle East*. London, 1952.
Despois, J. *L'Afrique du Nord*. 3rd edn. Paris, 1964.
Fisher, W. B. *The Middle East*. 4th edn. London, 1961.
Hogarth, D. G. *The Nearer East*. London, 1902.
Humlum, J. *La géographie de l'Afghanistan*. Copenhagen, 1959.
Montagne, R. *La civilization du désert*. Paris, 1947.
Planhol, X. de. *Le monde islamique: essai de géographie religieuse*. Paris, 1957. Eng. tr. *The World of Islam*. Ithaca, N.Y., 1959.
—— *Les fondements géographiques de l'histoire de l'Islam*. Paris, 1968.
Robequain, C. *Le monde malais*. Paris, 1946.
Spate, O. H. K. *India and Pakistan*. 3rd edn. London, 1967.
Weulersse, J. *Paysans de Syrie et du Proche-Orient*. Paris, 1946.

The Sources of Islamic Civilization

Aubin, H. *Vom Altertum zum Mittelalter. Absterben, Fortleben und Erneuerung*. Munich, 1949.
Bark, W. C. *Origins of the Medieval World*. Stanford, 1958.
Baumstark, A. *Geschichte der syrischen Literatur*. Bonn, 1922.
Bloch, M. 'Pour une histoire comparée des sociétés européennes (1928)', *Mélanges historiques*. Vol. I. Paris, 1963.
Brunschvig, R. and Grunebaum, G. E. von. (ed.). *Classicisme et déclin culturel dans l'histoire de l'Islam*. Paris, 1957.
Carra de Vaux, B. *Les penseurs de l'Islam*. Paris, 1921–26.

Dawson, G. *The Making of Europe*. London, 1932.
Dubler, C. E. 'Das Weiterleben der Antike im Islam', in Wehrli, F. (ed.) *Das Erbe der Antike*. Zurich and Stuttgart, 1963.
Durand, G. *Les structures anthropologiques de l'imaginaire*. Paris, 1963.
Grunebaum, G. E. von. *Kritik und Dichtkunst*. Wiesbaden, 1955.
—— 'Muslim world view and Muslim science', in *Islam: Essays in the Nature and Growth of a Cultural Tradition*. 2nd edn. London, 1961.
—— *Der Islam in Mittelalter*. Zurich and Stuttgart, 1963.
—— *Islam: Experience of the Holy and Concept of Man*. Los Angeles [1965].
Hartmann, L. *Ein Kapitel vom spätantiken und frühmittelalterlichen Staate*. Berlin, 1913.
Laistner, M. L. W. *Christianity and Pagan Culture*. Ithaca and New York, 1957.
Lot, F. *La fin du monde antique et le début du moyen âge*. 2nd edn. Paris, 1951.
Madkour, I. B. *L'Organon d'Aristote dans le monde musulman*. Paris, 1934.
Makdisi, G. *Ibn 'Aqīl et la résurgence de l'Islam traditionaliste au XIe siècle, Ve siècle de l'Hégire*. Damascus, 1963.
Menasce, J. P. de. *Une encyclopédie mazdéenne: le Dēnkart*. Paris, 1958.
Meyerhof, M. *Von Alexandrien nach Bagdad*. Berlin, 1930.
Misch, G. *Geschichte der Autobiographie*. 3rd edn. Vol. II, Part 1. Frankfurt, 1955. Vol. III, Part 2. Frankfurt, 1962.
Momigliano, A. D. (ed.). *The Conflict between Paganism and Christianity in the Fourth Century*. Oxford, 1963.
Moreno, M. M. *Mistica musulmana e mistica indiana*. Vatican City, 1946.
Pellat, C. *Le milieu baṣrien et la formation de Ǧāḥiẓ*. Paris, 1953.
Rahman, Fazlur. *Islamic Methodology in History*. Karachi, 1965.
Rosenthal, F. *Das Fortleben der Antike im Islam*. Zurich and Stuttgart, 1965.
Stein, E. and Palanque, J.-R. *Histoire du Bas-Empire*. Vol. I. Paris, 1959.
Stroheker, K. F. *Germanentum und Spätantike*. Zurich and Stuttgart, 1965.
Tavadia, J. C. *Die mittelpersische Sprache und Literatur der Zarathustrier*. Leipzig, 1956.
Watt, W. M. 'The tribal basis of the Islamic state', in *Dalla tribù allo stato*. Rome, 1962.
Widengren, G. *Mani and Manichaeism*. London, 1965.

Social, Economic and Institutional History

Arnold, T. W. *The Caliphate*. Oxford, 1924.
Ayalon, D. *L'esclavage du mamelouk*. Jerusalem, 1951.
—— *Gunpowder and Firearms in the Mamluk Kingdom*. London, 1956.
Baron, S. W. *A Social and Religious History of the Jews*. Vols. III, IV. New York, 1957.
Coulson, N. J. *A History of Islamic Law*. Edinburgh, 1964.
Dennett, D. C. *Conversion and the Poll-tax in Early Islam*. Cambridge, Mass., 1950.

Fattal, A. *Le statut légal des non-musulmans en pays d'Islam*. Beirut, 1958.
Fries, J. N. *Das Heereswesen der Araber zur Zeit der Omaijaden nach Tabarī*. Tübingen, 1921.
Gardet, L. *La cité musulmane*. 2nd edn. Paris, 1961.
Gaudefroy-Demombynes, M. *Muslim Institutions*. London, 1950.
Gibb, H. A. R. 'The armies of Saladin', in Shaw, S. J. and Polk, W. J. (edd.). *Studies on the civilization of Islam*. Boston, Mass., 1962.
Goitein, S. D. *Studies in Islamic History and Institutions*. Leiden, 1966.
—— *A Mediterranean Society*. Vol. I. Berkeley and Los Angeles, 1967.
Heyd, W. *Histoire du commerce du Levant au moyen-âge*. Paris, 1885; Leipzig, 1923.
Horn, P. *Das Heer- und Kriegswesen des Grossmoghuls*. Leiden, 1894.
Hourani, G. F. *Arab Seafaring in the Indian Ocean in Ancient and Early Medieval Times*. Princeton, 1951.
Irvine, W. *The Army of the Indian Moghuls*. London, 1903; New Delhi, 1962.
Juynboll, T. *Handbuch des islamischen Gesetzes*. Leiden, Leipzig, 1910.
Khadduri, M. *War and Peace in the Law of Islam*. Baltimore, 1955.
Kremer, A. von. *Culturgeschichte des Orients unter den Chalifen*. Vienna, 1875–77. Partial English tr. in Bukhsh, S.K. *The Orient Under the Caliphs*. Calcutta, 1920; *Studies, Indian and Islamic*. London, 1927..
Lambton, A. K. S. *Landlord and Peasant in Persia*. London, 1953.
Lapidus, I. M. *Muslim Cities in the Later Middle Ages*. Cambridge, Mass., 1967.
Le Tourneau, R. *Fès avant le protectorat*. Casablanca, 1949.
Levy, R. *The Social Structure of Islam*. Cambridge, 1957.
Lewis, A. R. *Naval Power and Trade in the Mediterranean* A.D. *500–1100*. Princeton, 1951.
Løkkegaard, F. *Islamic Taxation in the Classic Period with Special Reference to Circumstances in Iraq*. Copenhagen, 1950.
Mez, A. *The Renaissance of Islam*. London, 1937 (tr. from German).
Rodinson, M. *Islam et capitalisme*. Paris, 1966.
Sachau, C. E. *Muhammedanisches Recht*. Stuttgart, Berlin, 1897.
Santillana, D. 'Law and society', in Arnold, T. W. and Guillaume, A. (ed.). *The Legacy of Islam*. Oxford, 1931.
—— *Istituzioni di diritto musulmano malichita*. Rome, 1925–38.
Sauvaget, J. *Alep*. Paris, 1941.
—— *La poste aux chevaux dans l'empire des Mamelouks*. Paris, 1941.
Schacht, J. *An Introduction to Islamic Law*. Oxford, 1964.
—— (ed.). *G. Bergsträsser's Grundzüge des islamischen Rechts*. Berlin and Leipzig, 1935.
——*Origins of Muhammadan Jurisprudence*. 4th edn. London, 1968.
Sourdel, D. *Le vizirat 'abbaside de 749 à 936*. Damascus, 1959–60.
Tyan, É. *Institutions du droit public musulman*. Paris, 1954–7.
—— *Histoire de l'organisation judiciaire en pays d'Islam*. 2nd. edn. Leiden, 1960.

Religion

Abdel-Kader, A. H. *The Life, Personality and Writings of al-Junayd.* London, 1962.
Adams, C. C. *Islam and Modernism in Egypt.* London, 1933.
Affifi, A. E. *The Mystical Philosophy of Muḥyid Din-Ibnul Arabi.* Cambridge, 1939.
Ahmad, A. *Islamic Modernism in India and Pakistan, 1857–1964.* London, 1967.
Arberry, A. J. *Introduction to the History of Ṣūfism.* London, 1942.
—— *Sufism: An Account of the Mystics of Islam.* London, 1950.
—— *Revelation and Reason in Islam.* London, 1957.
Baljon, J. M. S. *Modern Muslim Koran Interpretation, 1880–1960.* Leiden, 1961.
Bausani, A. *Persia Religiosa.* Milan, 1959.
Corbin, H. *L'imagination créatrice dans la Soufisme d'Ibn 'Arabi.* Paris, 1958.
Dar, B. A. *Religious Thought of Sayyid Aḥmad Khān.* Lahore, 1957.
Depont, O. and Coppolani, X. *Les confréries religieuses musulmanes.* Algiers, 1897.
Fyzee, A. A. A. *A Modern Approach to Islam.* Bombay, 1963.
Gardet, L. and Anawati, G.-C. *Introduction à la théologie musulmane.* Paris, 1948.
Gibb, H. A. R. *Modern Trends in Islam.* Chicago, 1946.
—— *Mohammedanism.* London, 1949.
—— 'The structure of religious thought in Islam', in Shaw, S. J. and Polk, W. J. (ed.). *Studies on the Civilization of Islam.* Boston, Mass., 1962.
Goldziher, I. *Le dogme et la loi de l'Islam.* Paris, 1958.
Keddie, N. R. *An Islamic Response to Imperialism.* Berkeley and Los Angeles, 1968.
Kedourie, E. *Afghani and 'Abduh.* London, 1966.
Laoust, H. *Essai sur les doctrines sociales et politiques d'Ibn Taimiyah.* Cairo, 1939.
—— *Les schismes dans l'Islam.* Paris, 1965.
Lings, M. *A Moslem saint of the twentieth century.* London, 1961.
Macdonald, D. B. *Development of Muslim Theology, Jurisprudence and Constitutional Theory.* New York, 1903.
—— *The Religious Attitude and Life in Islam.* Chicago, 1912. Repr. Beirut, 1965.
—— *Aspects of Islam.* New York, 1911.
Massignon, L. *La passion d'al-Ḥallāj, martyr mystique de l'Islam.* Paris, 1922
—— *Essai sur les origines du lexique technique de la mystique musulmane.* Paris, 1922.
Nicholson, R. A. *The Mystics of Islam.* London, 1914.
—— *Studies in Islamic Mysticism.* Cambridge, 1921.
—— *The Idea of Personality in Ṣúfism.* Cambridge, 1923.
Rahman, Fazlur. *Islam.* London, 1966.
Seale, M. S. *Muslim Theology: A Study of Origins with Reference to the Church Fathers.* London, 1964.
Smith, M. *Studies in Early Mysticism in the Near and Middle East.* London, 1931.
—— *An Early Mystic of Baghdad.* London, 1935.
—— *Readings from the Mystics of Islām.* London, 1950.

Smith, W. C. *Modern Islām in India*. Revised edn. London, 1946.
—— *Islam in Modern History*. Princeton, 1957.
Wensinck, A. J. *La pensée de Ghazzālī*. Paris, 1940.
—— *The Muslim Creed, its Genesis and Historical Development*. Cambridge, 1932.
Zaehner, R. C. *Mysticism Sacred and Profane*. Oxford, 1957.
—— *Hindu and Muslim Mysticism*. London, 1960.

Architecture, Art and Literature

Ahmad, Aziz. 'Urdu literature', in Ikram, S. M. and Spear, P. *The Cultural Heritage of Pakistan*. Karachi, 1955.
Anthologie de la littérature arabe contemporaine. Paris, 1964–7.
Arberry, A. J. 'Persian literature', in Arberry, A. J. *The Legacy of Persia*. Oxford, 1953.
Arnold, T. W. *Painting in Islam*. 2nd edn. Oxford, 1965.
Bailey, T. G. *A History of Urdu Literature*. Calcutta, 1932.
Barrett, D. *Islamic Metalwork in the British Museum*. London, 1949.
Bausani, A. *Storia della letterature del Pakistan*. Milan, 1958.
Bombaci, A. *La letteratura turca*. Rev. ed. Milan, 1969.
Browne, E. G. *A Literary History of Persia*. Cambridge, 1928.
Cresswell, K. A. C. *Early Muslim Architecture*. Oxford, 1932–40.
—— *A Short Account of Early Muslim Architecture*. London, 1958.
—— *The Muslim Architecture of Egypt*. Oxford, 1952, 1959.
—— *A Bibliography of the Architecture, Arts and Crafts of Islam*. Cairo, 1961.
Dimand, M. S. *A Handbook of Muhammadan Art*. 3rd edn. New York, 1958.
Ettinghausen, R. *Arab Painting*. Lausanne, 1962.
Gabrieli, F. *Storia della letteratura araba*. Milan, 1962.
Gibb, E. J. W. *A History of Ottoman Poetry*. London, 1900–9.
Gibb, H. A. R. *Arabic Literature*. 2nd edn. Oxford, 1963.
Gray, B. *Persian Painting*. Lausanne, 1961.
Hill, D. and Grabar, O. *Islamic Architecture and its Decoration*. London, 1964.
Lane, A. *Early Islamic Pottery*. London, 1947.
—— *Later Islamic Pottery*. London, 1957.
Levy, R. *An introduction to Persian Literature*. Repr. New York, 1969.
Nicholson, R. A. *A Literary History of the Arabs*. Cambridge, 1907, etc.
Pagliaro, A. and Bausani, A. *Storia della letteratura persiana*. Milan, 1960.
Pellat, Ch. *Langue et littérature arabes*. Paris, 1952.
Pope, A. U. *Persian Architecture*. London, 1965.
Rypka, J. *History of Iranian Literature*. Dordrecht, 1968.
Sadiq, Muhammad. *A History of Urdu Literature*. London, 1964.
Saksena, R. B. *A History of Urdu Literature*. Allahabad, 1940.
Sarre, F. *Die Ausgrabungen von Samarra II: Die Keramik von Samarra*. Berlin, 1925.
Survey of Persian Art. Oxford, 1939.

Science and Philosophy

Boer, T. J. de. *The History of Philosophy in Islam*. London, 1903.

Bouyges, M. *Essai de chronologie des oeuvres de al-Ghazali, Algazel.* Beirut, 1959.
Carra de Vaux, B. *Les penseurs de l'Islam.* Paris, 1921–26.
—— 'Astronomy and mathematics', in Arnold, T. W. and Guillaume, A. *The Legacy of Islam.* Oxford, 1931.
Corbin, H. *Avicenna and the Visionary Recital.* London, 1960.
—— *Histoire de la philosophie islamique I: Des origines jusqu'à la mort d'Averroës.* Paris, 1964.
Gardet, L. *La pensée religieuse d'Avicenne.* Paris, 1951.
Gardner, W. R. W. *Al-Ghazālī.* Madras, 1919.
Gauthier, L. *Ibn Thofaïl, sa vie, ses oeuvres.* Paris, 1909.
—— *La théorie d'Ibn Rochd (Averroès) sur les rapports de la religion et de la philosophie.* Paris, 1909.
—— *Ibn Rochd, Averroès.* Paris, 1948.
Goichon, A. M. *La distinction de l'essence et de l'existence d'après Ibn Sīnā (Avicenne).* Paris, 1937.
Kraus, P. *Jābir et la science grecque.* Cairo. 1942.
McCarthy, R. J. *The Theology of al-Ash'arī.* Beirut, 1953.
Madkour, I. *La place d'al-Fârâbî dans l'école philosophique musulmane.* Paris, 1934.
Mahdi, M. *Ibn Khaldûn's Philosophy of history.* London, 1957.
Massignon, L. and Arnaldez, R. *La science antique et médiévale.* Paris, 1957.
Meyerhof, M. 'Science and medicine', in Arnold, T. W. and Guillaume, A. *The Legacy of Islam.* Oxford, 1931.
Mieli, A. *La science arabe et son rôle dans l'évolution scientifique mondiale.* Leiden, 1938.
Nader, A. N. *La système philosophique des Mu'tazila.* Beirut, 1956.
Nasr, S. H. *Science and Civilization in Islam.* Cambridge, Mass., 1968.
Pines, S. *Beiträge zur islamischen Atomenlehre.* Berlin, 1936.
Plessner, M. 'Storia delle scienze nell'Islam', in *La civiltà dell'oriente.* Vol. III. Rome, 1958.
Sarton, G. *Introduction to the History of Science.* Vols. I-III. Baltimore, 1931–47.
Steinschneider, M. *Die arabischen Übersetzungen aus dem Grieschischen.* Leipzig, 1889–96; Graz, 1960.
Walzer, R. *Greek into Arabic.* Oxford, 1962.
Watt, W. M. *Free Will and Predestination in early Islam.* London, 1948.
Wensinck, A. J. *La pensée de Ghazzālī.* Paris, 1940.
Yuschkevich, A. P. *Mathematik im Mittelalter.* Leipzig. 1964.

The Transmission of Learning and Literary Influences

Arnold, T. and Guillaume, A. (ed.). *The Legacy of Islam.* Oxford, 1931.
Cerulli, E. *Il Libro della Scala e la questione delle fonti arabo-spagnole della Divina Commedia.* Vatican City, 1949.
Daniel, N. *Islam and the West: The Making of an Image.* Edinburgh, 1960.
Fück, J. *Die arabischen Studien in Europa bis in den Anfang des 20. Jahrhunderts.* Leipzig, 1955.

Gabrieli, F. 'La poesia araba e le letterature occidentali'. *Storia e civiltà musulmana*. Naples, 1947.

Menéndez Pidal, R. *Poesía araba e poesía europea*. Madrid, 1941.

Monneret de Villard, U. *Lo studio dell'Islām in Europa nel XII e XIII secolo*. Vatican City, 1944.

Schaeder, H. H. *Goethes Erlebnis des Ostens*. Leipzig, 1938.

Schwab, R. *La renaissance orientale*. Paris, 1950.

Southern, R. W. *Western views of Islam in the Middle Ages*. Cambridge, Mass., 1962.

Steinschneider, M. *Die europäischen Übersetzungen aus dem Arabischen bis Mitte des 17. Jahrhunderts*. Repr. Graz, 1956.

Stern, S. M. *Les chansons mozarabes*. Oxford, 1964.

GLOSSARY

'ĀLIM (pl., *'ulamā'*). A scholar in the Islamic sciences relating to the Qur'ān, theology and jurisprudence.

BID'A. An innovation in Muslim belief or practice; the converse of *sunna,* the alleged practice of the Prophet. *Bid'a* thus tends to be regarded as blameworthy by Muslims.

DĀR AL-ḤARB. 'The abode of war', i.e. territory not under Muslim sovereignty, against which warfare for the propagation of the faith is licit; cf. *Jihād.* It is the converse of *Dār al-Islām,* 'the abode of Islam'.

DHIMMĪ. An adherent of a revealed religion (especially Judaism or Christianity) living under Muslim sovereignty, under the protection of the *Sharī'a* (q.v.).

DIHQĀN (Persian). A member of the lesser feudal nobility in the Sasanian empire. The *dihqāns* largely retained their positions after the Arab conquest, but declined in status from the fifth/eleventh century.

FATWĀ. A formal statement of authoritative opinion on a point of *Sharī'a* (q.v.) by a jurisconsult known as a *muftī.*

FERMĀN (Turkish, from Persian, *farmān*). An order or edict emanating from an Ottoman sultan.

GHĀZĪ. A frontier-warrior, taking part in raids (sing. *ghazā*) in the Holy War (*Jihād,* q.v.) against the infidel. The term was used as a title of honour, e.g. by Ottoman rulers.

ḤADĪTH (pl., *aḥādīth*). A Tradition of an alleged saying or practice of the Prophet. A *Ḥadīth* consists of a chain of oral transmitters (*isnād*) and the text transmitted (*matn*).

ḤAJJ. The Pilgrimage to the Holy Places of Mecca, which is a legal obligation upon individual Muslims. The rites of the *Ḥajj* take place between 8 and 12 Dhu'l-Ḥijja, the last month of the Muslim year. The 'Lesser Pilgrimage' (*'Umra*) may be performed at any time.

'ĪD AL-AḌḤĀ. 'The Feast of Sacrifices', or *al-'Īd al-Kabīr* (the Great Feast), held on 10 Dhu'l-Ḥijja, to coincide with the sacrifice which is one of the rites of the *Ḥajj* (q.v.).

'ĪD AL-FIṬR. 'The Feast of the Breaking of the Fast' or *al-'Īd al-Ṣaghīr* (the Small Feast), held after the end of Ramaḍān, the month of fasting.

ILTIZĀM. A farm of taxes of state-lands. The tax-farmer was known as a *multazim.*

IMĀM. The leader of a group of Muslims in ritual prayer (*ṣalāt*); more specifically, the head of the Islamic community (*Umma*). The title was particularly used by the Shī'ī claimants to the headship of the community.

IQṬĀʿ. A grant of state-lands or revenues by a Muslim ruler to an individual usually in recompense for service.

JIHĀD. The Holy War against infidels, which in some cirumstances is an obligation under the *Sharīʿa* for Muslims. See also *Ghāzī*.
JIZYA. Poll-tax paid to a Muslim government by the male members of protected non-Muslim communities (see *Dhimmī*).

KHUṬBA. The sermon delivered at the Friday congregational prayer in the mosque. Since it includes a prayer for the ruler, mention in the *khuṭba* is a mark of sovereignty in Islam.

MADHHAB. Sometimes translated 'rite' or 'school', a *madhhab* is one of the four legal systems recognized as orthodox by Sunnī (q.v.) Muslims. They are named after their founders—the Ḥanafī, Ḥanbalī, Mālikī and Shāfiʿī *madhhab*.
MADRASA. A school for teaching the Islamic sciences, frequently connected with a mosque.
MAMLŪK. A slave, usually white-skinned (especially of Turkish, Circassian or Georgian origin) and trained as a soldier.
MAWLĀ (pl., *mawālī*). A client of an Arab tribe; more especially a non-Arab convert during the first century of Islam, who acquired status by attachment to an Arab tribal group.
MIḤRĀB. A recess in the wall of a mosque to indicate the *qibla,* i.e. the direction of Mecca, for the correct orientation of ritual prayer.
MILLET (Turkish, from Arabic *milla*). A religious community in the Ottoman empire, usually used of the non Muslim (*dhimmī,* q.v.) communities, which had some measure of internal autonomy.
MINBAR. The pulpit in a mosque, from which the *khuṭba* (q.v.) is delivered.
MUJTAHID. A Shīʿī *ʿālim* (q.v.), exercising the functions of a jurisconsult.
MULLĀ (modern Turkish, *molla*, from Arabic, *mawlā*). A member of the *ʿulamāʾ*.
MURĪD. A disciple of a Ṣūfī (q.v.) teacher.

PĪR (Persian). The Persian equivalent of the Arabic term *shaykh,* in the sense of a Ṣūfī (q.v.) teacher.

QĀḌĪ. A judge in a *Sharīʿa* (q.v.) court.
QĀNŪN. A statement of administrative regulations in the Ottoman empire.

SAYYID. Literally, 'lord'. Used to signify a descendant of the Prophet, more specifically through al-Ḥusayn b. ʿAlī. See also *Sharīf*.
SHARĪʿA. The revealed Holy Law of Islam, derived in theory from the Qur'ān, *Ḥadīth* (q.v.), the consensus (*ijmāʿ*) of the *ʿulamāʾ*, and analogical reasoning (*qiyās*).

SHARĪF. Literally 'noble'. Used to signify a descendant of the Prophet, more specifically through al-Ḥasan b. 'Alī. See also *Sayyid*.
SHĪ'A. Literally 'party'. Originally the supporters of 'Alī's claims to the caliphate, the Shī'a evolved into the principal minority religious group of Muslims, with numerous branches including the Twelver Shī'a and the Ismā'īlīs.
SHĪ'Ī. A member of the Shī'a.
SIPAHI (Turkish, from Persian). In Persian a soldier. In the Ottoman state, a cavalryman, maintained by the grant of a *timar* (q.v.). From this term in Indian and North African usage are derived the English 'sepoy' and the French 'spahi'.
ṢŪFĪ. A Muslim mystic, more especially a member of a religious order (*ṭarīqa*), which has special liturgical and other practices as a means to mystical ecstasy.
SUNNĪ. A member of the majority group of Muslims (in contradistinction to the Shī'a), belonging to one of the four *madhhabs* (q.v.), which claim the authority of the *sunna* of the Prophet as transmitted in the *Ḥadīths* (q.v.).

TIMAR. The Turkish equivalent to *iqṭā'* (q.v.): in particular, the smallest type of Ottoman land-grant. See also *Sipahi*.

VILAYET. A province of the Ottoman empire.

WAQF (pl., *awqāf*). An endowment (usually of landed property) established for pious purposes (*waqf khayrī*), or for the benefit of the donor's family (*waqf ahlī*). In North Africa the equivalent term is *ḥubus*.

ZĀWIYA. A Ṣūfī convent.

INDEX

Note. al— : names *beginning* thus are indexed under the capital letter immediately following. Figures in bold indicate a main entry.

al-Azhar (*cont.*)
  Muslim reformism and modernism at, 183
  Council of Islamic Research at, 651
  modern subjects at, 656
  role in connection with Arabic, 668
al-Azharī, *see* Ismā'īl al-Azharī
'Azīz al-Dīn Nasafī, 586
'Azīz Khammār, 17–18

Bā Aḥmad b. Mūsā, 275
Bā Ḥassūn, 241, 242, 252
Bābā Muḥammad b. 'Uthmān, 278
Bābur, Mughal Emperor, 24, 35–6, 836
  memoirs by, 36, 58, 686, 696
Bacon, Roger, 857
Badakhshān, 43, 44
Badajoz, Spain, 421, 423
Badā'ūnī, 62
Bādi', Red Sea port, 327
Bādī I Abū Rubāṭ, Funj ruler, 332
Bādī II Abū Diqan, Funj ruler, 332
Bādi III al-Aḥmar, Funj ruler, 333
Bādī IV Abū Shulūkh, Funj ruler, 333, 336
Badī' al-Zamān, 662, 664, 665
Badibu, West Africa, 379
Bādīs, of Granada, 422
Bādr al-Dīn Ṭayyibjī, 82, 90
Bādr al-Jamālī, 714
Badr-i Chāch, 33
Baghdād
  founded as 'Abbasid capital, 51, 521, 708
  temporarily replaced as capital by Sāmarrā, 709
  physicians of, 483, 767–8; hospital in, 749
  as centre of trade, 523
  Persian influences in, 569–70
  teams of translators at, 581–2
  'House of Wisdom' at, 582, 748, 783
  Shi'ism and Sunnism in, 570, 585
  Sufism in, 606, 608
  as literary centre, 662
  reduced to provincial capital by Buyids, 665
  occupied by Seljuk Turks (1055), 666
  tomb of 'Abd al-Qādir in, 621
  Sultans of Delhi recognize suzerainty of Caliphs of, 30
  destroyed by Mongols (1258), 7, 571, 667, 708
  taken by Ottomans from Persia (1638), 835
  modern, 470, 779
al-Baghdādī, 595
Bagirmi, 358–9, 365, 372, 374
  French in, 381
Bahā' al-Dīn al-Multānī, 622
Bahā' al-Dīn Walad, 625–6
Bahā' al-Dīn Zuhayr, 882
Bahādur, of Bengal, 24
Bahādur Shāh II, of Delhi, 80
Bahādur Shāh, of Gujarāt, 27, 36–7, 64
Bahādur Shāh, of Khāndēsh, 27
Bahlūl Lodī, 23, 24
Bahmanī dynasty, Deccan, 15, 27, 28–9, 30, 64
Baḥr al-Ghazāl, 337, 338, 374
  Mahdia and, 339, 340
Bahrām, of Delhi, 6
Bahrām, of Ghazna, 4
Bakhtiyārīs, in Persia, 464
al-Bakrī, 762
  on North Africa, 221, 222
  on Western Sudan, 346, 347, 348n
al-Balādhurī, historian, 546
al-Balāgh, pan-Islamic journal, 94
Balban, 6, 7–8, 31
Balearic Islands, 423, 427
Bali, 146, 452
Balkan Wars (1912, 1913), 95, 97, 650
Balkans, 448, 451
  Christian reoccupation of, 458, 459
Balkh, Afghanistan, 35, 48
al-Balkhī, 762
Balkuwārā palace, Sāmarrā, 709
Balobbo, of Masina, 378
Balūchīs, in West Pakistan, 111
Bambara people, 362–3, 398
  defeated by Shehu Aḥmadu, 375, 376
Banādir coast, East Africa, 387
Banāras, India, 5
Bandjarmasin, Borneo, 137
banks
  in Baṣra (11th century), 526
  in North Africa, 276, 295, 302, 313
Bantam, Java, 133, 140, 143, 144, 148
Banten, Java, 173, 179
Banū 'Abd al Wād: *see* 'Abd al-Wadid dynasty
Banū Abī Ḥusayn, 435
Banū Ghāniya, 426
Banū Qasī, 416
Bāqī, 690
al-Baqillānī (*qāḍī*), 595
Baqqāra Arabs, in armies of Mahdia, 339, 340
Baranī, *see* Ẓiyā al-Dīn Baranī
Barār (India), 29, 64, 65
Barbahārī, 591
Bārbak, governor of Jawnpur, 23
Barbarossa, *see* Khayr al-Dīn
Barbary Company, 246–7
Barbieri, G. M., 871

Buyid dynasty, Persia and Iraq, 502, 570, 665, 850
Buzurg b. Shahriyār, 762
Byron, Lord, 886
Byzantine Empire
Muslim conquests from, xix, 211, 212, 214, 824
Muslim heritage from, xx, 569, 723; in art and architecture, 493; in law, 491, 492, 497
turning of Islam towards Persia, and away from, 495
in Sicily, 432, 433, 434, 435
Sayf al-Dawla at war with, 665

Cadiz, Spain, 414
Cagliari, Italy, 436
Cairo
Fatimids move from Ifriqiya to (973), 219, 713
as centre of trade, 523, 525
Fatimid culture in, 579, 586
mosques in, 579, 710, 713–14, Pls 7(a)(b), 10(a), 11
libraries in, 582, 748–9
madrasas in, 724
hospitals in, 749
relations of Kanem with, 355
under Mamluks, 667, 731–2
superseded as capital by Istanbul, on defeat of Mamluks (1516), 667
Caliphate Conference in (1926), 102
University and Centre of Research in, 779
see also al-Azhar
Calabria, Italy, 435, 436
Calcutta, India, 78, 111
calendar
of different peoples, al-Birūnī on, 763
Islamic, in Java, 149
caliphate, 52, 531
in pan-Islamic thought, 94, 99, 192
abolished by Turks (1924), 102
Caliphate Conference, Cairo (1926), 102
caliphs, in Islamic law, 491, 542–3, 557
calligraphy, 60, 580, 723, 727, 731, 735, Pl. 20(a)
Cambon, Paul, 311, 312
camels, 444, 448, 449, 517
in warfare, 825, 830
camera obscura, of Ibn al-Haytham, 755
Cameroon, 396
Canal Waters Dispute, 113–14
canals, in India, 13, 20
Candia, siege of (1667–9), 847
cannibals, visit Mali, 351
cannon, *see* artillery
cantillation of the Qur'ān, 578, 580
Canton, China, massacre of merchant colony in (9th century), 523
cantonment policy in Algeria, 300
Cap Nègre, Tunisia, 260, 261
Cape Juby, Morocco, 271
caravans, from Muslim cities, 453
caravanserais, 522, 713, 717, 719, 732, 734
Carmathians, 377, 583
carpets, weaving of, 580
Seljuk, 723, Pl. 20(b)
Mamluk, 733, Pl. 27(b)
Ottoman, 736
Persian, 738–9, Pl. 31(a)
Carthage, 211, 212, 214, 433
cartography, 597, 763
Casablanca, Morocco, 269
under French, 321, 322, 323, 324
Castile
intervenes in Morocco, 232
hostilities between Muslims and, 414, 417, 418, 421, 423, 424, 425
Castro, A., 888
Castrogiovanni, Sicilly, 433, 434, 436
Catholic priests
in discussions with Akbar, 62
as missionaries in Ethiopia, 386
Caucasus, 336n, 736, 837
soldiers from, 833, 838
cavalry, Indian, 32
see also sipahis
Cayor, West Africa, French in, 379
Celebes, 137–9, 197, 199
Central Asia, 3, 5, 523
influence of art of, 710, 723
Ceuta, Morocco
Byzantine governor at, 211
under Cordova, 417, 418; under Granada, 430
Portuguese at, 232, 239, 243
Ceylon, Muslim and Chinese traders meet in, 523
Chaghatay period of Turkish literature, 685–7
Chanakkale, Dardanelles, pottery centre, 735
Chānd Bībī, dowager queen of Aḥmadnagar, 65
Charlemagne, 409–10, 411
Charles V, Emperor, 251, 261
Charles of Anjou, 852, 861
Charles Martel, 408
Chateaubriand, F. R. de, 886
Chauri Chaura, India, riots at (1921), 101
Chawdharī Raḥmat 'Alī, 107
Chawsa, battle of (1539), 38–9
chemical industry, 527

Ibn Sīnā (Abū 'Alī: Avicenna) (*cont.*)
disciples of, 822; followed in east of Islamic area, 819
Latin translations of works of, 853, 854, 855, 856, 862
Ibn Su'ūd, 102, 182
Ibn Taymiyya (Taqī al-Dīn) 571, 575, 591, 600, 602, **635–7**
and Ṣūfīs, 609
Wahhābī revolt inspired by ideas of, 638
traditionalist; opponent of *kalām*, 822–3
Ibn Ṭufayl (Abū Bakr Muḥammad), **816–17**
at Marrakesh, 225, 583
in Spain, 426, 571, 599, 815
and astronomy, 760, 761
on al-Fārābī, 800
Latin translations of works of, 860, 878
Ibn Ṭūlūn, mosque of, 579, 714
Ibn Tūmart (Muḥammad b. 'Abd Allāh), **224–5**, 227, 234
Ibn Wāfid (Abenguefit), 863
Ibn Waḥshiyya, 517, 774
Ibn Zaydūn, 666, 872
Ibn Zuhr (Avenzoar), 771, 861
Ibn Zunbul, 841
Ibo people, 397
Ibrāhīm (Pasha), of Algeria, 256, 286
Ibrāhīm (Qāḍī), in Ambon, 136
Ibrāhīm, of Bījāpur, 64
Ibrāhīm II, of Bījāpur, 57
Ibrāhīm, of Lahore, 4
Ibrāhīm (Shaykh), in Minangkabau, 128
Ibrāhīm al-Nakha'ī, 554
Ibrāhīm al-Naẓẓām, 500, 593, 788, 792n
Ibrāhīm al-Sharīf, 259, 266, 285
Ibrāhīm b. Adham, 606, 614
Ibrāhīm b. Ḥabīb al-Fazārī, *see* al-Fazārī
Ibrāhīm b. Ḥajjāj, 415–16
Ibrāhīm b. Sinān, 752
Ibrāhīm Khān Sūr (Ibrāhīm Shāh), of Delhi, 40, 41
Ibrāhīm Lodī, of Delhi, 24, 35, 37
Ibrāhīm Muḥammad, of Darfur, 338
Ibrāhīm Mūsā, 365
Ibrāhīm Shāh, of Jawnpur, 24, 25
Ibrāhīm Shināsī, 694
Ibrāhīm Sori, 365
Ibrīm, Lower Nubia, 330
'id al-aḍḥā (feast of sacrifices), 18, 76, 907
'id al-fiṭr (feast at the end of Ramaḍān), 18, 76, 907
Idrīs b. 'Abd Allāh, 216, 218, 237
Idrīs Alawma, of Bornu, 356
Idrīs b. Idrīs, 216
al-Idrīsī, 221, 225, 438, 597, 762
Idrisid dynasty, Morocco, 418, 419
Ifat, Muslim kingdom, 383, 384
Ifni, Morocco, 271
Ifrīqiya (Tunisia), 211, 216
under Fatimids, 213–18, 237, 564
bedouin invade, 220
under Almohads, 425, 427
under Hafsids, 228, 229
rivalry between Spain and Ottoman empire in (1508–74), 253–4, 286
see further Tunisia
al-Ījī, 595
ijtihād (independent reasoning in Islamic law), 564, 565, 635
reform movements and, 638, 640, 642, 643, 644
Ikdalā, Bengal, 21, 22
Īl-Khān dynasty, Persia, 586
art and architecture under, 727–9
'ilm al-fiqh, *see* law
'ilm al-kalām, *see kalām*
Ilorin, West Africa, 371, 372
under British, 381, 396
iltizām (farm of taxes of state lands), 907
Iltutmish (Shams al-Dīn), of Delhi, **5–6**, 30, 31
Ilyās, of Bengal, 21
Ilyās, Turkish corsair, 219
Ilyās Shāhī dynasty, Bengal, 25
'Imād al-Mulk, of Barār, 29
imām (leader in prayer), 74, 400, 446, 907
al-Imām, Singapore newspaper, 184–5
Imāmī Shī'ism, 585, 586
Imru'l-Qays, 576, 659
'Ināyat, of Acheh, 142
India
and Islamic civilization, 448, 482, 483, 507–8
Muslim, before the Mughals, 3–34
under the Mughals, 35–66, 838
influence of, in Java, 189
breakdown of traditional society in, 67–92
preliminaries of partition in, 97–109
partition of, 109–10
princely states of, 114–16
Muslims in Republic of, 116–19
Muslim study of works of science from, 507–8, 747, 752, 758, 793
Indian Civil Service, examinations for, 84
Indian Independence Act (1947), 110
Indian National Congress, 84
rapprochement of Muslim organizations with, 96, 97, 99, 102
anti- and pro-Muslim trends in leadership of, 101–2
parting of Muslim League and, 105, 107
accepts partition, 109
Indian Nationalist Party, 102

Indian Patriotic Association, against Congress, 84
Indians, in East Africa, 388; in South Africa, 405
indigénat, legal system of French in Algeria, 303–4
indigo, cultivation of, 76
Indonesia
  to 1941, *see* South-East Asia
  Japanese and, 199, 201, 203
  independent, 203, 206, 207
Indo-Persian style of poetry (*sabk-i Hindī*), 690
Indragiri, Sumatra, 126
industry
  in Pakistan, 111, 114
  in Tunis, 260
inheritance, Islamic law of, 460, 536, 542, 545, 551, 561, 565
Inje Mināre, Konya, 718
Inshā', 698
inshā' form of prose, in Turkish literature, 692–3
instrumental sciences, 595–7
intellectual developments, in reform movements, 642–51
intelligence services, of Indian rulers, 7, 10, 23, 32
Iqbāl, 682
iqṭā' (concessions to soldier-officials), 460, 533, 536, 832, 844, 908
Iran, *see* Persia
'Irāq, 482, 497, 514, 516, 570
  schools of Islamic law in, 550, 551, 552–3, 575
  integration of Arabs and people of, 585
  contact between Greek and Arab thought in, 852
  doctors from, in Cordova, 417
  Seljuks in, 716
  modern, 465, 467, 472
'Irāqī, 675, 678
Irian Barat (West New Guinea), 207
iron, 520, 842; from North Africa, 302, 313, 315, 322
irrigation, 462, 512, 517
  deserts arising from failure of, 494
'Īsā b. Aḥmad al-Rāzī, 417–18
Isaac Judaeus, *see* Isḥāq b. Sulaymān al-Isrā'īlī
Isabella of Castile, 432
Isaurian dynasty, Byzantium, 493
Iṣfahān, Persia, 570, 586
  mosque at, 716, 727, 737, Pl. 30
  palaces at, 737–8, Pl. 28(a)
  craftsmen at, 738, 739, 740
Isḥāq II (Askiya), of Songhay, 359
Isḥāq, Turkish corsair, 249
Isḥāq b. Ḥunayn, 581
Isḥāq b. Sulaymān al-Isrā'īlī (Isaac Judaeus), 771, 852, 861
Ishrāqī philosophy, 809, 821–2
Iskak (Mawlānā), in Java, 134
Iskandar Muda, of Acheh, 127, 141
Iskandar Thānī, of Acheh, 127, 142
Islām Khān, governor of Bengal, 46
Islām Shāh, of Delhi, 39, 40, 61
Islamic Research, Council of (al-Azhar), and Central Institute of (Pakistan), 651
Isly, battle of (1844), 270, 273, 299
Ismā'īl, of Bījāpur, 64
Ismā'īl (Khedive), of Egypt, 337, 338
Ismā'īl II, of Granada, 431
Ismā'īl (Mawlāy), of Morocco, 245, **267–8**, 279
Ismā'īl al-Azharī, 343, 344
Ismā'īl al-Manṣūr, of Ifrīqiya, 219
Ismā'īl Mukh, of the Deccan, 18
Ismā'īl Shahīd, 73
Ismā'īlis (extremist Shī'a), 589, 602, 634, 794, 800, 909
  attack al-Rāzī, 801, 803
  theology of, **803–4**, 812
  in India, 5–6, 21, 34
  in Persia, 450, 570, 586
  in Spain, 571, 599
  in Baghdād, 585
Isqaf Banī Junayd, near Baghdād, mosque at, 704
Isrā'īliyyāt (tales attributed to Children of Israel), 488
al-Iṣṭakhrī, 507, 762
Istanbul, 667, 688
  houses in, 456, 458
  mosques in, 733, 734
  see also Constantinople
Iṣṭifan b. Basīl, 499
Istiqlāl party, Morocco, 325–6
Italians
  as traders, 235, 236, 524
  in North Africa, as slaves, 289; as colonists, 300, 313, 315
  in East Africa, 395
Italy, 434, 523
  and North Africa, 276, 295, 296, 297
  at war with Ottoman empire, 97, 314
  cultural contact between West and Muslims in, 852
  Arabic influences in literature of, 878–82
  study of Eastern literature in, 888
I'timād al-Dawla (Mīrzā Ghiyāṣ Beg), 45, 46

medicine, 765–74
  schools of, at Gondēshāpūr, 483, 765–7, 784; in Cordova, 417; in Baghdād, 483; in India, 507
  Ibn Sīnā's work in, 596
  philosophers in, 784–5, 860–1
  Arabic translations of Greek works on 493, 768–9, 861
  Latin translations of Greek and Arabic works on, 861
Medina, Arabia
  caliphs of, 542, 544, 547; religion and culture under, 569, 574, 588
  school of law in, 550, 551, 552, 553, 554 560, 575
  mosque at, 579, 703
  poetry in, 661
medreses, in Anatolia, 718, 733; *see also madrasas*
Meḥmed I, Ottoman Sultan, 834
Meḥmed II (the Conqueror) Ottoman Sultan, 688, 735, 834, 835
Meḥmed Emīn, 694
Meknès, Morocco
  under Marinids, 229, 233
  under ʿAlawīs, 268, 273
  European colonists round, 324
Melik Ghāzī, near Kayseri, buildings at, 716, 719
Melilla, Morocco, 239, 242, 254, 269
Mendès France, Pierre, 319, 326
Menelaus, 747, 768, 855, 864
Menelik, Emperor of Ethiopia, 390, 395
mercenaries
  Christian, 232, 235, 413
  Negro, 218
  see also armies
merchants, *see* trade
mercury (metal), 520, 775
Mérida, Spain, 406–7, 411, 428
Mers el-Kebir, Morocco, 242, 249, 252, 254
mesnevi form of poetry, *see mathnawī*
Mesopotamia, 493, 495, 852
Messahala, *see* Mā Shā' Allāh
Meston, Sir James, 95–6
Messali Hadj, Algerian leader, 308, 309
Messina, Sicily, 434, 436
metallurgy, 527
metalwork, 580; Umayyad, 707, Pl. 3(b); Fatimid, 715; Seljuk, 721–2, Pl. 18(a) and (b); Ayyubid, 724, Pl. 22(a); Moorish, 726; Mamluk, 732; Safavid, 739, Pl. 31(b)
metempsychosis, 508, 804
Mēwār, India, 46, 50
Michael Scot, 853, 856, 865
migration, to India, 34; from India, 119; of bedouin into North Africa, 220; from Algeria, 307; from Sicily, 439
miḥrābs (niches in mosques indicating direction of Mecca), 703, 704, 705, 725, 908
  semicircular, 706; rectangular, 708; doubled, 709
  marble, 707
  mosaic, 711, 731, Pl. 8(a)
  faience, 711, 719, 728, 733, Pl. 16(b)
  carved stone, 718
  stucco, 712, 714, 717, 727, Pls. 7(b), 9(b) 11, 15(a)
  with wood carvings, 732
Miletus ware, 734
military service, compulsory, in Algeria, 305
Mill, John Stuart, 86
millenarianism, 492
millet (non-Muslim community in Ottoman empire), 908
mills, wind- and water-, introduced by Muslims, 518, 753
minā'ī pottery, Persia, 721, 724, Pl. 17(a)
minarets, 579, 705
  helicoid, 709
  cylindrical Seljuk, 717
  square, in North Africa and Spain, 725, 726, Pl. 22(b)
  Ottoman, 733, Pls. 15(b), 23(b), 30
Minangkabau, Sumatra, **128**, 140
  under Dutch, **163–7**, 173, 196
  Muslim reformism in, 197
  under Japanese, 204
minbar (pulpit), in mosques, 703, 711, 732, 908, Pl. 9(b)
Mineo, Sicily, 433
miniature painting, 580, 735, 738
  Seljuk, 721, 722, Pl. 19(a) and (b)
  Timurid, 730, Pls. 25(a) and (b), 26
mining, 520; in North Africa, 302, 313, 315, 317, 322
minorities, in India, 103, 104, 118
Minto, Lord, Viceroy of India, 91
Mīr Amman, 701
Mīr Jumlā, 49, 66
Mīr Nithār ʿAlī (Tītū Mīr), 77
Mīr Sayyid ʿAlī, 58
Mīr Taqī 'Mīr', 78, 698
miracles, 139, 485–6, 794
  modernist thinkers and, 645
Mīrafāb tribe, Sudan, 333
Mīrānjī Shams al-ʿUshshāq, 696
Mirdasid dynasty, al-Jazīra, 827
Mīrghaniyya order, in East Africa, 390
Mīrzā Abū Ṭālib Khān, 75

reform, revival and, in Islam, 364, 632–6
pre-modernist, 636–41
modern, 641–2; intellectual developments in, 642–51; social developments in, 651–4; educational developments in, 654–6; in South-East Asia, 186–97
regions, Islamic organization of, 465–8
religious, condominium of army and, characteristic of Muslim countries, 537
religious sciences, 576, **587–95**, 600, 603
in classification of sciences, 743, 745–6
Rentjeh (Tuanku nan), 166
Reverter, Catalan general, 424
Rhazes, *see* al-Rāzī
Rhodes, 261, 432, 839, 847
Ribāṭ-i Malik caravanserai, Persia, 717
Ribaṭ-i Safid, fire-altar of, 712
Ribāṭ-i Sharīf caravanserai, Persia, 717
ribāṭs (fortified convents), 453
Ribera, J., 872–3
rice, cultivation of, 113, 452, 466, 771
Riḍwān, *wazīr* in Granada, 431
Rif War, in Morocco, 322
Rifā'iyya order, 621–2
Rīfīs, mountain Berbers, 234
Rijali (Imām), 138
Rikhtī, genre of Urdu verse, 698
Rio de Oro, Morocco, 271
Riżā (Imām), shrine of, at Mashhad, 738
Riżā Shāh, of Persia, 457
Riżā Tevfīq, 694
Robert of Chester, 855, 863, 864
Roderick, of Spain, 406, 407, 408
Rodrigo Jiménez de Rada, Archbishop of Toledo, 855
Roe, Sir Thomas, received by Jahāngīr, 46
Roger I, of Sicily, 436, 437–8
Roger II, of Sicily, 438
Rohīlkhand, India, 80
Rokan, Sumatra, 126
Roman Empire, xxii, 211–12, 471, 498
Roncaglia, A., 874
Roosevelt, President, 325
Round Table Conferences, on future of India, 104
Rowlatt Act, 99
rubā'ī, Persian form of poetry, 673
Ruckert, J. M. F., 885
Rūdakī, 672, 675
al-Rūdhābārī, 614
rulers, Muslim attitude to, 492, 531–2
Rūmī, *see* Jalāl al-Dīn Rūmī
Rūmī Khān, artillery expert, 838
Rūpmati, 42
Ruṣāfa, Syria, pottery centre, 720
al-Ruṣāfa, summer palace near Cordova, 410
Rūshanā'īs, 43
Russia
Muslim trade with, 524
at war with Ottoman empire, 180, 845, 848, 849, 850
Rustam, Persian general, 445, 674–5
Rustamid dynasty, Tāhart, 216
Rustem Pasha, *vezīr*, 837

Sabah, Borneo, 206
Ṣābi'a (Arabic term for pagan religion), 787
Sabians, 742, 786–7
Sa'd, potter in Egypt, 715
Sa'd al-Dīn, of Ifat, 384
Sa'd al-Dīn, *Shaykh al-Islām*, 693
Sa'dāb Ja'aliyyūn tribe, Sudan, 333
Sa'dī, 67, 586, 677, 679, 730
Gulistān by, 680, 883
Sa'did dynasty, Morocco, 238, **240–8**
firearms under, 835, 838
Ṣādiqiyya College, Tunis, 296, 314, 317
Ṣadr al-Dīn al-Shīrāzī, *see* al-Shīrāzī
Safavid dynasty, Persia, 35, 464, 568, 730
culture under, 602, 681, 737–40
philosophy under, 823
armies of, 838
Safi, Morocco, 239, 240, 247
Sahara
routes across, 231, 263, 345, 349, 374
trade across, 236, 345
Turkish expedition into, 252
Sahel, Tunisia, 290, 291, 295
olive groves of, 313, 466
Ṣāḥib Ata Jāmi', Konya, 719
Sahl b. 'Abd Allāh al-Tustarī, 612, 617
Sahlīs, Ṣūfī sect, 617
Ṣaḥnūn, 217, 435
Ṣā'ib, 57, 681
Ṣā'id, on Party Kingdoms, 422
al-Sa'īd, Almohad ruler, 228, 229
Sa'īd 'Aql, 570–1
Sa'īd Ṣarṣarī (Ḥājjī), 18
Saint, L., French Resident in Tunisia, 316
Sakızlı (Muḥammad), 263
Sakkārī of Samarqand, 685
Saladin, Ayyubid Sultan, 724, 749, 832
Salado, battle of (1340), 431
Salafiyya reform movement, 305, 314, 402, 403, 404
Ṣalāḥ b. Yūsuf, 319
ṣalāt (ritual prayer), 907
Sale, George, xxiv, 883
Salé, Morocco, 233, 424
privateering from, 238, 240, 247, 248, 266
Salerno, Italy, 852
al-Ṣāliḥ, Ayyubid Sultan, 724

Sebüktigin, of Ghazna, 3
secularization, of modern Arabic literature, 668
Sefawa people, Western Sudan, 357, 372
Segu, Bambara state, 362, 377, 378
Selangor, Malaysia, 186
Selānīkī, 693
Seleucia, near Ctesiphon, centre of Hellenic learning taken by Muslims, 483
Selīm I, Ottoman Sultan, 250, 667, 841
Selīm III, Ottoman Sultan, 850
Selīm Kapudan (Salīm Qabūdān), 337
Selīmiye Jāmi' mosque, Edirne, 734, 735, Pl. 28(b)
Seljuk Turks, 4, 536, 666
  Sunnism under, 570
  art and architecture under, 579, 716–23
  Persian and Arabic languages under, 687
Seljuk white ware, Pl. 17(b)
Senegal, 399, 462
  soldiers from, 397
Senegambia, 379
Sennar, Funj capital, 330
separatism (political), of Muslims in India, 103–106
separatists and reformists, Muslim, 398-402
Serbia, soldiers from, 835
Servet-i Fünūn, Turkish journal, 694
Seville, Spain, 414, 415
  falls to Arabs, 406; under 'Abbadids, 421; under Almoravids, 423; under Almohads, 426, 579, 725, 726
  retaken by Ferdinand III, 428, 429, 571
  translations from Arabic at, 856, 863
Sfax, Tunisia, 290, 313, 438
sgraffiato pottery, 720, 732, Pl. 17(a)
sha'ā'ir al-Islām (the marks of Islam), 573
Shābbiyya Arabs, Tlemcen, 253
Shādhiliyya order, 280, 622
al-Shāfi'ī (Imām), Traditionist, **559–60**
  mausoleum and mosque of, Cairo, 724, Pl. 21(b)
Shāfi'ī school of jurists, 560, 590, 591
  al-Ghazālī and, 600, 619
Shāh 'Abd al-Azīz, of Delhi, 73, 74
Shāh 'Abd al-Ghanī, of Delhi, 73, 74
Shāh 'Abd al-Qādir, of Delhi, 73
Shāh 'Ālam, Mughal Emperor, 73, 698
Shāh 'Ālam, son of Awrangzēb, *see* Mu'aẓẓam
Shāh 'Ālam Bahādur Shāh, Mughal Emperor, 69
Shāh Fakhr al-Dīn, 71
Shāh Ismā'īl, of Persia, 730–1, 737, 738, 838
  mausoleum of, Bukhārā, 711–12, Pl. 8(b)
Shāh Ismā'īl, son of 'Abd al-Ghanī of Delhi, 74
Shāh-i Zinda, mausoleum complex, Samarqand, 729, Pl. 24(b)
Shāh Jahān (Prince Khurram), Mughal Emperor, 45, 46, **47–9**, 55, 66
  painting under, 59
Shāh Kalīm Allāh Jahānābādī, 71
Shāh Mīr, of Swāt, *see* Shams al-Dīn Shāh
Shāh Rafī' al-Dīn, son of Shāh Walī Allāh, 73
Shāh Rukh, of Herat, 730
Shāh Ṣafī, of Persia, 835
Shāh Shujā', governor of Bengal, 49, 50
Shāh Walī Allāh, **71–3**, 96, 638–9
Shāhīs, 3
Shāhjī Bhonsle, Marāthā king-maker, 50
al-Shahrastānī, 595, 789
Shahristān bridge, near Iṣfahān, 719
Shahryār, son of Jahāngīr, 46, 47–8
Shajar al-Durr, mausoleum of, Cairo, 724
Shākir, minister in Tunis, 293
Shamanism, of Mongols, 622
Shambhūjī, Mārāthā leader, 51–2
Shams al-Dīn, theologian in Acheh, 141
Shams al-Dīn, wandering dervish, 626
Shams al-Dīn Fērōz Shāh, of Bengal, 13, 24
Shams al-Dīn Iltutmish, *see* Iltutmish
Shams al-Dīn Shāh (previously Shāh Mīr of Swāt), of Kashmir, 25
Shandī, capital of Sa'dāb Ja'aliyyūn, 333
Shaqīq of Balkh, 606, 607
share-cropping, 462, 519
Sharī'a (Holy Law of Islam), xx, xxi, 481, 539, 908
  power of ruler limited by, 52, 491
  revealed character of, 473, 488
  equilibrium between theory and practice of, 565–7
  in India, 71, 72
  in South-East Asia, 139–40
  in Morocco, 273, 274
  in Sudan, 331
  in Ottoman empire, 567–8
  reform movements and, 637
  see also law
Sharī'at Allāh (Ḥājjī), leader of Farā'iżī movement, **76–7**
Sharīf, title used for descendants of Prophet, 241, 274, 909
al-Sharīf (Mawlāy), of Tafilelt, 266
Sharīf al-Dīn, Fulani ascetic, 373
Sharifian empire, Morocco, *see* Sa'did dynasty
Sharqī kingdom, India, 20, 23
al-Shāṭir, 759n
Shaṭṭāriyya order of Ṣūfīs, 63, 153, 156, 173